AUGSBURG COLLEGE & SEMINARY
George Sverdrup Library
MINNEAPOLIS 4, MINNESOTA

WITHDRAWN

The Soviet Design
for a World State

STUDIES OF THE RUSSIAN INSTITUTE

COLUMBIA UNIVERSITY

The Soviet Design for a World State

ELLIOT R. GOODMAN

WITH A FOREWORD BY PHILIP E. MOSELY

Columbia University Press
1960 New York

The transliteration from the Cyrillic is based on the Library of Congress system with some modifications. The spelling of Slavic names that appear in quotations from English-language texts has likewise been brought into conformity with this system. However, some names have been retained in their common English forms. Thus Trotsky, for example, has not been rendered Trotskii.

For the sake of uniformity, all dates have been transposed into the Gregorian (New Style) calendar, which the Soviet government adopted on February 14, 1918. Where several dates appear in a footnote reference, the first indicates the date on which the work was written or, if this is unavailable, the date on which it was first published. The date appearing within the parentheses indicates the time of publication of the edition cited.

Unless otherwise noted, Lenin, *Sochineniia*, refers to the third Russian edition of Lenin's collected works (Moscow, 1934–1935). The first, second, and fourth editions have been checked for textual variations and omissions relevant to the topic. Stalin, *Sochineniia*, refers to the Russian edition of Stalin's collected works (Moscow, 1946–1951).

Italics within quotations are as in the original texts except as indicated. British spellings within quotations have been adapted to American usage.

Copyright © 1957, 1960 Columbia University Press, New York
First published in book form 1960

First printing April, 1960
Second printing October, 1960

Published in Great Britain, India, and Pakistan
by the Oxford University Press
London, Bombay, and Karachi

Library of Congress Catalog Card Number: 60-7625
Manufactured in the United States of America

The Russian Institute of Columbia University

THE Russian Institute was established by Columbia University in 1946 to serve two major objectives: the training of a limited number of well-qualified Americans for scholarly and professional careers in the field of Russian studies, and the development of research in the social sciences and the humanities as they relate to Russia and the Soviet Union. The research program of the Russian Institute is conducted through the efforts of its faculty members, of scholars invited to participate as Senior Fellows in its program, and of candidates for the Certificate of the Institute and for the degree of Doctor of Philosophy. Some of the results of the research program are presented in the Studies of the Russian Institute of Columbia University. The faculty of the Institute, without necessarily agreeing with the conclusions reached in the Studies, believe that their publication advances the difficult task of promoting systematic research on Russia and the Soviet Union and public understanding of the problems involved.

The faculty of the Russian Institute are grateful to the Rockefeller Foundation for the financial assistance which it has given to the program of research and publication.

Studies of the Russian Institute

SOVIET NATIONAL INCOME AND PRODUCT IN 1937　　*Abram Bergson*
THROUGH THE GLASS OF SOVIET LITERATURE: VIEWS OF RUSSIAN
　SOCIETY　　*Edited by Ernest J. Simmons*
THE PROLETARIAN EPISODE IN RUSSIAN LITERATURE, 1928–1932
　　　　Edward J. Brown
MANAGEMENT OF THE INDUSTRIAL FIRM IN THE USSR
　A STUDY IN SOVIET ECONOMIC PLANNING　　*David Granick*
SOVIET POLICIES IN CHINA, 1917–1924　　*Allen S. Whiting*
UKRAINIAN NATIONALISM, 1939–1945　　*John A. Armstrong*
POLISH POSTWAR ECONOMY　　*Thad Paul Alton*
LITERARY POLITICS IN THE SOVIET UKRAINE
　1917–1934　　*George S. N. Luckyj*
THE EMERGENCE OF RUSSIAN PANSLAVISM
　1856–1870　　*Michael Boro Petrovich*
BOLSHEVISM IN TURKESTAN, 1917–1927　　*Alexander G. Park*
THE LAST YEARS OF THE GEORGIAN MONARCHY
　1658–1832　　*David Marshall Lang*
LENIN ON TRADE UNIONS AND REVOLUTION
　1893–1917　　*Thomas Taylor Hammond*
THE JAPANESE THRUST INTO SIBERIA, 1918　　*James William Morley*
SOVIET MARXISM: A CRITICAL ANALYSIS　　*Herbert Marcuse*
THE AGRARIAN FOES OF BOLSHEVISM: PROMISE AND
　DEFAULT OF THE RUSSIAN SOCIALIST REVOLU-
　TIONARIES, FEBRUARY TO OCTOBER, 1917　　*Oliver H. Radkey*
SOVIET POLICY AND THE CHINESE COMMUNISTS
　1931–1946　　*Charles B. McLane*
PATTERN FOR SOVIET YOUTH: A STUDY OF THE
　CONGRESSES OF THE KOMSOMOL, 1918–1954　　*Ralph Talcott Fisher, Jr.*
THE EMERGENCE OF MODERN LITHUANIA　　*Alfred Erich Senn*
THE SOVIET DESIGN FOR A WORLD STATE　　*Elliot R. Goodman*

To my Father
Lazure L. Goodman

Acknowledgments

ONLY those who have had the privilege of close association with Professor Philip E. Mosely can appreciate the measure of gratitude that is owed him. His patient and precise guidance, even in the midst of a whirlwind of distracting pressures, almost exceeds belief. In the writing of the present work his contribution has been invaluable, thanks to his knowledge and judgment as a scholar, while his painstaking and skillful editorial suggestions resulted in a sharpening and a substantial shortening of the text. For all this I can only express my heartfelt appreciation.

At the inception of this study a number of years ago Professor Frederick C. Barghoorn showed a warm and lively interest which the author has not forgotten. In the latter stages of writing Professor Henry L. Roberts, Director of the Russian Institute, was both kind and helpful in smoothing out some troublesome textual wrinkles and in negotiating the publication arrangements. For their thoughtful, and sometimes elaborate, critique of the manuscript at various stages of preparation, my thanks also go to Professor Alexander Dallin, Professor Harold H. Fisher, Professor Leland M. Goodrich, and Professor Kenneth Waltz. I naturally assume full responsibility for the final shape of the text, including the conclusions and opinions that are not specifically attributed to others.

Various chapters draw upon material that appeared in a modified form in the *Journal of Politics* and the *Russian Review*. The author wishes to express his gratitude to the editors of these journals for their consent to incorporate such passages in this book.

As every researcher knows, librarians are the truly unsung heroes of the scholar's world, and I wish to thank the numerous librarians, especially at Butler Library of Columbia University, the Slavonic Division of the New York Public Library, and the John Hay Library of Brown University, for their quiet and tireless assistance in tracing down many rare but important items.

A word of appreciation is also surely due my colleagues at Brown University, and in particular Professor Guy Howard Dodge, for a sympathetic understanding of the birth pangs involved in getting this work to press. Special mention must also be made of the many kindnesses rendered me during the writing process by Mr. and Mrs. Abraham Feinberg of New York. Finally, this book would scarcely have been conceivable without the sustained encouragement of my father, Lazure L. Goodman. Nor could this work ever have been brought to a conclusion without the constant support of my wife, Norma Goodman, whose contributions ranged from help in the formulation of ideas to secretarial drudgery, as well as the numerous wifely ministrations beyond calculation.

ELLIOT R. GOODMAN

Brown University
Providence, Rhode Island
August, 1959

Contents

	FOREWORD, BY PHILIP E. MOSELY	xiii
	INTRODUCTION	xvi
I.	MARX AND ENGELS ON THE WORLD STATE	1
II.	THE WORLD STATE AS AN EXPLICIT SOVIET GOAL	25
III.	THE INFLUENCE OF RUSSIAN NATIONALISM TO 1934	50
IV.	THE INFLUENCE OF RUSSIAN NATIONALISM SINCE 1934	80
V.	THE MEANING OF SOCIALISM IN ONE COUNTRY	129
VI.	THE MEANING OF PEACEFUL COEXISTENCE	164
VII.	THE ISSUE OF CENTRALISM VERSUS FEDERALISM IN THE LENINIST ERA	190
VIII.	THE ISSUE OF CENTRALISM VERSUS FEDERALISM IN THE STALINIST ERA AND AFTER	239
IX.	WORLD STATE AND WORLD LANGUAGE	264
X.	THE ROLE OF WAR IN BUILDING THE SOVIET WORLD STATE	285
XI.	WAY STATIONS TO THE SOVIET WORLD STATE	326
XII.	SOVIET REACTIONS TO SUPRANATIONAL PLANS FROM THE NON-SOVIET WORLD	373
XIII.	THE WORLD STATE OF NO STATE	426
XIV.	THE RESPONSE OF THE WEST	472
	PRINCIPAL SOURCES	489
	INDEX	494

Foreword

THEORY or doctrine fulfills a unique function in Soviet and Communist policy, a function which it is difficult for those reared in a democratic society to appreciate without, so to speak, standing on their heads. In a freely developing society the techniques and rules of political and social action are fairly rigid, operating within a tradition of respect for the individual and his freedom of opinion, thought, and association, whereas the goals of a democratic society are usually defined or redefined piecemeal, as new needs and challenges become generally visible.

In a totalitarian system, on the other hand, no instruments or rules of power are sacrosanct except in so far as they assist and guide the self-appointed ruling group in maximizing its control over the individuals ruled and over all their thinking and actions. The goals of a totalitarian system of power, in contrast, are spelled out in great detail, and the ruling elite measures its successes and failures by the rate at which it approaches the fulfillment of those goals. Described in terms of process, a democratic elite develops through many self-generating and self-directing activities freely carried on within a permissive structure. A totalitarian elite is selected from above, indoctrinated massively and ceaselessly, disciplined by a central authority, and promoted to higher positions or thrust into outer limbo on the basis of both its efficiency and its zeal in achieving predetermined goals as defined at any given time in the monopolistic body of doctrine. This is what gives the driving force to Communist ideology and Soviet policy.

Among the goals which shape Soviet thinking and action the ultimate achievement of a Communist world state is of central significance. It molds the thinking of the Communist elite about the present world system of diverse states, the continuing conflict between the Communist and all other systems of states, and their duty to strive by any and all means to achieve the goal of an allegedly stateless and conflictless Communist world system. Oddly enough, this basic core of Communist thought and emotion has not previously been examined with all necessary care, in the light of the most authoritative Soviet statements of doctrine. For this reason, Professor Goodman's study fills a very serious gap in our studies of Communist theory and Soviet policy.

One question which readers inevitably ask of any study of Communist doctrine is: Is doctrine really important? Does doctrine "cause" Soviet leaders to act? Or do they merely use doctrine to justify whatever they pragmatically want to do at any given time? There is both a simple and a complex answer to this very legitimate query. Of course, the Soviet leaders do not simply open the sacred books of Marxism-Leninism at random in order to pick out a passage and then decide what to do that day or that month. On the other hand, it must not be forgotten that one of the requirements for survival on the Soviet Olympus is both to master and to "interpret creatively" the basic Communist doctrine, and that Leninism has always emphasized the fruitful interaction between doctrine and action. At the center of Soviet power, the attention to doctrine as a source of power and a broad guide to action remains strong, and access to the levers of power requires a long and disciplined immersion in doctrinal thinking, quite unfamiliar to people who achieve wealth or influence within democratic societies. If doctrine does not dictate Communist actions in a literal sense, it does define the channels or grooves of thought through which decisions are made and actions are taken. Like others who have spent many hours or days in trying to reach the minds of truly indoctrinated Communists, I can testify to the efficiency of doctrine in molding the views of the decision-makers and their apparatus of information and action. Its effects cannot be underestimated except at great peril to democratic societies.

A second question is: Has the author approached his study with his opinions already formed, merely seeking to substantiate ready-made conclusions? Or did he embark on it with the open but not vacant mind which a free society expects of its scholars? In this respect I am perhaps in a unique position to report on Professor Goodman's qualifications, for he first tackled one aspect of this complex problem quite a few years ago, in my seminar at the Russian Institute, and I have had the pleasure and sometimes the sympathetic discomfort of watching him wrestle with doctrinal subtleties and with a vast array of empirical evidence as he developed his investigation into this book. I can also certify that, in order to reduce his study to publishable and readable dimensions, the author has been obliged to omit a large amount of doctrinal and historical evidence that he would have preferred to include. I am therefore able to assure his readers that Professor Goodman approached his subject without predetermined conclusions, that he has built up his findings piecemeal through a conscientious examination of both ideology and action, and that the powerful structure of his analysis stands firmly on the bedrock of evidence.

PHILIP E. MOSELY

New York City
August, 1959

Introduction

THE Soviet regime seeks "world revolution," "world domination," "world hegemony." Such are the vague, indeterminate phrases usually employed to describe the world-wide ambitions of the Soviet Union. But these concepts do not take us very far when measured against the pressing need to define issues and sharpen the outlines of the Soviet grand design.

This study has two closely related aims. The first and principal one is to reduce to concrete terms the meanings concealed in the commonly repeated, but seldom examined, clichés about Soviet purposes and goals. The second basic aim is to question the adequacy of the existing pattern of interstate relations in the non-Soviet world when viewed in the light of the concrete Soviet plan for the future.

Some observers contend that the description of Soviet intentions must necessarily remain vague, since the Kremlin's original zeal for refashioning the entire world into an exclusive Soviet pattern has been attenuated by the conservatism and inertia that overtake any vast bureaucratic apparatus as it becomes enmeshed in the difficulties of running a modern industrial society. The logic of industrialization and the demands of an efficient rational administration, it is held, will mellow a militant totalitarian regime, even one infused with an inexorable drive for boundless expansion, into a regime that is mildly authoritarian and capable of accommodation to the prevailing nation-state system. The Soviet leaders are undoubtedly subjected to certain sobering restraints by impersonal social and economic forces. But could not these impersonal forces also be manipulated and directed by the personal force of a political elite dedicated to the achievement of its own grandiose vision? If so, it becomes imperative to know precisely what it is that the Soviet leaders want.

Another much wider audience, less steeped in the concepts of an

INTRODUCTION

academic discipline, arrives at roughly the same conclusion—that the present inquiry is not a meaningful activity. This view springs from the perilous habit of wishful thinking. The West in general, and Americans in particular, tend to display a psychological resistance to facing up to the facts when the facts are unpleasant and forebode the worst. The perennial longing for an untroubled world, or simply the desire to be left alone, finds expression in reassuring self-deception. The prestige acquired from recent scientific and economic achievements has also made the Soviet regime increasingly admired and, among the wishful thinkers, increasingly accepted as a respectable member of the international community.

This study, unfortunately, can give no encouragement for complacency, since an examination of the evidence supplied by the Marxist heritage and developed abundantly by Soviet leaders and spokesmen has led to the conclusion that Soviet expectations and intentions constitute a well-delineated design for a world state.

The opening chapters are concerned with examining some of the direct evidence on this basic issue, as well as with analyzing other major Soviet doctrines that might seem contradictory to the Soviet aim of creating a world state. Then an attempt is made to derive from authoritative Soviet writings a picture of the structure and content of the world state that would follow from the logic of Soviet ideology, taking into account the important modifications of Soviet ideology that have resulted from its practical applications. Some of the questions inherent in this discussion are: How will political power be organized? Will the crucial decision-making groups be concentrated at a single nodal point, or are they to be distributed throughout the world so as to be more responsive to local needs? Is there to be a single highly integrated world economy? Is there an image of a single world culture and a single world language, and if so, what influence will existing national cultures and languages be likely to exert upon the character of these ultimate products?

Soviet methods for creating their world state are considered next, by contrasting Soviet statements concerning the completely voluntary nature of an ever-expanding Soviet state with the Soviet practice, grounded in theoretical justifications for war, of subjugating nations by means of crude military force. The question of other and rival supranational plans originating in the non-Soviet world is then examined to determine whether or not the Soviet leaders believe that any such projects might be reconciled with their own design. The study finally rounds out the Soviet image of the future by picturing the ultimate destiny of their intended world state as it is expressed in the doctrine of the withering away of this state and its transformation into a stateless world community.

Drawing the outlines of the Soviet design for a world state is also intended to bring into focus the fate of the contemporary nation-state system and thereby to stimulate serious reappraisal of supranational projects. The Bolshevik Revolution has ejected the world state idea from the scholar's cloister and has thrust a particular version of it into the arena of practical politics. Whether or not it is palatable to examine this idea in no way alters the remarkable persistence of the Soviet regime in pursuing its vision of a world state. This persistence has created a force that must surely be reckoned with in the reshaping of the world community.

The non-Soviet world can no longer afford to ignore a design which is explicitly aimed at destroying the contemporary system of international relations. Nor can we adequately respond to the Soviet challenge by constantly being placed on the defensive and viewing with complacency a fragmented non-Soviet world in the grip of an endless crisis. Confronted with the Soviet design for a world state, can the non-Soviet world confine itself to a precarious patchwork of expedients, or must it not conceive of its future in positive, creative terms and hammer out some common plan for its own survival, which might ultimately foster the genuine integration of all nations? The final chapter of this work is a brief, suggestive sketch of certain steps that might promote the healthful expansion of a supranational community, without, in the process, risking national suicide or destroying the precious freedoms of Western civilization. This points to conclusions that are not commonly accepted in the popular forum. Yet to be a realist in politics should include not only the realm of what is possible today, but also a careful scrutiny of what may become possible tomorrow.

E.R.G.

The Soviet Design
for a World State

I. Marx and Engels on the World State

MARX lived in a world of nation-states, and yet it was not the struggle between nations but the class struggle that held his attention. He believed that the tangible economic interests that unite social classes are stronger and more important than the more intangible complex of interests and emotions called nationalism.

THE EVALUATION OF NATIONALISM

While ambiguity is perhaps inherent in the very language of nationalism, the preoccupation of Marx and Engels with class rather than nation tended to make their treatment of nationalism especially vague and frequently arbitrary. It is true that they once defined a nation as being a great historic political entity, as distinguished from an ethnic group that had a common language but not an independent political existence. An ethnic group might or might not be entitled to be called a "nation" depending upon its role in history.[1] But generally speaking, as one scholar of Marxism has observed, Marx and Engels "used terms like 'national' and 'nation' with considerable looseness. Sometimes 'nation' was synonymous for 'country'; sometimes, for the quite different entity 'state.' Occasionally 'nation' stood for the ruling class of a country."[2] In any event, Marx did not conceive of a nation as a God-given entity, but only as a passing phase in the march of history. Since Marx viewed society as a dynamic, constantly changing organism, nations would have an end, just as they had had a beginning. The material forces of history, not nations, were sovereign. Once international class warfare had engulfed all nations, the loyalties that bound men to nations would be

[1] Engels, "What Have the Working Classes to Do with Poland?" 1866, in *Russian Menace*, p. 99.
[2] Solomon F. Bloom, *The World of Nations* (New York, 1941), p. 16.

readily dissolved and absorbed by the higher interests of an international class.

It is not surprising that in *The Communist Manifesto* Marx and Engels raised the battle cry, "the workers have no country," but it would be a mistake to take this statement at face value. The *Manifesto* explains, "we cannot take from them what they have not got. Since the proletariat must first of all acquire political supremacy, must rise to be the leading class of the nation, must constitute itself *the* nation, it is, so far, itself, national, though not in the bourgeois sense of the word." [3] Apparently Marx and Engels meant that no worker could rightfully call his country his own until the exploiting bourgeoisie had first been overthrown. Only then would the worker have a country worth defending. "Though not in substance, yet in form, the struggle of the proletariat with the bourgeoisie is at first a national struggle. The proletariat of each country must, of course, first of all settle matters with its own bourgeoisie." [4]

THE WHOLE WORLD THE ARENA

National revolution, Engels went on to say, is, per se, almost without meaning; in fact, he even doubted that an isolated national revolution would be possible. In his *Principles of Communism*, written in 1847, Engels asked: "Can this [proletarian] revolution take place in merely one country?"

The answer is no. Large-scale industry, by creating the world market, has established so close a connection among all the peoples of the globe, especially in the case of the civilized peoples, that each of them depends on what happens to the other. Then, too, large-scale industry has so levelled the social development in all civilized countries that everywhere the bourgeoisie and the proletariat have become the two determining social classes, and the struggle between them is the chief struggle of our time. The Communist revolution, therefore, will not be merely national, but will take place simultaneously in all civilized countries; that is, at least in England, America, France and Germany. It will also exercise a considerable influence upon the other countries of the world and will completely change and much accelerate their former course of development. It is a world revolution and will, therefore, have the whole world as its arena.[5]

[3] Marx and Engels, *Communist Manifesto*, 1848, p. 28.   [4] *Ibid.*, p. 20.
[5] Engels, "Printsipy kommunizma," 1847, in Marx and Engels, *Sochineniia* (Moscow, 1929), V, 476.

Apparently Engels thought that those nations which were not at first included in the proletarian revolution would be unable to withstand the power of attraction which the example of socialism would exert on them, so that they would soon fall into the socialist orbit. It seems too that he did not think that the ruling classes of the non-socialist nations could hold out for long against the pressures of the oppressed classes within them, much less muster enough force to crush those nations that had already established socialism.

From the countries Engels names, it is clear that he and Marx did not expect the revolution to start in Russia, but in the advanced industrial nations of the world. But when Marx began to study conditions in Russia in his later years, he discerned so great a potential for revolution there that he had to reconsider the order in which revolutions might occur. Any shock to the Tsarist autocracy, he wrote hopefully at the time of the Russo-Turkish War of 1877, might permit the East to be more revolutionary than the West. "This time the revolution will begin in the East, hitherto the unbroken bulwark and reserve army of counter-revolution." [6] And on the eve of Marx's death, Marx and Engels recorded in their preface to the second edition of *The Communist Manifesto*, written in 1882, that "today . . . Russia forms the vanguard of the revolutionary movement in Europe." [7] In speculating upon the possibility of revolution sweeping from East to West instead of from West to East, however, Marx and Engels at no time abandoned their cardinal precept that once revolution had begun it would "have the whole world as its arena." While suggesting that revolution might break out first in Russia, they emphasized time and again that backward Russia could make a rapid transition to socialism only if it were supported immediately by truly proletarian revolutions in the West.[8] The idea that

[6] Marx to Sorge, Sept. 27, 1877, in *Selected Correspondence*, p. 349.
[7] Marx and Engels, "The Communist Manifesto in Russian," 1882, in *Russian Menace*, p. 228. See also Engels, "Slavianskomu mitingu 21 marta 1881 g. v chest' godovshchiny parizhskoi kommuny," in Marx and Engels, *Sochineniia* (Moscow, 1935), XV, 552: "When [about ten years ago] the Paris Commune was crushed . . . the conquerors least of all thought of what ten years would bring, such as the events in far-off Petersburg which, after a struggle, possibly a long and cruel struggle, in the end must inevitably lead to the creation of a Russian Commune." In 1887 Engels wrote with almost unbridled optimism that "when the revolution breaks out in Russia, which is probably only a question of months, it can immediately be started in Germany too." (Engels to Sorge, April 23, 1887, in Marx and Engels, *Letters to Americans, 1848-1895* [New York, 1953], p. 184.)
[8] Marx, "Letter on the Russian Village Community," 1881, in *Russian Menace*,

revolution might *start* in Russia, but could only be saved and brought to completion if it received timely support from the West, anticipated closely the position that Trotsky was later to assume.

The international socialism of Marx and Engels, which consciously emphasized socialism at the expense of nationalism, stood in clear opposition to the proposals of national socialism that were advanced by some contemporary German Social Democrats. Georg Vollmar, pointing to the uneven development of capitalism in different countries, flatly contradicted Engels when he declared: "The assumption of a simultaneous victory of socialism in all cultured countries is absolutely ruled out, as is also, and for the same reasons, the assumption that all the rest of the civilized states will immediately and inevitably imitate the example of a socialistically organised state." This led Vollmar to the concept of "the isolated socialist state" which he admitted was "not the only possibility" but "nevertheless the greatest probability." [9]

This approach to the socialist revolution, which foreshadowed Stalin's theory of "socialism in one country," only brought derision from Marx. While Marx did not specifically answer Vollmar, he did attack Ferdinand Lassalle who, like Vollmar, advocated a variety of national socialism. In his *Critique of the Gotha Program*, Marx reprimanded Lassalle for viewing "the labor movement from the most narrow national standpoint." [10] Marx granted that "it is perfectly obvious that to be able to fight at all, the working class must organize at home as a class and that its own country is the immediate

---

p. 222. See also Engels, "Russia and Revolution Reconsidered," 1894, in *ibid.*, pp. 233-34, 241. Marx considered Russia's position anomalous in more ways than one. In 1877 he hinted, somewhat darkly, that the existence of the village commune might permit Russia to escape "all the sudden turns of fortune of the capitalist system" and presumably to make a direct transition to socialism. In *Capital*, Marx later remarked with astounding casualness, "I claim only to trace the path by which the capitalist order in Western Europe developed out of the feudal economic order." He upbraided those who sought "to change my sketch of the origin of capitalism in Western Europe into an historico-philosophical theory of a Universal Progress, fatally imposed on all peoples, regardless of the historical circumstances in which they find themselves." (Marx, "Letter on the Economic Development of Russia," 1877, in *Russian Menace*, p. 217.)

[9] Quoted in Trotsky, *Revolution Betrayed*, 1936, pp. 293-94. Vollmar's article, "Der Isolirte Sozialistische Staat," appeared in *Jahrbuch fur Sozialwissenschaft und Sozialpolitik*, Ludwig Richter, ed. (Zurich, 1879), pp. 59-75; cited in Trotsky, *Third International After Lenin*, 1928, p. 316.

[10] Marx, *Critique of the Gotha Program*, 1875, pp. 35-36.

arena of the struggle."[11] But, Marx asked, how is it possible to contain the struggle within " 'the framework of the existing national state' " (as the *Gotha Program* had put it) since " 'the framework of the existing national state' . . . is itself, again economically 'within the framework' of the world market and politically 'within the framework' of the system of states."[12] Economically the world is tied together so closely that the proletariat cannot have its sights restricted by national boundaries. *The Communist Manifesto* specifically distinguished the Communists from all other working-class parties because, "in the national struggles of the proletarians of the different countries, they point out and bring to the front the common interests of the entire proletariat, independently of all nationalities."[13] Marx was most insistent that it was the task of the proletariat "to make the revolution permanent . . . until the proletariat has conquered state power . . . not only in one country but in all the dominant countries of the world."[14]

Marx and Engels believed that the economic forces that were destined to create a world-wide proletarian revolution were already at work under capitalism, undermining national boundaries and preparing the world for its future socialist unity. *The Communist Manifesto* announced that "the conditions of bourgeois society are too narrow to comprise the wealth created by it."[15] This was so because

> the need of a constantly expanding market for its products chases the bourgeoisie over the whole surface of the globe. . . . The bourgeoisie has, through its exploitation of the world market, given a cosmopolitan character to production and consumption in every country. . . . It has drawn from under the feet of industry the national ground on which it stood. All old established national industries have been destroyed or are daily being destroyed. They are dislodged by new industries . . . that no longer work up indigenous raw material, but raw material drawn from the remotest zones; industries whose products are consumed, not only at home, but in every quarter of the globe. . . . In place of the old local and national seclusion and self-sufficiency, we have intercourse in

---

[11] *Ibid.*, p. 36.   [12] *Ibid.*, p. 37.
[13] Marx and Engels, *Communist Manifesto*, p. 22.
[14] Marx, "Address of the Central Council to the Communist League," 1850, in *Selected Works* (New York, 1933), II, 161. The phrase "Permanent Revolution" became especially associated with Trotsky, but as a matter of fact all the leading Bolsheviks claimed this passage as their own, Stalin included, each insisting on his own "legitimate" interpretation. See Stalin, *Sochineniia*, VI, 99-106, 362-80; VIII, 18-20.
[15] Marx and Engels, *Communist Manifesto*, p. 15.

every direction, universal interdependence of nations. And as in material, so also in intellectual production. The intellectual creations of individual nations become common property. National one-sidedness and narrow-mindedness become more and more impossible, and from the numerous national and local literatures there arises a world literature.[16]

THE CONDITION FOR WORLD PEACE

When the world had become unified under a rule of socialism, all tensions between nations would be so diminished that all hateful differences, rivalries, national exploitation, and wars would be utterly erased from the face of the earth. While international socialism was not expected to produce a universal cultural uniformity, at least not at first, Marx and Engels apparently believed that all harmful differences between nations would soon be doomed to oblivion.

The national differences and antagonisms between peoples are daily more and more vanishing, owing to the development of the bourgeoisie, to freedom of commerce, to the world market, to the uniformity in the mode of production and in the corresponding conditions of life. The supremacy of the proletariat will cause them to vanish still faster. . . . In proportion as the exploitation of one individual by another is put to an end, the exploitation of one nation by another will also be put to an end. In proportion as the antagonism between classes within the nation vanishes, so will the hostility of one nation to another come to an end.[17]

This reduces all the causes that might lead to war to one phenomenon: the economic exploitation of man by man. Being an economic determinist, Marx believed that, at bottom, only economic exploitation really mattered, since the political and social forms of any society are dependent upon the economic base that supports those institutions. As soon as the "forces and relations of production" were brought into adjustment under a system of socialism, *all* types of exploitation must disappear. Marx could not conceive of the possibility of man being oppressed and exploited by the exercise of *political* power in a state that had socialized all forms of property, since, for him, political power did not exist as a force in its own right, capable of exploitation regardless of the economic base upon which it rested. He would not concede that the love of power might be more dangerous than the love of money, or that the two might ever be separated. The dangers of the love of money, rooted in the institutions of private property, would vanish with the socialization

[16] *Ibid.*, pp. 12–13. [17] *Ibid.*, p. 28.

of the means of production, and upon this new economic base the dangers of the love of power in all its forms would simply melt away as a matter of course. All that need be done was to establish socialism throughout the world and all the causes of war would automatically disappear.

Engels expressed the corollary of this idea, namely, that so long as capitalism existed, neither a just world order nor a lasting peace could be attained. He blamed the liberal, bourgeois democratic leaders of the Revolution of 1848 for dangling before the people a vision of world order which, he insisted, could only issue from a world proletarian revolution. "We have often enough called attention to the fact that the gentle dreams . . . such as the sentimental fantasies of a universal brotherhood of peoples, of a European Federative Republic and eternal world peace, were basically nothing more than the disguises for the boundless perplexity and inactivity of the spokesmen of the time." Such ideas would only take on meaning with a socialist revolution, but "instead of revolutionary deeds the people received only sentimental phrases." [18] Bakunin likewise came under attack for participating in the 1848 Slav Congress in Prague. The Congress issued a Manifesto which advocated not only a federation of Slav nations, but also a "general Federation of European Republics." Engels claimed that even though these proposals were clad in revolutionary terminology, they were only pseudo-revolutionary since all Slav nations, except the Poles, were in fact counterrevolutionary. Whether these fond hopes spring from East or West "the 'European brotherhood of peoples' will not come into being through empty phrases and pious wishes, but only through thoroughgoing revolutions and bloody struggles." [19] Engels explained that "the fantasy of a European Republic, of eternal peace under a political organization," was a typical product of "bourgeois phrasemaking."

The bourgeoisie has its own special interest in each country, and since this interest is always supreme, they can never go beyond the limitations of nationalism. . . . Proletarians, on the other hand, have one and the same interest, one and the same enemy, one and the same struggle before them in all countries. The great majority of proletarians are, by nature,

---

[18] Engels, "Democratic Panslavism," 1849, in *Russian Menace*, p. 67.
[19] *Ibid.*, pp. 68–69. Another caustic reference to "the bourgeois Peace League's 'United States of Europe'" may be found in Engels to Bebel, March 18, 1875, in *Selected Correspondence*, p. 334.

devoid of national prejudices, and their whole outlook and movement are essentially humanitarian and anti-national. None but the proletarians can destroy nationalism; only the awakening proletariat can establish the brotherhood of nations.[20]

THE FORM OF THE PROLETARIAN WORLD STATE

Engels alluded to the state form of this future brotherhood of nations as a "World Republic." During the lifetime of Marx and Engels, the abortive and scattered attempts of the proletariat to seize and organize state power in the Revolution of 1848 were crowned with the momentary success of the Paris Commune of 1871. Though this experiment in proletarian state rule was extremely short-lived, and though its writ of authority was confined to the city of Paris, Marx and Engels greeted it as "a new point of departure of world historic importance," [21] and as "the glorious harbinger of a new society." [22] The Paris Commune foreshadowed the coming of a proletarian world state, and for this reason Engels hailed the motto of the Communards that "the flag of the Commune is the flag of the World Republic." [23]

Marx characterized the state form of this World Republic as a "revolutionary dictatorship of the proletariat," designed to endure for a transitional interim, "a period of revolutionary transformation" lying "between capitalist and Communist society." [24] When the proletariat had established its revolutionary dictatorship throughout the world, would each nation have its own dictatorship of the proletariat, with the various nations loosely bound by some sort of confederate or federal tie in a World Republic, or would there be one highly centralized dictatorship of the proletariat for the entire world? If we were to frame an answer based solely on economic considerations, it would seem undeniable that Marx would have preferred centralization to federation. Capitalism had already made the existing national state obsolete, and national seclusion and self-

[20] Engels, "Das Fest der Nationen in London; zur Feier der Errichtung der Französischen Republik, 22 September 1792," in Franz Mehring, ed., *Aus dem Literarischen Nachlass von Karl Marx, Friedrich Engels und Ferdinand Lassalle, Vol. II, Gesammelte Schriften von Karl Marx und Friedrich Engels von Juli 1844 bis November 1847* (Stuttgart, 1902), pp. 405–6.
[21] Marx to Kugelmann, April 17, 1871, in *Selected Correspondence*, p. 311.
[22] Marx, *Civil War in France*, 1871, p. 81.
[23] Engels, "Introduction," 1891, in Marx, *ibid.*, p. 14.
[24] Marx, *Critique of the Gotha Program*, pp. 44–45.

sufficiency were becoming more and more impossible. Marx criticized Proudhon, who advocated a loose federalist structure for society, on the grounds that only a thoroughly integrated, centralized society could provide that highly productive economy upon which socialism was to be based. At one point Marx praised the Commune of 1871 for its alleged rejection of federalism. "The Communal Constitution has been mistaken for an attempt to break up into a federation of small states, as dreamt of by Montesquieu and the Girondins, that unity of great nations, which, if originally brought about by political force, has now become a powerful coefficient of social production." [25] Engels, in his 1891 introduction to this work, reiterated the importance of centralization:

> By far the most important decree of the Commune instituted an organization of large-scale industry and even of manufacture which was not based only on the association of workers in each factory, but also aimed at combining all of these associations in one great union; in short an organization which, as Marx quite rightly says . . . must necessarily have led in the end to communism, that is . . . the direct antithesis to the Proudhon doctrine.[26]

Engels concluded that "the proletariat can only use the form of the one and indivisible republic." [27]

Though Marx and Engels rejected federalism on economic grounds, it seems that in certain exceptional cases involving difficulties among ethnic groups Marx did condone federation as a second-best. But when Marx considered federation, it always seemed to come as an afterthought. Neither he nor Engels paid much attention to the possibilities of federalism as a serious political principle which could be used to ease the national problem within a multinational union. Nor did they show much interest in federalism as a means of linking together various independent nation-states of different ethnic origins. In fact Marx and Engels had no theory for the self-determination of nations which might point the way to the evolution of a higher unity of nations, no consistent policy for the liberation of subject nations to bring them to a status of independence, and no program for their further integration, as nations, into a world society. The explanation for this is quite simple: Marx and Engels

---

[25] Marx, *Civil War in France*, p. 59.
[26] Engels, "Introduction," in Marx, *ibid.*, p. 19.
[27] Engels, "K kritike proekta sotsial-demokraticheskoi programmy 1891 g.," June 29, 1891, in Marx and Engels, *Sochineniia* (Moscow, 1936), XVI, Part 2, 110.

were not interested in nations as ethnic groups but only as agents of revolution, and when they dealt with a problem of national independence or federalism it was only because it was forced upon them by the exigencies of the revolutionary situation. Their image of the world dictatorship of the proletariat did not accord any special role to nations, and it would seem that nations would be retained or disregarded according to the dictates of administrative efficiency. Certainly nationality would have no special claim in their world proletarian state, since Marx and Engels specifically stated that "the Communist revolution . . . is in itself the expression of the dissolution of all classes, nationalities, etc., within present society." [28]

This lack of regard for nationality is demonstrated by Engels's attitude toward Alsace-Lorraine while it was still a part of France before the Franco-Prussian War of 1870. Engels thought that it was ridiculous for Germany to demand Alsace-Lorraine "which in all respects belongs to France, under the pretext that the majority of the population there is Germanic." [29] In Eastern Europe, on the other hand, Marx and Engels championed the ethnic rights of the Poles and demanded the reemergence of an independent Poland. But this they did only because they felt that a united Poland would be a powerful revolutionary force which might strike a fatal blow at the heart of autocratic Russia and serve similarly to cripple the German and Austrian monarchies, the three beneficiaries of the successive partitions of Poland. As to the other Slavs of Eastern Europe, Engels stated his views quite frankly: "Now you may ask me whether I have no sympathy whatever for the small Slavic peoples, and remnants of peoples, which have been severed asunder by the three wedges driven into the flesh of Slavdom: the Germans, Magyars and Turks? In fact I have damned little sympathy for them." [30]

In the Austro-Hungarian Empire only the Germans, Magyars, and Poles were considered worthy of attention since they were advanced, revolutionary nations, "the carriers of progress." [31] To Engels it was inconceivable that a nation like Czechoslovakia could emerge from Austria-Hungary. "The Austrian Slavs never had a

---

[28] Marx and Engels, *German Ideology*, 1846, p. 69.
[29] Engels, "Democratic Panslavism," in *Russian Menace*, pp. 81–82; Engels, "What Have the Working Classes to Do with Poland?" in *ibid.*, p. 99.
[30] Engels, "Nationalism, Internationalism, and the Polish Question," 1882, in *ibid.*, p. 119.
[31] Engels, "Hungary and Panslavism," 1849, in *ibid.*, p. 59.

history of their own . . . they are historically, literarily, politically, commercially and industrially dependent on the Germans and Magyars. . . . Neither Hungary nor Germany can tolerate the secession and independent constitution of such tiny buffer states which would be unfit for life." [32] Rumania would come off no better since "the Roumans of Wallachia . . . never had a history, nor the energy required to have one." [33]

For the Slavs living under the rule of the Turkish Empire, Engels could only find contempt. He hardly bothered to cast a disparaging glance at "the almost nomadic barbarism of the Croats and the Bulgarians." [34] The question of the future of these peoples seems to have been one of the very rare instances in which the views of Engels differed somewhat from those of Marx. Marx reprimanded the Western powers on the eve of the Crimean War for not hastening the disintegration of feudal Turkey. He complained that they were "too timid to undertake the reconstruction of the Ottoman Empire by the establishment of a Greek Empire, or of a Federal Republic of Slavonic States," [35] that is, by the creation of independent states that would coincide roughly with present-day Greece, Bulgaria, and Yugoslavia (the latter two forming a single federal state). Apparently Marx felt that the liberation of these nations would be a step toward social revolution in the Ottoman Empire and that at the same time they could serve as effective advanced bases of the Western powers in their struggle with counterrevolutionary Russia.

In the case of Ireland's relations with England, Marx held contradictory views. During the 1840s he opposed Irish independence because he felt it was to Ireland's advantage to be an integral part of England's great industrial economy.[36] When no revolution occurred

[32] Engels, "Democratic Panslavism," in *ibid.*, p. 77.
[33] Engels, "What Have the Working Classes to Do with Poland?" in *ibid.*, p. 100.
[34] Engels, "Hungary and Panslavism," in *ibid.*, p. 62.
[35] Marx, "Traditional Russian Policy," 1853, in *ibid.*, p. 164. This disagreement between Marx and Engels was not very sharp, since at one point Engels came close to conceding that the South Slavs might be constituted as a nation: "Except for the Poles, the Russians, and at best the Slavs in Turkey, no Slavic people has a future"; Engels, "Democratic Panslavism," in *ibid.*, p. 72. Of all the South Slavs, Marx looked with particular favor upon the Serbs as the nucleus of the struggle for independence from Turkey. See Marx's article in the New York *Tribune*, April 21, 1853; quoted in D. Riazanov, ed., *Ocherki po istorii Marksizma* (Moscow, 1923), p. 600.
[36] Bloom, *World of Nations*, p. 38.

in England during the 1850s and 1860s Marx changed his mind. In 1867 he stated: "I used to think the separation of Ireland from England impossible. I now think it inevitable, although after the separation there may come *federation*." [37] Again, the reason that motivated this change of front was based solely upon considerations of revolutionary tactics. Marx explained that he had become convinced that the English proletariat could "never do anything decisive here in England until it separates its policy with regard to Ireland . . . from the policy of the ruling classes, until it not only makes common cause with the Irish, but actually takes the initiative in dissolving the Union established in 1801, and replacing it by a free federal relationship." [38] Realizing that sooner or later a break was inevitable, Marx wanted to use this issue as a means of intensifying class warfare in England. He did not advocate Irish independence because of his love of small or backward peoples nor because of a desire to break the world up into a number of small states. On the contrary, he hoped that Irish independence would be followed by federation with England, since his primary goal had always been a union that would not be complicated by the operation of any centrifugal forces. Federation for Marx was only an expedient and transitional measure for the reintegration of Ireland with England, and he resorted to it as a way of readjusting the unsatisfactory union then in existence.

Applying these attitudes on a world scale, once the world proletarian revolution had succeeded, it would seem that Marx favored a highly centralized world dictatorship of the proletariat, modified by the federal principle only if necessary, and then only as a transitory measure to complete centralism.

WORLD STATE TRANSFORMED INTO NO STATE

As all class contradictions disappeared and the world socialist society became productive enough to support an economy that could reward people according to their needs, rather than according to their ability, then the dictatorship of the proletariat would give way to full communism. At this point it would not be appropriate to call the Marxian vision a world state, since all economic exploitation of man by man would be eliminated, peace would reign su-

[37] Marx to Engels, Nov. 2, 1867, in *Selected Correspondence*, p. 228.
[38] Marx to Kugelmann, Nov. 29, 1869, in *ibid.*, p. 278.

preme, and the need for state power would have vanished. Rather, the world state would become no state.

Engels presented two contradictory explanations for the emergence of the state, but was unambiguous about its ultimate destiny. In 1877 he implied that the state, in some form, had always existed. "The state," he suggested, had first served "primitive groups of communities of the same tribe . . . only for safeguarding their common interests (such as irrigation in the East) and providing protection against external enemies." It was the emergence of class differences in society that transformed the state into an instrument for "maintaining by force the economic and political position of the ruling class against the subject class."[39] In 1884, however, Engels asserted flatly that "the state . . . has not existed from all eternity."[40] Here he pictured society as springing from primordial communism in which there was neither private property nor class distinctions, nor a state. The state came into being only as a coercive mechanism of the exploiting class after the stage of primitive communism had supposedly given way to a society torn by class antagonism based on the development of private property.[41] But irrespective of its origin, Engels's prediction on the future of the state was unvarying.

We are now rapidly approaching a stage in the development of production at which the existence of these classes has not only ceased to be a necessity, but becomes a positive hindrance to production. They will fall as inevitably as they once arose. The state inevitably falls with them. The society which organizes production anew on the basis of free and equal association of the producers will put the whole state machinery where it will then belong—into the museum of antiquities, next to the spinning wheel and the bronze axe.[42]

This new classless and stateless society was to be the fruit of the proletarian revolution, and it would be ready for plucking after a temporary proletarian semistate had performed its duties. Marx had pointed to the Paris Commune as the model for this transitional form of the dictatorship of the proletariat. It was organized on principles that were supposed to insure not only the destruction of bourgeois state power, but, after a transitional period, of proletarian state power as well. The first decree of the Commune abolished the standing army and put in its place a people's militia in which all would

[39] Engels, *Dühring's Revolution in Science*, 1877, p. 165.
[40] Engels, *Origin of the Family*, 1884, p. 158.
[41] *Ibid.*, pp. 6, 96–97, 154–55, 159. [42] *Ibid.*, p. 158.

serve "an extremely short term of service." The permanent "police was at once stripped of its political attributes, and turned into the responsible and at all times revocable agent of the Commune." The old permanent state bureaucracy was replaced by a public administration devoid of all privilege, in which all could participate, subject to immediate recall. To prevent the rise of a bureaucratic caste, all "public service had to be done at *workingmen's wages*." In like manner, "magistrates and judges were to be elected, responsible and revocable." The governing body of the Commune itself was to be chosen by universal suffrage and subject to recall on short notice. "The Commune was to be a working, not a parliamentary body, the executive and legislative at the same time." This was to be a kind of state power in which "the merely repressive organs of the old governmental power were to be amputated" and the rest of its functions performed with such full participation of the population that no new permanent state apparatus could be erected.[43]

Engels once expressed the fear that the old repressive state machinery used against the proletariat might make its reappearance in a new guise and that therefore the proletariat must "safeguard itself against its own deputies and officials by declaring them all, without exception, subject to recall at any moment." He wanted to avoid the danger of an untouchable state apparatus standing above society. In the United States, for example, Engels claimed that he had discerned "this process of the state power making itself independent in relation to society, whose mere instrument it was originally intended to be." But he was confident that if the proletarian state used the "infallible expedients" of the Commune, such as the right of immediate recall, placing all administrative, judicial, and educative posts on an elective basis, and paying "all officials, high or low" only the wages of other workers, then proletarian state power could never become detached from and stand above society. These devices would prevent the "transformation of the state and the organs of the state from servants of society into masters of society." [44]

If Engels had pursued this thought that the state sometimes detaches itself from society, becomes "independent in relation to society," logically he would have arrived at the conclusion that the state must be something more than the reflection of the economic

[43] Marx, *Civil War in France*, pp. 57–58.
[44] Engels, "Introduction," in Marx, *ibid.*, pp. 20–21.

interests of the ruling class, something more than a simple instrument of class oppression. Possibly aware of the contradiction involved, Engels did not pursue this idea, but added in almost the next breath that "in reality, however, the state is nothing but a machine for the oppression of one class by another." This was an inherited evil "whose worse side the proletariat, just like the Commune, cannot avoid having to lop off at the earliest possible moment, until such time as a new generation, reared in new and free social conditions, will be able to throw the entire lumber of the state on the scrap-heap." [45]

Engels also described the process by which state power would disappear: "The interference of state power in social relations becomes superfluous in one sphere after another, and then ceases of itself. The government of persons is replaced by the administration of things, and the direction of the process of production. The state is not 'abolished,' *it withers away*." [46] *The Communist Manifesto* described what remains as "an association in which the free development of each is the condition for the free development of all." "Public power will lose its political character. Political power, properly so called, is merely the organized power of one class for oppressing another." [47]

---

[45] *Ibid.*, p. 22. A more startling aberration on the function of the state appears in a passage in Marx, where one finds the curious question, "what change will the form of the state undergo in Communist society?" and the phrase, "the future forms of the state in Communist society." (Marx, *Critique of the Gotha Program*, pp. 44-45.) If here Marx actually meant to say that the state, in some form or other, would be needed in the future Communist society, then he stood in total contradiction to everything else he and Engels wrote on this subject. If one assumes that this was only a careless and inexact use of words, then that would only prove that Marx too could make errors. Lenin was obviously embarrassed by these passages and offered this reassuring interpretation that tried to obliterate the contradiction: "It might appear that Marx was much more 'pro-state' than Engels, and that the difference of opinion between the two authors on the question of the state was very considerable. Engels suggested . . . that the word 'state' be eliminated from the [Gotha] Program and the word 'community' be substituted for it. Engels even declared that the Commune was really no longer a state in the proper sense of the word, yet Marx spoke of the 'future state in Communist society,' i.e., apparently he recognized the need for a state even under communism. But such a view would be fundamentally wrong. A closer examination shows that the views of Marx and Engels on the state and its withering away were completely identical, and that Marx's phrase quoted above refers merely to the *withering away* of the state." (Lenin, "Gosudarstvo i revoliutsiia," Aug.-Sept., 1917, in *Sochineniia*, XXI, 427.)

[46] Engels, *Dühring's Revolution in Science*, p. 307.

[47] Marx and Engels, *Communist Manifesto*, p. 31.

This ideal of a stateless society differs from that of the anarchists in two fundamental respects. Marx revealed the first difference in his controversy with Bakunin. "The Alliance [Bakunin's group] has put the matter backwards. It proclaims anarchy in the ranks of the proletariat as the most infallible means of breaking up the powerful concentration of social and political forces in the hands of the exploiters." Marx explained that the powerful concentrations of social and political forces cannot simply be destroyed, but must be taken over by the proletariat and used by them as the basis for their transitional state, the dictatorship of the proletariat. Marx then defined in what way socialism coincides with anarchism.

What all socialists understand by anarchism is this: as soon as the goal of the proletarian movement, the abolition of classes, shall have been reached, the power of the state, whose function it is to keep the great majority of producers beneath the yoke of a small minority of exploiters, will disappear and governmental functions will be transformed into simple administrative functions.[48]

The second difference between the anarchists and Marx in their concept of a world proletarian stateless society is that the anarchists advocated a form of federalism, while Marx insisted upon centralism. This reflected their basic difference of emphasis, the anarchists centering their attention upon the "free personality" of the individual with little regard for the economic processes of society, Marx concentrating upon the organization of the economic forces of society as a means of freeing the individual. Marx equally disliked all schemes for a "free federation of communes," whether proposed by Proudhon, Bakunin, or any of their followers. Engels, in his *Socialism, Utopian and Scientific*, made Marx's centralist views quite explicit. One of the great benefits of proletarian society is that

social anarchy of production gives place to a social regulation of production upon a definite plan, according to the needs of the community and of each individual.

. . . . .

Socialized production upon a predetermined plan . . . makes the existence of different classes of society thenceforth an anachronism. *In proportion as anarchy in social production vanishes, the political authority of the state dies out.*[49]

[48] Marx, *Les prétendues scissions dans l'Internationale*, 1872 (Geneva, 1872), p. 37.
[49] Engels, *Socialism, Utopian and Scientific*, 1877, pp. 41, 47 (italics added).

That is, the state will die out at the very point when socialized production has reached the pinnacle of centralization, since the state can vanish only when all anarchy in production has been eliminated through the operation of a centrally planned economy. This is the Marxian view of the ultimate world society, highly centralized, but without any organs of political power, centralization without compulsion.

THE METAMORPHOSIS OF MAN

The prospect of this kind of a stateless world society did not seem the least bit incredible to Marx and Engels. As a matter of fact, they calmly asserted that "people will be able to manage everything very simply" by basing the economic plan directly upon the calculation of the labor value contained in different products. They believed that society would "arrange its plan of production in accordance with its means of production, which include, in particular, its labor forces. The useful effects of the various articles of consumption, compared with each other and with the quantity of labor required for their production, will in the last analysis, determine the plan." [50] This future planned society, while permitting people "to manage everything very simply," would, at the same time, require more stringent controls over the disposition of labor and a more exacting system of bookkeeping and economic calculation than had existed under capitalism. As Marx foresaw it in *Capital*, "after the abolition of the capitalist mode of production ... the determination of value continues to prevail in such a way that the regulation of the labor time and the distribution of the social labor among the various groups of production, also the keeping of accounts in connection with this, become more essential than ever." [51]

If it is true, as Marx noted, that "regulation and order are themselves indispensable elements of any mode of production," [52] then the future organization of the productive process must also be subject to strict regulation and discipline. "All labors," Marx generalized, "in which many individuals cooperate, necessarily require

[50] Engels, *Dühring's Revolution in Science*, p. 338.
[51] Marx, *Capital*, III, 992. I am indebted to Professor Solomon F. Bloom for bringing this reference, as well as the material cited in the two subsequent footnotes, to my attention.
[52] *Ibid.*, III, 921.

for the connection and unity of the process one commanding will, and this performs a function . . . in the same way as does that of a director of an orchestra."[53]

What was the significance of likening the joint labor process to the functioning of an orchestra? The orchestra metaphor was also the common property of the anarchists, who used it to imply that in the future society everyone would know his proper function and would voluntarily and automatically work in harmony with his fellow man in the absence of any external coercive authority. Marx seemed to be saying much the same thing when he remarked that under capitalism "the fanatic hankering of the capitalist after economies" was in part responsible for "the discipline exerted over them [the workers] by the capitalist." But, Marx added, "this discipline will become superfluous under a social system in which the laborers work for their own account."[54] That is, while all forms of the joint labor process demand discipline, or as Marx put it, "one commanding will," in the future society the exploitative discipline exercised by the capitalist over the workers would be replaced by an equally firm, but nonexploitative, self-discipline exerted by the workers over themselves. Upon such self-discipline would be founded the well-ordered, harmonious society of the future.

Marx and Engels were the first to admit that man in his presently debased condition would not be able to live in or successfully operate the future society. But they believed in the infinite perfectibility of man and were convinced that once socialism enveloped the world all of man's latent talents would blossom forth and all of his ugly habits quickly wither away. Just as socialism would remove the cause of collective strife, and thus render war obsolete, similarly socialism would remove all obstacles to man's individual development. They freely acknowledged that "the alteration of man on a mass scale is necessary," but added that it is "an alteration which can only take place in a practical movement, a *revolution* . . . only in a revolution [can the proletariat] succeed in ridding itself of all the muck of ages and become fitted to found society anew."[55]

The attainments of this new proletarian man can hardly be overestimated—in fact, he will become omnicompetent. Everyone will be able to do everything and no one will be expected to limit his

[53] *Ibid.*, III, 451. Marx repeats the orchestra metaphor in *ibid.*, I, 363; III, 455.
[54] *Ibid.*, III, 100.   [55] Marx and Engels, *German Ideology*, p. 69.

activity at any one pursuit. The institutionalized division of labor of bourgeois society stifles the worker's capacities and degrades his dignity as a human being. The future society will abolish the division of labor and, with it, "the distinction between manual and intellectual work." Instead of labor being merely a means of making a living, it will be elevated to the "prime necessity of life," [56] and all labor will become interchangeable.

In Communist society, where no one has an exclusive sphere of activity but each can become accomplished in any branch he wishes, society regulates the general production and thus makes it possible for me to do one thing today and another tomorrow, to hunt in the morning, fish in the afternoon, rear cattle in the evening, criticize after dinner, just as I have a mind, without ever becoming a hunter, fisherman, shepherd or critic.[57]

Marx and Engels apparently found no difficulty in reconciling the existence of this highly mobile man with the concomitant operation of a highly centralized, strictly regulated planned world society.

Another consequence of a society that develops "the harmonious cooperation of its productive forces on the basis of one single vast plan" is that it will make possible "the abolition of the antithesis between town and country." Engels insisted that the destruction of "the separation between town and country is not utopian, even insofar as it presupposes the most equal distribution possible of large-scale industry." At the same time, Engels admitted that this process might not be easy since "it is true that in the huge towns, civilization has bequeathed us a heritage to rid ourselves of, which will take much time and trouble. But this heritage must and will be got rid of, however protracted the process may be." [58]

What loyalties will this omnicompetent man hold, this man who cannot be characterized as a physical or a mental laborer, moving about in a society in which there is no separation between town and country? Will this man be a free-floating individual, devoid of any attachment to family or nation, will he be the ultimate cosmopolitan, or will he still retain some of these intermediate loyalties?

Certainly the bonds of the bourgeois family will be dissolved, for Engels thought of the bourgeois family as nothing more than a hypocritical commercial transaction. Under communism men and

[56] Marx, *Critique of the Gotha Program*, p. 31.
[57] Marx and Engels, *German Ideology*, p. 22.
[58] Engels, *Dühring's Revolution in Science*, pp. 323-24.

women would mate purely on the basis of desire, unencumbered by any economic considerations. As "the intense emotion of individual sex-love varies much in duration from one individual to another, especially among men," Engels concluded that "if affection definitely comes to an end or is supplanted by a new passionate love, separation is a benefit for both partners as well as for society." [59] It would seem that Engels's conception of marital love could be reduced to the word "lust." Under this arrangement society-at-large would assume many of the functions that formerly devolved upon the family. Engels envisioned a future in which "private house-keeping is transformed into a social industry. The care and education of children becomes a public affair." [60] If the family is to have this destiny, what will be the fate of nations?

THE FATE OF NATIONS

When Marx and Engels said that the state would wither away, it is not clear whether they assumed that the disappearance of the state would also mean the disappearance of nations. As Gsovski has pointed out, "It is somewhat uncertain whether Marx and Engels used the word 'state' (*der Staat, l'état*) to denote the nation as a separately existing body politic or as the governmental machinery." Gsovski feels that this "term is used to indicate both, because the Marxian philosophy is offered as an international plan, and hence the individually existing national states were supposed to merge in an international association of classless societies. Thus the proposition of the 'withering away of the state' apparently implied both the merger of national states and the end of government within the states." [61]

Bloom, on the other hand, does not believe that Marx anticipated such a merger of national states. He draws the conclusion that Marx "was decidedly not a cosmopolite in his picture of a world order although there were many traces of cosmopolitanism in his thought.... Marx rejected the vague and amorphous global society.... The socialist world of his imagination consisted of a limited number of advanced nations." [62] It would be surprising if there were not some disagreement among scholars on this point,

[59] Engels, *Origin of the Family*, p. 73.   [60] *Ibid.*, p. 67.
[61] Vladimir Gsovski, *Soviet Civil Law* (Ann Arbor, Mich., 1948), I, 171.
[62] Bloom, *World of Nations*, p. 207.

for neither Marx nor Engels clearly delineated the ultimate fate which they expected for nations.

It is clear, however, that Marx and Engels looked to a few great nations as carriers of civilization (i.e., revolution) and that all those nations not so classified were marked for obliteration. Engels, writing in 1849, described the role of different nations in this manner:

> There is no country in Europe which does not contain in some corner one or several ruins of peoples, left-overs of earlier inhabitants, pushed back by and made subject to the nation which later became the carrier of historical development. These remains of nations which have been mercilessly trampled down by the passage of history, as Hegel expressed it, this ethnic trash always becomes and remains until its *complete extermination or denationalization*, the most fanatic carrier of counterrevolution, since its entire existence is nothing more than a protest against a great historical revolution. Such in Scotland were the Gaels. . . . Such in France were the Bretons. . . . Such in Spain were the Basques. . . . Such in Austria are the Panslavist South Slavs, who are nothing more than the waste product of a highly confused development which has gone on for a thousand years.[63]

The only nations worth saving in the Austrian Empire were the Germans, Magyars, and Poles. "The chief mission of all the other races and peoples—large and small—is to perish in the revolutionary holocaust." [64]

A counterrevolutionary nation might "perish," according to Engels, either by its complete extermination or by denationalization. Denationalization had presumably occurred among the Slavic tribes, such as the Wends or Lusatian Sorbs, who had once filtered into central Germany. At first mercilessly subjugated by the German sword, their national culture had been progressively swallowed up in the dominant German cultural sea. Engels was gratified to observe that "these stretches of Slavic territory have been completely Germanized," and that "this conquest was in the interests of civilization." [65] The pressures set loose by denationalization, however, might easily spill over into extermination. When Engels praised the Germans and the Magyars for their services to the backward Slavs, for their binding "these tiny, crippled, powerless little nations together

---

[63] Engels, "Hungary and Panslavism," in *Russian Menace*, p. 63 (italics added).
[64] *Ibid.*, p. 59.
[65] Engels, "Democratic Panslavism," in *Russian Menace*, p. 75. Engels's claim was somewhat premature, since Wendish continued to be spoken for almost another century.

in a great Empire," he also indicated that he was not particular about the way in which this "ethnic trash" was dumped into the garbage can of history. "To be sure," Engels added, "such a thing is not carried through without forcibly crushing many a delicate little national flower. But without force and without an iron ruthlessness nothing is accomplished in history." [66] Mankind will be impelled toward its destiny of universal peace and brotherhood by revolutionary war and genocide. Engels predicted that

> with the first victorious uprising of the French proletariat . . . the Germans and Magyars in Austria will become free and will take bloody revenge on the Slavic barbarians. The general war which will then break out will explode this Slavic league [i.e., the Pan-Slav Movement] and these petty, bullheaded nations will be destroyed so that nothing is left of them but their names.
>
> The next world war will cause not only reactionary classes and dynasties but also entire reactionary peoples to disappear from the earth. And that too would be progress.[67]

It is undeniable that Marx and Engels glorified the role of a few great nations as agents of revolution, but does this necessarily mean that these nations were to maintain a position of glory which would be undiminished with the passage of time or the vital alteration of circumstance? Once these nations had performed their revolutionary tasks would they remain forever as powerful entities in a proletarian world state and even after that in a world stateless society? To return to our unanswered query: What is the Marxist image of the ultimate fate of nations?

The Communist Manifesto indicated that the proletariat, even in the few great revolutionary nations, had already discarded its attachment to a national group. "The proletarian is without property . . . modern subjection to capital, the same in England as in France, in America as in Germany, has stripped him of every trace of national character." [68] This description of the alleged strength of national feelings among the proletariat refers to the situation before the proletarian revolution. The revolution will presumably hasten this trend since "the Communist revolution," Marx and Engels prophesied in 1846, "is in itself the expression of the dissolution of all classes, nationalities, etc., within present society." [69]

[66] *Ibid.*, p. 76.
[67] Engels, "Hungary and Panslavism," in *Russian Menace*, p. 67.
[68] Marx and Engels, *Communist Manifesto*, p. 20.
[69] Marx and Engels, *German Ideology*, p. 69.

Some twenty years later Marx modified significantly this rather categorical judgment on the unimportance of nationality. Following a meeting of the General Council of the First International which had discussed the Austro-Prussian War of 1866, Marx faced up to the persistence of strong national antagonisms even among the "enlightened" representatives of the proletariat. He went further and chastised those who sought to ignore the nationality issue, or to define it out of existence. In a letter to Engels, Marx recorded how he had twitted those Frenchmen who "came out with the announcement that all nationalities and even nations were 'antiquated prejudices.'"

The English laughed very much when I began my speech by saying that our friend Lafargue, etc., who had done away with nationalities, has spoken "French" to us, i.e., a language which nine-tenths of the audience did not understand. I also suggested that by the negation of nationalities he appeared, quite unconsciously, to understand their absorption into the model French nation.[70]

Experience had apparently taught Marx that proletarians of different nationalities had not been entirely stripped of "every trace of national character" and that the Communist revolution could not therefore be expected instantly "to dissolve" all nationalities.

Neither Marx nor Engels gave any indication, however, that they had revised their long-range estimate of the significance of nationality and nations, nor had they altered their opinion of the ultimate cause of national conflicts. For them, class attachments remained primary, national affiliations accidental and secondary, so that once the proletarian revolution had removed the economic basis for national conflicts and had reorganized all life according to a new, harmonious, international proletarian plan, the importance attached to national differences would steadily decline. The assumption that world revolution would eventually diminish the strength and stature of all nations, as nations, would likewise be in line with the very pronounced centralist tendencies of Marxist thought, since the more each major nation retained its historic identity the more powerful would be the impetus toward a federalist rather than a centralist political structure. It is conceivable that in their view the proletarian world state might be forced to evolve through federal forms to achieve complete centralism, but they pointed clearly in the direc-

[70] Marx to Engels, June 20, 1866, in *Selected Correspondence*, p. 208.

tion of centralism and hence of the consequent dissolution and merger of all nations, including those few great historic bodies that once received their boundless praise. This "amorphous global society" would not be expected to materialize during the initial stages of the proletarian world state. But as the world state withered away, nations would fuse, and the ultimate world community would evolve from an international into a cosmopolitan world society.

THE SOVIET ELABORATION OF MARXIST DOCTRINE

How have the Soviet leaders developed their Marxist heritage? In order to answer such a comprehensive question satisfactorily, it is necessary to break it down into its major components and to examine each one in some detail.

1. Have the Soviet leaders made the world state an explicit and integral part of their ideology, or has it remained largely an implied goal, as in Marx and Engels?

2. What of the other, apparently contradictory, facets of Soviet ideology, such as the revival of nationalism or the theories of "socialism in one country" and "peaceful coexistence" with the capitalist world? Do these ideas actually negate the objective of a world state? If not, how can they be reconciled with it, and what influence have they upon the goal of a world state?

3. What kind of a world state do the Soviet leaders want? Is it to be a highly centralized, unitary world state, or will power be distributed throughout the world by means of a federal structure? Are any provisions made for local populations to give expression to the local will, and, if so, to what sort of matters will this self-determination apply? Do the Soviet leaders intend to preserve national cultures and national languages, or do they want a single, uniform world culture and world language?

4. Is this world state to be built up purely on the basis of voluntary consent, and, if not, what role will the use of force play?

5. What attitude do the Soviet leaders exhibit toward any other proposal for the creation of a world state? Do they indicate that any compromise solution might be acceptable to them?

6. How do the Soviet leaders apply the doctrine of the withering away of the state to their projected world state?

A discussion of these questions forms the body of this work.

II. The World State as an Explicit Soviet Goal

THE Bolsheviks inherited the Marxist belief that the age of nationalism was but a momentary stage in the march of history, and that the capitalist nation-state system was destined to be transformed into a socialist world state. This led the Bolshevik theoreticians to make a number of explicit pronouncements on the goal of a world state. In order to provide an unmistakable frame of reference for further discussion it is essential to consider a few of the more important forthright Bolshevik statements on this goal.

PREREVOLUTIONARY VIEW OF THE NATION-STATE SYSTEM

The early writings of Lenin and Stalin on the nationality problem were concerned primarily with the difficulty of organizing the proletariat on an international scale, and though the objective of a proletarian world state could be implied throughout, it was not Lenin or Stalin, but Trotsky who first began to articulate the goal of a world state. Though Trotsky was not even a Bolshevik at the time, and had many disagreements with both Lenin and Stalin, his views on the nature and ultimate fate of the bourgeois nation-state system largely coincided with those of the Bolsheviks. In June, 1905, Trotsky pictured the forces to which the bourgeois nation-states were being subjected: "Imposing its methods of production upon all countries, capitalism has converted the whole world into a single economic and political organism." Individual nations were no longer able to resist the organization of "all the forces of reaction into a kind of world-wide joint stock company," which not only undermined the old basis of national existence, "but also prepared the basis for a social crisis of unheard of dimensions." [1]

[1] Trotsky, "Europe and Revolution," June, 1905, in *A Review and Some Perspectives* (Moscow, 1921), p. 75. Trotsky did not formally join the Bolsheviks

It was not until January, 1913, that Stalin, writing under Lenin's tutelage, explicitly stated that a nation could be considered only as a transitory historical phenomenon. "A nation is not merely an historical category, but an historical category belonging to a definite epoch, the epoch of rising capitalism." The prototype of capitalist nation-states could be found in Western Europe, in France, England, Germany, and Italy. "In Eastern Europe matters proceeded differently. While in the West, nations developed into states, in the East multinational states were formed, each consisting of several nationalities." [2] Stalin attributed the multinational nature of the Austro-Hungarian and Russian empires to the fact that these states had been formed when the remains of feudalism were still quite strong and the development of capitalism rather weak. But with the further development of capitalism Stalin predicted the further growth of nationalism and the rise of national states. These new national states, in turn, would find the limits of their existence within the confines of the capitalist system, since the consolidation of nations and the development of nationalism were considered exclusively capitalist phenomena. As to the "fate of the national movement it is naturally connected with the fate of the bourgeoisie," [3] and since Stalin took it for granted that the bourgeoisie must be destroyed, the world of sovereign nation-states which it had created was likewise doomed to oblivion.[4] Stalin confirmed this prognosis by citing Marx's words in

---

until July, 1917. He disagreed with Lenin on Party structure, on the tempo of the bourgeois and proletarian revolutions, on the relative importance of the revolutionary peasantry and proletariat, and on various other questions. But Trotsky spoke as explicitly and as insistently as any Bolshevik about the necessity and inevitability of a proletarian world state. His views on this subject did not come into serious conflict with those of the Bolsheviks until 1924, when Trotsky met Stalin head-on over the question of socialism in one country.

[2] Stalin, "Marksizm i natsional'nyi vopros," Jan., 1913, in *Sochineniia*, II, 303.
[3] *Ibid.*, II, 311.
[4] Today, to say that every unit in the nation-state system is a purely national state must obviously stretch beyond recognition the original concept that each nation should have its own state. Due to the global intermixture of ethnic stocks and the consequent insoluble conflicts of national claims, the original idea lost all meaning as soon as the term was given wide application. On the other hand, we do not have a world state, and terms like "nation-state" and "nation-state system" have found wide acceptance—probably for lack of any better shorthand way of speaking. We have nothing against the continued use of these terms, so long as it is understood that they do not have an ethnic connotation, but denote effective units in international relations. Thus, for purposes of international politics both the United States and the USSR are nation-states. The United States is made up of many ethnic groups who all consider themselves "Americans," and the USSR, though

The Communist Manifesto that the national differences which were already vanishing under bourgeois rule would vanish much faster under the rule of the proletariat.[5]

In October, 1913, Lenin supplied an important insight into the complex development of national states, by emphasizing the dual and contradictory processes in their growth.

> Developing capitalism knows two historical tendencies in the national question. First, the awakening of national life and national movements, the struggle against all national oppression, and the creation of national states. Second, the development and acceleration of all kinds of intercourse between nations, the breakdown of national barriers, the creation of the international unity of capital, of economic life in general, of politics, science, etc. Both tendencies are a world-wide law of capitalism. The first predominates at the beginning of its development, the second characterizes mature capitalism that is moving towards its transformation into socialist society.[6]

This formula, like others before it, assumed that the nation-state was the highest political authority that the bourgeoisie was capable of producing and that the transformation of a world capitalist society into a world socialist society would elevate the level of highest political authority from nation-states to a world state. But Lenin went beyond this by drawing a distinction between an incipient and a mature nationalism under the bourgeoisie, indicating that a nation-state could be a progressive or a reactionary symbol, depending upon its stage of development. This subtlety was overlooked by some of Lenin's associates, who took little notice of the uneven rate at which different nations had developed. Their tendency to attribute virtue only to the proletarian world state, and evil to all bourgeois nation-states, led them into a violent conflict with him.

At the outbreak of the First World War in 1914, Lenin and Trotsky attacked the Social Democrats of the Second International who came to the defense of their bourgeois fatherlands, first, because it was a bourgeois fatherland that they were defending, and second, because these fatherlands were too small to encompass the

---

strictly speaking a multinational state, still reduces all its members to "Soviet citizens" and acts like a nation-state in the operation of the world nation-state system.

[5] Stalin, "Marksizm," in *Sochineniia*, II, 330.

[6] Lenin, "Kriticheskie zametki po natsional'nomu voprosu," Oct., 1913, in *Sochineniia*, XVII, 139–40.

forces of a world socialist revolution. "The proletariat can have no interest in defending the outlived and antiquated national 'fatherland,'" Trotsky asserted. "The task of the proletariat is to create a far more powerful fatherland . . . the republican United States of Europe, as the foundation of the United States of the World." [7] Similarly, Lenin insisted that "the proletariat must not participate in the defense of the old framework of bourgeois states, but must create a new framework of socialist republics." [8] That this did not mean simply the substitution of socialism for capitalism in the existing system of nation-states was made clear when he added:

It is impossible to pass from capitalism to socialism, without breaking national frameworks, as it was impossible to pass from feudalism to capitalism without adopting the idea of a nation.[9]

The socialist movement cannot be victorious within the old framework of the fatherland. It creates new, higher forms of human life under which the best demands and progressive tendencies of the laboring masses of all nationalities will be fully satisfied in an international unity while the present national partitions are destroyed.[10]

By August, 1915, Lenin was declaring that "the United States of the World . . . coincides with socialism." "The United States of the World (and not just of Europe) is that state form for the unification and freedom of nations which we identify with socialism." [11] However, he cautioned against using "the United States of the World" as an immediate tactical slogan, since it might cause some socialists to ignore the uneven rate at which different capitalist nations had developed, as well as the possible necessity for achieving the socialist world state only through a series of stages.

The idea of a socialist United States of Europe as a first, essential step toward a socialist United States of the World was again expounded by Trotsky with great force and clarity in a series of

[7] Trotsky, *The Bolsheviki and World Peace* (New York, 1918), p. 28. This was first published as an article in the Paris Russian-language paper *Golos* in November, 1914. (See Isaac Deutscher, *The Prophet Armed* [New York, London, 1954], p. 215.)

[8] Lenin, "Rech' na referate G. V. Plekhanova," Oct. 11, 1914, in *Sochineniia*, XVIII, 48.

[9] Lenin, "Referat na temu: proletariat i voina," Oct. 14, 1914, in *ibid.*, XVIII, 53.

[10] Lenin, "Polozhenie i zadachi sotsialisticheskogo internatsionala," Nov. 1, 1914, in *ibid.*, XVIII, 70.

[11] Lenin, "O lozunge Soedinënnykh Shtatov Evropy," Aug. 23, 1915, in *ibid.*, XVIII, 232.

articles in 1915–1916. Trotsky said that "no matter which side proves victorious" in the World War, "the fact remains that there can no longer be a return to independence for small states." [12] The forces of economic development had produced a

> centralist tendency of modern economy which is *fundamental* and which must be guaranteed the amplest possibility of executing its real historical liberating mission: *the construction of a united world economy*, independent of national frameworks, state and tariff barriers, subject only to the peculiarities of the soil and its contents, to climate and the requirements of the division of labor.[13]

So far as Europe was concerned, "the state unification of Europe was a prerequisite," not only for economic development, but also for the sake of national cultures, since "a national-cultural existence and development is only possible under the roof of a democratically united Europe, free from state tariff barriers and national economic antagonisms." [14] Trotsky predicted that "the living part of culture, such as a national language which is its living organ, will retain its significance for an indefinitely long historical period." [15] But that should not hinder the proletariat from advancing the slogan "the United States of Europe," which expressed "the fact that the national state has become obsolete—as a framework for the development of the productive forces, as a basis for class struggle, and thereby also as the state form of the proletarian dictatorship." [16]

The unfolding of inevitable economic forces was pushing all mankind toward a socialist unity organized in the form of a world state. But interlaced with the notion of irresistible objective forces was a subjective value judgment. What was objectively necessary was also supremely desirable. The creation of this world state was considered part of a preordained process of man's salvation. This was a secular vision of human redemption, since its appearance was to symbolize the end of all forms of human oppression and exploitation. It was this vision that infused the Bolshevik Revolution with its dynamic and universal character, and it was under the spell of this image that all sacrifices could be justified.

[12] Trotsky, "Programma mira," 1915–1916, in *Sochineniia*, III, Part I, 77.
[13] *Ibid.*, III, Part I, 83.
[14] *Ibid.*, III, Part I, 83–84.
[15] *Ibid.*, III, Part I, 82.
[16] *Ibid.*, III, Part I, 89.

THE BOLSHEVIK REVOLUTION AND THE IMMINENCE OF A
WORLD STATE

The Bolsheviks therefore assumed that their coup d'état in Russia was only the first step toward the creation of a Soviet world state. On November 8, 1917, Trotsky announced to the Second Congress of Soviets: "The union of the oppressed everywhere. That is our course." [17] Lenin similarly appealed to the proletariat of all countries to fight for a Soviet world state, since it alone could produce the millennium of world peace. "Only a socialist union of toilers of all countries will clear away the ground of national quarrels and emnities." [18] By the time the Third Congress of Soviets had convened in January, 1918, Lenin was predicting confidently that "a new era in the history of the world" had begun. He told the Congress that the state power that the proletariat had seized in Russia "pointed the way toward the future socialist structure of the whole world, for the toilers of all countries." [19] It was Lenin's expectation that "the time was not far distant when the toilers of all countries will unite in a single world state and together build a new socialist edifice." [20]

The Soviet leaders looked upon the Constitution of the newly formed Russian Soviet Federated Socialist Republic as a tangible symbol of their future world state. Steklov, who was entrusted with the honor of introducing the Constitution before the Fifth All-Russian Congress of Soviets in July, 1918, made it clear that this new state was to be more than a nucleus for reuniting those territories that had been torn away from Russia:

Our Constitution is of world-wide significance. As the workers and peasants from different countries take advantage of favorable circumstances and follow the example of Soviet Russia . . . the Russian Soviet Republic sooner or later will be surrounded by daughter and sister Republics, which uniting will lay the basis for a federation, first of Europe, and then of the entire world.[21]

[17] Trotsky, "Speech to Second All-Russian Congress of Soviets," Nov. 8, 1917; quoted in James Bunyan and H. H. Fisher, *The Bolshevik Revolution, 1917-1918* (Stanford, 1934), p. 137.
[18] Lenin, "Rech' na pervom vserossiiskom s"ezde voënnogo flota," Dec. 5, 1917, in *Sochineniia*, XXII, 101.
[19] Lenin, "Zakliuchitel'noe slovo, III vserossiiskii s"ezd sovetov," Jan. 31, 1918, in *ibid.*, XXII, 223.
[20] *Ibid.*, XXII, 225.
[21] Speech by Steklov, July 10, 1918, in *Piatyi vserossiikii s"ezd sovetov, stenograficheskii otchët* (Moscow, 1918), p. 186.

WORLD STATE AN EXPLICIT SOVIET GOAL

Lenin felt certain that the Soviet Constitution "reflects the ideals of the proletariat of the whole world," and that the task before the Russian workers was to "maintain the power of the Soviets till the working class of all countries revolts and raises aloft the banner of a World Socialist Republic!" [22]

Bukharin, in his widely distributed pamphlet of 1918, *Program of the Communists*, also called upon the proletariat of the world to revolt and create a world state: "Overthrow of the imperialist governments by armed uprisings and the organization of the International Republic of Soviets—that is the way to the international dictatorship of the working class." He particularly directed the messianic appeal of this world state to the backward and oppressed areas of the world. "The International Republic of Soviets will liberate from oppression the hundreds of millions of inhabitants in the colonies.... European civilization exists on the bodies of the mercilessly exploited and plundered nations in far-off overseas countries." "Sooner or later," he stated categorically, such deliverance will come, and "we shall have the International Republic of Soviets." [23]

The founding of the Communist International (Comintern) in March, 1919, supposedly marked another concrete step toward the founding of a Soviet world state. The Executive Committee of the Comintern plainly stated its aim: "Our Third International is an international association of the proletariat of all countries for the purpose of overthrowing the bourgeoisie and of laying the foundations for an International Soviet Republic." [24] The few documents issued by the First Comintern Congress, brief and declamatory in nature, emphasized the importance of the world state. The Manifesto of the Congress again recited the inadequacy of the national state, [25] and the Platform adopted by the Congress proclaimed that the proletariat must "wipe out boundaries between states, transform the whole world into one cooperative commonwealth, and realize the freedom and brotherhood of nations." [26] The Platform ended

[22] Lenin, "Rech' na mitinge v khamovnicheskom raione," July 26, 1918, in *Sochineniia*, XXIII, 150.
[23] Bukharin, *Programma*, May, 1918, pp. 73-74.
[24] "Long Live the First of May! Long Live Communism!" April 20, 1919, *Communist International* (London ed.), No. 1 (May 1, 1919), p. 24.
[25] "Manifest Kommunisticheskogo Internatsionala," March 2-6, 1919, in *Kom. Int. v dok.*, p. 56.
[26] "Platforma Kommunisticheskogo Internatsionala," March 2-6, 1919, in *ibid.*, p. 62.

with the salvo: "Long live the International Republic of Workers' Soviets."[27]

Each time Lenin appeared before the First Comintern Congress he exuded confidence over the possibilities of attaining a world state: "The founding of the Third, Communist International is the forerunner of the International Republic of Soviets, the international victory of communism."[28] As a matter of fact, all through 1919 there was hardly a public statement that Lenin made on any topic which did not include some reference to the world state. Lenin not only reflected a persistent enthusiasm for the idea, but even the expectation of its imminent realization.

On March 31, 1919, for example, he declared: "It will not be long and we shall see the victory of communism in the entire world, we shall see the founding of a World-wide Federal Republic of Soviets."[29] This outcome was inevitable for, as Lenin told the Eighth Party Congress, in March, 1919, "No force on earth can hold back the course of the world Communist revolution which will end in a World-wide Soviet Republic."[30] With the appearance of the short-lived Soviet Republics of Hungary and Bavaria in the spring of 1919 Lenin was sure that he saw the beginning of a rapid-fire chain reaction. "Every day brings news that the red flag of liberation has been raised first in one place and then in another. . . . You will soon see how the World Federal Republic of Soviets will come into being."[31] In the summer of 1919 Lenin even set a date by which the Soviet world state would be created. "We say with conviction . . . that this July is our last difficult July, and that by next July, we shall greet the victory of the International Soviet Republic, and that this victory will be complete and irreversible."[32] This probably marked the high point of Lenin's hopes. By the fall

---

[27] *Ibid.*, p. 66.
[28] Lenin, "Zavoevannoe i zapisannoe," March 5, 1919, in *Sochineniia*, XXIV, 26.
[29] Lenin, "III Kommunisticheskii Internatsional," March 31, 1919, in *ibid.*, XXIV, 194.
[30] Lenin, "Rech' pri otkrytii s"ezda," March 18, 1919, in *ibid.*, XXIV, 115.
[31] Lenin, "Rech' na pervykh moskovskikh sovetskikh komandnykh kursakh," April 15, 1919, in *ibid.*, XXIV, 215.
[32] Lenin, "Doklad o vnutrennem i vneshnem polozhenii respubliki na moskovskoi konferentsii RKP(b)," July 12, 1919, in *ibid.*, XXIV, 381. The Comintern's Executive Committee also proclaimed: "The great Communist International was born in 1919. The great International Soviet Republic will be born in 1920." ("Long Live the First of May!" *Communist International*, No. 1 [May 1, 1919], p. 28.)

WORLD STATE AN EXPLICIT SOVIET GOAL 33

of 1919 the Hungarian and Bavarian Soviet Republics had not only been crushed, but no new Soviet Republics had sprung up to take their places, and Soviet Russia was coming to terms with bourgeois governments in the Baltic states, where, the previous year, other Soviet Republics had been established briefly. Despite these reversals Lenin maintained that "this struggle will end in the victory of a World-wide Soviet Republic," adding somewhat apologetically, "it is only a question of time."[33]

At the end of 1919 Lenin addressed an appeal to the Ukraine, which was then a separate republic, urging it to prepare for a union with the RSFSR. "Let the Communists of the Ukraine . . . provide the toilers of the whole world an example of a really firm union of workers and peasants of different nations struggling for Soviet power and the creation of a World Federated Soviet Republic."[34] The union between the RSFSR and the Ukraine could only be considered a point of departure because

> capital is an international power. In order to conquer it we need an international union of workers, an international brotherhood of workers. We are opponents of national hostility, national antagonisms, and of national particularism. We are internationalists. We aim at the firm union and full fusion of the workers and peasants of all nations of the world into one World-wide Soviet Republic.[35]

When the Second Comintern Congress opened in July, 1920, and Lenin's prophecy of the previous July had proven false, Soviet leaders began lengthening the time span required for the birth of the world state. Zinoviev, as President of the Comintern, admitted that "perhaps we were carried away by our enthusiasm, perhaps it is true that not one year, but two or three years will be necessary before all Europe becomes Soviet." But beyond this Zinoviev no longer set any time limits for the achievement of a Soviet world state. He could only add that "whether it comes a year sooner or a year later . . . we *shall* have the International Soviet Republic toward which our Communist International guides us."[36]

The Second Comintern Congress was the scene of serious discus-

---

[33] Lenin, "Dva goda sovetskoi vlasti," Nov. 7, 1919, in *ibid.*, XXIV, 521.
[34] Lenin, "Pis'mo k rabochim i krestianam Ukrainy," Dec. 28, 1919, in *ibid.*, XXIV, 660.
[35] *Ibid.*, XXIV, 656.
[36] Speech by Zinoviev, July 19, 1920, in *Vtoroi kongress Kommunisticheskogo Internatsionala*, p. 11.

sion on the problem of integrating nations into a Soviet world state. The Congress adopted Lenin's Draft Resolution on the National Question which stated that "the task of transforming the dictatorship of the proletariat from a national one . . . into an international one . . . has become the question of the day." [37] It must be made clear to the masses of all countries that the imperialist powers only practice deception "by creating, in the guise of politically independent states, states which are absolutely dependent upon them economically, financially, and militarily." The illusion of freedom and independence for such national states under imperialism, the Theses continued, must be shattered once and for all, since "there is no salvation for dependent and weak nations except in a Union of Soviet Republics." The proletariat of the great powers were also reminded of their duties, since socialism cannot attain "its ultimate goal unless the proletariat and toiling masses of all nations of the world rally of their own accord into a concordant and close union." [38]

The Manifesto of the Second Comintern Congress laid heavy stress upon the important role of the colonial and semicolonial areas in the formation of the Soviet world state.

Egypt, India, Persia are convulsed by insurrections. From the advanced proletariat of Europe and America the toiling masses in the colonies are acquiring the slogan of Soviet Federation.

. . . .

On the experience of Soviet Russia the peoples of Central Europe, of the Southeastern Balkans, of the British Dominions, all the oppressed nations and tribes, the Egyptians and the Turks, the Indians and the Persians, the Irish and the Bulgarians have convinced themselves that the fraternal collaboration of all national units of mankind can be realized only through a Federation of Soviet Republics.[39]

The Manifesto ended with a vow of duty which the world proletariat held toward Russia as the nucleus of this world state. "The Communist International has proclaimed the cause of Soviet Russia as its own. The international proletariat will not sheath its sword

---

[37] Lenin, "Pervonachal'nyi nabrosok tezisov po natsional'nomu i kolonial'nomu voprosam," June 5, 1920, in *Sochineniia*, XXV, 288.
[38] *Ibid.*, XXV, 290; "Natsional'nyi i kolonial'nyi voprosy," July 19–Aug. 7, 1920, in *Kom. Int. v dok.*, pp. 128–30.
[39] "Manifest II kongressa Kommunisticheskogo Internatsionala," July 19–Aug. 7, 1920, in *Kom. Int. v dok.*, pp. 142, 151.

until Soviet Russia is incorporated as a link in the World Federation of Soviet Republics." [40]

The Second Congress also formally adopted the Statutes of the Comintern, which restated its aim as "the overthrow of capitalism, the establishment of the dictatorship of the proletariat and of the International Soviet Republic for the complete abolition of classes and the realization of socialism—this first step toward Communist society." [41] This declaration of purpose became a key statement which was repeated countless times, not only in Comintern literature, but also in a variety of other Soviet publications.

In preparation for the Tenth Congress of the Russian Communist Party, in March, 1921, Stalin sought to account for the disconcerting persistence of nationalism in the face of repeated Bolshevik predictions of the coming of the Soviet world state. True, Soviet Russia had emerged from the World War, but so had a number of new capitalist nation-states. He explained that this development in no way invalidated the progression of mankind toward a proletarian world state. Taking up his theoretical discussion where he had left off in 1913, Stalin repeated his major premise that "modern nations are a product of a definite epoch, the epoch of rising capitalism." [42] The multinational states of Eastern Europe, the Austro-Hungarian and Russian Empires, which were originally formed prior to the disappearance of feudalism, had by now felt the full impact of capitalism. As Stalin had prophesied, new national states arose out of these multinational empires, but "the formation of new bourgeois national states (Poland, Czechoslovakia, Yugoslavia, Finland, Georgia, Armenia, etc.) . . . did not and could not result in the peaceful coexistence of nationalities, and did not and could not eliminate national inequalities or national oppression." [43] According to Stalin, bourgeois national states could not become viable units, but would continue to create national strife on three levels: the dominant national group of each state would oppress its own national minorities, the great and powerful national states would oppress and dominate the smaller and weaker national states, and the national states that

[40] *Ibid.*, p. 152.
[41] "Ustav Kommunisticheskogo Internatsionala," July 19–Aug. 7, 1920, in *Vtoroi kongress Kommunisticheskogo Internatsionala*, p. 536.
[42] Stalin, "Ob ocherednykh zadachakh partii v natsional'nom voprose," Feb. 10, 1921, in *Sochineniia*, V, 15.
[43] *Ibid.*, V, 17.

owned colonies would continue to oppress the national-colonial liberation movements. Stalin considered all this an inevitable consequence of the capitalist system, and drew this comparison with socialism: "If private property and capital inevitably divide peoples, incite national enmity, and intensify national oppression, then collective property and labor just as inevitably draw peoples together, undermine national enmity, and destroy national oppression."[44] Thus Stalin pictured the integration of nations in terms of the traditional Marxist stages of development: the formation of multinational states under feudalism, their dissolution and the rise of national states with the rise of capitalism, and the reintegration of nations into a new multinational state, this time a world state, under socialism. Stalin pointed to the RSFSR as the "only country in the world in which the experiment of peaceful coexistence and fraternal collaboration of a large number of nations and peoples has succeeded." It is "only a federation of this kind," he concluded, "that can serve as the transitional stage to that supreme unity of the toilers of all countries, living in a single world economy, the necessity for which is growing more and more evident."[45]

This single world economy, the Fourth Comintern Congress noted in November, 1922, will spread the benefits now enjoyed by the privileged areas of the world. The proletariat of the West must seize power not only for its own sake, "but also because it is only from the victorious proletariat of the advanced countries that the workers of the East will receive unstinting aid for the development of their backward productive forces. The union with the proletariat of the West opens the way to the International Federation of Soviet Republics."[46]

THE SOVIET UNION AS THE PROTOTYPE OF THE WORLD STATE

The end of 1922 witnessed the historic steps toward the formation of the USSR. One theme ran through all the speeches and declarations which marked this event: the USSR is not an end in itself, but rather the embryo of a Soviet world state. In his speech of December 26, 1922, to the Tenth All-Russian Congress of Soviets, Stalin reiterated the proposition that the collective ownership of property

[44] *Ibid.*, V, 19.   [45] *Ibid.*, V, 23.
[46] "Vostochnyi vopros," Nov. 5–Dec. 5, 1922, in *Kom. Int. v dok.*, p. 321.

facilitates the collection of nations into a higher unity. Soviet power, based on collective property, "is so constructed that being international by its intrinsic nature, it systematically fosters the idea of unity among the masses and impels them toward amalgamation." [47] The unification of nations in a world state was depicted as part and parcel of the unraveling of the inexorable forces of history, destined to destroy private property and to create in its stead a world socialist brotherhood. Then, referring to the impending union of Soviet Republics, Stalin concluded "that the new union state will be another decisive step toward the amalgamation of the toilers of the whole world into a World Soviet Socialist Republic." [48]

Four days later, on December 30, 1922, the Congress of Soviets approved a treaty creating the USSR. The same day the First Congress of Soviets of the USSR was convoked. Before this gathering Stalin repeated his view of the meaning of the act of union.

Today is a day of triumph for the new Russia ... which has transformed the red flag from a Party banner into a state banner, and rallied around that banner the peoples of the Soviet Republics in order to unite them into a single state, the Union of Soviet Socialist Republics, the prototype of the future World Soviet Socialist Republic.[49]

Stalin then read to the Congress the Declaration of Union, which was subsequently incorporated as Part I into the Constitution of the USSR. The Constitution went through various stages of ratification, receiving its final approval at the Second Congress of Soviets of the USSR on January 31, 1924. The Declaration of Union anticipated the growth of the USSR into a world state by including the specific provision "that admission to the union is open to all Socialist Soviet Republics, both those now in existence and those which will arise in the future." The idea of a world state was further woven into the fabric of the Constitution of the USSR by the declaration that "the new union state is ... a new decisive advance toward the amalgamation of the toilers of all countries into a World Socialist Soviet Republic." [50]

In his speech on the national question before the Twelfth Party

[47] Stalin, "Ob ob"edinenii Sovetskikh Respublik," Dec. 26, 1922, in *Sochineniia*, V, 149-50.
[48] *Ibid.*, V, 155.
[49] Stalin, "Ob obrazovanii Soiuza Sovetskikh Sotsialisticheskikh Respublik," Dec. 30, 1922, in *Sochineniia*, V, 158.
[50] Stalin, "Deklaratsiia ob obrazovanii Soiuza Sovetskikh Sotsialisticheskikh Respublik," Dec. 30, 1922, in *ibid.*, V, 394.

Congress, in April, 1923, Stalin once more insisted that the Soviet Union was both "the first experiment on the part of the proletariat in regulating international relations among independent countries and the first step toward the creation of the future World Soviet Labor Republic." [51]

Stalin used the occasion of Lenin's death in January, 1924, to intone the solemn vow to expand the Soviet Union into a world state.

> In departing from us, Comrade Lenin bequeathed to us the duty of strengthening and expanding the Union of Republics. We vow to you, Comrade Lenin, that we will honorably fulfill this, your bequest. . . . Lenin never regarded the Republic of Soviets as an end in itself. He always regarded it as a necessary link for . . . facilitating the victory of the toilers of the whole world over capital. Lenin knew that only such an interpretation is the correct one, not only from the international point of view, but also from the point of view of preserving the Republic of Soviets itself. . . . *Lenin bequeathed to us the duty of remaining loyal to the principles of the Communist International. We vow to you, Comrade Lenin, that we will not spare our lives to strengthen and expand the union of the toilers of the whole world.*[52]

In April, 1924, Stalin delivered his lectures *On the Foundations of Leninism*, a work important not for originality of ideas, but for the ideas that he chose to reaffirm. On the national question Stalin repeated Lenin's thesis, expounded in October, 1913, on the duality of national development in the process of evolution toward a proletarian world state: the formation of national states in backward areas of the world occurring simultaneously with the breaking down of national barriers and a merger of national states in the advanced areas where nationalism had already matured. Only by grasping the dual nature of this process would it be possible to achieve "the amalgamation of nations into a single world economic system," and only through the application of this knowledge thus far has it been possible "to create that remarkable organization for the collaboration of peoples which is called the Union of Soviet Socialist Republics, which is the living prototype of the future amalgamation of nations in a single world economy." [53]

[51] Stalin, "Zakliuchitel'noe slovo po dokladu o natsional'nykh momentakh v partiinom i gosudarstvennom stroitel'stve," April 25, 1923, in *ibid.*, V, 273.
[52] Stalin, "Po povodu smerti Lenina," Jan. 26, 1924, in *ibid.*, VI, 49–51.
[53] Stalin, "Ob osnovakh Leninizma," April, 1924, in *ibid.*, VI, 147–48. The revised edition cited did not affect this particular passage; see Stalin, "Ob osnovakh Leninizma," April, 1924, in *O Lenine i Leninizme* (Moscow, 1924), p. 102, the first publication of the speech. Like many other works of both

WORLD STATE AN EXPLICIT SOVIET GOAL

In an article of November 7, 1927, commemorating the tenth anniversary of the revolution, Stalin once more held up the Soviet Union as a model of the future world state. It is only within the USSR that there exists *"for the first time* in the history of mankind . . . nations which are *really* free and *really* equal thereby setting a contagious example for the nations of the whole world." The Soviet Union has destroyed the idea "that the world was divided into inferior and superior races, into blacks and whites, and that the former are incapable of assimilating civilization and are doomed to be subject to exploitation." Only the Soviet regime had formed the correct method "of liberating oppressed nations," and "the existence of the Union of Soviet Socialist Republics, which is the prototype of the future amalgamation of the toilers of all countries into a single world economy, is the direct proof of this." [54]

When the definitive draft of the Comintern Program was presented to the Sixth Comintern Congress, in August, 1928, Stalin commended its formula for expanding the Soviet federation: "The draft puts in place of the slogan of the United States of Europe, the slogan of a federation of Soviet Republics of advanced countries and colonies that have fallen away or are falling away from the imperialist system." [55] The Program accordingly devoted special attention to the prospect of joining the colonial areas to the Soviet Union. "The Peasants' Soviets in the backward ex-colonies and the Workers' and Peasants' Soviets in the more developed ex-colonies, grouping themselves politically around the centers of proletarian dictatorship [will] join the growing federation of Soviet Republics, and thus enter the general system of the world proletarian dictatorship." [56] Ultimately the time will come when "the federation of these Repub-

---

Lenin and Stalin, this not only received wide circulation at the time of its appearance, but it has continued to be published in countless revised editions, and in millions of copies. This process of republication and continued distribution applies to a considerable part of the material presented in this and subsequent chapters. Therefore, the reader should keep in mind that, while we have presented material by and large chronologically, the original publication date is likely to represent just the beginning of the work's significance.

[54] Stalin, "Mezhdunarodnyi kharakter oktiabr'skoi revoliutsii," Nov. 7, 1927, in *Sochineniia*, X, 243–44.

[55] Stalin, "Ob itogakh iiul'skogo plenuma TsK VKP(b)," July 13, 1928, in *ibid.*, XI, 203. The full significance of this statement will become apparent in chapter 5 on socialism in one country.

[56] "Programma Kommunisticheskogo Internatsionala," Sept. 1, 1928, in *Kom. Int. v dok.*, p. 31.

lics has finally been transformed into a *World Union of Soviet Socialist Republics,* uniting the whole of mankind under the hegemony of the international proletariat organized as a state." [57] In the meantime the workers of all nations must look to the USSR which "is the prototype of those fraternal relations among nationalities of all countries which will exist in the World Union of Soviet Socialist Republics, the prototype of that economic unity of the toilers of all countries operating within a single world socialist economy, which the world proletariat must establish, once it has conquered state power." [58] The Sixth Comintern Congress also adopted a revised set of Statutes in which the Communist International was designated as "a World Communist Party" working for "the establishment of the world dictatorship of the proletariat, for the creation of a World Union of Socialist Soviet Republics, for the complete destruction of classes and the realization of socialism, the first stage of Communist society." [59]

In March, 1929, Stalin again wrote an essay on *The National Question and Leninism,* published for the first time only in 1949. Looking forward to "the period of the victory of socialism on a world-wide scale," Stalin said that this period would be distinguished by the fact that "nations will unite in one world socialist economic system and will thereby create the real conditions necessary for the gradual fusion of all nations into one whole." [60]

The idea of the fusion of nations in a world state was similarly reflected in the first edition of the *Small Soviet Encyclopedia,* issued in 1930. The proletariat, being international by nature, "knows no territorial boundaries," but has its destiny tied only to an ever-expanding Soviet Union. "That is why every country which has concluded a socialist revolution will enter the USSR." Then, when the world state has come into being, "when the socialist revolution is completed in all countries and a classless society has been built on a world scale, every border between countries will vanish, and the fatherland of the toilers' society will be the whole world." [61]

The contrast between a bourgeois fatherland, delimited by na-

[57] *Ibid.,* p. 18.   [58] *Ibid.,* p. 34.
[59] "Ustav Kommunisticheskogo Internatsionala," Sept. 1, 1928, in *Kom. Int. v dok.,* p. 46.
[60] Stalin, "Natsional'nyi vopros i Leninizm," March 18, 1929, in *Sochineniia,* XI, 343.
[61] M. Volfson, "Patriotizm," in *Malaia sovetskaia entsiklopediia* (Moscow, 1930), VI, 356.

WORLD STATE AN EXPLICIT SOVIET GOAL

tional boundaries, and the proletarian fatherland, limited only by the extent of the earth itself, was emphasized in Stalin's conversation with Emil Ludwig in December, 1931. Ludwig asked Stalin if he thought that there was any parallel between himself and Peter the Great. Stalin answered, "No, not in any way," and based his reply primarily upon the difference in attitude which each held toward the national state. "Peter did a great deal toward the creation and strengthening of a national state of landlords and merchants," whereas "the task to which I am dedicating my life consists in elevating another class—namely, the working class. That task does not consist in strengthening any sort of 'national' state, but in strengthening a socialist state, and that means an international state." [62]

THE WORLD STATE THEME IN SOTTO VOCE

Actually Ludwig's question was not as far-fetched as Stalin made it appear, nor was Stalin's disavowal of nationalism as clear-cut as he represented it. Because of the failure of the Soviet regime to fulfill its early expectations and to create a world state in short order, a gradual, but decided, change had taken place in Soviet thinking. Starting with the theory of "socialism in one country" and gaining momentum with the Five-Year Plans and the collectivization of agriculture, Stalin gave priority to building up a strong, highly industrialized state which, competing for survival in a world of nation-states, itself took on some of the familiar features of other nation-states. Part of the transformation involved a rebirth of Russian nationalism. It was no accident that this change of front was accelerated by the rise of Hitler Germany and the mounting threat of a militarist Japan in the Far East, for it was the Kremlin's sense of isolation and national weakness that forced the Soviet leaders to retreat from their early, overtly bellicose position. This shift in tactics had the effect of sharply reducing the number of forthright and explicit statements on the objective of a Soviet world state, since it led to an increasing reliance upon the traditional weapons of national diplomacy and, in general, the terminology of nationalism familiar to the non-Soviet world.

At this point the question might be raised as to whether this period

[62] Stalin, "Beseda s nemetskim pisatelem Emilem Liudvigom," Dec. 13, 1931, in *Sochineniia*, XIII, 104-5.

of retreat did not also symbolize an abandonment of the goal of a Soviet world state, in which case it would no longer be legitimate to apply the term "world state" to the ultimate objective of Soviet policy. The "united front" and even the "popular front" movements of the mid-1930s indicated a willingness on the part of the Kremlin to reconcile itself to cooperation with broadly based political forces in the non-Soviet world for the attainment of certain immediate aims. But can this policy of retreat be equated with abandonment of the fundamental, long-range objective of a world state? It would seem prudent to recall some of Stalin's prior theoretical pronouncements, such as, for example, his warning of 1924 that it was not enough to know how to attack. Citing a passage from Lenin, Stalin said that the proletariat "must understand that it is necessary to supplement this knowledge with the knowledge of how to retreat properly." Only by learning to use and to alternate both of these techniques will victory be possible. Stalin was very clear about the purpose of a period of retreat. It was "to gain time, to disintegrate the enemy, and to accumulate forces in order to assume the offensive later on." [63]

The Seventh Comintern Congress, meeting in July and August, 1935, epitomized the height of this conciliatory period. Its speeches were cast in the phraseology of nationalism and were preoccupied with the tactical questions of how to increase the national security of the existing Soviet state. A careful reading of this material, however, makes it apparent that while the Soviet leadership consciously played upon the terminology of nationalism, it was interpreted in the Soviet lexicon in a manner that made it entirely consistent with an abiding design for a Soviet world state. Here is how Dimitrov as head of the Comintern attempted to blend the defense of nationalism with the ultimate objective of creating a world state: "The interests of the class struggle of the proletariat against the exploiters and oppressors at home do not conflict with the interest of a free and happy future for their nation. On the contrary, the socialist revolution will bring *salvation for the nations* and open the road to a higher development for them." [64] Dimitrov then went on to state quite plainly in

[63] Stalin, "Ob osnovakh Leninizma," in *O Lenine i Leninizme*, p. 115. For one observer who understood perfectly the meaning of this retreat, see the prophetic report of July, 1935, by American Ambassador William Bullitt in *Foreign Relations of the United States: The Soviet Union, 1933–1939* (Washington, 1952), pp. 224–27.
[64] Dimitrov, *Nastuplenie fashizma*, Aug. 13, 1935, p. 79.

WORLD STATE AN EXPLICIT SOVIET GOAL 43

what this "higher development" consisted. "The wheel of history," he told the Congress, "is turning forward and will continue to turn forward toward a World-wide Union of Soviet Socialist Republics, toward the final victory of socialism throughout the whole world." [65]

The new 1936 Constitution for the USSR likewise reflected the period of retreat in which it was written. Gone was the open assertion of the 1924 Constitution that the USSR was the nucleus of a world state. The closest this idea came to receiving open expression in the 1936 version was Article 143, which provided that the official motto of the USSR remain, "Workers of All Countries, Unite!" However, Stalin continued to nurture the messianic image of the USSR as a model union of nations, as the fulfillment of what "millions of honest people in imperialist countries have dreamed of and still dream of." From this Stalin concluded that "what has been realized in the USSR is fully possible of realization in other countries," and therefore "the international significance of the new Constitution of the USSR can hardly be exaggerated." [66]

Even though Stalin began speaking more cautiously, lesser Party lights continued to keep alive his earlier, forthright statements. In 1937, for example, an article appeared in *The Communist International*, which recalled Stalin's boast of December 26, 1922, that the new union state of the USSR " 'will be another decisive step towards the amalgamation of the toilers of the whole world into a single World Socialist Soviet Republic'. . . . On the basis of the national policy of Lenin-Stalin," the article continued, "the Party [has] created an invincible friendship of peoples in which the world proletariat sees the prototype of the future Communist society." [67] Similarly, a volume of the *Large Soviet Encyclopedia*, published in 1938, reaffirmed that the Communist International was steadfastly devoted to the aim of creating "a World Union of Soviet Socialist Republics." [68]

With the signing of the Nazi-Soviet Pact in August, 1939, the period of retreat was transformed into a period of advance. Within a year the Soviet Union had swallowed a piece of Finland, the three

---

[65] *Ibid.*, p. 126.
[66] Stalin, "O proekte konstitutsii Soiuza SSR," Nov. 25, 1936, in *Doklad o proekte*, p. 50.
[67] S. Dimanshtein, "The Victory of Socialism and the Friendship of the Peoples in the U.S.S.R.," *Communist International*, XIV, No. 12 (Dec., 1937), 936-37.
[68] *Bol'shaia sovetskaia entsiklopediia* (Moscow, 1938), XXXIII, 715.

Baltic States, the western Ukraine, western Belorussia, northern Bukovina and Bessarabia, and was set for bigger stakes. An editorial in *The Communist International* of September, 1940, represented this expansion of the USSR as "an outstanding example of a genuine solution of the national question, making possible the peaceful and fraternal collaboration of numerous peoples within a multinational socialist state. The increase in the number of Soviet Constituent Republics from eleven to sixteen . . . is a brilliant confirmation of the correctness of the national policy of Lenin and Stalin." [69] But these limited accretions were considered merely the beginning of a process of indefinite expansion, according to another 1940 editorial in *The Communist International*. Recalling Stalin's vow "to strengthen and extend the Union of Soviet Socialist Republics, to strengthen and extend the union of the toilers of the whole world," the article declared that the First World War had only provided the opening by which Stalin had "snatched one-sixth of the earth from the imperialist world system." Now the hope was expressed that "under his banner the toilers of all countries will emerge victorious from the Second Imperialist War." [70]

Upon Hitler's attack in 1941, the Soviet regime was forced into a new period of retreat. It was so overwhelmed with the immediate problem of survival that all mention of the aggressive goal of a world state disappeared from Soviet writings. On May 15, 1943, Stalin dissolved the Comintern, a move most likely designed as a further encouragement to the Allies to give all-out aid in the common fight against the Axis.[71] Again, as in the mid-1930s, many non-Soviet observers declared that the Soviet Union was really just another national state, with no desire, either apparent or latent, to transform itself into a world state. For example, the leading editorial in the New York *Herald Tribune* of May 23, 1943, stated that "there is no reason to suspect that the dissolution of the Comintern is merely a gesture. Instead, it appears far more probable that it is the climax of the process that began when Stalin won his duel with Trotsky for leadership in Russia—the organization of that country into a national state, run on Communist lines, rather than a center of world revolution."

[69] "A Year of Imperialist War," *Communist International*, No. 9 (Sept., 1940), p. 574.
[70] "The Voice of Lenin," *ibid.*, No. 1 (Jan., 1940), p. 12.
[71] "Postanovlenie prezidiuma ispolnitel'nogo komiteta Kommunisticheskogo Internatsionala," May 15, 1943, *Pravda*, May 22, 1943, p. 1.

WORLD STATE AN EXPLICIT SOVIET GOAL

The precise fate that befell the Comintern is a matter of some conjecture.[72] But regardless of what happened to its organizational structure, the important question is whether the tactical retreat of 1943 implied an abandonment of the objective of a Soviet world state. If this fundamental principle was in fact abandoned, then it would have been consistent with the Soviet practice of periodically rewriting history to delete all reference to the Comintern from those editions of the official Party bible, *The History of the All-Union Communist Party (Bolsheviks), Short Course*, which were published after 1943. The 1952 edition of this Party history retains, verbatim,

[72] A German-Polish Communist agent who worked in the Comintern headquarters in Moscow dates the actual beginning of the liquidation of the Comintern organization from the Great Purges of 1937. When all foreigners, Communists included, were cast under the dark shadow of suspected treason, the ranks of the Comintern headquarters were so decimated that the organization lost all authority and became simply a minor foreign languages propaganda machine. These activities apparently continued after the Comintern's "dissolution" in 1943, under the guise of various names, such as Institute No. 205. Stalin reportedly drew upon this organization, and even the Comintern agents who had been banished to forced labor camps during the purges, to form the governing cadres for the postwar Soviet satellite states. (Alfred Burmeister, *Dissolution and Aftermath of the Comintern: Experiences and Observations, 1937-47* [New York, 1955], pp. 1-40.) Delgado, the Spanish Comintern functionary, who was in Moscow in 1943, also relates how the Comintern continued to function under other disguises. (Enrique Castro Delgado, *J'ai perdu la foi à Moscou* [Paris, 1950], pp. 217-31.) Ravines, one of the principal Comintern agents for Latin America, records that a meeting of high Comintern officials in Moscow toward the end of 1938 had already explored the possibility of dissolving the Comintern because of the threat of war and the dangers of Soviet isolation. He records this conversation between Georgi Dimitrov and Dimitri Manuil'skii: "'If the Communist International needs to be thrown overboard to save the ship,' said Dimitrov, clearly and emphatically, 'it will disappear as the First International, founded by Marx, disappeared once it had ceased to serve the purpose for which it was created.' 'It will disappear formally,' interrupted Manuil'skii, 'because the links we have formed across the world are now unbreakable. The Third International will die, but our bonds will grow stronger than ever, precisely because of that fact.'" (Eudocio Ravines, *The Yenan Way* [New York, 1951], p. 260.) The foreign Communist Parties could still form unbreakable links across the world without entrusting their supervision to the Comintern headquarters in Moscow. This function was very likely brought under Stalin's direct control through a department of the Central Committee of the CPSU. It was to these foreign operations that Igor Gouzenko, the Soviet embassy employee in Ottawa, referred when he testified that "only the name was liquidated, with the object of reassuring public opinion in the democratic countries. Actually the Comintern exists and continues its work." The Canadian Royal Commission which investigated these allegations added that "the documents which Gouzenko brought with him corroborate this testimony." (*The Report of the Royal Commission to Investigate the Facts Relating to and the Circumstances Surrounding the Communication, by Public Officials and other Persons in Positions of Trust of Secret and Confidential Information to Agents of a Foreign Power* [Ottawa, 1946], p. 37.)

Stalin's two vows of 1924 about "strengthening and expanding the Union of Republics," and of "remaining loyal to the principles of the Communist International." [73]

In one of his first major postwar pronouncements, his so-called electoral speech of February 9, 1946, Stalin returned to the theme that the USSR was singularly designed to solve the nationality problem and therefore admirably suited for expansion on an international scale. It was Stalin's claim that "the war showed that the Soviet multinational state system passed the test successfully, that it grew even stronger during the war and proved the state system perfectly capable of enduring." From this Stalin again concluded that "the Soviet state system has proved itself a model of a multinational state system where the national question and the problem of collaboration among nations are solved better than in any other multinational state." [74]

It was possibly in an effort to facilitate a Soviet solution to "the problem of collaboration among nations" that either were—or were soon likely to be—under Soviet influence that the Communist Information Bureau (Cominform) was founded in September, 1947. The objective of the Cominform appears to have been limited to the rather modest task of seizing or consolidating power in eight European states. Of its members at the moment of its founding, Soviet control appeared secure in Yugoslavia, Bulgaria, Rumania, Hungary, and Poland. Czechoslovakia was then still enjoying the twilight of freedom, while the sanguine Soviet expectations for France and Italy did not materialize. The sterility of the Cominform became apparent when its principal mission was soon reduced to waging Stalin's futile battle to unseat Tito. The utility of dissolving this embarrassing instrument in April, 1956, was likewise obvious in view of the efforts by Stalin's successors to woo the affections of Tito and other "neutralist" powers.[75]

[73] *Istoriia vsesoiuznoi*, p. 257.
[74] "Rech' tovarishcha I. V. Stalina na predvybornom sobranii izbiratelei Stalinskogo izbiratel'nogo okruga g. moskvy 9 fevralia 1946," *Bol'shevik*, No. 3 (Feb., 1946), p. 4.
[75] An editorial alongside the announcement of the dissolution of the Cominform made it clear that this act did not involve a loosening of Moscow's control over the Parties of the countries involved: "The decision to dissolve the Information Bureau by no means signifies that fraternal relations among the Communist and Workers' Parties will to any degree be weakened." ("For the Further Development and Strengthening of the International Communist Movement," *For a Lasting Peace*, April 17, 1956, p. 1.)

WORLD STATE AN EXPLICIT SOVIET GOAL 47

The limited scope and meager existence of the Cominform stands in bold contrast to the founding of the Comintern, whose extensive approach rested upon a belief in the imminence of a world state. The differences between the two bodies reflect the sobering influence of the difficulties in extending Soviet power in the intervening years. Yet it would be dangerous to assume that the goal of a world state is no longer of any importance to the Soviet leaders. It would seem, rather, that a Soviet world state is not a goal whose realization is anticipated in a matter of days, weeks, months, or at most, a brief span of years, as was the case in the early period of the Comintern. It is more likely that this goal is now regarded as the object of achievement of a number of generations of future Soviet citizens.

Though there has been a decided lowering in the level of expectation as to the immediate attainment of a world state, the goal itself remains as the polestar of Soviet policy. The years since the Second World War have been marked once more by a flurry of direct statements about a Soviet world state. On the occasion of Stalin's seventieth birthday in 1949 several works on the nationality problem were published by members of the Soviet Academy of Sciences, some of which were given a wide distribution both in the Soviet Union and in foreign languages, including English. One of these essays, by M. D. Kammari, eulogizing Stalin's "contribution" to Marxist theory on the national question, described the role of the USSR as the standard-bearer of the banner of proletarian internationalism: "This banner had rallied around itself the great commonwealth of socialist nations of the U.S.S.R.; it is rallying around the U.S.S.R. the People's Democracies. This banner will rally around itself the whole of toiling mankind and will lead to the creation of a great world commonwealth of socialist nations." [76] That the word "commonwealth" specifically meant a world state is beyond question, since elsewhere in the same work, Kammari stated that "J. V. Stalin appraised the creation of the U.S.S.R. . . . as a new and decisive step towards the amalgamation of the working peoples of all countries into a single World Socialist Republic, as the prototype of such an amalgamation." [77] In another essay E. A. Dunaeva quoted Stalin's statement that the USSR "is the prototype of the future

[76] Kammari, *Development by J. V. Stalin*, 1949, p. 86.
[77] *Ibid.*, pp. 44–45.

amalgamation of the toilers of all countries into a single world economic system."[78]

The official *Short Philosophical Dictionary*, published in 1952, again stressed explicitly the goal of a world state. "The solution of the national question in the USSR and the unification of all of its nations and peoples" was once more held up as "the prototype of the future unification of all the peoples of the world, once they are liberated from the slavery of imperialism."[79] "In the future, after the victory of socialism on a world scale," the *Dictionary* continued, "there will arise the proper conditions necessary for the gradual fusion of all nations into a single whole."[80]

The subsequent denigration of Stalin in no way affected the theme that the USSR is the model for the future organization of all mankind. In July, 1956, for example, *Pravda* pointed to "Lenin's concern about implementing a correct nationality policy, about the need to strengthen untiringly the Union of Soviet Socialist Republics . . . in the interests of all mankind. The relations among the peoples of the Soviet Union, based on equality and friendship, Lenin noted, will have enormous significance as the model for the peoples of the whole world."[81]

Similarly, in 1958 a Soviet ideologue reiterated the validity of Lenin's vision for the future of mankind.

Lenin repeatedly emphasized that Communists are confirmed opponents of national enmity, of national separation, of national isolation. "We are internationalists. We aim at the close union and full fusion of the workers and peasants of all nations of the world." . . . The fusion of nations remains the aim of the Communists. . . . The unification of peoples in a single world economy is conceivable only on the basis of the destruction of the entire imperialist system and the victory of socialism. . . . There can be no other basis for the future merger and union of nations.[82]

Finally, in March, 1959, Khrushchev speculated upon the nature of the future world Communist society in which nations would no longer be partitioned off from each other as sovereign independent units in a nation-state system.

[78] Dunaeva, *Collaboration of Nations*, 1949, p. 9.
[79] *Kratkii filosofskii slovar'* (Moscow, 1952), p. 157.   [80] *Ibid.*, p. 328.
[81] Z. Lëvina and A. Romanova, "Velikaia rol' V. I. Lenina v organizatsii Soiuza Sovetskikh Respublik," *Pravda*, July 11, 1956, p. 3.
[82] E. Modrzhinskaia, *Kosmopolitizm—imperialisticheskaia ideologiia poraboshcheniia natsii* (Moscow, 1958), pp. 160-61.

WORLD STATE AN EXPLICIT SOVIET GOAL

With the victory of communism on a world-wide scale, borders between states will disappear, as Marxism-Leninism teaches. In all likelihood only ethnic borders will survive for a time. . . . They will simply demarcate the historically formed location of a given people or nationality in a given territory. That this will be so is shown by the process going on in the Soviet Union, which is a multinational state.

Here again the organization of nations within the USSR was regarded as the prototype for the unification of nations on a world-wide scale upon the universal victory of communism. "In the Soviet Union each people and each nationality has its own historically formed boundaries, traditions and culture. But all the peoples of the Union and Autonomous Republics of our country are united in a single family." In a like manner, he looked forward to

the amalgamation of nations in a single Communist family. The question of borders as it is presently conceived will gradually cease to exist. No sovereign socialist country can shut itself up within its own borders and rely solely upon its own forces and its own wealth. If this were the case, we would not be Communist internationalists but would become national socialists.

Reiterating the familiar image of the future fusion of all nations into a single world economic unit, Khrushchev continued:

Speaking of the future, it seems to me that the further development of the socialist countries will in all probability proceed along the lines of the consolidation of a single world socialist economic system. The economic barriers that divided countries under capitalism will fall one after another. The common economic foundation of world socialism will grow stronger, eventually rendering pointless the question of borders.[83]

Thus, direct and open avowals on the objective of a Soviet world state and predictions of the ultimate reshaping of nations have continued to appear in official Soviet sources. This has been true despite the strong trend in recent years to disguise these intentions by the heavy use of national symbols and by reference to the theories of "socialism in one country" and "peaceful coexistence" with the non-Soviet world. It is to a discussion of these hidden and indirect methods of stating the goal of a Soviet world state that we now turn.

[83] "Rech' tovarishcha N. S. Khrushcheva na deviatoi obshchegermanskoi rabochei konferentsii v gorode Leiptsige 7 marta 1959 goda," *Pravda*, March 27, 1959, p. 2.

III. The Influence of Russian Nationalism to 1934

ON the basis of Marxian economics the Soviet leaders assert that bourgeois nation-states must be transformed into a single proletarian world state and that within this world state all nations eventually will lose their identity as nations and will merge into a single whole. If all phenomena ultimately could be reduced to economics and if, in fact, the Soviet leaders acted as if nationalism were some sort of outmoded bourgeois prejudice, then this alleged description of events might have some merit. But nationalism seems to be a stubborn force which has only a peripheral relationship to economics. Not only do bourgeois nations show a great reluctance to die, but strong national feelings persist in newly born proletarian states. In the Soviet Union, for example, the expression of nationalism and the use of national symbols and terminology have become stronger, not weaker, with the passage of time.

Thus we must now try to discover just what effect nationalism has had upon the formulation of the goal of a Soviet world state. Has the Soviet Union so thoroughly acclimatized itself to a world of bourgeois nation-states that it can, for all practical purposes, be equated to a bourgeois nation-state? Is this development of nationalism in the Soviet Union a denial of the earlier protestations of internationalism; does it indicate an abandonment of the desire to create an all-embracing International Soviet Republic? If this is not the case, if the Soviet leaders have not abandoned their goal of a world state, then what influence has nationalism exerted upon their image of a world state?

TWO ATTITUDES TOWARD NATIONALISM

Soviet leaders have always made an effort to adjust to the uncomfortable reality of nationalism in two ways. On the one hand, there has been a negative attitude toward nationalism, a decided tendency to deprecate and dismiss, or at least seriously to underestimate, its immense driving power. This approach tends to by-pass concrete thinking on the subject by assuming that "under socialism the national problem will solve itself"; an approach still evident in current Soviet statements to the effect that "the national problem does not exist in the Soviet Union," or that "the national problem has been solved in the land of socialism."

On the other hand, Soviet leaders have recognized that national feelings cannot be ignored, even within their own ranks. Consequently they have attempted to take nationalism in tow and to rationalize its manipulation as an instrument in the cause of socialism. This positive approach has always been a source of embarrassment to Soviet theoreticians, since it has meant that in some form or other they were encouraging nationalism, supposedly a remnant of bourgeois thinking, in the development of a socialist society. As a result, most Soviet statements dealing with nationalism are marked by a lack of candor and a sense of unreality. A Soviet discussion of nationalism is likely to be turned on its head: in Soviet parlance Soviet Russian nationalism becomes "proletarian internationalism"; similarly, internationalism in non-Soviet language becomes "bourgeois nationalism" in Soviet terminology.

Lenin's thinking on nationalism clearly combined both these negative and positive approaches. Though Lenin's negative statements were more temperate than those of his Bolshevik colleagues Bukharin and Piatakov, or of the Polish-German socialist leader Rosa Luxemburg, they still reflected a naive sort of cosmopolitan internationalism. "The proletarian," Lenin asserted in 1913, "welcomes every type of assimilation of peoples, except those based on coercion or privilege." For this reason, "the proletariat cannot support any effort to strengthen nationalism: quite the opposite, it supports everything that helps to erase national distinctions and to break down the barriers between nations, everything which makes the ties between nationalities tighter and tighter, everything that leads to the fusion of nations."[1] Being a Great Russian, Lenin added that it was necessary "to fight against all nationalism and, above all, against Great Russian nationalism."[2]

[1] Lenin, "Kriticheskie zametki po natsional'nomu voprosu," Oct., 1913, in *Sochineniia*, XVII, 146.
[2] Lenin, "O prave natsii na samoopredelenie," Feb., 1914, in *ibid.*, XVII, 474.

With the outbreak of the First World War, Lenin was subjected to strong pressures because of his antipatriotic views and found it necessary to qualify his attack on Great Russian nationalism. An explanation, written in December, 1914, revealed his positive approach to nationalism in general, and to Great Russian nationalism in particular. In phrases reminiscent of *The Communist Manifesto*, Lenin said that the majority of the Great Russian people would have a fatherland worth defending only when the oppressed became the ruling class and "constituted itself the nation." "It is impossible for the Great Russians to 'defend the fatherland' other than by wishing to defeat Tsarism in every war." In this respect his position differed from that of the Second International, whose members did not seek the defeat of their own national governments. But looking beyond the downfall of the Tsarist regime through war, he spoke in a different vein about the national feelings of the newly liberated masses, which he said constituted 90 percent of the Russian people. Here Lenin began spouting patriotic phrases that were all too similar to those "shameful" expressions of the Second International. He asked:

Are we enlightened Great Russian proletarians impervious to the feelings of national pride? Certainly not! We love our language and our motherland; we, more than any other group, are working to raise its laboring masses (i.e., nine-tenths of its population) to the level of intelligent democrats and socialists. . . . We, Great Russian workers, filled with national pride wish by all means to have a free and independent, sovereign, democratic, republican, proud Great Russia.[3]

Then came the link between Great Russian nationalism and the cause of socialism. "We are filled with national pride because of the knowledge that the Great Russian nation, too, has created a revolutionary class; that it, too, has proven capable of giving humanity great examples in the struggle for freedom and socialism."[4] Lenin carried this identification one step further and strongly suggested that which later became a Soviet dogma; namely, whatever was good for the Great Russian people was automatically "good" for a socialist of any nation. Here, as early as 1914, Lenin tied this knot by saying that "the national pride of the Great Russians (understood not in a debased way) coincides with the *socialist* interests of

---

[3] Lenin, "O natsional'noi gordosti velikorussov," Dec. 12, 1914, in *ibid.*, XVIII, 81–82.
[4] *Ibid.*, XVIII, 81.

the Great Russian (and all other) proletarians." [5] The words "and all other" Lenin put in parentheses, as if added as an afterthought. This assertion of the identity of interests between the Great Russian "and all other" proletarians was soon to become a fixed preoccupation for most Soviet leaders.

With the conquest of state power in Russia, the revolution had found a fatherland, which Lenin said it was the duty of proletarians everywhere to defend. "The worker has the right to defend his fatherland when it is for socialism, for the working class." [6] However, when Lenin said, "We are defenders of the socialist fatherland," he insisted in this ambivalent phrase that the interest of socialism dominated the interest of the Russian fatherland. This was in line with the traditional Marxist concept that the class struggle, rather than the struggle between nations, is the prime mover of history. "It is not a national interest that we are upholding, for we maintain that the interests of socialism, the interests of world socialism, rank higher than national interests, higher than the interests of the state." [7]

THE DILEMMA IN FOSTERING INTERNATIONALISM
FROM A NATIONAL BASE

Part of Lenin's justification for deprecating the interests of a national fatherland doubtless was based on the assumption that world socialism would soon triumph in the form of a world state. Consequently the contradiction between a national fatherland and world socialism would quickly disappear. But what would happen if the Soviet Russian state failed to expand into a world state? Stuchka, a leading Soviet legal authority, pointed to the abiding character of Article 19 of the 1918 Constitution of Soviet Russia, which stipulated that it was "the duty of all citizens of the Republic to come to the defense of their socialist fatherland." "Only the unification of the whole world into a single Union of Soviet Socialist Republics," Stuchka said, "will make this conception superfluous. Not before." [8] The only value capable of replacing the loyalty of the Russian proletariat to its national homeland would be the expansion of this loyalty

[5] *Ibid.*, XVIII, 83.
[6] Lenin, "Doklad o vneshnei politike," May 14, 1918, in *Sochineniia*, XXIII, 12.
[7] *Ibid.*, XXIII, 14.
[8] P. Stuchka, ed., *Entsiklopediia gosudarstva i prava* (Moscow, 1925), I, 681–82.

into the broader loyalty to a world state. So long as the "workers of the world" had not united in a Soviet world state, the proletariat, both within and beyond the confines of Russia, would owe its supreme allegiance to the Soviet Russian state.

The Treaty of Brest-Litovsk provided the first major, concrete test of the validity of Lenin's claim that "the interests of world socialism rank higher than national interests, higher than the interests of the state." A furious debate arose over how best to further the interests of world socialism in the face of rapacious German demands. Bukharin led a strong faction that wanted to reject the peace treaty and to wage an international class struggle through a revolutionary war against Germany—even at the risk of destroying the Soviet state in Russia. Lenin insisted that world socialism could only be advanced by saving the new state in Russia, even if it meant accepting an ignominious peace treaty with German imperialism. Lenin's policy was finally adopted, but only on the basis of a plurality (not an absolute majority) of the votes of the Party's Central Committee. Nor was this a clear-cut decision against Bukharin, for while the Central Committee gave its approval to signing the Treaty of Brest-Litovsk, at the same session it unanimously recommended that preparations for a revolutionary war be completed as soon as possible.[9] This indicates the ambivalence involved in the defense of "Soviet Russia." Which part of this phrase was more important, "Soviet" or "Russia"? After accepting the Treaty of Brest-Litovsk the Soviet regime held only the old Muscovite heartland of Great Russia, so that, despite its protestations of advancing the cause of an international class, the fate of "world socialism" was, however inadvertently, increasingly bound to the fate of the national fatherland of Great Russia.

THE REASSERTION OF RUSSIAN NATIONAL INTERESTS
IN THE EARLY 1920S

With the defeat of Germany in the World War, the Entente policy of blockade and intervention tended to push Russia and Germany together. Both were outcasts of the Versailles system, and their common hostility toward the Entente could easily create a common

[9] Trotsky, *Stalin*, p. 253. On February 23, 1918, the Central Committee voted seven to four, with four abstentions, to accept the Treaty of Brest-Litovsk.

policy toward it, based purely upon considerations of national interest. In October, 1919, this conclusion was drawn by a peculiar combination of forces in Germany, consisting of some extreme right-wing nationalist, militarist groups and a faction of German Communists led by Laufenberg and Wolffheim. The proposed policy, known as "National Bolshevism," sought to have Russia and Germany carry on a joint struggle against the Entente, even threatening to reopen a war against it. Radek, the highest Soviet representative in Berlin, rejected this idea for the time being, though he took careful note of it for the future.[10] When he carried this idea back to Moscow, Lenin considered it such a flagrant compromise of the international class struggle that he found it necessary "to repudiate the crying absurdity of 'National Bolshevism' (of Laufenberg and others) who have gone to the length of advocating a bloc with the German bourgeoisie for a war against the Entente." [11]

The Russo-Polish War of 1920 blurred class lines and rallied support for the Russian cause around the banner of national patriotism. The Soviet government accepted the offer of the former Tsarist Commander in Chief, General A. A. Brusilov, to form a special committee of prominent ex-Tsarist generals for the purpose of rousing the Russian people to the defense of their fatherland against the onslaught of a traditional national rival.[12] Radek consciously abandoned the language of the international class struggle: "We preach that this is a war for Russian independence; we assert that we are employing in this war every available source of aid, not primarily to defend the Soviet government and communism, but to defend the independence of Russia." [13] Even Zinoviev, the head of the Comintern, said that "the war is becoming national. . . . We Communists must be at the head of this national movement which embraces all classes of the population." [14] The struggle between the national and the inter-

[10] Ruth Fischer, *Stalin*, pp. 92–96; Carr, *Bolshevik Revolution*, III, 311–12, 319–22, 326; Lionel Kochan, *Russia and the Weimar Republic* (Cambridge, England, 1954), pp. 18–20.
[11] Lenin, "Detskaia bolezn' 'levizny' v kommunizme," April 27, 1920, in *Sochineniia*, XXV, 214. For the denunciation of Laufenberg and Wolffheim by the Comintern Executive Committee, see "Aux Membres du Parti Communiste Allemand," June 2, 1920, in *La IIIe Internationale Communiste*, pp. 266–76.
[12] D. Fedotoff White, *The Growth of the Red Army* (Princeton, 1946), pp. 210–11.
[13] *Freiheit*, July 27, 1920; quoted in Dennis, *Foreign Policies*, p. 151.
[14] "Tov. Zinoviev o bor'be s poliakami," *Pravda*, May 18, 1920, p. 1.

national factions of the Party during the Polish war recalled the struggle over the Treaty of Brest-Litovsk. Clara Zetkin reported Lenin as saying that "the conclusion of peace with Poland, in the beginning, met with serious opposition, in much the same way as the conclusion of the Brest-Litovsk Peace." Some Soviet leaders argued that the war should be continued in the hope that a prolonged revolutionary war might spread the class struggle to foreign lands. Lenin, who at first backed the gamble of a revolutionary war, was again unwilling to take undue risks with the security of the Russian state, when this gamble did not pay off. "I thought it wiser from a political standpoint," Lenin said, "to come to terms with the enemy; and the temporary sacrifice of a hard peace appeared to me preferable to the continuation of the war." [15] The tangible interests of the Russian state once more took priority over the theoretical interests of the international proletariat.

The rapprochement between Germany and Soviet Russia reached at Rapallo in April, 1922, again stimulated the latent current of National Bolshevism. In the fall of 1922 Bukharin moved from the left to the right wing of the Party, and joined Radek and the Soviet economist Varga in advocating an alliance between Soviet Russia and a united front of all classes in Germany. Varga's idea that the Entente was transforming Germany into an industrial colony through requiring reparations payments now provided the theoretical justification for such a policy.[16]

Rapallo also intensified the cooperation between the Reichswehr and the Red Army, by which the interests of the Russian state were clearly placed ahead of the class struggle in Germany. If there was any one force in Germany that was the special object of hatred of the German Communist Party, it was the Reichswehr. Yet the Soviet Russian state was helping to strengthen this right-wing military force, which could be used to crush an uprising of the German proletariat.[17]

[15] Clara Zetkin, *Reminiscences of Lenin* (New York, 1934), p. 19.
[16] Ruth Fischer, *Stalin*, p. 199; Kochan, *Russia and the Weimar Republic*, pp. 65–68.
[17] On Reichswehr–Red Army collaboration, see Cecil F. Melville, *The Russian Face of Germany: An Account of the Secret Military Relations Between the German and Soviet-Russian Governments* (London, 1932); Wollenberg, *Red Army*, pp. 234–39; Friedrich von Rabenau, *Seeckt: Aus Seinem Leben, 1918–1936* (Leipzig, 1940), pp. 305–19; Julius Epstein, Eugen Fischer-Baling, M. J. L., "Der Seeckt-Plan," *Der Monat*, I, No. 2 (Nov., 1948), 42–58; Ruth

In June, 1923, following the French occupation of the Ruhr, Radek openly presented the thesis of National Bolshevism to a meeting of the Comintern Executive Committee in Moscow. He argued that a German Communist revolution could not succeed at that time and that the Comintern should therefore play the German nationalist card, which would coincide with the interests of the Soviet Russian state. This time Radek's proposal for a Communist-led nationalist bloc found wide acceptance in the Russian Politburo, and he was entrusted with building up the "Schlageter movement," glorifying a German fascist martyr, as a means of popularizing National Bolshevism.[18]

The final episode of this German policy was acted out in August, 1923, with the fall of the Russian-oriented Cuno government. It was replaced by the Stresemann government, which hoped through British support to work out a settlement with France on the disputes over the Ruhr and reparations. The prospect of Germany abandoning the spirit of Rapallo and casting its lot with the Entente promptly forced the Russian Politburo to scuttle the policy of National Bolshevism. In October, 1923, Moscow ordered a revolution in Germany as a logical protest against Germany's turn toward the West. That is, a key consideration which touched off an ill-fated revolution in Germany was based, not on the plight of the German proletariat, but on the changed status of the relations between the German and Russian states.[19]

This same conflict between proletarian internationalism and Russian nationalism appeared in determining Soviet and Comintern policy in the Near and Middle East. At the Second Comintern Congress in 1920 the Theses presented by the Indian Communist M. N.

Fischer, *Stalin*, pp. 263–65, 527–36; George W. F. Hallgarten, "General Hans von Seeckt and Russia, 1920–1922," *Journal of Modern History*, XXI, No. 1 (March, 1949), 28–34; E. H. Carr, *German-Soviet Relations* (Baltimore, 1951), pp. 55–61, 93–96, 119–21; Carr, *Bolshevik Revolution*, III, 361–65, 370–72, 435–37; Gustav Hilger and Alfred G. Meyer, *The Incompatible Allies* (New York, 1953), pp. 187–208; Arthur L. Smith, "The German General Staff and Russia, 1919–1926," *Soviet Studies*, VIII, No. 2 (Oct., 1956), 125–33; Gerald Freund, *Unholy Alliance* (New York, 1957), pp. 85, 92–93, 112–13, 124–26, 201–12; Eudin and Fisher, *Soviet Russia and the West*, pp. 173–74, 205–9.

[18] Ruth Fischer, *Stalin*, pp. 266–73; Carr, *German-Soviet Relations*, pp. 71–72; Kochan, *Russia and the Weimar Republic*, pp. 71–78; Freund, *Unholy Alliance*, pp. 149–62; Eudin and Fisher, *Soviet Russia and the West*, pp. 171–72, 184.

[19] Ruth Fischer, *Stalin*, pp. 303–4, 312; Carr, *German-Soviet Relations*, pp. 73–75; Kochan, *Russia and the Weimar Republic*, pp. 80–85; Freund, *Unholy Alliance*, pp. 168–83.

Roy placed primary emphasis on establishing and strengthening revolutionary Communist Parties in the colonial and semicolonial areas.[20] Lenin's Theses, on the other hand, put greater emphasis on strengthening the national liberation movements through sanctioning temporary alliances between the Communist Parties and the rising bourgeoisie in the dependent areas.[21] Unlike Roy's Theses, Lenin's were compatible with the Soviet official policy of helping newly formed nationalist governments to eject the Western imperialist powers. The effect of Lenin's policy, as it turned out, was that official Soviet relations were developed with these new governments, based on the power interests of the Russian state, frequently at the expense of the local Communist movements.

This tendency was illustrated by the fate of the First Congress of the Peoples of the East, organized by the Comintern in September, 1920. The Congress, which was overflowing with direct revolutionary appeals to the colonial peoples, was intended to be the first of a series of such gatherings, and even established a permanent organization for future meetings. But as Louis Fischer pointed out, "the First Congress remained the only Congress. The establishment of normal diplomatic relations between the governments of Eastern countries and the government of Russia began to take precedence over the relations between the revolutionary movements in Eastern countries with the revolutionary movements of Russia." [22]

Soviet Russia eagerly embraced Kemalist Turkey, even though Ankara systematically undermined and then decimated the Turkish Communist Party.[23] When Kemal Pasha tore up the Treaty of Sèvres and raised an army against the invading Greeks, the Soviet leaders thought that the Russian state had found an ally. It was clear

[20] For a discussion of the differing versions of Roy's Theses, see Carr, *Bolshevik Revolution*, III, 252–57. Roy recalls: "My contention when I disagreed with Lenin in the Second World Congress was that, if the nationalist movement succeeded under the leadership of the bourgeoisie, it would only mean transfer of power to the native ruling class; there would be no social revolution." (M. N. Roy, "Joseph Stalin, Mephisto of Modern History," *The Radical Humanist* [Bombay], XIV, No. 49 [Dec. 10, 1950], 582.)

[21] Lenin, "Pervonachal'nyi nabrosok tezisov po natsional'nomu i kolonial'nomu voprosam," June 5, 1920, in *Sochineniia*, XXV, 285–90; "Natsional'nyi i kolonial'nyi voprosy," July 19–Aug. 7, 1920, in *Kom. Int. v dok.*, pp. 126–30.

[22] Louis Fischer, *Soviets in World Affairs*, I, 284. See also Carr, *Bolshevik Revolution*, III, 388–89, 468–70.

[23] For a documentary survey of these relations, see Eudin and North, *Soviet Russia and the East*, pp. 106–16, 184–91; "Documents from the History of Soviet-Turkish Relations," *International Affairs* (Moscow), No. 2 (Feb., 1958), pp. 123–29.

to all that, for the moment, France and Britain stood behind Greece and that victory for a newly united, nationalist Turkey would be a defeat for the Entente. Consequently when Kemal appealed to Lenin in April, 1920, for political support and material aid, he found a ready response. Friendly negotiations were opened in Moscow during July, 1920, and proceeded to the conclusion of the Soviet-Turkish Treaties of Friendship, signed in March and October, 1921.[24] In December, 1921, Frunze, the Soviet military leader, traveling in the guise of a representative of the Ukrainian SSR, visited Ankara "to arrange for heavy shipments of Russian munitions and for the mapping out of a detailed plan of campaign against the Greeks in which, if need be, Red officers would participate." [25]

All the while the fledgling Turkish Communist Party had been subjected to Kemal's severe harassment. In January, 1921, the top leadership of the Party was mysteriously drowned in the Black Sea off Trebizond. This was followed by a general repression of the remainder of the Communist movement in Turkey, so that by February, 1923, the Comintern acknowledged that "the Turkish Communist Party has been routed." [26] Moscow periodically protested against these Kemalist persecutions, but this in no way interfered with a policy of full Soviet support for Kemal's government vis-à-vis the Entente. At the Lausanne Conference, for example, which convened from November, 1922, until July, 1923, Chicherin insisted even more adamantly than the Turks that Turkey be given the right to fortify the Straits and to prohibit the passage of all warships.

A somewhat similar concession to Russian national interests occurred in neighboring Persia. The Soviet Republic of Ghilan, established in northern Persia in May, 1920, with Soviet military support, was dissolved on direct orders from Moscow in October, 1921. In order to forestall the creation of a British protectorate in southern Persia, which would have placed a great power within reach of the

[24] Degras, ed., *Soviet Documents*, I, 238, 264, 266. These treaties also temporarily resolved the conflicting Soviet-Turkish territorial ambitions in the Transcaucasus arising from the destruction and partial dismemberment of the independent states of Georgia and Armenia.

[25] Louis Fischer, *Soviets in World Affairs*, I, 393. See also I, 391, 394. On this trip, according to Frunze's own account, "The most important military secrets were made known to me." (M. V. Frunze, *Sochineniia*, I, 359; quoted in Eudin and North, *Soviet Russia and the East*, p. 113.) On January 2, 1922, Frunze also signed a Ukrainian-Turkish Treaty of Friendship.

[26] *Izvestiia*, Feb. 14, 1923; quoted in Eudin and North, *Soviet Russia and the East*, p. 191. See also Carr, *Bolshevik Revolution*, III, 298–301, 479–84.

border of the Russian state, Moscow chose to sacrifice its revolutionary foothold in Persia and to strengthen the hand of a unified nationalist government in Teheran, which would be capable of controlling provincial and tribal leaders who might otherwise come under British influence.[27]

The conflict between Russian national interests and revolutionary internationalism also affected Soviet relations with China. The status of Outer Mongolia and the future of the Chinese Eastern Railway were the two principal apples of discord.

By 1916 Outer Mongolia had fallen almost completely under Russian control, although Russia continued to recognize Chinese suzerainty over it. After the revolution in Russia, China eliminated Russian control and extended its own administration over Outer Mongolia. When, in the flush of revolutionary fervor, the Soviet government declared that "all previous treaties made between the Russian Government and China shall be null and void, and that the Soviet Government renounces all encroachments on Chinese territory and all concessions within China," the Chinese assumed that Soviet Russia had relinquished all Tsarist privileges in Outer Mongolia. This pledge had been offered as a gesture of genuine proletarian internationalism, as one of a series of anti-imperialist proclamations renouncing all of the national privileges of Tsarist Russia on foreign soil. In November, 1921, however, Soviet Russia signed a treaty with a Soviet-sponsored People's Revolutionary Government of Outer Mongolia. This treaty not only recognized the Soviet puppet regime as "the only legal government" of Outer Mongolia, but also completely ignored the rights of China. Peking responded with anger that "the Soviet Government has suddenly gone back on its own words and secretly and without any right concluded a treaty with Mongolia. Such action on the part of the Soviet Government is similar to the policy the former Imperial Russian Government assumed towards China." [28]

A like reversion to the Tsarist Russian mentality occurred in the case of the Chinese Eastern Railway. On July 5, 1918, Chicherin, the

[27] Louis Fischer, *Soviets in World Affairs*, I, 430, 463; Alexander Barmine, *One Who Survived* (New York, 1945), p. 143. See also, Eudin and North, *Soviet Russia and the East*, pp. 91–103, 175–81.
[28] Note of the Chinese Foreign Office, May 1, 1922, *Peking Daily News*, May 6, 1922; quoted in Dennis, *Foreign Policies*, p. 324; see also pp. 320–23. For the use of Russian national sentiment in the period of the Japanese intervention in Siberia, see p. 284.

Soviet Commissar of Foreign Affairs, told the Fifth Congress of Soviets that the Soviet government wished to expedite the return of the Chinese Eastern Railway to China. This offer was specifically extended to include return without compensation in a Manifesto of July 25, 1919, signed by Karakhan, Deputy Commissar of Foreign Affairs. But the Soviet government reconsidered, and the Manifesto appeared in *Izvestiia* on August 26, 1919, with no mention whatever of the Chinese Eastern Railway. When Joffe, the Soviet Ambassador to China, arrived in Peking in 1922, he specifically stated that the Chinese Eastern Railway had not been ceded to China, and in 1923 Karakhan himself denied that he had ever signed a document to that effect. Despite Chinese protests, the Chinese Eastern Railway continued to operate under Russian control until the Soviet government sold its rights to the Japanese puppet state of Manchukuo in the mid-1930s.[29] Once again the bonds of solidarity of an international class proved weaker than the material interests of the Soviet Russian state.

A DEFINITION OF PROLETARIAN INTERNATIONALISM

This very un-Marxist priority of nation above class was displayed by those Soviet leaders entrusted with the practical conduct of the affairs of the Russian nation. But during the first few years of the Comintern's existence there was still a strong current asserting the priority of class above nation. The Second Comintern Congress in 1920 dedicated itself to the cause of proletarian internationalism which was defined as: "(1) the subordination of the interests of the proletarian struggle in one country to the interests of the struggle on a world scale, and (2) the ability and readiness on the part of the nation which has gained a victory over the bourgeoisie to make the greatest national sacrifices for the sake of overthrowing international capitalism." [30]

This formula, which subordinated the interests both of the Russian nation and of the Soviet state to the goals of proletarian internationalism, came from the pen of Lenin, writing as a leader of the Comintern. In this capacity he stood in clear contradiction to the

[29] Allen S. Whiting, "The Soviet Offer to China of 1919," *The Far Eastern Quarterly*, X, No. 4 (Aug., 1951), 355–64; Ling Nai-jui, "Tsarist and Soviet Diplomacy in China," in Waldemar Gurian, ed., *Soviet Imperialism* (Notre Dame, 1953), pp. 117–21.
[30] "Natsional'nyi i kolonial'nyi voprosy," in *Kom. Int. v dok.*, p. 128; Lenin, "Pervonachal'nyi nabrosok," in *Sochineniia*, XXV, 288–89.

position he took as head of the Russian state. The contradiction was also evident in the twenty-one Conditions which he stipulated that foreign Parties must accept before joining the Comintern.[31] If Lenin were only interested in gaining support for the Russian state and not in building his own international class organization, he need not have split the world labor movement, as he did, by insisting upon the expulsion of all factions of the foreign socialist and Communist Parties which failed to measure up to his rigid ideological standards. The Western European Social Democrats, in particular, were one certain source of support upon which Lenin could have counted, if he had not chosen to reject them in this doctrinaire insistence on the purity of proletarian internationalism. Point Fourteen of the twenty-one Conditions, on the other hand, emphasized the importance of the Russian state by making it obligatory for the world proletariat to render every kind of assistance to that proletarian republic which had already achieved state power.[32] The 1920 Statutes of the Comintern also declared that "the Communist International fully and unreservedly upholds the gains of the great proletarian revolution in Russia." [33]

The tug between Russian nationalism and proletarian internationalism, which was evident even within the Comintern, was especially apparent in the conflicts between the Comintern and the Soviet Russian Commissariat of Foreign Affairs. Time and again Chicherin sought to hamper the activities of the Comintern agents that proved embarrassing to the conduct of the foreign relations of the Russian state, while Zinoviev, for the Comintern, protested against the primacy of interests claimed by the Commissariat. Carr places the end of this struggle as early as December, 1922, when a reorganization of the Comintern apparatus at the Fourth Comintern Congress lodged unchallengeable authority in the hands of the already dominant Russian contingent. "Henceforth the policy of Comintern would be fitted into a framework of Soviet foreign policy instead of Soviet foreign policy being fitted—as had once been the case, at any rate in form—into a framework of world revolution." [34]

[31] "Usloviia priëma v Kommunisticheskii Internatsional," July 19–Aug. 7, 1920, in *Kom. Int. v dok.*, pp. 100–4.
[32] *Ibid.*, p. 103.
[33] "Ustav Kommunisticheskogo Internatsionala," July 19–Aug. 7, 1920, in *Vtoroi kongress Kommunisticheskogo Internatsionala*, p. 536.
[34] Carr, *Bolshevik Revolution*, III, 451. On the reorganization of the Comintern's structure, see *Fourth Congress of the Communist International*, pp. 8–13, 181–88.

TWO APPROACHES TO A SOVIET WORLD STATE

This brief account of the forces at work in the early 1920s would indicate that proletarian internationalism was destined to wage a losing battle. But did the encroachments of Russian nationalism mean that the goal of an International Soviet Republic had given way to the more restricted goal of a nation-state operating in a predominantly bourgeois nation-state system? Is it possible that the *goal* of Soviet Russian nationalism was identical with the goal of proletarian internationalism, each tendency differing in the values emphasized and in the approach used toward the realization of a common objective? The purist advocates of proletarian internationalism had dedicated their lives to a world state and not to any particular nation-state. They demanded "the ability and readiness on the part of the nation which has gained a victory over the bourgeoisie to make the greatest national sacrifices for the sake of overthrowing international capitalism." Their world state would be one of genuine proletarian brotherhood and equality, with no one nation exalted above any other.

Those who were in charge of running the Russian state, however, found it difficult to implement these clear-cut prescriptions. While pursuing the same ultimate goal of a world state and professing to uphold the interests of world socialism, these statesmen were forced to maneuver the Russian state in the perilous balance-of-power game of international politics. These leaders, whom we may call partisans of Soviet Russian nationalism, therefore frequently demanded sacrifices on the part of non-Russian proletarian movements for the sake of aiding and strengthening the Soviet Russian fatherland, which they regarded as the *center* or the nucleus of an emergent world state. Progress toward a world state would then be synonymous with a process of continual aggrandizement and glorification of Soviet Russia. The end result of this process would be a world state in which all nations were equal, but in which Russia was "more equal" (to adopt George Orwell's phrase).

In the struggle between these two approaches to a Soviet world state, Soviet Russian nationalism took an early lead which it has never relinquished. Soviet leaders have always taken great pains to rationalize their Russian nationalism in the language of proletarian internationalism, since a naked, un-Marxist explanation of their conduct would undermine the basic class tenets of their regime and would strike a body blow at the legions of uncritical Soviet supporters throughout the world. The most common Soviet technique has been to identify the interests of Russian nationalism with those of the international proletariat and to assert that the two are indissolubly merged. In March, 1923, for example, Trotsky was asked by an English newspaper reporter in what way the interests of the Comintern contradicted those of Soviet Russia. Trotsky replied that "the contrast itself is possible only if one contrasts the 'national' interests of Russia with the international interests of the working class." This conflict of interests was nonexistent, Trotsky insisted, since "the national interests of Russia coincide with the interests of her ruling class, i.e., the proletariat. But the genuine interests of the working class cannot be satisfied otherwise than by international means, i.e., by means of the establishment of a World Federation of Republics based on labor and its solidarity." [35] That is, the national interests of Soviet Russia and the interests of the international proletariat are identical and can only be satisfied by the establishment of a Soviet world state.

With the development of Stalin's theory of "socialism in one country" in 1924, Trotsky soon shifted his position. He claimed that this theory marked a parting of the ways between the interests of the Russian state and those of the international proletariat, and contended that the theory of socialism in one country meant the abandonment of the international tasks of the proletariat and the eventual degeneration of the Soviet Union to the status of a bourgeois nation-state, in the stage of state capitalism.

In a speech of June, 1925, Stalin admitted that "the pressure exercised by the capitalist states upon the Soviet Union is tremendous and the officials who are working in our Commissariat of Foreign Affairs are not always able to withstand this pressure, but are tempted to adopt the line of least resistance, to enter the path leading to nationalism." He gave reassurance, however, that this pressure could and would be resisted, since "it is abundantly clear that the first proletarian state can retain its position of standard-bearer of the international revolutionary movement only on the condition that it retain a consistently internationalist outlook." [36] Then, in phrases

[35] "Interview by Trotsky on Russia and the European Situation," *Manchester Guardian*, March 1, 1923; in Degras, ed., *Soviet Documents*, I, 375.
[36] Stalin, "Voprosy i otvety, rech' v Sverdlovskom universitete," June 9, 1925, in *Sochineniia*, VII, 169.

very much like those used by Trotsky in 1923, he sought to identify the interests of Russian nationalism with those of proletarian internationalism. In a speech to a Comintern gathering in December, 1926, Stalin said that

> the Party proceeds from the assumption that the "national" and the international tasks of the proletariat of the USSR fuse into the one common task of the liberation of the proletariat of all countries from capitalism, that the interests of building socialism in our country completely and fully merge with the interests of the revolutionary movement in all countries, in the one general interest of the victory of the socialist revolution in all countries.

It followed from this that "to place the 'national' tasks of the proletariat of this or that country in opposition to its international tasks is to fall into the most serious error." [37] Again, the national tasks of the Russian state and the international tasks of the proletariat could only be fulfilled by the creation of a Soviet world state, and the identity of this goal was used to obscure the process by which Russian nationalism benefited at the expense of proletarian internationalism.

THE CHARACTER OF RUSSIAN HEGEMONY IN THE USSR

In support of its claim that the Soviet Union is "the prototype of the future World Soviet Socialist Republic," the Soviet leadership has constantly boasted of its achievements of genuine proletarian internationalism within the existing Soviet state. Even among those who are aware of the complex ethnic composition of the USSR, there is a widespread tendency to give credence to Soviet assertions concerning the existence of national equality in the Soviet Union and to underestimate the serious friction, both past and present, which has been generated between the Russian and the non-Russian peoples.

Several important factors not directly associated with Russian nationalism as such have contributed heavily to the sacrifice of non-Russian interests within the Soviet Union. The very fact that the Bolshevik Revolution was made primarily in the name of the proletariat and not primarily in the name of the peasantry automatically placed the Great Russians in a favored position. The proletariat as the new ruling class was predominantly Great Russian, not only in

[37] Stalin, "Eshchë raz o sotsial-demokraticheskom uklone v nashei partii," Dec. 7, 1926, in *ibid.*, IX, 27-28.

the heartland of Russia proper, but also to a large extent in the border areas, such as the Ukraine, Belorussia, and Soviet Central Asia.

Lenin's polemic with a Ukrainian Social Democrat in 1913 illustrates how emphasis upon the proletariat tended to carry with it a built-in bias in favor of the Great Russian. One could not be upset by the complaint, Lenin insisted, that the predominance of Great Russian proletarians in the Ukrainian urban centers threatened to obliterate the national culture of the Ukrainian workers. To be sure, Lenin sought to dissociate his nationality policy from that of the reactionary Great Russian chauvinists by urging a "resolute struggle against the incredible humiliation of the Ukrainians," demanding instead "complete equality for them." "But it would be an outright betrayal of socialism . . . to *weaken* the connection and union that presently exists between the Ukrainian and Great Russian proletariat," that is, it would be a betrayal of socialism to use the national culture of the Ukrainian worker as a barrier against strengthening the proletarian movement. Whoever would cast aside an overriding interest in the amalgamation of the proletariat of the two nations "for the sake of the momentary success of Ukrainian national glory," was castigated as "a short-sighted, narrow-minded, stupid bourgeois." The Ukrainian proletarian would apparently discover his "complete equality" with his Great Russian brother by immersing himself in the culture of the dominant Russian proletariat. "The Ukrainian *Marxist*," Lenin concluded, "will say to his workers: 'You must without fail, seize, use, and strengthen with all your might every opportunty for intimate contact with the Great Russian class-conscious workers, with their literature and with their range of ideas; the fundamental interests of *both* the Ukrainian and the Great Russian working class movements demand this.' " [38] But to what extent could the Ukrainian worker be immersed in the culture of the dominant Russian proletariat without being inundated by it? Lenin did not say, since he did not pursue the logical implication of his position.

Russian domination of the proletariat continued unabated following the Bolshevik Revolution. An official Party historian candidly described the situation, for example, at the time of the Twelfth Party Congress in 1923: "If we consider the whole composition of the population of the U.S.S.R., we find that the proletariat of our

[38] Lenin, "Kriticheskie zametki," in *Sochineniia*, XVII, 142-44.

country, not only in the central parts but in the outlying regions as well, is mainly Russian or Russianised." [39] Had a peasant party such as the Social Revolutionaries seized power, the rural non-Russian peoples would have had a better chance of resisting the pressure of Great Russian control.

A revolution based on large-scale industry instead of small-scale farming provided another subtle impetus to Great Russian domination. The Communists looked forward to a highly complex, but thoroughly integrated, planned and centralized industrial society. This made Moscow, as the administrative center of the Soviet Union, the integrating and planning center. It elevated the status of Moscow (the core of Great Russia) beyond what might have resulted from a more decentralized, agricultural based society, such as anticipated by the Social Revolutionaries.

Another factor arose specifically from the nature of the Bolshevik faction of Russian Social Democracy. The industrialized and centralized society was to be run by a Party organized upon highly authoritarian principles. The encouragement which the centralist Party structure gave to Great Russian nationalism was evident from the first, but the union of these two forces was not formally consummated until after the Party had become "monolithic" in fact. As power congealed in the Party, any type of freedom, either of individuals or of nationalities, was looked upon as a challenge to the centralized authority of the Party. Again the nub of Party authority rested in Great Russia and those who exercised this authority were Great Russians, or Russified non-Russians. This gave rise to suspicions in Moscow that those who resisted the influence of Great Russians were also resisting control by the centralized Party apparatus.

From the beginning the Bolshevik Party was predominantly Russian-based. Stalin readily acknowledged this when, in 1907, he admitted that "the overwhelming majority of the Bolshevik faction consists of Russians." [40] This Russian-based character of the Bolshe-

---

[39] N. Popov, *Outline History of the Communist Party of the Soviet Union*, 1927 (New York, 1934), II, 189.

[40] Stalin, "Londonskii s"ezd RSDRP," July 3, 1907, in *Sochineniia*, II, 50. By way of contrast, Stalin said that "statistics showed that the majority of the Menshevik faction consists of Jews (not counting the Bundists, of course), then come the Georgians and then the Russians." Stalin added that the Bolshevik Aleksinskii (later an open anti-Semite) might have hit upon something worth while in his joke "that the Mensheviks were a Jewish faction while the

vik Party naturally reinforced the tendency toward Great Russian control which, in any case, would have been produced by the centralized Party structure. The Mensheviks could point to a non-Russian nation like Georgia, for example, where an independent Georgian Republic was established and run by native Georgian Mensheviks. But when the Bolsheviks seized power among non-Russian peoples, they were invariably regarded as an alien Russian force. By 1922 only 24 percent of the Communist Party of the Ukraine consisted of Ukrainians, and only 21 percent of the Communist Party of Belorussia were Belorussians. It was not until after Stalin's death that a Ukrainian held the key position of First Secretary of the Central Committee of the Communist Party of the Ukraine, and in those instances in which native Communists have held the First Secretaryship in their Republics, their power has been more apparent than real, with a Russian Second Secretary wielding decisive authority.[41]

No one was more devoted to an authoritarian, centralized Party structure than Lenin. At the same time, though, he was aware of the danger of exciting Great Russian chauvinism, which he appeared to resist. He realized the difficulty of rallying into a large union many non-Russian peoples, who formerly had been antagonized by the Tsarist Russification policies. It was for this reason that Lenin complained: "Scratch some Communists and you will find a Great Russian chauvinist." [42]

Strangely enough many of the leading Communist Great Russian chauvinists were of non-Russian origin, and many of them were located in the Commissariat of Nationalities. Trotsky even expressed his sympathy for Stalin as the Commissar of Nationalities (1917–1923) because of the extreme pressure to which he was subjected by

---

Bolsheviks were a truly Russian one and that it might thus be a good idea for us Bolsheviks to start a pogrom within the Party." It appears that anti-Semitism was never really alien to Stalin and that the open Soviet anti-Semitism of Stalin's last years had roots in such crude jests as this.

[41] John S. Reshetar, Jr., "National Deviation in the Soviet Union," *American Slavic*, XII, No. 2 (April, 1953), 162–63, 170. See also George Fedotov, "The Fate of Empires," *Russian Review*, XII, No. 2 (April, 1953), 91. For an account of the severe frictions between the Russian and Ukrainian Communists in the early 1920s see Michael Pap, "Soviet Difficulties in the Ukraine," *Review of Politics*, XIV, No. 2 (April, 1952), 213–17. Finally on June 12, 1953, a Ukrainian, A. I. Kirichenko, was made First Secretary of the CC of the CP of the Ukraine: see "Plenum TsK KP Ukrainy," *Pravda*, June 13, 1953, p. 2.

[42] Lenin, "Zakliuchitel'noe slovo po dokladu o partiinoi programme," March 19, 1919, in *Sochineniia*, XXIV, 155.

his colleagues. The Collegium of Stalin's Commissariat consisted of Russified non-Russian Communists, who took the position that national oppression was only a manifestation of class oppression and that Soviet Russia, in destroying class oppression, therefore no longer needed to regard nationalities as serious entities. They opposed the creation of national republics and thought of dividing the state upon the basis of purely economic and administrative considerations.[43] Here is an example of doctrinaire Marxist internationalism, emphasizing centralism for economic reasons, but having the effect of undermining the status of the border nations and of elevating the authority of the Great Russian center. Perhaps the zeal of these non-Russian Communists to dissociate themselves from their native nationalists, who were almost always anti-Bolshevik, caused them to overshoot the mark and to fall into a posture of Great Russian chauvinism.

Though he did not accept the radical advice of his Collegium, Stalin, too, proved to be a Russified non-Russian. Stalin's Great Russian bias became obvious and indisputable only toward the end of his rule. During the first decade of Soviet power, in particular when the Soviet hold over the non-Russian regions was none too secure, he frequently condemned Great Russian chauvinism. At the same time, this early period revealed clear traces of his later shift to the position of a Russian chauvinist, which was a development of fundamental and lasting importance. Speaking in January, 1921, to a gathering of Turkic peoples, who vividly remembered the impact of Russian conquest, Stalin made this astounding assertion:

> Being in the past a governing nation the Russians in general, and the Russian Communists in particular, have not experienced national oppression, and generally speaking have not had to deal with any nationalistic tendencies in their midst, except for certain tendencies toward "great power chauvinism," and it was therefore not necessary, or almost not necessary, for them to overcome such tendencies.[44]

Another early evidence of Stalin's Russian nationalism appeared in his Draft Resolution on the formation of the USSR. Lenin circulated a letter of September 27, 1922, to the members of the Russian Politburo criticizing Stalin's Draft as being weighted in favor of the Great Russians. Lenin reported that "Stalin has already agreed to one

---

[43] Trotsky, *Stalin*, p. 257.
[44] Stalin, "Rech' pri otkrytii soveshchaniia kommunistov tiurksikh narodov RSFSR," Jan. 1, 1921, in *Sochineniia*, V, 2.

concession . . . instead of saying 'entry' into the R.S.F.S.R., to say 'formal unification' with the R.S.F.S.R. in a Union of Soviet Republics of Europe and Asia."[45] This would avoid the impression at least that Russia was swallowing up the other nations in this new union.

Then on December 31, 1922, Trotsky received a letter from Lenin, who was greatly disturbed by the ruthless measures that Stalin was using in subjecting his native Georgia to Soviet rule. Lenin said that "it is of course necessary to hold Stalin and Dzerzhinskii responsible for all this really Great Russian nationalistic campaign."[46] Lenin's personal secretary reported that "Vladimir Il'ich is preparing a bomb against Stalin" on the national question to be delivered at the forthcoming Twelfth Party Congress.[47] But before the Congress opened in April, 1923, Lenin had suffered another stroke and was unable to appear. Stalin quickly tried to repair his position by drafting the Theses for the Congress in which he called "the attention of the members of the Party to the particular danger of the deviation toward Great Russian chauvinism."[48]

In his speech to the Congress, however, Stalin relied heavily upon another Leninist tenet, namely, that the rights of nations must always be subordinated to the requirements of the class struggle. The effect of this argument substantially negated Stalin's disavowal of Great Russian chauvinism. "It is clear," Stalin noted, "that the political basis of the proletarian dictatorship is first of all and primarily in the central, industrial regions, and not in the borderlands which are peasant countries." While conceding that the non-Russian border nations must not be offended, Stalin warned that solicitude for the peasant borderlands must not be at the expense of the Great Russian industrial centers. "It is absurd to formulate a new theory that one must place the Great Russian proletariat in an inferior position

---

[45] Quoted in Trotsky, *Real Situation*, p. 294. Following Khrushchev's attack on Stalin this has finally been confirmed in the Soviet press. See "Neopublikovannye dokumenty V. I. Lenina," *Kommunist*, No. 9 (June, 1956), p. 26, n. 1.

[46] Trotsky, *Real Situation*, p. 298. The accuracy of Trotsky's documents on the Georgian question are confirmed in "Neopublikovannye," *Kommunist*, No. 9 (June, 1956), pp. 22-26. See also Pipes, *The Formation*, pp. 273-77. Dzerzhinskii, Polish by birth, was also a Russified non-Russian.

[47] Trotsky, *Real Situation*, p. 306. See also Trotsky, *My Life*, pp. 482-88; Trotsky, *Stalin*, pp. 360-64, 374.

[48] Stalin, "Natsional'nye momenty v partiinom i gosudarstvennom stroitel'stve," March 24, 1923, in *Sochineniia*, V, 193.

in relation to the formerly oppressed nations." [49] In the guise of placing the interests of class above nation Stalin was actually placing one nation above others by sanctioning the domination of a Great Russian, centralized, proletarian dictatorship over the non-Russian peasant masses in the borderlands.

Stalin soon made explicit the limitations beyond which he was unwilling to tolerate criticism of the Great Russians. In the spring of 1923 his protégé in charge of Moslem affairs, Sultan-Galiev, protested that "the policy of the Soviet government in regard to the non-Russian peoples differs scarcely at all from the policy of the Great Russian chauvinists," and that "the promises given in 1917 have remained only words." [50] The expression of this view prompted Stalin to arrest Sultan-Galiev, and subsequently to convoke a special conference of non-Russian peoples for the purpose of admonishing against further "counter-revolutionary deviations" in the Soviet nationality policy. Stalin bitterly attacked those Moslem Communists who "said that there was no difference between present-day Turkestan and Tsarist Turkestan." [51] On the other hand, he maintained the appearance of impartiality by chastising those Russian Communist officials in the borderlands who failed to "make concessions to those local national elements who are willing to work locally within the Soviet system." Stalin then revealed the conditional nature and the ultimate purpose of these concessions when he added, significantly: "Only in this way will it be possible successfully *to eliminate local nationalism* and to win the broad strata of the population to the side of the Soviet regime." [52]

During the 1920s and the early 1930s the most aggressive aspects of Russian nationalism were held in check. But even then loud complaints were raised against the Russian-dominated Party and state

[49] Stalin, "Zakliuchitel'noe slovo po dokladu o natsional'nykh momentakh v partiinom i gosudarstvennom stroitel'stve," April 25, 1923, in *ibid.*, V, 264-66.
[50] In the Turkish journal, *Yana Milli Vol*, No. 10 (1931), pp. 13-15, from the Tatar newspaper *Kzyl Tatarstan;* quoted in E. H. Carr, *The Interregnum, 1923-1924* (London, 1954), pp. 286-87. On Sultan-Galiev, see Pipes, *The Formation*, pp. 168-70, 190, 260-63; A. Bennigsen, "Sultan-Galiev: The USSR and the Colonial Revolution," in Walter Z. Laqueur, ed., *The Middle East in Transition* (New York, 1958), pp. 398-414; Walter Z. Laqueur, *The Soviet Union and the Middle East* (New York, 1959), pp. 19-26, 308-11.
[51] Stalin, "O pravykh i 'levykh' v natsrespublikakh i oblastiakh," June 10, 1923, in *Sochineniia*, V, 306.
[52] Stalin, "Proekt platformy po natsional'nomu voprosu k IV soveshchaniiu, odobrennyi Politbiuro TsK," end of May, 1923, in *ibid.*, V, 294 (italics added).

administrative apparatus in the non-Russian republics, as well as against the Red Army and the trade union organizations, which the non-Russian peoples widely regarded as agents of Russification.[53] The high-water mark of tolerance for the development of the non-Russian peoples was probably reached in 1926. In April of that year a furious debate over the tempo and extent of national development of non-Russian peoples occurred between the Russian Communists and a bloc of Ukrainian, Transcaucasian, and other non-Russian Communists.[54] Shumskii, the Ukrainian Commissar of Education, had led the fight for rapid "Ukrainization" of the Ukraine, but his demands were rebuffed by Moscow and he was soon dismissed from office. In a letter of April 26, 1926, to the Politburo of the Communist Party of the Ukraine, Stalin revealed his fears about Shumskii's demands and explained why he thought them excessive. "Shumskii does not see that this movement . . . could acquire the character of an estrangement of Ukrainian culture and Ukrainian society from an all-Soviet culture and society, the character of a struggle against 'Moscow' in general, against Russians in general, against Russian culture and its highest achievement—Leninism." [55]

The conflict between Russian nationalism and proletarian internationalism also flared up in an exchange of views between Stalin and the Ukrainian Communist writer Khvilevoi. In 1926 Khvilevoi published a frank statement rejecting the supremacy of things Russian. He asked:

From which world literature should our literature take its cue? *Under no conditions from Russian.* That is definite and without reservation. . . . From Russian literature, from its styles, Ukrainian poetry must flee as fast as it can! . . . We know the ideas of the proletariat without Moscow's art.[56]

[53] *Natsional'naia politika VKP(b) v tsifrakh* (Moscow, 1930), pp. 26, 48–50, 138–39, 199, 236; Kolarz, *Russia and Her Colonies*, pp. 8–9; Carr, *Bolshevik Revolution*, I, 367–71.
[54] Reshetar, "National Deviation," *American Slavic*, XII, No. 2 (April, 1953), 166. See also Alexander Ohloblyn, "Ukrainian Humanities and the Soviets," *Ukrainian Quarterly*, V, No. 1 (Winter, 1949), 10–19; Ilarion Ohienko, "Ukrainian Literary Language in the U.S.S.R.," *ibid.*, VI, No. 3 (Summer, 1950), 229–40.
[55] Stalin, "Tov. Kaganovichu i drugim chlenam PB TsK KP(b)U," April 26, 1926, in *Sochineniia*, VIII, 152. On Shumskii's "Ukrainization" program, see E. F. Girchak, *Na dva fronta v bor'be s natsionalizmom* (Moscow, Leningrad, 1930), pp. 99–109, 177–85, 216–19.
[56] Quoted in Girchak, *Na dva fronta*, p. 51. When transliterated from the Ukrainian, his name appears as Khvylovy

Khvilevoi thought of proletarian internationalism as giving to each nation the right to develop its own culture on a basis of equality with all others. Subservience to another nation was made no more palatable because such domination came from Moscow. Khvilevoi, in fact, was strongly oriented away from Moscow and toward the West, as are many Ukrainians. Through the old Kievan empire and then through the Ukrainian-Polish-Lithuanian commonwealth, the people of the Ukraine had for centuries established much deeper ties with the West than had Muscovy, which remained essentially Eastern in orientation.[57]

To all of this Stalin struck back sharply:

Whereas the proletarians of Western Europe and their Communist Parties are full of sympathy for "Moscow," the citadel of the international revolutionary movement and of Leninism, whereas the proletarians of Western Europe turn with joy to the banner waving over Moscow, the Ukrainian Communist, Khvilevoi, has nothing better to say for "Moscow" than to appeal to Ukrainian public men to get away from "Moscow" "as quickly as possible." And this is called internationalism! [58]

From this interchange it is apparent that Stalin equated "internationalism" with supreme loyalty to Moscow, which was not only a symbol of revolution, but also of the Russian nation.

After Stalin's chastisement, the Ukrainization program was allowed to continue until 1933, but at a more carefully regulated tempo. Shumskii's place was taken by the Ukrainian Communist Skrypnyk, who tried to carry on Shumskii's work under the increasingly watchful eye of Moscow. At the Sixteenth Party Congress in 1930 Stalin's official position remained that "the greatest danger is the *great-power deviation*" of Great Russian chauvinism.[59]

However, Stalin expressed another view in a private letter of De-

[57] Thus a Great Russian, the late George Fedotov, remarked: "We had outrageously neglected to acquaint ourselves with the Ukrainian past during those three or four centuries that had molded her nationality and culture in a way different from Great Russia. We assumed, in accordance with the historical scheme of Russian nationalists, that the Ukraine had languished under the Polish yoke and had been eager to be incorporated into the Muscovite realm. Actually the Ukrainians, while hostile to Catholicism, were by no means aliens within the Polish-Lithuanian state. They absorbed a great many elements of Polish culture and political tradition. It was rather Muscovy, with her Oriental despotism that was alien to them." (George Fedotov, "Fate of Empires," *Russian Review*, XII, No. 2 [April, 1953], 88).

[58] Stalin, "Tov. Kaganovichu," in *Sochineniia*, VIII, 153. On Khvilevoi, see Girchak, *Na dva fronta*, pp. 49–99, 211–14.

[59] "Shestnadtsatyi s"ezd VKP(b)," June 26–July 13, 1930, in *KPSS v rez.*, II, 564.

cember 12, 1930, to the Russian author Dem'ian Bednii (published for the first time in 1951). Here he specifically glorified Russia and the Russian workers in a way which strongly suggested no antipathy toward Great Russian chauvinism, which he supposedly was condemning:

> The whole world now recognizes that the center of the revolutionary movement has moved from Western Europe to Russia. . . . The revolutionary workers of all countries unanimously applaud the Soviet working class, and above all the *Russian* working class [Stalin's italics], the vanguard of the Soviet workers, as their recognized leader. . . . The leaders of the revolutionary workers of all countries eagerly study the instructive history of the Russian working class. . . . All this inspires (it cannot help but inspire) a feeling of revolutionary national pride in the hearts of the Russian workers who can move mountains and work miracles.[60]

The tide of Russian nationalism within the Soviet Union was clearly rising. By 1933 both Khvilevoi and Skrypnyk had committed suicide in a desperate attempt to protest the increasing Russification of their homeland, and Postyshev, who became known as "the hangman of the Ukraine," was sent down from Moscow to "control" Ukrainian national expression.[61] We have used the example of the Ukraine because the course of its development under Great Russian pressure is so easy to trace, but similar encroachment upon non-Russian peoples occurred in the other Soviet Republics as well.[62]

THE PERVERSION OF PROLETARIAN INTERNATIONALISM IN THE
LATE 1920S AND EARLY 1930S

The relations between the Russian and non-Russian peoples within the USSR were mirrored, to a large extent, in the relations that developed between the USSR and the world proletariat. In the period from the mid-1920s to the early 1930s the course of both relation-

[60] Stalin, "Tov. Dem'ianu Bednomu," Dec. 12, 1930, in *Sochineniia*, XIII, 24-25.
[61] Reshetar, "National Deviation," *American Slavic*, XII, No. 2 (April, 1953), 167-68; Pap, "Soviet Difficulties," *Review of Politics*, XIV, No. 2 (April, 1952), 220-23; Hryhory Kostiuk, *The Fall of Postyshev* (New York, 1954), pp. 1-25; "Mykola Skrypnyk and the Present Situation in Ukraine," *Ukrainian Quarterly*, XIV, No. 3 (Sept., 1958), 262-73.
[62] For a competent republic-by-republic, province-by-province survey of the pressure that the Great Russians have exerted upon the congeries of non-Russian peoples in the Soviet Union, see Kolarz, *Russia and Her Colonies*, and his *The Peoples of the Soviet Far East* (New York, 1954).

ships was set by the struggle for the consolidation of power within the Russian Party and by the steady growth of Russian nationalism within that controlling group. Every shift of power within the Russian Party was quickly reflected by purges and demotions in all foreign Communist Parties, so that the Comintern increasingly became the scene of intense factional strife which even further diverted it from its supposed cause of proletarian internationalism.

The Fifth Comintern Congress, held in June, 1924, Ruth Fischer observed, was but "an arena for the struggle between the various groups in the Politburo; it had no other meaning and it had little authority." [63] In the spring of 1925 the Fifth Enlarged Plenum of the Comintern adopted a lengthy and detailed Theses entitled "The Bolshevization of the Parties of the Communist International." [64] Ruth Fischer described the effect which this "Bolshevization" had wrought within the German Communist Party in 1928. "In place of the internationalist militant Communist of the Civil War times, there arose a new type of National Communist—the Stalinist, the Moscow agent. The new cadres did not feel that they represented an international workers party, but the Russian State Party; they were secret agents of a foreign state." [65] The Moscow-directed international class movement increasingly became a plaything of the Russian Party, losing any serious purpose of its own.

The factional struggle within the Russian Party and the conflicting interests of the Russian state vis-à-vis the international proletarian movement were clearly revealed in Soviet policy toward China in the late 1920s. The Trotsky-Stalin feud took on the appearance of Trotsky urging the formation of Chinese soviets of workers, peasants, and soldiers, with Stalin rejecting precipitate action and demanding instead a multiclass alliance with Chiang Kai-shek in the south and General Feng in the north, out of consideration of security for the Russian state. Russian policy logically could have followed either one of the two courses: back a revolutionary Chinese Communist Party, or abandon the Party for a state alliance with China, along the lines of Lenin's policy toward Turkey

[63] Ruth Fischer, *Stalin*, pp. 403–4.
[64] "Bol'shevizatsiia partii Kommunisticheskogo Internatsionala," March 21–April 6, 1925, in *Kom. Int. v dok.*, pp. 474–95. For Stalin's major pronouncements on "Bolshevization" of the Comintern, see Stalin, *Sochineniia*, VIII, 1–10, 100–7, 109–15; IX, 50–61, 147–48 (for 1926); X, 3–9, 57–59, 81–83, 89–90, 166–67 (for 1927); XI, 294–310 (for 1928).
[65] Ruth Fischer, *Stalin*, p. 510.

in the early 1920s. The resultant Russian policy was an uneasy compromise that invited disaster, for Stalin continued to cooperate with Chiang while making preparations for his ultimate destruction. The Communists' abandonment of their political and military independence led to their destruction, first in Canton in March, 1926, then in Shanghai in March, 1927, and later in 1927 in Wu-han. After the Wu-han disaster Moscow finally ordered civil war against the Kuomintang, but then it was too late.[66] In this early period Chiang succeeded in routing the Communists while not submitting to Stalin's terms of friendship required for the security of the USSR. Stalin promptly blamed this failure on Trotsky's "leftist" policy, and since Stalin emerged victorious over Trotsky, Stalin's Russian-oriented policy also emerged stronger than ever.

It was at the height of the Chinese crisis in August, 1927, that Stalin formulated his classic definition of proletarian internationalism. Now he said bluntly:

He is an internationalist who unreservedly, unhesitatingly and unconditionally is prepared to defend the USSR, because the USSR is the base of the world revolutionary movement, and it is impossible to defend, to advance this revolutionary movement without defending the USSR. Whoever thinks of defending the world revolutionary movement without, and against, the USSR, goes against revolution, and must slide to the camp of the enemy of the revolution.[67]

Revolution was only to be encouraged or permitted in so far as it fitted the interests of the Soviet state. Gone were the references to the primacy of the international class struggle and to the need of the "nation which has gained a victory over the bourgeoisie to make the greatest national sacrifices for the overthrow of international capitalism," as the 1920 Comintern Theses had demanded. Instead of subordinating the interests of the USSR to the interests of the proletarian struggle on the international scale, the interests of the international class struggle were subordinated to whatever would further the national interests of the Soviet Union. The flag of proletarian internationalism was still tacked to the mast of the Kremlin,

[66] Harold R. Isaacs, *The Tragedy of the Chinese Revolution* (rev. ed.; Stanford, 1951), pp. 41–52, 89–271; Borkenau, *Communist International*, pp. 309–16; F. F. Liu, *A Military History of Modern China* (Princeton, 1956), pp. 21–59; Eudin and North, *Soviet Russia and the East*, pp. 286–310, 343–85; Conrad Brandt, *Stalin's Failure in China, 1924–1927* (Cambridge, Mass., 1958).

[67] Stalin, "Mezhdunarodnoe polozhenie i oborona SSSR," Aug. 1, 1927, in *Sochineniia*, X, 51.

but clearly it was waving upside down. Those who resisted the idea that the best interests of the proletariat of all nations could be determined only by Moscow were branded "opportunists." In the words of a Comintern journalist, those who "stormed against the 'Moscow dictatorship' . . . revealed their national narrow-mindedness, their complete lack of understanding of international solidarity of action." [68] To say that those who resisted the Moscow dictatorship were guilty of national narrow-mindedness meant that no legitimate national interests could exist aside from those pursued by Moscow.

The duty of the international proletariat to further the state interests of the Soviet Union was emphasized in the Program of the Comintern, which was adopted at the Sixth Comintern Congress in 1928. This attitude was called for, the Program said, because in the USSR "the working class of the world now has its own state, the exclusive fatherland of the international proletariat." [69]

The Sixth Comintern Congress signalized a swing by Stalin to an extreme leftist phase. With the "left deviation" of Trotsky and Zinoviev in defeat, Stalin himself became "leftist" to discredit the right-wing group headed by Bukharin, who had in the meantime taken Zinoviev's place as head of the Comintern. It was not by accident that Bukharin was made to play such a leading part in the Sixth Comintern Congress, for Stalin quickly used the radical Program which Bukharin was forced to present as a weapon to discredit Bukharin's "right deviation."

The extreme purism of this leftist period had certain superficial similarities to the early days of proletarian internationalism, but closer examination shows that there is no real basis for such an identification. The early Comintern policy of proletarian internationalism was predicated upon invigorating the growth of the world proletarian movement, if need be, even at the expense of the Russian state. The extreme leftist Comintern policy of 1928 to 1934 sprang almost entirely from Stalin's attempt to monopolize power in the Soviet Union by destroying the last formidable opposition. Soon after the Sixth Comintern Congress Bukharin was deposed as head of the Comintern and no new president was nominated, the bulk

---

[68] J. Lenz, *The Rise and Fall of the Second International* (New York, 1932), p. 206.
[69] "Programma Kommunisticheskogo Internatsionala," Sept. 1, 1928, in *Kom. Int. v dok.*, pp. 13, 35.

of the work being handed over to Molotov, Manuil'skii, and Kuusinen. "The choice of this personnel," Borkenau remarks, "was a clear implication that international communism was no longer regarded as important in itself, but as a minor dependency of the Russian state," and, in particular, as an auxiliary instrument in the factional struggle within the Russian Party.[70] Stalin's "leftism," far from strengthening the international Communist movement, only brought renewed disaster to the major Communist movements in both China and Germany.

In China the extreme leftist policy forbade the Chinese Communists to cooperate with the Kuomintang on the basis of Chinese nationalism against the advance of the Japanese who set up the puppet state of Manchukuo in 1931. Then in 1933 the Chinese Communists again refused, in a doctrinaire way, to extend help to a part of the Kuomintang Army in Fukien province, which had revolted against Chiang Kai-shek. Had the Chinese Communists allied themselves with these Fukien rebels, as they could easily have done, the Communists could have enormously strengthened the position of their hard-pressed soviets in neighboring Kiangsi province. As it was, Chiang Kai-shek soon conquered both the rebels and Kiangsi province, forcing the Communists to start their Long March north to Shensi province in 1934. The privations of this march caused the Chinese Communists to lose some 70,000 of the original 90,000 who began the fantastic trek.[71]

A similar doctrinaire leftism dictated by Stalin's factional warfare within the Russian Party brought destruction to the German Communist Party. The German Communists dismissed Hitler's strongest opponents, the Social Democrats, as "Social Fascists," and the possibility of joint action to stop Hitler was summarily rejected.

The astonishing fact is not that Stalin's policy was out of touch with reality, but that he persisted in this policy for over a year after Hitler came to power. As soon as Hitler was master of Germany, he showed his appreciation for this divided opposition by promptly annihilating both the German Social Democrats and the German Communist Party. Yet Stalin's pseudo-leftism persisted. The German Communists continued to center their attack on the Social

[70] Borkenau, *Communist International*, p. 339.
[71] *Ibid.*, pp. 329–30; Edgar Snow, *Red Star over China* (New York, 1939), pp. 166–96, 381–83; Robert C. North, *Moscow and Chinese Communists* (Stanford, 1953), pp. 160–67.

Democrats, even though Communists and Social Democrats now met in Hitler's concentration camps. All the while the Communists pretended that Hitler was just a passing phase of reaction that would soon usher in a Communist revolution. Thus on October 10, 1933, almost eight months after Hitler's ascent to power, the Politburo of the German Communist Party declared: "A new upsurge of revolutionary mass movement in Germany is beginning." [72] And in December, 1933, Wilhelm Pieck, the German Communist leader, reported to the Comintern Executive Committee that "the prerequisites for the revolutionary crisis are increasing. Germany is marching towards the proletarian revolution." [73] By February, 1934, the truth could be denied no longer and Moscow was shaken to its roots, not because of the loss of the strongest Communist Party abroad, but because the Soviet leaders suddenly realized that their *state* was endangered by an aggressive nationalism. With this, the period of pseudo-leftism came to an end. It was replaced by the era of "united front," a decided shift to the right, in which national symbols were refurbished and brought into the open as never before in Soviet history.

[72] Quoted in Wilhelm Pieck, *We Are Fighting for a Soviet Germany*, Dec., 1933 (New York, 1934), p. 5.
[73] *Ibid.*, p. 10. See also Gordon W. Millikan, "The Science of Soviet Politics: 'Pravda' on Hitler in 1933," *Foreign Affairs*, XXXI, No. 3 (April, 1953), 472–85.

IV. The Influence of Russian Nationalism since 1934

WHILE Stalin did not lose sight of the goal of a Soviet world state, he adapted his policies to the climate of world politics in a way that caused many people to think that in fact he had forsaken it. The promotion of Soviet, and in particular Russian, nationalism was Stalin's response to the aggressive nationalism of Japan in the East and Germany in the West. Many observers began to equate the nationalism of the Soviet Union with the nationalism of a bourgeois nation-state and to draw the mistaken conclusion that the Soviet regime was no longer interested in the objective of a world state. This error could have been avoided if it had been generally realized that from the first days of the Soviet Republic there were two rival approaches to the objective of a world state: the approach of proletarian internationalism and that of Soviet Russian nationalism. Every delay in the process of creating a world state forced the advocates of proletarian internationalism to retreat before the protagonists of Soviet Russian nationalism. The idea of a genuine brotherhood of equal proletarian nations organized as a world state remained abstract and unrealized, while the problems of preserving and strengthening power in a Russian-based state were immediate and concrete. By the mid-1930s the pressing interests of the latter approach had won a clear and irreversible decision. Gone were the ambiguities about who would sacrifice for whom. The only criterion for one's "internationalism" was the glorification and aggrandizement of a Russian-based and Russian-dominated Union of Soviet Socialist Republics, the nucleus and prototype of a World Union of Soviet Socialist Republics.

THE TURN TOWARD OPEN NATIONALISM IN SOVIET FOREIGN
POLICY

When the Soviet leadership began openly to encourage the use of national symbols, the aggressive, long-range goal of a world state was played down, since the Soviet turn toward nationalism was occasioned by the weak and defensive position of the Soviet Union in the face of the threats of aggression from Germany and Japan. In an effort to counteract these threats, Stalin tried to follow the rules of power politics as he thought bourgeois nationalist diplomats conceived them. Stalin's biting commentary on bourgeois diplomacy, which he had recorded in 1913, goes a long way toward explaining his behavior as the head of the Soviet state in the 1930s. "For a diplomat," Stalin observed, "words *must* have no relation to actions —otherwise what sort of a diplomat would he be? Words are one thing, actions absolutely another. Good words are a mask for the concealment of unprincipled acts. To speak of a sincere diplomat is the same as talking about dry water or wooden iron." [1]

One of the first signs of Stalin's desire to don the striped pants of a bourgeois diplomat was his shift in attitude toward the hitherto much-reviled League of Nations. In an interview of December 25, 1933, Stalin said that "notwithstanding the withdrawal of Germany and Japan from the League of Nations, or perhaps just because of this, the League may be something of a brake to retard the outbreak of military actions or to hinder them." [2] If this were the case, Stalin hinted that the Soviet government might like to join the League, which it did in September, 1934. Soviet support of the League of Nations was widely interpreted, at the time, as a sincere effort to forge an anti-Fascist weapon of collective security. On the other hand, there have been many indications that Stalin never lost sight of the possibility of a compromise with Hitler, and that the Soviet role in the League of Nations was designed to improve Moscow's bargaining position with all the great powers.[3] In any

[1] Stalin, "Vybory v Peterburge," Jan. 25, 1913, in *Sochineniia*, II, 277.
[2] Stalin, "Beseda s korrespondentom gazety 'N'iu-Iork Taims' g. Diuranti," Dec. 25, 1933, in *ibid.*, XIII, 280.
[3] Krivitskii developed the thesis that from 1934 on it was Stalin's intent to make a deal with Hitler, and that the real meaning of Soviet support for a policy of collective security through the League of Nations was that he wanted to build up a position of strength from which he could induce Hitler to come to terms. The fact that Krivitskii first published this thesis in April, 1939, makes

event, Soviet membership in the League of Nations tended to push Soviet behavior even further toward the accepted norms of national interest as expressed by bourgeois diplomacy.

A content analysis of *Izvestiia* editorials clearly reveals that nationalistic, patriotic, fatherland-motherland symbols increased sharply starting about 1934. They climbed to a peak in 1939–1941, where they have more or less stayed ever since. It is interesting that the approval of these terms in *Izvestiia* was much more unequivocal than that given by the reactionary Russian *Novoe vremiia* during the First World War, and that in a survey of the world press for the first half of the twentieth century only "in Nazi Germany has there been such a one-sidedly nationalistic treatment of the news as in Bolshevik Russia since the late thirties." This rise in the use of nationalist terms was accompanied by a decline in the use of class terms, so that the basic conflicts in the world were less frequently put in terms of "proletariat" and "bourgeoisie," and increasingly cast in terms of a struggle between "fatherland" and "imperialists." This trend, which began in the mid-1930s, was of fundamental importance, for the investigators report that "the chauvinist character of *Izvestiia* has apparently become permanent." [4]

The way in which "proletarian internationalism" was grafted onto national symbols was made evident at the Seventh Comintern Congress, meeting in July and August, 1935. Dimitrov, the head of the Comintern, explained:

> Comrades, proletarian internationalism must, so to speak, "acclimatize itself" in each country in order to sink deep roots in its native soil. *National forms* of the proletarian class struggle . . . are in no contradiction to proletarian internationalism; on the contrary, it is precisely in

---

it something more than an ex post facto explanation for the Stalin-Hitler Pact. See W. G. Krivitskii, *I Was Stalin's Agent* (London, 1940), pp. 17–42, 91, 99, 134, 234–37, 248–49. For other indications of Soviet peace feelers to Berlin from 1934 to 1939, see Gustav Hilger and Alfred G. Meyer, *The Incompatible Allies* (New York, 1953), pp. 254–56, 263–71, 276–79, 283–96; William C. Bullitt, *The Great Globe Itself* (New York, 1946), p. 103; Alexander Barmine, *One Who Survived* (New York, 1945), pp. 308–9; John A. Lukacs, *The Great Powers and Eastern Europe* (New York, 1953), pp. 184–89; Robert Coulondre, *De Staline à Hitler: souvenirs de deux ambassades, 1936–1939* (Paris, 1950), p. 125. It would at least seem possible that Stalin was simultaneously entertaining two divergent policies and waiting to see which one would prove effective.

[4] Ithiel de Sola Pool, with the collaboration of Harold D. Lasswell and Daniel Lerner et al., *Symbols of Internationalism* (Stanford, 1951), pp. 48–52.

these forms that the *international interests* of the proletariat can be successfully defended.⁵

. . . .

The task of educating the workers and all toilers in the spirit of proletarian internationalism is one of the fundamental tasks of every Communist Party. But whoever thinks that this permits him . . . to sneer at all the national sentiments of the broad toiling masses is far from genuine Bolshevism, and has understood nothing of the teaching of Lenin and Stalin on the national question.⁶

The concluding session of the Seventh Comintern Congress adopted a resolution which stated that proletarian internationalism "is not only directed towards the defense of the Soviet country . . . it also protects the lives of the workers of all countries . . . it means the defense of the national independence of small nations, it serves the vital interests of humanity." ⁷ Proletarian internationalism now openly meant the defense of nationalism, first and foremost, a defense of the national independence of the USSR, but also a defense of the status quo generally, a defense of the national independence of all of those small states which were in danger of being overrun by Hitlerite aggression. This identification of the national interests, this simultaneous defense of the national independence of the Soviet Union with that of other states, began in a period of Soviet retreat. The startling consequences of this identification, when carried over into a period of Soviet advance, which opened with the Nazi-Soviet Pact, will be apparent shortly.

For the purpose of promoting the interests of the Soviet state, the Communist Parties of the West were assigned the tasks of defending the 1935 Mutual Assistance pacts concluded by the Soviet Union with France and Czechoslovakia, and of trying to keep an embarrassing civil war in Spain within manageable limits. While Soviet policy toward the Spanish Civil War implied a recrudescence of a genuine spirit of proletarian internationalism, in practice the Spanish Communists, with Moscow's obvious approval, made prolonged efforts to erect a façade of a broadly based coalition government in Spain. The Party Program, formulated in March, 1937, by José Diaz, the Secretary General of the Spanish Communist Party,

⁵ Dimitrov, *Nastuplenie fashizma*, Aug. 13, 1935, p. 79. ⁶ *Ibid.*, p. 77.
⁷ "Resolution Adopted by the Seventh World Comintern Congress," Aug. 20, 1935, *Communist International*, XII, No. 17–18 (Sept. 20, 1935), 959.

merely proclaimed that "we are fighting for a democratic republic, for a new type of democratic, parliamentary republic." It pointedly omitted all use of the words "Soviet" or "socialist." [8] This policy of moderation brought the Communists into sharp conflict with the radical platforms of the other proletarian parties, such as the Trotskyite POUM, the Syndicalists, and the Anarchists.[9] The power position of the Soviet state rather than the revolutionary potential of the Spanish proletariat dictated a cautious policy of Soviet intervention. An unlimited and undisguised Soviet military intervention might have catapulted the USSR into an unwanted war with the Axis, and an open Communist seizure of power in Spain would have risked a break with France, and potentially with Britain, to whom Moscow was looking for support to check the growth of Axis power. Social revolution was ordered or suppressed solely according to the effect it was calculated to have upon the national interests of the Soviet Union, and since revolution would embarrass Moscow's efforts to strengthen an anti-Fascist alliance, the Spanish Communists had to appear not only non-Bolshevik, but even non-socialist.

In the Far East, the protection of Soviet security made it essential to strengthen China's ability to resist Japanese expansion, and in order to develop a common front in China against Japan, the Comintern promoted compromise and cooperation between the Chinese Communists and the Nationalist regime. Temporarily, the Chinese Communists had to swallow the bitter pill of deferring to their arch rival, Chiang Kai-shek. In August, 1937, the Soviet Union concluded a nonaggression pact with Chiang and made arrangements to supply war materials for his armies. At the same time the Soviet government repeatedly offered to conclude a nonaggression pact with Japan. In both East and West the Soviet state demanded sacrifices of its foreign Communist movements for the national defense of the Soviet Union.

[8] José Diaz, "Report to the Enlarged Plenum of the Central Committee of the Communist Party of Spain," March 5, 1937, *ibid.*, XIV, No. 4 (March, 1937), 1001.
[9] Borkenau, *Communist International*, pp. 406–11. For a full account, see the two works by David T. Cattell, *Communism and the Spanish Civil War* (Berkeley, 1955); *Soviet Diplomacy and the Spanish Civil War* (Berkeley, 1957).

THE MOUNTING PRESSURE OF RUSSIAN NATIONALISM
WITHIN THE SOVIET UNION

The increasing emphasis in Soviet foreign relations upon national interest instead of class struggle found its counterpart within the Soviet Union, in terms of the growth of Soviet patriotism. Behind the mask of this all-inclusive word "Soviet" there stood the dominating reality of Great Russian nationalism. Through the use of "Soviet patriotism," it was possible to deemphasize the particularistic patriotisms of this or that nationality within the Soviet Union. It was as if all the various national patriotisms of the USSR which had been fostered since the revolution were dumped into the one vast sieve of Soviet patriotism. This sieve was then agitated until all the various nationalisms were jumbled together, and then one by one filtered out into semioblivion. There was only one nationalism too big to drop through this filter, or too tough to be fragmented into pieces of manageable size, and that was Great Russian nationalism, which remained and grew. This is not to deny the enormous impact of the common experience to which all nations in the USSR were subjected by living together under the Soviet regime. Unquestionably new attitudes and behavior patterns, common to all nations, grew up in response to the totalitarian pressures of Soviet society. But this does not justify the conclusion that national distinctions and strong national feelings were obliterated. If a new "Soviet patriot" or a new "Soviet man" arose, he was, at the same time, a member of a specific nationality.[10] And of all of these nationalities, the Great Russians maintained and strengthened their dominating position.

Even Stalin's official position on Great Russian nationalism underwent a change. In the past, Stalin's pronouncements at official gatherings, such as a Party Congress, invariably denounced the danger of Great Russian chauvinism, even though his acts and the expression of his private opinion contradicted his official, public

[10] According to a carefully conducted series of interviews of refugees from Soviet Central Asia who were found in the West after the Second World War, distinct national feelings remain firmly embedded even among the native intelligentsia, which is the most assimilated of all the strata of the non-Russian population. "The notion of an all-embracing 'Soviet' patriotism, fostered by the regime in its borderlands, apparently has had little if any success among the intellectuals." (Richard Pipes, "Muslims of Soviet Central Asia," *Middle East Journal*, IX, No. 3 [Summer, 1955], 306.)

stand. Stalin's last officially recorded condemnation of Great Russian nationalism was on January 26, 1934, in his report to the Seventeenth Party Congress. "Condemnation" is really too strong a word, for actually Stalin tried to evade the issue of Great Russian nationalism. He merely remarked that "there is a controversy as to which deviation represents a major danger: the deviation toward Great Russian nationalism, or the deviation toward local nationalism." To this question he replied: "Under present conditions this is a formal and therefore a pointless controversy." Stalin did dwell upon the dangers of Ukrainian nationalism, which would indicate that he was much more concerned about curbing the nationalism of a non-Russian people than that of the Great Russians. "The fall of Skrypnyk and his group in the Ukraine," Stalin observed, "is not an exception. Similar distortions have been observed among certain comrades in other national republics as well." [11]

To provide a firm base upon which Great Russian nationalism could be rebuilt openly, Stalin found it necessary to rewrite the Soviet interpretation of history. Ever since the revolution, Soviet historiography had been dominated by M. N. Pokrovskii, who interpreted all history according to allegedly "objective laws" based on the workings of economic forces and class warfare. Pokrovskii held that the feudal and capitalist stages of Imperial Russia had created a prisonhouse of nations in which the Great Russian jailors had ruthlessly suppressed all of the national liberation movements of the conquered non-Russian peoples. Socialism, Pokrovskii argued, could only be a negation of these miserable features of Tsarist Russia; to him it would have been blasphemy to draw a favorable comparison between the leaders of socialist Russia and Ivan the Terrible or Peter the Great. Actually Pokrovskii paid little attention to the role of the individual in history, since the evils of the Tsarist empire were explained by the operation of impersonal economic forces. This, too, Stalin found objectionable, for how could the growing Stalin cult flourish in such an atmosphere? Obviously the Pokrovskii school of history no longer served Stalin's needs. Consequently Pokrovskii's orthodox Marxism, which put class above nation, was replaced by a Stalinist interpretation of history, which, by implication, put nation above class, specifically the Great Russian nation

[11] Stalin, "Otchëtnyi doklad XVII s"ezdu partii o rabote TsK VKP(b)," Jan. 26, 1934, in *Sochineniia*, XIII, 361-62.

above the supposedly "international" proletarian class. And the leading role of "great men" took the place of Pokrovskii's economic "laws."

Criticism of Pokrovskii had begun in 1932, during the last days of his life, and it continued to grow in 1933. Finally on May 16, 1934, Molotov, as head of the government, and Stalin, as head of the Party, issued a joint decree, "On the Teaching of Civil History in the Schools of the USSR," which thoroughly demolished the Pokrovskii school.[12] A competition for new history textbooks was ordered, and at last in August, 1937, a textbook edited by A. V. Shestakov was officially sanctioned. Characteristic of this new approach to history was Shestakov's description of "the Time of Troubles" when the Poles invaded Moscow.

In the autumn of 1611 the whole people of Russia rose in rebellion against the Polish usurpers. The march against the Poles entrenched in Moscow was organized and led by a Nizhni Novgorod meat merchant, Koz'ma Minin. . . . The choice of commander of his army fell upon Prince Pozharskii, an experienced military leader. A number of the peasant detachments who were fighting the landlords joined his army. This decided the issue. The people's army marched to Moscow and besieged the Poles in the Kremlin. In 1612 the Kremlin was captured and the Poles fled from Moscow.[13]

Aside from the perfunctory remark about the "peasant detachments who were fighting the landlords," the emphasis was on the overriding importance of nation above class. Thus, the peasants joined with Minin, a merchant, and Pozharskii, a member of the military-landlord caste, and all acted like good Russians in throwing out the Poles. In a similar fashion the foreign conquests of Ivan the Terrible, Peter the Great, and other Tsars were given sympathetic treatment, since they had performed the service of building up a strong Russian Empire.

The growth of Great Russian nationalism during this period was largely obscured to the outside world, which had focused its attention upon the promulgation of the 1936 Stalin Constitution.

[12] "O prepodavanii grazhdanskoi istorii v shkolakh SSSR; postanovlenie SNK Soiuza SSR i TsK VKP(b)," May 16, 1934, *Istorik Marksist*, III, No. 37 (1934), 83–84. See also Akademiia nauk SSSR; institut istorii, *Protiv istoricheskoi kontseptsii M. N. Pokrovskogo*, Vols. I and II (Moscow, Leningrad, 1939–1940); Alexander Uralov [A. Avtorkhanov], *The Reign of Stalin* (London, 1953), pp. 104–20.

[13] A. V. Shestakov, *A Short History of the U.S.S.R.* (Moscow, 1938), pp. 57–58.

Stalin said that the Constitution marked the end of class antagonisms in the Soviet Union. In line with Marxist theory that antagonisms among nations would diminish in proportion to the elimination of class conflict, it was consistent Marxism for the Constitution to proceed "from the proposition that all nations and races have equal rights." [14]

What many observers neglected was the ugly reality of the purge trials of 1936–1938, which were behind the "liberal" face of the Stalin Constitution. It was an ironic, but by no means an accidental, fact that this "liberal" period opened the floodgates of terror for Soviet citizens, and first and foremost, for the members of the Communist Party. In the Great Purges, Stalin wiped out, almost without exception, the Communist leaders of all of the non-Russian peoples in the USSR and replaced them with agents more directly amenable to Moscow's Great Russian dictates. As Kolarz has observed, the purges, which deprived the "non-Russian peoples of an entire generation of the political leaders, economic experts and cultural workers," meant the triumph of the Russian language and of Russian civilization. "It is a striking coincidence that the decree on the obligatory teaching of Russian in all national minority schools was passed on the very day when Rykov and Bukharin were sentenced to death—on March 13, 1938." [15]

RESURGENT NATIONALISM IN THE ARENA OF THE SECOND WORLD WAR

Stalin also used the purge trials to refute Trotsky's insistent charges that the revival of nationalism in the Soviet Union proved that the USSR was, in fact, degenerating to the status of a bourgeois nation-state, and that it had abandoned the goal of a world state. Bukharin, in his final plea, spoke Stalin's words when he said, "Let it be clear to all that the counterrevolutionary thesis of the national limitedness of the USSR has remained suspended in the air like a wretched rag." [16]

[14] Stalin, "O proekte konstitutsii Soiuza SSR," Nov. 25, 1936, in *Doklad o proekte*, pp. 23–24.
[15] Kolarz, *Russia and Her Colonies*, pp. 11, 18. On the systematic decimation of the non-Russian leaders during the 1936–1938 purges, see Uralov, *Reign of Stalin*, pp. 67–73, 140–47; Zbigniew K. Brzezinski, *The Permanent Purge* (Cambridge, Mass., 1956), pp. 77–82, 180–89.
[16] *Report of Court Proceedings in the Case of the Anti-Soviet "Bloc of Rights and Trotskyites,"* Bukharin's Final Plea, March 12, 1938 (Moscow, 1938), p. 779.

Denials of the same charge that the Soviet state had become a purely "national" state, pursuing "national" goals, can be traced in Comintern writings that treated nationalism as a necessary and essential means to a universal end. A typical article, published in *The Communist International* in June, 1939, attempted to explain away the "dialectical contradiction" between Bolshevik internationalism and the new Soviet emphasis on national patriotism. The author speaks first of the necessity for the workers to defend the national independence of their countries against Fascist aggression, but then goes on, in Aesopean language, to indicate the role of nationalism in the progression toward a higher aim:

> For us, the nation is not the highest [aim]. For us the highest is socialism, communism. The nation is one stage towards humanity. . . . The nation outlasts capitalism . . . but, at the same time, in socialism there also develops a community which transcends all national limitations. . . . Upon the path out of the narrow confinement of the primitive forest towards the expanses of humanity, appeared the nation. . . . The working class marches in the vanguard of the nation in order to realize socialism and through socialism, humanity.[17]

If "world state" is substituted for "humanity" in the above quotation, the nature of the future "community which transcends all national limitations" becomes apparent. It may be objected that it is dangerous to supply synonyms for words in a Soviet text, for if the Soviet author had meant "world state" he would have said so explicitly. The most that one might claim, perhaps, is that the Soviet leadership continued to assert its drive to embrace all nations into a single socialist, and then communist, world system. The power relationships among the nations of the world, according to this view, need not be modified so as to obliterate their existence as independent national states through the formation of the new, all-encompassing state form of a world state.

Such a premise, while superficially attractive, does not seem to penetrate behind the Soviet manipulation of nationalist terminology nor grasp the connection between this nationalist terminology and the cause of socialism. The manner in which the peoples of the world are to achieve their fulfillment, as nations, specifically requires that they be incorporated into an ever-expanding Soviet state, the ultimate and logical extension of which is a Soviet world state.

[17] P. Wieden, "Changes in Bourgeois Nationalism," *Communist International*. XVI, No. 6 (June, 1939), 472–73.

The signing of the Nazi-Soviet Pact in August, 1939, permitted a practical application of this hybrid theory of nationalism and socialism serving the aims of an ever-expanding Soviet state. Prior to the Nazi-Soviet Pact, the Soviet Union had been defending the national independence of nations by defending the status quo. When Fascist aggression was turned away from the USSR, the Soviet leaders maintained their claim to be defending the independence of nations, now by upsetting the status quo. Dunaeva described the way in which the Soviet Union "defended the national independence" of nations as a result of the Nazi-Soviet Pact.

In 1939 the peoples of Western Ukraine and Western Belorussia joined the Union of Soviet Socialist Republics and in 1940 it was joined by the peoples of Latvia, Estonia and Lithuania. . . . These peoples found genuine national freedom and independence only after the establishment of Soviet government in their countries and their entry into the fraternal family of nations of the U.S.S.R.[18]

"Under socialism," Dunaeva remarked, "the tendency of nations to draw closer together and to unite combines harmoniously with the strengthening and development of the independence of the national Soviet republics." [19] Thus, Soviet theoreticians maintain that nations achieve their fullest measure of national independence only *after* they have been encompassed by a growing Soviet state, through "their entry into the fraternal family of nations of the U.S.S.R."

When Hitler turned against the Soviet Union, it was again around the banner of nationalism that Stalin rallied his people. In contradiction to the orthodox Marxist priority of class above nation, socialism came off a very bad second as a force which could attract and sustain the loyalties of Soviet citizens. On November 7, 1941, Stalin commemorated the anniversary of the revolution, not by recalling the goals of socialism, but by invoking purely Russian national heroes. "Let the manly images of our great ancestors—Alexander Nevskii, Dmitri Donskoi, Kuz'ma Minin, Dmitrii Pozharskii, Alexander Suvorov, Mikhail Kutuzov—inspire you in this war!" [20] Each of these figures represented a triumph of Russia over a foreign nation. The fact that Suvorov had crushed a peasant revolt of Pugachev

[18] Dunaeva, *Collaboration of Nations*, p. 18. This tract, written in 1949, would indicate that in the postwar world as well the best way for nations to "defend their independence" is by joining the USSR.
[19] *Ibid.*, p. 23.
[20] Stalin, "Rech' na parade Krasnoi Armii," Nov. 7, 1941, in *O velikoi otechestvennoi voine Sovetskogo Soiuza* (Moscow, 1950), pp. 71-72.

RUSSIAN NATIONALISM SINCE 1934

in 1774, twenty years later had suppressed a rebellion for Polish freedom led by the famous patriot Kosciuszko, and had attempted to stamp out the effects of the French Revolution throughout Italy and Switzerland was now conveniently forgotten. The memory of these counterrevolutionary activities was buried in an unequivocal assertion of the interests of nation above class.

The Soviet press overflowed with testimonials, such as the following from the leading Soviet author Alexei Tolstoy: "This is my birthplace, my native soil, my fatherland—there is not in life a more ardent, deeper, and holier feeling than my love for you." [21] It was not accidental that love for Mother Russia took on overtones of a religious supplication. Together with Russian nationalism the Russian Orthodox Church was lifted out of the "rubble-heap of history" and put in a prominent place in the showcase of Russian patriotism. In early 1939, in anticipation of the war, the Soviet government softened noticeably its policy towards the Church. In September, 1943, Stalin gave his personal blessing to the "patriotic endeavors" of the Orthodox Church, and the Metropolitan of Moscow was raised, amid solemn ceremony, to be Patriarch of All Russia. The Russian Church again became an active exponent of Russian nationalism and, in some respects, a useful instrument of Soviet policy.[22]

While it is true that during the war the Soviet regime made use, in varying degrees, of national symbols of the non-Russian peoples in the USSR, this should not obscure the fact that it was Great Russian nationalism which the Soviet leaders singled out and elevated above all others. The new national anthem of the Soviet Union, introduced on December 20, 1943, at the very height of the war, clearly reflected this policy of conscious discrimination. According to a verse in the anthem: "Great Russia has built an eternal and indestructible Union of Free Republics." The anthem remains a symbol of official policy and has frequently been praised in the postwar Soviet press.[23]

[21] Alexei Tolstoy, "What We Are Defending," in Lucien Zacharoff, ed., *The Voice of Fighting Russia* (New York, 1942), p. 25.
[22] Nicholas S. Timasheff, *The Great Retreat* (New York, 1946), pp. 225-40; Timasheff, "Religion in Russia, 1941-1950," in Waldemar Gurian, ed., *The Soviet Union* (Notre Dame, 1951), pp. 153-94.
[23] See for example, M. Kammari, "Tovarishch Stalin o natsiiakh burzhuaznykh i sotsialisticheskikh," *Bol'shevik*, No. 16 (Sept., 1949), p. 39; V. Galkin, *Vozniknovenie i razvitie sotsialisticheskikh natsii v SSSR* (Moscow, 1952), p. 63.

On May 24, 1945, Stalin celebrated the end of the war in Europe with a reception at the Kremlin for high officers of the Red Army. On this occasion he proposed this carefully worded toast:

> I would like to raise a toast to the health of our Soviet people, and first of all to the Russian people because it is the most outstanding nation of all of the nations which reside in the Soviet Union. . . . It deserves general recognition in the war as the leading force in the Soviet Union among all the peoples of our country. . . . It is the leading people, because it has a clear mind, firm character, and endurance.[24]

With this, the steam roller of Great Russian chauvinism shifted into high gear. The May, 1945, issue of *Bol'shevik* published Stalin's toast on its first page, and followed it by a ten-page editorial on "The Russian People—the Leading Force Among the Peoples of Our Country," in which the Great Russian nation, credited with every conceivable virtue, was described as the vanguard of civilization since the dawn of history.[25]

The end of the war in Asia also produced an outburst of purely Russian nationalism. Stalin, in an address to the peoples of the Soviet Union on September 2, 1945, revealed how far the values of Russian nationalism had displaced those of authentic proletarian internationalism. In a complete reversal of historical fact he recalled:

> The defeat of Russian troops in 1904 in the period of the Russo-Japanese War left grave memories in the minds of our people. It was a dark stain on our country. Our people trusted and awaited the day when Japan would be beaten and the stain wiped out. For forty years we, the men of the older generation, have waited for this day. And now this day has come.[26]

Actually, forty years before Stalin, like all Bolsheviks, had hailed each Japanese victory as a triumph for the revolutionary forces within Russia over their common enemy, the Tsarist Russian autocracy. To be specific, on January 21, 1905, Stalin wrote an article, "Workers of the Caucasus, It Is Time for Revenge," in which he rejoiced:

> The Tsarist autocracy is losing its principal base of support—its "faithful troops". . . . Defeat follows defeat. . . . It is time to demand that the

[24] "Vystuplenie tovarishcha I. V. Stalina na priëme v Kremle v chest' Komanduiushchikh Voiskami Krasnoi Armii," May 24, 1945, *Bol'shevik*, No. 10 (May, 1945), pp. 1–2.
[25] "Russkii narod—rukovodiashchaia sila sredi narodov nashei strany," *ibid.*, No. 10 (May, 1945), pp. 3–12.
[26] "Obrashchenie tov. I. V. Stalina k narodu," Sept. 2, 1945, *ibid.*, No. 16 (Aug., 1945), p. 2.

RUSSIAN NATIONALISM SINCE 1934

government account for the tens of thousands of innocent and unfortunate men who have perished on the battlefield in the Far East. . . . It is time to destroy the Tsarist government.[27]

The contrast between these two statements accurately indicates the depth of the transformation which had occurred in the Bolshevik attitude toward Russian nationalism during the intervening forty years.

DISAFFECTION AND PUNISHMENT OF NON-RUSSIAN NATIONS

In his toast of May 24, 1945, Stalin admitted that "we had some bad moments in 1941 and 1942." These perils were overcome, according to Stalin, because of the loyalty of the Great Russian people. It is significant that Stalin made no mention of the contribution of the non-Russian peoples. He said only: "This confidence on the part of the Russian people in the Soviet government proved to be the decisive force insuring our historic victory over mankind's foe, fascism. Let us thank them, the Russian people, for this confidence! Let us drink to the health of the Russian people." [28] Among the factors that gave rise to these "bad moments" was a widespread disloyalty of non-Russian groups. It would be a gross distortion to say that all disloyalty sprang from a desire of the non-Russian peoples to throw off the oppression of the Great Russians. When German troops marched into Soviet territory, large parts of the indigenous population displayed a disloyalty to the Soviet regime for a variety of reasons. General Vlasov, the most prominent anti-Soviet leader, was a Great Russian. But the non-Russian peoples had a double reason for disloyalty, for they not only shared the common dissatisfaction with the totalitarian Soviet regime, but each nation sought to replace the existing condition of national oppression with some new arrangement which would give its people a status of equality and freedom. Thus the national factor, while only one of many, was nevertheless of very great importance in breaking the fabric of a supposedly homogeneous Soviet society when subjected to the stress of crisis.

[27] Stalin, "Rabochie Kavkaza, pora otomstit," Jan. 21, 1905, in *Sochineniia*, I, 75; see also Lenin, "Padenie Port-Artura," Jan. 14, 1905, in *Sochineniia*, VII, 44–50.
[28] "Vystuplenie tovarishcha I. V. Stalina," *Bol'shevik*, No. 10 (May, 1945), p. 2.

The invading German forces reported an enormous and unexpected disaffection among both Soviet soldiers and civilians, particularly among the non-Russian nationalities. DeWitt C. Poole, who headed an American mission which interrogated some fifty top Nazi leaders immediately after the war, relates that the Germans found this revolt against Moscow particularly strong in the Ukraine. "During the opening weeks of the campaign, according to these Germans, soldiers deserted from the Soviet Armies by the hundreds of thousands." The same disaffection was found in the non-Russian civilian population. Poole reported: "A good many Ukrainians had at first shown a friendly readiness to volunteer for labor in Germany, our informants averred. . . . Volunteering among the Ukrainians for labor in Germany was alleged to have run as high as eighty percent."[29] But the brutal Nazi racist policy dispelled the illusion about the Germans being liberators, and armed resistance against the Germans by both the Red Army and its guerrilla detachments soon sprang up. As Goebbels wrote in his diary: "The inhabitants of the Ukraine were more than inclined at the beginning to regard the Fuehrer as the savior of Europe and to welcome the German Wehrmacht most cordially. This attitude has changed completely in the course of months. We have hit the Russians, and especially the Ukrainians, too hard on the head."[30]

Despite Nazi hostility toward the peoples of the East, the Wehrmacht did manage to recruit an estimated total of 800,000 Soviet citizens into their military units. A number of these were national "legions" enlisted from the non-Russian peoples of the Caucasus and Soviet Central Asia, as well as various units of Ukrainians. No similar policy of recruiting Russians into military units was permitted by Hitler until the closing months of the war.[31] Not all of the non-Russian military organizations, however, were formed with German help. There were also independent formations of non-Russian nationals, which were both anti-German and anti-

[29] DeWitt C. Poole, "Light on Nazi Foreign Policy," *Foreign Affairs*, XXV, No. 1 (Oct., 1945), 151–52.

[30] Louis P. Lochner, ed., *The Goebbels Diaries, 1942–1943* (Washington, New York, 1948), p. 185.

[31] On the non-Russian nationals enlisted in German-sponsored military units, see George Fischer, *Soviet Opposition to Stalin* (Cambridge, Mass., 1952), pp. 48–52, 207–8; Wladyslaw Anders, *Hitler's Defeat in Russia* (Chicago, 1953), pp. x–xii, 161–204; Caroe, *Soviet Empire*, pp. 246–56; John A. Armstrong, *Ukrainian Nationalism, 1939–1945* (New York, 1955), pp. 165–86; Alexander Dallin, *German Rule in Russia, 1941–1945* (London, 1957), pp. 533–52 and *passim*.

Soviet, particularly in the Ukraine and Lithuania. The Ukrainian Insurgent Army and the Lithuanian Resistance Movement even continued to harass the Soviet regime with acts of daring for many months after the end of the war.[32]

Stalin's resentment against the non-Russian nationalities was accompanied by drastic action. Six national units suffered a stroke of retaliation by the government, with large parts of their populations being deported, en masse, to Siberia and Central Asia. It was tragic irony that the Volga Germans, the first nationality organized as an autonomous republic on Soviet soil with Stalin's personal participation in 1918, also became the first national unit that Stalin formally disbanded. They were victims of suspected but unproved disaffection, since the German armies never reached their territory; victims of Stalin's open embrace of Hitler's precept that blood ties form a firmer bond than class ideology in determining group loyalties. In rapid order the Karachaev Autonomous Region, the Kalmyk ASSR and the Chechen-Ingush ASSR likewise disappeared, the Kabardinian-Balkar ASSR was reduced to a Kabardinian ASSR, and the Crimean Tatars suffered the demotion of their Crimean ASSR to the status of a nonautonomous region.[33] The reasons for the de-

[32] During the war, Khrushchev publicly acknowledged the considerable activity of the Ukrainian Insurgent Army (UPA), but sought to discredit it with the accusation that it was totally subservient to the Germans. See N. S. Khrushchev, "Osvobozhdenie ukrainskikh zemel' ot nemetskikh zakhvatchikov i ocherednye zadachi vosstanovleniia narodnogo khoziaistva Sovetskoi Ukrainy," *Bol'shevik*, No. 6 (March, 1944), pp. 15–16. For the most detached accounts of the anti-Soviet, anti-Nazi Ukrainian Resistance Movement, see Armstrong, *Ukrainian Nationalism*, pp. 98–100, 143–64, 176–78; Dallin, *German Rule*, pp. 621–25. Among those accounts available in English from Ukrainian sources, whose claims should be read with caution, see N. D. Czubatyj, "The Ukrainian Underground," *Ukrainian Quarterly*, II, No. 2 (Winter, 1946), 154–66; "The U.P.A. Fights the Kremlin," *ibid.*, III, No. 4 (Autumn, 1947), 355–63; Ukrainian Congress Committee of America, *Ukrainian Resistance* (New York, 1949), pp. 60–137; Lev Shankowsky, "Ten Years of the U.P.A. Struggle (1942–1952)," in *The Ukrainian Insurgent Army in Fight for Freedom* (New York, 1954), pp. 23–51. On the Lithuanian Resistance Movement, see "Five Years of Lithuanian Underground Resistance," *Lithuanian Bulletin*, III, No. 3 (May–June, 1945), 1–7; "The Birth of the Lithuanian Underground Resistance Movement as Documented by Secret Soviet Reports," *ibid.*, V, No. 9/10 (Sept.–Oct., 1947), 4–31; *Second Interim Report of the Select Committee on Communist Aggression*, 83d Congress, 2d Session, House Report No. 2650 (Washington, 1954), p. 20; *Fourth Interim Report of the Select Committee on Communist Aggression, Part 2*, 83d Congress, 2d Session (Washington, 1954), pp. 1369–74.

[33] Theodore Shabad, "Recent Changes in the Political Geography of the Soviet Union," *American Review on the Soviet Union*, VII, No. 2 (Feb., 1946), 26–34; Kolarz, *Russia and Her Colonies*, pp. 67–87, 146, 184–95; *Select Committee on Communist Aggression*, House Report No. 2650, pp. 10–14; *Forced*

struction of entire national units was plainly stated in the decree of the Supreme Soviet of the RSFSR of June 26, 1946, which ratified the elimination of the Chechen-Ingush and Crimean Tatar Republics:

> During the Great Fatherland War, when the peoples of the USSR heroically defended the honor and independence of their motherland against the German Fascist plunderers, many Chechens, and Crimean Tatars, at the instigation of German agents, joined German-organized volunteer detachments and fought with German troops against parts of the Red Army . . . moreover the bulk of the population of the Chechen-Ingush and Crimean ASSR showed no opposition to these traitors to the motherland. . . .
> According to a decree of the Presidium of the Supreme Soviet of the RSFSR, authorized by the laws of the Presidium of the Supreme Soviet of the USSR, the Chechen-Ingush ASSR was abolished and the Crimean ASSR was reorganized as a Crimean Region.[34]

The language of this decree is misleading in the case of the Chechen-Ingush peoples, since, like the Volga Germans, their national existence was obliterated without the Wehrmacht ever having entered their territory.[35] "The Ukrainians avoided meeting this fate," Khrushchev remarked in his "secret" speech to the Twentieth Party Congress, "only because there were too many of them and there was no place to which to deport them. Otherwise, he [Stalin] would have deported them also." [36]

A year later, in February, 1957, the Secretary of the Presidium of the USSR Supreme Soviet publicly acknowledged "gross violations" in the Soviet nationality policy which "took the form of the unfounded exile of entire peoples and the creation of a number of restrictions upon them in their areas of resettlement." Accordingly, he announced that this body had decreed the restoration of

---

Labor in the Soviet Union, Dept. of State Pub. 4716 (Washington, 1952), pp. 18–19; *Fourth Interim Report of the Select Committee on Communist Aggression,* Part II, pp. 1359–68, 1386–87; Nikolai K. Deker and Andrei Lebed, eds., *Genocide in the USSR* (New York, 1958), pp. 20–57.

[34] "Zakon ob uprazdnenii Checheno-Ingushskoi ASSR i o preobrazovanii Krymskoi ASSR v Krymskuiu oblast'," *Pravda,* June 28, 1946, p. 5.

[35] Uralov, *Reign of Stalin,* pp. 148–55; Lorimer, *Population of the Soviet Union,* Plate XXII at p. 194.

[36] "Secret Speech of Khrushchev Concerning the 'Cult of the Individual,' Delivered at the Twentieth Congress of the Communist Party of the Soviet Union," Feb. 25, 1956, in *The Anti-Stalin Campaign and International Communism: A Selection of Documents Edited by the Russian Institute, Columbia University* (New York, 1956), p. 57.

national autonomy for the Balkar, Chechen, Ingush, Kalmyk, and Karachai nations, and the return of the remnants of these peoples to their traditional homelands.[37] No mention was made of restitution for the Volga Germans and the Crimean Tatars, although these peoples have apparently been permitted the restoration of some of their linguistic rights in exile.[38]

Stalin had instituted similar drastic demographic policies in those Soviet territories annexed as a result of the Second World War. Large numbers of the indigenous populations were forcibly removed to eastern parts of the Soviet Union and their places systematically filled with Russians and other Slav settlers. A substantial proportion of the non-Russian Soviet citizens who managed to make their way to the West escaped a similar fate by refusing repatriation.[39] Mass deportations also occurred in those East European states which were not as yet formally incorporated into the Soviet Union. These Soviet-sponsored deportations reach such proportions that émigré representatives of the Baltic states, the Ukraine, Belorussia, and the East European satellites commenced bombarding various organs of the United Nations with detailed indictments of genocide.[40]

The violent nature of the Soviet nationality policy during and after the Second World War was merely a repetition of the treat-

[37] "Utverzhdenie Ukazov Prezidiuma Verkhovnogo Soveta SSSR, doklad Sekretaria Prezidiuma Verkhovnogo Soveta SSSR tov. A. F. Gorkina," *Pravda,* Feb. 12, 1957, p. 5.

[38] "Soviet Restores Crimean Tatars," New York *Times,* May 5, 1957.

[39] Albert Kalme, *Total Terror* (New York, 1951); Pranas Rupejko, "Progress of the Extermination of the Baltic Nations (1940–1950)," *The Eastern Quarterly,* V, No. 1/2 (Jan.–April, 1952), 33–40; Kolarz, *Russia and Her Colonies,* pp. 102, 110–12, 120; *Forced Labor,* Dept. of State Pub. 4716, pp. 31–34; *Report of the Ad Hoc Committee on Forced Labour,* Economic and Social Council and International Labour Office, UN Doc. E/2431 (Geneva, 1953), pp. 449–52, 507–10.

[40] *Appeal to the United Nations on Genocide,* Lithuanian Foreign Service (n.p., 1951); Roman Smal-Stocki, *The Nationality Problem of the Soviet Union* (Milwaukee, 1952), pp. 336–37; *Current News on the Lithuanian Situation,* VIII, No. 9 (Nov., 1951), 3–5. See also Philip E. Mosely, "Soviet Exploitation of National Conflicts in Eastern Europe," in Gurian, ed., *The Soviet Union,* pp. 68–71, 79–80; Eugene M. Kulischer, *Europe on the Move* (New York, 1948), pp. 282–301; C. L. Sulzberger, "Satellites Copy Russia on Population Policy," New York *Times,* April 20, 1952. On November 21, 1956, the UN General Assembly adopted a resolution associating the Soviet Union with the crime of genocide following the Soviet military intervention in Hungary which suppressed the anti-Communist revolt of October–November, 1956. (New York *Times,* Nov. 22, 1956. On the deportation of Hungarians to the Soviet Union, see *Report of the Special Committee on the Problem of Hungary,* UN General Assembly, Official Records, 11th Session, Supplement No. 18 [A/3592] [New York, 1957], pp. 123–27.)

ment that had been meted out to various non-Russian peoples from the founding of the Soviet regime. The Moslem peoples of the Soviet Union were brought under Soviet control only at the price of their systematic decimation. On April 12, 1921, Safarov, one of the Soviet policymakers for Central Asia, wrote that "more than a million Kirghiz [Kazakhs] died on the steppes of Turkestan, victims of the Bolshevik Juggernaut."[41] Similarly, the Bashkirs in the southern Urals, who had numbered about 2,000,000 in 1916, were reduced to a mere 700,000 by the time of the 1926 census.[42] The period of ruthless industrialization and collectivization of agriculture, beginning in the late 1920s, was especially harsh on the non-Russian peoples, since there has frequently been a close identification of social with national resistance to the Kremlin's policies. For example, the official Soviet census figures of 1926 and 1939 indicate that the destruction of nomad life in Kazakhstan cost the Kazakh people approximately 1,500,000 lives.[43] In a like manner, the stubborn resistance of the Ukrainian peasantry to collectivization resulted in a mass depopulation of the Ukrainian villages through deportations and an artificially created famine. The 1939 census showed an absolute loss of over 3,000,000 Ukrainians compared to 1926, and a total deficit of about 8,000,000 Ukrainians, when one calculates the expected growth of the Ukrainian population in terms of the average rate of increase for the whole Soviet population during this period.

[41] Quoted in Joseph Castagné, "Le Turkestan depuis la révolution Russe," *Revue du monde Musulman*, L (June, 1922), 60–61. This figure is supported by a standard Soviet reference work which records that in the area known as "Russian Turkestan" under the Tsarist administration (comprising what later became the four southern SSRs of Soviet Central Asia, plus 70 percent of the Kazakh SSR) there was a population of 10,664,800 in 1913 compared to 9,682,800 in 1926. The decline in the Turkic population was even greater considering the fact that the Slavic elements showed a modest increase during this period. (*Entsiklopedicheskii slovar' russkogo bibliograficheskogo instituta Granat* [7th ed.; Moscow, 1933], XLI, Part 10, 114.) See also Mustafa Chokaev, "Turkestan and the Soviet Regime," *Journal of the Royal Central Asian Society*, XVIII, No. 3 (July, 1931), 409–12; P. T. Etherton, *In the Heart of Asia* (London, 1925), pp. 154, 222.
[42] *Narodnost' i rodnoi iazyk naseleniia SSSR* (Moscow, 1928), p. 14; cited in Richard E. Pipes, "The First Experiment in Soviet Nationality Policy: The Bashkir Republic, 1917–1920," *Russian Review*, IX, No. 4 (Oct., 1950), 318.
[43] Lorimer, *Population of the Soviet Union*, p. 140. There was an absolute decrease of 869,000 Kazakhs, but a total deficit of 1,500,000, when calculating the population loss in terms of an expected growth of 15.9 percent for this period, which was the average rate of increase for the whole Soviet population. See also Kulischer, *Europe on the Move*, pp. 100–2, 116; Caroe, *Soviet Empire*, pp. 166–69.

Significantly, this same span of time showed an absolute increase of about 22,000,000 Great Russians.[44]

POSTWAR RUSSIAN CHAUVINISM WITHIN AND BEYOND THE SOVIET UNION

In addition to its ferocious punishment for real or suspected disaffection among the non-Russian peoples, the Soviet leadership felt the need to counteract the impact of the West upon Soviet citizens of all nationalities, both military and civilian, who had fought or lived in Central Europe as a result of the Second World War. At the close of the war elaborate Soviet "decontamination" measures were set in motion to "reeducate" and even severely punish those who were suspected of succumbing to "pernicious" and "decadent" Western influences. The Soviet regime now embarked upon an all-out campaign to prove the superiority, past and present, of Russia and things Russian. The cardinal sins against which this crude chauvinistic campaign was directed were a "cosmopolitan" outlook, "bourgeois objectivism," and "kow-towing" to the West.[45]

The Kremlin not only advanced aggressive assertions of Russian superiority over all nations outside the Soviet Union, but pressed

[44] Lorimer, *Population of the Soviet Union*, p. 138. There was an absolute decrease of 3,124,572 Ukrainians, and by extrapolating population growth on the basis of Lorimer's figures there was a total deficit of 8,084,571. Martschenko contests several aspects of Lorimer's calculations, claiming that there was a considerably greater population loss as a result of the 1932–33 famine which is not reported in Soviet statistics. (Basilius Martschenko, *Soviet Population Trends, 1926–1939* [New York, 1953].) See also Kulischer, *Europe on the Move*, pp. 93–97; N. Prychodko, "The Famine in 1932–33 in Ukraine," *Ukrainian Quarterly*, IX, No. 3 (Summer, 1953), 213–17. For the connection between collectivization and the suppression of "bourgeois nationalists" in the Ukraine, see P. P. Postyshev and S. V. Kossior, *Soviet Ukraine Today* (Moscow, Leningrad, 1934); Armstrong, *Ukrainian Nationalism*, pp. 16–17. To some small extent, the gigantic deficiency in the Ukrainian population might be accounted for by the changing criteria for nationality in the two censuses. In 1926 nationality was determined according to *narodnost'*, or the nationality of one's parentage, while the 1939 census used *natsional'nost'*, in which nationality was determined according to one's choice. The fact that some of Ukrainian descent would record themselves as Russians testifies to the advantages of identifying oneself with the dominant Russian nationality.

[45] The first signs of the trend "proving" Russian priority in science and inventions appeared in June, 1944, when a scientific congress in Moscow emphasized the Russian contribution to world science and world culture. (*Pravda*, June 5, 8, 14, 1944.) For one of the first articles denouncing "cosmopolitanism," see N. Baltiiskii, "Patriotism," *New Times*, No. 1 (June 1, 1945), pp. 3–10. In chapter 12 we shall consider "cosmopolitan" ideas for a non-Soviet world state.

strident claim for the superiority of the Great Russians over the non-Russians within the USSR as well. A key editorial in a 1948 issue of *Voprosy filosofii* stated this claim quite clearly:

All of the peoples of the Soviet Union recognize and appreciate the tremendous historical mission which the great Russian people is performing, as the outstanding people in the Soviet fraternity of nations. . . . The achievements of the Russian people, as the leading people in the Soviet family are dear and important to each Soviet citizen, whatever the nation to which he belongs.[46]

The position of the Russian nation in relation to the world at large is stated with equal modesty:

It is necessary to bear firmly in mind the indisputable proposition that Russian culture has always played a tremendous role, and now plays the leading role, in the development of world culture. . . . We must point out the tremendous role of Russian culture in the history of world culture, through the concrete materials of the history of philosophy, literature, science, technology, the state, and law—through all realms of the history of material and spiritual culture.[47]

What did this outburst of Great Russian chauvinism mean in terms of Soviet ambitions to create a world state? Was the assertion of the leading role of Russian culture in the development of world culture a passive statement of pride in a state with limited national ambitions? Or was this the statement of an active Russian nationalism, which remains harnessed to the original Leninist goal of a world state? An article in *Voprosy istorii* illustrates the blending of Russian nationalism with Leninism: "Our Soviet socialist culture is based on the very rich culture of the Russian people. . . . The apex of Soviet culture, as well as of world culture, is Leninism." [48] Whatever else may be true of "Leninism," it has never denied its world-wide mission. In the statement that Leninism is the apex of world culture lies the unmistakable hint that the exponents of Leninism expect it to become *the* world culture. This "world culture," of course, is to be "based on the very rich culture of the Russian people." And so the circle is closed.

[46] "Protiv burzhuaznoi ideologii kosmopolitizma," *Voprosy filosofii*, No. 2 (1948), pp. 27–28. Note that in this quotation the proper adjective, *Great Russian* (*velikorusskii*), has been changed to *great* Russian (*velikii russkii*). Following the Second World War this usage was commonly adopted in an effort to intensify the glorification of the Russian nation.
[47] *Ibid.*, p. 20.
[48] "Zasedanie uchënogo soveta Instituta Istorii AN SSSR, 24–28 marta 1949 g.," *Voprosy istorii*, No. 3 (March, 1949), p. 152.

This same idea is restated in terms of "proletarian internationalism," which has always had the creation of a world state as its objective. *Voprosy filosofii* gives this explanation: "The socialist internationalism of the citizens of the USSR is organically blended with Soviet patriotism. Precisely because Soviet patriotism is a patriotism of a new kind, it blends harmoniously with proletarian internationalism." [49] Proletarian internationalism is equated with Soviet patriotism, and behind Soviet patriotism stands the "leading role of the Russian nation." It is possible to strip this formula to its essentials by discarding the rather empty phrase of "Soviet patriotism." This formula could then read: "Proletarian internationalism equals Soviet Russian nationalism," an aggressive nationalism with unlimited aims. This frank equation amounts to saying: We will pursue the goal of a world state, but only in such a way as exalts the position of the Russian people. In this coming union, the interests of Russia rank first, and those who do not accept this are bourgeois nationalists.

As a result of this attitude, "bourgeois nationalists" were found on all sides, among Communists both within and outside the USSR. The Soviet press overflowed with exhortations to "love the great Russian people" and its "mighty achievements," but if similar language was used toward any non-Russian people, it was condemned as "bourgeois nationalism." Thus the Ukrainian poet V. Sosiura, who had the audacity to write a poem entitled "Love the Ukraine," was soon branded a "bourgeois nationalist." Sosiura's recantation is interesting as it provides an insight into the fear that the Moscow dictatorship holds toward the growth of any separatist trend, however slight, among the non-Russian peoples in the USSR, which might threaten Moscow's highly centralized control over the outlying regions. "I have profoundly grasped the fact," Sosiura apologized, "that the Soviet Ukraine cannot be thought of in separation from the mighty growth of our multinational state." Then, in characteristic style, Sosiura was made to praise his Russian masters for the beating which they had just administered to him: "The Ukraine, after all, won its happiness with the fraternal assistance of the great Russian people." [50] A careful reading of the postwar Soviet press

[49] "Protiv burzhuaznoi," *Voprosy filosofii*, No. 2 (1948), p. 28.
[50] V. Sosiura, "V redaktsiiu gazety 'Pravda,'" *Pravda*, July 10, 1951, p. 4. For the original censure of Sosiura, see "Protiv ideologicheskikh izvrashchenii v literature," *ibid.*, July 2, 1951, p. 2.

until Stalin's death revealed "bourgeois nationalist deviations" among almost every non-Russian people in the USSR, but never once was there a mention of a deviation toward Russian bourgeois nationalism. Moscow had set up a very clear double standard: what was condemned as bourgeois nationalism among non-Russian peoples, was called "genuine proletarian internationalism" when applied to the Russians.

The Stalinist concept of "proletarian internationalism," which had so antagonized the non-Russian peoples of the Soviet Union, evoked a similar response when it was extended beyond the Soviet borders to embrace the nations of East Central Europe. Apparently Tito had failed to understand that proletarian internationalism implied the total submission of the "lesser brothers" to Moscow's orders and whims. On April 13, 1948, just prior to the break between Moscow and Belgrade, Tito wrote Stalin: "No matter how much each of us loves the land of socialism, the USSR, he can, in no case, love his country less."[51] This, of course, was a fatal mistake, for it was the duty of a "genuine proletarian internationalist" to love Russia first, and his own country second, and then only within the limits that Moscow was prepared to tolerate. In an effort to check the spread of "Titoism" to the satellite Communist Parties, Stalin moved swiftly to strike down large numbers of potential "Titoists" who might place loyalty to their own country on a par with their allegiance to Soviet Russia.

POST-STALINIST "PROLETARIAN INTERNATIONALISM"

The bow of Russian nationalism which was drawn so taut in Stalin's last years appears to have been relaxed very slightly at intervals since his death. During Beria's struggle for supreme power within the Kremlin there were several indications that he sought to enlist the support of the non-Russians, or perhaps of the non-Russian components of the ruling Party. Immediately after his downfall, however, the Soviet press resumed its glorification of the Great Russians.[52] The official announcement of Beria's execution contained the following accusation:

[51] "Letter from J. B. Tito and E. Kardelj to J. V. Stalin and V. M. Molotov," April 13, 1948, in *Soviet-Yugoslav Dispute*, p. 19.

[52] At the apparent zenith of Beria's power, in June, 1953, the Communist leaders of Western Ukraine were rebuked for a policy of forcible Russification. On July 10, 1953, *Pravda* declared Beria "an enemy of the people." Two days

RUSSIAN NATIONALISM SINCE 1934

In his anti-Soviet, treacherous aims, L. P. Beria and his accomplices carried out a number of criminal measures to activize remnants of the bourgeois nationalist elements in the Union Republics, to sow hostility among the peoples of the USSR, and, in the first place, to undermine the friendship of the peoples of the USSR for the great Russian people.[53]

The aftermath of the Geneva Conference of July, 1955, provided another brief respite from the usual blatant assertions of Russian chauvinism. This was in line with the temporary toning down of all harsh and offensive Soviet ideological positions. It was also guided, no doubt, by the highly practical consideration that the self-imposed isolation from the West of the "anticosmopolitan" campaign had become self-defeating. If the various Soviet delegations sent abroad following Geneva were to search out superior techniques in Western agriculture and industry which might be adapted to Soviet conditions, they must, at least, be sufficiently open-minded to acknowledge frankly that there were some things in the world which were not invented and perfected by the Russians.

While the more absurd aspects of Stalinist chauvinism have been pushed into the background, the basic pattern persists. The speeches which shattered the Stalin cult at the Twentieth Party Congress in February, 1956, continued to be interlaced with the familiar tributes to the Great Russian people and the warnings against the revival of "bourgeois nationalism" in the other Union Republics. Khrushchev first spoke of the need to "repulse all manifestations of bourgeois ideology, including nationalism" and then proceeded to quote Lenin's famous phrase: " 'Is the feeling of national pride alien to us Great Russian, class-conscious proletarians? Of course not!' "[54] And three years later, at the Twenty-first Party Congress,

---

later it carried this dispatch from Lvov, the capital of Western Ukraine: "The toilers of the Western regions of the Ukraine know that for their happiness, for their free and joyous life, they are indebted to the great Russian people. Only with the help and support of the great Russian people, and under the wise leadership of the Communist Party, were the Ukrainian people able to unite in a single family. Never will any despicable Berias succeed in disrupting the sacred friendship of our fraternal peoples." ("Plenumy partiinykh komitetov sovmestno s partiinym aktivom," *Pravda*, July 12, 1953, p. 2.) *Izvestiia* likewise reaffirmed that in all the undertakings of the Soviet state "the decisive role belongs to the great Russian people. The Russian people truly deserves universal recognition as the outstanding leading nation of the USSR." ("Osnova prochnosti mnogonatsional'nogo sovetskogo gosudarstva," *Izvestiia*, July 12, 1953, p. 1.)

[53] "V Verkhovnom Sude SSSR," *Pravda*, Dec. 24, 1953, p. 2.
[54] "Otchëtnyi doklad Tsentral'nogo Komiteta Kommunisticheskoi partii, doklad pervogo sekretaria TsK KPSS, tovarishcha N. S. Khrushcheva," *ibid.*, Feb. 15, 1956, pp. 8–9. This double standard was echoed in the speeches of the

a delegate from Uzbekistan exclaimed characteristically: "The Uzbek nation owes its happy present and still finer future . . . to the ever-strengthening, indissoluble fraternal friendship of nations of the USSR, headed by the elder brother—the great Russian people!" [55]

The reversal of Stalin's futile policy toward Tito involved the rehabilitation of the reputations of many of the satellite "Titoists" whom Stalin had branded as "bourgeois nationalists." But even here reservations remained. In April, 1956, *Pravda* admitted that the Polish Communist leader Wladyslaw Gomulka had been jailed on a number of false charges, but continued to defend "the war on Gomulkaism." Gomulka's unforgiven sin was to oppose the "Party line with a nationalist interpretation of the Polish working-class movement." [56]

When the Polish Communists placed Gomulka at the head of their Party on October 19, 1956,[57] in open defiance of Soviet wishes, Moscow chose to avoid the risk of naked military intervention, such as followed in Hungary, by accommodating itself to the resurgence of Polish national communism. Face-saving phrases about "profound confidence" in the principles of cooperation between the Soviet Union and Poland emerged from the Soviet-Polish communiqué of November 18, 1956, but the subsequent bitter polemics between Party spokesmen in the Soviet and the Polish press over the exact meaning of this accord made it obvious that there was no agreement in substance, and that the Kremlin would have liked to move back toward a clear-cut Stalinist basis of "proletarian in-

---

Party representatives from Georgia, Tadzhikistan, and Lithuania (*ibid.*, Feb. 18, 1956, pp. 4, 6, 8), Azerbaijan and Dagestan (*ibid.*, Feb. 21, 1956, pp. 5, 7).

[55] "Rech' tovarishcha S. Kamalova," *ibid.*, Feb. 2, 1959, p. 4. A spokesman from the CP of Kazakhstan then complained, in a vein reminiscent of Stalin's later years, that some Kazakhs persist in glorifying Kazakh national traditions, which are outmoded "survivals of the past," and resist the "civilizing" influence of the Russians in their midst. After a ritualistic warning for Russians to avoid the "great-power deviation," he directed the non-Russians to step up the fight against "local nationalism" and to inculcate "a spirit of boundless love for and gratitude to the great Russian people." (N. Dzhandil'din, "Nekotorye voprosy internatsional'nogo vospitaniia," *Kommunist*, No. 13 [Sept., 1959], p. 43.)

[56] "Doklad Edvarda Okhaba ob itogakh XX s"ezda KPSS," *ibid.*, April 8, 1956, p. 5.

[57] Gomulka was not officially elected First Secretary of the Polish Party until October 21, but he was the chief spokesman for the Poles in their crucial meeting with the Soviet leaders on October 19, when Soviet demands were successfully resisted.

ternationalism." [58] Soviet condemnation of national Communist trends also spilled over on the Yugoslavs, thus deteriorating this recently cemented relationship.

Disagreement over the Soviet justification for its military interventions in Hungary was one of the issues which reopened the schism between Tito and the Kremlin. Although Soviet spokesmen acknowledged mistakes on the part of the preceding Rakosi regime, the Hungarian uprising was allegedly inspired solely by the counterrevolutionary agents of the bourgeoisie and their foreign accomplices, whom the Soviet Army crushed in a magnanimous, sacrificial demonstration of proletarian internationalism. "Soviet military ideology contains the ideas and maxims of cooperation between our armed forces," remarked *Krasnaia zvezda*, "and those of the People's Democracies, which are in complete accord with the spirit of proletarian internationalism."

Trained by the Communist Party, the armed forces of the USSR live up to their international duty. This was demonstrated by the aid they gave to the working people of Hungary in suppressing the counterrevolutionary rebellion organized by international imperialism. The armed forces of the USSR performed their international class duty with honor.[59]

The increasingly Stalinist interpretation of "proletarian internationalism," which caused the Yugoslavs to refrain from signing the Moscow Declaration of November, 1957, again became quite explicit in the Soviet critique of the Yugoslav Party Program in April, 1958. The essence of the differences between the Soviet and Yugoslav positions, *Kommunist* observed, was that for the Yugoslavs "proletarian internationalism is reduced *exclusively* to the principles of equality and noninterference in another's internal affairs, while the necessity of strengthening unity and cooperation among the socialist countries and Marxist-Leninist Parties is buried in oblivion." This was a typically petit-bourgeois nationalist attitude. "Under certain conditions," the Soviet spokesmen continued, "proletarian internationalism demands the subordination of the interests of the proletarian struggle in one country to the interests of the struggle

[58] See, e.g., A. Azizian, "O proletarskom internatsionalizme," *ibid.*, Dec. 23, 1956, pp. 3-4; Jerzy Wiatr, "Crisis of Internationalism," *Nowe Drogi* (Warsaw), Nov.–Dec., 1956, in *East Europe*, VI, No. 4 (April, 1956), 52–56.

[59] Colonel G. Fedorov, "O soderzhanii sovetskoi voennoi ideologii," *Krasnaia zvezda*, March 22, 1957, p. 3.

on a world-wide scale." Moscow was obviously given the prerogative to direct this world-wide struggle, since the "camp of socialist states is headed by the Soviet Union." [60]

STUFFING THE MEMORY HOLES WITH "OBSOLETE"
NATIONALIST IDEAS

From its beginning, the attack on the "nationalist" Communists of Eastern Europe involved the traditional Soviet campaign to rewrite history. The object of this operation was to reshape the national consciousness of all of the satellite countries, so that Russia would appear as their eternal savior. As Orwell said in *1984:* "All history was a palimpsest, scraped clean and reinscribed exactly as often as was necessary. . . . 'Who controls the past,' ran the Party slogan, 'controls the future.' " This process had assumed the following proportions during Stalin's last years:

The Poles today, for example, are told that their greatest poet and national hero, Adam Mickiewicz (1798–1855), was an ardent supporter of cooperation and friendship with Russia, while in fact, he was a nationalist who fought Russia all his life. "Anti-Russian" references in history books, fiction works, encyclopedias and dictionaries are drastically purged, even if they describe events which have taken place more than ten centuries ago.[61]

The national revolts in Poland and Hungary that ensued upon de-Stalinization give one pause as to the validity of Orwell's description of the infinite malleability of the human mind and soul, since these rebellions were led, in large measure, by the supposedly "reeducated" native intelligentsia. On the other hand, since these satellites could boast of a long history of independence and had only been under Soviet control for roughly a decade, there would seem to be insufficient evidence to discount altogether the ghoulish Orwellian vision, if it were given time to ripen.

[60] P. Fedoseev, I. Pomelov, and V. Cheprakov, "O proekte programmy Soiuza kommunistov Iugoslavii," *Kommunist,* No. 6 (April, 1958), pp. 33, 36.
[61] Michael Padev, "The Great Liquidation: Satellite Culture," New York *Times Magazine,* Feb. 10, 1952. See also *Russification of Poland,* Polish Section, National Committee for a Free Europe (New York, 1950), pp. 1–14; Wiktor Weintraub, "Soviet Cultural Imperialism in Poland," in Waldemar Gurian, ed., *Soviet Imperialism* (Notre Dame, 1953), pp. 91–111; Istvan Csicsery-Ronay, *Russian Cultural Penetration in Hungary* (New York, National Committee for a Free Europe, 1952), pp. 1–42; Dana Adams Schmidt, *Anatomy of a Satellite* (Boston, 1952), pp. 233–52; Leland Stowe, *Conquest by Terror* (New York, 1952), pp. 232–46.

A similar crude remodeling of the history and national consciousness of non-Russian peoples also occurred within the Soviet Union. While aimed at all non-Russian nationals, it has been especially hard upon those peoples who are least able to defend themselves against the onslaught of Great Russian chauvinism, namely, those small and backward peoples of the Caucasus and Central Asia, who were originally brought into the Tsars' empire through the military conquests of Russian arms. The national folklore of these peoples has been ruthlessly expunged and their Tsarist Russian conquerors have been presented as the carriers of civilization and progress. Their national epics and folklore have been condemned as signs of "bourgeois nationalism," even though many of these primitive peoples never produced a real bourgeoisie. This might be amusing were it not for the fact that such folklore often represents their greatest national treasury, since many of these peoples have only recently become literate.

Under the Pokrovskii school of historiography, which held sway until the early 1930s, the imperial conquests of Tsarist Russia were frankly condemned as an absolute evil. This simple formula, reflecting an international class ideology, was scrapped when it came into conflict with the open revival of Russian nationalism in the mid-thirties. A government decree of August 22, 1937, censured those who could not see the beneficial aspects of Russia's conquest of a country like Georgia, which "at the time, was confronted by the alternative of either being swallowed up by the Shah of Persia and the Sultan of Turkey, or coming under a Russian protectorate. They do not see that the second alternative was nevertheless the lesser evil." [62]

In April, 1951, this "lesser-evil" formula proved insufficient for the aggressive purposes of the Russian Communists, since the conquest of a foreign nation by Russian troops nonetheless remained an evil, however slight. According to this critique, evil might still be imputed to the Tsarist methods of colonial administration, but how, it was asked, could one disregard "the new and positive contributions made by the great Russian people, despite Tsarism, to the economic and cultural life of these peoples?" [63] The outcome of this discussion was to replace the "lesser-evil" theory with what might

[62] Quoted in M. Nechkina, "K voprosu o formule 'naimenshee zlo,'" *Voprosy istorii*, No. 4 (April, 1951), p. 44.
[63] *Ibid.*, pp. 46–47.

be called the theory of the "absolute good," in which no evil whatsoever might be attributed to the *Russian* element of these annexations. The objections to the Tsarist regime were, of course, overcome when it was replaced by the Soviet regime, so that now there were no longer any conceivable objections, according to this theory, to the forcible annexation of nations by a regime which is both Soviet and Russian in nature.

In the face of this logic, anyone who opposed the annexation of his native land by Russian troops was automatically condemned as "counterrevolutionary." Foremost among such non-Russian insurgent leaders was the legendary figure of Shamil, who led the people of the Caucasus in their fight against the forcible encroachments of Tsarist Russia in the middle of the nineteenth century. Shamil's sin lay in his blindness to the "fact" that for his people "the annexation to Russia of Dagestan, together with the rest of the backward regions of the Caucasus, was not only progressive, but the only possible exit from their slough." [64] All Shamil's celebrated exploits could be summarized by this simple motivation: "In his activities Shamil was guided, not by the interests of the masses, but by the desire to destroy his political enemies, who understood the necessity of union with Russia." [65] De-Stalinization permitted Soviet historians to correct some of the grossest misinterpretations of Shamil's role. Former charges, such as of Shamil's being an Anglo-Turkish secret agent rather than a native rebel fighting the oppression of the Tsarist autocracy, were now abandoned as false. "But no serious Soviet scholar," *Kommunist* remarked in March, 1957, "ever doubted that joining the peoples of the North Caucasus to Russia was progressive." [66]

A similar official reevaluation was ordered of those national rebels who resisted Tsarist Russian conquests in Central Asia. Kenesary

---

[64] A. Daniialov, "Ob izbrashcheniiakh v osveshchenie miuridizma i dvizheniia Shamilia," *Voprosy istorii*, No. 9 (Sept., 1950), p. 13.

[65] *Ibid.*, p. 9.

[66] "Strogo sobliudat' leninskii printsip partiinosti v istoricheskoi nauke," *Kommunist*, No. 4 (March, 1957), p. 26. This was intended as a special rebuke to A. M. Pikman, who, in an article in *Voprosy istorii*, No. 3 (March, 1956), went so far as to suggest that Shamil was not only properly opposing the Tsarist autocracy, but even rightfully fighting for the independence of the North Caucasians against the Russian people. See also G. A. von Stackelberg, "The Twentieth Party Congress and the Soviet Evaluation of Historical Figures," *Bulletin of the Institute*, IV, No. 6 (June, 1957), 30–39; Paul B. Henze, " 'Unrewriting' History—The Shamil Problem," *Caucasian Review* (Munich), No. 6 (1958), pp. 7–29.

Kasymov, the Central Asian counterpart of Shamil, was likewise branded an unprincipled bandit, fighting against Russian "enlightenment." The Secretary of the Central Committee of the Communist Party of Kazakhstan castigated all those who "ignored the indisputable proof that, without this annexation and without this fraternal aid of the great Russian people, Kazakhstan would have remained apart from the general democratic revolutionary movement in Russia and would have been left in the position of the countries of the East, oppressed by the American-British imperialists." [67] And the Secretary of the Central Committee of the Communist Party of Azerbaijan scolded those who attempted to belittle "the progressive, fruitful significance of the annexation of Azerbaijan by Russia." [68] The competition in self-abasement had begun, as the Communists of all the non-Russian peoples rushed their tribute to the shrine of Great Russia.[69]

Despite the slight abatement of Russian chauvinism following Stalin's death, *Pravda* of September, 1954, still saw fit to attribute the following exhortation to the prerevolutionary Kazakh philosopher Abai Kunanbaev:

Science, knowledge, discoveries, art—the Russians have all these. To avoid evil and achieve good you must know the Russian language and Russian culture. The Russians see the world. If you will learn their language, the world will open before your eyes. Study Russian culture and art. This is the key to life.[70]

Russia and the Great Russian people have been moved into the center of world history, representing the progress of civilization at every stage of development. The usefulness of this theory lies not in excusing Russia's past, but in presenting a carte blanche for the future by which any and every act of Russia, by definition, is automatically progressive. If nations in the past have been com-

[67] Zh. Shaiakhmetov, "O nekotorykh voprosakh ideologicheskoi raboty v Kazakhstane," *Pravda*, April 10, 1952, p. 2.
[68] "Rech' tov. Bagirova," *ibid.*, Oct. 7, 1952, p. 4.
[69] For more of the original denunciations of the "lesser-evil theory," glorifying the Russian annexations of Azerbaijan, Armenia, Georgia, Dagestan, the Kazan Tatars, and the Moslem peoples of Soviet Central Asia, see articles by M. Mustafaev, N. Tavakalian, K. Naiakshin, A. Zevelev, and S. Abdullaev in *Voprosy istorii*, No. 9 (Sept., 1951).
[70] Leonid Sololev, "Abai Kunanbaev," *Pravda*, Sept. 5, 1954, p. 3. See also "Kazakhstan," *Central Asian Review*, II, No. 4 (1954), 350–57. For a review of post-Stalinist nationality policy within the Soviet Union, see Walter Kolarz, "The Nationalities Under Khrushchev," *Soviet Survey*, No. 24 (April–June, 1958), pp. 57–65.

mitted to share the fruits of civilization by being joined to (i.e., conquered by) Russia, this is all the more true of Soviet Russia, which is represented as the pinnacle of development of all world history. Russia has been entrusted by history with "civilizing" the world, and this can only be brought to a conclusion when all other nations are joined to Russia in a Soviet world state so that they may partake of Russia's felicitous tutelage.

SOVIET ANTI-SEMITISM

Another cancerous expression of Russian chauvinism was unveiled with an unmistakable outbreak of government-sponsored anti-Semitism during the last years of Stalin's rule. Beginning in September, 1948, the Soviet attack on "homeless cosmopolitans" assumed a decidedly anti-Semitic character, with a disproportionate citing of Jewish names among the alleged culprits. This may, in part, have been the Kremlin's response to an awakening of Zionist sentiment which was stimulated by the arrival in Moscow of Golda Myerson, the first Israeli Minister to the Soviet Union. Soviet Jews greeted her appearance with an extraordinary emotional fervor, and the large number of them who began visiting the Israeli Legation to inquire about the possibility of emigration to Israel must have alarmed the Soviet authorities. Correctly appraising this as a verdict of no-confidence in the Soviet nationality policy, *Pravda* retorted: "The solution of the 'Jewish problem' depends not on military successes in Palestine, but on the victory of socialism over capitalism." [71] And the Soviet government quickly struck back by closing down the Yiddish publishing house, Der Emes, the last national Yiddish newspaper, *Einikeit*, the Yiddish theater, Yiddish schools, the Jewish Anti-Fascist Committee, and similar Jewish institutions. Reverberations of Soviet anti-Semitism were felt in the satellites, especially in Prague, where in November, 1952, the Czech Jew Slansky and ten others, mostly Jews, were condemned to death as "Zionist, bourgeois traitors." The high point of this campaign appears to have been reached on January 13, 1953, when *Pravda* made the sensational announcement that a group of nine doctors, six of them Jews, had been arrested for murdering former Politburo members, Shcherbakov, and Zhdanov, as well as for con-

[71] Il'ia Erenburg, "Po povodu odnogo pis'ma," *Pravda*, Sept. 21, 1948, p. 3.

spiratorial activity with an allegedly American-sponsored international Jewish spy ring. Following Stalin's death the "doctors' plot" was officially repudiated as a hoax, and Soviet anti-Semitism, superficially, at least, was damped down.[72]

In April, 1956, the desanctification of Stalin permitted the Polish Communist press to admit a hitherto denied "raving anti-Semitism."[73] Moscow's response was significantly different. The rehabilitation of Soviet Jews who had been persecuted as "cosmopolitans" proceeded gradually and quietly, without any explanation that these individuals had suffered because of their ethnic origin,[74] and a spokesman for the Soviet Foreign Ministry soon branded Warsaw's revelations as "slanderous and anti-Soviet."[75] When Gomulka came to power in October, 1956, he identified the so-called "Natolin group," or the unrepentant Moscow agents, as being "in favor of preserving the previous state of affairs," which included approaching the "democratization" of Poland "in a very simplified way which could be taken for anti-Semitism."[76] The strategy of the Polish "Stalinists," the Warsaw paper *Po Prostu* elaborated, involved spreading the lie that a "Jewish administration had pauperized Poland."[77] Following de-Stalinization in the Soviet Union,

[72] On the plight of the Jews until Stalin's death, see S. M. Schwarz, *Antisemitizm v Sovetskom Soiuze* (New York, 1952); Elliot E. Cohen, ed., *The New Red Anti-Semitism* (Boston, 1953); Peter Meyer et al., *The Jews in the Soviet Satellites* (New York, 1953); *Treatment of Jews by the Soviet: Seventh Interim Report of Hearings before the Select Committee on Communist Aggression*, House of Representatives, 83d Congress, 2d Session (Washington, 1954).

[73] On April 4, 1956, the Warsaw Yiddish-language paper, *Folks-Shtimme*, officially acknowledged previous reports of the systematic anti-Semitic campaign. See Harrison E. Salisbury, "Soviet Confirms Jews' Execution," New York *Times*, March 7, 1956, and "Reds Name Jews Purged by Soviet," ibid., April 12, 1956.

[74] Harrison E. Salisbury, "Jewish Writers in Soviet Active," New York *Times*, July 26, 1956.

[75] Harry Schwartz, "Red Paper Chides Soviet on Jews," ibid., Sept. 17, 1956. Similarly, on June 27, 1956, when *Pravda* reprinted a *Daily Worker* article of June 18 by Eugene Dennis, *Pravda* pointedly omitted Dennis's condemnation of Stalin for "snuffing out the lives of more than a score of Jewish cultural figures." (*The Anti-Stalin Campaign*, pp. 148, 151; see also ibid., pp. 92, 94–95, 272–73, 325.)

[76] "Address by the First Secretary of the Polish United Worker's Party, Gomulka, Before a National Conference of Party Activists, Warsaw, November 4, 1956," *Trybuna Ludu*, Nov. 5, 1956, in Zinner, ed., *National Communism*, pp. 289–90.

[77] Quoted in the Warsaw dispatch of Sydney Gruson, "Jews Leave Poland in a Vast 'Exodus,'" New York *Times*, Feb. 17, 1957. See also Czeslaw Milosz, "Anti-Semitism in Poland," *Problems of Communism*, VI, No. 3 (May–June, 1957), 35–40.

several interviews with the Kremlin potentates, including Khrushchev, revealed a continuing, noticeable anti-Jewish bias on the part of the Soviet leaders.[78]

Of all the national groups under Soviet domination, the future of the Great Russians seems to be the most secure. Any people, aside from the Great Russians, can become a pawn and a plaything in the hands of the Soviet leaders. The possibility of the uninterrupted national development of the non-Russians, both in the Soviet Union and the Soviet satellite states, stands under the constant threat of seemingly arbitrary decisions made in Moscow, which is the heart both of a highly centralized empire and of Great Russia. There are definite limits to the opportunities for the development of the non-Russian cultures beyond which the Soviet regime cannot afford to let them go without endangering the existence of its Russian-based centralized dictatorship. The Muscovite centralized dictatorship cannot, by its very nature, tolerate for any length of time diverse centers of freedom of any description, either the freedom of individuals or the freedom of nationalities, which might arise as centers for the disintegration of a monopoly of centralized power.

THE MANIPULATION OF NATIONAL SOVEREIGNTY

Just as Moscow has manipulated the concept of national cultures to serve its power aims, so it has laid great stress upon manipulating the concept of national sovereignty. It is a fundamental axiom of Soviet ideology that law is simply an instrument of policy. This is

---

[78] The New York Yiddish-language Communist paper, *Morgen Freiheit*, recorded an interview between Khrushchev and a leading Canadian Communist, in which the latter was convinced that Khrushchev was "infected with anti-Semitism." (Harry Schwartz, "Red Paper Scores Khrushchev View," New York *Times*, Dec. 25, 1956.) A French Socialist delegation reported a similar impression after its interview with Khrushchev. (Harry Schwartz, "A Yiddish Revival in Soviet Doubted," New York *Times*, June 23, 1957.) Then, in a subsequent interview, Khrushchev leveled a whole series of complaints against Soviet Jews, including the objection that Jews were incapable of adapting themselves to Soviet society, since "they dislike collective work and group discipline." (Serge Groussard, "Propos libres avec N. Krouchtchev," *Le Figaro* [Paris], April 9, 1958, p. 5.) American Jewish Communists gave Khrushchev a point-by-point rebuttal in *Morgen Freiheit*. (Harry Schwartz, "Khrushchev Gets a Red Reprimand," New York *Times*, April 20, 1958.) For a survey of Soviet policy toward the Jews with emphasis on the post-Stalinist period, see Judd L. Teller, *The Kremlin, the Jews and the Middle East* (New York, 1957); *Soviet Survey*, No. 18 (Aug., 1957), pp. 1-20; "Jews in the Soviet Union," *New Leader*, Sept. 14, 1959, pp. 3-34.

nowhere better illustrated than in the legal concept of sovereignty, which Soviet theoreticians either attack or defend as policy dictates.

On those occasions when sovereignty has been invoked by non-Soviet nations to the distinct disadvantage of the USSR, Soviet spokesmen have attacked national sovereignty as a reactionary concept. During the Soviet attempt to use the League of Nations to check the expansion of Axis power, Litvinov denied that those nations which held back from efforts of collective security had a right to do so because of their sovereign status. On July 1, 1936, Litvinov told the Assembly of the League of Nations that "an end must be put to the situation wherein pleas of sovereignty and constitutional formality are an obstacle to the performance of international obligations."[79]

In the postwar period the Soviet leaders continued to exhibit their hostility toward Franco Spain by insisting that the United Nations should not permit pleas for the integrity of Spanish sovereignty to stand in the way of acts detrimental to the Franco regime. The more the dissension-laden Spanish question could be kept in the spotlight of the United Nations, the greater the possibility of encouraging disunity in the non-Soviet world. Thus I. D. Levin, the Soviet legal authority, dismissed the argument that national sovereignty could serve as a justifiable defense against vigorous United Nations actions toward Spain:

It is characteristic of those leaders who demand a review of "the principle of sovereignty" that they have come forth as opponents of the United Nations' resolution condemning the Franco regime, by relying upon "the sovereignty" of Franco Spain, which would act as a barrier to any interference in its internal affairs. But this is an obvious attempt to distort the real meaning of sovereignty. . . . A regime born of aggression and representing a constant threat of renewed aggression, it stands to reason, cannot pretend to protect itself by hiding behind the principle of sovereignty.[80]

Neither can non-Soviet colonial powers like France and Britain take refuge behind the concept of sovereignty, the Soviet theoreticians contend, in an effort to suppress movements for national independence in Asia and Africa. Here Soviet spokesmen have taken

[79] Litvinov, "Speech on the Indivisibility of Peace and the Strengthening of Collective Security, Delivered at the XVI Plenum of the League of Nations," July 1, 1936, in *Against Aggression*, p. 43.
[80] I. D. Levin, *Printsip suvereniteta v sovetskom i mezhdunarodnom prave* (Moscow, 1947), p. 24.

full advantage of the almost unlimited possibilities to exploit grievances, both real and imaginary, which the colonial peoples hold toward their former and present imperial rulers. To exacerbate these conflicts obviously has a divisive and disintegrative effect upon the non-Soviet world. Consequently Soviet representatives have systematically attempted to belittle the national sovereignty of the imperial powers, while striving to enlarge the sphere of action of the dependent peoples. In the words of a Soviet writer, "sovereignty is the banner of struggle of colonial peoples against imperialist domination and for national independence." [81] This is clearly illustrated by Vyshinsky's position in the debate in the United Nations over the status of Indonesia:

We are being referred to Article 2, paragraph 7, of the Charter, in an attempt to prove that the events in Indonesia are an internal matter and that the Organization has no right to interfere in such matters, as otherwise, as Mr. Bevin put it, the sovereign rights of Holland would be impaired, but these objections are quite unfounded. . . . Does not the Charter represent certain limitations of sovereignty of sovereign states? I say: Yes.[82]

In apparent contradiction to this derogatory attitude toward national sovereignty, the Soviet leaders have also appeared in the role of the most uncompromising defenders of national sovereignty known to modern times. Stalin's very last public address, delivered to the closing session of the Nineteenth Party Congress on October 14, 1952, contained this admonition to Communists all over the world:

Today the bourgeoisie sells the rights and independence of nations for dollars. The banner of national independence and national sovereignty has been thrown overboard. There is no doubt that you, the representatives of Communist and Democratic Parties, will have to pick up this banner and carry it forward, if you want to be patriots of your own country, if you want to become the leading force of your nation.[83]

There are three basic reasons which would seem to account for this urgent Soviet defense of national sovereignty. The first is the desire to perpetuate the anarchy of the nation-state system in the

[81] I. D. Levin, "K voprosu o sushchnosti i znachenii printsipa suvereniteta," *Sovetskoe gosudarstvo i pravo*, No. 6 (June, 1949), p. 38.
[82] A. Vyshinsky, "Speech on the Indonesian Question," Feb. 10, 1946, in *United Nations Security Council, Official Records*, First Year, First Series, meetings of Jan. 17, 1946, to Feb. 16, 1946, pp. 206–7.
[83] "Rech' tovarishcha I. V. Stalina," *Pravda*, Oct. 15, 1952, p. 1.

non-Soviet world. The Soviet leaders are aware of the fact that they would have much to lose and the non-Soviet world much to gain if that anarchic system were overhauled and strengthened. This objective, of keeping the non-Soviet world divided by defending the principle of national sovereignty, coincides with their attempt to divide and disintegrate the strength of the non-Soviet world by belittling the importance of national sovereignty, as in the above-cited cases of Spain and Indonesia. That is why the contradiction between attacking on one occasion and on another defending national sovereignty is more apparent than real. The phenomenon of ideological plumbing with hot and cold running sovereignty thus becomes somewhat less bewildering.

Since the Second World War, the Soviet regime has tried to separate the United States from its allies by posing as the defenders of the national sovereignty of America's allies against the encroachment of "American imperialism." The bêtes noires of this drama have been the non-Soviet left, moderate leaders, like Schuman, and European Socialists, such as Spaak, Saragat, Renner, Blum, and so forth, to whom the necessity of integrating the non-Soviet world has been painfully apparent. This non-Soviet left-of-center, whom the Soviet spokesmen often call "right-Socialists," are denounced as "troubadours of national treason." Kuusinen, the Comintern veteran, ridicules a leader like Spaak, the head of the Belgian Socialists, because he "strives to prove that state sovereignty is an 'outdated' idea, which one must throw out like an old shirt." Kuusinen asserts that it is possible to gauge how far the

right-Socialists have already gone in their subservience to American imperialists, on the one hand, from their attempts to hitch their own countries to the yoke of "American aid," accepting any sort of conditions set by the money-lenders of Wall Street, and on the other hand, from the zeal with which the most prominent Social-Democratic leaders call upon their own countries to renounce their national sovereignty.[84]

Some interesting questions arise from the Soviet defense of the sovereignty of *bourgeois* European nations. Is this defense absolute or conditional, are the Soviet leaders really trying to preserve bourgeois nation-states, or are they only trying to preserve the status quo in an effort to block the integration of these nations into some larger non-Soviet unit? And do these Soviet leaders ever hope to

[84] O. Kuusinen, *Sovremennye pravye sotsial-demokraty* (Moscow, 1948), pp. 19–20.

substitute a "proletarian sovereignty" for the "bourgeois sovereignty" of these states? Korovin, the Soviet authority on international law, draws a contrast between "Soviet sovereignty," which he says is "a genuinely popular sovereignty," and "bourgeois sovereignty, which conceals behind the sovereign nation the class domination of the bourgeoisie." [85] Since the Soviet leaders intend to destroy "the class domination of the bourgeoisie," it must be assumed that "bourgeois sovereignty" must some day give way to "Soviet sovereignty," and that the Soviet defense of "bourgeois sovereignty" is therefore conditional, not absolute. This would seem to be confirmed by Levin's statement that "the principle of sovereignty is subordinated to the principle of democracy as a more general and universal principle of relations among states and relations within a state." [86] If it is understood that "democracy" to a Soviet author can only mean "Soviet democracy," then it should be clear that the concept of national sovereignty is but another tool to be manipulated for the advantage of the Soviet state, whose ultimate aim is to replace the "bourgeois sovereignty" of nations by a "Soviet sovereignty."

Korovin also supplies the second and third basic reasons for the Soviet leaders' adamant defense of national sovereignty:

> The principle of sovereignty as applied by the Soviet state has been called upon to serve as a legal bulwark for the protection of peoples from imperialistic encroachments and from military and economic aggression, and as a guarantee for the liberation of peoples of colonial and dependent countries from imperialist enslavement, as well as a means of guaranteeing the establishment of the most progressive social and political systems.[87]

Here is a frank statement of the two additional causes served by the Soviet defense of national sovereignty, two complementary purposes which form different sides of the same coin. On the one side is the use of national sovereignty "as a bulwark for the protection of peoples from imperialistic encroachments," as a barrier to prevent the influence of Europe and America from penetrating the dependent areas in Asia and Africa, and especially as a barrier to prevent any interference by the non-Soviet world in the affairs of the

[85] E. A. Korovin, "Vklad SSSR v mezhdunarodnoe pravo," *Sovetskoe gosudarstvo i pravo*, No. 11 (Nov., 1947), p. 25.
[86] Levin, *Printsip suvereniteta*, p. 24.
[87] Korovin, "Vklad SSSR," *Sovetskoe gosudarstvo i pravo*, No. 11 (Nov., 1947), p. 25.

RUSSIAN NATIONALISM SINCE 1934

Soviet Union and Soviet satellite states. The other side reveals the use of national sovereignty "as a guarantee for the liberation of the peoples of colonial and dependent countries" and as a means of establishing "the most progressive social and political systems," that is, as a means of "liberation" and Sovietization of those nations which can be detached from the core of the non-Soviet world.

The use of national sovereignty as a shield against unwanted outside interference appears in many forms. We have already indicated how the Soviet leaders magnify the sovereign status of dependent areas in an effort to detach them from the West. With the proposal of the Marshall Plan in June, 1947, the Soviet regime also became the foremost proponent of the sovereignty of the European nations, in an attempt to repulse American influence from Europe in general, and from Eastern Europe in particular. At the Paris Conference of European Foreign Ministers, called in response to Secretary Marshall's proposal, Molotov voiced his fear of American economic aid: "It is perfectly obvious . . . that the European countries will become subsidiary states and will forfeit their former economic independence and national sovereignty in favor of certain strong powers." The Marshall Plan proposal, in which both Poland and Czechoslovakia initially showed great interest (without the "benefit" of Moscow's advice), must have created panic among the Soviet leaders, who feared losing control of their East European preserve. Thus at the Paris Conference, Molotov made this revealing protest:

Where may this lead? Today pressure may be exerted on Poland to make her produce more coal. . . . Tomorrow it will be said that Czechoslovakia must be asked to increase her agricultural output and curtail her machine-building industry. . . . What then will remain of the economic independence and sovereignty of such European countries? [88]

The challenge of the Marshall Plan was undoubtedly a major reason for the creation of the Cominform, which had as its immediate objective the exclusion of all American influence and the tightening of Moscow's hold on Eastern Europe. The Declaration of the founding Cominform Conference warned that the Communists "must grasp in their hands the banner of national independence and sovereignty in their own countries," and conduct a "fight against

[88] V. M. Molotov, "Statement Made at the Paris Conference of the Three Foreign Ministers," July 2, 1947, in *Problems of Foreign Policy* (Moscow, 1949), p. 466.

attempts at the economic and political subjugation of their countries."[89]

Soviet legal theoreticians likewise showed a flurry of activity in their efforts to produce new and more exacting definitions of national sovereignty. The most widely accepted definition, devised by Vyshinsky, stated quite simply that "sovereignty is the status of independence of a given state power from any other power, either within or beyond the boundaries of that state."[90] A Soviet colleague, with an eye fixed on American activity in the Near East, described the type of things such sovereignty was intended to preclude:

Any attempts to direct affairs in the territory of a foreign state through military missions, unsolicited "advisors," the organization of military bases on the territory of a foreign state, etc. (as in Greece and Turkey), any attempts to limit the authority of the state over its own citizens constitutes a violation of sovereignty—a violation of international law which guards the sovereignty of states.[91]

The Korean War provided a new justification for invoking national sovereignty to exclude unwanted interference. Soviet theoreticians contended that when the United Nations intervened in the Korean War, it was violating international law "that guards the sovereignty of states," since the troublesome events in Korea were a matter of domestic concern. The Korean War could not be branded an act of aggression because "aggression is the armed attack of one *state* upon another." Since aggression is a term which may only be attached to states, "it is clear that the events in Korea are not aggressive war by one part of Korea against the other. Before us is a civil war." Consequently it was ridiculous, in the Soviet view, to "proclaim as 'aggression' the noble struggle of the Korean people for their national unification and independence."[92] This Soviet defense of national independence and national sovereignty, which served to sanction aggression, again suggests the close relationship which exists between the Soviet use of sovereignty as a shield to repel non-Soviet influence and the function which this shield per-

[89] "Deklaratsiia," Sept., 1947, in *Informatsionnoe soveshchanie*, p. 9.
[90] A. Vyshinsky, "O nekotorykh voprosakh teorii gosudarstva i prava," *Sovetskoe gosudarstvo i pravo*, No. 6 (June, 1948), pp. 7–8.
[91] Levin, "K voprosu o sushchnosti," *ibid.*, No. 6 (June, 1949), p. 37.
[92] I. Pereterkii, "Narushiteli mezhdunarodnogo prava," *Izvestiia*, Aug. 11, 1950, p. 3.

forms as a protective covering behind which Soviet agents are free to "liberate" and Sovietize nations.

Long before the Korean War the Soviet leaders had established numerous precedents for presenting an act of military aggression in the guise of defending the "national sovereignty" of a weaker neighbor. On the eve of the Soviet attack against Finland, on November 29, 1939, Molotov asserted that "irrespective of the regime existing in Finland, we consider her an independent sovereign state in her external and internal policies. . . . The peoples of our country are ready also in the future to render the Finnish people assistance in assuring its free and independent development." [93] On December 1, 1939, Kuusinen as head of the Soviet puppet government for Finland replied: "The People's Government of Finland being deeply convinced that the Soviet Union pursues no aims directed against the independence of our country fully approves and supports actions by the Red Army on the territory of Finland." [94] Due to unforeseen difficulties the Red Army was only able to "protect" a small portion of Finnish sovereignty by annexation.

The Soviet operation against the Baltic states in the summer of 1940 was much cleaner. When Estonia, Latvia, and Lithuania were incorporated into the USSR, once more Soviet puppet governments expressed their gratitude for the "protection" of the sovereignty of their nations by the Soviet Union. On July 21, 1940, the Estonian Duma, the Lettish Sejm, and the Lithuanian Sejm passed almost identical resolutions of which this excerpt from the Lithuanian resolution may serve as an example: "The People's Sejm of Lithuania is confident that only admission into the Union of Soviet Socialist Republics will insure the real sovereignty of the Lithuanian State." [95]

Since it is "only admission into the Union of Soviet Socialist Republics" that insures the fullest measure of a nation's sovereignty, the satellite states of East Central Europe have thus far experienced a slightly less advanced stage of Soviet "protection" of their national sovereignty. Levin describes the relations between the USSR

[93] "Molotov's Broadcast to the Soviet People," Nov. 29, 1939, in *The U.S.S.R. and Finland* (New York, 1939), p. 55.
[94] "Declaration of the People's Government of Finland," Dec. 1, 1939, in *ibid.*, p. 57.
[95] "Declaration of the Lithuanian Sejm on the Joining of Lithuania to the U.S.S.R.," July 21, 1940, *Communist International*, No. 10 (Oct., 1940), pp. 734-35.

and the so-called "People's Democracies" as founded upon "the basis of genuine equality of states and respect for their sovereignty, a model of consistent policy of respect for the sovereignty of all peoples and states, large or small." [96] And Răutu, a member of the Central Committee of the Rumanian Communist Party, responds for the satellite states: "Only now, when the reins of power are in the hands of governments led by Communists, have the peoples of these countries acquired, with the fraternal aid of the Soviet Union, genuine national independence and state sovereignty." [97]

Much is made of "the fraternal aid," that is, the unlimited interference, of the Soviet Union. "The powerful, selfless aid of the Soviet Union has been of tremendous importance in guaranteeing the sovereignty of the countries of the People's Democracy." [98] The Soviet press constantly asserts that "the powerful, many-sided support by the Soviet Union made it possible for the countries of the People's Democracy to create their new state machinery." [99] Furthermore the Communist Parties are acclaimed for their leading roles in the "sovereign" affairs of each satellite. "The People's Democracies, as a form of the dictatorship of the proletariat, cannot be considered apart from the guidance of the Communist Parties. During the process of the formation and development of the People's Republics, the Communist Parties became the guiding core of power, the directing and organizing force of the people's democratic society." [100]

By this time the familiar Soviet double standard should be fully apparent. When a non-Soviet power "attempts to direct affairs in the territory of a foreign state, through military missions, unsolicited 'advisors,' " and so forth, this is interference in the internal affairs of another nation and a violation of its national sovereignty. When the Soviet Union does exactly the same thing, only to a much greater extent, by creating a new state machinery and then operating it entirely with its avowed agents, this is called "noninterference"

[96] Levin, "K voprosu o sushchnosti," *Sovetskoe gosudarstvo i pravo*, No. 6 (June, 1949), p. 46.
[97] L. Răutu, "Mighty Force of Proletarian Internationalism," *For a Lasting Peace*, Feb. 2, 1951, p. 6
[98] L. Zhukova, "Voprosy gosudarstva i prava v stranakh narodnoi demokratii," *Sovetskoe gosudarstvo i pravo*, No. 6 (June, 1949), p. 71.
[99] G. A. Gmanaberov, "Voprosy gosudarstva i prava v stranakh narodnoi demokratii," *ibid.*, No. 5 (May, 1949), p. 65.
[100] *Ibid.*, p. 67.

in the internal affairs of another nation and supreme respect for its national sovereignty. Those who resist this "noninterference" are doomed to lose their "sovereignty." This, the Cominform insisted, after 1948 until May, 1955, was the fate of Titoist Yugoslavia: "The Yugoslav Government is in a state of complete dependence on foreign imperialist circles . . . which has resulted in the liquidation of the sovereignty and independence of the Yugoslav Republic." [101] When, in the spring of 1958, Moscow and Peking renewed their attacks on Tito as "a Trojan horse of imperialism," it was again claimed that Yugoslav sovereignty and independence had been compromised.

Khrushchev's attempted reconciliation with Tito, the liberalization of Soviet policy in Eastern Europe, and the resulting national explosions in Hungary and Poland provided the occasion for another spectacular demonstration of the Kremlin's avowed regard for national sovereignty. As Moscow sought vainly to keep the mounting satellite crisis in hand, the Soviet government issued a Declaration on October 30, 1956, which offered the reassurance that "the countries of the great commonwealth of socialist nations can build their mutual relations only on the principles of complete equality, of respect for territorial integrity, state independence and sovereignty, and of noninterference in one another's affairs." [102]

This announcement was accompanied by the withdrawal of Soviet troops in Hungary from the public view, especially in Budapest. But simultaneously, according to the UN Special Committee of Inquiry, there "was the dispatch of new [Soviet] forces from the East to certain strategic centers within Hungary," as well as "the massing on and within the Hungarian borders of heavy armored units which were to be called upon four days later to crush the Hungarian uprising." [103] This massive reprisal, *Izvestiia* maintained, was evidence of selfless aid to the Hungarian nation, whose sovereignty was scrupulously respected. "Could the Hungarian people in the recent days of the counterrevolutionary rebellion have curbed the Fascist

---

[101] "Resolution of the Information Bureau: Communist Party of Yugoslavia in the Power of Assassins and Spies," in *Meeting of the Information Bureau of Communist Parties in Hungary in the Latter Half of November 1949* (n.p. [Moscow], 1950), p. 23.

[102] "Deklaratsiia Pravitel'stva Soiuza SSR ob osnovakh razvitiia i dal'neishego ukrepleniia druzhby i sotrudnichestva mezhdu Sovetskim Soiuzom i drugimi sotsialisticheskimi gosudarstvami," *Pravda*, Oct. 31, 1956, p. 1.

[103] *Report of the Special Committee on the Problem of Hungary*, p. 26.

cutthroats so quickly and so decisively, had it not been for the timely help of the Soviet Union?" Such assistance was founded upon correct relations among socialist states which "guarantee the complete independence, the maintenance, and the strengthening of the sovereignty of each socialist state and a mutual respect for national interests and traditions." [104] At the same time, Soviet spokesmen consistently assailed all efforts by the UN to deal with the Hungarian revolt as an invasion of Hungarian sovereignty.

THE ULTIMATE STAGE IN THE "PROTECTION" OF NATIONAL SOVEREIGNTY

Soviet pronouncements make it quite clear that satellite status is not the ultimate form in which the national sovereignty of these states is to be "protected." "The solution of territorial questions," we are told, "will be made in accordance with the will of the peoples, and will guarantee the right of nations to self-determination or to voluntary adherence to other states." [105] This opens the door for the "will of the peoples" of satellite states, expressed, of course, through "the guiding core of power," the Communist Parties, at some later time to request the transformation of these states into Union Republics of the USSR. Presumably only then will their sovereignty be "fully realized."

Within the USSR sovereignty is supposedly lodged in "the multinational Soviet people," with the result that both the USSR as a whole and each Union Republic of the USSR are said to constitute a sovereign state. "Due to the singular nature of the Soviet federation," a Soviet legal textbook explains, "there is a joint and fully compatible sovereignty of the USSR with the sovereignty of the Union Republics." [106] This idea of the sovereignty of the constituent Republics actually goes back to the formation of the USSR in 1923, when Stalin spoke of the newborn federation as a "state whose existence does not diminish the sovereignty of the separate Re-

[104] N. Vasil'ev, "Protiv izvrashcheniia printsipov proletarskogo internatsionalizma," *Izvestiia*, March 9, 1957, p. 3.
[105] V. F. Generalov, "Ob osnovnykh chertakh mezhdunarodno-pravovoga sotrudnichestva Sovetskogo Soiuza i stran narodnoi demokratii," *Sovetskoe gosudarstvo i pravo*, No. 7 (July, 1950), p. 18.
[106] I. P. Trainin and I. D. Levin, eds., *Sovetskoe gosudarstvennoe pravo* (Moscow, 1948), p. 244.

publics." [107] Article 3 of the first Constitution of the USSR provided for the Union to "protect the sovereign rights of the Union Republics," and, except in so far as these rights were restricted, "every Union Republic shall enjoy the rights of an independent state." [108] This theme was elaborated in the 1936 Constitution so that today the Union Republics are credited with an impressive array of sovereign rights. The 1947 edition of the *Large Soviet Encyclopedia* provides this description:

The basic rights of the Union Republics which express their state character, sovereignty, and equality are the following: (1) The Union Republics have their own constitutions. . . . [which] take into account the historical and national characteristics of each Republic. (2) Each Union Republic has territorial sovereignty. Its territory cannot be altered without its consent. (3) Each Union Republic has the unimpeded right of secession from the Union. (4) Each Union Republic has the right to enter into direct relations with foreign states and to conclude agreements with them, and to exchange diplomatic and consular representatives. . . . (5) The Union Republics have the right to create their own military formations. . . . (6) Each Union Republic, regardless of its population, has the right, on an equal basis with other republics, to an independent representative in the Council of Nationalities of the USSR. (7) Each Union Republic has the right to be represented in the Presidium of the Supreme Soviet in the person of one of the deputy chairmen of the Presidium. (8) Each Union Republic has the right to demand the convocation of an extraordinary session of the Supreme Soviet of the USSR and the taking of a referendum. (9) Each Union Republic has the right to bestow citizenship. (10) Each Union Republic possesses competence equal to that of other Union Republics to legislate and govern, and within the limits of this authority it wields power independently. The sovereignty of the Union Republics is realized in these rights. . . . The Union Republics are sovereign Soviet states, whose sovereignty is restricted only within the limits of Article 14 of the USSR Constitution.[109]

Article 14 of the Soviet Constitution assigns such extensive functions to the All-Union government as to largely negate these elaborate claims of sovereignty ascribed to the Union Republics. However, the demagogic value of this catalogue of claims is startling and ingenious. According to Soviet theory, the most perfect way for

[107] Stalin, "IV soveshchanie TsK RKP(b)," June 12, 1923, in *Sochineniia*, V, 336.
[108] *The Fundamental Law (Constitution) of the U.S.S.R.* (Moscow, 1932), p. 11.
[109] *Bol'shaia sovetskaia entsiklopediia: Soiuz Sovetskikh Sotsialisticheskikh Respublik* (Moscow, 1947), pp. 37-38.

any nation to preserve its sovereignty is to become a Union Republic in the USSR. The Soviet manipulation of the terminology of nationalism is entirely consistent with the goal of a Soviet world state.

The claim that the ultimate protection of a nation's sovereignty is to be found in its incorporation into an expanded Soviet state remains an important and persistent theme in Soviet ideology. At the Nineteenth Party Congress in October, 1952, for example, Beria repeated the well-established proposition that "the outlying national regions of Tsarist Russia have been transformed under Soviet power from colonies and semicolonies into really independent states —Soviet Republics with their own territory, national autonomy, their own Constitution, their own legislation." The motivation for this assertion becomes apparent when the familiar contrast was drawn between the fate of a nation subjected to American influence, in which case the nation "rapidly loses its sovereign rights and independence and is reduced to the status of a vassal," and that of one coming under Soviet tutelage, where its "sovereignty" and "independence" are in no way impaired. The effects of this doctrine on non-Soviet nations are of crucial significance: "The successes of the system of the united multinational Soviet state are of great international importance. Our example shows the working class of the capitalist countries the way to their deliverance." [110]

"Deliverance" for capitalist states, we are told with surprising frankness, can come at the hands of an invading Soviet Army which will act as the guarantor of the "sovereignty" and "independence" of the invaded nation. Levin makes this quite clear in his article "On the Essence and Significance of the Principle of Sovereignty":

> The Communists of capitalist countries . . . who declare that in case of war they will give aid to the Soviet armed forces, if these forces are compelled to enter their territory in pursuit of aggressors—these Communists come forth simultaneously both as patriots of their fatherland, guarding its sovereignty and independence, and as genuine proletarian internationalists.[111]

Concretely, let us assume that the Soviet Army marched into France in answer to an act of "French aggression" (in the same way, let us say, that the North Koreans answered the "aggressive" act of South

[110] "Rech' tov. Beria," *Pravda*, Oct. 9, 1952, pp. 2–3.
[111] Levin, "K voprosu o sushchnosti," *Sovetskoe gosudarstvo i pravo*, No. 6 (June, 1949), p. 46.

Korea). Under these circumstances any Frenchman who would defend France would be denounced as a "bourgeois nationalist," while those who gave aid and comfort to the Soviet Army would be "defending the sovereignty and independence of France." The defense of national sovereignty, far from contradicting the goal of a Soviet world state, has actually become one of the most formidable weapons in the struggle for its attainment.

A distinguished American jurist, Judge John J. Parker, once remarked that "there has been much nonsense talked about sovereignty." [112] This Soviet concept of sovereignty is perhaps the most ingenious nonsense ever devised. Yet it would be a tragic error to dismiss it as a bad joke. For the uninitiated, who must be counted in the hundreds of millions (especially in Asia and Africa), this Soviet manipulation of the symbols of national sovereignty and national independence is enormously effective. Once the Soviet leaders had decided to adopt this new language they became adept at its use and doubtless discovered hitherto unsuspected advantages in not speaking plainly. This technique of "reverse Russian," which Soviet spokesmen have developed highly in all fields of activity, seems to be related to the need for making the bitter truth more palatable by giving it a sugar coating. There seems to be a recognizable inverse relationship between substance and form: the more bitter the substance, the sweeter the form. The early pattern of plain speaking on the goal of a world state probably alienated more people than it attracted to the Soviet cause. In an effort to manipulate the nations of the world toward this ominous goal, the Soviet leaders found that the iron hand had to be clothed with a silk glove, if people were not to retreat in fear.

The wholesale, unabashed use of national symbols climaxes the victory of Soviet Russian nationalism over the forces of genuine proletarian internationalism. This struggle began in the earliest days of the Soviet Republic when two basic approaches to the goal of a world state emerged. On the one hand, the proletarian internationalists conceived of a world state of genuine equality and brotherhood among nations in which no single nation could be placed in a position to dominate and control the lives and welfare of other nations. To this way of thinking, the Russian nation was endowed less with

---

[112] John J. Parker, "World Organization," *International Conciliation*, No. 397 (Feb., 1944), p. 158.

privileges than with responsibilities toward the non-Russian peoples still laboring under capitalism. The Russians were expected to make great national sacrifices for the purpose of stimulating international class struggle, since class ranked above nation in the minds of these people. On the other hand, there were the Soviet Russian nationalists who placed nothing above the welfare of their state, and in doing so increasingly put the interests of their Russian state above the claims of an international ideology based on class. What was good for the Soviet Russian state was automatically considered "good" for the international proletariat. Whatever strengthened Soviet Russia advanced world revolution, even if it meant the sacrifice of this or that foreign proletarian movement. This approach stemmed from the argument that the defense of the socialist fatherland of the world proletariat, this one tangible nucleus of a world state, must have priority over all other considerations. One consequence of this position has been the glorification, over all other nations, of the one particular national group, the Great Russians, who formed the core of the world-wide socialist fatherland. Whoever furthers the aggandizement and domination of the Great Russians, by definition, advances the cause of the Soviet world state. The final consequence of this logic is that if this goal were achieved, it would clearly be a Russian-dominated world state.

TSARIST AND SOVIET RUSSIAN NATIONALISM COMPARED

It has become a serious but commonplace error to miss the significance of Soviet Russian nationalism by assuming that it is simply a revival of the Russian nationalism of the Tsars. Naturally there are similarities, since Russia is the base of both of these operations, and an offensive Russian chauvinism permeates both movements. But there are also important differences.

The first and most important difference is that Tsarist Russian nationalism set geographical limits upon its objectives of expansion. It was always concerned with definite regions on the periphery of Tsarist power, such as the Balkans, the Near East, Central Asia, and definite spheres of influence in Mongolia and Manchuria. There were, to be sure, the vague Slavophile dreams of world mission of Dostoevsky and Khomiakov, aspirations which were more in the realm of mysticism than politics. There were even the fanciful projects of Pogodin, Danilevskii, Tiutchev, and Leontiev for the indefinite expansion of the Russian Empire.[113] But all of these dreams were never reduced to a single, coherent, state-sponsored plan for the creation of a Tsarist Russian world state. The contrast with the Soviet regime is obvious, for here the goal was and is the creation of a Soviet world state. Not that the Soviet leaders have abandoned interest in the traditionally Russian spheres of influence, or that they have not pursued those interests with a vigor which matches or even surpasses that of the Tsars, but this identity of imperial policy based on an identity of the geographical situation is far from the whole story. Soviet aims obviously go beyond those of Tsarist Russian imperialism, and it is therefore a grievous mistake to equate the two.

Another major difference between Tsarist and Soviet expansionism is that the Tsars pursued their aim only fitfully, and inconsistently. Some Tsars were more expansionist-minded than others, some sets of imperial advisors would press for foreign adventures, others would advise against them, and policies would alternate in no predictable fashion. The Soviet regime, on the other hand, while forced to make numerous tactical retreats from positions of weakness, never seems to have abandoned the goal of a Soviet world state. It has been a constant and consistent objective in which they have never lost interest. We might even go so far as to say that of all the major ingredients of Soviet ideology which still remain as operational objectives, the world state stands in the forefront. The socialization of the means of production is possibly the only other policy stemming from the original Soviet ideology that could rank with the world state idea as an objective which has been as faithfully pursued. Early Soviet equalitarianism, both social and national, the withering of coercive government and many other social and economic facets of the original ideology have, for all practical purposes, been abandoned as operational objectives. It is true that the methods now used to pursue the goal of a Soviet world state have little resemblance to those originally employed. But that does not alter the fact that, as an operational objective of present-day Soviet policy, the idea of a world state remains as firm as ever.

[113] Hans Kohn, "The Permanent Mission," *The Review of Politics*, X, No. 3 (July, 1948), 267-89; Hans Kohn, ed., *The Mind of Modern Russia* (New Brunswick, N.J., 1955), pp. 58-68, 91-115, 191-211; Nicholas V. Riasanovsky, *Russia and the West in the Teaching of the Slavophiles* (Cambridge, Mass., 1952).

The Russian nationalism of the Tsars is distinguished from that of the Soviet leaders not only with respect to the totality of the goal and the consistency with which it is pursued, but also with regard to the armory of weapons employed. The Soviet state makes use of a class doctrine which permits workers of all nationalities beyond the borders of the Soviet Union to be recruited into an arm of the Soviet foreign service. The Tsarist government had agents abroad, but they had no class doctrine or utopia with which they could enlist a veritable army of foreign agents. Then, too, the Soviet state is the product of the twentieth century, for it is unmistakably a total state, claiming allegiance of mind, body, and soul. Tsarist Russia had a secret police which was surely no angel of mercy for those unsympathetic to the regime, but its methods of repression were most slipshod and haphazard compared to those devised by the Soviet regime. While Soviet totalitarianism has posed as the legitimate inheritor of a substantial part of the Russian national tradition, this does not merit the conclusion that the present Soviet regime is merely a renewed version of the Tsarist regime.

We are now in a position to answer the two questions posed at the beginning of our inquiry on Soviet Russian nationalism. In response to the query: "Does the development of nationalism in the Soviet Union mean that the Soviet regime has abandoned its goal of a world state?" all evidence would force us to answer "No." This evidence also permits us to answer the second question. "If the Soviet leaders have not abandoned their goal of a world state, then what influence does such nationalism exert upon the image of this projected world state?" The answer to the kind of a world state they want to create seems appallingly stark: quite simply, they want a Russified world state.

V. The Meaning of Socialism in One Country

THE Soviet theory of socialism in one country, on the face of it, would seem to deny the Soviet goal of socialism in one world. The theory of socialism in one country must therefore be subjected to a dual scrutiny, similar to the preceding investigation of Soviet Russian nationalism. It must be determined (1) whether or not the theory of socialism in one country negates the goal of a Soviet world state, and (2) if it does not, what influence this theory exerts upon the goal of a world state, and what approach to the goal of a world state the theory implies.

THE WORLD STATE BY STAGES

The question of socialism in one country arose directly out of a discussion on the prospects of a socialist world state. In an article published on August 23, 1915, Lenin set forth the relationship between these two subjects:

The United States of the World . . . is that state form for the unification and freedom of nations, which we identify with socialism. . . . As a separate slogan, however, the United States of the World would hardly be correct, first because it means the same thing as socialism and second, because it might foster an incorrect interpretation about the possibility of the victory of socialism in one country, and about the relations of such a country to others. Unequal economic and political development is an unconditional law of capitalism. From this it follows that in the beginning, the victory of socialism is possible in a few, or even in one capitalist country, taken separately.[1]

Approximately a year later, during the autumn of 1916, Lenin substantially reaffirmed this view:

[1] Lenin, "O lozunge Soedinënnykh Shtatov Evropy," Aug. 23, 1915, in *Sochineniia*, XVIII, 232.

The development of capitalism proceeds very unevenly in various countries. . . . From this it inevitably follows that socialism cannot be victorious simultaneously in *all* countries. It will be victorious, in the beginning, in one, or several countries, while the others will for some time remain bourgeois or prebourgeois.[2]

These statements clearly reveal Lenin's "stadial" thinking. It is most likely, he conjectured, that the world state will not spring into being all at once; rather it will be a product of several stages of development, during which a few, possibly even a single country, may at first become socialist.

Soon after the seizure of power in Russia, Lenin defended this stadial conception. "I know, of course, that there are wiseacres who consider themselves very clever and even call themselves socialists, who assure us that we should not have taken power until the revolution had broken out in all countries." This would have been a stupid sort of perfectionism, Lenin insisted, since "to wait until the laboring classes make a revolution on a world scale means that all of us must be kept waiting in a state of petrified suspension." But then Lenin warned, with equal vigor, that a victory in one country could not be considered a self-sufficient end. The final goal was a world state. "Having begun with brilliant success in one country, it may have to pass through painful periods, for the final victory is possible only on a world scale, and only as the result of the joint effort of the workers of all countries." [3]

By the fall of 1918 Lenin felt that the joint effort of the workers of the major countries was a matter of great urgency, since he began to doubt the possibility of maintaining the victory which he had achieved in one country.

Either Soviet power triumphs in every advanced country of the world, *or* the triumph of the most reactionary, the most savage imperialism, which is throttling all the small and weak nationalities and reinstating reaction all over the world. . . . One or the other. There is no middle course.[4]

[2] Lenin, "Voennaia programma proletarskoi revoliutsii," autumn, 1916, in *ibid.*, XIX, 325.
[3] Lenin, 'Doklad o vneshnei politike," May 14, 1918, in *ibid.*, XXIII, 9.
[4] Lenin, "Tsennye priznaniia Pitirima Sorokina," Nov. 21, 1918, in *ibid.*, XXIII, 293.

SOCIALISM IN ONE COUNTRY

THE "COMPLETE" VICTORY OF SOCIALISM

Not only did Lenin believe that the *final* victory of socialism was possible only on a world scale, but he also held that it was impossible for any one country, alone, to build a *complete* socialist society. This was especially true of a backward country like Russia. In May, 1918, Lenin stated quite frankly: "We do not close our eyes to the fact that a socialist revolution in one country cannot be brought to completion wholly by our own efforts, even if that country had been much less backward than Russia, even if we were living in much better conditions than we are, after four years of unprecedented, painful, severe, and ruinous war."[5] Or again in November, 1918, Lenin declared: "The complete victory of the socialist revolution is unthinkable in one country as it demands the most active collaboration of at least several of the advanced countries, among which Russia cannot be counted."[6]

During 1919 Lenin continued to assert the impossibility of organizing a complete socialist society in Russia: "I have had occasion more than once to say that, compared with the advanced countries, it was easier for the Russians to *start* the great proletarian revolution, but that it will be more difficult for them to *continue* it and carry it to complete victory, in the sense of organizing a complete socialist society." Lenin contended that in order to continue "the work of building socialism for the purpose of completing the work of construction, a very great deal is still required." This meant, above all, that socialist construction in Russia could only be completed under the leadership and with the aid of the advanced countries of Western Europe. "The Soviet Republics of the more cultured countries, in which the proletariat has greater weight and influence, have every chance of overtaking Russia as soon as they take the path of the dictatorship of the proletariat."[7]

The first time that Lenin seemed to contradict his otherwise consistent view of the impossibility of building a complete socialist society in Russia was toward the end of his life, on January 4, 1923.

---

[5] Lenin, "Rech' na I s"ezde sovetov narodnogo khoziaistva," May 26, 1918, in *ibid.*, XXIII, 42.
[6] Lenin, "Rech' o mezhdunarodnom polozhenii," Nov. 8, 1918, in *ibid.*, XXIII, 261.
[7] Lenin, "Tretii Internatsional i ego mesto v istorii," April 15, 1919, in *ibid.*, XXIV, 250-51.

In a long and incoherent statement, which either reflected the haste with which it was composed, or Lenin's failing health, or possibly both, he dropped a few incidental phrases which probably would not have attracted any attention had Stalin not seen fit subsequently to pounce upon them and magnify their importance. For this reason, it is worth while to cite this meandering passage found in Lenin's article "On Cooperation," in which he was speaking of the desirability of using the various types of cooperative movements, particularly among the peasantry, as a transitional measure toward socialism:

> As a matter of fact, the power of the state over all large-scale means of production, the power of the state in the hands of the proletariat, the alliance of this proletariat with the many millions of small and very small peasants, the assured leadership of the peasantry by the proletariat, etc.— is not this all that is necessary from the cooperatives—from the cooperatives alone, which we formerly treated as huckstering, and which, from a certain aspect, we have the right to treat as such now under the NEP— is not this all that is necessary in order to build a complete socialist society? This is not yet the building of socialist society, but it is all that is necessary and sufficient for this building.[8]

When Lenin said that this "is all that is necessary and sufficient" for building a complete socialist society, the ingredients to which he referred were the political and social instruments for organizing society. This said nothing whatsoever of an adequacy of material resources required for such building.

There was another, much clearer statement by Lenin, made on January 16, 1923, of which Stalin at first strangely failed to take full advantage. Here Lenin made a positive statement of faith in Russia's ability to pull itself up by its bootstraps and build a socialist society, if necessary, without the aid of Western Europe. It was "infinitely commonplace," Lenin remarked, for Western European Social Democrats to repeat the argument that they had "learned by rote during the development of Western European Social Democracy that we are not yet ripe for socialism: that, as certain of the 'learned' gentlemen among them express it, we lack the objective economic premises for socialism in our country." These "gentlemen" were fond of saying that " 'Russia has not attained the level of development of productive forces that make socialism possible,' " but Lenin asked if backward Russia "by

[8] Lenin, "O kooperatsii," Jan. 4, 1923, in *ibid.*, XXVII, 392.

SOCIALISM IN ONE COUNTRY

stimulating the efforts of the workers and peasants tenfold" might not be able to create "the fundamental requisites of civilization in a way different from that of the Western European countries."

If a definite level of culture is required for the creation of socialism (although nobody can tell what the definite "level of culture" is), why cannot we begin by creating the prerequisites for that level of culture in a revolutionary way and *then*, with the aid of the workers' and peasants' government and the Soviet system, proceed to overtake the other nations? [9]

There are some indications that Lenin was whistling in the dark to keep up his courage, for even after these two statements of January, 1923, he expressed this serious reservation, in an article of March, 1923: "The worst thing of all would be to rely upon the assumption that . . . we possess any considerable quantity of the elements necessary for building a really new apparatus that would really deserve the name of socialist, Soviet, and so forth." [10]

Here the matter lay until after Lenin's death. Then, toward the end of 1924, Stalin cautiously advanced the feelers for his theory of socialism in one country. The use to which Stalin put this theory, as well as the highly selective way in which he chose his supporting "evidence" would suggest that Stalin did not consider this theory purely as an attempt to contribute a theoretical gem to the treasure house of Marxism-Leninism. Its value as a polemical weapon, used according to the dictates of political expediency in his personal struggle for power with Trotsky, was obvious. Stalin also turned this weapon against those like Zinoviev and Kamenev who at one time or another aligned themselves with Trotsky.

Stalin sensed that the weak spot of Trotsky's theoretical position lay in his insistence that Russia, by itself, could not build a complete socialist society. Until the last year of Lenin's life this was Lenin's position as well. So long as there was hope that revolution would break out in the advanced countries of the world, particularly in Western Europe, the belief in Russia's inadequacies was of no importance, since it was assumed that the addition of the advanced countries to backward Russia would present the possibility of building a complete socialist society. By 1923 it had become apparent that Western Europe could not be relied upon for help, and that, for a long time at least, Russia would have to "go it alone." Stalin

[9] Lenin, "O nashei revoliutsii," Jan. 16, 1923, in *ibid.*, XXVII, 399-400.
[10] Lenin, "Luchshe men'she, da luchshe," March 2, 1923, in *ibid.*, XXVII, 407.

perceived that Trotsky could only offer the discouraging vista of a declining world revolution and the theoretically pointless task of building a socialist society in the USSR that could not be "completed." Stalin cleverly branded Trotsky's view as one of "permanent hopelessness" and noted that "it was not without reason that last year Trotsky predicted the 'doom' of our country." [11]

In contrast to this pessimistic picture that he conjured from Trotsky's position, Stalin counterpoised an image of the Soviet Union as a country capable of building a complete socialist society. In asserting that the USSR could "go it alone" for a prolonged period, if necessary, Stalin shrewdly made a strength out of a weakness. In place of a feeling of isolation and abandonment, Stalin sought to trade upon a feeling of self-sufficiency and self-confidence, which his approach implied. This theme doubtless struck a responsive chord among the rank and file of the Party, which was tired of a perspective of endless sacrifices for an uncertain future.

In December, 1924, Stalin began citing the cautious and vague statement from Lenin's article "On Cooperation" about the possibility of building a complete socialist society in the USSR.[12] This possibility arose, Stalin asserted, because of the "law of uneven capitalist development," to which Lenin had referred in his very first article relating to socialism in one country, published on August 23, 1915.[13] While Lenin had originally conceded that the creation of a world state would proceed by stages, there is no evidence whatever that he then thought of each of these stages as a self-contained unit, in each of which "complete socialism" could be built. Only during the last year of his life could such an inference be drawn, and then only with considerable caution. This did not deter Stalin from digging up a variety of Lenin's statements on "the victory of socialism," and retroactively imputing to them the connotation of "complete socialism."

Stalin's efforts, initially confined to quoting Lenin, soon became bolder. He sponsored a resolution, adopted by the Fourteenth Party Conference of April 27–29, 1925, in which it was unequivocally stated that it was possible to build a complete socialist society in the USSR.[14] Stalin's own report on the work of the Party Conference

---

[11] Stalin, "Oktiabr'skaia revoliutsiia i taktika russkikh kommunistov," Dec. 17, 1924, in *Sochineniia*, VI, 377.
[12] *Ibid.*, VI, 378.   [13] *Ibid.*, VI, 371–72.
[14] "Chetyrnadtsataia konferentsiia RKP(b)," April 27–29, 1925, in *KPSS v rez.*, II, 46–49.

SOCIALISM IN ONE COUNTRY

specified that "the complete victory of socialism" meant the complete conquest of "the internal contradictions that exist between the proletariat and the peasantry" within the USSR.[15] Stalin expressed confidence that this could be accomplished since "under the dictatorship of the proletariat we possess everything that is needed to build a complete socialist society and to overcome every and all internal difficulties, for we can and we must overcome them by our own effort." [16]

Two observations are pertinent to this question of building "complete socialism." In the first place, who is to determine when "complete socialism" has been built? In a totalitarian society like the USSR it is obvious that the "completion" of anything is dependent upon a completely arbitrary standard that Stalin could adjust to suit his own needs. Socialism would be "complete" when Stalin said so. This is a typical Soviet device of "solving" a problem by definition. That is, "complete socialism" was an arbitrary semantic term with no fixed correlation to reality. Thus Stalin decided that the 1936 Constitution marked the completion of socialist society in the USSR. He simply proclaimed: "The complete victory of the socialist system in all spheres of the national economy is now a fact." [17] There are many socialists throughout the world who would deny that the Soviet Union has ever had "socialism," not to speak of "complete socialism." These critics frequently describe the Soviet system as a variety of state capitalism.

In the second place, it should be made clear that Trotsky was not opposed to building socialism in the USSR. As a matter of fact, compared to Trotsky, Stalin was cautious and conservative in his approach to socialist construction. Trotsky was habitually more radical than Stalin, always pressing for more extensive socialist planning and a faster pace for the industrialization and collectivization of the Soviet economy. But by Stalin's insisting and Trotsky's denying that a "complete" socialist society could be built in the USSR solely by its own efforts, Stalin succeeded in creating a widespread impression that Trotsky was opposed to building socialism in the USSR and that, in reality, Trotsky represented the stagnation of revolution. While Trotsky believed that the building of

[15] Stalin, "K itogam rabot XIV konferentsii RKP(b)," May 9, 1925, in *Sochineniia*, VII, 110–12.
[16] *Ibid.*, VII, 116.
[17] Stalin, "O proekte konstitutsii Soiuza SSR," Nov. 25, 1936, in *Doklad o proekte*, pp. 13–14.

socialism in the USSR should continue, he contended that it could be done without any special theoretical props such as Stalin's theory of socialism in one country. To Trotsky, complete socialism in one country was a theoretical absurdity.

The reason Trotsky could never come to accept the idea that the USSR, by itself, could build "complete socialism" stemmed directly from his belief in a world state. Trotsky relied heavily upon the traditional Marxist premise of the unity of the world economy, and claimed that it would be impossible for any one country, especially an economically backward country like the Soviet Union, to detach itself from the world economy so as to build a complete socialist society apart from the rest of the world. Trotsky maintained that

> the present productive forces have long outgrown their national limits. A socialist society is not feasible within national boundaries. Significant as the economic successes of an isolated workers' state may be, the program of "socialism in one country" is a petty-bourgeois Utopia. Only a European and then a World Federation of Socialist Republics can be the real arena for a harmonious socialist society.[18]

Trotsky was undeniably correct in stating that orthodox Marxism looked upon "the world economy, not as a sum of national parts, but as a mighty, independent reality, which is created by the international division of labor, and the world market, and, in the present epoch, predominates over the national markets." If capitalism had created such an interdependent world society, Trotsky insisted that "socialist society must represent a higher stage compared to capitalism. To aim at the construction of a *nationally isolated* socialist society means. . . . to pull the productive forces backward, even as compared to capitalism." [19]

Until the initiation of his theory of socialism in one country in December, 1924, Stalin likewise accepted this view of a world economy, which precluded the possibility of successful socialist construction in a single country. For example, in August, 1921, Stalin described what, in his opinion, was an irreconcilable conflict between a single world economy and the capitalist nation-state system, "a basic conflict between the modern forces of production and their development within the national-imperialist frameworks."

[18] Trotsky, *The Russian Revolution*, a lecture delivered in Copenhagen, Nov., 1932 (London, n.d.), p. 8.
[19] Trotsky, "Preface," March 29, 1930, in *Permanent Revolution*, p. 3.

SOCIALISM IN ONE COUNTRY

The imperialist frameworks and the capitalist form of economy suppressed the productive forces rather than developing them. The only solution is the organization of the world economy on the principle of economic cooperation between the advanced (industrial) and the backward (raw-material producing) countries (and not on the principle of plunder by the latter of the former). In order to achieve this, an international proletarian revolution is necessary. Without this it is pointless to think of the organization and normal development of the world economy. But for this, in order to begin (at least *to begin*) the construction of a proper world economy, the victory of the proletariat is necessary in at least several of the advanced countries.[20]

As late as April, 1924, Stalin asserted that "individual countries and individual national economies have ceased to be self-sufficient units, and have become links in a single chain called a world economy." From this Stalin drew the conclusion that "the union and collaboration of nations within a single world economy is the material basis for the victory of socialism." [21]

When Stalin decreed that it was possible to build a complete socialist society in one country, he split the supposedly unified world economy into two parts: the Soviet socialist economy and the economy of the non-Soviet world, which, despite its wide variations in economic forms, he generally called "the world capitalist economy." "We must build our economy," Stalin declared in December, 1925, "as an independent economic unit, based mainly on the home market." [22] At the same time the weakness of the Soviet economy was so apparent, especially during the 1920s, that Stalin could not and did not deny the need to rely upon contacts with the world capitalist economy. But he maintained that it was possible to keep these contacts within such bounds as to preserve the independence of the USSR, and yet to enable it to build a complete socialist society. In December, 1926, he freely admitted that "no one denies there is a certain dependence of our national economy on the world capitalist economy." Then he asked: "Does that mean that dependence of our national economy on capitalist countries precludes the possibility of building a socialist economy in our country? Of course not." Stalin followed this assertion by

[20] Stalin, "Partiia do i posle vziatiia vlasti," Aug. 28, 1921, in *Sochineniia*, V, 109–10.
[21] Stalin, "Ob osnovakh Leninizma," April, 1924, in *O Lenine i Leninizme*, pp. 48, 99–100.
[22] Stalin, "Politicheskii otchët Tsentral'nogo Komiteta," Dec. 18, 1925, in *Sochineniia*, VII, 298.

a direct blow at Trotsky's assumption of the unbreakable unity of the world economy. "But Trotsky speaks not only of the dependence of our national economy, but he converts this dependence into a merger of our economy with the world capitalist economy. . . . This idea is stupid, Comrades." [23]

Actually Stalin did not succeed in creating a consistent view of a world economy to take the place of the orthodox Marxian position, which he was forced to abandon. Instead, he devised a hybrid formula which was full of contradictions. The Program of the Comintern, which was adopted in 1928, best illustrates this ambivalent striving both to retain the appearance of orthodoxy and to incorporate the new tenets of his theory of socialism in one country.

On the one hand, the Comintern Program spoke of "the sharp contradiction between the growth of the productive forces of the world economy and the barriers erected by national states," which has proved "that the shell of capitalism has become an intolerable fetter upon the further development of mankind." [24] This would suggest the unity of a world economy, which is artificially divided by national states. This unity is even more strikingly described in a passage relating to the underdeveloped areas of the world:

> Colonies and semicolonies . . . constitute the *world rural district* in relation to the industrial countries, which function, as it were, as the *world urban center*. Consequently, the problem of organizing a socialist world economy, of properly combining industry with agriculture, is, to a large extent, the problem of the relation toward the former colonies of imperialism.[25]

On the other hand, the Comintern Program declared that "within the framework of what was formerly a single world economy two antagonistic systems now struggle against each other. . . . The world economy has split into two fundamentally hostile camps: the camp of the imperialist states and that of the dictatorship of the proletariat in the USSR." [26] The Soviet camp was declared to have everything necessary for the building of a complete socialist society, though the break between the two world economies was not considered so complete as to require no further contact. "The simultaneous

---

[23] Stalin, "Zakliuchitel'noe slovo, VII rasshirenny plenum IKKI," Dec. 13, 1926, in *ibid.*, IX, 131–33.

[24] "Programma Kommunisticheskogo Internatsionala," Sept. 1, 1928, in *Kom. Int. v dok.*, pp. 1–2.

[25] *Ibid.*, p. 31.   [26] *Ibid.*, p. 13.

SOCIALISM IN ONE COUNTRY

existence of two economic systems" compelled the USSR "to resort to economic maneuvering and utilizing economic contacts with capitalist countries . . . but only within the limits useful to the USSR" so that the USSR would not be transformed "into an appendage of the world capitalist system." [27]

This position, which half affirmed and half denied the unity of a world economy, had a curious effect upon the Soviet approach toward a world state. Trotsky's stand was simple and clear-cut: a unified world economy demanded a world state, or at least, as a necessary first step, a union of Europe and Russia. He maintained that socialism in one country, which rejected his unambiguous unity of the world economy, of necessity, rejected his goal of a world state.

The Stalinist position, as written into the Comintern Program, retained the goal of a world state, but combined it with the theory of socialism in one country. This, Trotsky ridiculed as childish nonsense. According to the Comintern Program "socialism may be victorious at first in a few or even in one single capitalist country." Building upon this victory of a complete socialist society in one country, a world dictatorship of the proletariat would be realized

> when the victory of socialism has been achieved in certain countries or groups of countries, when the newly formed proletarian republics enter into a federal union with those proletarian republics already in existence, when the chain of these federative unifications grows . . . into a *World Union of Soviet Socialist Republics,* uniting the whole of mankind under the hegemony of the international proletariat, organized as a state.

Only *after* the creation of a world state, "only after the proletariat has achieved a victory and consolidated its power all over the world will a prolonged period of intensive construction of a world socialist economy set in." [28] The unity of a world economy remained as the ultimate goal, but it was to be achieved in a piecemeal, step-by-step fashion. In the meantime the USSR was the prototype of "the World Union of Soviet Socialist Republics, the prototype of that economic unity of the toilers of all countries operating within a single world socialist economy, which the world proletariat must establish, once it has conquered state power." [29]

Trotsky characterized this method of building a world state as hopelessly utopian, since "we would obtain not a world socialist

[27] *Ibid.,* pp. 34–35.   [28] *Ibid.,* pp. 17–18.   [29] *Ibid.,* p. 34.

economy based on an international division of labor, but a federation of self-sufficing socialist communes in the spirit of blissful anarchism, the only difference being that these communes would be enlarged to the size of the present national states." This Stalinist position, Trotsky asserted, offered the following perspective: "Up to the complete world victory of the world proletariat, a number of individual countries build socialism in their respective countries, and subsequently out of these socialist countries there will be built a world socialist economy, after the manner in which children erect structures with ready-made blocks." [30]

What has actually happened as a result of the expansion both of the Soviet Union and the Soviet sphere of influence cannot be described adequately in the original terms of the Stalin-Trotsky controversy. The Soviet regime has obviously rejected Trotsky's premise of the unbreakable unity of a world economy, but at the same time it has not strictly applied the "building block" theory, of which Trotsky accused Stalin. Instead, socialism in one country has been transformed into "socialism in one sphere," with the various countries in the Soviet sphere being ever more tightly integrated around Moscow as the nodal point. Stalin recognized this development in his last important theoretical statement, made in October, 1952, when he said that "the most important economic consequence of the Second World War . . . was the disintegration of a single, all-embracing world market." Formerly the world economy was split into two parts, but the Second World War had drastically reduced both the need for contacts between these two parts, and the consequent dependence, however limited, of the USSR upon the world capitalist economy. "China and the other People's Democracies in Europe," Stalin asserted, "had fallen away from the capitalist system and together with the Soviet Union, had formed a united and powerful socialist camp, confronting the camp of capitalism. The economic consequence of the existence of two opposing camps was the disintegration of a single all-embracing world market so that now we have two parallel world markets, also confronting one another." [31] Apparently socialism in one sphere has evolved as the intermediate step from socialism in one country to "socialism in one world."

[30] Trotsky, *Third International After Lenin*, 1928, pp. 54–55.
[31] Stalin, "Zamechaniia po ekonomicheskim voprosam, sviazannym s noiabr'skoi diskussiei 1951 goda," Feb. 1, 1952, in *Ekonomicheskie problemy*, p. 30.

SOCIALISM IN ONE COUNTRY

THE "FINAL" VICTORY OF SOCIALISM

The question naturally arises: If it is possible to build complete socialism in one country, or even complete socialism in one sphere, then why is it still necessary to talk about socialism in one world? Does not this theory render obsolete the demand for a world state? Stalin gave a negative answer to this question when he first devised the theory of socialism in one country. His answer lay in the distinction he drew between a "complete" and a "final" victory of socialism.

This distinction between a "complete" and a "final" victory evolved gradually. As late as April, 1924, Stalin treated the two terms with indifference, stating quite unequivocally that neither a complete nor a final victory of socialism was possible in one country. This was made clear when he asked:

> But overthrowing the power of the bourgeoisie and establishing the power of the proletariat in a single country does not yet guarantee the complete victory of socialism. The chief task of socialism—the organization of socialist production, has still to be fulfilled. Can this task be fulfilled, can the final victory of socialism be attained in a single country without the joint efforts of the proletariat in several advanced countries? No, it cannot. . . . For the final victory of socialism, for the organization of socialist production, the efforts of a single country, and particularly of such a peasant country as Russia, are inadequate.[32]

By December, 1924, Stalin had partially reversed himself, when, on the basis of Lenin's article "On Cooperation," he came to the conclusion that the USSR possessed "all that is necessary and sufficient" for the building of a "complete" socialist society in one

---

[32] Stalin, "Ob osnovakh Leninizma," in *O Lenine i Leninizme*, p. 60. This first edition of 1924 was withdrawn from circulation when Stalin decreed that socialism in one country was possible, and reissued in revised editions in which the crucial part of this passage was doctored up to read: "But does this mean that it will thereby achieve the complete and final victory of socialism, i.e., does it mean that with the forces of only one country it can finally consolidate socialism and fully guarantee that country against intervention and, consequently, also against restoration? No, it does not." Here no distinction was drawn between a "complete and final victory," as both terms were used solely to refer to the need of overcoming the dangers of foreign intervention. This patched-up version appears in Stalin's *Collected Works*. (Stalin, "Ob osnovakh Leninizma," in *Sochineniia*, VI, 107.) However, the original version is reprinted in another article found in his *Collected Works*, where he cited this passage for the purpose of repudiating it. (Stalin, "K voprosam Leninizma," Jan. 25, 1926, in *Sochineniia*, VIII, 61.)

country.³³ However, in this same article Stalin also used the word "complete" in an entirely different sense. "For the *complete* victory of socialism," Stalin said, "for *complete* security against the restoration of the old order, the united efforts of the proletariat of several countries are necessary." ³⁴ The threat of foreign intervention and the restoration of the old order, a matter of *international* relations, apparently had no relevance to Stalin's statement that the USSR had everything that was necessary, in terms of *domestic* resources, for building a "complete" socialist society in the USSR. Then to add to the confusion, Stalin stated as a truth "the proposition that the *final* victory of socialism in the first country to liberate itself is impossible without the combined efforts of the proletariat of several countries." ³⁵ Here Stalin's thinking is so unclear that it is difficult to tell what "final" means. Does a "final victory" mean the same thing as a "complete victory," and if so, in which sense of the word "complete"? Stalin repeated this indiscriminate use of the words "complete" and "final" in an article of January, 1925.³⁶

It was not until the spring of 1925 that Stalin began to draw a clear distinction between a "complete" and a "final" victory of socialism. This distinction first appeared in a resolution adopted by the Fourteenth Party Conference in late April, 1925:

> Leninism teaches that the *final* victory of socialism, in the sense of a full guarantee against the restoration of bourgeois relations, is possible only on an international scale. . . . But this does not mean that it is impossible to construct a complete socialist society in a backward country like Russia, without the "state aid" (Trotsky) of the technically and economically more highly developed countries.³⁷

Stalin explained that this resolution was based on the assumption that the internal contradictions of the USSR, between the proletariat and the peasantry, could be overcome without outside aid, and that consequently this would permit the building of a complete socialist society in the USSR. But the external contradictions, between the Soviet and the non-Soviet worlds, could be overcome "only as a result of the joint efforts of the proletariat of a series of countries, or, better still, only as a result of the victory of the proletariat of several countries. . . . That is why Lenin says that 'a final vic-

---

³³ Stalin, "Oktiabr'skaia revoliutsiia," in *ibid.*, VI, 378.
³⁴ *Ibid.*, VI, 374.   ³⁵ *Ibid.*, VI, 399.
³⁶ Stalin, "Pis'mo t. D-ovu," Jan. 25, 1925, in *Sochineniia*, VII, 17.
³⁷ "Chetyrnadtsataia konferentsiia RKP(b)," in *KPSS v rez.*, II, 46, 49.

SOCIALISM IN ONE COUNTRY

tory is only possible on a world scale and only by the joint effort of the workers of all countries.' " [38] Even in this supposedly definitive statement, Stalin asserted that a final victory would result from the "joint efforts . . . of a series of countries," from victory in "several countries," and from victory in "all countries." But it would seem safer to attribute these discrepancies to Stalin's fuzzy thinking, rather than to assume that he had abandoned the goal of a world state. In any event, the distinction between a complete and a final victory had become firmly established, and it quickly reappeared in a series of Stalin's pronouncements.[39]

The meaning of this rather academic distinction was either entirely missed or widely misunderstood beyond the borders of the Soviet Union, with the result that many foreign observers actually came to the conclusion that Stalin no longer sought to create a world state. This was the case, for example, with Thomas D. Campbell, an American agricultural engineer who had an interview with Stalin in January, 1929, and who, upon returning to the United States, circulated the report that Stalin was no longer interested in the objective of a world state. This brought a denial from Stalin:

Mr. Campbell romances again and again when he attributed to Stalin the statement that "it was Trotsky who really tried to spread communism over the whole world, and this was the primary cause of the split between Trotsky and himself (i.e., Stalin); that Trotsky believed in world communism, while he, Stalin, wanted to limit his activities to his own land."

Campbell's allegation Stalin dismissed as an "absurd fiction." [40]

Even within the Soviet Union, the difference between a complete and a final victory was not always clearly understood. After the adoption of the 1936 Constitution, which supposedly signified the triumph of a complete socialist society in the USSR, some Communists apparently held the view that their tasks had substantially come to an end. In order to dispel this delusion Stalin published his correspondence with a certain Comrade Ivanov who had been

[38] Stalin, "K itogam rabot XIV konferentsii RKP(b)," May 9, 1925, in *Sochineniia*, VII, 118–19.
[39] For other articles in which Stalin drew a clear distinction between a "complete" and a "final" victory of socialism, see: Stalin, "K voprosam Leninizma," Jan. 25, 1926, in *Sochineniia*, VIII, 64, 71; "O sotsial-demokraticheskom uklone v nashei partii," Nov. 1, 1926, in *ibid.*, VIII, 261–67; "Zakliuchitel'noe slovo po dokladu 'O sotsial-demokraticheskom uklone v nashei partii,'" Nov. 3, 1926, in *ibid.*, VIII, 326–28; "Eshchë raz o sotsial-demokraticheskom uklone v nashei partii," Dec. 7, 1926, in *ibid.*, IX, 24–25.
[40] Stalin, "Gospodin Kempbell priviraet," Nov. 30, 1932, in *ibid.*, XIII, 147

accused of "Trotskyism" for asserting that a complete victory of socialism was not the same thing as a final victory. Ivanov appealed to Stalin: "I said, basing myself on your works, that the final victory of socialism can only be on a world scale." Ivanov explained that when he began quoting Stalin's works on the subject he was rebuffed by his accusers, who asserted that " 'Comrade Stalin was speaking in 1926, whereas we are now in 1938; then we did not have a final victory, but now we have and there is no need at all for us to think about intervention and restoration.' "

Stalin's reply opened with the brusque judgment: "Of course, you are right, Comrade Ivanov, and your opponents . . . are wrong." It is true, Stalin declared, that a complete socialist society had been built in the USSR. "We call this the victory of socialism, or, to be more exact, the victory of socialist construction in one country. We could say that this victory was final if our country were situated on an island, and not surrounded by a number of other capitalist countries." Since this was not the case, it was still necessary to hold on to the fundamental tenet of Leninism which "teaches that 'the final victory of socialism, in the sense of complete security from the restoration of bourgeois condition, is only possible on a world scale'. . . . This means that the serious help of the international proletariat is that force without which the problem of a final victory of socialism in one country cannot be solved." [41] So that there could be no further misunderstanding, this formulation was repeated in the authoritative *History of the All-Union Communist Party (Bolsheviks), Short Course,* which likewise appeared in 1938.[42]

In March, 1939, Stalin told the Eighteenth Party Congress that it was even possible for one country, taken alone, to build a complete *Communist* society (as the higher stage of complete socialism.) But this again could not be considered the end of the process, so long as the Soviet Union was surrounded by hostile capitalist states.[43]

That the fate of revolution in one country is inextricably bound up with the fate of revolution in all countries remains one of the indestructible propositions of Soviet ideology. After the Second

---

[41] "Pis'mo t. Ivanova i otvet t. Stalina," *Bol'shevik*, No. 4 (Feb. 15, 1938), pp. 12–15.
[42] *Istoriia vsesoiuznoi*, pp. 261–62.
[43] Stalin, *Otchëtnyi doklad na XVIII s"ezde*, March 10, 1939, pp. 139–50.

SOCIALISM IN ONE COUNTRY

World War, for example, a theoretical statement in *Bol'shevik* reiterated this premise as follows:

"The Party," said Comrade Stalin, "proceeds from the fact that the 'national' and the international tasks of the proletariat of the USSR are merged in the one general task of liberating the proletariat of all countries from capitalism, that the interests of constructing socialism in our country are wholly and entirely merged with the interests of the revolutionary movement of all countries in the one common interest in the victory of revolution in all countries." [44]

This would indicate that Stalin advocated a program of continuous revolution until the Soviet regime had finally achieved its goal of a world state. Here again the clarity of this position has frequently been obscured because, in the process of defending his theory of socialism in one country, Stalin attacked Trotsky's theory of "permanent revolution."

THE DISPUTE OVER "PERMANENT REVOLUTION"

Even before Lenin's mummified body had gone on display in his massive tomb on Red Square, Stalin was casting about for weapons with which he could embarrass and discredit potential rivals for Lenin's mantle. Stalin thought that in Trotsky's theory of "permanent revolution" he had found a wedge which he could use to drive between Trotsky and Lenin's sacred heritage.

Trotsky had devised his theory of "permanent revolution" to guide the role of the proletariat in the Russian Revolution of 1905. In a backward country like Russia, Trotsky contended, the bourgeoisie was so weak and timid that "the revolution will not be able to solve its immediate bourgeois tasks, except by putting the proletariat in power." [45] Once the proletariat has risen to power as the leader of the bourgeois democratic revolution, it is "inevitably and very quickly placed before tasks that are bound up with deep inroads into the rights of bourgeois property." In an effort to resolve these conflicts, "the democratic revolution grows over immediately into the socialist, and thereby becomes a *permanent* revolution." [46]

Lenin tended to believe that the bourgeois democratic revolution

---

[44] Iu. Frantsev, "Natsionalizm—oruzhie imperialisticheskoi reaktsii," *Bol'shevik*, No. 15 (Aug. 1, 1948), p. 46.
[45] Trotsky, *Permanent Revolution*, p. 120.   [46] *Ibid.*, p. 168.

would require a prolonged period of consolidation before passing into the stage of the socialist revolution. In July, 1905, Lenin wrote on the revolutionary situation: "But of course it will be a democratic, not a socialist dictatorship. . . . As yet such a victory will by no means transform our bourgeois revolution into a socialist revolution."[47] However, in apparent contradiction to this, Lenin wrote an article in September, 1905, which almost coincided with Trotsky's view: "from the democratic revolution we shall at once—according to the extent of our strength, the strength of the class-conscious, organized proletariat—begin to pass to the socialist revolution. We stand for an uninterrupted revolution. We shall not stop half-way."[48]

From 1905 on Trotsky also believed that the world revolution might very likely begin in backward Russia. "In an economically backward country, the proletariat can come to power sooner than in the economically advanced countries."[49] Yet Trotsky never maintained that Russia, by itself, was ready for socialism. "The socialist revolution begins on national grounds, but it cannot be completed on these grounds."[50] It is the "world economy as a whole, and [the] European economy in the first place, which is completely ripe for the socialist revolution. Whether the dictatorship of the proletariat in Russia leads to socialism or not, and at what rate and over what stages, will depend upon the further fate of European and international capitalism."[51] Thus the revolution would also become permanent in the international arena, in the sense that no one country could achieve a successful proletarian revolution and construct a complete socialist society without the aid of supporting revolutions in other countries. In the case of Russia a socialist revolution could be saved only by timely aid from Western Europe.

Looking at the 1905 Revolution, Lenin again expressed a view which came very close to that of Trotsky's. Lenin said that if the Russian proletariat and peasantry succeeded in taking the leadership in the bourgeois democratic revolution, then "the revolutionary

[47] Lenin, "Dve taktiki sotsial-demokratii v demokraticheskoi revoliutsii," July, 1905, in *Sochineniia*, VIII, 62.
[48] Lenin, "Otnoshenie sotsial-demokratii k krest'ianskomu dvizheniiu," Sept. 14, 1905, in *ibid.*, VIII, 186–87. See also Lenin, "Proletarskaia revoliutsiia i renegat Kautskii," Nov. 10, 1918, in *ibid.*, XXIII, 391.
[49] Trotsky, *Permanent Revolution*, p. 61.   [50] *Ibid.*, p. 25.
[51] *Ibid.*, p. 21.

SOCIALISM IN ONE COUNTRY

conflagration will spread all over Europe; the European worker, languishing under bourgeois reaction, will rise in his turn, and will show us 'how it is done'; then the revolutionary wave in Europe will sweep back again into Russia and will convert an epoch of a few revolutionary years into an epoch of several revolutionary decades." [52]

The views of Lenin and Trotsky tended to diverge over what Trotsky termed "the political mechanics of the collaboration of the proletariat and the peasantry" in the 1905 Revolution. A slight difference in emphasis was reflected in Trotsky's slogan calling for "the dictatorship of the proletariat supported by the peasantry," as contrasted with Lenin's slogan of "the democratic dictatorship of the proletariat and the peasantry." [53] It is likely that this difference would have remained buried in the Party archives if Stalin had not chosen to dig it up and make political capital out of it. In April, 1924, Stalin used this controversy over the role of the peasantry as a pretext for attacking Trotsky's theory of permanent revolution. At the time, Stalin had not yet formulated his theory of socialism in one country. Consequently he did not challenge the fact that, despite their differences over the peasantry, both Lenin and Trotsky shared the opinion that the building of socialism in Russia by the victorious proletariat would require the assistance of the victorious socialist regimes in the more advanced countries. Stalin even specifically affirmed that Lenin's views coincided with Trotsky's on the issue of an uninterrupted revolution. "Lenin fought the adherents of 'permanent' revolution," Stalin asserted, "not over the question of 'uninterruptedness,' for he himself maintained the point of view of uninterrupted revolution, but because they underestimated the role of the peasantry, which is the greatest reserve force for the proletariat." [54]

Launching his theory of socialism in one country in December, 1924, Stalin broadened his attack on Trotsky so as to discover "a great chasm dividing the Leninist theory of the dictatorship of the proletariat from Comrade Trotsky's theory of 'permanent revolu-

[52] Lenin, "Sotsial-demokratiia i vremennoe revoliutsionnoe pravitel'stvo," April 12, 1905, in *Sochineniia*, VII, 191. See also Lenin, "Dve taktiki," in *ibid.*, VIII, 62, 82–84; "Etapy, napravlenie i perspektivy revoliutsii," end of 1905 or beginning of 1906, in *ibid.*, VIII, 427.
[53] Trotsky, *Permanent Revolution*, pp. 70, 79.
[54] Stalin, "Ob osnovakh Leninizma," in *O Lenine i Leninizme*, p. 56.

tion.'"[55] Not only did the theory of permanent revolution demonstrate a "lack of faith in the revolutionary possibilities inherent in the peasant movement," it also indicated a "lack of faith in the strength and capacities of the proletariat in Russia."[56] "According to Lenin," Stalin now declared, "the revolution draws its forces chiefly from among the workers and peasants of Russia itself; according to Trotsky, the necessary forces can be found *only* 'on the arena of the world proletarian revolution.'" Therefore, Stalin claimed that Lenin believed in the idea of building socialism in one country, while Trotsky rejected it.[57]

Trotsky challenged Stalin's conclusion that socialism in one country was possible by relying solely on the forces of the proletariat and peasantry in the USSR. He maintained that, regardless of how "correct" the relations between these two forces might be, they could not, of themselves, furnish enough strength to complete a socialist revolution in Russia. It was a simple matter for Trotsky to counter with citations from Lenin stating that, in addition to a proper correlation of the forces of the Russian proletariat and peasantry, the complete success of revolution in Russia was also dependent upon receiving timely aid from Western Europe. For example, Lenin had told the Tenth Party Congress in March, 1921:

In Russia the industrial workers are in the minority, and the small farmers are in the overwhelming majority. In such a country the socialist revolution can be completely successful only on two conditions: first, on the condition that it receives timely support from the socialist revolution in one or several of the advanced countries. . . . The other condition is the agreement between the proletariat that is realizing its dictatorship, or that holds political power, and the majority of the peasant population.[58]

The meaning of this controversy over the theory of "permanent revolution" should now become apparent. Basically it was a means by which Stalin undertook to discredit Trotsky, for Stalin's attack began before he launched his theory of socialism in one country. His assault on the theory of "permanent revolution" soon became an additional method of affirming the possibility of building a complete socialist society in the USSR. Trotsky's reliance upon "timely aid" from the West now became very untimely, since no such aid

[55] Stalin, "Oktiabr'skaia revoliutsiia," in *Sochineniia*, VI, 367.
[56] *Ibid.*, VI, 378.   [57] *Ibid.*, VI, 368.
[58] Lenin, "Doklad o natural'nom naloge," March 15, 1921, in *Sochineniia*, XXVI, 237–38.

SOCIALISM IN ONE COUNTRY

had developed. Stalin could conveniently claim that, by waiting for revolution in the West, while denying the Russian proletariat and peasantry the possibility of building "complete socialism," Trotsky was dooming the Soviet Union to a program of inaction and stagnation.

CAPITALIST AND SOCIALIST ENCIRCLEMENT

In attacking Trotsky's theory of permanent or uninterrupted revolution, Stalin was *not* counterpoising a theory of a "permanently interrupted revolution," or revolution in Russia alone. "To win a final victory," Stalin declared, "it is necessary for the present capitalist encirclement to be replaced by a socialist encirclement." [59] "Socialist encirclement" would appear to be a euphemism for "world state." While Stalin never said this in so many words, it seems rather obvious that this is what "socialist encirclement" was meant to imply. For example, in one and the same work, Stalin conjectured about what would happen "if the present capitalist encirclement is replaced by a socialist encirclement," and then specified the ultimate form that this socialist encirclement would assume by referring to "the Union of Soviet Socialist Republics, the living prototype of the future union of all nations in a single world economy." [60]

On one aspect of socialist encirclement Stalin was quite explicit. In his report to the Sixteenth Party Congress in June, 1930, he explained that "the capitalist encirclement is not simply a geographic concept." [61] If a capitalist encirclement is to be replaced by a socialist encirclement, this would mean not simply ringing the Soviet Union with noncapitalist states, but destroying capitalist states wherever they might be located, that is, destroying capitalist states on a world scale.

The enlargement of the Soviet Union and the Soviet sphere of influence as a result of the Second World War did not alter this view. An article "On Capitalist Encirclement" in *Bol'shevik* for August, 1951, stated that "capitalist encirclement is a political concept. Comrade Stalin has pointed out that capitalist encirclement

[59] Stalin, "O sotsial-demokraticheskom uklone," in *Sochineniia*, VIII, 263.
[60] Stalin, "Ob osnovakh Leninizma," in *O Lenine i Leninizme*, pp. 70–71, 102.
[61] Stalin, "Politicheskii otchët Tsentral'nogo Komiteta XVI s"ezdu VKP(b)," June 27, 1930, in *Sochineniia*, XII, 303.

cannot be considered simply in geographic terms." This article proudly pointed to the Soviet borders, solidly rimmed by "friendly" powers; the "People's Democracies" on the Western European border, the "Mongolian People's Republic," the "Chinese People's Republic," and the "Korean People's Republic" on the southern and eastern Asiatic borders. "The camp of countries which have freed themselves from the rule of imperialism stretches from the shores of the Pacific Ocean to Central Europe, uniting 800,000,000 people." In spite of this, capitalist encirclement was found to be as dangerous as ever. "The change in the relative strength of the two systems does not mean that capitalist encirclement no longer exists." [62] If capitalist encirclement was a political and not a geographic concept, then theoretically the Soviet Union could be "encircled" by a single capitalist country, even though this one remaining capitalist country might in reality be encircled by the USSR.

Following Stalin's death the meaning of the idea of capitalist encirclement underwent a gradual but basic change. At the Twentieth Party Congress in 1956 Mikoyan indicated that this doctrine was outmoded: "The time is past when the Soviet land of socialism was in isolation, when we were an oasis in a capitalist encirclement. Now there can be no such talk." [63] Both he and Khrushchev emphasized the continuing shift in the balance of forces on a world scale against capitalism and in favor of socialism. "The chief feature of our epoch," Khrushchev had boasted in his speech to the Congress, "is the emergence of socialism from the confines of one country and its transformation into a world system." However, he was more cautious than Mikoyan in viewing capitalist encirclement as a thing of the past. Khrushchev stressed the need for the services of the "honest officials" of the secret police, since "the capitalist encirclement has sent a considerable number of spies and saboteurs into our country." [64]

During 1958 Khrushchev aired further doubts about the validity of this idea. "The very concept of 'capitalist encirclement' of our country," he acknowledged, "is in need of serious clarification." Since the situation in the world had "changed radically" in favor

[62] V. Mekheev, "O kapitalisticheskom okruzhenii," *Bol'shevik*, No. 16 (Aug., 1951), pp. 58, 61.
[63] "Rech' tovarishcha A. I. Mikoyana," *Pravda*, Feb. 18, 1956, p. 5.
[64] "Otchëtnyi doklad Tsentral'nogo Komiteta Kommumisticheskoi partii, doklad pervogo sekretaria TsK KPSS, tovarishcha N. S. Khrushcheva," *ibid.*, Feb. 15, 1956, pp. 1, 9.

SOCIALISM IN ONE COUNTRY

of socialism, "it is not now known who encircles whom: whether the capitalist states encircle the socialist states or vice versa. It is impossible to regard the socialist states as some kind of island in a seething capitalist ocean." The radical alteration of the geographic setting, Khrushchev hinted, might also affect the meaning of capitalist encirclement as a political concept. "It is impossible to speak of capitalist encirclement in the same sense as it was used formerly." [65]

Finally, in his speech to the Twenty-first Party Congress in 1959, Khrushchev removed all ambiguity when he declared bluntly: "The capitalist encirclement no longer exists for our country. Two world social systems are in existence: capitalism, living out its last days, and the ever-growing, vital forces of socialism, which has the sympathy of the toilers of all countries." [66]

The optimism of this assertion was characteristic of the enormous surge of self-confidence demonstrated by Khrushchev's entire report, which exalted the prospect of the Soviet Union crossing the threshold into the period of building the glorious future Communist society. This exuberance not only obliterated the capitalist encirclement, but spilled over to extinguish another long-standing Stalinist tenet on the nature of socialism in one country. As will be recalled, Stalin had affirmed that the Soviet Union could both achieve a complete victory of socialism and construct a complete Communist society. But so long as the capitalist encirclement remained, it was only possible to speak of the complete, not the final, victory of socialism and communism. Now, having decreed the end of capitalist encirclement, Khrushchev logically abolished the distinction between a complete and a final victory. The correlation of forces in the world was now considered such that the Soviet Union would be able to repel any attack upon it. "The danger of a capitalist restoration in the Soviet Union is ruled out. This means that *the victory of socialism is not only complete but final.*" [67]

In seeming to repudiate Stalin, Khrushchev borrowed the technique that Stalin had employed when he first advanced the theory of socialism in one country. This theory, Stalin had contended, was a positive affirmation of faith in the ability of the Soviet Union to overcome all obstacles and to achieve a complete victory of so-

---

[65] "Beseda tovarishcha N. S. Khrushcheva s korrespondentom frantsuzskoi gazety 'Figaro,'" March 19, 1958, *ibid.*, March 27, 1958, p. 2.
[66] "Doklad tovarishcha N. S. Khrushcheva, *ibid.*, Jan. 28, 1959, p. 9.
[67] *Ibid.*, p. 9.

cialism. By declaring that the victory was now also final, Khrushchev was adding an equally positive affirmation of faith in the ability of the Soviet Union and the whole socialist camp to surmount all threats to their continued existence. As a result of the great strength of the socialist camp, "the idea that war is inadmissible will take ever-firmer roots in the minds of peoples. The new balance of forces will be so evident that even the most die-hard imperialists will clearly see the futility of any attempt to unleash war against the socialist camp." And should some mad adventurers "plunge into a hopeless venture," by so doing "they will only bring nearer the ultimate downfall of the capitalist system. Any attempt at aggression will be stopped short and the adventurers put where they belong." [68]

Khrushchev's doctrinal innovation on the achievement of the final victory of socialism therefore assumed the character of a boastful and aggressive assertion of the indestructibility of the Soviet Union and a promise of the indefinite expansion of the Soviet system. As a leading Soviet theorist promptly explained: "the thesis concerning the final and complete victory of socialism in our country is of enormous scientific importance." By excluding the possibility of a capitalist restoration "history has once and for all answered the question 'Who will win, socialism or capitalism?' *on a world-wide scale.*" [69] Khrushchev's own similar pronouncements continue to be given wide circulation, making it evident that the final victory of socialism in the Soviet Union does not represent the full and final scope intended for such victory. On the contrary, the confidence in the assertion of this victory serves to reinforce the drive toward the still more final aim of world-wide socialism and then world-wide communism. "We are living in a remarkable time," Khrushchev rejoiced typically, "when history is moving inexorably toward the ultimate victory of socialism and communism throughout the world." [70]

It is apparent that at no point during the evolution of the theory of socialism in one country has the goal of a world state been negated. But to determine what this theory has not done is to tell only half the story. We must also inquire about what positive in-

[68] *Ibid.*, p. 7.
[69] "Rech' tovarishcha P. F. Iudin," *ibid.*, Feb. 6, 1959, p. 5 (italics added).
[70] "Vyshla iz pechati kniga tovarishcha N. S. Khrushcheva 'K pobede v mirnom sorevnovanii s kapitalizmom,'" *ibid.*, April 17, 1959, p. 1.

SOCIALISM IN ONE COUNTRY

fluence this theory has had upon the goal of a world state, what approach it has implied, what values it has emphasized that would influence the kind of world state likely to result should the Soviet leaders succeed in their strivings.

THE CONTROVERSY OVER THE "UNITED STATES OF EUROPE"

The approach toward a world state implicit in Stalin's theory of socialism in one country only becomes clear when it is examined in connection with Trotsky's slogan of a "United States of Europe." Trotsky first set forth his arguments for a socialist United States of Europe at the outbreak of the First World War. "The creation of a stable regime of the proletarian dictatorship," Trotsky then asserted, "would only be conceivable for all of Europe, organized in the form of a European Republican Federation." [71] After the Bolshevik seizure of power, Trotsky became the outstanding advocate of a Soviet United States of Europe, which was meant to save Soviet Russia as well as Europe. Writing a postscript in 1922 to the republication of his 1915–1916 articles on European federation, Trotsky declared that "a genuine advance in the construction of a socialist economy in Russia will become possible only after the victory of the proletariat in the most important countries of Europe." For the salvation of both Russia and Europe, "the European proletariat must advance the program of a Federal European Soviet Republic." [72] Trotsky anticipated that "this federation will extend across the great bridge of the Soviet Union to Asia and will then effect a Union of the World Socialist Republics." [73] This would be possible because in a union with Asia "the European revolutionary proletariat will wrest from American capital the control of the world economy and will lay the foundations for the Federation of Socialist Peoples of the whole earth." [74]

Stalin recognized the pivotal position that the United States of Europe held in Trotsky's thinking. He also realized that it was a

[71] Trotsky, "Programma mira," 1915–1916, in *Sochineniia*, III, Part I, 88.
[72] Trotsky, "Posleslovie," 1922, in *ibid.*, III, Part I, 93.
[73] Trotsky, *Third International After Lenin*, p. 15. See also Trotsky, "V poriadke mezhdunarodnoi diskussii," June 30, 1923, in *Piat' let Kominterna*, p. 571.
[74] Trotsky, "Whither Europe," Feb. 15, 1926, in *Europe and America*, p. 71. See also *ibid.*, pp. 66–67, 70; "Perspectives of World Development," July 28, 1924, in *ibid.*, p. 33.

direct challenge to his own theory of socialism in one country. In December, 1924, Stalin sharply contrasted these two concepts:

Trotsky criticizes the Leninist theory of the proletarian revolution regarding the victory of socialism in one country, and opposes to it the slogan of the United States of Europe. He asserts that the victory of socialism in one country is impossible, that the victory of socialism is possible either as a victory in several principal states of Europe (England, Russia, Germany) united in the United States of Europe, or else it is quite impossible. He openly declares that "a victorious revolution in Russia or in England is unthinkable without a revolution in Germany and vice versa." [75]

Stalin directed the attention of the Russian Communists to the inescapable fact that Trotsky's United States of Europe remained a dream. "There is no question but that the widely held theory that revolution must take place simultaneously in the principal countries of Europe, a theory which denied the possibility of the victory of socialism in one country, has turned out to be an untenable and lifeless contention." [76] Stalin claimed that Lenin had foreseen the failure of simultaneous revolutions on the basis of his study of capitalism at its highest stage of development, capitalism in the "era of imperialism." As a result of this study "Lenin arrived at the law of the unevenness, of the spasmodic character of the economic and political development of the capitalist countries." [77] Lenin's discovery of this law of uneven development opened the way to the victory of socialism in one country, a conclusion that Stalin was frank to admit ran counter to the beliefs of Marx and Engels. "All we Marxists, beginning with Marx and Engels, maintained the opinion that the victory of socialism in one country, taken separately, was impossible, and that in order for socialism to win, simultaneous revolutions were necessary in a series of countries, at least in the more developed, civilized countries." [78] But Stalin maintained that this belief in simultaneous revolutions was a product of the preimperialist era of capitalism, when the law of uneven development was supposedly unknown to Marx and Engels. "The difference between Lenin and Engels is a difference between two historical periods." [79] Stalin then took the liberty of bringing Engels back to life, so that he might sanction his theory of social-

[75] Stalin, "Oktiabr'skaia revoliutsiia," in *Sochineniia*, VI, 373.
[76] *Ibid.*, VI, 395. [77] *Ibid.*, VI, 369.
[78] Stalin, "O sotsial-demokraticheskom uklone," in *ibid.*, VIII, 247.
[79] Stalin, "Pis'mo t. Ermakovskomu," Sept. 15, 1925, in *ibid.*, VII, 233.

ism in one country. "Of course, if Engels were alive he would not cling to the old formula, but on the contrary, he would greet our revolution in every way saying: 'To hell with all the old formulas, long live the victorious revolution in the USSR.' " [80]

Trotsky claimed that Stalin was making a wholly spurious use of the law of uneven capitalist development. In 1878 the German Social Democrat Vollmar based his theory of the "isolated socialist state" on the law of uneven capitalist development. This work, Trotsky noted, was "written when Lenin was eight years old." Moreover, in describing this law, Vollmar "was only paraphrasing the thoughts of Engels, to whom, we are told, the law of the unevenness of capitalist development remained 'unknown.' " [81] Not only was this law well known before Lenin "discovered" it, but Lenin's own writings on imperialism further demonstrated the impossibility of socialism in one country. Trotsky held that "imperialism links up incomparably more rapidly and more deeply the individual national and continental units into a single entity, bringing them into the closest and most vital dependence upon each other, and rendering their economic methods, social forms, and level of development more identical." That is, imperialism increases the interdependence of nations while the law of uneven development only tends to *"upset* but in no case to *eliminate* the growing economic bonds and interdependence between those countries." [82]

Trotsky had long maintained the view that the law of uneven capitalist development confirmed, rather than denied, the reality of his slogan of the United States of Europe. As far back as 1915 he had criticized those who believed that the law of uneven capitalist development justified the conclusion

that the victory of socialism in one country is possible, and that therefore there is no point in making the dictatorship of the proletariat in each separate country conditional upon the creation of a United States of Europe. That capitalist development in different countries is uneven is an absolutely incontrovertible fact. But this very unevenness is itself extremely uneven. The capitalist level of England, Austria, Germany, or France is not identical, but compared with Africa and Asia, all these countries represent capitalist "Europe," which has grown ripe for socialist revolution.[83]

[80] Stalin, "Zakliuchitel'noe slovo po dokladu," in *ibid.*, VIII, 303.
[81] Trotsky, *Revolution Betrayed*, 1936, p. 294.
[82] Trotsky, *Third International After Lenin*, pp. 20–21.
[83] Trotsky, "Programma mira," in *Sochineniia*, III, Part I, 89–90.

Europe is a unit, whose problems cannot be solved separately. "Europe is not a geographic term; it is an economic term, something incomparably more concrete . . . than the world market." [84]

While such units as Europe, Asia, and America were all ultimately to be found on the master timetable of world revolution, each area was also assigned its own immediate schedule. For Trotsky, there was no question but that Europe came first. "Naturally," Trotsky remarked, "the Workers' and Peasants' Federation will not stop in its European phase," since this would only be a transitional step toward a world state. "We are, therefore, envisaging here only a stage, but a stage of great historical importance, through which we must first pass." [85]

The closest Stalin ever came to giving priority to Europe was his statement of February 10, 1926:

It will be possible to conquer international capitalism only with the forces of the working class of all countries, or at least, of the principal countries of Europe. . . . We cannot do without the victory of the revolution in several countries of Europe, without that, the final victory of socialism cannot be assured.[86]

On the whole, this is an atypical statement, since Stalin tended to discard the traditional priority that orthodox Marxism had always assigned to Europe.

THE "WEAKEST LINK" THEORY

In the main, Stalin relied on the "weakest link" theory, which specifically stated that revolution need not be expected next in the most industrially advanced areas of the world. Referring to the national links in a single world chain, a metaphor that was common property of all of the Bolsheviks, Stalin introduced an idea that upset Trotsky's schemata of revolutionary development. Revolution occurs "as a result of the snapping of the chain of the world imperialist front in one country or another." But Stalin asked, "Where will revolution begin? Where, in what country, can the front of capital be pierced first?" The customary answer, Stalin admitted, was "where industry is more developed, where the proletariat constitutes the majority, where there is more culture, where

[84] Trotsky, "V poriadke," in *Piat' let Kominterna*, p. 571.   [85] *Ibid.*, p. 575.
[86] Stalin, "O vozmozhnosti postroeniia sotsializma v nashei strane," Feb. 10, 1926, in *Sochineniia*, VIII, 97.

there is more democracy." This answer was no longer valid, since revolution might next be expected "not necessarily where industry was most developed," but "where the chain of imperialism is the weakest." In 1917 Russia proved to be the weakest link even though it was less developed than Western Europe.

Where will the chain break in the near future? Again where it is the weakest. It is not precluded that the chain may break, let us say, in India. . . . It is also possible that the chain may break in Germany. Why? Because the factors which are operating, let us say, in India, are beginning to operate in Germany as well.[87]

Stalin expounded this view in April, 1924. It was subsequently incorporated as part of his theory of socialism in one country, which made its appearance in December, 1924.[88] Thereafter the "weakest link" idea was given wide circulation, to the point that Stalin found it necessary to set aright some distortions which had developed during its popularization. Stalin criticized Bukharin (who was also the great popularizer of Stalin's theory of socialism in one country) for having carried the "weakest link" idea too far. "According to Bukharin, the imperialist front breaks in the country with the weakest economic system. This, of course, is not true. If it were true, the proletarian revolution would have begun somewhere in Central Africa and not in Russia." It was not a question of the weakest country, but of the "imperialist chain breaking where it (i.e., the chain) is the weakest." In order to avoid further misunderstanding, Stalin then added these minimal conditions which a country must meet before it could qualify as a link in this chain:

What determines the weakness of the imperialist chain in a given country? The presence of a certain minimum of industrial development and culture in that country. The presence there of a certain minimum of industrial proletariat, the revolutionary spirit of the proletariat, and the proletarian vanguard in that country. The presence there of a serious ally of the proletariat (the peasantry, for example) capable of following the proletariat in the decisive struggle against imperialism.[89]

This attempted refinement was still the epitome of vagueness, for it might apply to almost any part of the world. It was really a theory of no theory. Stalin excluded the jungles of Africa, but he still gave no indication where the weakest links might be

[87] Stalin, "Ob osnovakh Leninizma," in *O Lenine i Leninizme*, pp. 49–50.
[88] Stalin, "Oktiabr'skaia revoliutsiia," in *Sochineniia*, VI, 370.
[89] Stalin, "Neobkhodimaia popravka," Dec. 18, 1929, in *ibid.*, XII, 138–39.

found, or where revolution might first be expected. The "weakest link" theory really amounted to a tautology: revolution would first occur in the country that was the weakest link, which was where revolution would first occur. But the impact of the "weakest link" theory was not so indecisive as the theory itself, since it had the definite and decisive effect of destroying Trotsky's concept of the United States of Europe.

The idea of the United States of Europe did not die easily. It hung on with especial tenacity in the Comintern, which Stalin did not fully succeed in bringing under his control until the late 1920s. The United States of Europe slogan was first accepted by the Comintern at its Fourth World Congress, held at the end of 1922.[90] It continued to appear in Comintern documents until the end of 1926.[91] As a matter of fact, it was during 1926 that the United States of Europe slogan received its fullest exposition by a Comintern body.[92] Only with the writing of the definitive Comintern Program in 1928 did Stalin finally bury Trotsky's pet idea of the United States of Europe. In commenting on the draft Program of the Comintern, Stalin noted with approval that "the draft puts in place of the slogan of the United States of Europe, the slogan of a federation of Soviet Republics of advanced countries and colonies that have fallen away or are falling away from the imperialist system, and are placing themselves in opposition to the world capitalist system in their struggle for world socialism." [93] Here was Stalin's answer to Trotsky's United States of Europe. The theory of socialism in one country rejected the rigid, orthodox, programmatic approach of the United States of Europe, and put in its place the thoroughly flexible, pragmatic formula of "a federation of both advanced countries and colonies," striving for the goal of "world socialism." Stalin simply welcomed revolution anywhere as logical and correct. To him, the

---

[90] "Taktika Kommunisticheskogo Internatsionala," Nov. 5–Dec. 5, 1922, in *Kom. Int. v dok.*, p. 295: "America will enslave capitalist Europe unless the European working class seizes political power . . . and begins to create a Federal Soviet Republic of Europe."

[91] "Mezhdunarodnoe polozhenie i zadachi Kommunisticheskogo Internatsionala," Nov. 22–Dec. 16, 1926, in *ibid.*, p. 638: "As a counterpart to a [bourgeois] Pan-Europe, advance the slogan of the Socialist United States of Europe."

[92] "Ocherednye problemy mezhdunarodnogo kommunisticheskogo dvizheniia," Feb. 17–March 15, 1926, in *ibid.*, p. 547.

[93] Stalin, "Ob itogakh iiul'skogo Plenuma TsK VKP(b)," July 13, 1928, in *Sochineniia*, XI, 203.

SOCIALISM IN ONE COUNTRY

only test of a proper revolution was whether or not it succeeded.[94] And again the explanation of a successful revolution was simply that it had broken through the weakest link in the imperialist chain. The actual pattern of Soviet expansion would indicate that, with the exception of a country like Czechoslovakia, the weakest links in this chain have thus far been found primarily in the backward areas of the world, or, put another way, at least the first broken links in this chain have not resulted in a Soviet United States of Europe. Not that this is rejected as a future goal, but history has refuted Trotsky's rigid priority for Western Europe.

THE "BASE" FOR WORLD SOCIALISM AND RUSSIAN NATIONALISM

The only clear priority that emerged from Stalin's theory of socialism in one country was a priority for the Soviet Union itself. Stalin's approach was intensive; a revolution already in hand is worth several in the bush. Trotsky's approach tended to be extensive; only by constantly exploiting revolution outside of Russia could the revolution in Russia find the security and support needed to develop to completion. This gave Stalin the opportunity to accuse Trotsky of defeatism on a national scale, but it also gave Trotsky the opportunity to accuse Stalin of defeatism on an international scale. Whenever Stalin spoke of the need to build up socialism in one country as a mighty bastion for world socialism, Trotsky charged that Stalin was really building up an immense national bureaucratic regime that had abandoned the international tasks of the revolution.

From his very first utterance on socialism in one country, Stalin explicitly denied this accusation. He remonstrated sharply that "those who are forgetful of the international character of the October Revolution, and declare that the victory of socialism in one country is purely a national and only a national phenomenon, are wrong." The purpose of this socialist construction in one country was to create a base from which revolution could be spread into

---

[94] This pragmatic approach is reminiscent of Lenin's remark: "Where, in what books, have you read that such variations of the customary historical order of events are impermissable, or impossible? I remember that Napoleon once wrote: 'On s'engage et puis . . . on voit.'" (Lenin, "O nashei revoliutsii," Jan. 17, 1923, in *Sochineniia*, XXVII, 401.)

all countries. "The world significance of the October Revolution," Stalin declared, "lies in its constituting the first stage of the world revolution, and a powerful base for its further development." [95]

The victory of socialism in one country is not an end in itself; it must be looked upon as a support, as a means for hastening the proletarian victory in all other countries. For the victory of the revolution in one country, in this case Russia . . . is the beginning and the advanced base for the world revolution.

. . . .

It is likewise beyond doubt that the very development of the world revolution, the very process of the breaking away of a number of new countries from imperialism, will be more rapid and more thorough, the more thoroughly socialism fortifies itself in the first victorious country, the faster this country is transformed into a base for the further unfolding of the world revolution, into a lever for the further disintegration of imperialism.[96]

The Soviet Union is the "base" for world revolution, the magnet to which all those countries "breaking away from imperialism" will be attracted, and to which they will finally become attached. This is the image of the Soviet Union, sketched by Stalin on numerous occasions, and which became, and today remains, a permanent feature of Soviet ideology.[97]

While Trotsky's charges were doubtless overdrawn, they cannot be dismissed altogether. Trotsky was undoubtedly correct in saying that the emphasis Stalin placed upon this "base" meant the creation and entrenchment of a new nationalist-minded Soviet bureaucracy, which would become petrified in the pose of a permanent

---

[95] Stalin, "Oktiabr'skaia revoliutsiia," in *Sochineniia*, VI, 400–1.
[96] *Ibid.*, VI, 396, 399.
[97] For other occasions on which Stalin used the "base" idea, see: Stalin, "Ob osnovakh Leninizma," in *O Lenine i Leninizme*, pp. 60, 108; "O zadachakh komsomola," Oct. 29, 1925, in *Sochineniia*, VII, 242; "Politicheskii otchët Tsentral'nogo Komiteta," Dec. 18, 1925, in *ibid.*, VII, 295; "Eshchë raz o sotsial-demokraticheskom uklone," Dec. 7, 1926, in *ibid.*, IX, 28; "Mezhdunarodnyi kharakter oktiabr'skoi revoliutsii," Nov. 7, 1927, in *ibid.*, X, 245–46; "Politicheskii otchët Tsentral'nogo Komiteta," Dec. 3, 1927, in *ibid.*, X, 340; "O programme Kominterna," July 5, 1928, in *ibid.*, XI, 152. The idea that the Soviet Union is the base for world revolution was repeated endlessly in the Soviet press. A postwar example from the Cominform journal stated: "The thesis that the victory of socialism in one country is not an end in itself, but a means for developing and supporting the struggle for socialism in other countries, permeates all the works and all the speeches of Comrade Stalin. In the Soviet Union the Bolshevik Party built a mighty stronghold of the world liberation movement of the proletariat and the oppressed peoples." (L. Răutu, "Mighty Force of Proletarian Internationalism," *For a Lasting Peace*, Feb. 2, 1951, p. 6.)

SOCIALISM IN ONE COUNTRY

genuflex to the cult of Russian nationalism. If the international tasks were not forgotten, then at least they would be accomplished at a time and in the manner that would suit the convenience of the Russian Communists. Trotsky predicted the effect that this encouragement of Russian nationalism would have upon the non-Russian Communist Parties throughout the world. "The task of the Comintern," Trotsky asserted, would simply be reduced to playing "the role of a frontier guard," protecting the construction of socialism in the USSR.[98] Again, if this blast was somewhat wide of the bull's-eye, it was still very much on the target, for our discussion of Soviet Russian nationalism has already recorded how the Comintern was reduced from a serious revolutionary instrument in its own right to a mere tool of Soviet foreign policy.

The Stalin-Trotsky conflict was, in some respects, a modern re-enactment of the old Slavophil-Westernizer controversy. Stalin's entire experience and training had produced a Russian-centered view of the world. Trotsky, on the other hand, did not look upon Moscow as the capital of the future Soviet world state. Viewing the Comintern soon after its founding in 1919, he commented: "If today Moscow is the center of the Third International, tomorrow, we are profoundly convinced, this center will move to the West: to Berlin, Paris, London."[99] Trotsky made no pretense about the unsuitability of primitive Russia as the leader of the civilized world:

> Our country is still very backward, our country is barbarian. . . . But we are defending this bulwark of the world revolution since, at this moment, it is the only one in the world. When another stronghold is erected in France, or in Germany, then Russia will lose nine tenths of its significance, and then we shall come to you in Europe to defend this other, more important stronghold. It would be a sheer absurdity, Comrades, to think that we consider this Russian revolutionary stronghold the center of the world.[100]

No such words ever escaped Stalin's lips. Long before he voiced his theory of socialism in one country, and even before the Bolshevik Revolution, he had rejected the alleged superiority of Europe over Russia. Speaking on August 3, 1917, he took issue with Preobrazhen-

[98] Trotsky, *Permanent Revolution*, p. 8.
[99] Trotsky, "Mysli o khode proletarskoi revoliutsii," May 1, 1919, in *Sochineniia* (Moscow, 1926), XIII, 28.
[100] Trotsky, "Rech' po ital'ianskomu voprosu na III kongresse Kominterna," June 29, 1921, in *Piat' let Kominterna*, p. 222.

skii, who promulgated the commonly held view that Russia could only make a real advance toward socialism "provided there is a proletarian revolution in the West." Stalin objected:

> I am against such a conclusion. . . . The possibility is not excluded that Russia may be the very country that will pave the way to socialism. . . . We must reject the outworn conception that only Europe can show us the way. There is dogmatic Marxism, and creative Marxism. I stand on the side of the latter.[101]

This "creative Marxism," which upset the orthodox view of Western European superiority, was in reality an assertion of Russian nationalism.

After the Bolshevik Revolution, but again before the appearance of his theory of socialism in one country, Stalin gloated over the inaccuracy of the "dogmatic" Marxist prediction that "a socialist revolution would run its course, and be crowned with success, first of all, in countries of highly developed capitalism." Speaking in October, 1920, Stalin expressed his satisfaction that "the October Revolution has disproved this view, for the socialist revolution began precisely in a country backward in point of capitalist development, i.e., in Russia." Not only did it begin in Russia, but there was also no basis for the belief that "the socialist revolution in Russia could be crowned with success, and that this success could endure, only in the event that revolution in Russia was immediately followed by a more profound and more serious revolutionary explosion in the West." Stalin displayed almost unlimited faith in Russia when he stated that "this view has also been disproved by events, for socialist Russia has been successfully continuing to exist and develop for three years now without having received any direct support from the Western proletariat." The consequence of this situation, Stalin boasted, was that the West must look to Russia, and not Russia to the West. "It turned out that it is not only possible for a socialist revolution to begin in a backward country, but also for it to be crowned with success, to go forward and serve as an example for countries with developed capitalism." [102] This poor, much maligned, "backward" Russia, Stalin exulted, turned out to be an example for the "advanced" countries.

[101] Stalin, "Vystupleniia na VI s"ezde RSDRP(b)," Aug. 9, 1917, in *Sochineniia*, III, 186–87.
[102] Stalin, "O politicheskom polozhenii respubliki," Oct. 27, 1920, in *ibid.*, IV, 374.

SOCIALISM IN ONE COUNTRY

This view, it must be remembered, was expressed more than four years before Stalin introduced his theory of socialism in one country. The Russian-centered emphasis of this theory, once adopted, obviously developed the already latent feelings of Russian national pride. It was the Russian nation that had made the first successful revolution, and therefore there was something intrinsically good, if not superior, about the Russian nation. The more widely the theory of socialism in one country was accepted, the more profound these feelings became.

Summarizing the effects of the theory of socialism in one country upon the goal of a world state, we can say (1) that this theory does not negate the goal of a world state, (2) that it implies a thoroughly pragmatic approach toward this goal, and (3) that it emphasizes the values of Russian nationalism, which would only reinforce the tendency, described in preceding chapters, to create a Russified world state.

VI. The Meaning of Peaceful Coexistence

THE concept of peaceful coexistence of the Soviet and non-Soviet worlds seemingly stands in contradiction to the goal of a Soviet world state. The world cannot be molded into a Soviet world state and at the same time be divided into two opposing and unintegrated blocs. One of these two concepts must lie closer to the core of Soviet thought. Does the concept of peaceful coexistence negate the goal of a Soviet world state, and, if not, what bearing has it upon this goal?

THE ORIGIN OF THE PEACEFUL COEXISTENCE THEORY

The theory of peaceful coexistence was born of desperation. In the early days of the Soviet Republic, when the survival of the new regime was still very much in doubt, Soviet leaders were divided over the methods of dealing with the hostile capitalist environment. Bukharin, heading a doctrinaire but influential faction, regarded all capitalist states with an unvarying and implacable animosity. He proposed a "holy" revolutionary war against capitalism wherever it might exist. He considered the suggestion of any sort of compromise with any capitalist state as treason to the cause of international socialism. Lenin represented a more realistic faction that saw the necessity for coming to some sort of working agreement with part of the non-Soviet world in order to save the Soviet regime. The root of the coexistence idea was the willingness to deal with and make use of forces which were nevertheless considered deadly enemies. "When in February, 1918," Lenin related, "the German imperialist robbers led their troops against unarmed, demobilized Russia . . . I did not hesitate in the least to enter into a 'compromise' with the French monarchists." The French officer de

Lubersac told Lenin, "I am a monarchist, and my sole object is to defeat Germany." Lenin understood perfectly the Frenchman's distaste for revolution. "This did not in the least prevent me from 'compromising' with de Lubersac concerning the services which French officers, expert sappers, desired to render us in blowing up railway tracks to hinder the German advance." This "compromise" was permissible, Lenin maintained, because it furthered the cause of socialism. "The French monarchist and I shook hands, knowing that each of us would willingly have hanged his 'partner.' For a time, however, our interests coincided." [1]

In pressing his colleagues to "compromise" with Germany by signing the Treaty of Brest-Litovsk, Lenin explained again that this was only a temporary concession which was necessary if the Soviet state was to fulfill its future tasks. "We must make use of this breathing spell, which circumstance has given us, to heal the wounds that war has inflicted on the social organism of Russia and to raise the economic level of the country. . . . In so far as we solve the problem of organization, so far shall we be in a position to assist the socialist revolution in the West, which is late in arriving." [2] With the beginning of the Entente's military intervention in Soviet Russia in 1918, the Soviet government signed three supplementary agreements with Germany covering a variety of political and financial matters. Chicherin defended these agreements as perfectly proper and feasible "in spite of the great difference between the regimes of Russia and Germany and the fundamental tendencies of both governments." [3] In August, 1918, Lenin sought to arrange what would have amounted to a military alliance between Imperial Germany and Soviet Russia, in order to stop the Entente's advance. "After a lengthy consultation with Vladimir Il'ich," Chicherin recalled, "I personally went to the new German Ambassador, Helfferich, with a proposition that we work out the conditions for joint action against Alexeev in the South, and to consider the possibility of dispatching a German detachment, with our consent, to attack the troops of the Entente near the White Sea." [4] These attempts to come

---

[1] Lenin, "Pis'mo k amerikanskim rabochim," Aug. 20, 1918, in *Sochineniia*, XXIII, 182.
[2] Lenin, "Ocherednye zadachi sovetskoi vlasti," March–April, 1918, in *ibid.*, XXII, 440.
[3] Quoted in Carr, *Bolshevik Revolution*, III, 86.
[4] Georgii Chicherin, "Lenin i vneshniaia politika," *Izvestiia*, Jan. 30, 1924, p. 2.

to terms with a part of the non-Soviet world were cut short by Germany's defeat in the war.

It was not until 1920 that Soviet Russia and a bourgeois power concluded an agreement that was destined to have a reasonable span of life. Chicherin characterized the peace treaty with Estonia of February 2, 1920, as "the first experiment in peaceful coexistence with bourgeois states." [5] This treaty marked the formal recognition of a stalemate of forces, in which Soviet Russia could neither be crushed nor expand further, and thus opened what proved to be a prolonged period of relatively normal relations with capitalist states. From this time onward, the subject of peaceful coexistence acquired a prominent status in Soviet thought.

THE "TWO CAMPS" THEORY

The real meaning of the theory of peaceful coexistence with the non-Soviet world only becomes clear in the context of that more encompassing Soviet belief of the ultimate irreconcilability of the two worlds, as expressed in the "theory of the two camps." In February, 1919, Stalin recorded the axiomatic Soviet position that "the world is decisively and irrevocably split into two camps: the camp of imperialism and the camp of socialism. . . . The struggle between these two camps forms the axis around which all contemporary life revolves." [6] In March, 1919, Lenin emphasized the irreconcilable nature of the conflict between these camps when he said: "We live not only in a state, but in a *system of states*, and the existence of the Soviet Republic side by side the imperialist states for a prolonged period of time is unthinkable. In the end either one or the other will conquer." [7] Though this statement was made at the height of the interventionist period, it acquired the character of a classic expression of an enduring Soviet belief. Stalin continued to cite it for decades after Lenin's death, and the Soviet press has reprinted it countless thousands of times.[8] Lenin reiterated this idea in

---

[5] Quoted in Louis Fischer, *Soviets in World Affairs*, I, 254.
[6] Stalin, "Dva lageria," Feb. 22, 1919, in *Sochineniia*, IV, 232.
[7] Lenin, "Otchët Tsentral'nogo Komiteta," March 18, 1919, in *Sochineniia*, XXIV, 122.
[8] Stalin, "K itogam rabot XIV konferentsii RKP(b)," May 9, 1925, in *Sochineniia*, VII, 119; "K voprosam Leninizma," Jan. 25, 1926, in *ibid.*, VIII, 66; "O sotsial-demokraticheskom uklone v nashei partii," Nov. 1, 1926, in *ibid.*, VIII, 263; "Pis'mo t. Ivanova i otvet t. Stalina," *Bol'shevik*, No. 4 (Feb. 15, 1938), p. 14.

a number of less well-known statements, such as that of November, 1920: "So long as capitalism and socialism remain, we cannot live peacefully: either one or the other will conquer in the end—either a funeral dirge will be sung over the Soviet Republic, or over world capitalism." [9]

In signing a peace treaty with Estonia, the Soviet leaders did not envisage an eternal collaboration of peaceful partners, but were simply looking forward to a time when Estonia would drop from the non-Soviet world into the Soviet world which would be marching in a steady progression toward a Soviet world state. Lenin acknowledged that the peace treaty with Estonia contained many concessions. "But we do not want to spill the blood of workers and Red Army men for the sake of a piece of land, the more so since this concession will not last forever." Lenin expressed the conviction that the workers "will soon overthrow this power and create a Soviet Estonia, which will then conclude a new peace with us." [10] This frank statement by Lenin stands in bold contrast to the text of the treaty, which proclaimed that "Russia unreservedly recognizes the independence and autonomy of the state of Estonia, and renounces voluntarily and forever all rights of sovereignty formerly held by Russia." [11] The word "forever" obviously meant "until such time as Soviet Russia has the power to alter the situation." The independence of Estonia, like all other non-Soviet states, was not intended to last forever, since such states were someday destined to be incorporated in a "World Union of Soviet Socialist Republics." Behind the pledge of eternal peaceful coexistence there stood an undefined, but very real, time limit. On another occasion Lenin offered this rationalization for granting independence to the states bordering on Russia:

By our recognizing the state independence of Poland, Latvia, Lithuania, Estonia, and Finland we are slowly but surely winning over the confidence of the oppressed toiling masses of these little neighboring states. In this way we are surely tearing them away from the influence of "their"

[9] Lenin, "Rech' na sobranii sekretarei iacheek moskovskoi organizatsii RKP(b)," Nov. 26, 1920, in *Sochineniia*, XXV, 512. See also Lenin, "Doklad o voine i mire," March 7, 1918, in *ibid.*, XXII, 317; "Tsennye priznaniia Pitirima Sorokina," Nov. 21, 1918, in *ibid.*, XXIII, 293; "Novaia ekonomicheskaia politika i zadachi politprosvetov," Oct. 17, 1921, in *ibid.*, XXVII, 45.

[10] Lenin, "Rech' na bespartiinoi konferentsii rabochikh i krasnoarmeitsev presnenskogo raiona," Jan. 26, 1920, in *ibid.*, XXV, 16.

[11] *Sbornik deistvuiushikh dogovorov, soglashenii i konventsii, zakliuchennikh RSFSR s inostrannimi gosudarstvami* (Moscow, 1921), I, No. 17, 100.

national capitalists, and surely leading them to a condition of full confidence in us, and leading them to the future united International Soviet Republic.[12]

"PERFECT" AND IMPERFECT COEXISTENCE

Stalin stated the relationship between the "two camps" idea and that of a Soviet world state in an unmistakable manner to the First Congress of Soviets of the USSR, on December 30, 1922. In his Declaration on the Formation of the USSR, which later became Part I of the 1924 Constitution of the USSR, he maintained that "since the formation of the Soviet Republics the states of the world have been split into two camps: the camp of capitalism and the camp of socialism." The contrast between these two camps was based on the allegation that the non-Soviet camp was "powerless to organize the collaboration of nations," whereas the Soviet camp had successfully solved this problem. For this reason, the USSR, "built on the basis of the peaceful coexistence and fraternal collaboration of nations . . . will mark a new decisive advance toward the amalgamation of the toilers of all countries into a World Socialist Soviet Republic." Of these two camps, only the Soviet camp was to survive, and it was to result in a Soviet world state. In this world state there would be genuine "peaceful coexistence and fraternal collaboration of nations," in contrast to the relations among nations existing under capitalism, where "we find national animosities and inequality, colonial slavery and chauvinism, national oppression and pogroms, imperialist brutality and wars." [13]

When the Soviet leaders speak of the peaceful coexistence of nations, it is apparent that they have two types of coexistence in mind:

[12] Lenin, "Pis'mo k rabochim i krest'ianam Ukrainy po povodu pobed nad Denikinym," Dec. 28, 1919, in *Sochineniia*, XXIV, 657.
[13] Stalin, "Deklaratsiia ob obrazovanii Soiuza Sovetskikh Sotsialisticheskikh Respublik," Dec. 30, 1922, in *Sochineniia*, V, 159, 393-94. For similar statements by Stalin on the "two camps," see: Stalin, "Ob ob"edinenii Sovetskikh Respublik," Dec. 26, 1922, in *ibid.*, V, 154-55; "Oktiabr'skaia revoliutsiia i taktika russkikh kommunistov," Dec. 17, 1924, in *ibid.*, VI, 400; "K itogam rabot XIV," in *ibid.*, VII, 95; "Politcheskii otchët Tsentral'nogo Komiteta," Dec. 18, 1925, in *ibid.*, VII, 281-82; "Mezhdunarodnoe polozhenie i oborona SSSR," Aug. 1, 1927, in *ibid.*, X, 51; "Beseda s pervoi amerikanskoi rabochei delegatsiei," Sept. 9, 1927, in *ibid.*, X, 135; "Ob itogakh iiul'skogo Plenuma TsK VKP(b)," July 13, 1928, in *ibid.*, XI, 203; "Politicheskii otchët Tsentral'nogo Komiteta XVI s"ezdu VKP(b)," June 27, 1930, in *ibid.*, XII, 255.

the "perfect" type, when all nations will be united in a Soviet world state; and that precarious, unstable type of coexistence in which no real confidence can be placed so long as any capitalist nation survives. Thus, even if the Soviet leaders should want to coexist peacefully with non-Soviet states for an indefinite period, they believe that the nature of capitalism makes such an arrangement impossible.

The Soviet theoreticians do not regret the existence of the supposedly war-producing tensions within the non-Soviet world. On the contrary, it is the prime duty of the Soviet regime to exploit them, so as to avoid the emergence of a strong, purposeful, and united non-Soviet world. The more the states within the non-Soviet camp are prodded to fight each other, the more this camp will be torn to pieces from within, and the closer the day will come when it will no longer be necessary to speak of two camps and of this distasteful type of peaceful coexistence.

Lenin repeatedly insisted: "So long as we have not conquered the whole world, so long as we remain economically and militarily weaker than the capitalist world . . . we must know how to use the contradictions and oppositions among the capitalists." [14] Similarly, in March, 1921, Stalin chided Chicherin for underestimating the contradictions within the non-Soviet world. "The whole purpose of the existence of the People's Commissariat of Foreign Affairs," Stalin lectured, "is to take account of these contradictions, to base ourselves upon them, and to maneuver among these contradictions." [15] Stalin listed these contradictions as (1) between the proletariat and the bourgeoisie within capitalist countries, (2) among the imperialist powers struggling for the conquest of foreign territories, (3) between the imperial powers and their colonial and dependent peoples, (4) between the victorious and vanquished powers and their colonial and dependent peoples, (5) among the victorious powers themselves.[16]

---

[14] Lenin, "Rech' na sobranii sekretarei," in *Sochineniia*, XXV, 498.

[15] Stalin, "Doklad ob ocherednykh zadachakh partii v natsional'nom voprose," March 10, 1921, in *Sochineniia*, V, 42.

[16] Stalin listed these contradictions in various ways with various degrees of completeness on the following occasions: "Ob osnovakh Leninizma," April, 1924, in *O Lenine i Leninizme*, pp. 24–26; "K itogam rabot XIV," in *Sochineniia*, VII, 96; "Politicheskii otchët," Dec. 18, 1925, in *ibid.*, VII, 262–81; "Eshchë raz o sotsial-demokraticheskom uklone v nashei partii," Dec. 7, 1926, in *ibid.*, IX, 26; "Politicheskii otchët," June 27, 1930, in *ibid.*, XII, 248–54.

COEXISTENCE AND TRADE

By maneuvering among these contradictions the Soviet leaders hope to gain a "breathing spell" from capitalist attack and to provide themselves with the opportunity to so strengthen the Soviet camp that it can meet any eventuality. Consequently talk of peaceful coexistence has always been especially closely associated with Soviet efforts to stimulate those economic ties with the non-Soviet world which are essential for the construction of the Soviet fortress. When Soviet delegates attended the International Economic Conference at Genoa in April, 1922, they displayed a conciliatory attitude calculated to produce trade. Lenin freely acknowledged that it would be better business to supplant talk of revolution by that of peaceful coexistence. "We welcomed Genoa," Lenin stated, "we understood perfectly well, and did not conceal it that we were going there as merchants because trade with capitalist countries is absolutely essential for us (so long as they have not yet collapsed)." [17] Chicherin, who headed the Soviet delegation at Genoa, made an effort to speak like a merchant without ceasing to be a Communist: "While remaining faithful to the principles of communism, the Russian delegation recognizes that in the present historical period in which there is the possibility of the parallel existence of the old and the new expanding socialist order, economic competition between states representing the two systems of property is imperatively necessary for general economic reconstruction." [18] This economic cooperation, based on the peaceful coexistence of two differing world systems, was imperative "in the present historical period." But there was the unmistakable inference that in the next historical period such peaceful coexistence would not be a subject for discussion, since there would only be one world system in operation.

Just when this historical period would come to a close was a matter of considerable speculation. In the early days of Soviet power it was calculated in terms of months, or at most, in terms of a few years. But these early expectations remain unfulfilled. By 1925 Stalin had admitted that "what at first seemed to be a short breathing spell after the war has turned into a whole period of respite." This pro-

[17] Lenin, "O mezhdunarodnom i vnutrennem polozhenii Sovetskoi Respubliki," March 6, 1922, in *Sochineniia*, XXVII, 169.
[18] Speech by Chicherin, April 10, 1922, quoted in V. P. Potëmkin, ed., *Istoriia diplomatii* (Moscow, Leningrad, 1945), III, 170.

PEACEFUL COEXISTENCE

longed breathing spell resulted from "a temporary equilibrium of forces" between the two camps.[19] The non-Soviet camp, headed by an Anglo-American bloc, had achieved an illusory stabilization (since it was really being torn apart by internal contradictions). The strength of the Soviet camp, on the other hand, was depicted as steadily increasing. As a result of the forces at work in each camp, the coexistence between them was considered, at best, as a provisional and unstable arrangement.[20] Stalin summarized the situation: "Thus we have two stabilizations.... Who will conquer whom —that is the essence of the entire matter." [21]

By December, 1927, Stalin was offering this alarming report of an impending test of strength between the two camps:

> If two years ago it was possible and necessary to speak of a period of a certain equilibrium and "peaceful coexistence" between the USSR and the capitalist countries, now we can assert that *the period of "peaceful coexistence" is receding into the past,* and giving way to periods of imperialist surges and preparation for an intervention against the USSR.[22]

Stalin cited England, which had just broken off diplomatic relations with the USSR, as the spearhead of this supposedly ensuing capitalist attack. To what extent Stalin believed in the imminence of this foreign threat or to what extent this danger was consciously exaggerated to meet the needs of his domestic situation remains an open question. At this time Stalin was preparing to launch his campaign against the right wing within the Party by inaugurating a doctrinaire, pseudo-leftist period of hostility toward all non-Soviet powers. The fact that Stalin's expressed fears did not materialize need not detract from the value of this incident, since it sheds additional light on Soviet thinking on the nature and purpose of peaceful coexistence. Peace must be maintained, Stalin insisted, because the USSR was still weak and it needed time to build up a position of strength from which it would later fight the non-Soviet world. Stalin recalled Lenin's warning that "very much in our work of construction depends upon whether we succeed in putting off war with the capitalist world, which is inevitable." For the time being, Stalin added, peaceful construction must continue and war "must be postponed either until the moment when the proletarian revolution in

---

[19] Stalin, "Politicheskii otchët," Dec. 18, 1925, in *Sochineniia*, VII, 262.
[20] *Ibid.*, VII, 281–88. [21] Stalin, "K itogam rabot XIV," in *ibid.*, VII, 95.
[22] Stalin, "Politicheskii otchët Tsentral'nogo Komiteta," Dec. 3, 1927, in *ibid.*, X, 288.

Europe matures, or until the moment when the colonial revolutions have fully matured, or lastly, until the moment when the capitalists fight among themselves over the division of colonies." [23]

Stalin repeated this analysis in his comments on the Comintern Program in July, 1928, adding that the leadership of the non-Soviet camp, which had formerly been under an Anglo-American alliance, was now the object of a struggle between England and America.[24] The Comintern Program itself unequivocally placed America at the head of the non-Soviet camp, stating that among the capitalist powers "the economic center has shifted to the United States of America making the 'Dollar Republic' the chief exploiter." [25] The subject of peaceful coexistence between these two camps was described as a matter of "the transition from the world dictatorship of imperialism to the world dictatorship of the proletariat which extends over a long period of proletarian struggle, of its defeats and victories." This prolonged period, the Comintern Program declared, "will include the coexistence of both capitalist and socialist socio-economic systems within the world economy," since "the international proletarian revolution cannot be conceived of as a single event occurring simultaneously all over the world." [26] Until the capitalist camp has been annihilated, "the simultaneous existence of two economic systems . . . compels the USSR to resort to economic maneuvering and utilizing economic contacts with the capitalist countries." [27]

The attempt to develop economic contacts with capitalist countries continued to coincide with Soviet insistence upon peaceful coexistence. At the International Economic Conference, which met in Geneva in May, 1927, Obolenskii-Ossinkii, the chief Soviet delegate, at once introduced this draft resolution: "With regard to the great importance of full participation of the U.S.S.R. in world trade, the Conference recommends to all states to develop their relations with

---

[23] *Ibid.*, X, 288–89.
[24] Stalin, "Ob itogakh iiul'skogo Plenuma," in *Sochineniia*, XI, 198–202.
[25] "Programma Kommunisticheskogo Internatsionala," Sept. 1, 1928, in *Kom. Int. v dok.*, p. 13. The Soviet economist, Eugene Varga, had adopted this view as early as 1925: "The counter pole of Soviet Russia in the capitalist world is the United States of America. . . . The final struggle between the bourgeoisie and the proletariat on an international scale will be carried out under the leadership of the United States and the Union of Soviet Socialist Republics." ("Ways and Obstacles to the World Revolution," *Communist International*, No. 18/19 [Dec., 1925–Jan. 1926], pp. 78–79).
[26] "Programma," in *Kom. Int. v. dok.*, pp. 16–17.　　　　[27] *Ibid.*, p. 34.

PEACEFUL COEXISTENCE

the Soviet Union on the basis of a pacific coexistence of two different economic systems." [28] Under the threat of the withdrawal of further Soviet participation, the Conference substantially adopted this resolution. Such protestations of the Soviet desire for peaceful coexistence were not without their embarrassments. Sokol'nikov, another Soviet delegate, likewise pleaded for economic cooperation between the two systems, but then prophesied that this would end in the "happy elimination" of capitalism.[29] Statements such as these provoked Jouhaux, the French trade union leader, to protest that "it is inconsistent to condemn, *ex cathedra,* systems other than one's own and then to suggest cooperation with those very systems that have been condemned." [30] When Stalin was asked about these economic contacts with capitalism, in an interview of September, 1927, he again indicated the ambivalent nature of the Soviet effort to coexist. He affirmed that "such agreements are possible and expedient under conditions of peaceful development," and that "import and export arrangements are appropriate subject matter for such agreements." But such agreements could not be of an unequivocal nature, since there are "limits set by the different nature of the two systems, and the competition and struggle between them. Agreements are entirely possible within the limits that are permitted by these two systems, but only within these limits." [31]

These declarations of 1927 served as a point of reference for continuing appeals for trade and peaceful coexistence. In his speech to the Sixth Congress of Soviets in March, 1931, Molotov recalled the position of the Soviet delegates at the 1927 Geneva Conference. " 'The contradictions between the two economic systems, which during a certain historical period must unavoidably coexist, do not exclude the possibility of some practical arrangement between them.' " "Today," Molotov added, "we still hold the same view." Each camp drew its own conclusions from this uneasy truce. "Our conclusions are that this historical period must be used to the utmost to gain a victory for our system. The purpose of our enemy is to wipe off the face of the earth the Soviet state, the socialist state. Two worlds are brought face to face." [32] "Peaceful coexistence" was but an oblique

[28] *Records of the International Economic Conference of 1927,* quoted in Davis, *Soviets at Geneva,* p. 201.
[29] *Ibid.,* p. 203.   [30] *Ibid.,* p. 207.
[31] Stalin, "Beseda s pervoi amerikanskoi," in *Sochineniia,* X, 123.
[32] "Doklad Predsovnarkoma tov. Molotova VI s"ezdu sovetov SSSR," *Izvestiia,* March 12, 1931, p. 3.

way of stating the ultimate irreconcilability of these two worlds.
Litvinov echoed this call for peaceful coexistence at Geneva in
May, 1931, in a more diplomatically worded statement intended for
foreign consumption. He hoped to facilitate trade with the non-
Soviet world by proposing that the Commission of Inquiry for European Union adopt an economic nonaggression pact. Such a pact,
Litvinov asserted, "would be fresh confirmation of the principle
adopted by the 1927 Conference as to the peaceful coexistence, at
the given historical stage, of two economic systems." [33] Even this
purposely polite approach retained the reference to coexistence at
"the given historical stage." Litvinov renewed his plea for this pact
at the World Monetary and Economic Conference at London in
June, 1933, though as at Geneva in 1931, nothing came of it.[34] In
January, 1934, Stalin reaffirmed the connection between trade and
peaceful coexistence when he stated that Soviet foreign policy was
one "of preserving peace and of strengthening trade relations with
all countries. . . . Those who want peace and seek business ties
with us will always receive our support." [35]

POLITICAL COEXISTENCE IN THE 1930S

Soviet entry into the League of Nations in September, 1934,
marked the culmination of a series of political gestures toward peaceful coexistence. These activities became associated in the public
mind with the effort of Maxim Litvinov. They had begun with the
so-called "Litvinov Protocol" of 1929 which applied the principles
of the Kellogg-Briand Pact about the peaceful settlement of disputes to the Soviet Union and its western neighbors.[36] This was reinforced by the negotiation of a series of nonaggression and neutrality pacts [37] and by efforts to get an international agreement on
the definition of aggression, which also was put in the form of a
separate treaty between the USSR and the states on its western and
southern borders.[38] Yet if one reads with care the speech delivered

[33] "Statement by Litvinov on the Soviet Draft for a Pact of Economic Non-
Aggression," May 21, 1931, in Degras, ed., *Soviet Documents*, II, 501.
[34] Davis, *Soviets at Geneva*, pp. 246–47.
[35] Stalin, "Otchëtnyi doklad XVII s"ezdu partii o rabote TsK VKP(b),"
Jan. 26, 1934, in *Sochineniia*, XIII, 305.
[36] Louis Fischer, *Soviets in World Affairs*, II, 782–84.
[37] Litvinov, *Against Aggression*, pp. 135–69; T. A. Taracouzio, *War and
Peace in Soviet Diplomacy* (New York, 1940), pp. 319–21.
[38] Litvinov, *Against Aggression*, pp. 170–80; Davis, *Soviets at Geneva*, p. 190.

by this chief apostle of peaceful coexistence on the occasion of the entry of the Soviet Union into the League of Nations, certain limitations and reservations about peaceful coexistence become apparent. As to "the peaceful coexistence of different social-political systems at a given historical stage," Litvinov asserted, "we have advocated it again and again at international conferences. . . . The invitation to the Soviet Union to join the League of Nations may be said to represent the final victory of this principle." However, he added that the "Soviet Union is entering into the League today as a representative of a new social-economic system, not renouncing any of its special features." Litvinov elaborated on these "special features":

> In order to make our position quite clear, I should like further to state that the idea in itself of an association of nations contains nothing theoretically inacceptable for the Soviet state and its ideology. The Soviet Union is itself a league of nations in the best sense of the word, uniting over two hundred nationalities, thirteen of which have a population of not less than one million each, and others such as Russia and the Ukraine, a population running into scores of millions. I will make so bold as to claim that never before have so many nations coexisted so peacefully within a single state.[39]

Here is a revival of the familiar Soviet distinction between two types of peaceful coexistence. The nations within the USSR had found the secret of true peaceful coexistence within the confines of a single state, and represented coexistence "in the best sense of the word." As the Soviet Union was not renouncing its role as a representative of this new system, it was but a short step to the assertion that all nations must someday so coexist within a single state, this time a world state. The USSR represented the "perfect" type of coexistence and as such the prototype of a world state. Until the arrival of this golden day, it was necessary, at this "given historical stage," to endure that far from perfect type of coexistence of two contradictory world systems.

During the latter 1930s the rising menace of Germany forced the Soviet regime to concentrate all its efforts on maneuvering within the confines of this imperfect type of coexistence. In March, 1936, Stalin told the American newspaper publisher Roy Howard: "We can peacefully coexist if we do not indulge in too much faultfinding

[39] "Litvinov's Speech at the League Assembly on the Entry of the U.S.S.R. into the League of Nations," Sept. 18, 1934, in Degras, ed., *Soviet Documents*, III, 92–93.

about all sorts of petty matters." But even while stating that "American democracy and the Soviet system can peacefully coexist and cooperate," Stalin warned that "one cannot develop into the other. The Soviet system will not grow into American democracy and vice versa." [40]

As the war approached Stalin experimented with any kind of coexistence that showed promise of permitting the Soviet state to escape the blows of military attack; if coexistence should prove impossible, he would seek involvement in the war only under the most favorable circumstances. On the eve of intensive negotiations with both sides, in March, 1939, Stalin assumed a noncommittal position: "We stand for peace and the strengthening of business relations with all countries." [41] When the Soviet Union finally struck a bargain with the Nazis, Molotov defended it in terms of "Lenin's well-known principle regarding the peaceful coexistence of the Soviet state and capitalist countries." So long as this coexistence served the aims of Soviet policy, the nature of these capitalist countries was of no consequence. "People ask, with an air of innocence," Molotov chided, "how the Soviet Union could consent to improve political relations with a Fascist state." Molotov pointed to the nonaggression and neutrality treaty which the Soviet Union had maintained with Fascist Italy ever since 1933. "It has never occurred to anybody as yet to object to this treaty, and that is natural, for inasmuch as this pact meets the interests of the USSR, it is in accord with our principle of peaceful coexistence of the USSR and capitalist states." [42]

DECEPTIVE POSTWAR STATEMENTS

Hitler's invasion of the USSR forced the Soviet Union into an unanticipated cooperation with the Western Allies. This excited uncritical, yet widespread and fervently held expectations that once the Soviet Union was freed of mortal danger, this cooperation, born of crisis, would stretch into an indefinite postwar period of peaceful

[40] "Beseda tovarishcha Stalina s predsedatelem amerikanskogo gazetnogo ob"edineniia 'Skripps-Govard Niuspeipers,' g-nom Roi Govardom," March 1, 1936, *Pravda*, March 5, 1936, p. 2.
[41] Stalin, *Otchëtnyi doklad na XIII s"ezde*, March 10, 1939, p. 40.
[42] "O ratifikatsii sovetsko-germanskogo dogovora o nenapadenii, soobshchenie tov. Molotova na zasedanii Verkhovnogo Soveta Soiuza SSR 31-go avgusta 1939 goda," *Pravda*, Sept. 1, 1939, p. 1.

PEACEFUL COEXISTENCE

coexistence. This prayerful hope was, from the beginning, doomed to disappointment because of the failure to understand that this imperfect type of coexistence was not a long-range Soviet goal. It had to be pursued under conditions that offered no alternative, but a release from peril meant a renewed opportunity to pursue aggressive policies which would someday lead the Soviet regime to the "perfect" type of coexistence among nations.

At the same time, the longer the Soviet leaders succeeded in keeping alive these false expectations, the greater would be the tendency of the West to underestimate, or explain away, any aggressive Soviet acts. Following the war, Stalin made a series of statements on the cooperation and peaceful coexistence of the two systems, which no longer contained the reservations characteristic of his prewar pronouncements. This could be accounted for either by the assumption that Stalin no longer had any reservations about peaceful coexistence, or by the assumption that these reservations remained, but that Stalin was speaking with greater dishonesty.

In September, 1946, an English newspaperman, Alexander Werth, asked Stalin: "Do you believe in the possibility of a friendly and lasting collaboration of the Soviet Union and the Western Democracies despite the existence of ideological discord, and in friendly competition between the two systems?" Stalin's reply was generally printed in the English-speaking world as "I do, unconditionally." "Unconditionally" would appear to be a mistranslation, since Stalin's reply of *bezuslovno verno* is an idiomatic Russian expression which might more accurately be rendered as, "Yes, surely," or "Why, yes, of course."[43] But even this corrected translation borders on a categorical and unconditional affirmation of the possibility of the coexistence between the two systems. Substantially, the same question-and-answer sequence took place in an interview between Stalin and Elliott Roosevelt on December 21, 1946.[44]

When the question of peaceful coexistence was again raised in an interview between Stalin and Harold Stassen, on April 9, 1947, Stassen began prodding in the right direction, though he stopped short. Stassen recalled his impression that in the past various state-

[43] "Otvety tov. Stalina I. V. na voprosy, zadannye moskovskim korrespondentom 'Sandei Taims,' g-nom Aleksandrom Vert v svoei zapiske na imia t. Stalina ot 17 sentabria 1946 g.," *Izvestiia*, Sept. 24, 1946, p. 1.
[44] "Zhurnal 'Luk' opublikoval interviu tovarishcha Stalina s Elliotom Ruzveltom," *Bol'shevik*, No. 1 (Jan., 1947), pp. 1-4.

ments had been made "about the impossibility of cooperation" between the two systems, adding that "Stalin himself had made such assertions." Stalin's reply was obviously calculated to foster a misconception. He denied flatly that he had ever had any reservations about cooperation between the two different economic systems. "The idea of cooperation between the two systems was first expressed by Lenin. Lenin is our teacher . . . and we, the Soviet people, are Lenin's pupils. We have never departed and shall never depart from Lenin's teachings." Stalin said that he might have indicated "that one system, for example, capitalism, does not want to cooperate, but that refers to desire, not the possibility of cooperating." Reiterating that he "held the point of view of Lenin on the possibility and desirability of cooperation between the two economic systems," Stalin affirmed "that the Russians had the desire to cooperate." [45]

The previous statements of Lenin and Stalin to which Stalin referred always emphasized the ultimate impossibility of cooperation between the two world systems. They had consistently held that the world was split into two irreconcilable camps. Consequently the relations between them, euphemistically labeled "peaceful coexistence," were always circumscribed by the contradictory nature of the two systems and by a limitation of time, beyond which only one of the two systems was expected to survive. By failing to mention any of these reservations, Stalin quite dishonestly conveyed the impression that both he and Lenin had always believed in the indefinite coexistence of two compatible world systems.

THE REASSERTION OF ORTHODOXY

With the founding of the Cominform in September, 1947, the reservations were once more explicitly stated. Perhaps the Soviet leaders recognized that their untempered pronouncements on collaboration with capitalist states were incompatible with the Soviet rejection of the Marshall Plan offer. In addition, there were dangers in relying solely upon expressions of peaceful intention, which traded upon an ever shrinking reservoir of wartime good will. A reassertion of orthodox Communist doctrine was necessary, both as

[45] "Zapis' besedy tov. I. V. Stalina s deiatelem respublikanskoi partii SShA, Garaldom Stassenom, 9 aprelia 1947 goda," *Pravda*, May 8, 1947, p. 1.

a measure for eliminating ideological confusion and as a means of tightening control over the "faithful" throughout the world who had become accustomed to collaborating with non-Communist elements. Accordingly, the Declaration of the founding Cominform Conference announced that "two opposite political lines have crystallized." Returning to familiar terminology, these were described as "two camps—the camp of imperialism and antidemocratic forces, whose chief aim is the establishment of a world-wide American imperialist hegemony and the crushing of democracy; and the anti-imperialist, democratic camp, whose chief aim is the elimination of imperialism." [46] The world was once again divided into two irreconcilable parts. America had been officially reinstated as the leader of the "imperialist" camp, and the Soviet regime had taken as its "chief aim . . . the elimination of imperialism." Zhdanov's speech to the Cominform Conference restated the premise that this coexistence was conceived of within certain time limits: "Soviet foreign policy proceeds from the fact of coexistence for a long time of the two systems—capitalism and socialism." [47] This coexistence might be lengthy, but as Korovin stated in November, 1947, "the Soviet people know that time is working in their favor and that each additional year of peaceful coexistence of the two systems, the socialist and the capitalist, strengthens the former and undermines the latter." [48] An editorial in the Soviet press, commemorating the thirtieth anniversary of the Bolshevik Revolution, likewise warned that while the coexistence of the two systems is inevitable "for a fairly long time . . . the capitalist system, as a historically transitory form of society, is nearing its end. It will be replaced by a more perfect order of social relations such as has already been inaugurated in the Soviet Union." [49] With the elimination of capitalism, a new world order would be patterned on the Soviet Union: again the theme that the USSR is the prototype of a world state.

Once orthodoxy had been reinforced in Party circles, the unconditional type of coexistence statements continued to be directed at a diminishing, but still sizable, audience of uncritical observers in the non-Soviet world. As before, Stalin periodically exchanged views

---

[46] "Deklaratsiia," Sept., 1947, in *Informatsionnoe soveshchanie*, pp. 6–7.
[47] A. Zhdanov, "O mezhdunarodnom polozhenii," in *ibid.*, p. 27.
[48] E. A. Korovin, "Vklad SSSR v mezhdunarodnoe pravo," *Sovetskoe gosudarstvo i pravo*, No. 11 (Nov., 1947), p. 30.
[49] "Thirty Years," *New Times*, Nov. 7, 1947, p. 3.

on the possibility of peaceful coexistence. In May, 1948, Stalin obligingly answered an inquiry of Henry A. Wallace, who was running for President on a "get-soft-with-Russia" policy, by providing the assurance that "the government of the USSR believes that, despite the difference in economic systems and ideology, the coexistence of these systems and the peaceful settlement of differences between the USSR and the USA are not only possible but absolutely necessary in the interests of universal peace." [50] In April, 1952, Stalin told a group of American newspaper editors that "the peaceful coexistence of capitalism and communism is quite possible provided there is a mutual desire to cooperate, a readiness to carry out undertaken commitments, and observance of the principle of equality and noninterference in the internal affairs of other states." [51] These reservations were widely interpreted as a request that the West live up to the Soviet versions of the various wartime agreements, and as a veiled demand for withdrawal of all American power throughout the world, wherever the Soviet regime considered it an "interference." Though these reservations somewhat pared down the scope of Stalin's previous postwar statements, they still neglected to mention the two fundamental reservations of the irreconcilability of the two systems and the limitation of time during which coexistence could continue. Stalin's last coexistence epistle came as a Christmas present to James Reston of The New York *Times*, on December 25, 1952. In response to Reston's query as to whether the USSR and the United States "can live peacefully in the coming years," Stalin replied that "our countries can continue to live in peace." [52]

THE SOVIET "PEACE" MOVEMENT

The manipulation of an officially sponsored Soviet "peace" movement has been an important and long-standing tactic of struggle, dating back to the Peace Decree of November 8, 1917.[53] The systematic elaboration and broadcasting of post–Second World War

[50] "Otvet I. V. Stalina na otkrytoe pis'mo G. Vollesa," May 17, 1948, *Bol'shevik*, No. 10 (May, 1948), p. 2.
[51] "Otvet tovarishcha Stalina no voprosy gruppy redaktorov amerikanskikh gazet," *Pravda*, April 2, 1952, p. 1.
[52] "Otvety tov. Stalina I. V. na voprosy diplomaticheskogo korrespondenta 'N'iu-Iork Taims,' Dzheimsa Restona, poluchennye 21 dekabria 1952 g.," *ibid.*, Dec. 26, 1952, p. 1.
[53] See the beginning of chapter 10 below.

"peace" pronouncements was entrusted to a number of Communist-created organizations, the most important of which has been the World Congress of Peace Partisans, first convened in April, 1949, and its Permanent Committee, now called the World Peace Council.[54] Amid the gentle cooing of Picasso's dove of peace, these organizations have pressed upon world opinion such propagandistic devices as the Stockholm Peace Petition and a Pact of Peace to be signed by the five Great Powers. A close reading of this postwar "peace" propaganda reveals two basic and familiar Soviet motivations: to provide a "breathing spell" at home and to exploit divisions in the non-Soviet world abroad.

This was a period in which the regime hoped to relieve domestic tensions and consolidate its rule. Even in a war-devastated country, the Soviet government persisted in a policy of allocating a disproportionately large share of its production to capital goods (and militarily useful) industries. The strain on the Soviet economy was increased by the cold war embargo on strategic goods enforced by the United States and its allies. It should not be surprising that the cry of peaceful coexistence was used to renew demands for increased trade with the non-Soviet world. For example, the International Economic Conference held at Moscow in April, 1952, issued a communiqué complaining that "traditional trade ties between nations have been severed, the geographical area in which commerce is conducted has been limited, and trade between East and West drastically curtailed." The Conference abounded in assurances of the possibility of peaceful coexistence, insisting that "differences in economic and social systems need not be an obstacle to the expansion of international economic relations."[55]

While demanding freedom of East-West trade, the Soviet Union

[54] The forerunners of the First Congress of Peace Partisans were the August, 1948, Congress of Cultural Leaders in Defense of Peace (Wroclaw, Poland) and the March, 1949, Cultural and Scientific Conference for World Peace (New York). "Peace" proclamations similar to those of the World Congress of Peace Partisans and the World Peace Council are constantly issued by such Soviet-controlled organizations as the World Federation of Trade Unions, World Federation of Scientific Workers, World Federation of Democratic Women, World Federation of Democratic Youth, International Union of Students, International Organization of Democratic Journalists, International Association of Democratic Lawyers, and so forth. For a history of the postwar Soviet "peace" movement, see A. I. Oparin, *Narody mira v bor'be za mir* (Moscow, 1951), pp. 1–23.
[55] "Communiqué of the International Economic Conference in Moscow," April 3–12, 1952, *News*, No. 8 (April 15, 1952), p. 4.

also posed as the protector of Europe against America. The European countries which stood to lose by restrictions on trade with the Soviet bloc had frequently accepted this policy of restraint only with reluctance and only after American urging. The call for peaceful coexistence and East-West trade was therefore a way to separate America from its allies. All of the arguments used against the Marshall Plan, about the American "enthrallment" of Europe, were revived as a salt treatment for this irritated and tender spot. But it was not enough to separate America from Europe, for peaceful coexistence also meant that the various countries of Europe must be kept apart from each other. Europe could only live "peacefully" if if abandoned all efforts at integration. The same Soviet periodicals that devotedly espoused peaceful coexistence invariably condemned the political federation of Europe, the Council of Europe, the Schuman Plan, the European Defense Community, the Organization for European Economic Cooperation, the European Payments Union, the European Economic Community, and Euratom.[56]

The attack on the European Defense Community and the integration of West Germany into NATO has perhaps been the most sustained, since it is associated with the rearmament of the West, and it is this which talk of peaceful coexistence is especially designed to forestall. Expressions of peaceful intention were meant to persuade a body of sympathetic, or at least neutralist, opinion that there is no need to rearm. A variant, designed for the same audience, is that the Soviet Union means "peace," and that therefore its terms ought to be accepted, whatever they might be. The Soviet leaders have effectively exploited man's fear of war and his deep-seated longing for peace, which in this atomic age frequently takes the form of a desire for peace at any price. When successful, this peace propaganda has the effect of distracting attention from war-like Soviet acts and immobilizing resistance to Soviet moves. Thus Stalin's letter to Henry Wallace closely preceded the Berlin blockade and the Stockholm Peace Petition, and agitation for a Pact for Peace coincided with war in Korea and Indochina. The "peace" movement is calculated to prevent an effective collective response from the non-Soviet world to an aggressive Soviet policy.

Stalin emphasized the importance of perpetuating these divisions in the non-Soviet world in his last major theoretical work, *The*

[56] This is documented in chapter 12 below.

PEACEFUL COEXISTENCE

Economic Problems of Socialism in the USSR. In what amounted to a repudiation of the theory of capitalist encirclement, Stalin pointed out that the Second World War had not found the Soviet Union surrounded by a solidly united capitalist camp. On the contrary, the war began among members of the capitalist camp. First it was a struggle between Germany and the Anglo-French-American bloc. Then, "when Hitler Germany declared war on the Soviet Union, the Anglo-French-American bloc, far from joining with Hitler Germany, was compelled to enter into a coalition with the USSR against Hitler Germany." From this Stalin drew the conclusion that "the struggle of the capitalist countries for markets and their desire to crush their competitors in practice proved to be stronger than the contradictions between the capitalist camp and the socialist camp." This was a startling statement, since it apparently invalidated the assumption that the *basic* division in the world was between the irreconcilable camps of capitalism and socialism. By magnifying the divisions within the capitalist camp, Stalin was appealing both to Communists and non-Communists in the West. He was warning the Communists that they must not sit idly by waiting for the "inevitable" collapse of the non-Soviet world as a result of the conflict between the two camps. Instead, the process of disintegrating the capitalist camp from within must be speeded up by exploiting its existing divisions to full advantage. Moreover, by playing up the conflicts in the West, Stalin was inviting the non-Communist, but non-American, leaders to break away from Washington's "dictation." Stalin confidently predicted that these divisions would some day develop into an open conflict and that consequently "the inevitability of wars between capitalist countries remains in force." [57] That is, by emphasizing peaceful coexistence between the USSR and the West, while at the same time inflating the conflicts within the West, Stalin was urging one Western power to weaken or to kill off another by war. This is the real import of this refurbished version of "peaceful" coexistence.

Though Stalin had given the "two camps" theory a new twist, he did not destroy the premise of the ultimate irreconcilability of the two camps. While the Soviet "peace" movement was bent on maintaining peace, "it is possible," Stalin said, "that in a certain con-

[57] Stalin, "Zamechaniia po ekonomicheskim voprosam, sviazannym s noiabr'skoi diskussiei 1951 goda," Feb. 1, 1952, in *Ekonomicheskie problemy*, pp. 33–35.

fluence of circumstances, the fight for peace will somewhere develop into a fight for socialism. But this will no longer be the present-day peace movement, but a movement for the overthrow of capitalism." This development would be unavoidable, since despite "all the successes of the peace movement, imperialism will remain . . . and consequently so will the inevitability of wars. To eliminate the inevitability of wars, it is necessary to destroy imperialism." [58] The peaceful coexistence of the two camps was still expected to come to an end with the downfall of the non-Soviet world.

In his report to the Nineteenth Party Congress in October, 1952, Malenkov presented the traditional Soviet version of the two camps theory.[59] He also repeated the usual avowals of peaceful coexistence, but then added this significant prospect:

While it steadfastly pursues its policy of peaceful cooperation with all countries, the Soviet Union takes into account the existence of the threat of new aggression on the part of the warmongers who have lost all restraint. . . . The facts of history cannot be ignored. And the facts show that as a result of the First World War Russia dropped out of the capitalist system, while as a result of the Second World War a whole series of countries in Europe and Asia dropped out of the capitalist system. There is every reason to assume that a Third World War will bring about the collapse of the world capitalist system.[60]

According to this view, which the Soviet leaders continue to reiterate,[61] a third world war will destroy one of these two irreconcilable systems.

The struggle for power within the Soviet hierarchy following Stalin's death produced a series of conciliatory moves on both the domestic and foreign fronts, including a renewed clamor for peaceful coexistence. This could have been expected, since all the rival factions locked in the joust for power at the Party summit had the common need of a new, prolonged "breathing spell" and a release

[58] *Ibid.*, p. 36.
[59] Malenkov, *Otchëtnyi doklad XIX s"ezdu*, Oct. 5, 1952, p. 6.
[60] *Ibid.*, pp. 31–33. For the first reference to the three-stage elimination of world capitalism by war, see "32-ia godovshchina Velikoi Oktiabr'skoi sotsialisticheskoi revoliutsii, doklad G. M. Malenkova na torzhestvennom zasedanii moskovskogo soveta 6 noiabria 1949 goda," *Pravda*, Nov. 7, 1949, p. 4.
[61] "Rech' Predsedatelia Soveta Ministrov SSSR, deputata G. M. Malenkova," *ibid.*, April 27, 1954, p. 5; "Rech' pervogo sekretaria TsK KPSS, deputata N. S. Khrushcheva," *ibid.*, April 27, 1954, p. 8; "Rech' G. M. Malenkova," *ibid.*, Feb. 19, 1956, p. 8; "Rech' tovarishcha N. S. Khrushcheva na deviatoi obshchegermanskoi rabochei konferentsii v gorode Leiptsige 7 marta 1959 goda," *ibid.*, March 27, 1959, p. 2.

from unnecessary, distracting pressures. At Stalin's funeral, Malenkov promised to follow "a policy of international cooperation and development of business relations with all countries, a policy based on the Leninist-Stalinist position of the possibility of a prolonged coexistence and peaceful competition between the two different systems—the capitalist and socialist." [62] The Soviet propaganda machine continues to grind out a spate of similar assurances.

Soviet campaigns of peaceful coexistence have traditionally been designed as a trap to halt the further integration of the non-Soviet world, and, if possible, to promote its active disintegration, thus preparing the way for a renewed period of Soviet advance. Malenkov frankly revealed these Soviet hopes in a speech of August, 1953, when he read the following fears into the minds of NATO's leaders: "The aggressive circles fully understand that if the North Atlantic bloc is already torn by internal conflicts and contradictions during this period of international tension, then it might disintegrate totally if that tension is relaxed." [63] The Soviet cry for peaceful coexistence was accompanied by an unabated assault upon the Western "positions of strength," in which Moscow explicitly demanded the dissolution of NATO, and, by implication, envisaged for the West what must logically be termed "positions of weakness."

At the Twentieth Party Congress, in February, 1956, Khrushchev gave several twists of his own to the coexistence doctrine. He granted that "so long as the economic base giving rise to wars remains, imperialism will also continue to exist." But he then revised the traditional Leninist-Stalinist view of war by asserting that in the present era "war is not fatally inevitable." This innovation, which perhaps acknowledged the dangers of total atomic war to the Soviet regime, also strengthened the appeal of Soviet "peace" propaganda by removing the basic contradiction of a "peace" movement that simultaneously asserted the fatal inevitability of war.[64] The choice, said Khrushchev, was simple: "either peaceful coexistence or the most destructive war in history. There is no third way." In responding to this proposition it is obvious that no nation would choose war,

[62] "Traurnyi miting na krasnoi ploshchadi vo vremia pokhoron Iosifa Vissarionovicha Stalina, rech' tovarishcha G. M. Malenkova," March 9, 1953, *Kommunist*, No. 4 (March, 1953), p. 13.
[63] "Rech' Predsedatelia Soveta Ministrov Soiuza SSR tovarishcha G. M. Malenkova," *Pravda*, Aug. 9, 1953, p. 3.
[64] The implications of this doctrinal innovation regarding the use of force are more fully developed at the end of chapter 10.

but not quite so obvious is the implication of choosing "peaceful coexistence." The latter condition was imperiled by the Western military alliances and could be satisfied only by their abandonment. This was an appeal especially designed for the neutralist nations with whom Moscow seeks to make common cause on the basis of a shared antagonism toward the "imperialist" West and "militarist" America. Khrushchev praised those "peace-loving European and Asian states which have proclaimed nonparticipation in blocs," or, more specifically, "closed military imperialist alignments." Those "neutralist" states, Khrushchev indicated somewhat prematurely, have already slipped under Moscow's tutelage by joining the vast, Soviet-led "zone of peace," embracing "nearly 1,500,000,000—that is, the majority of the population of our planet." Soviet opposition to "military blocs" can be overcome, it seems, by joining the Soviet "peace bloc." By refusing to admit the possibility of a third way between his two alternatives Khrushchev was, despite his seeming solicitude for neutralism, still posing the ultimate choice between war and peaceful submission to Soviet control. It has been characteristic of Soviet thought not to be embarrassed by advocating two seemingly contradictory ideas, since each idea can be aimed at a different audience with the same basically consistent purpose of maximizing Soviet power. In this instance, it is not difficult to reconcile the short-range appeal to neutralism with the long-range goal of a Soviet world state.

"Peaceful coexistence," Khrushchev continued, far from seeking a peaceful reconciliation of the two systems, is itself a tool of ideological warfare. He reprimanded those who confused the temporary coexistence of different systems with the peaceful coexistence of Soviet and non-Soviet ideologies. "That we support peaceful coexistence and economic competition with capitalism certainly does not mean that we can relax the struggle against bourgeois ideology and the remnants of capitalism in the people's minds." [65]

It is evident that the Soviet leaders have in no way retracted their basic reservations about the nature of the coexistence of the two worlds. Khrushchev's pronouncements have repeatedly exuded a self-confident, boastful attitude towards the "inevitable" world

[65] "Otchëtnyi doklad Tsentral'nogo Komiteta Kommunisticheskoi partii, doklad pervogo sekretaria TsK KPSS, tovarishcha N. S. Khrushcheva," *Pravda*, Feb. 15, 1956, pp. 3, 4, 11.

triumph of the Soviet cause that is reminiscent of an earlier era. His remarks of November, 1955, for example, are refreshingly frank:

I, personally, dislike very much the capitalist system. I speak of coexistence not because I want capitalism to exist, but because I cannot help recognizing that this system does exist. . . . But despite this, we are confident that, even as things are now, in peaceful competition between the capitalist and socialist systems, it is we, socialism, that will win.

I happened to say this publicly at one of the receptions in the Kremlin. The bourgeois correspondents blazoned it around the world that Khrushchev had been "incautious" and let out that the Bolsheviks had not abandoned their political plans. No, I was not incautious and had not let out anything, but said what we think and what we confidently believe. We have never abandoned, and never will abandon, our political line, which was mapped by Lenin; we have never abandoned, and never will abandon, our political program. . . . And so we say to the gentry who are expecting the Soviet Union to change its political program: "Wait until the crab whistles!" [66]

To those who remain in doubt of Soviet intentions, one can only say that candor is, indeed, the best form of deception.

Although "we, on our part, believe that communism is invincible and that the future belongs to the Communist system," Khrushchev stated in February, 1955, the coexistence of the two systems will nevertheless be "prolonged." "As to how long this coexistence can last, the answer is that this will depend on historical conditions, on historical development. . . . The Soviet people believes that communism will triumph. When this will come about, is not known." [67]

THE ANTICIPATED END OF COEXISTENCE

Despite this disavowal of an exact knowledge of when coexistence will come to an end, there have been various attempts by Soviet theoreticians to pin-point the target date. Or, put another way, the Soviet leaders have endeavored, from time to time, to set a deadline for the establishment of the Soviet world state.

During the first years of Soviet power the idea of prolonged co-

[66] "Speech by N. S. Khrushchev at Reception in Indo-Soviet Cultural Society, in Bombay," Nov. 24, 1955, *International Affairs* (Moscow), No. 1 (Jan., 1956), p. 195.
[67] "Beseda N. S. Khrushcheva s amerikanskimi zhurnalistami V. R. Kherstom, Kingsberi Smitom i F. Konniform, 5 fevralia 1955 goda," *Pravda*, Feb. 11, 1955, p. 1.

existence was rejected. In March, 1919, Lenin said that "the existence of the Soviet Republic side by side the imperialist states for a prolonged period of time is unthinkable. In the end either one or the other will conquer." [68] In July, 1919, he predicted that "by next July we shall greet the victory of the International Soviet Republic, and that this victory will be complete and irreversible." [69] When 1920 failed to produce a Soviet world state, Soviet theoreticians began redefining Lenin's words. A Party resolution of April, 1925, cited Lenin's statement of March, 1919, and held that "these fundamental propositions of Leninism remain entirely true today. The whole question lies in how one must interpret the words 'a prolonged period' or 'in the end.' At first it appeared that 'in the end' would be only a matter of years or even a matter of months." The resolution suggested that the basis of a more reasonable estimate might be Lenin's statement of 1921. Then, Lenin asserted that "ten to twenty years of correct relations with the peasantry and our victory on a world scale is assured . . . otherwise it may be necessary to suffer through another twenty to forty years of White Terror." [70] According to this view, "victory on a world scale" might be expected by 1931 at the earliest, or 1961 at the latest.

In 1935 the Comintern veteran, Wilhelm Pieck, told the Seventh World Comintern Congress that, as compared to the lapse of time between the bourgeois revolutions of 1789 and 1848, "not a longer, but a considerably shorter period of time will be required from the victory of the first socialist revolution, the great October Revolution of 1917, to the victory of socialism throughout the world." [71] This would still place the world victory of the Soviet camp somewhere around 1960.

A more recent estimate has been given by a Soviet economist, G. V. Kozlov, in *Voprosy ekonomiki* of April, 1952. Kozlov concluded that "the general crisis of capitalism" had gone through two stages. "The first stage ran from the First World War and the

[68] Lenin, "Otchët Tsentral'nogo Komiteta," March 18, 1919, in *Sochineniia*, XXIV, 122.
[69] Lenin, "Doklad o vnutrennem i vneshnem polozhenii respubliki na moskovskoi konferentsii RKP(b)," July 12, 1919, in *ibid.*, XXIV, 381.
[70] "Chetyrnadtsataia konferentsiia RKP(b)," April 27-29, 1925, in *KPSS v rez.*, II, 48.
[71] W. Pieck, "The Activities of the Executive Committee of the Communist International," July 26, 1935, in *VII Congress of the Communist International*, p. 66.

October Revolution to the Second World War. . . . A new, second stage of the general crisis of capitalism began after the Second World War, and was characterized by a new round of wars and revolutions." The decisive feature in this new stage was found in "the sharp alteration in the balance of forces between the two systems, in favor of socialism and to the detriment of capitalism." [72] Although the scales were tipping in favor of world socialism, it was unlikely that the balance would be entirely upset at once, hence the Soviet leaders looked to the "inevitability of a lengthy coexistence of the two systems." Kozlov then ventured this definiton of the word "lengthy":

> In the first half of the twentieth century the great October Socialist Revolution conquered in our country. . . . China and a series of countries of Central and Southeastern Europe have fallen out of the capitalist system. . . . The second half of the twentieth century will produce the complete victory of communism throughout the entire world.[73]

First Deputy Premier L. M. Kaganovich confirmed this prediction in a speech of November 6, 1955:

> Revolutionary ideas know no frontiers. . . . The immortal ideas of Marx and Engels penetrated all corners of the earth and entered into the consciousness of the working masses of all countries. . . . If the nineteenth century was the century of capitalism, the twentieth century is the century for the triumph of socialism and communism.[74]

These latest forecasts for the complete world victory of the Soviet camp envisage the end of peaceful coexistence by the year 2000.

Whether the end comes sooner or later, an end to the coexistence of the two worlds is unquestionably anticipated. And this end will mark the beginning of the Soviet world state.

[72] G. V. Kozlov, "Obshchii krizis kapitalizma i ego obostrenie na sovremennom etape," *Voprosy ekonomiki*, No. 4 (April, 1952), pp. 76–77.
[73] *Ibid.*, pp. 85–86.
[74] "Doklad tovarishcha L. M. Kaganovicha na torzhestvennom zasedanni moskovskogo soveta 6 noiabria 1955 goda," *Pravda*, Nov. 7, 1955, p. 2.

VII. The Issue of Centralism versus Federalism in the Leninist Era

WHAT image do the Soviet theoreticians project for the future of man under the rule of their world state? What sort of society, what type of cultural pattern or patterns, do they anticipate? Do they desire a unitary, centralized world state with a single world culture, or a diversified, loosely knit world state, consisting of many national cultures? Will all of humanity be poured into a single mold, and if so, will this mold be cast at a single world center? Will every clerk have to dip his pen in the inkwell in Red Square? Will the pattern-forming and decision-making processes of the Soviet world state be concentrated in the hands of a small central body, or will they rest among many decentralized groups scattered throughout the world? In political terminology, this image polarizes around the concepts of centralism and federalism.

THE SETTING FOR THE CENTRALIST-FEDERALIST CONTROVERSY

Soviet views on centralism and federalism in a world state are largely a projection of their attitude toward the centralist-federalist issue as it arose in the building of the Russian Party and state. Hence it is necessary to point up underlying concepts and motivations, derived from Soviet experiences in Russia, which in turn affect the concept of a Soviet world state. In discussing the clash between centralism and federalism within Party and state, it is only intended here to clarify the basic ideas, without attempting a comprehensive description or history of either the Communist Party or the Soviet state.

The structure of the Party is relevant to our topic for three principal reasons. The Party was the first concrete Soviet experiment in organizing power relations among different national groups. The

CENTRALISM V. FEDERALISM

attitude toward centralism and federalism which emerged in the development of the Party provides important insights, for the Party was the model, the ideal type of organization, which, it was hoped, could be applied on an ever-widening scale as the framework of power expanded from Party to nation-state to world state. The Party, being small and subject to strict control, was more immune from the pressures that later watered down, in form at least, the centralized organization of state power. The purity of Party organization therefore continues to express Soviet aspirations for the ultimate organization of a world society.

Second, the very nature of the Party as a vanguard group, a self-proclaimed repository of truth, automatically assigned the Party a vital role in the future Soviet state. No effort was made to conceal this anticipated development. For example, in 1927 Stalin declared:

Our Party guides the government. . . . The Party supervises the work of the administration, the work of the organs of power, it corrects their errors and shortcomings, which are unavoidable, helps them to carry out the decisions of the government, and tries to secure for them the support of the masses, since there is not any important decision taken by them without the direction of the Party.[1]

Or again, in 1939, Stalin reasserted this relation between Party and state, this time restricting effective control to an even smaller group within the Party:

The Party cadres constitute the commanding staff of the Party, and since our Party is in power, they also constitute the commanding staff of the leading organs of the state. After a correct political line has been worked out and tested in practice, the Party cadres become the decisive force in the work of guiding the Party and the state.[2]

Obviously, the influence that radiates from the Party, especially from the nub of Party power, has a determining effect upon the Soviet state. As the present Soviet state is the avowed prototype of a world state, it must be assumed that the Party would play a similar role in the Soviet world state.

Finally, the Soviet attitude toward centralism and federalism is nowhere developed with such clarity and frankness as in the early debates over the Party structure. Here Lenin's centralist philosophy is revealed in its most uncompromising form.

[1] Stalin, "Beseda s pervoi amerikanskoi rabochei delegatsiei," Sept. 9, 1927, in *Sochineniia*, X, 101–2.
[2] Stalin, *Otchëtnyi doklad na XVIII s"ezde*, March 10, 1939, p. 116.

LENINIST AND JACOBIN CENTRALISM

Lenin's centralism was, of course, based on that of Marx, but Marx's centralism was largely limited to economic considerations, to an appreciation of the merits of the tight integration of large territorial units made possible by the Industrial Revolution. While Lenin certainly accepted this idea, it cannot be considered an adequate explanation of the centralist principles upon which he founded the Party. For this, it is necessary to look to another source of inspiration which struck a deeply responsive chord in Lenin: namely, the Jacobin tradition of the French Revolution.[3]

The principal source of Jacobin doctrine was Rousseau's *Social Contract*, which predicated the existence of an infallible general will. An enigmatic and controversial theorist, Rousseau has become all things to all men. Partisans of liberal democracy tend to see the general will as the legal expression of man's reason and conscience and the guarantor of his moral integrity and individual freedom. For society as a whole it becomes the expression of justice and of the general moral consensus which binds a community together. The general will is formulated through the constant interaction of the individual wills of free citizens.[4] "Nor is there any other way of making sure that the will of the individual is in conformity with the general will," Rousseau stipulated, "save by submitting it to the free votes of the People."[5]

The Jacobins, and their fellow advocates of what has aptly been termed totalitarian democracy, pieced together the numerous illiberal elements in Rousseau and pounced upon his statements that reflect a deep mistrust of the people. "The general will is always right and ever tends to the public advantage. But it does not follow

---

[3] Lenin, of course, was not the only, nor even the first, "Russian Jacobin." An extremist tradition in the Russian intelligentsia of which Lenin was a part, formed of such figures as Bakunin, Nechaev, Zaichnevskii, and Tkachëv, had posited many of the revolutionary axioms that Lenin systematically elaborated. It is extremely difficult, if not impossible, however, to document the extent of Lenin's indebtedness to them. On the roots of Russian Jacobinism, see the doctoral thesis of Miriam Haskell Berlin, The Jacobin Tradition in the Russian Revolutionary Movement, 1860-1880 (Radcliffe, 1957). V. Varlamov, *Bakunin and the Russian Jacobins and Blanquists as Evaluated by Soviet Historiography* (New York, 1955), is useful for its extensive bibliography.
[4] For an interpretation that stresses the liberal democratic elements, see John W. Chapman, *Rousseau—Totalitarian or Liberal?* (New York, 1956).
[5] Rousseau, "The Social Contract," in *Social Contract: Essays by Locke, Hume and Rousseau*, Bk. II, ch. 7, p. 207.

CENTRALISM V. FEDERALISM

that the deliberations of the People are always equally beyond question. It is ever the way of men to wish their own good, but they do not at all times see where that good lies." [6] When the state is originally constituted, or when it needs to be reconstituted, Rousseau turns to a legislator who must be a "superior intelligence," an "extraordinary figure," a "genius" who can "make the Gods speak." The lawgivers are "wise men . . . speaking to the vulgar herd." [7] "How can the blind multitude, which often does not know what it wants because only rarely does it know what is for its own good, undertake, of itself, an enterprise so extensive and so difficult as the formulation of a system of law?" [8] Even after the state is a going concern, Rousseau finds that "it is the best and most natural arrangement that can be made that the wise should govern the masses, provided that they govern them always for their own good, and not selfishly." [9] And in times of crisis, when the existence of the state is threatened, all power can be invested in a single dictator, who will become the protector of the general will. "A Dictator might, in certain circumstances, defend the public liberty without ever constituting a serious threat to it." [10] Rousseau also recommends official censorship of ideas, for "censorship maintains manners by preventing opinions from growing corrupt, by intervening to keep them on the right lines." [11] The state ideology must be codified as a civil religion, whose basic tenets cannot be taken lightly. "Any man who, after acknowledging these articles of faith, proceeds to act as though he did not believe them, is deserving of the death penalty." [12] Rousseau's social order was theoretically dedicated to the achievement of individual freedom, but it was also clearly empowered "to compel a man to be free" [13] if he should lack insight into the general will.

Robespierre, the exponent of Jacobin authoritarianism, concluded that the people cannot be trusted to will their own good, but that this must be done for them by an enlightened vanguard, which alone possesses true insight into the general will. All effective power must naturally reside in a tiny central beacon of omniscience. His prin-

[6] *Ibid.*, Bk. II, ch. 3, p. 193.   [7] *Ibid.*, Bk. II, ch. 7, pp. 204–8.
[8] *Ibid.*, Bk. II, ch. 6, p. 204.   [9] *Ibid.*, Bk. III, ch. 5, p. 235.
[10] *Ibid.*, Bk. IV, ch. 6, p. 292. It is true that Rousseau also specifically affirms the right of revolution to overthrow a tyrant. But if the people may not be trusted to perceive the general will, which may be expressed through a dictator, how, then, does one determine when the people have the right to revolt?
[11] *Ibid.*, Bk. IV, ch. 7, p. 294.   [12] *Ibid.*, Bk. IV, ch. 8, p. 306.
[13] *Ibid.*, Bk. I, ch. 7, p. 184.

cipal opponents, the Girondins, were inclined to deny that truth could be the exclusive preserve of any elite, but rather that it would emerge from the balancing of many diverse views and interests. The Girondins, quite logically, were federalists.

After welcoming the forcible expulsion of the legally elected Girondin leaders from the National Convention on June 2, 1793, Robespierre undertook the relentless process of making the "general will" an actuality. "True law-givers," he declared, "ought not to subordinate their laws to the corrupt morality of the people for whom they are destined," but promulgating just and virtuous laws, they must "know how to surmount every difficulty in order to impose them upon men."[14] Since the general will was one and indivisible, all opposing parties must be outlawed, and all factions within the Jacobin Party itself must be annihilated. The power for discovering and suppressing agents of "partial wills" was centralized in the hands of the Committee of Public Safety, and doctrinal purity was maintained in the Jacobin ranks by a constant process of self-purification. It was left to "the Incorruptible," as Robespierre called himself, to purge the "corrupt" within this elite. A state of permanent warfare existed between this incorruptible vanguard and everyone who might disagree with it. Robespierre believed that those who differed with him did so out of stupidity, or more likely malice, and so must be declared "enemies of the people." These dissidents had to be "re-educated" until they too acclaimed the general will, and in the interim, all means, the guillotine included, were valid instruments to force men to be "free." The Reign of Terror was to usher in the Reign of Virtue.

It is not at present fashionable for the Soviet leaders to afford excessive praise to Rousseau and the Jacobin dictatorship under Robespierre, since they stood in the forefront of a bourgeois, not a proletarian, revolution.[15] But the centralist philosophy and the

[14] Quoted in Talmon, *Totalitarian Democracy*, p. 211. This volume is confined to the period of the French Revolution. The promised appearance of two volumes developing this theme in nineteenth-century Western Europe and twentieth-century Eastern Europe is awaited with great interest.

[15] "Russo," in *Kratkii filosofkii slovar'* (Moscow, 1952), pp. 445–47; "Robesp'er," in *Politicheskii slovar'* (Moscow, 1940), pp. 486–87; "Iakobintsy" in *Politicheskii slovar'*, p. 666; Vyshinsky, *Sovetskoe gosudarstvennoe pravo*, pp. 162–65. Vyshinsky objected to Rousseau's general will because it was applied to a society rent by class conflict, and so served as a disguise for the will of the bourgeoisie, rather than on the grounds that it is impossible for any society to be guided by a single will. In the "classless" Soviet society, Vyshinsky asserted, there is but a single will, which is authoritatively interpreted by the Party. While

totalitarian principles of political organization which the Jacobins used in a bourgeois revolution are directly relevant to the subsequent development of Soviet theory and institutions. Lenin frankly recognized this affinity and early in his career openly embraced the Jacobin experiment.

When the Russian Social Democratic Labor Party split into its Bolshevik and Menshevik factions in 1903, the term "Jacobin" was freely hurled at Lenin by those who resisted his demands for an authoritarian, highly centralized Party. This centralism was the foundation rock of Lenin's Bolshevism, to which he forever remained firmly attached. Instead of retreating before the charge of "Jacobinism," Lenin took up the challenge and answered the Menshevik leader, Axelrod, from whom it was heard most frequently. "Comrade Axelrod is probably aware that the division of present-day Social Democracy into revolutionary and opportunist has long since given rise—and not only in Russia—to 'historical parallels with the era of the great French Revolution.' " [16] In analyzing this historical parallel, Lenin arrived at these definitions of a Jacobin and a Girondin:

These "dreadful words"—Jacobinism and the rest—are only expressions of opportunism. A Jacobin who maintains an inseparable bond with the *organization* of the proletariat, *conscious* of its class interests, is a *revolutionary Social Democrat*. A Girondin who yearns for professors and high school students, who is afraid of the dictatorship of the proletariat and who sighs about the absolute value of democratic demands, is an *opportunist*.[17]

Rousseau is given credit for condemning the social ills of inequality that result from the growth of private property, he is accused of not recognizing that the origin of the state can be traced to the birth of private property and the creation of antagonistic classes. Nor is he said to acknowledge that the state functions as an organ of class oppression. However, one should recall these famous sentences of Rousseau: "The first man who, having enclosed a piece of ground, bethought himself of saying 'This is mine,' and found people simple enough to believe him, was the real founder of civil society. . . . Such was, or may well have been, the origin of society and law, which bound new fetters on the poor, and gave new powers to the rich; which irretrievably destroyed natural liberty, eternally fixed the law of property and inequality, converted clever usurpation into unalterable right, and, for the advantage of a few ambitious individuals, subjected all mankind to perpetual labor, slavery and wretchedness." (Rousseau, "A Discourse on the Origin of Inequality," in *The Social Contract and Discourses*, Everyman's Library, No. 660 [London, New York, 1947], pp. 192, 205.) See also Engels's favorable comment on Rousseau in *Dühring's Revolution in Science*, pp. 24, 26, 108, 113, 152–54.

[16] Lenin, "Shag vperëd, dva shaga nazad," Feb.–May, 1904, in *Sochineniia*, VI, 301.
[17] *Ibid.*, VI, 303.

Trotsky, who at the time considered himself a protégé of Axelrod, pounced upon Lenin's definition of a Jacobin. "This formula," Trotsky said in 1904, "is supposed to sanction all the political and theoretical conquests of the Leninist wing of our Party. In this little formula is hidden the theoretical roots of our disagreement." [18] Lenin's arbitrary objection to the "absolute value of democratic demands" evoked an angry response from Trotsky, who accused Lenin of transforming the idea of the dictatorship of the proletariat into "a dictatorship over the proletariat." [19] Trotsky countered with this prophetic vision of the Bolshevik Party, organized on the principles of Jacobin centralism: "These methods will lead, as we shall yet see, to a situation in which the Party organization replaces the Party itself, then the Central Committee replaces the Party organization, and finally a Dictator replaces the Central Committee." [20] In the end, Trotsky joined the Bolshevik Party and, ironically, became a victim of the Dictator whose appearance he had foreseen.

His faith in Jacobinism unshaken, Lenin continued to apply this term to his defense of centralism. In 1913, for example, he argued, "we are against federalism, we are for the Jacobins and against the Girondins." [21] On the eve of the Bolshevik Revolution in 1917 he specifically envisioned the extension of Jacobin organizational principles to the entire world. "In the twentieth century," Lenin conjectured, it "could not only achieve the same great, ineradicable, unforgettable things that were achieved by the Jacobins of the eighteenth century, but could also lead to a permanent triumph of the toilers on a universal scale." [22]

Lenin also adapted the theory of the general will to the requirements of a proletarian revolution in Russia. His conception of the Russian Revolution of 1905 provides a clear illustration of this application. According to Lenin, this revolution would pass through two stages: first, that of a democratic republic, installed at the instigation of the proletariat and the bourgeois peasantry, and second, a socialist regime in which the interests of the proletariat would clearly predominate. During the first phase of this revolution it would be possible to speak of "the united will" of the forces striv-

[18] Trotsky, *Nashi politicheskie zadachi*, 1904, p. 90.   [19] *Ibid.*, pp. 101 ff.
[20] *Ibid.*, p. 54.
[21] Lenin, "Pis'mo S. G. Shaumianu," Dec. 6, 1913, in *Sochineniia*, XVII, 90.
[22] Lenin, "Mozhno li zapugat' rabochii klass 'iakobinstvom'?" July 7, 1917, in *ibid.*, XX, 556.

ing to create a democratic republic, because of "the *general* character of the democratic revolution: If it is 'general' it means there *must* be a 'unity of will' precisely in so far as this revolution satisfies general needs and requirements." The word "general" is a translation of the Russian *obshchenarodnyi*, which literally means "all people's." This unity of will which satisfies the needs and requirements of all people is almost indistinguishable from the Jacobin general will. But where Robespierre stopped Lenin continued. "Beyond the boundaries of democracy there can be no unity of will between the proletariat and the peasant bourgeoisie." That is, "will may be united in one respect and not in others." While there would be "unity of will on questions of democracy and the struggle for a republic," this unity would not survive the second stage of the revolution.[23] "The time will come when the struggle against the Russian autocracy will be over, when the period of democratic revolution in Russia will also be over, and then it would be ridiculous to talk about 'unity of will' of the proletariat and the peasantry." [24] Starting from an "all people's" or general will, Lenin foresaw the evolution of a *class will* which would strive to satisfy the needs and requirements of the proletariat alone. Even this was very much in the Jacobin tradition, for this refinement had been introduced into Robespierre's doctrine by Babeuf, his proletarian disciple. Babeuf's abortive revolution of 1796 sought to superimpose a class doctrine on Rousseau's general will and so arrive at a new general will, which would have been an approximation of a proletarian class will.[25]

THE STRUGGLE FOR CENTRALISM IN THE PARTY

The instrument for giving expression to Lenin's class will was a highly disciplined, centralized Party elite, since the masses could not be trusted to will their own good. "The history of all countries shows," Lenin wrote in 1902, "that the working class, exclusively by its own efforts, can only develop a trade-union conscious-

---

[23] Lenin, "Dve taktiki sotsial-demokratii v demokraticheskoi revoliutsii," July, 1905, in *ibid.*, VIII, 84.
[24] *Ibid.*, VIII, 86.
[25] Talmon, *Totalitarian Democracy*, pp. 167-247. See also Ernest Belfort Bax, *The Last Episode of the French Revolution* (London, 1911); David Thomson, *The Babeuf Plot* (London, 1947).

ness."[26] Marx's expectation that an increasing pauperization of the masses would spontaneously develop a well-defined, revolutionary proletarian consciousness had remained unfulfilled. How then can the worker's class consciousness ever be raised to the point of staging a revolution? "Political class consciousness can be instilled in the worker *only from without*,"[27] that is, by a tiny, centrally commanded vanguard group with true insight into the class will. When objections were raised that this autocratic centralism would lead to "the ossification of thought" among the rank and file, Lenin retorted that freedom of criticism could only sow confusion among the rank and file. "Freedom of criticism means . . . freedom from any complete and thought-out theory; it means eclecticism and absence of principle."[28] Lenin added that the members of a revolutionary organization "do not have time to think about the toy forms of democracy."[29] Part of his defense for this attitude rested, quite understandably, upon the need for a conspiratorial type of Party, which could operate in complete secrecy under the nose of the Tsarist autocracy. But this Russian environment could only be considered a partial explanation, since Lenin's Jacobin-like distrust of the common man caused him to reject under *any* conditions a decentralized, democratically organized Party.

Lenin had put these views on record even before the convocation of the Second Party Congress, where he was to stand out as the most implacable foe of federalism. Among his opposition, the stronghold of federalist sentiment was located in the General Jewish Worker's League of Lithuania, Poland, and Russia, or "the Bund." Founded in 1897, one year before the First Congress of the Russian Social Democratic Labor Party, the Bund had become a constituent part of the latter on special terms giving it autonomy in questions relating to the Jewish proletariat. Early in 1903, just prior to the Second Party Congress, Lenin noted with anguish a Bund resolution which sought "to introduce new *federal* relations into the

---

[26] Lenin, "Chto delat'?" 1902, in *Sochineniia*, IV, 384.   [27] *Ibid.*, IV, 422.
[28] *Ibid.*, IV, 379.
[29] *Ibid.*, IV, 469. Similarly, Lenin told the old Bolshevik Valentinov in March, 1904: "The Social Democratic Party is not a seminar where various ideas are confronted. It is a militant class organization of the revolutionary proletariat. It has its own program and philosophy, a system of thought exclusively its own. Within the Party you cannot expect any particular freedom to criticize and to compare ideas. He who has joined the Party has to accept its ideas, has to share them, not tamper with them." (N. Valentinov, "Encounters with Lenin," *Russian Review*, XIII, No. 3 [July, 1954], 178.)

CENTRALISM V. FEDERALISM

rules of the Russian Party." [30] By seeking to organize the workers according to nationality, the Bund "has planted in the minds of the Jewish workers ideas which will serve to *replace* their class consciousness." [31] Lenin was operating on the assumption that the class will was one and indivisible, and that it could only be authoritatively interpreted by one centralized organization which would speak for the workers of all nationalities. "We must act as a single, centralized, fighting organization, we must have behind us the entire proletariat, without distinction of nationality and language . . . we must not breed estrangement and isolation and then have to cure an artificially inoculated disease with the aid of those famous 'federation' plasters." [32]

One of the first resolutions introduced by Lenin at the Second Congress was directed against the Bund. He proposed that "the Congress resolutely reject the federal principle for the structure of the Russian Party and reaffirm the organizational principle laid down in the 1898 rules, namely, autonomy for national Social Democratic organizations in matters immediately concerning them." [33] Even the word "autonomy" was unsatisfactory; while the Bund wished to expand autonomy into federalism, Lenin wished to diminish autonomy to the vanishing point. The breach between the two points of view was complete. The Party rejected federalism and the Bund seceded from the Party.

Stalin's writings of this period also reflect an uncompromising centralism. As early as 1901 Stalin asserted that "for the realization of the socialist ideal, it is necessary to unite the workers into a force organized without regard to nationality and country." [34] When the question of federalism in the Transcaucasus was raised by a section of the Georgian and Armenian Social Democrats in 1904, Stalin promptly protested. The purpose of the Party was to

---

[30] Lenin, "Nuzhna li 'samostoiatel'naia politicheskaia partiia' evreiskomu proletariatu," Feb. 15, 1903, in *Sochineniia*, V, 245.

[31] *Ibid.*, V, 248.

[32] *Ibid.*, V, 248-49. See also Lenin, "Natsional'nyi vopros v nashei programme," July 15, 1903, in *Sochineniia*, V, 344.

[33] Lenin, "Proekt rezoliutsii o meste Bunda v partii," n.d., in *ibid.*, VI, 6. See also Lenin, "Rech' po voprosu o meste Bunda v RSDRP," Aug. 2, 1903, in *ibid.*, VI, 18-20; Lenin, "Polozhenie Bunda v partii," Oct. 22, 1903, in *ibid.*, VI, 78-86; "Rezoliutsii II s"ezda RSDRP, 1. O meste Bunda v partii," Aug., 1903, in *ibid.*, VI, 398.

[34] Stalin, "Rossiiskaia Sotsial-Demokraticheskaia Partiia i eë blizhaishie zadachi," Nov.-Dec., 1901, in *Sochineniia*, I, 12.

demolish, not reinforce, national barriers. " 'National distinctions,' which are only of minor interest for centralists, have become the foundation upon which national Parties can arise for federalists." [35] "At the very time when we need a single, flexible, centralized Party, whose Central Committee should be able to rouse the workers of the whole of Russia at a moment's notice . . . we are offered a monstrous 'federal league' broken up into separate Parties." [36] Stalin then set forth this dictum which future developments caused him to repudiate: "The science of dialectical materialism has long ago proved that the existence of any sort of 'national spirit' is no longer possible." [37]

About this time Lenin also assumed his most fanatically centralist stand, from which he too was forced to make at least a tactical retreat. As a result of the bitter factional struggle of the Second Party Congress, which had placed in jeopardy his sacred centralism, Lenin struck back in 1904 with an acid diatribe which even bypassed an attack on federalism and struck directly at the minimal freedom of autonomy. In upholding the authority of the central organ of the Party bureaucracy, Lenin frankly admitted his antipathy toward democracy:

Bureaucracy versus democracy is precisely the same thing as centralism versus autonomy; it is the organizational principle of revolutionary Social Democracy as opposed to the organizational principle of opportunist Social Democracy. The latter strives to proceed from the bottom upwards, and therefore, wherever possible and as far as possible, insists upon autonomy and "democracy," which is carried (by the overzealous) to the point of anarchy. Revolutionary Social Democracy seeks to proceed from the top downwards, and insists upon an extension of the rights and full powers of the center against the parts.[38]

This bold statement of autocratic centralism called forth a torrent of abuse by Lenin's colleagues.

When Lenin's precepts were largely disregarded during the spontaneous mass movement of the 1905 Revolution, he found it necessary to restyle his autocratic centralism "democratic centralism," a phrase appearing for the first time in a Party resolution of the

---

[35] Stalin, "Kak ponimaet sotsial-demokratiia natsional'nyi vopros?" Sept. 14, 1904, in *ibid.*, I, 38.
[36] *Ibid.*, I, 41.   [37] *Ibid.*, I, 53.
[38] Lenin, "Shag vperëd," in *Sochineniia*, VI, 313-14. This entire 183-page work is a polemic against democratic federalism.

Tammerfors Conference of December, 1905.[39] From this time onward, "democracy" became a more positive symbol in Lenin's polemical vocabulary, but this concession in language was to have slight effect on his organizational principles and Party structure. If more autonomy was accorded to local Party organs, if more Party officials were elected from below, rather than appointed from above, this was not, in the long run, to alter the hard core of Lenin's autocratic centralism which was destined to register a total victory under Stalin.

While placating the demand for autonomy, the Party remained unalterably opposed to federalism. In the spring of 1905 the Third Party Congress, a purely Bolshevik affair, again condemned federalism,[40] and on the basis of the resolution, Lenin appealed to the Bund to mend its ways.[41] The reconciliation of dissident factions was speeded up by the 1905 Revolution in which the activity of the masses blurred factional lines. As a result, the Party held a Fourth or Unity Congress at Stockholm in the spring of 1906. Lenin's terms for unification were democratic centralism and territorial autonomy, not federalism.[42] Territorial autonomy meant that all the workers of a given territory, regardless of nationality, would be united in a territorial subdivision of the All-Russian Party. In this way the workers would be organized into tidy territorial units which would facilitate firm control from the center; at the same time workers of different nationalities would be mixed together in an effort to weaken national sentiments and so to avoid the splintering of the Party into a federation of national entities. A group of Polish, Lithuanian, and Latvian Social Democrats agreed to join the Party on the basis of territorial autonomy,[43] and the Bund rejoined the Party after acceding to a special, but uneasy, compromise, which did not recognize it as the exclusive representative of all Jewish workers.[44] A decision to admit a group of Armenian

[39] "Pervaia konferentsiia RSDRP," Dec. 25–30, 1905, in *KPSS v. rez.*, I, 99.
[40] "Rezoliutsii III S"ezda RSDRP, 8. Ob otnoshenii k natsional'nym sotsial-demokraticheskim organizatsiiam," April–May, 1905, in Lenin, *Sochineniia*, VII, 435.
[41] Lenin, "K evreiskim rabochim," summer, 1905, in *ibid.*, VIII, 24–26.
[42] Lenin, "Takticheskaia platforma k ob"edinitel'nomu s"ezdu RSDRP," March, 1906, in *ibid.*, IX, 47.
[43] "Usloviia sliianiia SDP i L s RSDRP"; "Proekt uslovii ob"edineniia Lat. SDRP s RSDRP," May, 1906, in *ibid.*, IX, 468–70.
[44] "Proekt usloviia ob"edineniia Bunda s RSDRP," May, 1906, in *ibid.*, IX, 470–71.

Social Democrats on similar terms was taken at the Fifth Party Congress, meeting in London in May, 1907.[45] The strength of federalist sentiment among all these nationalities prevented the faithful execution of these agreements, so that a Party Conference, meeting in December, 1908, found it necessary to scold the groups that had retained federal ties "in spite of the decisions of the Stockholm Congress." The national groups were once more ordered to unify on the basis of territorial autonomy, since the Party "decisively rejects unification on the basis of federalism." [46] Even this did not eliminate federalist influence, and complaints continued to be heard.[47]

The matter finally came to a head in 1912 with a new burst of federalist demands from the Transcaucasian Social Democrats. Lenin decided that unity with non-Leninists had become an unbearable burden and that an end must be put to all compromise. He promptly held a rump Conference of Leninist Social Democrats at Prague, claiming that it was the sole and legal spokesman for the entire Party. The Prague Conference was naturally confined to those of undiluted centralist sentiment.[48]

In reply to this, Trotsky organized the so-called "August Bloc," a loose congeries of forces including the Bund and other federalists.[49] This Bloc was held together by a shared antipathy toward Lenin's rigid orthodoxy and his autocratic methods, but otherwise was too varied and unstable to unite on any positive program. As a result, it soon disintegrated. Lenin interpreted this failure as a vindication of his centralism:

[45] "Priniataia s"ezdom rezoliutsiia ob ob"edinenii s armianskoi s d organizatsiei," May, 1907, in *ibid.*, XI, 536–37.
[46] "Rezoliutsii vserossiiskoi (dekabr'skoi) konferentsii RSDRP, 7. Ob ob"edinenii natsional'nykh organizatsii na mestakh," Dec., 1908, in *ibid.*, XIV, 450. See also "Primechaniia," in *ibid.*, XIV, 487.
[47] Stalin, "Anarkhizm ili sotsializm?" 1907, in *Sochineniia*, I, 349; "Platforma gruppy 'Vperëd,'" early 1910, in Lenin, *Sochineniia*, XIV, 456–57: "Full unity on the local level has not been realized: national parties have not become regional organizations of a single All-Russian Social-Democracy. . . . National centers must be reduced to the status of regional groups." While Lenin criticized the platform of this Bolshevik group in many respects, he did not take issue with the above views. See Lenin, "O 'platforme' storonnikov i zashchitnikov otzovizma," March 19, 1910, in *Sochineniia*, XIV, 291–99.
[48] "Rezoliutsii Prazhskoi konferentsii RSDRP," Jan., 1912, in *ibid.*, XV, 375–76.
[49] Trotsky's "August Bloc" did not consist entirely of federalists. It had four representatives of the Left Polish Social Democrats, whose denunciation of national sentiment was more violent than Lenin's. See Olga Gankin and H. H. Fisher, *The Bolsheviks and the World War* (Stanford, 1940), p. 504, n. 23.

CENTRALISM V. FEDERALISM 203

The destruction of the Party program in favor of the nationalism of the August (1912) Conference of Liquidators, Bundists, and Latvian Social Democrats revealed with especial clarity the full bankruptcy of the federal principles in building a Social Democratic Party, and the profound harm that the parcelization of "national" Social Democratic organizations does to the cause of the proletariat.[50]

Meanwhile Lenin's Bolshevik Party had been successfully reborn. It was this highly centralist vanguard group which was destined both to seize state power in Russia and to project the seizure of state power throughout the world.

PLANS FOR CENTRALISM IN THE ORGANIZATION OF STATE POWER

Lenin's plan for the integration of different national groups in a reshaped Russian state foreshadowed his concept of the integration of nations in a world state. As in the case of the Party, these nations were to be rallied around centralist, not federalist, principles.

The Party Program, adopted at the Second Party Congress in 1903, contained four items that outlined the changes envisaged for the various nations within the Russian Empire, once the Tsarist regime had been replaced by a democratic republic. Three of these, though seemingly federalist in character, were based on strictly centralist assumptions, as Stalin explained in 1904.[51] The fourth was intended as a reluctant gesture in the direction of federalism. The Party Program listed the first three items as:

(3) Broad local self-government and regional self-government for those localities that are distinguished by a special way of life, local conditions and composition of the population.

(7) ... Complete equality of rights for all citizens, regardless of sex, religion, race, or nationality.

(8) The right of the population to receive education in its native language ... and the use of the native language on a par with the state language in all local, public, and state institutions.

If only these basic democratic rights were accorded to those nations presently suffering national oppression, and if allowances were made

[50] "Rezoliutsii soveshchaniia TsK RSDRP s partiinymi rabotnikami," Jan. 14, 1913, in Lenin, *Sochineniia*, XVI, 234.
[51] Stalin, "Kak ponimaet sotsial-demokratiia," in *Sochineniia*, I, 49-50.

in the administrative structure of the state for variations in local conditions, then, it was argued, no further concessions to national sentiment would be needed. This approach pointedly rejected the concept of the state as a federation of national states.

A fourth item in the Party Program held out a somewhat different prospect for the fate of these nations. It was contained in the celebrated Point 9, which demanded "the right of self-determination for all nations living within the state." [52] The severity of Great Russian oppression in the Tsarist Empire had long ago forced Russian Social Democracy to grant at least nominal recognition to the right of the downtrodden nations to determine their own future status, a concession to a centrifugal force which obviously had more federalist than centralist possibilities. The idea of national self-determination had been first introduced in the world socialist movement by Plekhanov at the 1896 Congress of the Second International,[53] and it was accepted by the Russian Social Democratic Labor Party at its founding Congress in 1898.[54] At the Second Party Congress in 1903 Plekhanov explained that the right of self-determination of nations "is obligatory for us as Social Democrats. If we should forget about this right . . . then the battle cry of international social democracy, 'Proletariat of all countries, unite!' would become a shameful lie on our lips." [55] This would indicate that the Party was championing the liberation of oppressed nations as a means of *uniting* the proletariat of all nations. Self-determination was never intended to give unlimited encouragement to the separate national ambitions of any people, but rather was looked upon as a lever for the amalgamation of liberated nations.

The ultimate purpose of self-determination was the integration of all nations under proletarian rule. But what of its immediate utility under the rule of the bourgeoisie? Speaking in 1903, Lenin warned that the recognition of this right "does not commit us to support every demand for national self-determination." The erection of national state barriers breaks the ties between the proletariat of different nations, and strengthens the ties between the proletariat

---

[52] "Programma Rossiiskoi Sotsial-Demokraticheskoi Rabochei Partii, priniataia II s"ezdom," 1903, in Lenin, *Sochineniia*, V, 386.
[53] Lenin, "O prave natsii na samoopredelenie," Feb., 1914, in *ibid.*, XVII, 455.
[54] "Pervyi s"ezd RSDRP," March 13–15, 1898, in *KPSS v rez.*, I, 15.
[55] Quoted in Lenin, "O natsional'noi programme RSDRP," Dec. 28, 1913, in *Sochineniia*, XVII, 120.

CENTRALISM V. FEDERALISM

and the bourgeoisie of the same nation. "We must always and unconditionally strive for the tightest union of the proletariat of all nationalities, and only in some exceptional circumstance should we propose and actively support demands for the creation of a new class state, or for replacing the complete political unity of a state by weaker federative ties." [56] Elsewhere Lenin stated that self-determination might be interpreted as the right of national autonomy within a state, but, again, sanctioning this type of arrangement "would be required only in separate, special circumstances." [57] In 1904 Stalin explained that it was possible for a bourgeois national liberation movement "to prove favorable for the development of the class consciousness of the proletariat.... It is precisely with such possible cases in view that Point 9 was included in our Program." In such cases "nationalities are accorded a right that will prompt them to strive to arrange their national affairs in accordance with their own wishes ('liberate themselves' completely, to secede)." [58] Evidently the meaning of self-determination was not settled, as it could be stretched to connote anything from national autonomy to federation, or even secession and the creation of an independent national state. The sole point clearly made was that any decentralized state structure, or secession, could only be recommended in the most exceptional circumstance, and that generally speaking a centralist state was highly preferable.

Lenin's basic consideration was that "the demand for national self-determination must be *subordinate* to the interests of the class struggle." Building upon the assumption that national self-determination was always conditioned by the interests of the proletariat, Lenin concluded, in July, 1903, that Social Democracy could only have "as its real and chief aim, the use of the principle of self-determination not for peoples and nations, but for the proletariat within each nation." [59] Thus, Lenin said that he was really not talking about the self-determination of *nations* at all, but only about the self-determination of the proletariat of each nation. He was not interested in the will of a nation, but only in the *class will* of the

[56] Lenin, "Natsional'nyi vopros v nashei programme," July 15, 1903, in *ibid.*, V, 337.
[57] Lenin, "O manifeste armianskikh sotsial-demokratov," Feb. 1, 1903, in *ibid.*, V, 243.
[58] Stalin, "Kak ponimaet sotsial-demokratiia," in *Sochineniia*, I, 49–50.
[59] Lenin, "Natsional'nyi vopros v nashei programme," in *Sochineniia*, V, 337–38.

proletariat of a nation. And who would interpret this class will? Obviously the Party elite, and in the last analysis, Lenin himself. It would be more accurate to call Lenin's 1903 formula not a policy of self-determination of a nation's state form, but a policy of *Lenin's* determination of a nation's state form. While this might appear to be an extraordinary conclusion, it should come as no surprise to those familiar with the Jacobin tradition.

Lenin's specific interpretations of self-determination at this time were strictly centralist. He told the Armenian Social Democrats that they "must remove from their Program the demand for a *federal* republic and limit their demands to a democratic republic in general." [60] The right-wing Polish Socialists were denounced for their unqualified demand for the secession of Poland from Russia, and the Russian Social Revolutionaries came under attack for advocating the transformation of the Russian Empire into a federal state.[61] Similarly, Stalin rejected the demands by Georgian and Armenian Social Democrats for a federal structure of the future Russian state. Stalin explained that the phrases in the Party Program about local and regional self-government made the demand for a federation superfluous.

You want specified localities to have the right to apply *general* state laws to their own peculiar conditions? If that is so, if that is the substance of your demand. . . . we have nothing against it. We do not doubt that different localities of the Russian state, distinguished from one another by their way of life, local conditions, and the composition of the population, cannot all apply the state constitution alike, that such localities need the right to apply the general state constitution in that *form* which will be most useful.[62]

This centralist argument of 1904 clearly adumbrated Stalin's formula of two decades later, i.e., "national in form, socialist in content."

THE REJECTION OF NATIONAL CULTURAL AUTONOMY

The centralists also found it necessary to combat the Austro-Marxist theory of national autonomy, which spread with increasing approval during the first decade of the twentieth century among

[60] Lenin, "O manifeste armianskikh," in *ibid.*, V, 243.
[61] Lenin, "Natsional'nyi vopros v nashei programme," in *ibid.*, V, 338.
[62] Stalin, "Kak ponimaet sotsial-demokratiia," in *Sochineniia*, I, 45 (first italics, Stalin's; second italics added).

the federalist circles of Russian Social Democracy. The intermixture of nationalities in the Austro-Hungarian Empire prevented any clear division of its territory into a federation of national states, without leaving sizable national minorities within each constituent unit. Federalist thought among Austrian Social Democrats therefore turned to a conception of national cultural autonomy, whereby the political and economic unity of the multinational state would be preserved, but within it the members of each nationality would receive full rights of cultural autonomy. These rights were to inhere in the individual of a given nationality, regardless of where he lived within the state, rather than to belong solely to those members of a nationality who lived within a specific territorial subdivision. This plan appealed strongly to the Bund, for the Russian Jews were everywhere a minority people, and therefore without territorial ambitions in a future Russian state. By 1912 this idea had also taken hold in the Transcaucasus, where there was also an extensive mixture of ethnic stocks.[63]

The advocates of national cultural autonomy within the state were likewise supporters of federalism within the Party, and the combined impact of these views impelled Lenin to reassert his centralism in respect to both Party and state. In addition to his drastic expulsion of the federalists from the Party in 1912, Lenin was equally vigorous in denouncing his opponents of centralism in the state, above all, the partisans of national cultural autonomy. Lenin did this both through his own writings and by making use of Stalin who, as a native Georgian and as a centralist, could more effectively counter the views of the Transcaucasian federalists.

Stalin attempted to destroy the concept of national cultural autonomy by defining it out of existence. He postulated that "a nation is a historically evolved, stable community of people, arising on the basis of a common language, territory, economic life, and psychological makeup, manifesting itself in a community of culture." [64] This formulation sought to check the "exaggerated"

---

[63] For the views of the Austro-Marxist theorists Bauer and Renner and the Bundist Medem, see Velikovskii and Levin, eds., *Natsional'nyi vopros*, I, 7-10, 18-39, 137-39, 146-71; Robert A. Kann, *The Multinational Empire* (New York. 1950), I, 44-45, 103-8, 194-95; II, 40-51, 154-78. For the debate among the Transcaucasian Marxists, see Mary Matossian, "Two Marxist Approaches to Nationalism," *American Slavic*, XVI, No. 4 (Dec., 1957), 489-500.

[64] Stalin, "Marksizm i natsional'nyi vopros," Jan., 1913, in *Sochineniia*, II, 296 (italics omitted).

definition of nationalism inherent in personal cultural autonomy by insisting that a nation must inhabit a common territory and participate in a common economic life. The proletariat, Stalin reasoned, must not seek to extend nationalism, which was only the product of rising capitalism, but rather must look forward to a state form in which the workers of all nations would be organized along lines facilitating the operation of a highly integrated, highly centralized economy, unencumbered by the disintegrative pulls of separate nationalisms.

Stalin's principles for the organization of state power were the same as Lenin's terms for the organization of the Party: namely, democratic centralism and territorial autonomy. If only each nation were granted the basic democratic rights to use its own language, possess its own schools, have assured its freedom of conscience, and maintain its own habits and customs without the threat or use of force being exerted on it by some powerful neighboring nation, then the cry for special institutional safeguards, such as national autonomy or a federation of national states, would vanish overnight.[65] Stalin argued that

> the advantage of regional autonomy consists, first of all, in the fact that it does not deal with a fiction deprived of territory, but with a definite population inhabiting a definite territory. Secondly, it does not divide people according to nation, it does not strengthen national partitions; on the contrary, it only serves to break down these national partitions and unites the population in such a manner as to open the way for . . . division according to class. Finally, it provides the opportunity of utilizing the natural wealth of a region and of developing its productive forces in the best possible way . . . functions which are not suitable to national cultural autonomy.[66]

In 1913 Lenin elaborated the meaning of democratic centralism and territorial autonomy. "Marxists, it stands to reason, are hostile to federation and decentralization," but, Lenin added, this should not sanction a centralism that would be confused with the arbitrary rule of the Tsarist bureaucracy. "It is essential to remember that while insisting upon centralism, we insist exclusively upon *democratic* centralism."[67] This would "*not* exclude local self-government in an autonomous territory, set up because of its peculiar

---

[65] *Ibid.*, II, 310, 362–63.   [66] *Ibid.*, II, 361–62.
[67] Lenin, "Kriticheskie zametki po natsional'nomu voprosu," Oct., 1913, in *Sochineniia*, XVII, 154.

CENTRALISM V. FEDERALISM

economic and traditional circumstances, or due to the national composition of its population, etc." On the contrary, democratic centralism meant both central control and limited self-government in a territorial unit. Lenin then indicated what types of matters should fall within each jurisdiction.

> Marxists must recognize that all the most important and essential questions concerned with the operation of capitalist society must not be within the jurisdiction of the autonomous assemblies of the separate regions, but belong exclusively to the central government. Questions of this category should include: tariff policy, trade and industrial legislation, the means of communication and transportation (the railroads, post, telegraph, telephone, etc.), the military establishments, the tax system, civil and criminal laws, general principles of education . . . legislation about safeguards for labor, about political freedom (the right of association), etc., etc.[68]

Those questions falling within the jurisdiction of local authorities would be matters of purely local significance, *as determined by the central government.* "The central government will define the boundaries of the autonomous regions, and limit the jurisdiction of the autonomous assemblies." [69] In questions of state structure as in questions of Party organization, Lenin's democratic centralism was preoccupied with centralism and very little concerned with democracy. What Lenin objected to was the "bureaucratic interference in *purely* local (regional, national, etc.) affairs," since this serves as "one of the greatest obstacles to economic and political development in general, and especially one of the obstacles to *centralism* in important, large, and basic matters." [70] The purpose of eliminating the arbitrary interference of the centralized bureaucracy was really to increase the efficient operation of the whole economy, and thereby to aid centralism.

A SINGLE UNIVERSAL CULTURE AND THE FUSION OF
NATIONS

If the workers were not to be encouraged to foster their own national cultures, then what type of culture should they have? Lenin explained that while he was opposed to any sort of national oppression that would forcibly deprive a nation of a right to express itself in accordance with its own national traditions, that did not mean

[68] *Ibid.,* XVII, 155.   [69] *Ibid.,* XVII, 158–59.   [70] *Ibid.,* XVII, 156.

that national cultures should necessarily be sanctioned as good and progressive forces. "As to a struggle *for* any sort of national development, *for* a 'national culture' in general," Lenin answered: "unconditionally no." [71] "We are against national culture—as one of the slogans of bourgeois nationalism. *We are for an international culture of a thoroughly democratic and socialist proletariat.*" Lenin foresaw the creation of an "*international* culture, in which only a part of each national culture will enter, namely, only the consistently democratic and socialist content of each national culture." [72] The whole course of history was moving toward this objective "since the entire economic, political, and spiritual life of mankind has become more and more internationalized under capitalism. Socialism will internationalize it completely." [73] A Party resolution of October, 1913, alleged that the process of forming the future world culture was already underway: "the world-wide worker's movement creates and, with every passing day, develops more and more the international (world) culture of the proletariat." [74]

Talk of a future international culture raised loud protests from the Bund which had supported the idea of national cultural autonomy as a means of preventing the cultural assimilation of nations. Lenin quickly retorted that he favored the assimilation of nations, defining assimilation as "the loss of national characteristics and the subsequent transition into a new nation." Such a development was inherent in the basic economic forces bred by capitalism, which simultaneously produced two contradictory historical tendencies. One was the awakening of national life and the fight to throw off every sort of national yoke. During this phase the proletariat must insist upon equal rights for all nations and their national cultures, so as to destroy all national privileges of the past. The second phase was that of mature capitalism "in the process of being transformed into a socialist society." This phase expressed "a universal historical tendency to break down national barriers, to wipe out national differences, a tendency toward the *assimilation* of nations, which with each decade becomes all the more powerful, and which presents

[71] *Ibid.*, XVII, 146.
[72] Lenin, "Proekt platformy k IV s"ezdu sotsial-demokratii Latyshskogo Kraia," Nov. 20, 1913, in *Sochineniia*, XVII, 66.
[73] Lenin, "Tezisy po natsional'nomu voprosu," July, 1913, in *ibid.*, XVI, 510.
[74] Lenin, "Rezoliutsii letnego 1913 goda soveshchaniia TsK RSDRP," Oct. 5–14, 1913, in *ibid.*, XVII, 12.

one of the greatest moving forces transforming capitalism into socialism." Such a process represented "the greatest historical progress." [75] Thus, as early as 1913, Lenin projected the ultimate fusion of all nations under the world rule of socialism. It is clear that Lenin intended this to be a unitary, centralized world state, with a single world culture, not a diversified, decentralized, federalized world state, consisting of many distinct national cultures.

LENIN'S DEFINITION OF NATIONAL SELF-DETERMINATION

Lenin's thinking on the methods of achieving this future integration of nations also became more concrete. In July, 1913, he clarified the meaning of self-determination of nations by two important innovations, which the Party formally adopted at a Conference in October, 1913. The first extended the exercise of the right of self-determination from the proletariat of each nation to the entire national population, which would determine its future by means of a plebiscite. Now Lenin asserted that a nation should determine its future status "exclusively on the basis of a general, direct, equal, and secret voting of the population of a given territory."

His second refinement established the previously unsettled meaning of self-determination as the right of secession. As recently as January, 1913, Stalin had declared that the meaning of self-determination "must not be restricted, it may include both autonomy and federation, as well as secession." [76] But now Lenin stipulated: "The right of self-determination can only be interpreted to mean the *political* right of self-determination, i.e., the right of separation and the formation of an independent state." [77] This squeezed the concept of self-determination into a neater, more manageable package. It also produced a sharper weapon against the theory of national cultural autonomy, which did not challenge the political unity of a state, and so, in effect, denied the right of secession. If such a state were divided into oppressor and oppressed nations, a denial of the right to secede might mean an indefinite sanction of this injustice. Lenin did not want to throw away the tremendous psychological appeal of the right to form an independent national state, nor did

[75] Lenin, "Kriticheskie zametki," in *ibid.*, XVII, 139-40.
[76] Stalin, "Na puti k natsionalizmu," Jan. 25, 1913, in *Sochineniia*, II, 286.
[77] Lenin, "Tezisy po natsional'nomu voprosu," in *Sochineniia*, XVI, 507-8. See also, Lenin, "Rezoliutsii letnego 1913 goda," in *ibid.*, XVII, 12.

he want to lose his freedom to maneuver this right by denying its use, especially during the incipient, disintegrative phase of capitalist development when the acceleration of national movements might advance the class struggle.

Both of these innovations appeared to be gestures toward democracy and away from centralism. But a closer examination revealed that the Party had not abdicated its former guiding role. The mere recognition of the right of self-determination must not "be confused with the question of the expediency of the secession of this or that nation." The Party must make the decision "in each individual case, taken separately from the point of view of the interests of the general development of society and the interests of the class struggle of the proletariat for socialism." [78] Lenin drew the analogy that "the *right* of nations to secede in no way precludes *agitation* against secession by Marxists of a particular *oppressed* nation, just as the recognition of the right of divorce does not preclude agitation against divorce in a particular case." [79]

It was equally clear that Lenin did not consider the right of self-determination incompatible with the goal of a centralized world state:

To defend this right does in no way mean to encourage the formation of small states, but on the contrary it leads to a freer, more fearless, and therefore wider and more universal formation of larger states and unions of states which are more advantageous for the masses and more in accord with economic development.[80]

Lenin believed that the very offer of self-determination would inspire such confidence in the formerly oppressed nations that they would voluntarily choose not to exercise this right, but would rather speedily enter a new and larger union of nations. The only reason the Bolsheviks demanded the right of self-determination is

not because we dream of an economically atomized world, nor because we cherish the ideal of small states, but on the contrary because we are for larger states, and for a drawing together, even a fusion of nations, but on a truly democratic, truly international basis, which is *unthinkable* without the freedom of separation.[81]

[78] Lenin, "Rezoliutsii letnego 1913 goda," in *ibid.*, XVII, 13.
[79] Lenin, "O prave natsii na samoopredelenie," in *ibid.*, XVII, 472.
[80] Lenin, "Sotsializm i voina," Aug., 1915, in *ibid.*, XVIII, 206.
[81] Lenin, "Revoliutsionnyi proletariat i pravo natsii na samoopredelenie," Nov., 1915, in *ibid.*, XVIII, 328.

CENTRALISM V. FEDERALISM

Lenin realized that this renewed interest in self-determination would activate federalist sentiment. He admitted that while, fundamentally, "the right of self-determination is an *exception* to our general premise of centralism," it must nevertheless be carefully dissociated from federalism. The meaning of self-determination had been strictly confined to the right of state secession, which the Party would agitate for or against as each case required. "Do not think that you have a *'right'* to federation," Lenin wrote a colleague. "We are in principle against federation—it weakens the economic bond, it is unsuitable for a unified state." [82] Viewed in its historical perspective, Lenin insisted, the present "large, centralized state is an immense historical step forward from the dispersal of political power in feudal times to the future socialist unity of the whole world." [83] The future socialist world state should not regress by introducing federalism.

THE BOLSHEVIK CONCEPTION OF FEDERALISM

In denouncing "the philistine ideal of federation," [84] Lenin revealed his own understanding, or misunderstanding, of this concept. "Federation is a union of equals, a union demanding general agreement. Under these conditions, how can one side expect that the other side will always agree with it? This is absurd." [85] Or again: "the right to federation is, in general, an absurdity, as federation is a two-sided agreement." [86] Lenin was actually describing a league of sovereign states, in which each state holds a veto power over every act, so that nothing can be accomplished except by continual general agreement. Such a condition does not prevail in a federal structure where certain matters of overriding importance fall under the exclusive and unimpeded jurisdiction of the federal government, while other matters are reserved for the jurisdiction of the constituent states. Apparently this idea of a division of authority was so repulsive to Lenin that he had either erected a mental block against it, and so entirely failed to understand it, or he purposely exaggerated the weakness inherent in a delimitation

---

[82] Lenin, "Pis'mo S. G. Shaumianu," in *ibid.*, XVII, 90.
[83] Lenin, "Kriticheskie zametki," in *ibid.*, XVII, 154.
[84] Lenin, "O natsional'noi gordosti velikorussov," Dec. 12, 1914, in *ibid.*, XVIII, 82.
[85] Lenin, "Pis'mo S. G. Shaumianu," in *ibid.*, XVII, 90.
[86] Lenin, "O prave natsii na samoopredelenie," in *ibid.*, XVII, 463.

of authority, so as to ridicule and discredit the idea of federation.

Stalin's grasp of federalism was equally appalling. He displayed this ignorance most conspicuously in an essay on federalism in March, 1917, which included this rather startling account of the origin and development of the federal government of the United States. Stalin insisted that American federalism arose when

> in the sixties of the nineteenth century a break in the political life of the country occurred; the northern states demanded a closer political union in spite of the protests of "centralism" from the southern states, which reflected the old order. The "Civil War" broke out and the North won. A *federation* was created in America, that is, a union of sovereign states . . . but such an order did not last long. Federation proved to be just as transitional a measure as was confederation. The struggle between the states and the central government continued, dual power became unbearable, and as a result of further evolution the United States was transformed from a federation into a unitary state.[87]

Federalism could only be "a transitional form," Stalin explained, "since the development of capitalism in its highest forms is bound up with the expansion of the territorial framework of the economy, and with it comes a centralizing tendency, which demands not federation, but a unitary form of state life." It was imperative that the Bolsheviks "take account of this tendency if we do not want to turn back the wheels of history." [88]

Lenin left only a tiny crack through which federalism might enter the structure of the future socialist state. On several occasions prior to the Bolshevik Revolution, he noted that Marx and Engels, though partisans of a centralist, unitary state, had considered federation as a step forward in certain exceptional circumstances involving conflicts between national groups (recommending, for example, a federation of Ireland and England).[89] But Lenin gave no indication that he intended to apply the federal principle freely; if possible he would resist its application altogether.

On the very eve of the Bolshevik Revolution Lenin wrote in *State and Revolution* that "federalism arises, as a principle, from the petty-bourgeois views of anarchism" of Proudhon and Bakunin.

[87] Stalin, "Protiv federalizma," March 28, 1917, in *Sochineniia*, III, 24–25.
[88] *Ibid.*, III, 25.
[89] Lenin, "Revoliutsionnyi proletariat i pravo natsii na samoopredelenie," in *Sochineniia*, XVIII, 325; Lenin, "Sotsialisticheskaia revoliutsiia i pravo natsii na samoopredelenie," March, 1916, in *ibid.*, XIX, 40; Lenin, "Gosudarstvo i revoliutsiia," Aug.–Sept., 1917, in *ibid.*, XXI, 418–19.

CENTRALISM V. FEDERALISM

Following the destruction of the bourgeois state, the proletariat will not be organized on the principle of a free federation of communes, but on the principle "of voluntary centralism, of a voluntary union of communes." Those who found it difficult to accept this view were dismissed as "philistines," who "can only imagine centralism as coming from above, imposed and maintained solely by means of bureaucracy and militarism." [90]

LENIN'S STRUGGLE WITH THE RITUALISTIC CENTRALISTS

Lenin's fight with the federalists was only half the story. Oddly enough, he also found it necessary to dispute with equal vehemence the beliefs of a group of doctrinaire centralists, who denied that the right of national self-determination could have any meaning whatever for the proletariat. At the beginning of the First World War this extreme centralist opposition had developed around two groups: in Russian circles, around Bukharin and Piatakov, and in the left wing of Polish Social Democracy, around Radek and Rosa Luxemburg.

Radek feared that agitation for self-determination of nations would deflect the proletariat from its struggle for a world socialist revolution and lead it to defend "the anachronistic ideal of national states." [91] The imperialist era of capitalism had already "outgrown the framework of national states," and it was the duty of socialism to abolish national states altogether. "*Social Democracy must not advocate under any conditions either the erection of new boundary posts in Europe or the reestablishment of those destroyed by imperialism.*" The proletariat could only cry "*down with boundaries!*" [92] The advanced countries that were ripe for socialism, that is Europe and North America, would form one great socialist state, immediately renounce all colonies and, by abolishing colonial oppression, hasten the attraction of the backward areas into a socialist world state.

This impatience with national boundaries was perhaps an exaggerated expression of the Marxist belief that it was class and not

---
[90] Lenin, "Gosudarstvo i revoliutsiia," in *ibid.*, XXI, 406.
[91] Quoted in Lenin, "Revoliutsionnyi proletariat i pravo natsii na samoopredelenie," in *ibid.*, XVIII, 323.
[92] "Tezisy ob imperializme i natsional'nom ugnetenii 'Gazety rabotnichei,'" Oct., 1916, in *ibid.*, XIX, 438-39.

nation that decided everything. The federalists had tempered this view by insisting that nations were serious entities, whose existence deserved respect, apart from considerations of the class struggle. The extreme centralists, on the other hand, wished to organize the future socialist state upon centralist principles, dictated purely by economic considerations. The Polish centralists conceded that a nation might possess "the character of a cultural and linguistic unit," but that it could not form the basis of an economic-political unit, since the territorial subdivision of the socialist state "can result only by virtue of the demands of production."

If self-determination of nations was meaningless under socialism, it was all the more senseless under capitalism. A "national" policy was, in reality, only the policy of a ruling class of a nation, and could not express the interests of the proletariat. In any event, capitalist control of the press, schools, and church rendered the proletariat incapable of making a wise choice about the future of its nation. Doubtless mindful of the traditional hatred between Poles and Russians, these Polish extremists thought it senseless to preach the right of secession of Poland from Russia, based upon the unrealistic expectation that a liberated Poland would immediately seek re-union with its former oppressor. They did not want to risk the chance of dismembering a large economic unit by entrusting the fate of Poland, or any other nation, to a plebiscite. "It is totally impossible to make the will of nations a deciding factor in questions concerning the changing of boundaries, as the so-called right of self-determination demands." [93]

Lenin stigmatized these sneerings at the national problem as "Imperialist Economism." They supposedly represented a revival, in

[93] Theses of the Luxemburgist organ of Polish Social Democracy, "Tak nazyvaemoe pravo natsii na samoopredelenie," April, 1916, in Velikovskii and Levin, eds., *Natsional'nyi vopros*, I, 317–18. A distinction must be drawn between the theories for the organization of a socialist state offered by the Austrian and the Polish Social Democrats. The theories present superficial similarities, since the Austrian theory of national cultural autonomy assumed that a nation would only form a cultural-linguistic unit and not an economic-political unit in the socialist state. However, this plan was devised for an area of hopelessly intermixed ethnic groups, and so represented a maximal claim for all national groups (since the formation of economic-political units based on nations would necessarily have sacrificed the interests of some national minorities). The plan of left-wing Polish Social Democracy, on the other hand, denied that a nation should form the basis of an economic-political unit under any circumstances—even if a nation formed a coherent territorial bloc untroubled by national minorities. This represented a minimal claim for national entities. See also *ibid.*, I, 139–41, 215–46, 312–24, 382–91.

CENTRALISM V. FEDERALISM

the era of imperialism, of that school of socialist "Economists" who were so concerned with the economic struggle against capitalism that they tended to dismiss the importance of all noneconomic factors. Lenin denied "that 'only' 'economics' is important for Marxists," since this distorts "Marxism into a caricature." "Although based on economics, socialism is by no means exclusively economics." [94]

The Polish opposition, however, did not repudiate the political struggle; just the contrary, it looked upon world revolution as the only solution for all present disorders, the national problem included. But they dismissed nationalism and national oppression as by-products of class warfare. These phenomena would simply evaporate under a socialist society, which, by definition, would remove all forms of oppression. In the interim, the problems of nationalism should not divert the efforts of the workers from making a socialist revolution.

It would seem that Lenin had become more sensitive to the realities and complexities of the national problem and had tried to make systematic allowances for these forces in the body of his Marxist doctrine. He protested that nations could not be wished out of existence, and so "the proletariat cannot pass over in silence the question of state *boundaries* based on national oppression." [95] "The slogan, 'down with boundaries,' is an utter absurdity." [96] National boundaries exist, and so long as they remain, they must be determined by the will of the nation involved. Lenin pointed out that Radek demanded an end to annexations and a renunciation of colonies, yet he sanctioned the perpetuation of past annexations in Europe by opposing the restoration of boundaries based upon the freely expressed will of nations. Poland, in particular, must be offered the right to secede (a right that need not be used), for otherwise Social Democracy would be identified with the Tsarist Great Russian annexationists.

Self-determination was not only obligatory for nations under socialism, but it was fully feasible under capitalism. Lenin cited the peaceful secession of Norway from Sweden in 1905 as a successful example of self-determination under capitalism, and added that

[94] Lenin, "Itogi diskussii o samoopredelenii," autumn, 1916, in *Sochineniia*, XIX, 244–45.
[95] Lenin, "Sotsialisticheskaia revoliutsiia i pravo natsii na samoopredelenie," in *ibid.*, XIX, 41.
[96] Lenin, "Rech' po natsional'nomu voprosu," May 12, 1917, in *ibid.*, XX, 277.

a slight change in the great power relations might easily cause "the formation of new states, Polish, Indian, etc." [97] He admitted that the right of self-determination was not an absolute, self-sufficient demand, but was only a small part of the whole program for socialism. "Possibly, in individual concrete cases the part may contradict the whole; if so, it must be rejected." [98] It is doubtful if this argument won over any of those who already considered self-determination a meaningless and unreliable doctrine.

The debate with Rosa Luxemburg provided another insight into Lenin's view of the role that nation-states would play in their development toward a world state. History unfolds by stages, and the stage of rising capitalism is identified with the rise of independent national states. Lenin pinpointed the era for the creation of national states in Western Europe as lying between 1789 and 1871. "In Eastern Europe and in Asia the period of bourgeois democratic revolutions started only in 1905. . . . It is precisely and solely because Russia and the neighboring countries are passing through this epoch that we need an item in our Program on the right of nations to self-determination." [99] Lenin expressed doubt as to "whether Asia will have time before the downfall of capitalism to become crystallized into a system of independent national states like Europe." At least, "the tendency of these movements is toward the creation of national states in Asia," the prototype being Japan, which was both the most-developed capitalist state and the only independent national state in Asia.[100] The birth of capitalist nation-states must not be rejected out of hand, since this was but the first stage in their life cycle. Elsewhere in the world the death of capitalist nation-states was well underway. Eventually, all capitalist nation-states would be transformed into a socialist world state, but each nation was moving toward this common destiny at its own rate, and in an often seemingly contradictory way.

Most of the arguments advanced by the Polish opposition were also voiced by Bukharin and Piatakov. In addition, the latter raised

[97] Lenin, "Sotsialisticheskaia revoliutsiia i pravo natsii na samoopredelenie," in *ibid.*, XIX, 38.
[98] Lenin, "Itogi diskussii o samoopredelenii," in *ibid.*, XIX, 256–58.
[99] Lenin, "O prave natsii na semoopredelenie," in *ibid.*, XVII, 435–36. At this point Lenin held that the Western European Social Democratic Parties need not have a provision for self-determination in their programs, though later he insisted that the principle of self-determination should be recognized by all of Europe.
[100] *Ibid.*, XVII, 430–31.

CENTRALISM V. FEDERALISM

one objection to self-determination which Lenin was hard-pressed to answer. At the Zimmerwald Conference in September, 1915, Lenin had urged that the World War be transformed into an international class war, by initiating a civil war between classes within each nation.[101] Bukharin and Piatakov claimed that this demand was rendered meaningless if the proletariat must cooperate with the bourgeoisie in fighting for the reestablishment of independent nation-states, determined by a national, not a class, will. Either the proletariat fights a civil war against its own bourgeoisie, or it fights in the defense of a bourgeois state, in which case it is defending the "fatherland" in the same manner as the "social chauvinists." The proletariat must assume an attitude of *"indifference* with respect to the 'fatherland,' to the 'nation,'" since it is absurd to believe in "the 'liberation of nations' *within* the realm of capitalist civilization." They granted that in backward and colonial countries where capitalism was very little developed, it was necessary to support movements for national liberation. This would weaken the bourgeois imperial powers in Europe, without undermining the struggle for socialism, since the proletariat in these areas was almost nonexistent. But wherever there was a well-developed proletarian movement, as in Europe, talk of "liberating nations" would kill the prospect of class warfare.[102]

Lenin countered with the bald assertion that "without a really *democratic* organization of relations among nations, and consequently without the freedom of state secession—a civil war of the workers and the toiling masses of all nations against the bourgeoisie is *impossible.*"[103] Just how, or why, self-determination of nations would precipitate an international civil war Lenin did not say. Furthermore, Lenin defended self-determination for capitalist Europe on the rather curious grounds that self-determination was one of the general demands of democracy and that no aspect of democracy could be abrogated in the process of working toward socialism, which represented the highest fulfillment of democracy.

---

[101] Lenin, "Vsemirnaia voina i zadachi sotsial-demokratii," Sept. 5–8, 1915, in *Sochineniia*, XVIII, 417.
[102] Bukharin and Piatakov, "Tezisy o lozunge prava natsii na samoopredelenie," Nov., 1915, in Velikovskii and Levin, eds., *Natsional'nyi vopros*, I, 358–60. See also *ibid.*, I, 356–57, 404–7, 417–18; "Proekt rezoliutsii po natsional'nomu voprosu, predlozhennyi G. Piatakovym," April, 1917, in Lenin, *Sochineniia*, XX, 625–26.
[103] Lenin, "Otvet P. Kievskomu (Iu. Piatakovu)," Aug.–Sept., 1916, in *ibid.*, XXX, 261.

Again, Lenin did not indicate in what way the application of this democratic right of self-determination would hasten the advent of socialism.

Behind these polemical sparrings lay Lenin's expectation that nations would not exercise the right of self-determination, once it had been offered, so that, practically speaking, this right would not interfere with the proletarian struggle for socialism. Lenin held that the mere offer of self-determination would dissipate the demand for its use. Simply posing the right of secession would be such a demonstration of democracy that it would dispel national animosities and create a feeling of mutual confidence among nations, which would then see the wisdom of remaining united. He predicted that "the more closely the democratic structure of the state comes to providing complete freedom of secession, the rarer and the weaker will these strivings for secession be in practice; for the advantages of large states, both from the point of view of economic progress and from the point of view of the interest of the masses, are beyond doubt." [104] Although Lenin was more aware of the difficulties of the national problem than was his extreme centralist opposition, he still grossly underestimated the strength of nationalism. He failed to foresee the impact that national feelings would exert upon the organization of society under a bourgeois democratic regime, as well as under future Soviet rule. Stalin shared this shortcoming, for as late as May, 1917, he said, with reference to the Russian Empire, that "after the overthrow of Tsarism nine tenths of the nationalities will not want to secede." [105]

The ultimate purpose of granting the right of secession was to create a socialist world state based on the consent of the constituent nations. Lenin demanded that bourgeois governments grant "the colonies complete *freedom* of secession," promising that "we *shall grant* it when we ourselves are in power." However, "when we demand freedom of secession for the Mongolians, Persians, Egyptians, and *all* oppressed and disfranchised nations without exception, *we do so, not because we want them to secede*, but *only because* we are in favor of a *free, voluntary*, and not a forcible coming together and amalgamation of nations." Lenin anticipated that this amalga-

[104] Lenin, "Sotsialisticheskaia revoliutsiia i pravo natsii na samoopredelenie," in *ibid.*, XIX, 39–40.
[105] Stalin, "VII (aprel'skaia) konferentsiia RSDRP(b)," May 12, 1917, in *Sochineniia*, III, 53.

CENTRALISM V. FEDERALISM

mation of socialist nations would start among the advanced nations and then spread to the backward areas of the world. "The Poles and Finns are highly cultured," and if they should decide to secede, "the secession of Poland and Finland, after the victory of socialism, can only be of very short duration. The Egyptian fellaheens, the Mongolians and the Persians, who are infinitely less cultured, may secede for a longer period; but we shall try to shorten this period by unselfish aid." [106]

Because of the different heritages of the oppressor and the oppressed nations, "the road to the single goal, to full equality, the closest intimacy, and the subsequent *fusion of all* nations obviously proceeds by different concrete routes," and calls for different attitudes on the part of the proletariat of different nations. Thus, Lenin proposed the seemingly contradictory formulas: "Social Democrats of oppressing nations must insist on 'freedom to *secede*,' while Social Democrats of oppressed nations must insist on 'freedom to *unite*.'" [107] On the very brink of seizing power in October, 1917, Lenin added one final clarifying note about this future amalgamation of nations. He explained that he had not issued a demand "for unification of states in general." On the contrary, "social revolution demands the unification *only* of those states which have gone over or are going over to socialism, colonies which are gaining their freedom, etc." [108] The processes of secession and amalgamation were to be applied selectively, in order to produce the disintegration of the capitalist nation-state system and the subsequent formation of a socialist world state.

NATIONAL SELF-DETERMINATION REINTERPRETED

The metal of these theories on the amalgamation of nations was soon tested by the fire of revolution. How much of this grand scheme was tempered and hardened, and how much was melted into a new and almost unrecognizable form?

Lenin had predicted that amalgamation would proceed on the basis of voluntary centralism. By the term "voluntary" he clearly

[106] Lenin, "O karikature na marksizm i ob 'imperialisticheskom ekonomizme,'" Oct., 1916, in *Sochineniia*, XIX, 228.
[107] Lenin, "Itogi diskussii o samoopredelenii," in *ibid.*, XIX, 261-62.
[108] Lenin, "K peresmotru partiinoi programmy," Oct. 19-21, 1917, in *ibid.*, XXI, 316-17.

denoted the will of an entire nation expressed in the form of a plebiscite. The day after the seizure of power, Lenin stated that a nation must be "given the right to determine the form of its state life by free voting." Otherwise any union consummated "without the precisely, clearly, and willingly expressed consent and desire of that nation" would be considered a "forcible annexation."[109] This was quickly followed by the Declaration of Rights of the Peoples of Russia of November 15, 1917, signed by Lenin and Stalin, granting "the right of free self-determination of peoples, even to the point of secession and the formation of an independent state."[110]

When applied to the concrete historical situation, the meaning of "the will of a nation" underwent a fundamental transformation. At first the shift was almost imperceptible, but within a few months it became quite clear. Perhaps this can best be illustrated by the Soviet attitude toward Finland. On November 27, 1917, Stalin told the Finnish Social Democratic Party:

> We would not be democrats (to say nothing of socialists) if we did not recognize the right of self-determination for the peoples of Russia. I declare that we can bring about socialism only if we exert every effort to build up brotherly confidence between the Finnish and Russian workers. But it is obvious that it is impossible to create such confidence without decisive recognition of the right of free self-determination for the Finnish people.[111]

What did this mean, to speak at one moment in terms of the Finnish workers, and in the next moment in terms of the Finnish people? Was it a slip, or could it possibly mean that only the workers were "the people"? In a statement of November 30, 1917, Stalin still maintained that "the will of the nation is defined by referendum or by a national constituent assembly."[112] On December 16, 1917, the

[109] Lenin, "Doklad o mire," Nov. 8, 1917, in *ibid.*, XXII, 13–14.
[110] "Deklaratsiia prav narodov Rossii," Nov. 15, 1917, *Izvestiia*, Nov. 16, 1917, p. 4.
[111] Stalin, "Rech' na s"ezde Finliandskoi Sotsial-Demokraticheskoi Rabochei Partii v Gel'singforse," Nov. 27, 1917, in *Sochineniia*, IV, 3.
[112] "Tekst razgovora po priamomu provodu Predstavitelia Sovnarkoma I. Stalina s Predstavitelem TsK USDRP Porshem i oblastnoi organizatsii RSDRP(b) Bakinskim 30 (17) noiabria," in V. Manilov, ed., *1917 god na Kievshchine, khronika sobytii* (Kiev, 1928), p. 532. Excerpts from both of these conversations were reprinted in Stalin, *Stat'i i rechi ob Ukraine* (Kiev, 1936), pp. 14–17, but under a misleading title and incorrect date: "Sovet Narodnykh Komissarov ob Ukraine, beseda s tov. Sergeem Bakinskim, 23 noiabria (6 dekabria) 1917 g.", which was first published in *Pravda* on Nov. 24/Dec. 7, 1917. Neither version is found in Stalin's *Sochineniia*.

CENTRALISM V. FEDERALISM

Council of People's Commissars assured the entire Finnish people that its national wishes would be respected: "Against the bourgeois Finnish Republic, which still remains bourgeois, we have not taken one step in the sense of limiting its national rights or the national independence of the Finnish people, and we shall take no such steps." [113] Soviet Russia formally recognized the independence of the Finnish Republic on December 31, 1917.

It soon became apparent that the bourgeois Finnish state had no intentions of abdicating power to a Soviet Finland, which would rejoin Soviet Russia as the nucleus of a Soviet world state. It was to this disagreeable situation that Stalin turned in an address of January 4, 1918. He began with the customary assurance that, "if a people, through its representatives, categorically demands recognition of its independence, then a proletarian government, operating on the principle of self-determination for all peoples, must decide wholly in favor of Finland." This seemed innocuous enough until Stalin suddenly added:

But if we look more closely into the picture of the independence received by Finland, we shall see that in fact the Council of People's Commissars has, contrary to its own wishes, given freedom not to the people, not to the representatives of the Finnish proletariat, but to the Finnish bourgeoisie which by a strange coincidence seized power and received independence from the hands of the socialists of Russia.[114]

Now Stalin openly identified "the people" with "the representatives of the Finnish proletariat," who alone should have received the right of self-determination. It was apparently through some accident that this right had been granted to the entire Finnish nation, contrary to the wishes of the Council of People's Commissars. This evolution in the meaning of "the people" was also occurring elsewhere. For example, as early as December 25, 1917, Stalin had informed a group of Ukrainians that the Council of People's Commissars "is ready to recognize the Republic of any national region of Russia, *on the wishes of the toiling population* of that region." [115]

Rosa Luxemburg considered this shift in emphasis from nation to class as a vindication of her views on self-determination. The Bolsheviks had discovered that they had strengthened the forces of

[113] Lenin, "Manifest k ukrainskomu narodu s ul'timativnymi trebovaniiami k ukrainskoi rade," Dec. 16, 1917, in *Sochineniia*, XXII, 121.
[114] Stalin, "O nezavisimosti Finliandii," Jan. 4, 1918, in *Sochineniia*, IV, 23.
[115] Stalin, "Otvet tovarishcham ukraintsam v tylu i na fronte," Dec. 25, 1917, in *ibid.*, IV, 8 (italics added).

counterrevolution "by their hollow nationalistic phraseology concerning the 'right of self-determination to the point of separation.' . . . By this nationalistic demand they brought on the disintegration of Russia itself and pressed into the enemy's hand the knife which it was to thrust into the heart of the Russian Revolution." She repeated that "under the rule of capitalism there is no self-determination of peoples, that in a class society each class of the nation strives to 'determine itself' in a different fashion." [116] The Soviet leaders had, in reality, shifted their stand on self-determination in the direction of Rosa Luxemburg's. But there was nothing essentially alien to the Leninist tradition in this move, since as early as 1903 Lenin had declared that Social Democracy could only have "as its real and chief aim, the use of the principle of self-determination not for peoples and nations, but for the proletariat within each nation." [117] Subsequently Lenin had talked in terms of self-determination for an entire nation, since this was an effective way of embarrassing the rulers of the bourgeois nation-states. The essential demagoguery of this position was revealed when the Soviet leaders themselves came to the helm of state power and, after a brief but disastrous trial period, rejected the very theory of national self-determination that they had so long and so ardently defended.

THE SOVIET ADOPTION OF FEDERALISM

The shift in the second half of Lenin's premise of "voluntary centralism" was wholly alien to the Leninist tradition. The Soviet leaders reluctantly acknowledged the need of substituting federalism for centralism as the method of amalgamating nations.

A half dozen years after the Bolshevik Revolution, from the vantage point of hindsight, Stalin explained the Soviet acceptance of federalism. He frankly admitted that "the strength of the national movement was much greater, and the road to the unification of nations was much more complicated than had been earlier supposed." Nine tenths of the nationalities of the Russian Empire had not declined secession as Stalin had predicted. Instead, Stalin was obliged to record that "a whole series of nationalities in Russia were, in fact, in a state of complete separation, and in view of this, federation be-

[116] Rosa Luxemburg, *The Russian Revolution*, early 1918, trans. with an Intro. by Bertram D. Wolfe (New York, 1940), pp. 26, 29.
[117] Lenin, "Natsional'nyi vopros v nashei programme," in *Sochineniia*, V, 337.

CENTRALISM V. FEDERALISM

came a step forward . . . to their drawing together, to their unity." He added that the introduction of federalism had not been so disastrous after all, since "the forms of federation created in the Soviet structure were not as contradictory to the aims of the economic unity of the toiling masses of the nationalities of Russia as had earlier been supposed."[118] This strictly ex post facto rationalization had the merit of revealing the basic Soviet attitude toward federalism, once it had been forced upon them, namely: the aim of filling the federalist forms with a centralist content.

The first official hint that federation might be an acceptable solution for the national problem came on November 30, 1917, when Stalin stated that "if the will of a nation should be expressed in favor of a federal Republic, then the government can have nothing against it."[119] On December 16, 1917, Lenin announced that Soviet Russia would be willing to enter into negotiations with the Ukrainian People's Republic "concerning a federative, or some similar, relationship."[120] By December 25, 1917, Stalin acknowledged the willingness of the Council of People's Commissars "to recognize a federal structure for the political life of our country, if the toiling population of the regions of Russia desire it."[121]

This offer was formally embodied in the Declaration of the Rights of the Toiling and Exploited People, authored largely by Lenin, and approved by the Central Executive Committee of the Congress of Soviets on January 16, 1918. It stated that "the Russian Soviet Republic is founded on the basis of a free union of free nations as a federation of Soviet national Republics." It was left "to the workers and peasants of each nation to decide independently, at their own plenipotentiary Soviet Congresses whether or not they desire, and if so, on what conditions, to take part in the federated government and other federal Soviet institutions."[122] The Declaration was first submitted to the Constituent Assembly, which rejected it. After the Soviet government had forcibly dissolved the Constituent Assembly on January 19, 1918, it was reintroduced into the Third Congress of

[118] Stalin, "Primechanie avtora," Dec. 1924, in *Sochineniia*, III, 30–31.
[119] "Tekst razgovora," in Manilov, ed., *1917 god*, p. 532.
[120] Lenin, "Manifest k ukrainskomu narodu," in *Sochineniia*, XXII, 121. See also Lenin, "Postanovlenie Soveta Narodnykh Komissarov," Jan. 12, 1918, in *ibid.*, XXII, 151.
[121] Stalin, "Otvet tovarishcham ukraintsam," in *Sochineniia*, IV, 8–9.
[122] Lenin, "Proekt deklaratsii prav trudiashchegosia i ekspluatiruemogo naroda," early Jan., 1918, in *Sochineniia*, XXII, 174, 178; "Deklaratsiia prav trudiashchegosia i ekspluatiruemogo naroda," Jan. 16, 1918, in *ibid.*, XXII, 553–54.

Soviets, which officially adopted the principle of federation on January 24, 1918. Subsequently, part of the Declaration found its way into the first section of the Constitution of the RSFSR, adopted on July 10, 1918.[123] In addition to this Declaration, at the Third Congress of Soviets Stalin introduced a resolution propounding, in rough outline, the principles of Soviet federalism, which helped guide the drafting of the first Constitution.[124]

Despite the official adoption of federalism, it was obvious that the Soviet leaders had not abandoned their centralist convictions. In March, 1918, Lenin stated that it was necessary to look upon the Soviet "federation of nations as a transition to a *conscious* and closer union of toilers who will have learned to rise *willingly* above national differences."[125] He attempted to reconcile the federalism at hand with the centralism of the future:

> We stand for democratic centralism. . . . But federation need not contradict democratic centralism, if federation operates within reasonable limits from an economic point of view and if it is based upon serious national distinctions. . . . Time and again, given a really democratic order, especially one such as exists under the Soviet organization of state, federation is only a transitional step toward real democratic centralism. In the example of the Russian Soviet Republic we see most clearly that the federation we are now introducing, and which we will develop in the future, will serve as the surest step to the most solid unification of the different nationalities of Russia into a unitary, democratic, centralized Soviet state.[126]

Stalin warned against being swept away by the federalist tide. Federalist demands must be subjected to careful scrutiny in order to avoid a needless decentralizing of the Soviet state. "Obviously, not every sort of district and unit, and not any kind of geographical territory, is a proper subject for federation, but only certain definite regions which naturally combine a distinct way of life, a singularity of national composition, and a certain minimal completeness of

---

[123] "Primechaniia," No. 80, in *ibid.*, XXII, 596–97.
[124] Stalin, "Vystupleniia na III vserossiiskom s"ezde sovetov r.s. i k.d.," Jan. 28, 1918, in *Sochineniia*, IV, 32–33; "O federalnykh uchrezhdeniakh Rossiiskoi Respubliki," Jan. 31, 1918, in *Tretii vserossiiskii s"ezd sovetov rabochikh, soldatskikh i krest'ianskikh deputatov* (Petersburg, 1918), pp. 93–94.
[125] Lenin, "Chernovoi nabrosok proekta programmy," March 8, 1918, in *Sochineniia*, XXII, 372.
[126] Lenin, "Nabrosok stat'i 'Ocherednye zadachi sovetskoi vlasti,'" March 28, 1918, in *ibid.*, XXII, 415–16.

CENTRALISM V. FEDERALISM

economic territory." [127] Federalism must be endured, limited where possible, and ultimately abolished. This objective was recorded in the Party Program which was adopted formally by the Eighth Party Congress in March, 1919. The Party approved "a federative union of states, organized on the Soviet model, as one of the transitional forms leading to complete unity." [128]

NATIONAL SELF-DETERMINATION IN PRACTICE

The Party Program also officially recorded the conclusions that the Soviet government had drawn from its practical experience with self-determination of nations. The Soviet rulers had learned that in areas already under Soviet domination, or on the brink of falling under Soviet control, it had been disastrous to rely upon the will of a nation for a favorable decision. The fate of these non-Russian peoples was therefore taken out of the hands of the nation and given to "the representatives of the proletariat," who became "the nation." Practically speaking, this meant that the Communist Parties of the non-Russian nations, acting under the control of the Russian Communist center, agitated for reunion with Soviet Russia. Stalin formulated this new position on January 28, 1918, when he told the Third All-Russian Congress of Soviets that it was necessary to interpret "the principle of self-determination as the right of self-determination not of the bourgeoisie, but of the toiling masses of a given nation." [129] The Congress subsequently adopted a resolution approving "the principle of self-determination of nations, in the sense of self-determination of the toiling masses of all nationalities living in Russia." [130] Martov, speaking at the Congress, objected that the Soviet leaders had erected a double standard. In such areas as the Ukraine, the Caucasus, and Finland, the exercise of self-determination must be entrusted solely to the toilers. On the other hand, Trotsky had demanded at Brest-Litovsk that areas under German control, such as Poland, Courland, and Lithuania, be permitted to determine their future by plebiscites, which would record the will

[127] Stalin, "Organizatsiia Rossiiskoi Federativnoi Respubliki," April 3, 1918, in *Sochineniia*, IV, 69.
[128] "Vosmoi s"ezd RKP(b)," March 18–23, 1919, in *KPSS v rez.*, I, 417.
[129] Speech by Stalin, Jan. 28, 1918, in *Tretii vserossiiskii s"ezd sovetov*, p. 73.
[130] "Obrashchenie priniatoe 3-m vserossiiskim S"ezdom v natsional'nykh delakh," Jan. 31, 1918, in *ibid.*, p. 94.

of the entire nation. Preobrazhenskii and Stalin defended the double standard. It reflected realistically the power situation existing in each region. There was no immediate prospect of Soviet rule in the territory under German occupation, and therefore it was unnecessary to demand self-determination solely for the workers. But in areas beyond the reach of German troops, where it was possible to pass from the bourgeois to the proletarian stage of historical development, the exercise of self-determination must be put into the hands of the proletariat alone.[131] Essentially this was an attempt to get the best of both worlds: to encourage the disintegration of the non-Soviet world into new national units, but, as soon as it appeared likely that a nation might join the Soviet world, to entrust the right of self-determination solely to those who were committed to integrate their nation with Soviet Russia. Stalin later illustrated this double standard when he said that "in so far as Soviet states unite in a federation on a voluntary basis, the right to secede is not invoked," supposedly because this expressed the will of the proletariat. "However, in so far as we are dealing with the colonies in the clutches of England, France, America, Japan, in so far as we are dealing with oppressed countries like Arabia, Mesopotamia, Turkey, Hindustan, etc. . . . then the slogan of the right of peoples to secede is revolutionary." [132]

When this matter was reviewed at the Eighth Party Congress in March, 1919, Piatakov and Bukharin remained unreconciled even to this highly manipulative use of "self-determination." Piatakov still totally rejected the right of self-determination, while Bukharin now insisted that if it must be retained, it must be granted only to the toiling masses and never to nations. Lenin defended the concept of progression by stages, saying that first "every nation must secure the right to self-determination, and that this will facilitate the self-determination of the toilers." [133] Lenin's views prevailed and they were given this formulation in the Party Program:

On the question of who is to express the will of a nation to secede, the Russian Communist Party adopts the class-historical viewpoint, taking

[131] Speeches by Martov, Preobrazhenskii, and Stalin, Jan. 28, 1918, in *ibid.*, pp. 75–80.
[132] Stalin, "Doklad ob ocherednykh zadachakh partii v natsional'nom voprose," March 10, 1921, in *Sochineniia*, V, 43. See also Stalin, "Ot avtora," Oct., 1920, in *ibid.*, IV, 372–73.
[133] Lenin, "Doklad o partiinoi programme," March 19, 1919, in *Sochineniia*, XXIV, 138.

CENTRALISM V. FEDERALISM

into consideration the stage of historical development of the given nation; whether it is evolving from medievalism to bourgeois democracy, or from bourgeois democracy to Soviet or proletarian democracy, etc.[134]

This theory of self-determination was grounded in the Jacobin premises that underlay the entire structure of Soviet society. When it was a question of establishing Soviet power, neither whole nations nor the "toiling masses" could be trusted to will their own good. Such wisdom was the monopoly of the leaders of the Communist Party, that tiny elite, vanguard group, which alone possessed insight into the class will. Thus, when popular movements demanded secession from Soviet Russia, Stalin lectured the masses as to where their best interests lay:

> The demand for secession of the border regions from Russia must be rejected . . . first of all because it contradicts the essential interests of the popular masses both of the center and of the border regions. . . . The interests of the popular masses render the demand for secession of the border regions at this stage of the revolution profoundly counter-revolutionary.[135]

This all-embracing wisdom of the Party elite presumably included the ability to determine the exact point at which a revolution had moved from the bourgeois to the proletarian stage, so that self-determination could be removed from the hands of a nation and placed in the hands of the "representatives of the proletariat."

Events proved that the judgment of the Party leaders was not infallible in determining just when this great divide had been reached. In the case of Finland, Stalin declared in January, 1918, that self-determination should be given to "the representatives of the Finnish proletariat," and on March 1, 1918, the Soviet government recognized the insurgent Finnish Communists by signing a Treaty of Friendship with the so-called "Finnish Socialist Worker's Republic." [136] A year later, in March, 1919, when the Finnish revolution had proved illusory, Lenin insisted that the right of self-deter-

[134] "Vosmoi S"ezd RKP(b)," in *KPSS v rez.*, I, 417.
[135] Stalin, "Politika sovetskoi vlasti po natsional'nomu voprosu v Rossii," Oct. 10, 1920, in *Sochineniia*, IV, 352-54. The Jacobin attitude toward the self-determination of non-French areas was almost exactly parallel to the Soviet attitude toward the self-determination of non-Russian areas, with bourgeois France occupying a position in the bourgeois revolution comparable to that occupied by proletarian Russia in the proletarian revolution. See Talmon, *Totalitarian Democracy*, p. 110.
[136] "Treaty of Friendship with the Finnish Socialist Worker's Republic," March 1, 1918, in Degras, ed., *Soviet Documents*, I, 47-48.

mination should rest with the entire Finnish nation. "If we were to declare that we do not recognize the Finnish nation, but only the toiling masses, that would be sheer nonsense." [137] This was the same Lenin who, a year before, had signed a treaty with the Finnish Communist "government." Similar developments followed in the Baltic states, where the Communists got one foot across the great divide only to lose their foothold.[138] Apparently revolutions could not only advance from the bourgeois to the proletarian stage, but they could also regress from the proletarian to the bourgeois stage. It seemed that the omniscient Soviet leaders were not only unable to mark the transition from one stage to another, but they could not even determine the direction in which a given stage was moving.

Even more bewildering was the phenomenon of a revolution that could skip stages. In 1920 Lenin predicted that "with the aid of the proletariat of the advanced countries, the backward countries may make a transition to the Soviet system, and, after passing through a definite stage of development, to communism, without ever passing through the capitalist stage of development." [139] In 1921 Stalin said that the backward peoples of Central Asia "will have to pass from primitive forms of economy to the stage of Soviet economy without passing through the stage of industrial capitalism." [140] Some of these Central Asian peoples were incorporated directly into Russian Turkestan, which at first was part of the RSFSR. During 1920 Khorezm and Bokhara became Soviet, though supposedly not yet

[137] Lenin, "Doklad o partiinom programme," in *Sochineniia*, XXIV, 138.
[138] "Resolution of the All-Russian Central Executive Committee on the Recognition of the Soviet Republics of Estonia, Lithuania, and Latvia," Dec. 23, 1918, in Degras, ed., *Soviet Documents*, I, 129. See also *ibid.*, I, 126–27.
[139] Lenin, "Doklad komissii po natsional'nomu i kolonial'nomu voprosam," July 26, 1920, in *Sochineniia*, XXV, 354. This represented a fundamental *volte-face*, since Lenin had long maintained that backward countries must go through the capitalist stage of development before reaching socialism. In 1905 he asserted that "Marxism has broken irrevocably with all the nonsense talked by the Narodniki and the Anarchists about Russia, for instance, being able to avoid capitalist development, jump out of capitalism, or skip over it, by some means other than the class struggle on the basis and within the limits of capitalism." (Lenin, "Dve taktiki sotsial-demokratii v demokraticheskoi revoliutsii," June–July, 1905, in *ibid.*, VIII, 56–57.) Following the 1911 revolution in China, Lenin branded Sun Yat-sen a "Chinese Narodnik" because he entertained "the hope that China will be able to avoid the path of capitalism. . . . The possibility of 'preventing' capitalism in China, of the greater ease of a 'socialist revolution' in China, because of its backwardness, etc., is a completely reactionary dream." (Lenin, "Demokratiia i narodnichestvo v Kitae," July 28, 1912, in *ibid.*, XVI, 28–29.)
[140] Stalin, "Doklad ob ocherednykh zadachakh," in *Sochineniia*, V, 41.

CENTRALISM V. FEDERALISM

socialist, Republics, since their Constitutions recognized capitalist private property. By 1925 these Republics had been dissolved and their peoples had joined the Uzbek and Turkmen Socialist Soviet Republics, which became Union Republics of the USSR.[141] How was it possible for some of these peoples to jump from their Asiatic order or from a feudal society [142] directly into socialism while others had to pass through a five-year period of capitalist development? If the capitalist stage of historical development was necessary at all, then why not ten, twenty, or one hundred years for it? It would seem that the decision as to when a nation had passed from one stage to another did not depend upon elaborate theoretical considerations, but purely upon the balance of forces controlling the expansion of Soviet power. If a nation, whatever its stage of historical development, could successfully repulse a Soviet power thrust, then it had "freely" and "voluntarily" exercised its right to remain in the non-Soviet world. If a nation temporarily resisted total subjugation, it might enter a transitional, satellite stage. At this point it was inexpedient to absorb such a nation as a full-fledged Soviet Socialist Republic. But if a nation were completely overwhelmed by Soviet power, then it would immediately enter the proletarian stage of development, and the "representatives" of the "toiling masses" would henceforth bear that nation's mandate. After decades of theoretical hairsplitting, the Soviet doctrine of self-determination of nations had been reduced to this simple pragmatic equation of raw power.

By the application of the Soviet version of self-determination, it was hoped to federate one nation after another with Soviet Russia and so to arrive at a World Soviet Federation. Lenin's draft Theses for the Second Comintern Congress in 1920 forecast the process of piecemeal "liberation." Soviet Russia must bind to itself both "the Soviet movement of the advanced workers of all countries and all the national liberation movements of the colonies and the oppressed countries." The strength of these ties will be "determined by the stage of development of the Communist movement" in each country, but at some point each nation will become ripe for plucking

---

[141] Batsell, *Soviet Rule*, pp. 346–48, 356–65.
[142] For a discussion of the highly significant but little noted attempt of Soviet historiography to obscure the original Marxist distinction between an Asiatic and a feudal society, see Karl A. Wittfogel, *Oriental Despotism* (New Haven, 1957), pp. 369–412, 438–46.

and will be attached to Soviet Russia by means of an ever-expanding federation. "Federation has already demonstrated its expediency as a means of establishing relations between the RSFSR and other Soviet Republics." (This statement, made in 1920, was factually incorrect, though it accurately anticipated the formation of the USSR several years later.) "The task of the Communist International, in this regard, consists both in the further development of this federation, and in the study and testing by experience of those new federations that will arise on the basis of the Soviet order and the Soviet movement." [143]

Lenin warned that the World Soviet Federation could only be constructed by taking into account the national peculiarities of each people. By 1920 he had acquired considerable respect for the enduring strength of national traditions. If these were ignored, then it would be impossible "to create a really centralized, leading center, capable of directing international tactics of the revolutionary proletariat in its struggle for a World Soviet Republic." The approach toward different nations could not be based on "stereotyped, mechanically equalized, and identical tactical rules of struggle."

So long as national and state differences exist among peoples and countries, and these differences will continue to exist for a very long time, even after the dictatorship of the proletariat has been established on a world scale—the unity of international tactics of the Communist working-class movement of all countries demands, not the elimination of variety, not the abolition of national differences (that is a foolish dream at the present moment), but such an application of the *fundamental* principles of communism . . . as will *correctly modify* these principles in *certain particulars,* correctly adapt and apply them to national and national-state differences.[144]

Stalin had become even more apprehensive about the residual strength of nationalism, and the obstacles to be overcome in creating a federation of Soviet nations. He suggested that the Second Comintern Congress approve confederation as an alternate method of amalgamating nations, should federation pose too many difficulties. "For the nations already found in the framework of the old Russian Empire our Soviet-type federation must be considered the most

[143] Lenin, "Pervonachal'nyi nabrosok tezisov po natsional'nomu i kolonial'nomu voprosam," June 5, 1920, in *Sochineniia,* XXV, 287; "Natsional'nyi i kolonial'nyi voprosy," July 19–Aug. 7, 1920, in *Kom. Int. v dok.,* p. 127.
[144] Lenin, "Detskaia bolezn' 'levizny' v kommunizme," April–May, 1920, in *Sochineniia,* XXV, 227.

CENTRALISM V. FEDERALISM

expedient path toward international unity." However, other nations that have previously lived as independent national states would be likely to resent this type of federation. "Take, for example, the future Soviet Germany, Poland, Hungary, Finland. These nations, having their own state institutions, their own armed forces, their own finances, would hardly consent to an immediate federation with Soviet Russia . . . since they would consider this an encroachment upon their state independence." Stalin concluded that "the most acceptable way of drawing together these nations would be through a confederation (i.e., an alliance of independent states)." [145]

THE LONG-RANGE GOAL OF A CENTRALIST WORLD STATE

Lenin rejected this proposal, and the Comintern Theses of 1920 mentioned only federation as the accepted method for joining nations to Soviet Russia. The Theses then looked beyond the time when a World Soviet Federation will have come into being, and foresaw the transformation of this federation into a unitary world state. "It is necessary to strive for an ever closer and closer federal union, recognizing federation as a transitional form toward complete unity." Federation will evolve toward complete unity by fostering "the tendency toward the creation of a single world economy regulated by the proletariat of all nations according to one common plan. This tendency is already clearly and fully revealed under capitalism, and must definitely be further developed and fully perfected under socialism." [146] A Comintern Manifesto asserted that releasing "the productive forces of all countries from the tentacles of national states, and unifying all peoples in the closest economic cooperation on the basis of a common economic plan," will, at the same time, permit "the weakest and smallest people freely and independently to direct the affairs of their own national culture, without any detriment to the unified and centralized European and world economy." [147]

Extremists like Piatakov wanted to write a provision into the Program of the Russian Communist Party for the immediate creation

[145] Stalin's letter to Lenin, June 12, 1920, quoted in "Primechaniia," in Lenin, *ibid.*, XXV, 624, n. 141.
[146] "Natsional'nyi i kolonial'nyi voprosy," in *Kom. Int. v dok.*, p. 127; Lenin, "Pervonachal'nyi nabrosok," in *Sochineniia*, XXV, 287.
[147] "Manifest Kommunisticheskogo Internatsionala," March 2–6, 1919, in *Kom. Int. v dok.*, pp. 56–57.

of a "World Council of People's Economy." Lenin opposed this on the grounds that the Program being written in 1919 "must be based on what actually exists." He did not deny that "we shall have a Program applicable to the entire world, when the World Soviet Republic is created," but by that time "we shall doubtless have written several more programs." [148] Despite this note of caution, a Comintern document of 1920 demanded that "the Supreme Economic Council of the imperialist Entente must be replaced by a Supreme Economic Council of the world proletariat for the centralized exploitation of all the economic resources of mankind." The goal of Soviet power was "a reconstruction of national and world economy on the basis of a single economic plan, created and realized by a unified society of producers." [149] A Party resolution of 1921 reiterated that this could only be realized through a federation of Soviet Republics. "Only a federation of this kind can serve as a transitional stage to that supreme unity of the toilers of all countries bound together in a single world economic system, the necessity for which is growing more and more evident." [150] This was the expectation. Soviet Russia would be joined by other Soviet Republics in a federation that would grow into a World Soviet Federation. This, in turn, would be transformed into a unitary, highly centralized world state.

The concessions to federalism dealt exclusively with the structure of the Soviet state. At no time did the Soviet leaders introduce federalism into the structure of the Party, which monopolized effective power in the Soviet state. The Eighth Party Congress, meeting in March, 1919, drew a distinction between the structure of state and Party. Federalism had been introduced, at least in name, if not in fact, into the structure of the RSFSR, and federalism had been approved as the method of joining new states to Soviet Russia. But, the Eighth Party Congress warned, "this in no way implies that the Russian Communist Party in turn must be organized as a federation of independent Communist Parties. . . . There must be *one* centralized Communist Party with one Central Committee directing the entire work of the Party in all parts of the RSFSR." The resolution further noted that "at the present time the Ukraine, Lithuania,

---

[148] Lenin, "Zakliuchitel'noe slovo po dokladu o partiinoi programme," March 19, 1919, in *Sochineniia*, XXIV, 149–50, 153.
[149] "Manifest II kongressa Kommunisticheskogo Internatsionala," July 19–Aug. 7, 1920, in *Kom. Int. v dok.*, pp. 146, 151, 157.
[150] "Desiatyi s"ezd RKP(b)," March 8–16, 1921, in *KPSS v rez.*, I, 558.

CENTRALISM V. FEDERALISM

Latvia, and Belorussia exist as separate Soviet Republics. For the present moment these are the forms in which the state has to exist." Even though these Soviet states have not yet reached the transitional stage of federation, the Party must remain a centralized entity, exercising strict control over the Communist Parties in these nominally independent states:

All decisions of the Russian Communist Party and its directing organs are unconditionally binding upon all parts of the Party, regardless of their national composition. The Central Committees of the Ukrainian, Latvian, and Lithuanian Communist Parties are accorded the rights of regional committees of the Party, and are entirely subordinated to the Central Committee of the Russian Communist Party.[151]

The unified Party's demand for the unconditional subordination of the non-Russian periphery to the will of the Russian center provides a perfect illustration of the tie between centralism and the rise of Soviet Russian nationalism.[152]

Party centralism, which excluded federalism, was soon to condemn all types of Party factionalism. The prohibition against factionalism was precipitated by the Kronstadt rebellion of March, 1921, a revolt that was interpreted by Party leaders as a warning of the dangers inherent in demands for free discussion by organized groups of workers, including organized groups within the Party.[153] Accordingly, Lenin's resolution drafted for the Tenth Party Congress in March, 1921, stipulated that "the Party must take strict measures to prevent any factional conduct whatsoever." In order to insure this, "the Congress authorizes the Central Committee to apply all Party penalties, including expulsion, in cases of breach of discipline or reviving or engaging in factionalism." [154] All dissident

---

[151] "Vosmoi s"ezd RKP(b)," in *ibid.*, I, 443.

[152] The objection might be raised that the word "Russian" in the title of the Russian Communist Party was the territorial term "rossiiskaia," not the ethnic term "russkaia." But this is an academic quibble, since the exclusion of areas like the Ukraine and Belorussia from the Russian CP made "rossiiskaia" roughly equivalent to "russkaia." In any event, the bulk of the membership of the Russian CP was ethnically Russian, and policy for Communists of all nationalities was formulated in and directed from the Kremlin, in the ethnic heart of Great Russia.

[153] Many of the important documents on Kronstadt are reproduced in Alexander Berkman, *The Kronstadt Rebellion* (Berlin, 1922). See also Robert V. Daniels, "The Kronstadt Revolt of 1921," *American Slavic*, X, No. 4 (Dec., 1951), 241–54; Leonard Schapiro, *The Origin of the Communist Autocracy* (Cambridge, Mass., 1955), pp. 296–342.

[154] Lenin, "Pervonachal'nyi proekt rezoliutsii X s"ezda RKP o edinstve partii," March, 1921, in *Sochineniia*, XXVI, 260–61.

Party factions (The Worker's Opposition, Democratic Centralism, etc.) were ordered dissolved. This blow to intra-Party democracy was at first kept secret. However, factional activity continued and Lenin's authority began to wane, as illness increasingly removed him from active direction of the Party. As he lay on his deathbed, in January, 1924, the Thirteenth Party Conference complained: "The Bolshevik view of the Party as a monolithic whole is replaced by the view that the Party is the sum of every possible tendency and faction." Consequently, "the Conference suggests that the Central Committee publish the hitherto unpublished Point 7 of the resolution on unity adopted at the suggestion of Comrade Lenin at the Tenth Congress of the RCP," which authorized the expulsion of Party members for factionalism.[155]

The designation of the Party as "a monolithic whole" in fact marked its entry into the political stone age. In theory, the Party remained faithful to the principle of "democratic centralism." [156] Party centralism was undoubtedly firmly and permanently implanted, but Party democracy, which had always been precarious at best, was now pulled up by the roots. How could democracy operate with a prohibition against the formation of factions represented different points of view? James Madison long ago observed that "liberty is to faction what air is to fire," and therefore, "it could not be less folly to abolish liberty, which is essential to political life, because it nourishes faction, than it would be to wish the annihilation of air, which is essential to animal life, because it imparts to fire its destructive agency." [157] Madison assumed that no one individual or no one clique could possess a monopoly of truth, and that liberty and democracy could only result from the free interplay of ideas. Lenin operated upon the Jacobin assumption that there was only one valid will in all society, and that this will could be expressed accurately by a tiny vanguard elite which would insure "democracy" for the inarticulate masses. From this point of view it was logical to abolish factions. How could several divergent factions interpret

---

[155] "Trinadtsataia konferentsiia RKP(b)," Jan. 16–18, 1924, in *KPSS v rez.*, I, 781, 785. It was Stalin who described the Party as a "monolithic organization, hewed from a single block," and it was at Stalin's instigation that the secret resolution against factions was published. (Stalin, "Doklad ob ocherednykh zadachakh partiinogo stroitel'stva," Jan. 17, 1924, in *Sochineniia*, VI, 22–24.)

[156] "Desiatyi s"ezd RKP(b)," in *KPSS v rez.*, I, 519–20.

[157] James Madison, "The Federalist, No. 10," Nov. 23, 1787, in Hamilton, Jay, and Madison, *The Federalist* (Modern Library ed., New York, n.d.), p. 55.

CENTRALISM V. FEDERALISM

a single will, which was one and indivisible? When introducing his resolution against factions, Lenin said it was necessary to consider the Party as "the genuine embodiment of the unity of will of the vanguard of the proletariat."[158] Soon afterwards Stalin echoed: "The Party is a unity of will, precluding all factionalism and division of authority in the Party."[159]

Along with the prohibition of factions, Party centralism had been further strengthened by the creation of the Politburo, Orgburo, and Secretariat, which began to function in March, 1919. These three small, interlocking groups, perched at the pinnacle of the Party structure, served to concentrate effective power in the hands of a few Party leaders, who likewise dominated the structure of the Soviet state. In March, 1920, Lenin reported that "the Politburo decided all questions of international and domestic policy."[160] And in April, 1923, a Party resolution demanded "an improvement in the work of the Politburo in the realm of the planned direction by the Politburo of the organs of state power."[161] The centralized, monolithic Party more and more tended to fill the federal forms of the Soviet state with a single, unitary content.

This relationship between Party and state within the Soviet Union supposedly anticipated the relationship between the World Communist Party and the Soviet world state. Just as the federalism of the Soviet state was held up as the prototype for a World Soviet Federation, so the centralism of the Party was used as a model for a centralized World Party. With the founding of the Comintern, this World Party was proclaimed to have sprung into existence. The Statutes of the Communist International, adopted at the Second Comintern Congress in 1920, declared that "the Communist International must be one universal Communist Party, of which the Parties operating in each country form only individual sections."[162] The Third Inter-

---

[158] Lenin, "Pervonachal'nyi proekt rezoliutsii X S"ezda RKP," in *Sochineniia*, XXVI, 259.
[159] Stalin, "Ob osnovakh Leninizma," April, 1924, in *O Lenine i Leninizme*, p. 139.
[160] Lenin, "Doklad Tsentral'nogo Komiteta," March 29, 1920, in *Sochineniia*, XXV, 95.
[161] "Dvenadtsatyi S"ezd RKP(b)," April 17-25, 1923, in *KPSS v rez.*, I, 724. On the origin of the Politburo, Orgburo, and Secretariat, see "Vosmoi s"ezd RKP(b)," in *ibid.*, I, 443; Carr, *Bolshevik Revolution*, I, 94, 96, 193-95, 204, 212-13.
[162] "Ustav Kommunisticheskogo Internatsionala," July 19-Aug. 7, 1920, in *Vtoroi kongress Kommunisticheskogo Internatsionala*, p. 536.

national was described as "a single World Communist Party, as contrasted with the Second International, which was built upon the principles of 'federalism.'" [163] Apparently the Russian model of a federal state with a centralized Party was not clearly understood by all foreign Communists. The Comintern leaders warned:

> The principle of federalism is absolutely incompatible with the true interests of a revolutionary organization. All references to the federal Constitution of the Soviet Republics are absolutely misleading, since the structure of the Communist Party cannot be compared to that of the Soviet state in any respect. The Communist Party is one and the same in all of the federal Republics, for it is a strictly centralized Party.... The International, in the same categorical fashion, must reject the application of the principles of federalism.[164]

Zinoviev, as head of the Comintern, complained that experienced Party workers already knew "how difficult it is to establish correct relations between the center and the local organizations, even within the limits of one country. How much more difficult is this task when it is a question of more than fifty Parties, comprising the Comintern? The federalist traditions are much stronger than there was reason to believe." However, the avowed aim remained "a centralized International Communist World Party. This is an absolute principle, and we must abide by it. But we require years in order to carry it out thoroughly." [165]

If it was to take years to create a single, centralized World Party out of a relatively small number of highly disciplined individuals, then how much longer would it take to create a centralized, unitary Soviet world state, which was the ultimate object of the World Communist Party? Yet it was precisely this goal which the Soviet leaders posed before all humanity. They sought to pour the diverse and inchoate masses of the entire world into but a single mold.

---

[163] *Malaia sovetskaia entsiklopediia* (Moscow, 1937), V, 693.
[164] "Vtoroi rasshirennyi plenum," July 7–11, 1922, in *Kom. Int. v dok.*, p. 285.
[165] Speech by Zinoviev, Nov. 9, 1922, in *Fourth Congress of the Communist International*, pp. 8, 15. See also Carr, *Bolshevik Revolution*, III, 448–51.

VIII. The Issue of Centralism versus Federalism in the Stalinist Era and After

ACCORDING to Soviet testimony, the existing Soviet federation is a pilot plant, whose principles of operation will be extended to the entire world, in the form of a "World Federation of Soviet Republics." Since the Soviet federation portends the shape of the future, it would seem worth while to examine briefly the evolution and nature of Soviet federalism.

FEDERALISM IN THE RSFSR

In 1918 Stalin reminded those who were drawing up the Constitution for the first Soviet state that faith in "the growth of federalism is not justified by history."[1] Repeating the "historical" lecture that he delivered prior to the revolution, he maintained that the American and Swiss federations had "developed through confederation to federation, and, going beyond that, they have, in fact, become unitary states, retaining only the forms of federalism."[2] "Federalism in Russia," Stalin concluded, "as in America and Switzerland, is destined to play a transitional role—to a future *socialist* unitary state."[3] He specifically condemned the federalist device of a second chamber to express the will of the different nations in Russia, on the model of bourgeois second chambers, which provided for representation by states or cantons. "This bicameral system leads to nothing but the usual bourgeois legislative dilly-dallying," which is obviously "unsuitable for the toiling masses of Russia."[4] The crea-

---
[1] Stalin, "Organizatsiia Rossiiskoi Federativnoi Respubliki," April 3, 4, 1918, in *Sochineniia* IV, 72.
[2] *Ibid.*, IV, 66. This distortion of bourgeois federalism was repeated continually: see Vyshinsky, *Sovetskoe gosudarstvennoe pravo*, pp. 229-32; M. P. Kareva, "Stalinskaia Konstitutsiia i sotsialisticheskaia federatsiia," *Sovetskoe gosudarstvo i pravo*, No. 2 (Feb., 1952), pp. 13-14.
[3] Stalin, "Organizatsiia Rossiiskoi," in *Sochineniia*, IV, 73.
[4] *Ibid.*, IV, 71.

tion of "sovereign local and regional organs of power operating parallel with the power of the center," Stalin feared, "would in fact bring about the disintegration of all power and a return to capitalism." [5]

Though the word "federal" appeared in the official title of the Russian Socialist Federal Soviet Republic, there was precious little federalism in its Constitution. While regions that were distinguished by a "national character" could participate in the RSFSR "upon a federal basis," the Constitution did not provide for any specific territorial arrangements, nor accord delimited but exclusive rights to the autonomous national units in the Republic. The various national minorities simply received *ad hoc* grants of autonomy; this could be equated roughly with the administrative subdividing of a unitary state.[6]

FEDERALISM IN THE TRANSCAUCASUS

Constitutionally speaking, the first Soviet federation was hammered out, in a series of stages from April, 1921, to December, 1922, among the Transcaucasian Soviet Republics of Georgia, Armenia, and Azerbaijan.[7] What motivation lay behind the formation of this federation? Clearly, the initiative did not come from Transcaucasia but from Moscow. On November 28, 1921, for example, Lenin drafted a directive, in the name of the Central Committee of the Russian Communist Party, approving the creation of a Transcaucasian federation, and instructing "the Central Committees of Georgia, Armenia, and Azerbaijan to carry out this decision." [8] Stalin and his aide-de-camp, Ordzhonikidze, who was largely entrusted with supervising this task, urged such a federation as the best way of taming the nationalism of the three Transcaucasian republics. In July, 1921, Stalin complained of "the nationalism—Georgian, Armenian, and Azerbaijanian—which has been terribly strengthened over the past few years in the Transcaucasian Republics, and which is hindering

[5] Stalin, "Vystupleniia na soveshchanii po sozyvu uchreditel'nogo s"ezda Tataro-Bashkirskoi Sovetskoi Respubliki," May 10, 1918, in *Sochineniia*, IV, 89.
[6] "Constitution of the Russian Socialist Federal Soviet Republic," adopted July 10, 1918, Article II, Paragraph 11, in *Decrees and Constitution of Soviet Russia* (New York, n.d.).
[7] Pipes, *The Formation*, pp. 252-54; Batsell, *Soviet Rule*, pp. 401-25.
[8] Lenin, "Proekt predlozheniia ob obrazovanii federatsii Zakavkazskikh Respublik," Nov. 28, 1921, in *Sochineniia*, XXVII, 94.

CENTRALISM V. FEDERALISM

the process of unification." [9] The Transcaucasian federation was this instrument of unification; a federal form serving the cause of centralism. Through it Moscow could funnel the various national strivings so as to make them amenable to centralist control.

Opposition at once developed in the Transcaucasus, spearheaded by the Georgian Communists Mdivani and Makharadze. In December, 1921, Makharadze, the Chairman of the Council of People's Commissars of Soviet Georgia, argued that, while "we have nothing against our organizational merger with Russia," it was harmful to create a federation "at a time when we have not yet succeeded in drawing near to the masses, when we have not yet had time to call a Congress of Soviets. I declare that a unification of this kind, *dictated from above*, not only will do us no good, but will still further remove us from the people." In vain he protested that

federation under such circumstances will mean the creation of yet one more new bureaucratic organ, absolutely unconnected with the people, completely unpopular. Of course, it would be quite another matter if Georgia and Armenia had already organized Soviets, and if this federation had been arranged by the Executive Committees of the Soviets of Georgia, Armenia, and Azerbaijan.[10]

After the creation of the Transcaucasian federation, Makharadze reiterated these objections, adding his resentment against Russian control through "a whole series of artificial, bureaucratic organs and apparatuses in which only specialists with clearly colonizing and great-power tendencies are given full play." [11]

[9] Stalin, "Ob ocherednykh zadachakh kommunizma v Gruzii i Zakavkaz'e," July 6, 1921, in *Sochineniia*, V, 95. See also Stalin, "Doklad o natsional'nykh momentakh v partiinom i gosudarstvennom stroitel'stve," April 23, 1923, in *ibid.*, V, 248-57.

[10] F. Makharadze, Doklad Tsentral'nomu Komitetu RKP(b) otnositel'no raboty v Gruzii, Dec. 6, 1921, pp. 7-8 (italics added). An authenticated copy of a document from the archives of the Georgian government in exile, Paris, with a notation indicating that another copy was deposited in the files of the Central Committee of the RCP. This report was first published in *Independent Georgia*, Paris, No. 24, 1922, and was transmitted to the present writer by Dr. D. Chatara, ed., *The Voice of Free Georgia* (New York). Pipes, who has likewise examined this document, states that "its authenticity cannot be doubted." (Pipes, *The Formation*, p. 265.)

[11] F. Makharadze, "Nado razobrat'sia," *Pravda*, April 19, 1923, p. 4. For the rebuttal see S. Ordzhonikidze, "Deistvitel'no nado razobrat'sia," *ibid.*, April 19, 1923, p. 5; Stalin, "Zakliuchetel'noe slovo po organizatsionnomu otchëtu TsK," April 19, 1923, in *Sochineniia*, V, 227-34.

THE REBUFF TO FEDERALISM IN SOVIET CENTRAL ASIA

By way of contrast, it is interesting to speculate on why a regional federation was never formed among the various nations of Soviet Central Asia. A regional federation among these Moslem peoples, who, except for the Tadzhiks, were all of Turkic origin, would have seemed both natural and beneficial for the solution of their common problems. The Second All-Moslem Congress, meeting in Tashkent at the end of September, 1917, elaborated a plan for a "Turkestan Federal Republic," composed of the various regions of Russian Turkestan, which would enter "the Russian Republic as a separate autonomous territorial federation, organized on the basis of national-cultural self-determination for all the nationalities inhabiting these regions." [12] Safarov, the Central Asian specialist of the Russian Communist Party, revealed why this proposal was unacceptable:

A single Republic of all Turkic peoples within the RSFSR would, according to the defenders of this scheme, serve as a powerful counterweight to "Moscow." They do not talk about this, but it is understood and it would be quickly revealed by the further course of events.[13]

The consolidation of ties around Tashkent would not only produce a rival to Moscow, as the repository for the supreme loyalty of the Moslem peoples, but it would also provide a powerful impetus to Pan-Islamic and Pan-Turkic sentiments, also directed away from Moscow—in this case, toward areas beyond the borders of the Soviet Union. The Soviet leaders clearly feared the plans, however vague, of Enver Pasha for a Pan-Turkic federation of Turkey, Afghanistan, and the Turkic peoples of what later became Soviet Central Asia.[14] To this day, even the suggestion of a Pan-Turkic idea is denounced as treason to the USSR.[15] Consequently, the Russian Communists rejected a regional federation in Central Asia for exactly the same reason they created a regional federation in Transcaucasia. In both cases their desire was to enhance the power of Moscow, to

[12] Quoted in G. Safarov, *Kolonial'naia revoliutsiia (opyt Turkestana)* (Moscow, 1921), p. 63.
[13] *Ibid.*, p. 112. See also Kolarz, *Russia and Her Colonies*, pp. 259–60, 275, 282, 285.
[14] Dennis, *Foreign Policies*, pp. 253, 257–58; Louis Fischer, *Soviets in World Affairs*, I, 386–89; II, 789.
[15] G. A. von Stackelberg, "The Tashkent Conference on the History of the Peoples of Central Asia and Kazakhstan—1954," *Bulletin of the Institute*, I, No. 2 (May, 1954), 8–12.

CENTRALISM V. FEDERALISM

strengthen the control of the center over the outlying regions. Federalism was employed only if it could be a tool of centralism.

FEDERALISM IN THE 1923 CONSTITUTION OF THE USSR

The debates that accompanied the drafting of the 1923 Constitution of the USSR brought into focus divergent attitudes concerning the merits of federalism. One group of Communists, who recalled Lenin's advice of as late as September, 1917, that "the proletariat can only use the form of the one and indivisible Republic," [16] wished to abandon federalism altogether. In rebuttal, Stalin sharply condemned as "anti-proletarian and reactionary"

> the considerable section of Soviet officials, both in the center and on the local level, who consider the Union of Republics not as a union of state entities with equal rights, dedicated to guarantee the free development of national Republics, but as a step toward the liquidation of those Republics, as the beginning of the formation of the so-called "one and indivisible" Republic.[17]

The Ukrainian representatives, Skrypnik and Rakovskii,[18] took seriously the pledge "to guarantee the free development of national Republics," by demanding a substantial grant of power for the non-Russian periphery so that it could better forestall dictation from the Russian center. Specifically, they proposed a bicameral Central Executive Committee of the Congress of Soviets of the USSR, with one chamber providing representation on the basis of population, the other on the basis of the contracting states. So that the RSFSR would not dominate the other Union Republics, Rakovskii commended the provision in the Weimar Constitution which prohibited any one state from having more than two fifths of the total votes. The Ukrainians also sought to protect the independence of each chamber by permitting each body to have its own Presidium. Finally, they demanded that each Union Republic retain its own Commissariats of Foreign Affairs and Foreign Trade, operating under the general direction of Moscow.

As late as November, 1922, Stalin was on record as maintaining

---

[16] Lenin, "Gosudarstvo i revoliutsiia," Aug.-Sept., 1917, in *Sochineniia*, XXI, 418.

[17] Stalin, "Natsional'nye momenty v partiinom i gosudarstvennom stroitel'stve," March 22, 1923, in *Sochineniia*, V, 190.

[18] Rakovskii's defense of Ukrainian nationalism was newly found; see John S. Reshetar, Jr., *The Ukrainian Revolution* (Princeton, 1952), pp. 225, 258.

that a second chamber "in which all nationalities are given equal representation . . . is incompatible with the Soviet system." [19] But by April, 1923, he had conceded the need for a bicameral institution, in which one chamber "would reflect the specific interests of the nationalities, peoples, and tribes inhabiting the territories of the Union of Republics." [20] The second chamber he envisaged was not to be a deliberative body expressing the interests of the constituent states, but a showplace for all the various nationalities in the Soviet Union. Stalin explained that by thinking only in terms of state units, Rakovskii had completely missed the point of such a chamber, which was especially calculated to inflate the prestige of the backward Asiatic nationalities, that were, in large measure, within the RSFSR.[21] The center of the national question, Lenin had rightly insisted, was not in the West, "but in the colonial and semicolonial countries of the East." "The Eastern peoples [of Russia], organically tied to China, to India, bound to them by language, religion, habits, etc., are supremely important for the revolution. The relative importance of these little nationalities is much greater than that of the Ukraine." [22] The Soviet federation must excite the interest and enthusiasm of the traditionally downtrodden nations of the East, so that the bulk of humanity may quickly be incorporated in the USSR. "The fact of the matter is that the whole East regards our union of Republics as an experimental station." If the Soviet Constitution would give a conspicuous place to the oppressed and backward nationalities, then, Stalin predicted, "the entire East will see that our federation is the banner of its liberation, the advanced guard, in whose steps it must follow." [23] Consequently, "we must here, in Russia, in our federation, solve the national problem in a

[19] Stalin, "Vopros ob ob"edinenii nezavisimykh natsional'nykh respublik," Nov. 18, 1922, in *Sochineniia*, V, 143. See also Trotsky, *Real Situation*, p. 295.
[20] Stalin, "Doklad o natsional'nykh momentakh," in *Sochineniia*, V, 259.
[21] In 1923 most of Soviet Central Asia was in the RSFSR. The following Union Republics were successively carved out of it: 1925, the Uzbek and Turkmen SSRs; 1929, the Tadzhik SSR; 1936, the Kazakh and Kirghiz SSRs. In 1925 the Soviet Republics of Khorezm and Bukhara, which were not part of the RSFSR, were incorporated in the Uzbek and Turkmen SSRs. A number of smaller Asiatic peoples still remain in the RSFSR with varying degrees of national autonomy. The three Transcaucasian Republics also have numerous nationalities with racial and religious ties in the East.
[22] Stalin, "Otvet na popravki k rezoliutsii," April 25, 1923, in *Sochineniia*, V, 276–77.
[23] Stalin, "Doklad o natsional'nykh momentakh," in *ibid.*, V, 238.

correct, a model way, in order to set an example to the East, which represents the heavy reserves of our revolution, and thus increase confidence in and the urge toward our federation." [24]

Rakovskii's other demands for dual Presidiums and for according each Union Republic a voice in foreign affairs and foreign trade were likewise rebuffed. "We are not creating a confederation, but a federation of Republics, a single union state," Stalin asserted, "a state that in no way diminishes the sovereignty of the individual Republics." [25]

The startling contradiction of this last statement summarized Stalin's attitude toward Soviet federalism. He wanted to create a federation, which, in substance, would be a "single union state," while appearing to leave intact the sovereignty of the individual Republics. The conflict between appearance and reality was written into Article IV of the 1923 Constitution of the USSR by providing that "each Union Republic shall retain its right freely to secede from the union." [26] The right of secession, emphasizing the independence of the constituent states and the voluntary nature of their decision to federate, at the same time raised doubts as to whether the Soviet Union was really a federation. Stalin admitted that he had been questioned about the reality of this provision, since some Comrades wondered "whether, after unification, the Republics remained independent." This question was "resolved" in the following manner: "Their independence is restricted, for every unification involves a certain restriction of the former rights of those who unite. But the basic elements of independence undoubtedly remain, for each Republic has the right to secede from the union at its own discretion." Stalin then tried to dismiss the subject by saying that "this is a scholastic question." [27] This question was indeed purely academic, since Stalin had previously stated, with great frankness, that while the secession of a nation from the non-Soviet world was "revolutionary," the secession of a nation from Soviet Russia was "pro-

[24] *Ibid.*, V, 261.
[25] Stalin, "Zakliuchitel'noe slovo," June 12, 1923, in *Sochineniia*, V, 335-36.
[26] *The Fundamental Law (Constitution) of the U.S.S.R.* (Moscow, 1932), ch. 2, Article 4. This has been referred to as the 1923 Constitution because it was adopted by the Central Executive Committee of the Congress of Soviets of the USSR on July 6, 1923, although the formality of final approval by the Congress of Soviets itself was not registered until Jan. 31, 1924.
[27] Stalin, "Doklad o natsional'nykh momentakh," in *Sochineniia*, V, 243.

foundly counterrevolutionary." And woe unto those who sought to test the "voluntary" basis of this federation by proposing a counterrevolutionary idea.

Article 3 of the 1923 Constitution seemed equally bold in proclaiming that "except as so restricted, every Union Republic shall enjoy the rights of an independent state." [28] An examination of the remainder of the Constitution revealed the meaning of the qualification "except as so restricted." The state budgets of the Union Republics were not determined by these Republics, but were incorporated as sections of the single state budget of the USSR, which operated on a single financial plan. The central All-Union government had the power to veto any act whatsoever of the supreme organs of authority in the Union Republics. The government of the USSR operated through three types of Commissariats: an All-Union, or strictly centralist type; a Union Republic, or indirect centralist type, in which there was dual subordination to the Union Republic's Council of People's Commissars and to the head office of the Commissariat in Moscow; and a Republic type of Commissariat, which was nominally responsible only to the Union Republic. All the "commanding heights" of government were lodged in the first two categories, but even those affairs relegated to the Republic level were governed by the norms of the general economic plan, the principles of civil, criminal, and labor legislation, and the principles of public education and health as established by the supreme organs of the USSR. In addition, those activities allocated to the lower categories of administration did not indicate an inalienable right of self-government for the Union Republics. No functions were permanently frozen at any one level, but could be shifted from one type of Commissariat to another to suit the convenience of the center.

If federalism means a substantial degree of independence for the constituent subdivisions, immune from the arbitrary encroachment of the center, then it would seem best to call the Soviet state something other than federal. The Soviet state was essentially centralist, not federalist, and any decentralization of authority seems to have derived from considerations of expediency for the center, rather than from a basic respect for the rights of the periphery. Perhaps Gsovski comes close when he characterizes Soviet "federalism" as a system of bureaucratic decentralization, or a system of deconcen-

[28] *Fundamental Law*, ch. 2, Article 3.

CENTRALISM V. FEDERALISM

trated power.[29] Whatever it is called, it would seem that Soviet "federalism" was more shadow than substance.

THE VOLTE-FACE ON NATIONAL DEVELOPMENT

The Soviet leaders had adopted these federalist trappings with considerable reluctance. Federalist forms in the Soviet state owed their origin (unlike federalism in the United States) to an attempt to solve a nationality problem and integrate distinct ethnic groups. These concessions in form were inescapable, for as Stalin explained, "the strength of the national movement was much greater, and the road to the unification of nations was much more complicated than had been earlier supposed."[30] Before the Bolshevik Revolution the Soviet theorists had envisaged a unitary, centralized world state with a single world culture, rather than a federal world state composed of many distinct and diverse national cultures. The forces unleashed by the revolution quickly shattered this simple image of world unity. To their dismay, the Bolsheviks were propelled not only into a social revolution, but also into the midst of many *national* revolutions, which issued from the disintegration of power in the Russian Empire. They discovered that national strivings could not be neutralized or placated by a few demagogic slogans about national self-determination. This caused them to reevaluate the strength of national sentiment and concede that nationalism was a force that could be ignored only at great peril. The basic Soviet response to this challenge was not to ignore or suppress but to manipulate this resurgence of national feeling. In defiance of their prerevolutionary tradition, they took up the cry of national development and sought to guide it into channels compatible with Soviet power.

Whereas prior to the revolution, Lenin answered "unconditionally no" to the demand "*for* any sort of national development, *for* a 'national culture' in general,"[31] the Tenth Party Congress, meeting in March, 1921, resolved that "the right of national minorities to free national development is guaranteed by the very nature of the Soviet system." The non-Russian peoples were encouraged to de-

[29] Vladimir Gsovski, *Soviet Civil Law* (Ann Arbor, Mich., 1948), I, 83-85.
[30] Stalin, "Primechanie avtora," Dec., 1924, in *Sochineniia*, III, 31.
[31] Lenin, "Kriticheskie zametki po natsional'nomu voprosu," Oct., 1913, in *Sochineniia*, XVII, 146.

velop their own administrative, economic, educational, and cultural institutions, functioning in the native language and staffed by those familiar with the psychology of the indigenous population.[32] The Twelfth Party Congress, in March, 1923, again urged the Russian proletariat to foster the economic and cultural advancement of the non-Russian nations.[33]

The sudden solicitude for national sensitivities was based upon certain practical considerations. The rapid industrialization of the Soviet Union required the services of a large number of technicians of all nationalities. This, in turn, depended upon the rapid elevation of educational standards for all peoples. The impact of Soviet industrialization upon the non-Russian nations was undoubtedly beneficial in so far as it raised their level of literacy and opened up other previously withheld opportunities for cultural development. At the same time, great caution must be exercised in using the rate of industrial development as an index to the general cultural growth of the non-Russian peoples. To a very large extent, Soviet industrialization pumped Russian officialdom and Russian cadres of skilled workers into the non-Russian areas, while the vast reservoir of unskilled labor in the non-Russian areas was drawn into Russian centers of industrial development. This intermingling of populations has tended to break down the traditional native way of life, increase Great Russian domination, and gradually lead to the Russification of the non-Russian nations.

The Soviet promises of national development were also designed to win over various national groups within the USSR who were of uncertain or wavering allegiance. In many instances these peoples could also serve as showcase nations for their fellow nationals who lived immediately beyond the borders of the Soviet Union, and so to facilitate the future expansion of the USSR. Finally, this policy of promising national cultural and economic development was designed to reverberate in areas of emergent nationalism throughout the entire world. Stalin asserted that the aid which the Russian proletariat had pledged to the non-Russian nations presently under Soviet rule anticipated the world-wide pattern of development un-

[32] "Desiatyi s"ezd RKP(b)," March 8–16, 1921, in *KPSS v rez.*, I, 559–62; Stalin, "Ob ocherednykh zadachakh partii v natsional'nom voprose," Feb. 10, 1921, in *Sochineniia*, V, 24–27.

[33] "Dvenadtsatyi s"ezd RKP(b)," April 17–25, 1923, in *KPSS v rez.*, I, 713–18; Stalin, "Natsional'nye momenty," in *Sochineniia*, V, 188–94.

CENTRALISM V. FEDERALISM

der a Soviet world state. The advanced nations of the world will have to "render aid, real and prolonged aid to the toiling masses of the backward nations in their cultural and economic development"; otherwise "it will be impossible to bring about the peaceful coexistence and fraternal collaboration of the toilers of the various nations and nationalities within a single world economic system, which are so essential for the final triumph of socialism." [34] By May, 1925, Stalin had arrived at a formula that claimed to reconcile this program of national development with the international tasks of socialism. He denied that there was any contradiction between these two objectives.

> We are building a proletarian culture. That is absolutely true. But it is also true that proletarian culture, which is socialist in content, assumes different forms and modes of expression among the various peoples that have been drawn into the work of socialist construction, depending on differences of language, way of life, and so forth. Proletarian in content and national in form—such is the universal human culture toward which socialism is marching.[35]

Mankind was marching toward a universal human culture, which would be national in form and socialist in content. This contrasted sharply with Lenin's prerevolutionary image of a single, universal proletarian culture. Stalin acknowledged that this discrepancy had been called to his attention by "some Buriat Comrades," who had asked him to explain "the relationship between this universal human culture and a national culture." These Buriats had inquired:

> The ultimate aim of the Communist Party is a single universal culture. How do you conceive of the transition from the national cultures, which we are developing within the limits of our separate autonomous Republics, to a single universal culture? How must the peculiarities of the separate national cultures (language, etc.) be assimilated?

Stalin did not squarely reject Lenin's prediction of the future assimilation of national cultures. But he chose to interpret this assimilation in a way that would be consistent with the fostering of separate national cultures. Stalin implied that Lenin was only con-

---

[34] Stalin, "K postanovke natsional'nogo voprosa," May 2, 1921, in *Sochineniia*, V, 58–59. The idea of encouraging the national development of backward nations as preparation for their federation with an ever-expanding USSR was written into the Comintern Program; see "Programma Kommunisticheskogo Internatsionala," Sept. 1, 1928, *Kom. Int. v dok.*, pp. 18, 24.

[35] Stalin, "O politicheskikh zadachakh Universiteta Narodov Vostoka," May 18, 1925, in *Sochineniia*, VII, 138.

cerned with the assimilation of some minor national cultures, for the purpose of strengthening other national cultures. "This process of the assimilation of certain nationalities does not exclude, but rather presupposes the opposite process of the strengthening and development of a number of vital and powerful nations, since the partial process of assimilation of various nationalities is a result of the general process of the development of nations." Therefore, these partial assimilations confirm the proposition "that a universal proletarian culture does not exclude, but presupposes and fosters national culture." [36] On a later occasion, Stalin decided to repudiate entirely the idea of assimilation by arbitrarily identifying it with an "attempt to bring about the amalgamation of nations by decree from above, by compulsion." Such a policy meant that "assimilation is unconditionally excluded from the arsenal of Marxism-Leninism, as an antipopular, counterrevolutionary policy, as a fatal policy." [37]

When Lenin advocated the assimilation of nations and national cultures, he was not speaking of a process of partial assimilation, confined to minor nationalities, nor did he identify assimilation with coercive amalgamation. Lenin had conceived of assimilation as "a universal historical tendency" that would "wipe out national differences, a tendency toward the assimilation of nations which, with each decade, becomes all the more powerful, and which presents one of the greatest moving forces transforming capitalism into socialism." Socialism would speed up this process of assimilation, which Lenin defined as "the loss of national characteristics," [38] so that the proletariat would create an "*international* culture, in which only a part of each national culture will enter, namely: only the consistently democratic and socialist content of each national culture." [39] Stalin later protested that "it would be foolish to imagine that Lenin conceived of socialist culture as a *non-national* culture, not possessing a definite national form." [40] The fact is that prior to the revolution, Lenin made no reference whatever to the preservation and strengthening of national forms in the future universal proletarian culture.

[36] *Ibid.*, VII, 139–40.
[37] Stalin, "Natsional'nyi vopros i Leninizm," March 18, 1929, in *Sochineniia*, XI, 347.
[38] Lenin, "Kriticheskie zametki," in *Sochineniia*, XVII, 139–40.
[39] Lenin, "Proekt platformy k IV s"ezdu sotsial-demokratii Latyshskogo Kraia," Nov. 20, 1913, in *ibid.*, XVII, 66.
[40] Stalin, "Politicheskii otchët Tsentral'nogo Komiteta XVI s'ezdu VKP(b)," June 27, 1930, in *Sochineniia*, XII, 368.

CENTRALISM V. FEDERALISM

His disregard of national forms was premised on the basic assumption, which Stalin had elaborated in 1913, that a nation was merely "a historical category, belonging to a definite epoch, the epoch of rising capitalism." Consequently, "the fate of the national movement is naturally connected with the fate of the bourgeoisie." [41] The very idea of a socialist nation bordered on a contradiction in terms.

After the revolution, when the Soviet leaders had sanctioned the idea of national development, Stalin complained of those Communists who believed that "the elimination of the nations existing under capitalism is equivalent to the elimination of nations in general, to the elimination of all nations." Now Stalin berated those who could not see the "obvious" fact that his earlier statement about the disappearance of nations referred only to the disappearance of *capitalist* nations.

But there are other nations. These are the new, Soviet nations, which have developed and taken shape on the basis of the old bourgeois nations after the overthrow of capitalism. . . . The fact of the matter is that the elimination of bourgeois nations signifies the elimination, not of nations in general, but only of bourgeois nations.[42]

Stalin fortified this retroactive interpretation of his original position with Lenin's assertion that "national and state differences . . . will continue to exist for a very long time, even after the dictatorship of the proletariat has been established on a world scale." [43] But this statement, which Lenin made in 1920, again reflected the postrevolutionary Soviet accommodation to nationalism. Stalin would not concede the *volte-face* on national development that had occurred since the revolution.

THE FUSION OF NATIONS STILL THE FINAL TASK OF SOCIALISM

If the Soviet leaders now anticipated the perpetuation of national distinctions for a considerable period of time, even after the creation of the Soviet world state, did this mean a complete abandonment of the earlier vision of the assimilation of all nations and the formation of a single, international (really non-national), universal culture? Stalin asked what meaning should be attributed to Lenin's belief

[41] Stalin, "Marksizm i natsional'nyi vopros," Jan., 1913, in *ibid.*, II, 303, 311.
[42] Stalin, "Natsional'nyi vopros i Leninizm," in *ibid.*, XI, 339-40.
[43] *Ibid.*, XI, 346.

"that the ultimate goal of socialism is the fusion of nations"? Interpreting this statement in a letter of 1927, Stalin explained that "Lenin had in mind the fusion of nations as the final task of socialism which would be realized as a result of the victory of socialism *in all countries*, after 'a very long' period of time, 'after the dictatorship of the proletariat has been established on a world scale.' " [44] Subsequently, Stalin enlarged upon this by saying that a world ruled by socialism "will radically undermine national enmity, will unite nations into one world socialist economic system, and will thus create the real conditions necessary for the gradual fusion of all nations into one whole." [45] He affirmed that Communists are "advocates of the future *fusion* of national cultures into a single common culture (common both in form and in content)," but "for the present we are advocates of the *flowering* of national cultures." "National cultures must be allowed to develop and unfold, to reveal all their potentialities, in order to create conditions for fusing them into one common culture with one common language in the period of the victory of socialism on a world scale." In this apparently contradictory formula "lies the dialectical approach of the Leninist presentation of the question of national culture." [46] Prior to the revolution, Lenin had conceived of the fusion of nations and national cultures in terms of a straight-line progression; it was a process already "evident" under capitalism, which socialism would bring to rapid fruition. When the residual strength of nationalism forced the Soviet regime to make concessions to national culture, at least in form, the zigzag was conveniently explained as an example of Marxian dialectics. However, the ultimate goal remained as before, to pour all humanity into a single mold, common both in form and in content. The Stalinist formula for the ultimate fusing of all national cultures, both in form and in content, has been explicitly reaffirmed in the post-Stalinist period.[47]

Like the introduction of federalism, the encouragement of national development represented a tactical deviation from the objective of a unitary world state. But just as Soviet federalism was disguised centralism, so the formula for promoting national culture

[44] Stalin, "Tovarishchu M. I. Ul'ianovoi," Sept. 16, 1927, in *Sochineniia*, X, 151.
[45] Stalin, "Natsional'nyi vopros i Leninizm," in *ibid.*, XI, 343.
[46] Stalin, "Politicheskii otchët," in *ibid.*, XII, 369.
[47] A. Egorov, "O natsional'nykh osobennostiakh iskusstva," *Kommunist*, No. 9 (June, 1956), p. 87; B. Gafurov, "Uspekhi natsional'noi politiki KPSS i nekotorye voprosy internatsional'nogo vospitaniia," *ibid.*, No. 11 (Aug., 1958), pp. 16–17.

CENTRALISM V. FEDERALISM

was basically an attempt to control, and ultimately to abolish, national culture. Never, at any time, did Stalin advocate the spontaneous and unhampered growth of national cultures. As in the case of federalism, the concession to national culture extended to form, but not to substance. Defining Soviet culture as national in form, but socialist in content, was an attempt to keep the meaning of "national culture" within manageable bounds and to restrict its undesirable extension. It is worth while recalling the precursor of Stalin's 1925 formula on national culture, when in 1904 he suggested, as part of an argument for state *centralism*, that general laws be applied "in that form which will be most useful."[48] Similarly, in the case of national cultures, the form could assume local variations, but the content was to be one and the same for all, emanating from a single centralized source—the Party. And what if it should prove impossible to separate form and content into two neat packages? What if a national form should influence content? Who then should decide whether this aspect of national form should be encouraged or repressed? Obviously, the Party was to be the arbiter of this minimal right of national expression.

THE EFFECT OF INCREASING PARTY CENTRALISM ON THE MEANING OF "NATIONAL IN FORM, SOCIALIST IN CONTENT"

Freedom of national expression turned in large measure upon the struggle for freedom of individual expression, and the latter progressively contracted with the consolidation of power in the Party. The heyday of cultural development for all Soviet nationalities occurred in the 1920s, which was precisely the period in which Stalin was still involved in his intra-Party intrigues, eliminating first one "deviation," then another. The conversion of the Party into a totally centralized monolith also radically transformed and restricted the character of national development.

In his pursuit of a monolithic Party, Stalin was never embarrassed by the need to pay lip service to federalism. In Party affairs federalism forever remained a term of violent abuse, and after the Tenth Party Congress, in 1921, "factionalism" underwent the same fate. What a telling condemnation was intended when Stalin claimed that "for Trotsky the Party is something in the nature of a federation of

[48] Stalin, "Kak ponimaet sotsial-demokratiia natsional'nyi vopros?" Sept. 14, 1904, in *Sochineniia*, I, 45.

factional groups with separate factional centers."[49] The elimination of Stalin's rivals under the accusation of factionalism was accompanied by a constant strengthening of centralism at the expense of the "democracy" that was implied in the Party's formula of "democratic centralism." The increasing restrictions upon discussion within the Party inevitably weakened, or even eliminated, the opportunity for the dissident members to resist the authority of the Party center.

It was left for the Great Purges of 1936–1938 to put the capstone on the victory of Party centralism. The stronghold of federalist sentiment was found among the leaders of the non-Russian peoples, who wanted fewer political restraints from Moscow, and more freedom to develop their native, non-Russian cultures. It was precisely this group which the Great Purges almost entirely obliterated. To be sure, the purges made heavy inroads on the Russian leadership as well, but there were two differences in the long-range results. The recuperative power of the Russian nation was higher. As Kolarz has noted: "It is true that Stalin's purges affected both Russians and non-Russians alike, but the non-Russians, having only a limited reserve of educated persons at their disposal, suffered proportionally much heavier losses than the Great Russians who numbered 100,000,000."[50]

The purges also accelerated the movement down the path, by then well marked, toward an open revival of Great Russian chauvinism, since Russian chauvinism was the national expression of political centralism. The elevation of Russian national prestige at the expense of the non-Russian peoples gradually transformed the meaning of a "culture, national in form, and socialist in content." As part of the program to glorify the Tsarist Russian past, Russian conquerors and empire builders were resurrected and made "national" heroes for all the peoples of the USSR, while at the same time those indigenous national heroes of the non-Russian peoples, who had fought the encroachments of Russian imperialism, were denounced as "counterrevolutionary and unprogressive." These attempts to recreate the past in a Russian image were designed to extend the "leading role" of the Russian "elder brother" in the future. As a result, the "socialist" content, which was obligatory for all Soviet nations, was increasingly infused with Great Russian symbols, while

[49] Stalin, "Rech' 5 avgusta," Aug. 5, 1927, in *ibid.*, X, 79.
[50] Kolarz, *Russia and Her Colonies*, p. 11.

the scope of the traditional non-Russian national forms was correspondingly restricted. Soviet culture ever tended to become Russian nationalist in form and Russian socialist in content.

FEDERALISM IN THE 1936 CONSTITUTION OF THE USSR

The beginning of the Great Purges also coincided with the adoption of the 1936 Constitution of the USSR, which remains the constitutional basis of the present Soviet federation. Like the 1923 Constitution before it, the new Constitution claimed to embody the model of a federal state. But just as the Great Purges made a mockery of the elaborate constitutional provisions "guaranteeing" the inviolability of person and home, so fundamental governmental decisions continued to be made in the highest Party circles in an extra-legal manner, without regard to the constitutional formalities of state federalism. The new Constitution, Stalin professed, was called forth by the abolition of all antagonistic classes in the Soviet Union. This was an indirect way of stating that the federal forms were now totally filled with the "monolithic" content of Soviet society. Vyshinsky described this new polity in the Jacobin-like terms of the "one and indivisible" general will, which was rephrased, after the fashion of Babeuf, in class terminology. In Soviet society, he asserted, "the will of the working class and the peasantry fundamentally coincided, blending into the general will of the overwhelming majority of the toilers." [51] Soviet statutes express "the will of the working class," which in turn "merges with the will of the entire people. This provides the basis for speaking of our Soviet socialist law as the expression of the will of the whole people." [52]

The contrast between form and substance presented the paradox of federalist forms continuing to blossom from the ever-hardening core of centralist power. When the USSR was first organized, for example, it was composed of four Union Republics and ten Autonomous Republics,[53] while the 1936 Constitution provided for eleven Union Republics and twenty Autonomous Republics. This was accomplished by creating new Republics and by dissolving the Trans-

[51] Vyshinsky, *Sovetskoe gosudarstvennoe pravo*, p. 164.
[52] A. Ia. Vyshinsky, *Osnovnye zadachi nauki sovetskogo sotsialisticheskogo prava* (Moscow, 1938), p. 40.
[53] Batsell, *Soviet Rule*, p. 124. This calculation is based on dating the formation of the USSR from the treaty of union of Dec. 30, 1922.

caucasian federation into its constituent units. By this time the centralist pull in the Soviet state was so strong that Georgia, Armenia, and Azerbaijan could enter the USSR directly, without presenting a serious threat to Moscow's control. In the words of the Soviet legal authority, Denisov, "the extraordinary development of Soviet forms of state life" were accompanied "by a parallel process of political centralization, by a strengthening of the unity of Soviet statehood." [54]

In some respects even the forms of the 1936 Constitution were more centralist than those of the 1923 document. While retaining the centralist features of its predecessor, the 1936 Constitution included several legal innovations that augmented the central power. The Procurator General of the USSR, for example, was empowered to supervise the execution of laws at all levels of government, without regard to federal distinctions, and to bring to trial any citizen or state official within any Union Republic, his agents on the local level performing "their functions independently of any local organs whatsoever." [55] The supreme organs of the All-Union government were also granted additional authority over ethnic and geographic units within each Union Republic by requiring that the central government approve "the formation of new Territories and Regions and also of new Autonomous Republics and Autonomous Regions within Union Republics." [56]

Stalin insisted upon the continued need for a bicameral body (now renamed the Supreme Soviet) in which the Council of Nationalities would have full equality with the Council of the Union. But the Council of Nationalities remained, as before, ornamental in character.[57] As part of this program of window dressing, Stalin again focused attention upon the right of each Union Republic to secede from the Soviet federation, scolding those who said this provision was but an empty verbalism. "To delete from the Constitution the article providing for the right of free secession from the USSR would violate the voluntary character of this union." So that "this right does not become a meaningless scrap of paper," he suggested

[54] A. I. Denisov, *Sovetskoe gosudarstvennoe pravo* (Moscow, 1947), p. 222.
[55] *Constitution (Fundamental Law) of the Union of Soviet Socialist Republics* (Moscow, 1954), Articles 113, 117.
[56] *Ibid.*, Article 14(f).
[57] See Charles Bohlen's colorful report of a meeting of the Council of Nationalities in 1938: *Foreign Relations of the United States: The Soviet Union, 1933-1939* (Washington, 1952), pp. 509-10.

CENTRALISM V. FEDERALISM

that the creation of Union Republics be limited to the border regions of the USSR. This would permit a Union Republic to "be in a position, logically and actually, to raise the question of secession from the USSR." Moreover, to qualify as a Union Republic "the nationality which imparts its name to a given Soviet Republic must constitute a more or less compact majority within that Republic," which should have "a population of at least a million inhabitants." Such considerations were again designed to give meaning to the right of secession, since "it would be wrong to assume that a small Soviet Republic with a very small population and a small army could hope to maintain its existence as an independent state." [58]

If taken seriously, these propositions would violate two conceptions that are basic to the Soviet goal of a world state. In the first place, it had always been assumed that the Soviet leaders would work ceaselessly for the disintegration of the capitalist nation-state system, and the reintegration of these nations into a World Soviet Federation. Could it be assumed that Stalin had any intentions whatever of reversing this process by genuinely contemplating the secession of a Union Republic from the Soviet Union? He attempted to cover this objection by adding that "of course, none of our Republics would actually raise the question of seceding from the USSR," since "there is not a single Republic that would want to secede from the USSR." [59] The Great Purges, hot on the heels of the 1936 Constitution, provided conclusive proof, if any were needed, that the very suggestion of secession was an act of treason. For example, the former Chairman of the Central Executive Committee of the Uzbek SSR was accused of plotting the secession of Uzbekistan from the USSR, and of making it an unofficial British protectorate, like Afghanistan. Vyshinsky, the State Prosecutor, jumped at this "confession" of criminal plans: "And so, secession from the Soviet Union, the independence of Uzbekistan, an agreement with England, means that Uzbekistan reaches another shore?" [60] The defendants in the March, 1938, trial were accused, among other things, of desiring the "dismembering of the USSR, and severing from it the Ukraine, Belorussia, the Central Asiatic

---
[58] Stalin, "O proekta Konstitutsii Soiuza SSR," Nov. 25, 1936, in *Doklad o proekte*, pp. 41–43.
[59] *Ibid.*, pp. 41–42.
[60] *Report of Court Proceedings in the Case of the Anti-Soviet "Bloc of Rights and Trotskyites,"* March 2–13, 1938 (Moscow, 1938), p. 229.

Republics, Georgia, Armenia, Azerbaijan, and the Maritime Region of the Far East." [61]

Second, if these qualifications for a Union Republic were observed faithfully, it would mean that no new Union Republics could be added onto the present Soviet federation, since this would deprive the existing Union Republics of their "position, logically and actually, to raise the question of secession." This prospect runs counter to all other Soviet expectations that are premised on the growth of the present Soviet federation into a World Soviet Federation. There is the possibility that the present Union Republics could be dissolved or assigned some other status as new Union Republics were added to the growing periphery of the Soviet federation. This too would seem to be going to preposterous lengths to justify a few sentences that Stalin uttered in 1936. It is more likely that if and when a propitious time comes to add Union Republics to the Soviet federation, these sentences will conveniently fade into oblivion, and will become just as dangerous to quote as Stalin's initial statements about the impossibility of socialism in one country, or the early withering away of the state.

The original conditions that supposedly governed the creation of a Union Republic have already been violated, or replaced by new circumstances. How realistic is it, strictly from a geographic point of view, for the present Union Republics to raise the question of secession, when the Soviet Union is ringed by Eastern European satellite states and by Communist China? On the contrary, would it not seem more logical some day for these states to join the present Soviet federation? [62] And did not the existence of the Karelo-Finnish Union Republic, formed in 1940 and arbitrarily dissolved in 1956, violate the requirements that the nationalities giving their names to a Soviet Republic should constitute a majority within that Republic, which should have a total population of at least one million? According to official Soviet statistics the total population of the Karelo-Finnish SSR in 1941 was 606,333, the majority of whom were Russians, not Karelians and Finns.[63] Similarly, it is dubious whether

[61] *Ibid.*, p. 5. See also *Report of Court Proceedings in the Case of the Anti-Soviet Trotskyite Centre,* Jan. 23–30, 1937 (Moscow, 1937), pp. 8, 58, 64, 113, 115, 153, 172, 184, 491, 575.
[62] This point is developed more fully in chapter 11 below.
[63] *Bol'shaia sovetskaia entsiklopediia: Soiuz Sovetskikh Sotsialisticheskikh Respublik* (Moscow, 1947), p. 1938. The percentage figures given here (63 percent Russian, 23 percent Karelian, 14 percent others) were those within

CENTRALISM V. FEDERALISM

the Kazakhs comprised even a bare majority of the population of the Kazakh SSR, on the basis of the 1939 Soviet census.[64] The 1959 census placed both Kazakhs and Kirghiz in minority positions in their own Republics.[65] And what a curious interpretation of a border Republic was devised in August, 1945, when the Koenigsberg Area of East Prussia was added to the RSFSR, not to the Lithuanian SSR, with which it was contiguous. Moscow doubtless preferred to control this region of untested reliability directly, rather than through Vilna. When this area is well in hand, in part due to the influx of Russian settlers, it is possible that it might be attached to the Lithuanian SSR, in the same way that the Crimean Region was transferred in February, 1954, from the RSFSR, with which it was not contiguous, to the Ukrainian SSR, as a result of the mass deportation of the Crimean Tatars.[66] All this would indicate that there is nothing very sacred about the borders of a Union Republic, which have been, and will likely continue to be, subject to arbitrary manipulation to meet the needs of the moment. Vyshinsky stated the matter succinctly when he said that "Soviet federation is not dogma; its forms cannot be frozen and established once and for all, but must evolve, changing to the extent required by the concrete environment." [67] There is no inherent rigidity in Soviet federalism which could prevent it from expanding, if the "concrete environment" permitted.

The highly manipulative quality of Soviet federalism was graphically demonstrated by the constitutional amendment of 1944. This authorized each Union Republic "to enter into direct relations with foreign states," and to create "its own Republican military forma-

---

the 1939 borders, before the addition of some Finnish territory as a result of the Soviet-Finnish War of 1939-1940. But even within the expanded borders Towster estimates that the Republic was 57 percent Russian. (Julian Towster, *Political Power in the U.S.S.R., 1917-1947* [New York, 1948], p. 338.) See also A. V. Iurchenko, "The Liquidation of the Karelo-Finnish S.S.R.," *Bulletin of the Institute*, III, No. 10 (Oct., 1956), 28-32.

[64] The Soviet claim that the Kazakhs accounted for 57.1 percent of the population of the Kazakh SSR is misleading, since the census figures show that the total population of the Kazakh SSR was 6,146,000, while the total number of Kazakhs for the entire USSR, not all of whom lived within the Kazakh SSR, was only 3,098,800. (*Bol'shaia*, pp. 60, 62, 1843.) Thus the Kazakhs probably did not comprise 50 percent of the population of Kazakhstan in 1939.

[65] According to *Pravda*, Feb. 4, 1960, the Kazakhs comprise only 29.6 percent and the Kirghiz only 40.5 percent in their respective Republics.

[66] "The Transfer of the Crimea to the Ukraine," *Bulletin of the Institute*, I, No. 1 (April, 1954), 30-33.

[67] Vyshinsky, *Sovetskoe gosudarstvennoe pravo*, p. 216.

tions," both activities to be pursued within the framework of policy established by the higher organs of state power in the USSR.[68] Molotov hailed this amendment as a "great expansion in the activities of the Union Republics, which had become possible as a result of their political, economic, and cultural growth, or in other words, as a result of their national development." It was "a new, important step in the practical solution of the national problem in the multinational Soviet state, a new victory for our Leninist-Stalinist national policy." [69] He failed to note that this amendment was closely patterned after the proposal of Rakovskii and Skrypnik, advanced prior to the adoption of the 1923 Constitution, when it was suggested that each Union Republic retain its Commissariats of Foreign Affairs and Foreign Trade, operating under the general direction of Moscow. At that time Stalin protested: "Where could we find this single union state, if each Republic had its own Commissariat of Foreign Affairs and Foreign Trade? . . . We are not creating a confederation, but a federation of Republics, a single union state, uniting Military Affairs, Foreign Affairs, Foreign Trade, and other matters." [70] What happened between 1923 and 1944 to cause this about-face? It would seem that in 1923 any participation by the Union Republics in foreign relations might have created genuine obstacles to the formulation and implementation of a single, centrally controlled foreign policy. The 1944 amendment reflected the measure of confidence that the center had acquired to proliferate forms bordering on confederation, which could no longer present any threat whatever to the centralist substance of Soviet policy.

This amendment was widely interpreted as a gesture to facilitate the expansion of the Soviet Union, by permitting additional states to be transformed into Union Republics, while retaining their accustomed voice in international politics. This speculation has so far been unfounded, though the possibility of its future usefulness for this purpose remains. Its immediate purpose was to obtain membership in the United Nations for every Union Republic in the USSR. Edward Stettinius reported that when he met the Soviet representa-

[68] *Constitution,* Articles 14(a), (g); 18(a), (b); 60(e), (f); 68(d), (e).
[69] "O preobrazovanii Narkomata Oborony i Narkomindela iz Obshchesoiuznykh v Soiuzno-Respublikanskie Narkomaty; doklad tov. V. M. Molotova v Verkhovnom Sovete SSSR 1 fevralia 1944 goda," *Pravda,* Feb. 2, 1944, p. 1.
[70] Stalin, "Zakliuchitel'noe slovo," in *Sochineniia,* V, 336.

CENTRALISM V. FEDERALISM

tives at Dumbarton Oaks in August, 1944, they proposed "that all sixteen Soviet Republics be admitted as members of the world organization." This request was transmitted to Secretary of State Hull who asked, "are these Russians going to break up our hopes of a world organization?"[71] At Yalta, in February, 1945, the Soviet negotiators pared down their request for UN membership to the Ukrainian, Belorussian, and Lithuanian Soviet Socialist Republics (in addition to membership for the USSR), and then settled for supplementary seats for the Ukraine and Belorussia.[72]

Beyond the rather modest accomplishment of permitting a single foreign policy to be issued in triplicate, what evidence is there that this federalist gesture has kindled any genuine activity in the Union Republics? Towster observed that the achievements of this new policy could be summed up in a "few minor agreements between Soviet border Republics and such satellites as Poland," which were concluded soon after the adoption of the 1944 amendment. No Ukrainian officials participated in the negotiation and signing of the Soviet-Czechoslovak Treaty of June, 1945, by which Sub-carpathian Ruthenia was transferred to the Ukrainian SSR. In August, 1947, the Soviet authorities rejected a British proposal to establish diplomatic relations with the Ukraine. In August, 1948, Vyshinsky waived the right of Ukrainian representation on the Danubian Commission, and in May, 1951, the exchange of strips of Ukrainian and Polish territory was conducted without the benefit of a Ukrainian delegation.[73] In the post-Stalinist period Moscow has assigned some Union Republics quasi-diplomatic functions, such as the establishment of extensive contacts between representatives of the Uzbek Republic and leading figures of the Afro-Asian world, and the expansion of this type of activity is distinctly possible.[74] As to the Union Republican military formations authorized by the

[71] Quoted in Edward R. Stettinius, Jr., *Roosevelt and the Russians* (New York, 1949), p. 17.
[72] *Ibid.*, pp. 191–92, 196–98, 202–3, 281–83, 296–97; Winston S. Churchill, *Triumph and Tragedy* (Boston, 1953), pp. 357–60; James F. Byrnes, *Speaking Frankly* (New York, 1947), pp. 40–42.
[73] Julian Towster, "Recent Trends and Strategies in Soviet Federalism," *The Political Quarterly*, XXIII, No. 2 (April–June, 1952), 167–68.
[74] For an examination of the juridical basis and the diplomatic potentialities of the Union Republic Ministries of Foreign Affairs, see Vernon V. Aspaturian, "The Union Republics and Soviet Diplomacy: Concepts, Institutions, and Practices," *American Political Science Review*, LIII, No. 2 (June, 1959), 383–411.

1944 amendment, nothing whatever has been heard of that, nor is such a development likely in view of the mass defection of non-Russian nationalities during the Second World War.

In the light of the foregoing survey, what meaning should be attached to the assertion in Article 13 of the Soviet Constitution that "the Union of Soviet Socialist Republics is a federal state"? The Soviet leaders have contrived elaborate federalist-appearing devices that have attempted to take advantage of and to give a minimal play to national sentiment, not only for the nations under their control, but also for those nations that they seek to attach to their self-proclaimed embryo of a world federation. But using the vocabulary of federalism has never touched the core of their political philosophy, which is thoroughly centralist, nor would it seem to have altered their ultimate aim of a unitary world state.

NATIONAL LANGUAGE AS THE FORM OF NATIONAL CULTURE

The last refuge from Soviet centralism in the field of national expression has been the continued existence of a certain diversity in the forms of national culture. Here, too, there has been an ever-mounting pressure for conformity on the part of all non-Russian nations to the requirements of Great Russian chauvinism. In 1949 Dunaeva expressed this growing conformity in euphemistic terms when she wrote: "In the Soviet Union a significant process of the drawing together of the cultures of the different nationalities is going on." [75] By 1950 Stalin had reduced all the differences in national cultures to the single element of national language. During the linguistics discussion of that year Stalin asked: "Are not our Comrades familiar with the well-known formula of the Marxists that the present Russian, Ukrainian, Belorussian, and other cultures are socialist in content and national in form, i.e., in language?" [76] This was not an idle statement, nor a slip of the tongue, for Kammari reiterated quite plainly: "Language is the national form of a given culture." [77] This blunt formulation affirms that the content of all national cultures is identical and that the difference in form can be equated quite simply with the difference in language. Put another

---

[75] Dunaeva, *Collaboration of Nations*, 1949, p. 40.
[76] Stalin, "Otnositel'no Marksizma v iazykoznanii," June 20, 1950, in *Marksizm i voprosy*, pp. 17–18.
[77] Kammari, *Development by J. V. Stalin*, 1949, p. 70.

CENTRALISM V. FEDERALISM

way, the Soviet development of national cultures has culminated in the right to read *Pravda* in many languages, but no matter how you slice it, it is still *Pravda*.

If national languages have become the last decisive sanctuary from Soviet centralism, what future do the Soviet theoreticians project for national languages? Would the creation of a Soviet world state lead to the formation of a single world language, and if so, what language would this likely be? It is to this question that we now turn.

IX. World State and World Language

THE Soviet grand design for transforming the present nation-state system into a Soviet world state envisages a fundamental reshaping of national languages. A national language, as the nerve center of a national memory, is probably the most important single medium through which national traditions are nurtured and transmitted. Of all of those ingredients producing a sense of national cohesion, a national language is doubtless the fundamental element, although the existence of several multilingual nation-states would indicate that national languages need not be an insuperable barrier to the growth of broader loyalties. Yet even here the continued use of national languages imparts a sense of national distinctiveness which cannot be obliterated, except through the destruction of the various national languages. If the time should ever come when all national languages are merged and transformed into a single world language, then the last glimmering of nationalism will have flickered out. The fate of national languages can therefore serve as a barometer marking the rise and fall of the very concept of a nation.

As the ultimate destiny of nations is a matter for the distant future, no Soviet theoretician has ever indicated that the extinction of all national languages or the adoption of a single world language is prerequisite to the creation of a world state. The question of a world language has therefore not been among the first problems with which the Soviet regime contended in projecting the image of a world state. But as this subject was bound to arise from any serious consideration of a world state, the Stalinist era produced a number of striking and explicit statements which both foretold the doom of national languages and predicted the formation of a single world language.

LENINIST ASSUMPTIONS ABOUT NATIONAL LANGUAGES

Stalin's contributions were based upon assumptions implicit in Lenin's vision of a socialist world state. Lenin foresaw the assimilation of nations and the formation of a single proletarian, non-national world culture. However Lenin's actual statements on the anticipated role of national languages were confined to his experience in the multilingual Russian Empire. He recognized "the unquestionably progressive significance of centralization, of large governmental units, and of a single language," yet he opposed the mandatory adoption of Russian as the official state language.[1] The compulsory teaching of Russian in schools in non-Russian areas, and the obligatory use of Russian in the official institutions of non-Russian regions, were part of the hated Russification policy of the Tsars. This, Lenin rightly perceived, only served to drive nations apart and retarded the process of their assimilation. Consequently, Lenin pleaded for the right of each nation to use and freely develop its own language as the first step toward the voluntary adoption of a language common to all nations. With the abolition of privileges for any one language, the objective forces of economic development would do the rest. "The demands of the economic factors will, of their own, *determine* which language of a given country the majority would *profitably* learn in the interests of trade. This determination will be the more certain and the populations of different nations will voluntarily adopt it the more quickly and widely, the more democracy will be consistently introduced."[2]

THE BOLSHEVIK REVOLUTION AND THE FOSTERING OF NATIONAL LANGUAGES

This position, which Lenin assumed before the Bolshevik Revolution, underestimated the strength and tenacity of the national sentiment of the oppressed nations which were soon to be set free by the

[1] Lenin, "Pis'mo S. G. Shaumianu," Dec. 6, 1913, in *Sochineniia*, XVII, 89. On the other hand, Lenin specifically favored the widespread use of Russian within the Empire, if it could be introduced without compulsion: "The progressive significance of the *Russian* language for a vast number of miserable and backward nations is indisputable."
[2] Lenin, "Liberaly i demokraty v voprose o iazykakh," Sept. 18, 1913, in *ibid.*, XVI, 596. See also, "Nuzhen-li obiazatel'nyi gosudarstvennyi iazyk?" Jan. 31, 1914, in *ibid.*, XVII, 179–81; "Razvrashchenie rabochikh utonchënnym natsionalizmom," May 23, 1914, in *ibid.*, XVII, 361.

disintegration of the Russian Empire. The first few years after the revolution were consumed with the implementation of the first phase of development in which each nation rediscovered its own national traditions and language. At this point there was little talk of the second stage of development in which a common language would supersede the newly revitalized national languages. The suggestion of one common language for the Soviet Union was condemned as a deviation of Great Russian chauvinism, and even the very prospect of a single world language came under attack. At the height of this period, in May, 1925, Stalin said:

Certain persons (Kautsky, for example) talk of the creation of a single universal language and of the dying away of all other languages in the period of socialism. I have very little faith in this theory of a single all-embracing language. Experience, in any case, does not speak for, but against, this theory. Up until now the socialist revolution has not diminished, but increased the number of languages, since it has aroused the broad masses of humanity, pushed them onto the political stage and awakened a new life in a whole series of new nationalities, which were formerly unknown or almost unknown.[3]

This statement was made on the same occasion that Stalin introduced the idea of a "culture, national in form and socialist in content." This formula was intended to set limits upon the further development of nationalism, by standardizing the ideological content of each culture. Though it was somewhat less obvious, the formula also provided the basis for confining the development of national forms, among which language was the most important, to those modes of expression which Moscow chose to tolerate. The "national form" of a given culture, like its ideological content, was a highly manipulative concept, subject to official definition by Moscow. The handwriting on the wall now clearly warned that henceforth the integrative, not the disintegrative, phase of national development would gradually assume paramount importance. While in 1925 this formula was first directed toward integrating the content of each national culture, within a decade it was also aimed at integrating the forms of national cultures, including, first and foremost, the integration of national languages. Soon the script, vocabulary, and even the syntax of these national languages were all subjected to violent and arbitrary alterations. Thus, when Stalin re-

[3] Stalin, "O politicheskikh zadachakh Universiteta Narodov Vostoka," May 18, 1925, in *Sochineniia*, VII, 138-39.

turned to the language discussion in 1929 and 1930, he no longer rejected the idea of a world language.

STALIN'S CONCEPT OF A NON-NATIONAL WORLD LANGUAGE

Stalin expounded his views on a world language in an article written in March, 1929, though it was not published until 1949. It is difficult to explain the delay in its publication, since he repeated the essence of these ideas publicly in his report to the Sixteenth Party Congress in June, 1930. In these declarations Stalin claimed to revert to the Leninist tradition by acknowledging "Lenin's theses, namely, that with the victory of socialism on a *world scale*, national differences and national languages will begin to die away, that after this victory national languages will begin to be supplanted by one common language." [4] Stalin neglected to mention that this was not Lenin's original position, but only the one forced upon him by the revolution. Before the revolution Lenin had held that the process of assimilation of nations was already in progress under the bourgeoisie, and that it would be greatly accelerated by the advent of socialism. He did not then believe that national differences would only *begin* to die away *after* the formation of a socialist world state. Stalin accurately cited Lenin's statement that "national and state differences . . . will continue to exist for a very long time even after the dictatorship of the proletariat has been established on a world scale," [5] but failed to note that this statement, made in 1920, was at variance with Lenin's prerevolutionary views. Nor did Stalin indicate that this 1920 statement contradicted his own prerevolutionary position. In 1913 Stalin had agreed fully with the Marxian premise that " 'national differences . . . are now more and more vanishing,' and that 'the supremacy of the proletariat will cause them to vanish still faster.' " [6] By 1929–1930 Stalin sought to extricate Lenin and himself from this contradiction, as well as to obscure his own openly heretical position of 1925, when he denounced the idea of a world language, by shifting the blame for these ideological confusions onto a scapegoat.

Stalin again dragged Kautsky onto the stage and carefully propped him up as a straw man whom he could blow over as a tour de force.

[4] Stalin, "Natsional'nyi vopros i Leninizm," March 18, 1929, in *ibid.*, XI, 342.
[5] *Ibid.*, XI, 346.
[6] Stalin, "Marksizm i natsional'nyi vopros," Jan., 1913, in *Sochineniia*, II, 330.

Stalin now criticized Kautsky for suggesting that a revolution in the Austro-Hungarian Empire of the nineteenth century would have led to the Germanizing of the Czechs and the adoption of German as a common language. "The mere force of unshackled intercourse," Kautsky maintained, "the mere force of modern culture of which the Germans were the vehicles, without any forcible Germanization, would have converted into Germans the backward Czech petty bourgeoisie, peasants, and proletarians who had nothing to gain from their decayed nationality." [7] This statement closely paralleled Lenin's assertion that the effect of economic factors, by themselves, would determine which language would be adopted by the majority in any given mixture of peoples. It was also practically a verbatim quotation from Engels, who had looked upon the Germans as agents of progress and dismissed the Czechs as an ethnic by-product.[8]

Now Stalin called Kautsky "a dilettante in the national question," since he "praises the assimilating 'work' of the Germans among the Czechs, and casually asserts that the Czechs . . . have no future as a nation." [9] Getting to the heart of the matter, Stalin said that Kautsky "does not understand the mechanics of the development of nations and has no inkling of the colossal power of stability possessed by nations, and believes that the fusion of nations is possible long before the victory of socialism." Here Stalin obviously shifted the onus of the prerevolutionary Bolshevik views onto Kautsky, since it is abundantly clear that, until hit by the actual impact of the revolution, neither Lenin nor Stalin had a real "inkling of the colossal power of stability possessed by nations."

This assertion of faith in the enormous staying power of nations furnished Stalin a convenient pretext for explaining away his condemnation, in 1925, of the concept of a world language. Stalin said that in excluding the possibility of a world language it must have been "evident that what I had in mind in my speech was not the period of the victory of socialism on a *world scale*, but exclusively the period of the victory of socialism in *one country*." [10] Stalin's actual statement of 1925 was that "certain persons (Kautsky, for example) talk of the creation of a single universal language and of

[7] Quoted in Stalin, "Politicheskii otchët Tsentral'nogo Komiteta XVI s"ezdu VKP(b)," June 27, 1930, in *ibid.*, XII, 364 (italics omitted).
[8] Engels, "Hungary and Panslavism," 1849, in *Russian Menace*, p. 59; Engels, "Democratic Panslavism," 1849, in *ibid.*, p. 77.
[9] Stalin, "Natsional'nyi vopros," in *Sochineniia*, XI, 344.
[10] *Ibid.*, XI, 344-45.

the dying away of all other languages in the period of socialism. I have very little faith in this theory of a single all-embracing language." From this it is by no means evident that Stalin was drawing a distinction between the periods of the victory of socialism in one country and the victory of socialism on a world scale, and thereby endorsing the idea of the emergence of a world language after the creation of a Soviet world state. But it was just this distinction upon which Stalin now wished to rest his theory of a world language. He looked forward to "the flowering of national cultures (and languages) in the period of the proletarian dictatorship in one country with the object of preparing the conditions for their dying away and merging into one common socialist culture (and into one common language) in the period of the victory of socialism in the entire world." [11] Stalin indicated that the ultimate world language could not be identified with any one of the presently existing national languages, for "national languages must inevitably fuse into one common language, which, of course, will be neither Great Russian nor German, but something new." [12] Barmine reports that Stalin once considered Esperanto as this future non-national world language, but abandoned the idea after an unsuccessful attempt to master it.[13]

Whatever this new world language might be, Stalin warned that it could not be hurried into existence immediately after the victory of world socialism, "at one stroke, by decree from above." [14] This world language must evolve without coercion, and through a gradual series of stages. "It is a mistake to think that the first stage of the period of the world dictatorship of the proletariat will mark the beginning of the formation of a single common language." At this point the hitherto oppressed national cultures and national languages will find full freedom of expression. Only in the second stage of world socialism, when a single world socialist economy has been successfully constructed, "only in that stage will something in

[11] Stalin, "Politicheskii otchët," in *Sochineniia*, XII, 370.
[12] Stalin, "Zakliuchitel'noe slovo po politicheskomu otchëtu TsK XVI S"ezdu VKP(b)," July 2, 1930, in *ibid.*, XIII, 5.
[13] Alexander Barmine, *One Who Survived* (New York, 1945), p. 260. On the fluctuation of Soviet linguistic theory toward Esperanto and the Soviet attempt to make use of the Esperanto movement, see George P. Springer, *Early Soviet Theories in Communication* (MIT Center for International Studies, Cambridge, Mass., 1956), pp. 1, 11–16, 28–37; E. Bokarev, "Esperanto—vspomogatel'nyi mezhdunarodnyi iazyk," *Literaturnaia gazeta*, July 18, 1957, p. 2.
[14] Stalin, "Natsional'nyi vopros," in *Sochineniia*, XI, 347.

the nature of a common language begin to take shape, for only in that stage will nations feel the need to have a common international language in addition to their own national languages, as a convenience of intercourse and as an aid to economic, cultural, and political cooperation." In the beginning, Stalin anticipated that there might be several common international languages existing alongside national languages. "It is probable that, at first, not one economic center will be formed, common to all nations and with one common language, but several zonal economic centers for separate groups of nations, with a separate common language for each group of nations, and that only later will these centers combine into one common world socialist economic center, with one language common to all nations." The final stage will arrive when the world socialist economic system has fully consolidated its gains and "when practice has convinced nations of the superiority of a common language over national languages." Only at this point will "national differences and languages begin to die away and make room for a world language, common to all nations." [15]

These views, expressed in 1929, were fully upheld in the Soviet linguistics discussion of 1950, at which time Stalin further refined his description of the fate of national languages, both before and after the creation of a Soviet world state. *"Prior to the victory of socialism on a world scale* . . . when national and colonial oppression remains in effect, when national isolation and mutual distrust of nations are reinforced by state differences," Stalin held that the crossing of two languages "does not yield some new, third language" but rather "one of the languages usually comes out the victor, whereas the other dies away." On the other hand, *"after the victory of socialism* on a world scale . . . when national and colonial oppression has been liquidated, when national isolation and mutual distrust of nations have been replaced by mutual confidence and a drawing together of nations," then "national languages will have the opportunity freely to enrich one another on the basis of cooperation."

In this case we will not have two languages, one of which is suffering defeat while the other emerges victorious from the struggle, but hundreds of national languages from which at first the most enriched single zonal languages will emerge as a result of lengthy economic, political, and

[15] *Ibid.*, XI, 348-49.

cultural cooperation of nations, and subsequently the zonal languages will fuse into one common international language, which, of course, will be neither German, nor Russian, nor English, but a new language which has absorbed the best elements of the national and zonal languages.[16]

It would seem that the limits of this inquiry had been reached, as this view offers no prospect of further identifying this future world language. Continued probing would be pointless if, in fact, the Soviet leadership considered all the existing major languages on a par, as being equally eligible to shape the form of this future common world tongue. But closer examination shows that this is clearly not the case. In the struggle for world supremacy between East and West the roles of Russian and English are cast in entirely different lights.

RUSSIAN AND ENGLISH COMPARED AS
INTERNATIONAL LANGUAGES

The Soviet regime claims that "American colonizers, aspiring to world domination, are seeking to have English recognized as the world language which should replace all other languages." Accordingly, the American motto "E Pluribus Unum" means "from the separate sovereign states to a single world government, with English as the single world language." [17] To facilitate this conquest "American linguists are hastily preparing plans for the 'simplification' of the English language in order to make it the single international tongue." These efforts are producing "the poisonous bacteria of cosmopolitanism" intended to "destroy a feeling of national dignity in the soul," and thereby to promote the capitulation of nations to the "American imperialists." [18] But such strivings will be of no avail, since an attempt "to force the English language upon all peoples" is sure to meet with "utter failure and defeat." [19]

The prospect for Russian is depicted in precisely the opposite

[16] Stalin, "Tovarishchu A. Kholopovu," July 28, 1950, in *Marksizm i voprosy*, pp. 45-47.
[17] T. P. Lomtev, "I. V. Stalin o razvitii natsional'nykh iazykov v epokhu sotsializma," *Voprosy filosofii*, No. 2 (1949), pp. 136-37.
[18] A. Elistratova, "Izmenniki narodu," *Literaturnaia gazeta*, March 2, 1949, p. 2.
[19] M. Kammari, "An Outstanding Contribution to the Science of Marxism," *New Times*, No. 26 (June 27, 1951), p. 7. See also G. Serdiuchenko, "O vrednoi teorie v iazkoznanii," *Kultura i zhizn'*, June 30, 1949, p. 3.

manner. Russian is credited with a constant accretion of strength through its supposedly voluntary adoption by an ever-mounting number of non-Russian peoples. This process began in the multilingual Soviet Union and has spread to large areas outside the Soviet Union.

During the 1920s attempts to force the adoption of Russian among non-Russian peoples in the USSR were officially condemned out of consideration for the newly aroused sensitivities of the non-Russian nationalities. But even this earliest period was marked by relapses into Russification. For example, from 1920 until August, 1923, the Soviet government sanctioned the application in the Ukraine of Lebed's so-called "theory of the struggle of two cultures." In the Ukraine, Russian was widely spoken in the cities, while Ukrainian was the language of the countryside. Under the cover of proposing a natural struggle between them, Lebed's theory was really intended to produce the victory of Russian over Ukrainian, on the ground that the future belonged to the Russian-speaking urban proletariat which possessed a culture superior to the backward-looking, Ukrainian-speaking peasantry.[20]

The rediscovery of the various national languages in the Soviet Union came as a mixed blessing to the national minorities, since it often had the curious effect of elevating the importance of Russian among the non-Russian peoples. Instead of creating a common language for ethnically related peoples who were hitherto largely illiterate, Soviet policy elevated dialects into languages, even, if need be, at the cost of inventing new, written alphabets. This conscious policy of fragmentation might be explained, in large part, by the fear that large, cohesive blocs of non-Russians, speaking a common tongue, would present a formidable threat to the centralized, Russian-based dictatorship. The treatment of the Moslem peoples of the Soviet Union provides the clearest illustration of this policy of parcelization. In an effort to avoid the creation of a large Moslem state in the Volga-Urals region, the Soviet regime created separate Bashkir and Tatar ASSRs, and enlarged upon the somewhat artificial distinction between the Bashkir and Tatar languages. More-

---

[20] E. F. Girchak, *Na dva fronta v bor'be s natsionalizmom* (Moscow, Leningrad, 1930), pp. 18–22; Ilarion Ohienko, "Ukrainian Literary Language in the U.S.S.R.," *Ukrainian Quarterly*, VI, No. 3 (Summer, 1950), 231; Roman Smal-Stocki, *The Nationality Problem of the Soviet Union* (Milwaukee, 1952), pp. 94–96.

over, Moscow was happy to encourage the Turco-Tatar "Latinizers," since writing these languages in the Arabic script would have encouraged Pan-Islamic and Pan-Turkic ties, which were far more deadly sins than a tie between the Bashkirs and the Tatars. This pattern of linguistic development was later repeated among the numerous peoples of Turkic stock in Central Asia and in the Northern Caucasus.[21] While non-Russian languages were codified by the score, their development was carefully channeled and their divergencies inflated so that no new regional non-Russian language could evolve among them. The logical result of this policy was that Russian increasingly became the lingua franca of the non-Russian peoples.

THE RUSSIFICATION OF LANGUAGES IN THE SOVIET UNION

Stalin expressed opposition to Russian as an official state language for the last time in 1930. Those who urged its adoption were still condemned as Great Russian chauvinists. "Is it not evident," Stalin asked, "that those who advocate one common language within the borders of *one* state, within the borders of the USSR, are, in essence, striving to restore the *privileges* of the formerly predominating language, namely the *Great Russian* language?"[22] But the trend toward Great Russian chauvinism was, in fact, well under way. The tempo of introducing the study of Russian among non-Russian peoples was increasingly stepped up during the 1930s, and on March 13, 1938, the Soviet government and the Central Committee of the Communist Party of the Soviet Union jointly decreed the obligatory teaching of Russian in all non-Russian schools.[23]

[21] Kolarz, *Russia and Her Colonies*, pp. 32–33, 41–44, 202–4, 259–62, 275, 282, 294–95; Smal-Stocki, *Nationality Problem*, pp. 152–53; Stefan Wurm, *The Turkic Languages of Central Asia: Problems of Planned Cultural Contact* (Oxford, 1953), pp. 1–53; Stefan Wurm, *Turkic Peoples of the U.S.S.R.* (Oxford, 1954), pp. 10–51; G. A. von Stackelberg, "The Second Turkmen Linguistic Congress and Its Political Significance," *Bulletin of the Institute*, II, No. 1 (Jan., 1955), 24–28; Richard Pipes, "Muslims of Soviet Central Asia," *The Middle East Journal*, IX, No. 2 (Spring, 1955), 159–62.
[22] Stalin, "Politicheskii otchët," in *Sochineniia*, XII, 365.
[23] "O prepodavanii russkogo iazyka v nerusskikh shkolakh," *Pravda*, April 10, 1938, p. 6; A. M. Danev, ed., *Narodnoe obrazovanie: osnovnye postanovleniia, prikazy i instrukstii* (Moscow, 1948), p. 86; N. K. Dmitriev and V. M. Chistiakov, eds., *Rodnoi i russkii iazky v natsional'noi shkole* (Moscow, 1953), p. 3. Isolated Union Republics, such as the Ukraine and Belorussia, made the teaching of Russian compulsory before this. In the Ukraine, for example, Russian was

The latter half of the 1930s also marked the conversion from the use of the Latin to the Cyrillic (or Russian) alphabet for the languages of numerous non-Russian peoples. During the 1920s the Latin script had been introduced, on the theory, most sharply expressed by Trotsky, that Western Europe and not Russia would be the heart of the Soviet world state. It was assumed that the future world language would be based upon Western European, rather than Russian, roots. Furthermore, the adoption of the Latin, instead of the Cyrillic, script within the Soviet Union avoided the odious connotation of Great Russian chauvinism, an attitude that was still officially condemned during this early period.

Stalin's counterattack in the linguistic field was delayed until the mid-1930s. As late as 1933 a Soviet source reported that "72 nationalities of the USSR, formerly without alphabets, had received them, of which 64 were based on the Latin script."[24] Many more languages previously written in another script, for example, Arabic, had also been Latinized. Within a decade virtually a complete transformation occurred in all these languages. Only a few peoples who had for centuries maintained a vigorous literary language in a non-Cyrillic script (the Georgians, Armenians, Finns, Estonians, Latvians, and Lithuanians) were left untouched. Yiddish was also unaffected, but the Yiddish press in the Soviet Union was almost completely closed down by 1949.[25] All the remaining non-Russian languages in the Soviet Union went through a second painful metamorphosis, this time as part of an undisguised program of Russification. The Soviet leaders frankly stated that the purpose of forcing these non-Russian

obligatory as early as 1923: see Harold R. Weinstein, "Language and Education in the Soviet Ukraine," in *The Slavonic Year-Book, American Series*, I (1941), 144–48. Despite such scattered laws, the teaching of Russian in non-Russian schools was haphazardly executed. The Soviet press continually complained of the lack of qualified teachers and the absence of any unified methods for teaching Russian. It was not until 1938 that the teaching of Russian in all non-Russian schools began in earnest.

[24] L. Slavin and T. Khodzhaev, "Natsional'nye raiony na rubezhe dvukh piatiletok," *Planovoe khoziaistvo*, No. 3 (March, 1934), pp. 177–78.

[25] In the summer of 1956 Soviet authorities indicated that a limited revival of Yiddish literary activity could be expected, but, as a Communist source admitted, after more than a year these promises remained unfulfilled. ("Soviet Outlines Yiddish Revival," New York *Times*, Aug. 11, 1956; Chaim Suller, "Jewish Culture in USSR Today: Another Look One Year Later," *The Worker* [New York], Sept. 22, 1957.) Finally, in 1959 the Kremlin sanctioned the celebration of the centennial of Sholom Aleichem's birth by reissuing his writings in Russian and in Yiddish. (Harry Schwartz, "Yiddish Writer Hailed in Soviet," New York *Times*, March 8, 1959.)

peoples to adopt the Cyrillic script was to accelerate their learning of Russian and to broaden the influence of Russian culture.[26] The Soviet press abounded in expressions of gratitude for the "service" that this second alphabet reform had rendered. Thus a group of Kirghiz declared: "The adoption of a new alphabet based on the Russian script has played a tremendous role in elevating the culture of the Kirghiz people by bringing them into closer association with the great Russian culture." [27]

An Estonian philologist, Alo Raun, summarized the impact of this linguistic Russification. "Examining any one of the languages of the Soviet Union, e.g., Mordvinian, one is shocked by the discovery that it swarms with Russian words, and that often only the suffixes are Mordvinian. The word order, use of cases, etc., are a poor imitation of Russian." [28]

Soviet authorities, far from objecting to this characterization of their policy, only found fault with those who obstructed its implementation. A long article in *Voprosy filosofii* in 1949 complained of resistance from "local bourgeois nationalists," who were accused of "masquerading as defenders of their national language." Their treachery "consisted first of all, in attempts to eliminate international and particularly sociopolitical terminology, and to replace it by a provincial, nationalist terminology." That is, the non-Russian languages of the Soviet Union were required to use international terms of foreign origin in the form in which they have been adopted in the Russian language. Second, these bourgeois nationalists

sought to use foreign languages as their models, persistently trying to minimize the importance of the Russian language. Belorussian and Ukrainian nationalists injected into their native speech elements of the Polish gentry's speech; the Moldavian nationalists tried to drag into their language aristocratic Rumanian drawing-room words; and the Latvian nationalists, carrying out the orders of the German gentry, attempted to Germanize their tongue. The bourgeois nationalists of our Eastern Re-

[26] A. E. Mordinov, "O razvitii iazykov sotsialisticheskikh natsii v SSSR," *Voprosy filosofii*, No. 3 (1950), p. 92; Kolarz, *Russia and Her Colonies*, pp. 34–38; Alo Raun, "National in Form, Socialistic in Content," *Ukrainian Quarterly*, VI, No. 2 (Spring, 1950), 115–21; E. Koutaissoff, "Literacy and the Place of Russian in the Non-Slav Republics of the U.S.S.R.," *Soviet Studies*, III, No. 2 (Oct., 1951), 124–26.

[27] "Velikomu vozhdiu sovetskogo naroda I. V. Stalinu, ot Kirgizskogo naroda," *Pravda*, Feb. 1, 1951, p. 2.

[28] Raun, "National in Form," *Ukrainian Quarterly*, VI, No. 2 (Spring, 1950), 115–16. See also Ohienko, "Ukrainian Literary," *ibid.*, VI, No. 3 (Summer, 1950), 229–40.

publics infused their native languages with Persian-Arabic and Turkish elements. In essence, this was a policy of betrayal of national interests, a policy of cosmopolitanism.

Only by using the Russian language as their model could these non-Russians defend their "national interests." Russian, of course, had no objectionable history, since it had never been the language of the Tsars and the Russian gentry who gathered in their drawing rooms to plot the forcible Russification of the Belorussian, Ukrainian, Polish, and other languages! And how could one resist the obvious logic of the assumption that Russian was the natural model for the languages of the peoples of Central Asia rather than Persian, Arabic, or Turkish! A third and final accusation rested on the charge that "bourgeois nationalists artificially bred local words and forms to obstruct the penetration of Russian words and forms."[29] Again, was it not obvious that the use of local words and forms in a non-Russian language was "artificial," while the use of Russian words and forms was "natural"? In contrast to the petty, narrow-minded mentality nourished by the non-Russian languages, Russian was portrayed in the following manner:

> The great Russian language has become the source of enrichment and flowering for the different national languages. . . . The Russian language is great, rich, and mighty. It is the instrument of the most advanced culture in the world. From its inexhaustible treasures, the national languages of the USSR draw a life-giving elixir.[30]

RUSSIAN AS THE FUTURE WORLD LANGUAGE

This Soviet conception of the role of Russian, both within the USSR, and in the development of a world language, found its theoretical justification by means of a distorted interpretation of the works of Nicolai Ia. Marr, the father of Soviet linguistics. Marr had died in 1934, leaving a collection of linguistic theories, many of which rested upon arbitrary assumptions lacking proof or consistency. In broad outline, Marr postulated the operation of a single world glottogonic, or language-forming, process. Though all languages are related, they are divided into four classes, representing four chronological strata, or stages of development. Those languages which somehow got stuck at a lower level are without a future,

[29] Lomtev, "I. V. Stalin," *Voprosy filosofii*, No. 2 (1949), p. 135.
[30] *Ibid.*, p. 136.

while those in the fourth stage of development represent the material for a future world language. Russian was placed in this highest stage along with all Indo-European languages. Marr considered language as an element in the Marxist superstructure dependent upon the economic base of society. Consequently, the creation of a single world socialist economy was expected to produce a single world language. Just as this base might be changed by force, so, Marr thought, the linguistic superstructure should be impelled to develop toward its ultimate goal. "Mankind, proceeding toward economic unity and a classless society, cannot help applying artificial means, scientifically worked out, in order to accelerate this broad process." [31]

By 1930 Marr had firmly grafted Marxism onto his prerevolutionary linguistic theories,[32] and depicted himself as an orthodox Marxist who put class above nation. He was interested in the evolution of a future proletarian world language, rather than in the aggrandizement of any single national language, Russian included. But the elements of Marr's theories, and the vagueness with which they were stated, lent themselves to easy perversion by his disciples, who, in the guise of following Marr's linguistic theories, joined other Soviet linguists in the systematic glorification of the Russian language.

We have already indicated the application of "artificial means" to favor the victory of Russian in the Soviet Union, where Russian was clearly considered the language of a chosen people who would assume the directing role in the future socialist world society. From this it was an easy step to assert that Russian would likewise be the future world language. As early as 1937 *Pravda* had boasted: "We love our Russian language, which is great, powerful, and rich. It is already becoming an international language. It is being studied by the leaders of humanity." [33] By 1949 Soviet theoreticians were asserting categorically that Russian was predestined to be the future world language. One Soviet writer recalled that "one world language has replaced another time and again throughout the thou-

[31] Quoted in A. Chikobava, "O nekotorykh voprosakh sovetskogo iazykoznaniia," *Pravda*, May 9, 1950, p. 3. See also Smal-Stocki, *Nationality Problem*, pp. 79–86; D.B.Y., "The Stalin-Marr Philological Controversy in the U.S.S.R.," *The World Today*, VI (Aug., 1950), 355–64.
[32] Lawrence L. Thomas, "Some Notes on the Marr School," *American Slavic*, XVI, No. 3 (Oct., 1957), 338–44.
[33] "Velikii russkii narod," *Pravda*, Jan. 15, 1937, p. 1.

sands of years of the history of mankind," with the economic base of each era raising a different language to world supremacy.

Latin was the language of the ancient world and the early middle ages. French became the language of the ruling classes in the feudal era. It was maintained for a long time together with feudal traditions and customs, and became the language of international diplomacy. English became the world language of capitalism. . . . Looking to the future, we see that the Russian language is the world language of socialism.[34]

THE LINGUISTICS DISCUSSION AND THE DISAVOWAL OF MARR

This simple schematic view appeared to have been upset by Stalin's abrupt intervention in the Soviet linguistics discussion in the summer of 1950. Stalin unceremoniously provided Marr with a second funeral—this time, an ideological one. Suddenly Soviet philologists "discovered" that the basis of their entire linguistic work had been unscientific. What caused this disavowal of Marr, and what effect did this have both upon the Soviet concept of a world language, and upon the role of Russian in the development of this world language?

The denunciation of Marr was explained, first of all, on the ground that his theories had introduced such chaos into Soviet linguistics that most serious linguistic work had been brought to a standstill. No doubt there was considerable justification in this complaint.[35] The newly found critics of Marr's followers charged that the literacy of the non-Russian peoples had unmistakably suffered as a result of the crude attempts to Russify the non-Russian languages.

N. Ia. Marr's followers completely ignored the specific features of national languages and, in an oversimplified and vulgarized manner, interpreted the leading role of the Russian language in the development of national languages as a mechanical hybridization of the two. The practical results of such a vulgarized approach to the development of

[34] D. Zaslavskii, "Velikii iazyk nashei epokhy," *Literaturnaia gazeta*, Jan. 1, 1949, p. 3.
[35] For a discussion of the charges leveled against Marr, see Jeffrey Ellis and Robert W. Davies, "The Crisis in Soviet Linguistics," *Soviet Studies*, II, No. 3 (Jan., 1951), 209–64. Aspects of this interpretation are sharply challenged by Thomas, "Some Notes," *American Slavic*, XVI, No. 3 (Oct., 1957), 323–48. For additional material on the Marr controversy, see the numerous references listed in the footnotes on page 323 of the Thomas article, and Jindrich Kucera, "Soviet Nationality Policy: The Linguistic Controversy," *Problems of Communism*, III, No. 2 (March–April, 1954), 24–29.

national languages was the discarding from some alphabets of a number of letters that reflected phonetic peculiarities of the national languages. . . . This harmful approach, involving a break with the existing laws of the national languages, led to anarchy in orthography, to inumerable difficulties in mastery of the grammar of the native language, in the work of local newspapers and magazines, etc.[36]

But the damage was not confined to non-Russian languages, since these methods had also led to an estrangement of these languages from Russian.

The "drawing together" of languages, recommended by the followers of N. Ia. Marr, actually only hampers their real harmonizing. . . . Destroying historically developed rules of pronunciation does not make it easier, but harder for the working people to master new words borrowed from Russian, i.e., yields results contrary to the aims proclaimed by the supporters of the "new teaching" on language.[37]

These critics did not object to the principle of altering these non-Russian languages so as to draw them closer to Russian, but only to the use of harsh and clumsy methods which had, in fact, obstructed the attainment of this goal. This sudden abuse of Marr was a tactical concession to the development of non-Russian languages, but it was by no means a clear-cut defeat for the Russian language. Subsequent comments make it clear that Russian was not expected to lose its dominant position, nor was the idea of its eventual victory disowned. These goals would be pursued, but with greater caution and by more skillful means. Thus, the Ministry of Education of the Uzbek SSR reported: "Thanks to the reorganization of teaching on the basis of J. V. Stalin's brilliant works on linguistics, the teaching of the Russian language and literature has been improved in Uzbek and other non-Russian schools in the Republic." [38] The subsequent denigration of Stalin left the Russifying impact of Stalin's linguistic policy intact, for the post-Stalinist period has seen a continuation, and even an intensification, of attempts to step up the teaching of Russian in non-Russian schools.[39]

[36] Mordinov, "O razvitii," *Voprosy filosofiii*, No. 3 (1950), p. 82.
[37] *Ibid.*, p. 83.
[38] "V ministerstve prosveshcheniia Uzbekskoi SSR," *Uchitel'skaia gazeta*, Nov. 15, 1952, p. 4.
[39] At the Twentieth Party Congress a Party spokesman from Dagestan, for example, simply substituted Lenin for Stalin: "An ever-increasing number of people in the Republic know Russian, the language of the great Lenin. The Russian language has become the international language of the peoples of Dagestan, and through it they gain contact with the advanced Russian Soviet

Arbitrary interference with the non-Russian languages had proceeded from the assumption that language was part of the superstructure and therefore subject to artificial manipulation. Stalin attacked this practice by denying the premise that language was part of the superstructure, or for that matter, that language was even a class phenomenon. This "revelation" had long been a commonplace assumption among those who did not pretend to understand the mysteries of dialectical materialism, but for good Marxists it came as a blow. Language, Stalin announced,

> was created not by any class, but by all society, by all classes of society, by the efforts of hundreds of generations. . . . Language is the product of a whole series of epochs, in the course of which it takes shape, is enriched, develops, and is polished. A language therefore exists immeasurably longer than any base or any superstructure.

Stalin said that Pushkin's language "has been preserved in all essentials as the basis of modern Russian," and that "the Russian language has remained essentially what it was before the October Revolution."[40] Thus belatedly he did for language what he had previously done for the teaching of history, namely: assert the interests of nation above class. Far from destroying the prestige of the Russian language, he was fortifying it by drawing upon the endless stream of historical memories and traditions of Russian nationalism.

---

and world culture." ("Rech' tovarishcha A. D. Daniialova," *Pravda*, Feb. 21, 1956, p. 7.) Typical of efforts to strengthen the position of Russian in the non-Russian Republics was the announcement in the spring of 1956 of a forthcoming "interrepublican scientific conference in Tashkent on the problems of studying the Russian language in national schools." It was necessary to make "decisive improvements in this important matter. The tremendous significance of teaching the Russian language in national schools is well known, since it is the means of communication among the fraternal peoples of the Soviet Union." (M. Ismatullaev and I. Gimil'shtein, "Uchashchimsia—prochnye znaniia," *Kommunist Tadzhikistana*, May 11, 1956, p. 2.) See also H. Carrère d'Encausse, "Linguistic Russification and Nationalist Opposition in Kazakhstan," *The East Turkic Review* (Munich), I, No. 1 (April, 1958), 96–100. A Secretary of the CC of the CP of Kazakhstan then revealed that, in addition to Russian having become "a second native language for the Kazakh people" through its study in Kazakh schools, "at the present time approximately one fourth of the Kazakh children attend schools where instruction is conducted in Russian." He berated those parents who "think it necessary to establish a system under which the children of Kazakhs could attend only Kazakh schools. This view is nothing but a manifestation of bourgeois nationalism." (N. Dzhandil'din, "Nekotorye voprosy internatsional'nogo vospitaniia," *Kommunist*, No. 13 [Sept., 1959], p. 36.)

[40] Stalin, "Otnositel'no Marksizma v iazykoznanii," June 20, 1950, in *Marksizm i voprosy*, pp. 4–7.

There were doubtless other unspoken reasons for the renunciation of Marr's theories. Not only did their distorted application provoke resistance among the non-Russian peoples in the Soviet Union, but they also served to insult many nations outside the USSR. In Marr's four stages of linguistic development, for example, Chinese was permanently "frozen" at the lowest level. The embarrassments which this held for Soviet relations with Communist China are obvious.

Moreover, Marr repudiated the validity of comparative philology, and the classification of languages into separate linguistic families. This obviously contradicted the development of Pan-Slavic studies in the East European satellite states of Slavic origin, thus hindering their Russification.

AGAIN, RUSSIAN AS THE FUTURE WORLD LANGUAGE

What effect did the discrediting of Marr's theories have upon the Soviet concept of a world language? Chikobava, developing the newly accepted position, noted that "Marr expressed himself in favor of a single common language for future mankind. This is the only matter of principle on which, it would seem, Academician N. Ia. Marr's views are in accord with the theses of Marxism-Leninism." The prospect of a single world language was still upheld, but the "dying away of national languages and the formation of a single common world language will take place gradually, without any 'artificial means' invoked to 'accelerate' this process." [41]

One should add that the idea of "hybridization" or fusion of languages, which Stalin continued to use, was Marrist in origin. Stalin made this idea his own, in his characteristic fashion, by "reinterpreting" it to apply only to a given historical period. His distinction between the fate of national languages before and after the worldwide victory of socialism must be recalled. National languages will fuse in a gradual peaceful manner, without the application of "artificial means," only *after* the creation of a Soviet world state has made possible a condition of mutual confidence and harmony among nations. Before this time, however, the crossing of national languages under conditions of national oppression will not produce peaceful fusion, but a mortal struggle in which "one of the languages usually

[41] Chikobava, "O nekotorykh," *Pravda*, May 9, 1950, p. 3.

comes out the victor, whereas the other dies away."[42] "Such was the case, for instance, with the Russian language, with which the languages of a number of other peoples mixed in the course of historical development, and which always emerged the victor." The effect which this struggle had upon the Russian language was to enlarge its vocabulary, "but this not only did not weaken, but on the contrary enriched and strengthened the Russian language."[43] Stalin gave no indication that Russian would not continue to emerge the victor in future struggles that are predicted up until the very moment of the creation of the Soviet world state.

Soviet theorists have already clearly nominated Russian as a zonal language with unlimited prospects for expansion. "In the formation of a zonal language common to many nations, Russian will undoubtedly play the decisive role in many socialist nations. With the appearance of new socialist nations the world-historic role and influence of the Russian language will steadily increase."[44] This view, expressed in 1949, does not seem to have been repudiated in the linguistics discussion of 1950. Following this discussion the importance of Russian was reaffirmed both within and beyond the borders of the Soviet Union.

The role of the Russian language in the development of the languages and cultures of all the peoples of the USSR constantly increases. . . . Russian has therefore become an *international language* for the peoples of the USSR. But the significance of the Russian language is not limited to this. The great Russian language is becoming a second native language for the liberated peoples of the countries of the New Democracies as well as for the Chinese People's Republic. . . .

In our time the Russian language is becoming the most popular and widespread language in the world. The process of steady growth of the world significance of the Russian language reflects the vanguard role of our country . . . in the struggle for the liberation of all mankind from the yoke of exploitation and oppression.[45]

The satellite states duly echoed this glorification of Russian. The Czechoslovak press supported the demand of "giving the Russian language the same rights as our own Czech and Slovak languages. . . . It is for us the world language . . . the language of world-

[42] Stalin, "Tovarishchu A. Kholopovu," in *Marksizm i voprosy,* pp. 45–47.
[43] Stalin, "Otnositel'no Marksizma," in *ibid.,* p. 25.
[44] Lomtev, "I. V. Stalin," *Voprosy filosofii,* No. 2 (1949), p. 140.
[45] Mordinov, "O razvitii," *ibid.,* No. 3 (1950), p. 91.

wide brotherhood."[46] And Chervenkov, the Premier of Bulgaria, hailed Russian as the language of "the richest and most outstanding culture in the whole world. This imbues the Russian language with a world-historic significance and makes a knowledge of it vital to every advanced fighter for the happiness of his people."[47] This bowing and scraping by provincial satraps before the mother tongue of Moscow is a meaningful part of a larger design, for Stalin was quite aware of the importance of a single language in the process of building a world empire. He specifically noted that "the empires of Cyrus or Alexander the Great or of Caesar and Charles the Great . . . were transitory and unstable military and administrative unions. These empires not only did not have, but they could not have, a single language common to the whole empire and understood by all members of the empire."[48]

It would seem that there is a fundamental contradiction in Stalin's position on a world language. On the one hand, he declared that the ultimate world language will be neither German, nor Russian, nor English, but something new. On the other hand, Russian has been accorded a favored and privileged position denied to all other major languages. The Soviet leadership has already designated Russian, but *only* Russian, as one of the world's zonal languages. Some of the offensive, chauvinistic overtones of the campaign to force the adoption of Russian by non-Russian peoples may have been eliminated by the benign assurance that the ultimate world language will not be Russian. But along with this goes the expectation that Russian will continually fight and conquer as many non-Russian languages as possible during the period before the victory of world socialism. Theoretically, Russian is only supposed to enter into open combat with other languages in the arena of national oppression and inequality, that is, in the non-Soviet world. Within the Soviet world, where, by definition, national harmony reigns supreme, the struggle for the domination of one language over others has been replaced by the mutual enrichment of one language by another. Yet it is evident that this "mutual enrichment" has been largely a one-way

[46] "What the Russian Language Meant and Means to Us," *Slovanský přehled*, No. 7/8 (1949); quoted in *News from Behind the Iron Curtain*, II, No. 10 (Oct., 1953), 41.
[47] "Vsemirno-istoricheskoe znachenie russkogo iazyka," *Pravda*, Oct. 1, 1952, p. 4.
[48] Stalin, "Otnositel'no Marksizma," in *Marksizm i voprosy*, p. 10.

proposition in which Russian has been elevated, consciously and conspicuously, above all other languages.

This encouragement of the victory of Russian both within and beyond the confines of the Soviet world has definite implications for a future world language. If Russian gains a constant series of victories over non-Russian languages in the process of subduing non-Soviet nations to Soviet rule, then at the moment of the creation of the Soviet world state, Russian will have achieved an almost impregnable position of universal supremacy. Nor should this position diminish after the Soviet world state has come into operation. The "mutual confidence" and "national equality" among nations, such as is claimed for the present Soviet world, will then be of universal scope. Behind a smoke screen of verbiage about the "mutual enrichment" of languages, Russian will then be given the opportunity to triumph on a world scale. This creates the distinct possibility that Russian will, in fact, be the future world language, should the Soviet regime succeed in its ambitions.

Since the fate of national languages is intimately connected with the ultimate fate of nations, this would mean that the world would become the Russian nation writ large. Lenin predicted the assimilation of nations under the world rule of socialism, but Stalin developed this into the prospect of the assimilation of all nations by the Russian nation ruling a Soviet world state.

X. The Role of War in Building the Soviet World State

THE Soviet theory of self-determination of nations has always emphasized consent as the basis for the affiliation of nations with an ever-expanding Soviet federation. In 1913 Stalin affirmed flatly that "the right of self-determination means that only a nation itself has the right to determine its destiny, that no one has the right *forcibly* to interfere in the life of a nation."¹ On November 8, 1917, just one day after the Bolshevik seizure of power, Lenin issued the Decree on Peace, which condemned the forcible annexation of nations, and demanded the right of nations to determine the form of their existence in accordance with their freely expressed will.² It is the Soviet boast that the present Soviet federation rests purely and entirely upon the voluntary consent of its member nations, and that the World Soviet Federation will likewise be a product of the freely expressed will of all of the nations of the world. The supposed freedom of Union Republics to secede from the USSR is offered as "proof" of the voluntary nature of Soviet federalism, while the Soviet press continually asserts that the USSR has not been created by the use of force. On December 30, 1952, for example, *Pravda* stated:

The Soviet Union has not expanded its membership by means of the forced annexation of foreign territories as was done, for example, by the U.S.A. in relation to the state of Texas, which was torn from Mexico. . . . The Soviet Union resulted from the free expression of will of equal peoples.³

How do these assertions square with Soviet theory on the use of force which has served as a guide for Soviet practice?⁴ To

¹ Stalin, "Marksizm i natsional'nyi vopros," Jan., 1913, in *Sochineniia*, II, 310.
² Lenin, "Doklad o mire," Nov. 8, 1917, in *Sochineniia*, XXII, 13-14.
³ A. Poskrebyshev, "Velikoe mnogonatsional'noe sovetskoe gosudarstvo," *Pravda*, Dec. 30, 1952, p. 2.
⁴ This writer plans to publish as a separate study a country-by-country survey

what extent do the specific theoretical propositions which the Soviet leaders have developed with regard to the use of force indicate a desire or intention to build up a world state purely on the basis of voluntary consent?

LENINIST THEORY ON THE USE OF FORCE

Early in his career Lenin acknowledged the need to employ all conceivable forms of struggle. In 1906 he held that

Marxism is distinguished from all primitive forms of socialism by the fact that it does not tie the movement to any particular form of struggle. It recognizes the most varied forms of struggle. . . . At different moments of economic evolution, and depending upon varying political, national, cultural, and other social conditions, different forms of struggle assume prominence, become the chief forms of struggle, and in turn, cause the secondary and supplementary forms of struggle to change their appearance.[5]

The selection and use of weapons from the Leninist arsenal depended entirely upon considerations of expediency, upon a calculation of what method of struggle would prove most fruitful at any given moment. Under certain circumstances this would exclude the use of force. But in answer to the question, "Can Social Democrats be opposed to the use of force in general?" Lenin replied, "Obviously not!"[6]

The approved scope of violence ranged from terror, or violence against the individual, to the mass violence of organized war. In a discourse on tactical weapons in 1901 Lenin asserted that "we have never rejected terror on principle, nor can we do so. Terror is a form of military operations which may be entirely useful, or even essential, at a certain moment of combat."[7] He objected only to untimely, uncoordinated, adventuristic acts of terror, which resulted in disorganizing the revolutionary movement. An individual weapon like terror must be a subordinate part of over-all military plans, which specifically contemplate full-scale war. Still speaking

---

of the actual use of crude military coercion in the Soviet attempt to build a world state.

[5] Lenin, "Partizanskaia voina," Oct. 13, 1906, in *Sochineniia*, X, 80-81.

[6] Lenin, "Itogi diskussii o samoopredelenii," autumn, 1916, in *ibid.*, XIX, 247.

[7] Lenin, "S chego nachat'?" May, 1901, in *ibid.*, IV, 108. See also "To Franz Koritschoner," Oct. 25, 1916, in Elizabeth Hill and Doris Mudie, eds., *The Letters of Lenin* (New York, 1937), pp. 400-2.

prior to the Bolshevik Revolution, Lenin warned: "Whoever expects that socialism will be achieved *without* social revolution and a dictatorship of the proletariat is not a socialist. Dictatorship is state power, based directly upon *force*. In the twentieth century force . . . does not mean the fist or the club, but *troops*." [8] Since the "state power" that Lenin sought was that of a world state, it would seem that he anticipated the use of troops, of military force, as a method of attaining the world dictatorship of the proletariat. Just how this forcible interference in the affairs of the different nations of the world could be reconciled with the Soviet theory of self-determination of nations, which denied "the right *forcibly* to interfere in the life of a nation," is not clear.

The outbreak of the First World War stimulated Lenin to study Clausewitz's classic work, *On War*. Its basic premise that war is the continuation of politics by other means agreeably reinforced Lenin's previous views on the use of force.

"War is the continuation of politics by other (namely, violent) means." This famous dictum belongs to Clausewitz, one of the most profound authors on military questions. Marxists have always correctly considered this proposition as the theoretical basis for understanding the significance of any given war.[9]

The validity of this proposition has never been questioned by the Soviet leaders. In February, 1946, Stalin affirmed that "Clausewitz substantiated in his works the familiar Marxist thesis that there is a direct connection between war and politics, that politics gives birth to war, that war is the continuation of politics by violent means." [10]

Soviet theoreticians have improved upon this "bourgeois" thesis by radically extending the concepts both of politics and of war. In creating a total state, politics embraces all life. There is no pri-

[8] Lenin, "O lozunge 'razoruzheniia,'" Oct., 1916, in *Sochineniia*, XIX, 315.
[9] Lenin, "Sotsializm i voina," Aug., 1915, in *ibid.*, XVIII, 197.
[10] "Otvet tov. Stalina na pis'mo tov. Razina," Feb. 23, 1946, *Bol'shevik*, No. 3 (Feb., 1947), p. 7. Clausewitz could not have "substantiated" a familiar Marxist thesis, since he began to write *On War* in 1818, that is, the year that Marx was born. In this article Stalin was attempting to disavow the importance of any non-Russian military authority, specifying, "We are not only obliged to criticize Clausewitz, but also Moltke, Schlieffen, Ludendorff, Keital, and other bearers of German military ideology." The attack on foreign influences was part of the campaign against "cosmopolitanism," but it did not effect Stalin's acceptance of Clausewitz's basic thesis that war is the continuation of politics by other means.

vate, inviolable sanctuary above and beyond politics. Everything must be public and everyone must be partisan. To be apolitical, or even impartial and objective, borders on treason. Similarly, the role of war has been expanded so as to militarize this all-embracing concept of politics. The Party is organized on military lines, with a military-type chain of command, and a military-type discipline. The Party sets the tone for a society which produces "shock workers" in industry and "brigade leaders" in agriculture. All Soviet society is cast in the role of perpetual conflict with the non-Soviet world. Whether or not this conflict assumes military form is the only distinction between "peace" and war. The Soviet leaders feel that the world is irreconcilably divided into two hostile, armed camps, engaged in a permanent struggle which will cease only with the disappearance or destruction of the non-Soviet world and the creation of a Soviet world state. War is clearly considered a valid instrument which may be employed to achieve this end. When Lenin stated that "the existence of the Soviet Republic side by side the imperialist states for a prolonged period of time was unthinkable," he added, in the very same speech, that "we condemn imperialist war, but we do not reject *war in general*." [11]

Long before the Bolshevik seizure of power, in his Theses of October, 1915, Lenin illustrated his grasp of the interrelationship between politics and war, and the use of war in laying the basis for creating a world state.

As to the question of what the Party of the proletariat would do if a revolution placed power in its hands in the present war, we answer: we would propose peace to *all* belligerents on the conditions that they liberate their colonies and *all* dependent, oppressed, and disfranchised peoples. Under their present governments neither Germany, nor England and France would accept this condition. Then we would be obliged to prepare and wage a revolutionary war, i.e. . . . we would systematically raise revolts among all the peoples presently oppressed by the Great Russians, all those oppressed in all the colonial and dependent countries of Asia (India, China, Persia, etc.), and also of principal importance we would rouse to insurrection the socialist proletariat of Europe against their own governments.[12]

A "peace" movement was designed to flow precipitously into a war movement that would place power in the hands of the revolu-

[11] Lenin, "Otchët Tsentral'nogo Komiteta," March 18, 1919, in *Sochineniia*, XXIV, 121–22.
[12] Lenin, "Neskol'ko tezisov," Oct. 13, 1915, in *ibid.*, XVIII, 313.

WAR AND SOVIET WORLD STATE 289

tionary proletariat in vital areas throughout the world. Lenin's Decree on Peace of November 8, 1917, followed this pattern closely. It sought to capitalize on the prevailing war weariness by demanding an immediate peace, on condition that all annexations be annulled and all small and weak nations be given the right to decide their future by plebiscite. As Lenin had anticipated, this appeal was rejected by all the belligerents, but he was unable to execute his further plans for a revolutionary war because of the disintegration of the fighting front, the general chaos and demoralization of the home front, and the relative great strength of the belligerent states. Instead he found it necessary to oppose plans for an immediate revolutionary war and to urge the signing of the Treaty of Brest-Litovsk. He did this, not because he was opposed in principle to revolutionary wars, but because he felt that this venture, under the prevailing circumstances, would bring disaster to the Soviet cause.

The concept of a revolutionary war was described in Lenin's Theses of October, 1915, primarily in the form of a vast international civil war. This picture was supplemented by another statement of 1915 that envisioned a revolutionary war waged between the *state or states* seized by the proletariat, and the remaining *states* of the world. Lenin held that

in the beginning, the victory of socialism is possible in a few, or even in one capitalist country taken separately. The victorious proletariat of that country, having expropriated the capitalists and organized its own socialist production, would rise up *against* the remaining capitalist world, attracting to itself the oppressed classes of other countries, raising in them revolts against the capitalists, if need be, even *launching armed forces against the exploiting classes and their states.* . . . The free unification of nations in socialism is impossible without a more or less prolonged, stubborn battle between the Socialist Republics and the other states.[13]

After the Bolshevik Revolution Stalin frequently quoted, with approval, Lenin's injunction about the possible need of "launching armed forces against the exploiting classes and their states."[14] Sim-

[13] Lenin, "O lozunge Soedinënnykh Shtatov Evropy," Aug. 23, 1915, in *ibid.*, XVIII, 232-33 (first italics Lenin's; second italics added).
[14] Stalin, "Oktiabr'skaia revoliutsiia i taktika russkikh kommunistov," Dec. 17, 1924, in *Sochineniia*, VI, 400; Stalin, "Ob oppozitsionnom bloke v VKP(b)," Oct. 26, 1926, in *ibid.*, VIII, 217; Stalin, "O sotsial-demokraticheskom uklone v nashei partii," Nov. 1, 1926, in *ibid.*, VIII, 252; Stalin, "Zakliuchitel'noe slovo," Dec. 13, 1926, in *ibid.*, IX, 112.

ilarly, Bukharin and Preobrazhenskii echoed this view in their book, *The ABC of Communism*, which appeared shortly after the seizure of state power in Russia:

> Those countries in which the bourgeoisie has been conquered and put under the control of the workers must either conduct a war, or be ready to go to war, with the bourgeoisie of those states which do not yet have a dictatorship of the proletariat, or give armed assistance to the proletariat of those countries where the dictatorship of the proletariat has been proclaimed, but where the fight with the bourgeoisie has not yet come to an end.[15]

Such postrevolutionary statements merely elaborated the basic position set forth by Lenin in 1915. During 1916 Lenin rounded out and summed up his theoretical considerations on the "legitimate" use of war, enumerating three approved types of war. "Socialists cannot, without ceasing to be socialists, oppose every kind of war. In the first place, socialists have never been, nor can they be, opposed to revolutionary wars." An example of such a war would be "a war with the bourgeoisie, waged for the liberation of oppressed, dependent, or colonial peoples." He then recalled that, "in the second place, civil wars are also wars. . . . To repudiate or forget about civil wars is to fall into extreme opportunism and to renounce the socialist revolution." Finally, Lenin warned that the victory of socialism in one country would not eliminate the need for further wars.

> On the contrary, it presupposes such wars. . . . This situation must not only create friction, but direct attempts by the bourgeoisie of the other countries to crush the victorious proletariat of the socialist state. Under these conditions, war on our part would be legitimate and just. It would be a war for socialism, for the liberation of other nations from the bourgeoisie.[16]

War begets revolution, and, in turn, revolution produces war. Lenin asked: "Was there ever in history an example of a great revolution occurring by itself, not tied to war? Of course not." [17] Not only does revolution instigate and issue from war, but one type of war readily flows into another. Lenin recounted the experience of the French Revolution, which had produced a revolutionary war against the counterrevolutionary monarchies, but

---

[15] Bukharin and Preobrazhenskii, *Azbuka*, p. 145.
[16] Lenin, "Voennaia programma proletarskoi revoliutsii," autumn, 1916, in *Sochineniia*, XIX, 323–25.
[17] Lenin, "Otchët Tsentral'nogo Komiteta," in *ibid.*, XXIV, 122.

turned into a war for a Napoleonic Empire, and so engendered a new series of wars of national liberation against French imperialism. Failure to understand the way one kind of war can be transformed into another can be "very harmful in a tactical political sense, for it gives rise to stupid propaganda about 'disarmament' as if no other wars but reactionary wars are possible." [18]

It was the duty of the proletariat both to turn "reactionary" wars into wars of "liberation" and to start wars of "liberation" wherever possible. This specifically sanctioned launching aggressive war, since any war supported by the proletariat, or any war in which the proletarian state was engaged was automatically "just," regardless of how such a war began or who fired the first shot. "It is not the defensive or offensive character of a war," Lenin explained, "but the interests of the international proletarian movement," which determined whether or not a war was just.[19] "For instance, if Morocco were to declare war against France, or India against England, or Persia or China against Russia, etc., those wars would be 'just,' 'defensive' wars, no matter which one was the first to attack." [20] Or again:

The socialist, the revolutionary proletarian, the internationalist, considers that the character of a war (whether it is reactionary or revolutionary) does not depend upon who started it, on whose territory the "enemy" has occupied, but *upon which class* wages the war, and the politics of which this war is a continuation.[21]

The wars that Lenin sanctioned as "revolutionary" and "just" served two related purposes. One was the use of war to disintegrate the bourgeois nation-state system. This could be done through wars of liberation by colonial and dependent peoples and through civil wars within the bourgeois states. The other general purpose of a "just" war was to integrate nations into a proletarian world state. If, at first, the proletariat could only capture power in a single state, this single proletarian state could "justly" attack and attempt to conquer the surrounding bourgeois states. War was essential to the attainment of a proletarian world state, which alone could produce a peaceful world. "Only after we have overthrown, finally

[18] Lenin, "O broshiure Iuniusa," Aug., 1916, in *ibid.*, XIX, 181, 184.
[19] Lenin, "Voinstvuiushchii militarizm i antimilitaristskaia taktika sotsial-demokratii," Aug. 5, 1908, in *ibid.*, XII, 318.
[20] Lenin, "Sotsializm i voina," in *ibid.*, XVIII, 194.
[21] Lenin, "Proletarskaia revoliutsiia i renegat Kautskii," Oct.–Nov., 1918, in *ibid.*, XXIII, 380.

conquered, and expropriated the bourgeoisie of the entire world, and not just of one country," Lenin warned, "will wars become impossible." The need for wars would vanish only in the future socialist world, but "class *wars* are necessary for the achievement of this beautiful future." [22]

Lenin had sketched this picture in all its essential details well before the Bolshevik Revolution. Looking at the world from the seat of power, Lenin made only one significant alteration in his theoretical justification for the use of war. Before the revolution he had flatly condemned as reactionary a war between two imperialist blocs, unless it could be turned into some form of revolutionary war. Speaking in May, 1918, in defense of the Treaty of Brest-Litovsk, Lenin noted that this treaty had removed Soviet Russia from the field of combat, but had left the Entente and the Central Powers locked in battle, making the struggle between the imperialist blocs increasingly acute. Under these circumstances, the proletarian state should "wait until the imperialists weaken themselves *still more* by this conflict, and so bring revolution still closer in other countries." [23] In 1920 Lenin made explicit the potential advantage to the world revolution of conflicts between non-Soviet states. "What would have saved us still more would have been a war among the imperialist powers. If we must tolerate such scoundrels as the capitalist thieves, each of whom is preparing to plunge a knife into us, it is our primary duty to make them turn their knives against each other. When thieves quarrel, honest men win out." [24]

Lenin's article of May, 1918, explaining why Soviet Russia must remain outside the imperialist war, also foresaw a time when the new proletarian state would be able to wage a revolutionary war to expand its frontiers. "If the proletariat wages war, having conquered the bourgeoisie of its own country, if it wages war in the interests of strengthening and expanding socialism, then war becomes legitimate and 'holy.' " [25]

[22] Lenin, "Voennaia programma," in *ibid.*, XIX, 325.
[23] Lenin, "O 'levom' rebiachestve i o melkoburzhuaznosti," May 3, 1918, in *ibid.*, XXII, 506.
[24] Lenin, "Rech' na sobranii sekretarei iacheek moskovskoi organizatsii RKP(b)," Nov. 26, 1920, in *ibid.*, XXV, 505.
[25] Lenin, "O 'levom' rebiachestve," in *ibid.*, XXII, 510. See also Lenin, "Tezisy po voprosu o zakliuchenii separatnogo mira," Jan. 20, 1918, in *ibid.*, XXII, 196, 198-99.

WAR AND SOVIET WORLD STATE

Moscow began formulating plans for a military offensive that could exploit the collapse of the Central Powers in anticipation of the armistice of November 11, 1918, ending the First World War. On October 4, 1918, the Soviet government ordered "the Revolutionary War Council to adopt at once an extensive program of Red Army organization to meet the new international situation." [26] This resolution was adopted in response to Lenin's estimate that "the time is approaching when circumstances will require us to give aid to the German people. . . . The Russian proletariat must realize that it will soon be necessary to make great sacrifices in the cause of internationalism." Lenin exhorted, "Let us increase our efforts to organize the Red Army. . . . It was our intention to have an army of a million men by spring, but now we need an army of three million." [27]

The significance of this statement was elaborated by Nikolai Podvoiskii, a member of the directing Collegium of the Commissariat of Military Affairs. In a series of articles written toward the end of 1918, published under the imprint "The Supreme Military Inspection of the Worker's-Peasant's Red Army," Podvoiskii indicated the vital role to be played by the Red Army in creating a world state.

Our Red Army must become the nucleus of a World Proletarian Army, the core to which the revolting masses of other countries and the "defectors" of bourgeois armies must subsequently be added. But for such an accumulation of revolutionary force, we must act quickly and decisively, with an army of millions; we must throw against the oppressors such masses as the world has known only in the era of the great invasions, as in the time of Attila and Alaric, when the Roman legions were torn apart and destroyed by millions of "barbarians." [28]

The Red Army must not stop halfway, it must plant its red banners over the entire world. . . . Lenin has ordered us to create an army of three

---

[20] *Piatyi sozyv Vserossiiskogo Tsentral'nogo Ispolnitel'nogo Komiteta Sovetov Rabochikh, Krest'ianskikh, Kazachikh i Krasnoarmeiskikh Deputatov* (Moscow, 1919), Resolution of Oct. 4, 1918, pp. 251–53; quoted in James Bunyan, ed., *Intervention, Civil War, and Communism in Russia, April–December 1918* (Baltimore, 1936), pp. 151–52.

[27] Lenin, "Pis'mo ob"edinënnomu zasedaniiu VTsIK, moskovskogo soveta s predstaviteliami fabrichno-zavodskikh komitetov i professional'nykh soiuzov," Oct. 3, 1918, in *Sochineniia*, XXIII, 216–17.

[28] N. Podvoiskii, "Opyt voenno-revoliutsionnoi taktiki," Dec., 1918, in N. Podvoiskii and M. Pavlovich, eds., *Revoliutsionnaia voina* (Moscow, 1919), p. 49. Podvoiskii indicated that if only the difficulties of training, organization, and equipment could be overcome, the RSFSR alone should be able to supply "7,000,000 contingents for the Red Army." (*Ibid.*, p. 49).

million by spring. . . . A three-million-man army is necessary, because through this war we shall construct our Socialist World Republic.[29]

Following the armistice the Red Army pushed into the Baltic states as the German forces began their withdrawal. On December 25, 1918, *Izvestiia* frankly explained the larger design behind this move:

Lithuania, Latvia, and Estonia stand astride the roads over which we can push our revolution into Western Europe. These regions stand between Soviet Russia and revolutionary Germany. . . . The wall separating the Russian and German revolutionary workers must be destroyed. Soviet Russia must occupy with its own troops Lithuania, Latvia, and Estonia. The Russian working class must have the opportunity to influence directly the course of development of the German revolution, so that then, having created a genuine Soviet Germany, it may merge with it in the general union of a Central and Eastern European Socialist Federation. The conquest of the Baltic Sea and its littoral will also give Soviet Russia the opportunity to influence the socialist revolution in the Scandinavian states.[30]

These grandiose plans were frustrated when the Red Army proved unable to keep its foothold in the Baltic states. However, most of the other non-Russian nations of the former Tsarist Empire were again forcibly subjected to rule from Moscow, in large measure, through the military successes of the Russian Red Army.

The scope of Soviet Russian military ambitions definitely extended beyond reassembling the patrimony of the Tsars. In March, 1919, Lenin again tied the use of war to the objective of uniting all nations, prefacing this union with the ritualistic word "voluntary." "We must declare to other nations that we are complete internationalists, striving for a voluntary union of workers and peasants of all nations. This in no way precludes wars. . . . War may be a necessity under certain conditions."[31] As a result of "all the conquests by our Red Army in the Ukraine and on the Don," Lenin rejoiced in April, 1919, "we have the most serious chances

[29] N. Podvoiskii, "Osnovy revoliutsionnoi voiny i taktiki v internatsional'noi mezhduklassovoi bor'be," 1918, in Podvoiskii and Pavlovich, eds., *Revoliutsionnaia*, pp. 65, 69. Podvoiskii repeated: "When we have victoriously concluded this war, there will be no more wars. . . . There will be a World Labor Republic." (*Ibid.*, p. 67). For a sketch of Podvoiskii, see "Slovar'-ukazatel' imen," in Lenin, *Sochineniia*, XXII, 646–47.
[30] T. Draudin, "Bor'ba za Baltiiskoe more," *Izvestiia*, Dec. 25, 1918, p. 1.
[31] Lenin, "Zakliuchitel'noe slovo po dokladu o partiinoi programme," March 19, 1919, in *Sochineniia*, XXIV, 155.

for victory, not only in Russia, but in the entire world." [32] As Trotsky had just told the founding Comintern Congress, Red Army men "feel that they are not only the soldiers of the Russian Socialist Republic, but also the Red Army of the Third International." When called upon for "help by our Western brothers, we shall respond: 'We are here, we have learned how to bear arms, we are ready to fight and die for world revolution!'" [33] A mood of jubilation prevailed, when in the words of the former Red Army officer, Erich Wollenberg, "the Red Army began to prepare itself for its mission of carrying the banner of the international proletarian revolution into the lands of the West. . . . In the spring of 1919 direct military intervention by the Red Army in the international arena of the class war appeared to be only a matter of days." [34]

The fleeting appearance of Soviet Republics in Hungary and Bavaria led Lenin to believe that a westward push by the Russian Red Army could buttress these islands of Soviet power and touch off further revolutionary upheavals throughout Europe.

Although Lenin was rebuffed in his attempt to march the Red Army to the aid of Soviet Hungary, the Soviet-Polish War of 1920 provided Moscow with a new opportunity to attempt a breakthrough into Western Europe. Lenin left no doubt that the thrust into Poland was a gamble calculated to create a Soviet Europe. He recalled that "when Russian troops advanced on Warsaw, all Germany began to boil." [35] Victory had been so near, Lenin maintained, that it could almost be tasted, and yet it slipped away. "Several days more of victorious advance by the Red Army and not only Warsaw would have been taken (that would not have been so important), but the Versailles Peace would have been destroyed." [36]

Stalin admitted that "we undertook a task that was beyond our strength, the task of breaking into Europe through Warsaw." [37]

[32] Lenin, "Doklad o vneshnem i vnutrennem polozhenii Sovetskoi Respubliki," April 3, 1919, in *ibid.*, XXIV, 207–8.
[33] Trotsky, "Doklad ob RKP i Krasnoi Armii na 1-m zasedanii 1-go kongressa Kominterna," March 2, 1919, in *Piat' let Kominterna*, pp. 16–17.
[34] Wollenberg, *Red Army*, pp. 93–94.
[35] Lenin, "Doklad o kontsessiiakh na fraktsii RKP(b) VIII s"ezda sovetov," Dec. 21, 1920, in *Sochineniia*, XXVI, 14.
[36] Lenin, "Rech' na s"ezde rabochikh i sluzhashchikh kozhevennogo proizvodstva," Oct. 2, 1920, in *ibid.*, XXV, 402.
[37] Stalin, "K voprosu o strategii i taktike russkikh kommunistov," March 14, 1923, in *Sochineniia*, V, 167.

He also acknowledged that this attempt was not in accord with the declaration that the Council of People's Commissars had sent to Poland on January 28, 1920, in which the principle of self-determination of nations was recognized as "inviolable." Should this right come into conflict with the right of the Red Army to conquer foreign nations, a right which Stalin euphemistically termed "the right of the working class to strengthen its power," then

it must be said frankly—the right of self-determination cannot and must not obstruct the working class from realizing its right to dictatorship. This former right must yield to the latter. Such was the case, for instance, in 1920, when, in the interests of defending the power of the working class, we were obliged to march on Warsaw.[38]

Although the strength of the Red Army was not sufficient to carry through its avowed objective, Tukhachevskii, the Red Army Commander in Chief during the Polish war, defended the gamble of a bold military offensive.

In 1920 we had a situation when all of Western Europe was in the throes of a bitter class struggle. The revolutionary movement was growing. In Germany, Italy, and even in England the working class came into movement. It was in these circumstances that our offensive on Warsaw was undertaken for the destruction of the bourgeois-szlachta Polish state. This was a revolutionary act.[39]

He added that, if the Red Army had fulfilled its mission in Poland, "the conflagration would not have stopped at the frontiers of Poland. Like a furious torrent, it would have invaded all of Western Europe." Tukhachevskii then predicted that "the Red Army will not forget this experience of exporting revolution, and if the European bourgeoisie ever invites us to renew battle, the Red Army will succeed in crushing it and in supporting and spreading revolution in Europe." [40]

The acceptance of war as a means of creating a Soviet world state was officially acknowledged in the Statutes of the Communist International, adopted by the Second Comintern Congress in August, 1920: "In order to overthrow the international bourgeoisie and to create the International Soviet Republic . . . the Com-

[38] Stalin, "Zakliuchitel'noe slovo po dokladu o natsional'nykh momentakh v partiinom i gosudarstvennom stroitel'stve," April 25, 1923, in *ibid.*, V, 265.
[39] "Doklad M. N. Tukhachevskogo," in *Vestnik Kommunisticheskoi Akademii* (Moscow), XXXIX (1930), 207-8.
[40] M. N. Tukhachevskii, "La Marche au-delà de la Vistule," Feb., 1923, in Joseph Pilsudski, *L'Année 1920: édition complète avec le texte de l'ouvrage de M. Toukhatchevski* (Paris, 1929), p. 255.

WAR AND SOVIET WORLD STATE

munist International will use all means at its disposal, including armed force."[41]

As a temporary balance of forces between the Soviet and non-Soviet worlds was coming into existence in the early 1920s, Bukharin reminded the Fourth Congress of the Comintern that the Soviet regime continued to reserve the right to launch military excursions into foreign lands. In a speech of November 18, 1922, he insisted:

> We should make it plain in our program that every proletarian state has the right of Red intervention. . . . In the Communist Manifesto we were told that the proletariat should conquer the whole world. . . . This has to be done with bayonets and rifles. For this reason the spread of the system on which the Red Army is based is also the spread of socialism, of the proletarian might, of the revolution. This gives the basis to the right of Red intervention under special circumstances which makes the technical realization of it possible.[42]

Zinoviev, as head of the Comintern, likewise emphasized the duty of Soviet Russia to aid foreign Communist movements by armed assistance. In June, 1925, he noted that the victory of "socialism on a world scale" could not be assured simply by building socialism in the USSR. The situation of the Soviet Union in the proletarian revolution was comparable to that of France in the bourgeois revolution:

> Did not the great French Revolution conduct a number of wars? For what purpose? It is perfectly well understood that if France was to be surrounded by feudal countries the bourgeois revolution could not stand. It had to see that a number of neighboring countries should be formed on its own pattern. . . . That was how the bourgeois revolution came about. Still more is it true of the proletarian revolution.[43]

This view coincided perfectly with Stalin's declaration of May, 1925, that the Soviet Union "can and must build socialism, organize its own socialist economy, and create an armed force for the purpose of going to the aid of the proletarians in surrounding countries, who are struggling for the overthrow of capital."[44] During 1925 Stalin made two other significant statements in which he left

---

[41] "Ustav Kommunisticheskogo Internatsionala," July 19–Aug. 7, 1920, in *Vtoroi kongress Kommunisticheskogo Internatsionala*, p. 535.

[42] Speech by Bukharin, Nov. 18, 1922, in *Fourth Congress of the Communist International*, p. 171.

[43] G. Zinoviev, "Partial Capitalist Stabilization and Our Tasks," *Communist International*, I, No. 12 (June, 1925), 73.

[44] Stalin, "K itogam rabot XIV konferentsii RKP(b)," May 9, 1925, in *Sochineniia*, VII, 114.

no doubt that he banked upon "exporting revolution" with the aid of the Red Army. According to a plausible account by M. N. Roy, the former Indian Communist leader, Stalin told a closed meeting of high Comintern officials:

> Europe is in decay; no revolution can succeed unless the Red Army brings it there. Having captured power and consolidated our position in one country, now it is our task to build up an army which will be able to meet and defeat the combined might of the capitalist world.[45]

Skepticism concerning the ability of foreign Communist movements to achieve and preserve victory without the direct help of the Red Army was likewise reflected in Stalin's speech to high Party officials in January, 1925. While conceding that "the forces of the revolutionary movement in the West are strong" and "here or there may succeed in crushing the bourgeoisie," Stalin feared that

> it will be very difficult for the proletariat to retain power. The examples on our frontier, for instance, our experience in Estonia and Latvia, clearly show this. The question of our army, of its power and its preparedness in case of complications in bordering countries, will necessarily arise among us as the most decisive question.

Stalin cautioned against the precipitous commitment of the Red Army in the event of such foreign "complications." The Red Army must be used, but only in a way that will pluck the most fruit with the least effort. "If war breaks out we shall not be able to sit with folded arms. We shall have to take action, but we shall be the last to do so. And we shall do so in order to throw the decisive weight on the scales, the *weight* that will tip the balance." [46] This was apparently the strategy that Stalin had in mind in 1939 when he sought to contract the Soviet Union out of the hostilities that opened the Second World War. However, Hitler's attack in 1941 denied the Soviet Union the choice of committing the Red Army to battle only after the non-Soviet world had reduced itself to a state of mutual exhaustion.

When and how the Red Army is to be employed depends upon the balance of forces that vary with each situation. But the basic nature and mission of the Red Army is unvarying. Speaking on

[45] M. N. Roy, "Joseph Stalin, Mephisto of Modern History," *The Radical Humanist* (Bombay), XIV, No. 49 (Dec. 10, 1950), 584.
[46] Stalin, "Rech' na plenume TsK RKP(b)," Jan. 19, 1925, in *Sochineniia*, VII, 13–14.

WAR AND SOVIET WORLD STATE

the tenth anniversary of the Red Army in February, 1928, Stalin noted those special features of the Red Army that set it apart from other armies.

> Our Red Army has this peculiar quality, that it is a weapon . . . for the liberation of the workers and peasants from the yoke of the landlords and capitalists. Our army is an army for liberating the toilers.
>
> . . . .
>
> The power of our Red Army is due to the fact it was educated, from the very first day of its birth, in a spirit of internationalism. . . . It is precisely because our army was nurtured in the spirit of internationalism, in the spirit of the unity of interests of the workers of all countries, that our army is the army of the world revolution, the army of the workers of all countries.[47]

Not only did the Red Army have a world-wide mission, not only was it "the army of the world revolution," but the workers of all countries, in turn, owed certain duties to the Red Army. The 1928 Theses of the Sixth Comintern Congress explained that "the Red Army is not the army of the 'enemy,' but the army of the international proletariat." In the event that the Soviet Union becomes involved in war, the workers of all countries must consider the Red Army as "their own." "The proletariat of capitalist countries must not permit the bourgeoisie to frighten it by accusations of treason, nor should it refuse to support the Red Army under the threat of such accusations." [48]

THE MEANING OF SOVIET DISARMAMENT PROPOSALS

The 1928 Comintern Theses also provided a frank reformulation of Soviet theory on the use of force, in the light of a decade of practical experience. The Soviet government had long since learned the value of appealing to world public opinion with dramatic proposals for disarmament. As early as July 19, 1921, Chicherin informed the non-Soviet world that "the very idea of disarmament can only seem to the Soviet government as worthy of approval." [49]

---

[47] "Desiatiletie Krasnoi Armii, torzhestvennoe zasedanie mossoveta, rech' tov. Stalina," Feb. 25, 1928, *Pravda*, Feb. 28, 1928, p. 3. When reprinted in Stalin, *Sochineniia*, XI, 25, the phrase "army of the world revolution" was omitted.
[48] "Mery bor'by s opasnost'iu imperialistskikh voin, tezisy," July 17–Sept. 1, 1928, in *Kom. Int. v dok.*, p. 810. (This volume mistakenly assigns the beginning of the Sixth Comintern Congress to August 17 instead of July 17, 1928).
[49] "Telegram from G. Chicherin, People's Commissar for Foreign Affairs, to the Governments of Great Britain, France, the United States of America,

In the following years Chicherin and Litvinov elaborated bold schemes for world-wide disarmament at international conferences and in the League of Nations.[50] These proposals had apparently sown considerable confusion among Communists throughout the world, for some tended to accept these offers at face value. The Comintern found it necessary to clarify the intent and meaning behind these proposals and it did so with refreshing candor. The same basic reasoning continues to underlie the numerous disarmament proposals that the Soviet regime has subsequently advanced in the United Nations and through other channels.

"The aim of Soviet disarmament proposals," the 1928 Comintern Theses explained, "is not to spread pacifist illusions, but to destroy them . . . to propagate the fundamental Marxist postulate that disarmament and the abolition of war are possible only with the fall of capitalism." Soviet disarmament proposals were not intended to result in "replacing the slogan of arming the proletariat by the slogan of disarming the proletariat. This would be a rejection of civil war and the struggle for socialism. Hence, Communists must strenuously combat the wrong conclusions drawn from the Soviet government's disarmament proposals."[51] This brought the disarmament discussion back to the bedrock Communist position that Lenin had assumed in 1916. At that time Lenin held that "only *after* the proletariat has disarmed the bourgeoisie will it be able, without betraying its world-historical mission, to throw all armaments on the scrap heap; the proletariat will undoubtedly do this, but *only after this condition has been fulfilled, and under no conditions before then.*"[52] Since fulfillment of the "world-historical

---

China and Japan," July 19, 1921, in *The Soviet Union and Peace*, Intro. by Henri Barbusse (New York, 1929), p. 79.

[50] Early Soviet disarmament proposals may be found in *ibid.*, pp. 85, 111–244; *The Soviet's Fight for Disarmament*, Intro. by A. Lunacharskii (New York, 1932), pp. 1–44; Jane Degras, ed., *Soviet Documents on Foreign Policy* (London, New York, Toronto, 1951–1953), I, 250–51, 297, 321–22, 336–37, 346, 350–53, 381–82, 430–32; II, 65, 78, 86, 96, 101, 104–5, 188, 278–80, 304–13, 336–37, 344–45, 369–72, 410, 462–63, 468–69, 474–75, 520; III, 2–3, 7, 42, 83–84, 93, 105, 143, 208. See also Davis, *Soviets at Geneva*, pp. 75–76, 115–93, 208; E. A. Korovin, "The U.S.S.R. and Disarmament," *International Conciliation*, No. 292 (Sept., 1933), pp. 293–351; Wilbur Lee Mahaney, Jr., *The Soviet Union, the League of Nations and Disarmament: 1917–1935* (Philadelphia, 1940); Marina Salvin, "Soviet Policy Towards Disarmament," *International Conciliation*, No. 428 (Feb., 1947), pp. 43–82.

[51] "Mery bor'by," in *Kom. Int. v dok.*, pp. 825–26.

[52] Lenin, "Voennaia programma proletarskoi revoliutsii," autumn, 1916, in *Sochineniia*, XIX, 326.

WAR AND SOVIET WORLD STATE

mission" of the Soviet regime requires the creation of a Soviet world state, the Soviet regime cannot have a genuine interest in any disarmament proposal, short of the creation of a Soviet world state. Nor did the Soviet regime seriously expect other governments to act upon its proposals. "It goes without saying," the Comintern Theses continued, "that not a single Communist thought for a moment that the imperialists would accept the Soviet disarmament proposals." The utility of these proposals lay in their manipulation

for the purpose of (1) recruiting sympathizers for the Soviet Union as the fighter for peace . . . and (2) making use of the *results* of the Soviet disarmament policy to expose the imperialists . . . and explain to the broad masses that there is only one possible way to disarmament and the abolition of war: through the arming of the proletariat, the overthrow of the bourgeoisie and the establishment of the proletarian dictatorship.[53]

The "fight for peace" was intended to recruit Soviet partisans for war.

Comintern comment on the Kellogg-Briand Pact was in a similar vein: "The Soviet Union is taking part in the Pact to outlaw war in the same way as it is taking part in the disarmament negotiations of the League of Nations."[54] This Pact was "nothing but an ingenious form of camouflage for an imperialist policy of war." Nevertheless, "that the Soviet Government has been the first to ratify the Kellogg Agreement was a correct and clever step in the peace policy of the Soviet Union."[55]

SOVIET "PEACE" MOVEMENTS AND REVOLUTIONARY WAR

The Soviet regime has sought to exploit every conceivable "peace" project, but not out of devotion to pacifist principles. The years that have passed since 1928 do not seem to have altered this fundamental position. In February, 1952, *Bol'shevik* cautioned: "Certain demands of the fighters for peace—for example, the reduction of armaments and the peaceful settlement of international

---

[53] "Mery bor'by," in *Kom. Int. v dok.*, pp. 825–27.
[54] Ernst Schneller, "The Soviet Union and the Kellogg Pact," *International Press Correspondence*, VIII, No. 60 (Sept. 6, 1928), 1050.
[55] W. Stoecker, "The Ratification of the Kellogg Agreement and the Communist Parties," *ibid.*, IX, No. 7 (Feb. 8, 1929), 103–4. See also *The Soviet Union and Peace*, pp. 245–69.

conflicts—are outwardly similar to the slogans of the pacifists. But in spite of this similarity it would be a mistake to equate the present-day movement of the Partisans of Peace with pacifism." [56] The Communist-led Partisans of Peace, Stalin noted in 1952, might suddenly find themselves confronted with new tasks, since "it is possible that in a certain confluence of circumstances, the fight for peace will somewhere develop into the fight for socialism. But this will no longer be the present-day peace movement, but a movement for the overthrow of capitalism." [57] Similarly, *Pravda* commented in August, 1954, that in the event of a new war "there will rise up in the rear of the imperialist aggressors a mighty antiwar movement that will strive no longer merely to halt the war, but to end the system that gives rise to war." [58] And, added the neo-Cominform journal in September, 1958, history has "fully confirmed the correctness of the basic Marxist principles that the working class must carry on the fight for peace as part of the general liberation movement against capitalism, resorting if necessary to all possible means." [59]

These recent statements, that "peace" and "antiwar" movements are inseparable from the violent destruction of the non-Soviet world, faithfully reflect the definitive 1928 Comintern Theses, which could discern no contradiction "between the Soviet Government's preparations for defense and for revolutionary war, and a consistent peace policy. The revolutionary war of the proletarian dictatorship is but a continuation of the revolutionary peace policy 'by other means.'" [60]

What do these revealing 1928 Theses say of the role of revolutionary war? The Soviet Union knows that "an imperialist attack on Soviet power is inevitable, and that, in the process of the world proletarian revolution, wars between the proletarian and bourgeois states for the liberation of the world from capitalism are *inevitable*

---

[56] A. Beliakov, "Pod znamenem bor'by za mir," *Bol'shevik*, No. 3 (Feb., 1952), p. 49.
[57] Stalin, "Zamechaniia po ekonomicheskim voprosam, sviazannym s noiabr'-skoi diskussiei 1951 goda," Feb. 1, 1952, in *Ekonomicheskie problemy*, p. 36.
[58] B. Ponomarev, "Uroki istorii," *Pravda*, Aug. 1, 1954, p. 4.
[59] Antonin Novotny, "For the Triumph of Peace and Socialism," *World Marxist Review*, I, No. 1 (Sept., 1958), 8.
[60] *The Struggle Against Imperialist War and the Tasks of the Communists: Resolution of the VI World Congress of the Communist International, July–August, 1928* (New York, 1932), p. 31. The second sentence was omitted from *Kom. Int. v. dok.*, p. 811.

WAR AND SOVIET WORLD STATE

and necessary." [61] This suggests that a war in which the Soviet Union became involved "for the liberation of the world from capitalism" would start as a result of "an imperialist attack" upon the Soviet Union. But elsewhere the Theses recall the Leninist tenet that it is the nature of the war, not the way it begins, which is decisive. "The unjust war is not that waged by the one who is first to attack, but by the one who represents reaction, counterrevolution, exploitation and imperialism against national or proletarian revolution." The Theses likewise recapitulated Lenin's definition of "just" or "revolutionary" wars.

> The overthrow of capitalism is impossible without force, without armed uprisings and proletarian wars against the bourgeoisie. . . . Proletarian civil wars against the bourgeoisie, wars of the proletarian dictatorship against bourgeois states and world capitalism, and national-revolutionary wars of oppressed peoples against imperialism are inevitable and revolutionary.[62]

The Comintern Theses, designed primarily for the eyes of devoted Communists throughout the world, did not receive a careful examination in the world press, and Soviet official spokesmen continued to profess their peaceful intentions and to denounce the use of force among nations. In a much-quoted public statement of June, 1930, Stalin declared: "We do not want a single foot of foreign territory." [63] In May, 1932, responding to the question of an American newspaper man concerning the possibility of armed conflict between the USSR and the United States, Stalin asserted: "So far as the USSR is concerned, there is hardly any need to prove that the people and the government of the USSR likewise wish that 'an armed conflict between both countries would never under any circumstances' take place." [64] During 1930–1933 Litvinov busied himself devising elaborate definitions of aggression which aimed to eliminate all justifications for the use of force, either direct or indirect. These definitions, offered to the League of Nations in February, 1933, were incorporated in the conventions of July, 1933, which the Soviet Union signed together with eleven other states.[65]

---
[61] "Mery bor'by," in *Kom. Int. v dok.*, p. 811.
[62] *Ibid.*, pp. 797–98.
[63] Stalin, "Politicheskii otchët Tsentral'nogo Komiteta XVI s"ezdu VKP(b)," June 27, 1930, in *Sochineniia*, XII, 261.
[64] Stalin, "Otvety na voprosy Ral'fa V. Barnesa," May 3, 1932, in *ibid.*, XIII, 139.
[65] Litvinov, *Against Aggression*, pp. 170–80; T. A. Taracouzio, *War and Peace in Soviet Diplomacy* (New York, 1940), pp. 127–28; Julius Stone, *Ag-*

Stalin's highly publicized interview with Roy Howard, the head of the influential Scripps-Howard newspaper chain, in March, 1936, also expressed an unconditional rejection of the use of force. "If you think," Stalin asserted, "that the Soviet people have any desire to alter the face of things by the use of force or to change the established order in surrounding states by force, you are strictly mistaken." When Howard inquired if this meant an abandonment of previous Soviet plans and intentions concerning the use of force on a world scale, Stalin retorted wryly, "We never had any such plans and intentions." Howard prodded Stalin further by suggesting that "the world has long held another impression," but Stalin replied categorically: "This is the result of a misunderstanding. . . . The export of revolution is nonsense." [66]

During the 1930s Stalin presented another picture to his Communist audience. In a private letter of January, 1930, to Maxim Gorky, Stalin reiterated that he could only be opposed to "imperialist" wars. "We are *for* a liberating, anti-imperialist, revolutionary war despite the fact that such a war, as is known, not only is not free from 'the horrors of bloodshed' but abounds in them." [67] Stalin's report to the Seventeenth Party Congress in January, 1934, contained this unmistakable hint concerning the "export of revolution" through war: "It can hardly be doubted that a second war against the USSR will lead to the complete defeat of the aggressors, to revolution in a series of countries of Europe and Asia, and to the destruction of the bourgeois-landlord governments of these countries." [68] During the middle and late 1930s the Comintern press conspicuously played up Stalin's phrases that the Red Army was "an army for liberating the toilers" and "the army of the world revolution." [69] These ideas were echoed in the official 1938 Party his-

---

gression and World Order (Berkeley, Calif., 1958), pp. 34–40, 212–13. For the Soviet attitude toward a definition of aggression following the Second World War, see John N. Hazard, *Law and Social Change in the USSR* (London, 1953), pp. 292–94; George C. Guins, *Communism on the Decline* (New York, 1956), pp. 236–43; Stone, *Aggression*, pp. 46–48, 88, 111–18, 201–2.

[66] "Beseda tovarishcha Stalina s predsedatelem amerikanskogo gazetnogo ob"edineniia 'Skripps-Govard Niuspeipers,' g-nom Roi Govardom," March 1, 1936, *Pravda*, March 5, 1936, p. 2.

[67] Stalin, "Pis'mo A. M. Gor'komu," Jan. 17, 1930, in *Sochineniia*, XII, 176.

[68] Stalin, "Otchëtnyi doklad XVII s"ezdu partii o rabote TsK VKP(b)," Jan. 26, 1934, in *ibid.*, XIII, 297.

[69] See, for example, "The Seventeenth Anniversary of the Red Army," *Communist International*, XII, No. 4 (Feb. 20, 1935), 156, 161; Joseph Stalin,

WAR AND SOVIET WORLD STATE

tory, which again defined just wars as "wars of liberation, waged . . . to liberate a nation from the slavery of capitalism" or "to liberate colonies and dependent countries from the yoke of imperialism." This Party bible also cited Lenin's warning about those conflicts that would arise from the inescapable frictions generated by the coexistence of the Soviet and non-Soviet worlds: "Under these conditions, war on our part would be legitimate and just. It would be a war for socialism, for the liberation of other nations from the bourgeoisie." [70] These pronouncements kept intact the theoretical framework within which the Red Army would move at that propitious future date of reckoning which, it was felt, must inevitably arrive.

With the foreboding of a world war clearly in the air, Stalin's speech of March 10, 1939, provided important clues to the momentous onrushing events. After making perfunctory remarks about defending the principles of collective security, Stalin assumed a startling position with regard to Germany. He insisted that there was no substance to Hitler's long-publicized plans to annex the Soviet Ukraine. Moreover, it was the policy of the Soviet Union to establish friendly ties with all countries, and not "be drawn into conflicts by warmongers who are accustomed to have others pull the chestnuts out of the fire for them." [71] Available documents now leave no doubt that these remarks of Stalin were intended to pave the way for a partnership with Hitler, and that this intention was fully grasped in Berlin.[72] A careful reading of another section of this speech reveals the use to which Stalin hoped to put the Nazi-Soviet Pact, which was finally consummated in Moscow on August 23, 1939. In it Stalin accused France and Britain of a nonintervention policy that was designed to spread and deepen the Sino-Japanese War so as to lead to a conflict between Japan and the Soviet Union. In Europe this policy was intended to incite a conflict between Germany and the Soviet Union. It would now appear that

---

"Three Peculiarities of the Red Army," *ibid.*, XV, No. 3 (March, 1938), 219–21; O. Kuusinen, "The Army of the Land of Socialism," *ibid.*, XV, No. 4 (April, 1938), 335; Speech of Comrade Stalin, "Three Peculiarities of the Red Army," *International Press Correspondence*, XVIII, No. 8 (Feb. 26, 1938), 157; O. Kuusinen, "An Invincible, Heroic Army," *ibid.*, XVIII, No. 8 (Feb. 26, 1938), 158.

[70] *Istoriia vsesoiuznoi*, pp. 161, 163.
[71] Stalin, *Otchëtnyi doklad na XVIII S"ezde*, March 10, 1939, pp. 33–43.
[72] A. Rossi, *The Russo-German Alliance, 1939–1941* (Boston, 1951), pp. 7–10.

such Machiavellian thinking was much more a projection of Stalin's own attitudes, than a precise description of French and British policy. In Stalin's words, this was a strategy

> to allow all the belligerents to sink deeply in the mire of war, to encourage them surreptitiously in this; to allow them to weaken and exhaust one another; and then, when they have become weak enough, to appear on the scene with fresh strength, to appear, of course, "in the interests of peace," and to dictate conditions to the enfeebled belligerents. Cheap and easy! [73]

This strategy coincides almost exactly with the prescription for the use of the Red Army which Stalin had laid down as early as 1925. The records of the Nazi-Soviet negotiations give every indication that Stalin hoped that the partnership between Germany and the USSR would be a long-term proposition, and that he felt genuinely betrayed when Hitler turned on him. The painless expansion of the Soviet orbit while the major non-Soviet powers were sinking deeply in the mire of war had only a brief, though spectacular, success in Europe, but this strategy succeeded completely in Asia.

The secret telegrams Moscow sent to the Soviet Ambassador in Tokyo in 1940 revealed the purpose of the Soviet effort to arrive at a *modus vivendi* with Japan. In return for alleviating Soviet pressure on the Soviet-Manchurian border, "Japan plans intensifying pressure on foreign interests in China and southeast Asia by securing the safety of Manchuria. We considered that this action on part of Japan would collide with foreign nations to advantage of the Soviet Union and China." On the other hand, Moscow warned against a comprehensive agreement with Japan that would involve a peace settlement in China, since this would alienate the United States, whose aid might be needed in the event of a future rupture in Nazi-Soviet relations. "Also, such overall agreement with Japan might destroy our work proceeding among the suppressed peoples of Asia," that is, it would deprive Communists of the opportunity of placing themselves at the head of revolutionary, national liberation movements. Moscow also feared that "it would not instigate the Japanese-American War which we desire. So we are planning not to develop the negotiation into an agreement but merely to alleviate tension between Japan and the Soviet Union. We concluded an 'Agreement with Germany' because a war is required

[73] Stalin, *Otchëtnyi doklad na XVIII s"ezde*, pp. 30-31.

in Europe."[74] The Nazi-Soviet Pact was required in Europe, it would seem, to start a war, but in Asia, where war was already underway, a similar pact dividing the spoils might have limited and ultimately halted war, and this ran counter to the long-range Soviet calculation. The Soviet-Japanese Neutrality Pact, concluded on April 13, 1941, turned Japanese aggression away from the Soviet borders as desired, and then in August, 1945, when Japan was already on its knees, principally as a result of the war effort of the United States, Stalin was able to march the Red Army into Northeast Asia to pick up "cheap and easy" gains.

The prospective use of the Red Army in Europe was elaborated by Lev Mekhlis, Chief of the Political Administration of the Red Army and Assistant People's Commissar of Defense, in an address to the Eighteenth Party Congress four days after Stalin's speech of March 10, 1939. Mekhlis explained frankly that sooner or later the Red Army would see action, and that its mission could not be confined to a defense of the existing boundaries of the Soviet Union. The Red Army would, as a minimum, add new Union Republics to the USSR, and beyond that, it might completely destroy the "capitalist encirclement." Mekhlis predicted:

If the edge of the second imperialist war should be turned against the first socialist state in the world, we must carry military hostilities into the enemy's territory, perform our international duty, and increase the number of Soviet Republics. (*Applause*)

. . . .

The time is not far off, Comrades, when our army will, in retaliation to the insolent attack of the enemy, help the workers of the aggressor countries to emancipate themselves from the yoke of fascism, from the yoke of capitalist slavery, and to eliminate the capitalist encirclement of which Comrade Stalin spoke. (*Loud applause*)[75]

Over twenty years of experience had taught the Soviet regime that the destruction of this "capitalist encirclement" could scarcely be expected to result from indigenous revolutionary movements operating *within* each capitalist country. The Soviet leadership now

[74] These telegrams were intercepted by the Imperial Japanese government's Consul General in Harbin. Japanese copies were examined and accepted as authentic by Allen S. Whiting, and quoted in Ernst B. Haas and Allen S. Whiting, *Dynamics of International Relations* (New York, Toronto, London, 1956), p. 326.
[75] Speech by L. Mekhlis, March 14, 1939, in *The Red Army Today: Speeches Delivered at the Eighteenth Congress of the C.P.S.U.(B.), March 10-21, 1939* (Moscow, 1939), pp. 42, 54.

frankly anticipated that foreign "revolutions" would have to be imposed from *without*, by the use of armed force.

Sooner perhaps than Mekhlis had imagined, the Red Army was set into motion to add Union Republics to the USSR. However, this action was not in response to an "insolent attack of the enemy." The Nazi-Soviet Pact of August 23, 1939, which unleashed the Second World War, successfully contracted the Soviet Union out of immediate conflict with the major European powers while a secret protocol marked out a "sphere of interest" into which the Red Army could march with impunity.

Finland was among those hapless nations assigned to the Soviet sphere. The aggressive warfare launched across the Finnish border on the morning of November 30, 1939, has been accorded this curiously candid justification by F. I. Kozhevnikov, the eminent Soviet legal authority, and later Soviet representative on the World Court:

> The U.S.S.R. has a right to defend itself by shifting the boundaries of that state which constitutes an immediate menace to it. In order to secure the frontiers of the U.S.S.R., the territorial problem can be solved by means of a just war, which is the self-defense of the socialist state.[76]

Between August, 1939, and August, 1940, the Nazi-Soviet partnership had produced substantial results: some 23,000,000 people had been added to the Soviet Union, and the number of Union Republics in the USSR had been increased from eleven to sixteen. Each step in this process of adding Union Republics was a renewed test of the Soviet allegation that the Soviet federation rests purely and entirely upon the voluntary consent of its member nations. Historical evidence, however, would impose the conclusion that the affiliation of these nations in no way rested upon genuine expressions of national self-determination. At each stage in this drama the Red Army played the decisive role, for each acquisition was accompanied either by the direct threat or the actual use of armed force.

[76] F. I. Kozhevnikov, "The Creative Contribution of the U.S.S.R. to the Equitable Solution of Territorial Problems" (English summary), *Państwo i Prawo* (Warsaw), V, No. 12 (Dec., 1950), 1.

THE PROSPECT OF CARVING UP THE WORLD

Yet these gains seemed extremely modest when compared with the vista that was opened by the Nazi suggestion that the USSR join the Axis in dividing up the world. Molotov explored this possibility with Hitler and Ribbentrop during his visit to Berlin in November, 1940. Hitler specifically held out the prospect of Soviet participation in the liquidation of the British Empire. He told Molotov that "all the countries which could possibly be interested in the bankrupt estate would have to stop all controversies among themselves and concern themselves exclusively with the partition of the British Empire." According to the minutes of this conference of November 13, "Molotov replied that he had followed the arguments of the Führer with interest and that he was in agreement with everything that he had understood." Hitler indicated the need to determine "in bold outlines the boundaries for the future activity of peoples and of assigning to nations large areas where they could find an ample field of activity for fifty to a hundred years."[77] Hitler and Ribbentrop suggested that Soviet expansion might be directed variously toward the Persian Gulf, the Arabian Sea, and the Indian Ocean.[78] While Molotov did not renounce ambitions in Asia, he indicated that the immediate center of Soviet aspirations should be in the direction of the Persian Gulf, and, in addition, that the Soviet Union was vitally interested in the fate of all of East Central Europe.[79]

Though Moscow exhibited a definite desire to come to an agreement along these lines, the benefits of this partnership were already at an end, and on December 18, 1940, Hitler ordered full-scale preparations for the invasion of the Soviet Union.[80] The conversations between Hitler and Molotov are nevertheless revealing in that they demonstrated a willingness on the part of the Soviet Union to expand its frontiers by the use of force wherever an opportunity might appear. In this case the Soviet leaders contemplated the prospect

[77] Raymond James Sontag and James Stuart Beddie, eds., *Nazi-Soviet Relations, 1939–1941: Documents from the Archives of the German Foreign Office* (Washington, 1948), pp. 243–44.
[78] *Ibid.*, pp. 222, 243, 257.   [79] *Ibid.*, pp. 252, 258, 259, 270.
[80] *Ibid.*, pp. 260–64. Hitler had begun formulating plans for the invasion of the Soviet Union as early as July, 1940; see John A. Lukacs, *The Great Powers and Eastern Europe* (New York, 1953), pp. 318–20.

of driving into an area extending from Eastern Europe through the Near East and far into Asia.

THE RED ARMY AND THE WAR WITH GERMANY

When Hitler invaded the USSR on June 22, 1941, the primary mission of the Red Army was, naturally enough, cast in terms of defending the Soviet homeland. However it is astonishing to find that, even at this low point in the destiny of the Soviet regime and with the Red Army in full retreat, the aggressive, "liberating" mission of the Red Army continued to be mentioned. On October 1, 1941, Molotov projected this bold vision:

> The time will come when nations will pronounce their weighty judgment on that mission of liberation in which the Soviet Union, under the guidance of its great leader, Comrade Stalin, is now engaged, not only in the interests of the emancipation of the peoples of Europe, but in the interests of freedom for the peoples of the whole world.[81]

Stalin reiterated that the Soviet armed forces must look forward to this mission of liberation beyond the boundaries of the Soviet Union, in his speech of November 7, 1941:

> Comrades Red Army and Red Navy men. . . . The enslaved peoples of Europe, who have fallen under the yoke of German occupation, look upon you as their liberators. A great mission of liberation has fallen to your lot. Be worthy of this mission! The war you are waging is a war of liberation, a just war.[82]

When the tide of battle had finally turned, Molotov again reminded the Red Army of the tasks of national liberation which lay before it. Speaking on February 1, 1944, Molotov hailed the Red Army's campaigns to clear foreign troops off the territory of the prewar Soviet Union, as well as from those Union Republics created during the Nazi-Soviet honeymoon. In addition, Molotov continued, who could not fail to understand "that the Red Army fulfills its mission of liberation, not only with regard to its own motherland, but also with regard to all democratic countries" endangered by fascism?[83] These pronouncements, issued in the context of a war-

---
[81] "Rech' V. M. Molotova na zakliuchitel'nom zasedanii konferentsii predstavitelei SSSR, Velikobritanii i SShA," Oct. 1, 1941, *Pravda*, Oct. 2, 1941, p. 1.
[82] Stalin, "Rech' na parade Krasnoi Armii," Nov. 7, 1941, in *O velikoi Otechestvennoi voine Sovetskogo Soiuza* (Moscow, 1950), p. 71.
[83] "Doklad tov. V. M. Molotova v Verkhovnom Sovete SSSR, 1 fevralia 1944 goda," *Pravda*, Feb. 2, 1944, p. 1.

WAR AND SOVIET WORLD STATE 311

time alliance, did not seem threatening to the Western Allies, and it was only subsequently that their sinister meaning became evident.

During 1944-1945 the Red Army spilled over Eastern Europe, establishing Soviet political control in its wake. Among the satellite leaders Tito alone owed little to the Red Army for the seizure of state power, and it was, significantly, in Yugoslavia that Stalin met with failure when his will clashed with that of Tito. The Stalin-Tito correspondence, which attempts to justify Soviet demands on Yugoslavia by stressing the services of the Red Army, is of particular interest because it reveals Stalin's frank emphasis on the role assigned to the Soviet armed forces. In his letter to Tito of May 4, 1948, Stalin asserted that Tito's success was due, not to any special qualities of the Communist Party of Yugoslavia, but to the fact that "the Soviet Army came to the aid of the Yugoslav people, crushed the German invaders, liberated Belgrade, and in this way created the conditions which were necessary for the CPY to achieve power." [84] Tito proceeded to draw this significant political conclusion: "According to the views expressed in the Soviet Communist Party letters to the CP of Yugoslavia, it would appear that a revolutionary transformation is impossible without the assistance of the Red Army." Stalin held "the belief that only occupation by the Red Army may bring the new socialist order." [85] Except for the anomalous case of eastern Austria, the history of postwar Europe would, indeed, support the conclusion that a nation placed under Red Army occupation was destined for integration into the Soviet orbit.

By way of contrast, the Soviet-Yugoslav correspondence contains an enlightening Soviet explanation for the failure of the Communists to seize power in Western Europe. Stalin insisted that, "even though the French and Italian CPs have so far achieved less success than the CPY," this was due not to the virtues of the Yugoslav Party, but to the fact that Yugoslavia was liberated by the Red Army. The Soviet communication concludes: "Unfortunately the Soviet Army did not and could not render such assistance to the French and Italian CPs." [86] Leaving aside the argument over

[84] *Soviet-Yugoslav Dispute*, p. 51.
[85] "Marshal Tito Replies to French Journalist Louis Dalma," *Yugoslav Fortnightly* (Belgrade), I, No. 17 (Jan. 13, 1950), 2.
[86] *Soviet-Yugoslav Dispute*, p. 51.

who liberated Yugoslavia, there is much logic in Stalin's view that France and Italy would also probably have become "People's Democracies" if they had been "liberated" by the Red Army.

The specter of the Soviet armed forces appearing as the "savior" of Western Europe was not abandoned. At the end of February, 1949, Thorez and Togliatti touched off a chain reaction of manifestos by the Communist Parties of Western Europe, resolving that the peoples of these countries

> will not fight against the Soviet Union. . . . If the warmongers succeed in unleashing a new war, the people will fight on the side of the USSR in this war. They will fiercely support the Soviet Army when, in pursuit of the imperialist aggressors, it enters the territories of these states. The people will greet it in the same way as they greeted it in the countries of the People's Democracies during the course of the past war.[87]

To be sure, these declarations sanctioned the invasion of Western Europe by the Soviet Army only "in pursuit of the imperialist aggressors." But as the "aggressor" in Communist doctrine is not determined by who launches an armed attack, but by the class interest that each armed force represents, it is conceivable that the Soviet Army might *begin* the pursuit of the "imperialist aggressors," or even act to forestall an "invasion." This possibility was no doubt examined frankly in the Communist circles of Western Europe. It was this issue that precipitated the expulsion of two prominent Communist leaders, Valdo Magnani and Aldo Cucchi, from the Italian Communist Party in January, 1951. Magnani deplored the fact that "there is widespread opinion in the Communist Party that revolution can take its flag forward only by means of war." He denied that "a revolution can only win on the bayonets of an army which crosses our frontier." His unpardonable sin came in the form of a demand that the Italian Communists "stand for the defense of the national territory against an army, which from any

[87] I. Chashnikov, *Sovetskaia Armiia—armiia osvoboditel'nitsa* (Moscow, 1952), p. 65. This is reminiscent of earlier Comintern resolutions; for example, the one of 1935 issued by the Communist Parties of Europe which stated: "In case of a counter-revolutionary war against the fatherland of socialism, we will support the Red Army by all means in our power and will fight . . . for the defeat of any state which begins war against the Soviet Union." (*Communist International*, XII, Nos. 17–18 [Sept. 20, 1935], 918.) A significant difference is that the 1935 resolution spoke in terms of the armies of the West invading the Soviet Union, while the 1949 resolution pictured the army of the Soviet Union invading the West.

WAR AND SOVIET WORLD STATE

side whatsoever . . . might cross the frontiers and invade the country."[88]

SOVIET DIRECTIVES FOR THE USE OF ARMED FORCE IN ASIA

The increasing success of the Communist forces in the Chinese civil war coincided with the hardening of the Communist line in favor of the use of armed force throughout Asia. During the spring and summer of 1947 the prominent Soviet economist, Eugene Varga, was sharply rebuked for suggesting that national independence movements in Asia would probably proceed for some time along peaceful lines under native, non-Communist leadership.[89] Then Zhdanov officially proclaimed the turn toward armed struggle in his speech to the founding Cominform Conference in September, 1947.

> The Second World War aggravated the crisis of the colonial system as expressed in the rise of a powerful movement for national liberation in the colonies and dependencies. . . . The attempt to crush the national liberation movement by military force now increasingly meets armed resistance on the part of colonial peoples and produces prolonged colonial wars.[90]

This new "forward" policy was elaborated at two Communist conclaves held in Calcutta during February, 1948. The first was the Southeast Asia Youth Conference, sponsored by two international Communist-front youth organizations and attended by 900 delegates from various Asian countries. The second, also attended by Communist representatives of different lands, was a Congress of the Indian Communist Party at which the Party Secretary, P. C. Joshi, was deposed from the Party leadership for "gradualism." Following these gatherings Communist guerrilla warfare was triggered off in many parts of Southeast Asia, while those uprisings already in progress were intensified in scope.[91]

---

[88] Francis Noel-Baker, "Italy's Red Front Begins to Crack," *Life*, XXX, No. 9 (Feb. 26, 1951), 114, 119.
[89] Frederick C. Barghoorn, "The Varga Discussion and Its Significance," *American Slavic*, VII, No. 3 (Oct., 1948), 214–36; Ruth T. McVey, *The Soviet View of the Indonesian Revolution* (Cornell Modern Indonesia Project, Ithaca, N.Y., 1957), pp. 5–7.
[90] A. Zhdanov, "O mezhdunarodnom polozhenii," Sept., 1947, in *Informatsionnoe soveshchanie*, p. 17.
[91] John F. Cady, "Southeast Asia," in George B. de Huszar and associates, *Soviet Power and Policy* (New York, 1955), pp. 498–532; Milton Sacks, "The

It was the completion of the Communist conquest of the Chinese mainland and the proclamation of the People's Republic of China in October, 1949, which shifted the armed struggle in Asia to a vastly more threatening stage. Wishing to capitalize on the prestige of the Chinese military victory, Moscow chose to speak to the Communists of Asia through the Chinese Communist leaders. In accordance with the familiar practice of disseminating settled policy through an international Communist-front organization, the World Federation of Trade Unions called a Conference of Trade Unions of Asia and Australasia in Peking in November, 1949. At the suggestion of the Soviet delegate, this gathering of top Communist functionaries in Asia established a Permanent Liaison Bureau in Peking, through which the Sino-Soviet program of armed struggle could be popularized, and perhaps even supervised and guided.

China's chief spokesman at this Conference was Liu Shao-chi, who was introduced as Vice President of the WFTU and Honorary Chairman of the Chinese Trade Unions. Liu, long acknowledged as one of the outstanding theoreticians of the Chinese Communist Party, spoke with authority. He had been a member of the Party Politburo since 1932, was made a Vice Chairman of the Central People's Government of China in 1949, and in 1959 succeeded Mao Tse-tung as the titular chief of state. In his speech of November 16, 1949, to the opening session of the Conference, Liu quickly dispelled any illusions about an interest in trade unionism. "I consider that the work of our Conference of the Trade Unions of Asia and Australasia has as its principal aim the struggle against the yoke of imperialism and feudalism and the conquest of national independence and a people's democracy." He surveyed the armed struggle going on in the various Asian countries and held up China as the model for emulation. "The path chosen by the Chinese people for the victory over imperialism and its servants and for the creation of a Chinese People's Republic—this is the path that must be followed

---

Strategy of Communism in Southeast Asia," *Pacific Affairs*, XXIII, No. 3 (Sept., 1950), 227–47. The decision to shift the line in India was taken in December, 1947, but this turning point was slow in being accepted and publicized. See John H. Kautsky, *Moscow and the Communist Party of India* (New York, 1956), pp. 41–42; Gene D. Overstreet and Marshall Windmiller, *Communism in India* (Berkeley, Los Angeles, 1959), pp. 267–75, who emphasize the role of the Yugoslavs in transmitting the "forward" policy to Asia. See also Ruth T. McVey, *The Calcutta Conference and the Southeast Asian Uprisings* (Cornell Modern Indonesia Project, Ithaca, N.Y., 1958).

WAR AND SOVIET WORLD STATE

by the peoples of many colonial and semicolonial countries in their struggle to win national independence and a people's democracy." Then came this specific set of instructions:

> It is necessary to create, wherever and whenever possible, strong people's armies of liberation, skilled in fighting the enemy, under the leadership of the Communist Parties. It is necessary to create supporting bases for the operation of these armies, as well as to combine the struggle of the masses in the areas controlled by the enemy with this armed struggle. Moreover, *armed struggle is the main form of struggle in the national liberation movement in many colonies and semicolonies.*

And finally this blast: "The people's democratic and national liberation movement in the colonies and the semicolonies will not cease until it is crowned with total victory." [92]

To hasten the "liberation" of Asia, the Soviet delegate, Solovëv, called upon the French, Dutch, British, and American workers to "urge their governments to stop immediately the intervention in Indonesia, Vietnam, Burma, Malaya, and South Korea, and to withdraw their troops from these countries." [93] The West was invited to withdraw from Asia at the very moment that Communist-led "people's armies of liberation" were scheduled to accelerate the armed conquest of power. Liu Shao-chi then arose once more to acknowledge the special burden that had been assigned to Communist China in this process. Addressing his "trade union" colleagues on November 23, Liu vowed:

> The Chinese working class has to shoulder the grave responsibility of rendering assistance to the working class and working people of capitalist countries in the world, especially the colonial and semicolonial countries in Asia and Australasia. The victorious Chinese working class cannot, and should not, evade such an international responsibility.

Liu urged a quick consolidation of power in China so that "we will be able to encourage the oppressed nations to rise up and fight for their own liberation. This is what we can and should do." [94]

This was a rather straightforward exposition of Soviet directives

---

[92] "Rech' Liu Shao-chi na konferentsii profsoiuzov stran Azii i Okeanii," *Pravda*, Jan. 4, 1950, p. 3 (italics added).
[93] New China News Agency (NCNA), Peking Radio, Nov. 19, 1949, recorded in *Foreign Broadcast Information Service*, Washington, D.C., Nov. 22, 1949; quoted in Sacks, "The Strategy," *Pacific Affairs*, XXIII, No. 3 (Sept., 1950), 235.
[94] NCNA, Peking Radio, Nov. 24, 1949, recorded in *Foreign Broadcast*, Nov. 25, 1949; quoted in Sacks, "The Strategy," *Pacific Affairs*, XXIII, No. 3 (Sept., 1950), 236.

for Asia. China was the model. The Communists were to set up "liberated areas" and wage protracted civil wars, gradually expanding their state within a state until they vanquished all their foes. Communist China was pledged to feed the flames of these wars with whatever guidance and material assistance it could make available. And behind China stood the Soviet Union. With Soviet help and guidance, China was to grow into a strong, industrialized country capable of sustaining a high level of military activity. The Sino-Soviet Treaty of Friendship and Mutual Assistance of February 14, 1950, served to bolster China's military role in Asia, while committing the Soviet Union to the military defense of China in case it was subjected to attack.

Soviet-Chinese military coordination was evident when the Soviet-sponsored adventure of the Korean War made generous use of Chinese Communist "volunteers." However, Stalin's willingness to permit Mao's crack troops to be bled white in Korea undoubtedly created strains in this partnership. It would seem plausible that Peking's pressure on Moscow influenced heavily the Soviet declaration of June 23, 1951, in which the Soviet Union indicated that it was interested in fostering truce negotiations.[95] This was followed, in November, 1951, by an authoritative Soviet pronouncement that the "Chinese path" of conquering state power through armed force was not necessarily a " 'stereotype' for popular democratic revolutions in other countries of Asia," since they could not definitely "calculate on acquiring . . . a revolutionary army such as there is in China."[96] By 1951 the attempts of the various Asian Communist Parties to seize power by force of arms had begun to reach the limits of profitable ventures. The following years witnessed a gradual shift toward the struggle for power by "peaceful" means, which was best symbolized, perhaps, by the Bandung Conference of 1955.

That this shift reflected calculations of expediency rather than renunciation of principles was made perfectly obvious by the developments in Indochina. Here, the prospects of a Communist military victory remained highly promising, and both Soviet and

[95] Iuri A. Rastvorov, "Red Fraud and Intrigue in Far East," *Life*, XXXVII, No. 23 (Dec. 6, 1954), 176.
[96] Speech of E. M. Zhukov to the Institute of Oriental Studies, USSR Academy of Sciences, Nov. 12, 1951; cited in "Khronika v Institute vostokovedeniia," *Izvestiia Akademii Nauk SSSR; seriia istorii i filosofii*, IX, No. 1 (Jan.-Feb., 1952), 81.

WAR AND SOVIET WORLD STATE

Chinese ideological and material support were made available to Ho Chi Minh in his military conquest of North Vietnam. At the height of the battle for the vital French fortress of Dienbienphu, on April 21, 1954, *Pravda* invoked the memory of the revolutionary wars waged by the Russian Red Army:

> The young defenders of the Democratic Republic of Vietnam are reading the words which the great commander of the revolution spoke in November, 1919. V. I. Lenin said at that time: "I think that what the Red Army has done, its struggle and history of victory, will have great, universal significance for all peoples of the East. It will show the peoples of the East that, weak as they may be and invincible as may seem the power of the European oppressors, who employ all the marvels of technology and military arts, nevertheless a revolutionary war waged by the oppressed peoples, if this war really succeeds in arousing the millions of toilers and exploited, holds within itself such potentialities, such miracles, that the liberation of the peoples of the East is now quite practically attainable." [97]

Though the opportunity to launch war will vary with the individual circumstances and the particular balance of forces existing within each country, it is clear that, in principle, the Soviet leaders continue to sanction and stimulate armed aggression both in the East and in the West.

THE PROSPECT OF TOTAL ATOMIC WAR

Inherent in all situations involving the use of armed force in the atomic era is the threat that some "incident" might touch off a chain of events that would result in the holocaust of total atomic annihilation. General MacArthur's removal from the command of the UN troops in the Korean War was primarily attributable to President Truman's determined refusal to countenance the advice of those who wished to strike at the "privileged sanctuaries" of the Chinese Communist mainland, possibly with atomic bombs. Despite this rebuff, American extremists have periodically continued to advocate the dropping of nuclear bombs, without regard for the possibility of precipitating a general war.[98] The official United States position

---
[97] Nikolai Tikhonov, "Lenin ozaril put' k schast'iu narodov," *Pravda*, April 21, 1954, p. 3.
[98] For example, on March 27, 1955, Senate Republican Leader William Knowland announced that he "would favor defending Quemoy and Matsu even if it meant touching off a general war," and Senator Styles Bridges declared that he "would favor the use of atomic weapons to attack concentrations

has never embraced this view, although the doctrine of "massive retaliation," elaborated in 1954, had a threatening ring in much of the world. Since the Geneva Conference of 1955, however, the American government has repeatedly emphasized the unthinkability of general nuclear warfare.

The record of the Soviet attitude toward nuclear war has been more checkered and less reassuring. During Stalin's lifetime the truly catastrophic nature of such a war was never publicly acknowledged by any Soviet leader. This may have been motivated, in part, by the need to minimize the importance of a weapon that was being stockpiled by the West at a greater pace than by the Soviet Union. On September 24, 1946, Stalin remarked contemptuously that "atomic bombs are intended to frighten the weak-nerved but they cannot decide the outcome of war." [99] In major speeches of November 6, 1949, and October 5, 1952, Malenkov cheerfully contemplated "that a third world war would bring about the collapse of the world capitalist system," without hinting that such a war would simultaneously wipe out the Soviet state.[100]

President Truman's "State of the Union Message" of January 7, 1953, appealed directly to the Soviet leaders to recognize that atomic war could destroy civilization, and to reconsider the

belief in Lenin's prophecy that one stage in the development of Communist society would be war between your world and ours. But Lenin was a pre-atomic man, who viewed society and history with pre-atomic eyes. Something profound has happened since he wrote. War has changed its shape and its dimensions. It cannot now be a "stage" in the development of anything save ruin for your regime and your homeland.[101]

---

of military power on the Chinese mainland." ("Biggest Barriers to the Big Four Talks Believed Removed," New York *Times*, March 28, 1955.) In this instance, both the President and Secretary of State hinted broadly that the use of "tactical" atomic weapons might be permissible. See "Text of Broadcast by Dulles," *ibid.*, March 9, 1955; Elie Abel, "Dulles Says U.S. Pins Retaliation on Small A-Bombs," *ibid.*, March 16, 1955; "Transcript of Presidential Press Conference," *ibid.*, March 17, 1955. For a sharp critique of this proposal see Hanson W. Baldwin, "An Atomic Strategy," *ibid.*, March 17, 1955.

[99] "Otvety tov. Stalina I. V. na voprosy zadannye moskovskim korrespondentom 'Sandei Taims,' g-nom Aleksandrom Vert v svoei zapiske na imia tov. Stalina ot 17 sentiabria 1946 g.," *Pravda*, Sept. 25, 1946, p. 1.

[100] "32-ia godovshchina Velikoi Oktiabr'skoi sotsialisticheskoi revoliutsii, doklad G. M. Malenkova na torzhestvennom zasedanii moskovskogo soveta, 6 noiabria 1949 goda," *ibid.*, Nov. 7, 1949, p. 4; Malenkov, *Otchëtnyi doklad XIX s"ezdu*, Oct. 5, 1952, p. 33.

[101] "Truman Tells Stalin Either Side Could Be Destroyed in Atom War," New York *Times*, Jan. 8, 1953.

This grim truth was at last openly recognized by Malenkov after Stalin's death. In a speech of March 12, 1954, Malenkov admitted that a new world war, "waged with the modern implements of warfare, means the destruction of world civilization." [102] Following this pronouncement the Soviet press began revealing to the Soviet public for the first time the elementary atomic facts of life, including some notion of the destructive power of nuclear weapons. On March 31 Molotov elaborated the new position:

There can be no doubt that the use of atomic and hydrogen weapons in a war would bring untold suffering. It would mean a wholesale annihilation of civilians and the destruction of big cities, the centers of present-day industry, culture and science, including such old centers of civilization as the leading capitals of the world.[103]

Since Molotov obviously considered Moscow one of the "leading capitals of the world," the Soviet Union was not expected to escape such destruction. Similarly, on April 2, *Pravda* published a resolution of the World Peace Council stating that atomic weapons must not be used "for the purpose of annihilating mankind and destroying the many fruits of his thousands of years of toil." [104]

This clear-cut position was promptly compromised by some peculiar backsliding. On April 26, 1954, Malenkov told the Supreme Soviet of the USSR that if some "aggressive circles, putting their trust in atomic weapons," should decide to "test the strength and power of the Soviet Union—then it is not possible to doubt that . . . such an adventure would inevitably lead to the downfall of the capitalist social system." [105] This view was immediately seconded by Khrushchev, who repeated the threadbare phrase that a third world war "will inevitably end in the destruction of the entire capitalist system." [106] First Deputy Premier Kaganovich also reflected no fear of a new war. In his speech published in *Pravda* on May 24 he denied that Soviet railway transport would be an "Achil-

[102] "Rech' tovarishcha G. M. Malenkova na sobranii izbiratelei Leningradskogo izbiratel'nogo okruga g. Moskvy, 12 marta 1954 goda," *Pravda*, March 13, 1954, p. 2.
[103] "Nota Sovetskogo pravitel'stva pravitel'stvam Frantsii, Velikobritanii i SShA," *ibid.*, April 1, 1954, p. 2.
[104] "Deklaratsiia Biuro Vsemirnogo Soveta Mira ob atomnom oruzhii," *ibid.*, April 2, 1954, p. 4.
[105] "Rech' Predsedatelia Soveta Ministrov SSSR, deputata G. M. Malenkova," *ibid.*, April 27, 1954, p. 5.
[106] "Rech' pervogo sekretaria TsK KPSS, deputata N. S. Khrushcheva," *ibid.*, April 27, 1954, p. 8.

les' heel, i.e., a weak spot in a future war. . . . We reached Berlin on this heel, and, if an imitator of Hitler is found, then, relying on the might of our great Soviet Army we will go even farther on this heel." [107] Finally on February 8, 1955, when Bulganin and Khrushchev deposed Malenkov, the fleeting sanity of Malenkov's onetime position was explicitily disavowed. Now Molotov repudiated his recent statement: "It is not 'world civilization' that will perish, however much it might suffer from new aggression. Rather what will perish is the rotten social system with its blood-soaked, imperialist base, which has already outlived its day." [108] The Soviet state was expected to emerge battered but unbowed, from a full-scale atomic war.

This bellicose pose was promptly reversed by a Soviet "peace" offensive that culminated in the Geneva Conference of July, 1955. The Soviet understanding reached there was formally acknowledged by Bulganin and Khrushchev during their meeting with Nehru in December, 1955: "The Conference of heads of Government held in Geneva last July resulted in recognition by the Great Powers represented there of the senselessness of war which, owing to the development of atomic and hydrogen weapons, can only bring disaster to humanity." [109] Bulganin reaffirmed, in his letter of January 23, 1956, to President Eisenhower, that "the newest implements of war . . . place the peoples of all countries in an equally dangerous situation in the event that international peace is disturbed." [110]

KHRUSHCHEV'S "REVISIONS" OF LENIN ON THE USE OF FORCE

It was in this setting that Khrushchev delivered his report of February 14, 1956, to the Twentieth Party Congress, in which he reputedly abandoned orthodox Leninist tenets concerning the use

[107] "Rech' pervogo zamestitelia Predsedatelia Soveta Ministrov Soiuza SSR, tovarishcha L. M. Kaganovicha na vsesoiuznom soveshchanii aktiva rabotnikov zheleznodorozhnogo transporta," *ibid.*, May 24, 1954, p. 3.
[108] "Doklad pervogo zamestitelia Predsedatelia Soveta Ministrov i Ministra innostrannykh del SSSR, deputata V. M. Molotova," *ibid.*, Feb. 9, 1955, p. 4. See also "*Kommunist* Repudiates the 'End of Civilization' Argument," *Soviet Studies*, VII, No. 1 (July, 1955), 87–91.
[109] "Joint Statement by N. A. Bulganin, Chairman of the Council of Ministers of the USSR, N. S. Khrushchev, Member of the Presidium of the Supreme Soviet of the USSR, and Jawaharlal Nehru, Prime Minister of India," Dec. 13, 1955, *For a Lasting Peace*, Dec. 16, 1955, p. 1.
[110] "Bulganin-Eisenhower Letter," Jan. 23, 1956, *New York Times*, Jan. 29, 1956.

of force. Lenin's belief that "wars are inevitable so long as imperialism exists," Khrushchev explained, was valid at the time it was formulated, but today imperialism is no longer a world-embracing system and its war-producing tendencies are subject to restraints by the Soviet-sponsored "peace bloc." Therefore, while war is still possible, "war is not fatally inevitable." What is inevitable, Khrushchev continued, is that "all nations will arrive at socialism," but they may reach this goal by various paths, "and it is not true that we regard violence and civil war as the only way to remake society." In the present era one of the possible methods for installing the dictatorship of the proletariat is "by using parliamentary means." [111]

On the face of it, Khrushchev would seem to have abandoned Lenin's major prescriptions for the use of force. Closer scrutiny, however, reveals a series of important qualifications. The nonviolent extension of the Soviet system throughout the world is apparently premised on the assumption that the peoples outside the Soviet bloc will realize the hopelessness of resistance to "the wave of the future," and will therefore submit peacefully to it. "Of course, in those countries where capitalism is still strong, where it possesses a tremendous military-police apparatus," Khrushchev noted, "there, serious resistance by reactionary forces is inevitable. There, the transition to socialism will proceed by way of an acute revolutionary class struggle." [112] The use of force had not been abandoned, *Kommunist* explained, rather "the solution of the question of the relationship between the use of peaceful and forcible means which the working class will apply in the course of the socialist reorganization of society will depend wholly and entirely upon the degree and the ferocity of the opposition offered by the bourgeoisie." [113] To the extent that non-Soviet nations can be quietly subverted, or will voluntarily surrender, force will not be necessary. Thus the Soviet renunciation of the use of force was made wholly conditional upon the weakness and failure of will of the non-Soviet world.

The meaning of a nonviolent transition to socialism was illustrated by the postwar transformation of Eastern Europe. "The establish-

[111] "Otchëtnyi doklad Tsentral'nogo Komiteta Kommunisticheskoi partii, doklad pervogo sekretaria TsK KPSS, tovarishcha N. S. Khrushcheva," *Pravda*, Feb. 15, 1956, p. 4.
[112] *Ibid.*, p. 4.
[113] A. Sobolev, "Vsemirno-istoricheskoe znachenie sotsialisticheskogo lageria," *Kommunist*, No. 3 (Feb., 1956), p. 32.

ment of the dictatorship of the proletariat in the European countries of the People's Democracies," *Kommunist* elaborated, "proceeded without an armed uprising. . . . In a series of countries, as for example Czechoslovakia, the struggle for the establishment of the dictatorship of the proletariat was conducted by the use of parliamentary forms." Not only was the Czech coup d'état considered "peaceful," but the Red Army was blithely credited with being the major factor in the "peaceful" reshaping of those countries where it remained in occupation.

True, the bourgeoisie of Poland, Rumania, Hungary, and other countries, supported by foreign imperialists, wanted to unleash a civil war, but the decisive resistance of the people and the presence in these countries of the Soviet armed forces, which had come there during the war in the process of fulfilling their great liberating mission, undermined the counterrevolutionary plans of domestic and foreign reaction.[114]

Politburo-member Constantinescu promptly responded for the Rumanian Communists:

The peaceful development of the revolution was facilitated by the fact that at that period the Soviet Army was stationed on Rumanian territory and, without interfering in the internal affairs of our country [sic], by its mere presence paralyzed the action of the reactionary forces.[115]

Both past and possible future services of the Soviet armed forces in wars of liberation were explicitly sanctioned when *Kommunist* added: "The Leninist proposition concerning just and unjust, progressive and reactionary, liberating and enslaving wars remains in effect." [116]

Presumably Khrushchev's dictum that war was no longer a fatal inevitability was motivated, in part, by his recognition of the threat that nuclear warfare posed for the Soviet state. Yet here again, remarks of the Soviet leaders to the Twentieth Party Congress in February, 1956, would not substantiate this comforting assumption. Khrushchev ridiculed those "prominent bourgeois figures" who "frankly acknowledged that 'there can be no victor in an atomic war.' These public figures still do not venture to state that *capitalism*

[114] *Ibid.*, p. 19.
[115] M. Constantinescu, "Forms of Transition to Socialism in Different Countries," *For a Lasting Peace*, March 9, 1956, p. 2.
[116] A. Nikonov, "V sovremennuiu epokhu voiny mogut byt' predotvrashcheny," *Kommunist*, No. 6 (April, 1956), p. 42.

will find its grave in another world war, should it unleash one, but they are already obliged to admit openly that the socialist camp is invincible!" [117] Mikoyan was even less reassuring: "Hydrogen and atomic war can result in vast devastation, but it cannot result in the destruction of mankind or its civilization; it will destroy that obsolete and pernicious system, capitalism in its imperialist stage." [118] Similarly, Suslov declared that if the imperialists commence a war, there will be mighty forces "for crushing the aggressors and for burying forever both war and the capitalist system." [119] Malenkov was content simply to repeat the standard phrase: "There is no doubt that a third world war would lead to the total destruction of the world capitalist system." [120]

On the other hand, during his visit to England in April, 1956, Khrushchev stated that it is impossible "to subject the world to the danger of war. . . . Today, as a result of the development of technology, war will not be profitable for either side." [121] This view was again maintained only momentarily, for in a pair of interviews during the fall of 1957 Khrushchev was willing to envisage nuclear warfare. The socialist countries would admittedly suffer "colossal losses. . . . But we are convinced that socialism will live on, while capitalism will not remain. For despite great losses mankind will not only survive, but will continue to develop." The outbreak of a nuclear war would be the signal for people everywhere "to do away once and for all with the social structure that gives rise to wars, and the people will establish socialist orders in their own countries." [122]

---

[117] "Doklad . . . tovarishcha N. S. Khrushcheva," *Pravda*, Feb. 15, 1956, p. 3 (italics added).
[118] "Rech' tovarishcha A. I. Mikoyana," *ibid.*, Feb. 18, 1956, p. 6.
[119] "Rech' tovarishcha M. A. Suslova," *ibid.*, Feb. 17, 1956, p. 8.
[120] "Rech' G. M. Malenkova," *ibid.*, Feb. 19, 1956, p. 8.
[121] "Quoted in Nikonov, "V sovremennuiu epokhu," *Kommunist*, No. 6 (April, 1956), p. 43.
[122] "Otvety N. S. Khrushcheva na voprosy glavnogo diplomaticheskogo korrespondenta amerikanskoi gazety 'N'iu-Iork Taims' Dzh. Restona," Oct. 7, 1957, *Pravda*, Oct. 11, 1957, p. 1. This idea was repeated in "Beseda N. S. Khrushcheva s korrespondentom amerikanskogo agentstva Iunaited Press Genri Shapiro," Nov. 14, 1957, *ibid.*, Nov. 19 1957, p. 2. Subsequently, Khrushchev continued to assert: "We are convinced that if the imperialists unleash a war, it will end with the destruction of capitalism." ("Rech' tovarishcha N. S. Khrushchev na deviatoi obshchegermanskoi rabochei konferentsii v gorode Leiptsige 7 marta 1959 goda," *ibid.*, March 27, 1959, p. 2.)

A CAUTIOUS CONCLUSION

It is difficult to determine the pressures, domestic and external, that have been responsible for the fluctuations of these Soviet pronouncements,[123] just as it is dangerous to draw any firm conclusion from them. One can only reason modestly from the total body of Soviet theory and practice concerning the use of force. Traditionally, the Soviet leaders have always encouraged armed conflicts among members of the non-Soviet world, while seeking to reserve for the Soviet Union a policy of noninvolvement until such time as its intervention could prove decisive and could enable it to reap the fruits of victory with the smallest possible risk. Two new elements have now altered this formula: the shift in the balance of power resulting from the Second World War has now made the Soviet Union one of the two major global antagonists, so that in the event of a general war the USSR itself would unavoidably and instantaneously become a direct object of attack, while the very destructiveness of all-out nuclear warfare would leave little, if any, fruits of victory, even supposing the Soviet state managed to survive such a war.

This would lead to a conclusion, which must remain highly tentative in a world where rational thought is not at a premium. It would seem likely, or at least logical, that the Soviet Union would aim for a policy of permanent noninvolvement in a general nuclear war. It would, however, continue to promote, under the cover of a nuclear stalemate, those profitable, localized conflicts that could be confined to members of the non-Soviet world or to wars between the Soviet and non-Soviet worlds which could be conducted by proxy on the periphery of Soviet power, as for example, in the Middle East or in Asia.[124] Both types of conflict would strain the resources and dissipate the strength of the non-Soviet world, with a minimum of risk and sacrifice on the part of the Soviet Union.

Short of armed conflict, the Soviet leaders repeatedly have been willing to exploit to the fullest the fear of general nuclear warfare

[123] For a well-informed speculation, see Herbert S. Dinerstein, "The Revolution in Soviet Strategic Thinking," *Foreign Affairs*, XXXVI, No. 2 (Jan., 1958), 241-52.

[124] Note that Soviet agents were consummating an arms deal with Egypt at the very moment of the Geneva "peace" conference in July, 1955, and that the Khrushchev-Bulganin "peace" mission to Asia in the fall of 1955 resulted in the introduction of Soviet arms into Afghanistan.

WAR AND SOVIET WORLD STATE 325

in order to advance their power positions throughout the world. In the Syrian-Turkish war scare of October, 1957, for example, the Soviet Union sought to deepen its influence in the Middle East by posing as the fearless champion of the Arab cause, professing to support Syria, if need be, at the risk of plunging the world into a general war. Simultaneously, Moscow played upon the fear of nuclear war in an attempt to disrupt NATO. Membership in NATO was a liability, Moscow insisted, since "it must be recognized that an armed attack on Syria by Turkey, a member of the North Atlantic bloc (NATO), cannot fail to extend the conflict to other countries." [125] Khrushchev supplemented this with threatening letters to seven Western European socialist parties, hoping that they would promote the disengagement of their countries from NATO. In his message to the British Labor Party, for example, he said: "Any widening of the conflict around Syria may drive Britain into the abyss of a new destructive war with all its terrible consequences for the population of the British Isles." [126]

The Soviet policy of bluster and nuclear blackmail poses severe new problems for the West.[127] If, through some miscalculation, an aggressive-sounding Soviet move can no longer be contained as a bluff, then the whole world will, in fact, be facing the ultimate Armageddon.

[125] "Text of the Soviet Letter to the United Nations on Syria," New York *Times*, Oct. 17, 1957.
[126] "Text of Khrushchev Letter to British Labor Party on Mideast," *ibid.*, Oct. 16, 1957.
[127] See Henry A. Kissinger, *Nuclear Weapons and Foreign Policy* (New York, 1957); Hans Speier, "Soviet Atomic Blackmail and the North Atlantic Alliance," *World Politics*, IX, No. 3 (April, 1957), 307–28; Robert E. Osgood, *Limited War: The Challenge to American Strategy* (Chicago, 1957); Raymond L. Garthoff, *Soviet Strategy in the Nuclear Age* (New York, 1958); Robert Strausz-Hupé et al., *Protracted Conflict* (New York, 1959).

XI. Way Stations to the Soviet World State

WHAT are the prospects for assimilating into the body politic of the Soviet Union the recent enormous territorial gains, made largely through the use of force? Is this vast extension of Soviet power, both in Europe and in Asia, unrelated to the goal of a Soviet world state? Or are these congeries of nations presently passing through various stages of gestation, moving toward birth as new Union Republics in an ever-expanding federation of Soviet Republics—the self-avowed nucleus of a "World Federation of Soviet Republics"?

EARLY COMMUNIST PLANS FOR A FEDERATION OF
EASTERN EUROPE

Soviet theorists have long advocated integrating the nations of Eastern Europe into a larger political entity. Even during the Balkan Wars of 1912–1913 Lenin repeatedly called for a Balkan federation as the best means of liberating the downtrodden peasantry and solving the tangled nationality conflicts within that region. "The Balkan peoples could resolve these problems ten times easier and with one hundred times less sacrifice than at present by the creation of a Federal Balkan Republic."[1] Trotsky, who was a firsthand witness to the Balkan Wars as a correspondent for a Kiev newspaper, concurred in this view: "The slogan of *national independence* of Serbs, Bulgarians, Greeks, and others remains an empty abstraction without the supplementary slogan of a *'Federal Balkan Republic.'*"[2]

[1] Lenin, "Balkanskaia voina i burzhuaznyi shovinizm," April 11, 1913, in *Sochineniia*, XVI, 356. See also Lenin, "Balkanskie narody i evropeiskaia diplomatiia," Oct. 29, 1912, in *ibid.*, XVI, 158; "Pozornaia revoliutsiia," Oct. 31, 1912, in *ibid.*, XVI, 161; "Sotsial'noe znachenie Serbsko-Bolgarskikh pobed," Nov. 20, 1912, in *ibid.*, XVI, 187.
[2] Trotsky, "Programma mira," 1915–1916, in *Sochineniia*, III, Part I, 85. Trotsky's articles on the Balkan Wars are collected in *Sochineniia*, Vol. VI.

During the First World War he widened the scope of this union by saying that "the solution of the Balkan question is unthinkable without . . . the democratic federation of the Danube and Balkan nations."[3]

Following the Bolshevik Revolution, the concept of an Eastern European federation was incorporated into Soviet plans for constructing a Soviet World Federation. Zinoviev, as head of the Comintern, was committed to pursue both the all-encompassing goal of an International Soviet Republic and the regional unification of Eastern European states, which would form a component part of this over-all world state. In March, 1920, Zinoviev recorded that "only the victory of the proletarian dictatorship can unite the masses in a Balkan (or Balkan and Danubian) Federal Socialist Soviet Republic," and so save them from capitalist enslavement and national disputes.[4] On January 15, 1920, the Communist Parties of Bulgaria, Yugoslavia, Greece, and Rumania met in Sofia and formed the so-called "Balkan Communist Federation." This organ was intended to coordinate strategy for a proletarian revolution which "will liberate the Balkan nations from all oppression and will afford them a possibility of self-determination, uniting them all into one Balkan Socialist Soviet Republic."[5] The Program of the Yugoslav Communist Party, adopted in June, 1920, anticipated this stadial process of integration: it called for "a Yugoslav Soviet Republic which would join in a Balkan Soviet federation and then eventually in a universal Communist union."[6]

Both the scope (Balkan, or Balkan and Danubian) and the identity of the federating units remained unsettled. The prominent Bulgarian Communist, Vasil Kolarov, writing in a Comintern journal in 1924, offered an array of solutions. Compact national irredenta, "the Hungarians in Transylvania, the Bulgarians in Dobrudja, the Albanians in Serbia, etc.," could rejoin their kinsman, or the various national minorities could disintegrate the existing state structures and "constitute themselves as separate states, as, for instance, the Macedonians, Montenegrins, etc." Moreover, it was suggested, while

[3] Trotsky, *The Bolsheviki and World Peace* (New York, 1918), p. 60.
[4] G. Zinoviev, "Au prolétariat des pays Balkano-Danubiens," March 5, 1920, in *La IIIe Internationale Communiste*, p. 230.
[5] "The Resolutions of the Balkan Socialist Conference," *Communist International*, Nos. 11-12 (June-July, 1920), p. 2456.
[6] Adam B. Ulam, *Titoism and the Cominform* (Cambridge, Mass., 1952), p. 5.

these diverse national groups might first want to form a regional federation among themselves, they might, on the other hand, conceivably skip this stage and federate directly with the Soviet Union: "For instance the Croatians, Slovenians and Bessarabians are undoubtedly striving to federate with the Union of Socialist Soviet Republics." [7] In general during the 1920s the Communists put more emphasis on manipulating the explosive nationality problems of Eastern Europe for the purpose of destroying the existing states than upon working out a viable solution that would give the maximum satisfaction possible to all of the conflicting national claims. The only point clearly understood was that all of these nations, at one stage or another, would, by one means or another, inevitably find themselves in the embrace of an expanding Soviet Union.

During the 1930s, and especially after the adoption of the united front policy of 1935, the Comintern dropped its revisionist demands and replaced it by talk of the patriotic defense of the existing Eastern European states. This turn was occasioned by the threat that Hitler posed for the Soviet Union in the area. It was now Hitler, rather than the Communists, who exploited the cry of national self-determination and demanded the revision of the boundaries of the Eastern European states to suit his purposes.

THE SECOND WORLD WAR AND THE REVIVAL OF FEDERALIST
PLANS FOR EASTERN EUROPE

With the outbreak of the Second World War the Soviet Union again became a revisionist power. From 1939 to 1945 it expanded its federation of Soviet Republics by annexing outright a number of states and other areas lying along the Eastern European frontier. In addition, the question of incorporating still other Eastern European states apparently was also discussed actively.

On May 9, 1941, the Executive Committee of the Comintern reportedly sent Tito a set of instructions for his guidance after a Communist seizure of power. These much-publicized instructions of disputed authenticity included this provision: "The country where

[7] V. Kolarov, "The National Question in the Balkans," *Communist International*, No. 4 (1924), pp. 83–84. Perhaps the most authoritative statement on the future of the East European nationalities during the 1920s was made by the Fifth Comintern Congress, meeting in June–July, 1924. See *V vsemirnyi kongress Kommunisticheskogo Internatsionala*, pp. 137–45.

the Central Committee has recently assumed power should not apply for inclusion in the Soviet Union until necessary instructions to this effect have been received from the Executive Committee of the Comintern."[8] The idea that the Balkan nations could realistically anticipate their incorporation into the Soviet Union was undoubtedly given wide circulation in the Communist ranks during the war. On February 8, 1942, for example, an exuberant group of Montenegrin Communists reflected this belief when they proclaimed that "the liberated territory of Montenegro constituted an integral part of the Union of Soviet Socialist Republics."[9] From Macedonia came rumors of an agreement in July, 1943, between the Bulgarian and Greek Communists for the postwar creation of a Macedonian state that would be incorporated directly into the Soviet Union.[10] Perhaps the clearest statement of this expectation is found in the conversation between Sadchikov, the Soviet Ambassador to Yugoslavia, and Kardelj, the Yugoslav Minister of Foreign Affairs, of June 5, 1945, made public after the Stalin-Tito break.

Kardelj said he would like the Soviet Union to regard them [the Yugoslavs], not as representatives of another country, capable of solving questions independently, but as representatives of one of the future Soviet Republics, and the CPY as a part of the All-Union Communist Party, that is, that our relations should be based on the prospect of Yugoslavia becoming in the future a constituent part of the USSR.[11]

The fact that in their letter of May 4, 1948, the Soviet leaders castigated Kardelj's view as "primitive and fallacious" does not necessarily invalidate the Yugoslav expectation. The Soviet rebuff was written on the eve of the break in Soviet-Yugoslav relations, when, in anticipation of future recriminations, the Soviet leaders

[8] Quoted in Stephen Clissold, *Whirlwind: An Account of Marshal Tito's Rise to Power* (New York, 1949), p. 240. In reply to an inquiry from the present writer, Clissold stated that the source of this "directive" was a Serbian typescript document found in the archives of the pro-German, Serbian police. Clissold expressed strong conviction as to its authenticity. An inquiry was also addressed to the Yugoslav government, and a reply received, dated Jan. 10, 1952, signed by Mosha Pijade, in which this "directive" was dismissed as a pure forgery. The document was reproduced by Bogdan Raditsa in "The Sovietization of the Satellites," *The Annals*, CCLXXI (Sept., 1950), 124-26. An interview with Raditsa revealed that the source which he had cited (*Komunist*, 1948) was a misprint. He claimed to have seen the document from another source, which he was unable to identify, while in Belgrade as a minister in Tito's first postwar coalition government.
[9] Clissold, *Whirlwind*, p. 84.
[10] Hamilton Fish Armstrong, *Tito and Goliath* (New York, 1951), p. 190.
[11] *Soviet-Yugoslav Dispute*, p. 38.

might have wished to put themselves on record as seeking to uphold the independence of Yugoslavia. Another plausible explanation is that while both Kardelj and Sadchikov were aware of the May 9, 1941, Comintern directive, Kardelj, by raising the question of incorporation prematurely, was violating the instruction that a country should not apply for admission to the Soviet Union "until the necessary instructions to this effect have been received" from Moscow. Following the war, Moscow may have considered it inexpedient to proclaim the sudden annexation of its Eastern European satellites in the same manner in which it had annexed the Baltic states. Precipitous action was feasible in the Baltic because, in the words of a Soviet writer, "it was possible to take advantage of a favorable international situation at that time." [12] The Hitler-Stalin Pact had neutralized German opposition, and the Western powers were too preoccupied with their own survival to do more than utter feeble protests. After the Second World War a swift incorporation of the Eastern European satellites might have precipitated a sharp reaction on the part of the Western powers and destroyed the benign illusions of those legions of fellow travelers so useful to Moscow in delaying and disorganizing the defenses of the non-Soviet world.

Again in 1950 a corroborating piece of testimony came out of Yugoslavia with the release from prison of Sreten Žujović, the former Yugoslav Communist leader who had sided with the Cominform against Tito. Among the views he disavowed as part of his rehabilitation was his former belief that "Yugoslavia would become eventually a part of the Soviet Union." Ulam comments that "the whole history of the Yugoslav Party is an incontrovertible testimony to the fact that Žujović's beliefs were shared by the Party hierarchy until it dawned upon them that in the process of 'becoming worthy' of the merger with the Union of Soviet Socialist Republics their own positions and eventually their own necks would have to be sacrificed." [13]

Both the timing and the exact method of incorporating the Eastern European nations into the Soviet Union have remained in flux. Alongside the sporadic rumors of direct incorporation of this or that region there was a revived interest in the old plans of a re-

[12] J. Kalnberzins, *Ten Years of Soviet Latvia* (Moscow, 1951), p. 7.
[13] Ulam, *Titoism and the Cominform*, p. 112.

WAY STATIONS TO SOVIET WORLD STATE

gional federation as an intermediary step toward this same end. During the war, stories of a forthcoming Communist Balkan federation were openly discussed by such unofficial Communist spokesmen as Louis Adamic. In mid-1943 he spoke of the aspirations of the Communist underground of Yugoslavia and Bulgaria: "The Yugoslav or the Balkan federation would become a Republic within the Soviet Union, and would most likely be headed by Tito or Dimitrov." However, as a matter of timing, "it seems probable that the situation immediately following liberation would favor a federation which is not immediately incorporated into the Soviet Union." [14]

Concrete, preparatory steps for creating a Balkan federation were taken in the spring of 1943 when Tito began laying the groundwork for a united Macedonian state which would form a constituent unit within the federation. Some solution for Macedonia, which lay divided among Yugoslavia, Bulgaria, and Greece, was surely necessary before a regional federation could come into being. In May, 1943, Tito's chief Macedonian agent, Tempo (Svetozar Vukmanović), helped set up in Greek Macedonia, Slav Partisan detachments pledged to fight for a united Macedonia.[15] In January, 1944, a deal of uncertain authenticity was reported between the Greek and Bulgarian Communists, "ceding" Greek Macedonia to the future united Macedonian state.[16] In April, 1944, Josip Smodlaka, Tito's Minister of Foreign Affairs, stated that "we must have a Balkan federation, and the first step would be a union of Yugoslavia and Bulgaria. Second, we will invite Albania to enter with full and equal rights." So far as Greece is concerned, "Greece must either be included in the federation or we must have a permanent alliance with her." [17] Immediately following the Communist seizure of power in Bulgaria on September 9, 1944, Tempo led a Yugoslav delegation to Sofia to open the way for the cession of Pirin or Bulgarian Macedonia to a united Macedonia. Following the Tito-Stalin break the Bulgarian Communist press spoke frankly of this Bulgarian obligation: "After September 9, 1944, the Bulgarian Communist

---

[14] Louis Adamic, *My Native Land* (New York, 1943), pp. 447-50.
[15] Clissold, *Whirlwind*, pp. 144-47.
[16] C. M. Woodhouse, *Apple of Discord* (London, 1946), p. 297; Elizabeth Barker, *Macedonia* (London, New York, 1950), p. 82; John A. Lukacs, *The Great Powers and Eastern Europe* (New York, 1953), p. 638.
[17] C. L. Sulzberger, "Tito's Group Seeks Slavic Federation," *New York Times*, April 11, 1944.

Party confirmed many times, in conformity with the wish of the Macedonian population, its agreement to unite the Pirin region with the People's Republic of Macedonia within the framework of a South Slav federation with the participation of the Bulgarian People's Republic." [18]

TITO, DIMITROV, AND STALIN SPARRING OVER FEDERALIST PROJECTS

Hard bargaining over the details of federation began in November and December, 1944, when another Yugoslav delegation traveled to Sofia. In January, 1945, Stalin had the discussions transferred to Moscow, where he personally arbitrated the question of the relative weight of each partner in the projected union. The Bulgarians wanted to federate on the basis of parity with the Yugoslav state, while the Yugoslavs proposed that Bulgaria become a seventh constituent unit in an expanded Yugoslav state, being placed on a par with Serbia, Croatia, Slovenia, Bosnia-Herzegovina, Montenegro, and an enlarged Macedonia. At first, Stalin favored the Bulgarian proposal and then backed the Yugoslav position. On January 26 a British protest abruptly halted progress toward federation. Britain objected that Bulgaria was in no position to dispose of its territory as it was an ex-enemy state, theoretically under the control of a three-power armistice regime. Moreover, the British specifically opposed the creation of a united Macedonia, which would alienate Greek territory to a Communist federation. If any Balkan union were contemplated it would have to include non-Communist Greece and Turkey, Britain insisted. With the war still in progress, larger considerations prevailed over the immediate formation of a Communist Balkan federation. The Yugoslav and Bulgarian delegations left Moscow after the Premiers of the two states had exchanged a statement in which they acknowledged that "the main aim" of their policy was "the realization of a federation of the South Slav peoples in the shortest possible time." [19]

[18] Dino G. K'osev, "Zavetite na goliamoto Makedonsko-Ilindensko v"stanie,' *Rabotnichesko delo* (Sofia), Aug. 1, 1948, p. 1.
[19] Mosha Pijade, "The Truth About the Federation of Southern Slav States," *Yugoslav Fortnightly*, (Belgrade), I, No. 18 (Jan. 27, 1950), 1-2. See also Aleksandar Rankovich, "Who Is Responsible for Bulgaria's Not Entering South Slav Federation?" *ibid.*, I, No. 2 (Feb., 1949), 2; Vladimir Dedijer, *Tito* (New York, 1953), p. 304.

WAY STATIONS TO SOVIET WORLD STATE 333

Federalist plans were conspicuously revived after the Bled Agreement of August 1, 1947, between Yugoslavia and Bulgaria. A part of this accord, kept secret at the time, permitted Tito's agents to enter Pirin Macedonia freely in order to prepare the cession of that area to the Yugoslav Macedonian Republic in connection with a forthcoming Balkan federation.[20] Bulgaria's compensation, as Mosely suggests, would presumably have been provided at the expense of Greece, in the form of western Thrace, which Bulgaria had sought to annex during 1941–1944. In addition, the projected Greater Macedonia would never be complete without Greek Macedonia, which meant that the federation planned anew at Bled would, besides Yugoslavia and Bulgaria, also surely include Greece—provided the Communists could win the civil war then raging there.[21] This assumption was strengthened by the fact that in December, 1947, immediately after Bled, a "Free Greek Government" was proclaimed under General Markos Vafiades. The tie between Tito and Markos became indisputable when Markos was allowed to operate from Yugoslav territory *after* the Tito-Stalin break, until Markos himself was purged.[22]

It soon became apparent that Tito and Dimitrov were thinking in much broader terms than a strictly Balkan federation. Following Bled both Tito and Dimitrov began a series of triumphal tours to the capitals of the various Eastern European satellites, as part of a splurge of treaties of mutual assistance. By the end of 1947 Tito had distinguished himself as the only satellite ruler who had signed such pacts with every European "People's Democracy," and Dimitrov was hurrying to emulate him. Following the signing of a pact between Bulgaria and Rumania in January, 1948, Dimitrov spoke in an expansive and self-confident mood: "I do not consider that our

[20] Barker, *Macedonia*, pp. 103–7.
[21] Philip E. Mosely, "Soviet Policy and Nationality Conflicts in East Central Europe," in Waldemar Gurian, ed., *The Soviet Union* (Notre Dame, 1951), pp. 73–74, 82.
[22] Barker, *Macedonia*, pp. 117–19. There is evidence that Tito several times restrained his agents in non-Yugoslav Macedonia, holding that the creation of a united Macedonia must be subservient to the larger issue of a Communist victory in Greece; see *ibid.*, pp. 98, 112, 117. See also Svetozar Vukmanović, *How and Why the People's Liberation Struggle of Greece Met with Defeat* (London, 1950), pp. 71–77, 85; Joseph Scholmer, *Vorkuta* (New York, 1955), pp. 151–52; Sydney Gruson, "Purged Greek Red Turns Up in Poland," New York *Times*, Feb. 7, 1957; "VII rashirennyi plenum TsK Kommunisticheskoi partii Gretsii," *Pravda*, March 21, 1957, p. 3.

treaties between Bulgaria and Yugoslavia, between Bulgaria and Albania, and now between Bulgaria and Rumania, and, in addition those to be signed in the near future between Bulgaria and Czechoslovakia, between Bulgaria and Hungary, and between Bulgaria and Poland are ordinary pacts, but treaties concerning union." *Pravda*, in printing this statement on January 23, 1948, included the commentary that "Dimitrov emphasized that he had not accidentally used the word 'union.'" Dimitrov added that while the question of "creating a federation or a confederation . . . is not an immediate prospect," nevertheless,

when the question matures, as it inevitably will, then our peoples, the countries of the People's Democracies—Rumania, Bulgaria, Yugoslavia, Albania, Czechoslovakia, Poland, Hungary, and Greece—note that, and Greece!—will solve it. To them belongs the decision of whether it will be a federation or a confederation, when and how it will be created. It is possible to say that what our peoples have already done makes it considerably easier to solve this problem in the future.[23]

This was a remarkable pronouncement in at least three respects. First, it was a frank statement of intentions to expand a Balkan federation to grandiose proportions: a single Communist state of 100,000,000 people stretching from the Baltic to the Mediterranean. Second, the boldness of this statement was emphasized by the inclusion of two countries that were not yet "People's Democracies." Dimitrov's special reference to Greece confirms the above analysis of Greece as an essential ingredient in an Eastern European federation. In addition, his statement included Czechoslovakia, although it preceded by about a month the Communist coup d'état in Prague. Third, this bold and aggressive design for the organization of Eastern Europe was presented almost without reference to the Soviet Union. Dimitrov's statement, which occupied almost fully a half page of *Pravda*, was completely devoid of the usual panegyrics to Stalin, and the Soviet Union was only mentioned twice—and that in passing.

Stalin evidently concluded from this that Tito and Dimitrov were getting too big for their satellite britches. On January 28, 1948, *Pravda* neatly squelched their whole idea by a brief announcement that "these countries are not in need of a problematical and farfetched federation or confederation, nor a customs union, but the

[23] "Press-konferentsiia u G. M. Dimitrova," *Pravda*, Jan. 23, 1948, p. 4.

strengthening and the defense of their own independence and sovereignty."[24] The prospect of the formation of a large multinational state and a new hub of power on the periphery of the Soviet empire could hardly appeal to Stalin's deep-seated centralist proclivities. Within the Soviet Union there was a vast, multinational unit, the RSFSR, but it was at the heart of the Soviet state, and, if anything, reinforced the authority and prestige of Moscow over the outlying nations. There is some evidence to substantiate Stalin's fears that Tito and Dimitrov had illusions of becoming masters of their own realm. For example, Stalin never recognized the Markos "government" in Greece, which Tito and Dimitrov had encouraged as an essential partner in their prospective Balkan federation. This divergence may also have reflected, as Borkenau suggests, serious policy differences at the summit of Soviet power—between Stalin and Zhdanov. As head of the Cominform Zhdanov's special domain was Eastern Europe, and he was also known as an uncompromising advocate of an aggressive "forward" policy.[25] It may be no coincidence that Tito's expulsion from the Cominform was, in short order, conveniently followed by Zhdanov's death, the disappearance of Markos and the removal of Dimitrov to a Soviet sanatorium, where he soon died.

Pravda's denunciation of an Eastern European federation did not lay the idea to rest. Dimitrov dutifully recanted, although not totally. He indicated that Bulgaria should still seek to arrange a customs union with Yugoslavia, Rumania, and Albania. The Yugoslav retreat was even more equivocal. A "diplomatic source" in Belgrade agreed that federation was unnecessary—or, "at least it is not necessary to go much further, because with the exception of an outright organizational set-up creating a central executive body, federation virtually exists."[26] On February 10, 1948, Stalin called the

[24] "K voprosu ob interviu tov. Dimitrova na press-konferentsii v Sofia 21 ianvaria sego goda," *ibid.*, Jan. 28, 1948, p. 4.
[25] Franz Borkenau, *European Communism* (London, 1953), pp. 511–13, 531, 540–42. This view is supported by Boris Nicolaevskii, "A New Phase in the Development of Soviet Dictatorship," in *Proceedings of the Conference of the Institute for the Study of the History and Culture of the USSR*, March 20–22, 1953 (New York, 1953), pp. 114–15. This explanation would certainly seem more plausible than the exaggerated picture Ruth Fischer draws of Tito's and Dimitrov's aim "to build a Red Third Force" standing "alone between East and West." (Ruth Fischer, "Conspiracy Inside Communism," *Life*, XXVIII, No. 19 [May 8, 1950], 111.)
[26] "Sofia Denies Plan for Eastern Union," *New York Times*, Jan. 30, 1948.

Bulgarian and Yugoslav leaders to the Kremlin, and in their assemblage mercilessly pilloried Dimitrov for issuing his statement.[27] Then, according to the Yugoslav account, Stalin strangely countered with his own plan for three Eastern European federations between, respectively, Poland and Czechoslovakia, Rumania and Hungary, and Bulgaria and Yugoslavia. "Bulgaria and Yugoslavia should create their federation tomorrow," Stalin demanded. "The matter is ripe. First, Bulgaria and Yugoslavia should unite and then they should annex Albania." The Yugoslavs reacted with caution, sensing that this *volte-face* might have been made for the purpose of inserting a Stalinist Trojan horse into the joint state as a means of ousting Tito, since the strain in Soviet-Yugoslav relations was by then well advanced.[28]

Even several years after the Stalin-Tito break the idea of a Balkan federation was still being kept alive by Stalinist agents. The Bulgarian and Greek Communist Parties advocated it in connection with a renewed demand for the creation of a united Macedonia as a component part of a Balkan federation. Only now the transparent aim of this demand was to dismember Yugoslavia by cleaving Tito's Macedonian Republic from the Yugoslav state.[29] Following the Kremlin's rapprochement with Tito, rumors circulated concerning a renewed interest in a Balkan federation, but in August, 1956, *Pravda* again disavowed the idea.[30] A conspicuous campaign for the closer integration of Poland and Czechoslovakia was carried on from 1947 until the middle of 1949, but by 1950 this program had been quietly abandoned.[31]

[27] Dedijer, *Tito*, pp. 314–18.
[28] *Ibid.*, pp. 321–24, 328; "Speech of Marshal Tito Before National Assembly, April 26, 1950," *Yugoslav Fortnightly*, I, No. 25 (May 5, 1950), 1.
[29] K'osev, "Zavetite," *Rabotnichesko delo*, Aug. 1, 1948, p. 2; Wayne S. Vucinich, "Bulgaria: A Balkan Soviet, Part II," *Current History*, XX, No. 116 (April, 1951), 209; Barker, *Macedonia*, pp. 108, 120–25, 128–29; Vukmanović, *How and Why*, pp. 53–55.
[30] Anton Iugov, "Za ukreplenie mira na Balkanakh," *Pravda*, Aug. 7, 1956, p. 3. On September 10, 1957, Rumanian Premier Stoica advanced a Soviet-sanctioned feeler for a Balkan entente that would include not only Yugoslavia, but also Greece and Turkey. Tito, still operating in the twilight of the Soviet-Yugoslav rapprochement, indicated a cautious willingness to go along, while Greece and Turkey rejected the scheme totally. For the text of the Rumanian notes, see "Proposal for Balkan Entente," *East Europe*, VI, No. 11 (Nov., 1957), 55–56. See also *ibid.*, p. 35; Stefan Yowev, "Soviet Activity in the Balkans," *Bulletin of the Institute*, IV, No. 10 (Oct., 1957), 22–25.
[31] Alexander W. Rudzinski, *The Myth of Satellite Sovereignty* (New York, 1954), pp. 17–20.

WAY STATIONS TO SOVIET WORLD STATE

STALIN'S ALTERNATIVE OF THE CONFEDERAL APPROACH

The various schemes for regional federation among the Eastern European states were finally buried. The question of the further integration of these nations was then reduced to the prospect of their direct incorporation into the Soviet Union. As far back as June, 1920, Stalin had suggested a highly prophetic plan for the direct but gradual amalgamation of the states lying along Soviet Russia's western periphery. He advanced this proposal, significantly enough, when he was a political commissar in the Red Army, then beginning its march on Warsaw. The political reorganization of Eastern and Central Europe resulting from the export of revolution by force of arms, though frustrated at the time, was realized as a result of the Second World War, and the development of the satellites has closely adhered to the pattern he projected in 1920. For states such as "the future Soviet Germany, Poland, Hungary, Finland," Stalin had suggested "confederation, as one of the transitional forms for merging the toilers of various nations." This intermediate stage toward outright federation he defined as "an alliance of independent states." The use of this form would provide greater flexibility of maneuver and "make it easier for those nationalities not formerly included in the Russian Empire to achieve their state amalgamation with Soviet Russia." [32] Stalin advanced this proposal as an amendment to Lenin's Theses on the national question prepared for the Second Comintern Congress, in which Lenin had held that federation alone was the appropriate method for integrating nations into a World Soviet Federation. One indication that Stalin had not lost interest in his 1920 confederation proposal is shown by a fulsome reference to it in Denisov's *Soviet State Law*, published in Moscow in 1947—without any notation that Lenin had once rejected the idea.[33]

The confederal pattern, i.e., the tightening of Russian control over its outlying satellites in the guise of maintaining their sovereignty and independence, has definite tactical advantages: it flatters the sensitivities of the peoples concerned; it encourages the emergence of new satellites, particularly in Asia, where "independent" states are "liberated" from their former "imperialist captivity"; and it

[32] Letter from Stalin to Lenin, June 12, 1920; quoted in "Primechaniia," Lenin, *Sochineniia*, XXV, 624, n. 141.
[33] A. I. Denisov, *Sovetskoe gosudarstvennoe pravo* (Moscow, 1947), pp. 224-25.

stresses the disintegrative symbols of national sovereignty that Moscow finds so useful in its campaign to keep the non-Soviet world weak and divided. The comment frequently heard that the Soviet satellites are not incorporated into the Soviet Union for fear of losing votes in the United Nations is not convincing. A few votes more or less in the Soviet bloc would not be of such consequence, and, furthermore, these states could presumably federate with the provision that they retain their international status, like the Ukraine and Belorussia, for purposes of UN representation.

PREPARATION OF THE SATELLITES FOR "PROMOTION" TO UNION REPUBLICS

Meanwhile, in fact if not in name, the European satellites are being prepared for their transformation into Union Republics of the Soviet Union. Rudzinski quite properly objects to the term "satellite" as implying too much independence, "i.e., small states influenced in their foreign policy by a great power." These nations could more accurately be likened to protectorates or to puppet states, such as Japan created in Manchukuo in 1932, since Moscow seeks total control over their domestic life as well as their foreign relations.[34]

Following his return to power in October, 1956, Gomulka provided a candid description of how the Stalinist chain of command operated in the People's Democracies. "The essence of this system," Gomulka complained, was a "hierarchic ladder of cults." Stalin stood at the top, and "all those who stood on lower rungs of the ladder bowed their heads before him." These hand-picked satraps "in turn donned the robes of infallibility and wisdom. But their cult radiated only on the territory of the countries where they stood at the top of the national cult ladder." Their authority had the character of "a reflected brilliance, a borrowed light. . . . Nonetheless it was all powerful in the sphere of its action." [35]

Gradually, Stalin had been eliminating the discrepancies between the state structures of the People's Democracies and those of a Union Republic in the USSR. For example, on October 5, 1951, *Izvestiia* commented on the formation of local organs of administra-

[34] Rudzinski, *The Myth*, p. 13.
[35] "Address by Wladyslaw Gomulka before the Central Committee of the Polish United Worker's Party, October 20, 1956," *Trybuna Luda*, Oct. 21, 1956, in Zinner, ed., *National Communism*, p. 228.

WAY STATIONS TO SOVIET WORLD STATE 339

tion called "People's Soviets." "The establishment of People's Soviets in Bulgaria, Rumania, Hungary, and Albania, and of National Committees in Czechoslovakia, which perform the function of People's Soviets, was an important step forward in the further democratization of these states." [36] This "democratization" is simply another signpost in the transformation of a People's Democracy into a Soviet Republic. When, at the appropriate moment, Moscow decides to announce that these states have also "achieved socialism," then as Soviet Socialist Republics they would deserve to be treated as full-fledged members of the Union of Soviet Socialist Republics.[37]

The Council for Mutual Economic Aid has apparently been used, since its creation in January, 1949,[38] as an instrument for fostering the integration of the economies of the Eastern European satellites with that of the Soviet Union. In June, 1954, Moscow announced that the economic plans of these satellites would be coordinated fully with the sixth Five-Year Plan of the Soviet Union, scheduled to run from 1956 to 1960.[39] Then in June, 1955, Communist spokesmen revealed cryptically that China's economic needs would be included in a single, over-all economic plan "under the leadership of the Soviet Union," extending from Peking to Berlin.[40]

According to the testimony offered by the Rumanian Communist leader Gheorghiu-Dej, in February, 1956, the European satellites rely upon the Council for Mutual Economic Aid for "allocating to the particular countries assignments for producing particular items." This has resulted in a "new, socialist division of labor on an international scale." [41] Khrushchev hailed this arrangement in his speech

[36] "Narodnye sovety v stranakh narodnoi demokratii," *Izvestiia*, Oct. 5, 1951, p. 3.
[37] It is held that in the "People's Democracies" of Eastern Europe "the foundations of socialism are being laid successfully." ("The People's Democracies on the Road to the Victory of Socialism," *For a Lasting Peace*, April 1, 1955, p. 1.)
[38] "Creation of Mutual Economic Aid Council," *ibid.*, Feb. 1, 1949. p. 1. Details of the Council's organizational structure, as drawn from an East German source, are reported in Harry Schwartz, "New Paths Open to Red Economy," New York *Times*, May 25, 1958.
[39] "Satellite Integration," New York *Times*, June 15, 1954; Harry Schwartz, "Russia to 'Integrate' Satellites," *ibid.*, June 20, 1954; Clifton Daniel, "Soviet Hails Unity in Bloc's Economy," *ibid.*, Nov. 13, 1954.
[40] M. S. Handler, "Communist Lands Form Top Agency to Link All Action," *ibid.*, June 5, 1955; Harry Schwartz, "Red Coordination Faces Difficulties," *ibid.*, June 6, 1955.
[41] Gh. Gheorghiu-Dej, "Immense Contribution to the Strengthening of the Socialist Camp," *For a Lasting Peace*, Feb. 10, 1956, p. 4.

to the Twentieth Party Congress: "Now, when there is a powerful community of socialist countries, and their defense potential and security are based on the industrial might of the whole socialist camp, each European People's Democracy can specialize in developing those industries and producing those goods for which it has the most favorable, natural economic conditions." [42] In a detailed progress report of July, 1956, on the meshing of this international economic specialization, *Pravda* concluded that "in order to strengthen the position of socialism . . . it is necessary to intensify the coordination of the national economic plans of the USSR and the countries of the People's Democracies." [43]

In the spring of 1956 Moscow also revealed that it had become the seat of a newly created Joint Nuclear Research Institute, presumably for the development of peaceful uses of atomic energy, in which the Soviet Union, China and the People's Democracies of Europe and Asia were listed as members.[44]

On December 2, 1954, representatives from the Soviet Union, Poland, Czechoslovakia, East Germany, Hungary, Rumania, Bulgaria, and Albania assembled in Moscow to announce their intention of forming a unified military command for all of these states, should West Germany become a member of NATO. West Germany joined NATO and the Soviet bloc responded by signing a military pact in Warsaw on May 14, 1955.[45] The establishment of

[42] "Otchëtnyi doklad Tsentral'nogo Komiteta Kommunisticheskoi partii, doklad pervogo sekretaria TsK KPSS, tovarishcha N. S. Khrushcheva," *Pravda*, Feb. 15, 1956, p. 1.
[43] "Novye formy ekonomicheskogo sotrudnichestva stran sotsializma," *ibid.*, July 27, 1956, p. 5. See also A. Zakharov, "Economic Cooperation in the Socialist Camp," *International Affairs* (Moscow), No. 4 (April, 1956), pp. 21-31.
[44] "Zakliuchitel'noe soobshchenie o Mezhdunarodnom soveshchanii po voprosu ob organizatsii Ob"edinennogo instituta iadernykh issledovanii," *Pravda*, March 27, 1956, p. 3. The Soviet press was simultaneously denouncing Euratom, the proposed European atomic pool, "as a new step in the direction of knocking together the so-called political-economic 'unification of Europe,' that is, the creation of a closed group of Western European states under the control of the U.S.A. . . . The broad masses of Western Europe are extremely opposed to it, being disturbed by the prospect of losing their national sovereignty." (M. Sturua, "Chto skryvaetsia za shirmoi 'Evratoma'?" *Izvestiia*, March 28, 1956, p. 3.)
[45] "Deklaratsiia Pravitel'stv SSSR, Polskoi Narodnoi Respubliki, Chekhoslovatskoi Respubliki, Germanskoi Demokraticheskoi Respubliki, Vengerskoi Narodnoi Respubliki, Rumynskoi Narodnoi Respubliki, Narodnoi Respubliki Bolgarii i Narodnoi Respubliki Albanii," *Pravda*, Dec. 3, 1954, p. 2; "O sozdanii ob"edinënnogo komandovaniia vooruzhennymi silami gosudarstv-uchastnikov Dogovora o druzhbe, sotrudnichestve i vzaimnoi pomoshchi," *ibid.*, May 15, 1955, p. 2.

this single all-embracing military organization was certainly no sudden innovation in Soviet policy, since Moscow had long been the seat of command for the armed forces of these People's Democracies. This move was nonetheless significant as another integrative step within the Soviet orbit, placing the military resources of these states in formal subjection to the authority of a single political center at Moscow. This arrangement also provided for the participation of a Chinese military "observer," and formally extended the obligation of the Soviet Union to the defense both of Albania and of East Germany. The Soviet Union had not previously concluded a mutual assistance pact with Albania, which, until the Stalin-Tito break, was a Yugoslav satellite. On March 26, 1954, the Soviet Union granted "full sovereignty" to the "German Democratic Republic,"[46] thus completing the legal detachment of East Germany from the West and placing it on the same level as the other captive states of Eastern Europe. The Soviet-East German Treaty of September, 1956, however, provided for the continued stationing of Soviet troops on East German soil.[47] The military contribution of the East Germans was temporarily held in abeyance, perhaps in the hope of inducing West Germany to abandon its NATO obligation, but in January, 1956, the contingents of an East German army were formally placed at the disposal of Soviet Marshal Konev, the Commander in Chief of the Warsaw Treaty powers.[48]

In addition to these political, economic, and military measures, the people of Eastern Europe have been receiving their ideological preparation for the full embrace of Soviet Russia. Among other things, Muscovite agents have continuously rewritten their histories to demonstrate that Russia, from the beginning of recorded time, has exerted a wholly benign influence upon them. All of these omens presage the formal annexation of the captive European states by the Soviet federation at some undefined future moment that Moscow will regard as expedient. The strength of national sentiment in countries where the memory of national independence is still fresh

[46] "Zaiavlenie Sovetskogo Pravitel'stva ob otnosheniiakh mezhdu Sovetskim Soiuzom i Germanskoi Demokraticheskoi Respublikoi," *ibid.*, March 26, 1954, p. 1.
[47] "Dogovor ob otnosheniiakh mezhdu Soiuzom Sovetskikh Sotsialisticheskikh Respublik i Germanskoi Demokraticheskoi Respublikoi," *ibid.*, Sept. 21, 1955, p. 1.
[48] "Session of the Political Consultative Committee of the Warsaw Treaty Powers," Jan. 27-28, 1956, *For a Lasting Peace*, Feb. 3, 1956, p. 1.

and the benefits of exploiting the political folklore of national sovereignty will probably delay the final act for a number of years.

UPSETTING THE TIMETABLE WITH NATIONAL REVOLTS

The "liberalization" of the rigid Stalinist controls following Stalin's death and demotion, and the violent revolt against Moscow which this program unleashed when it obviously got out of hand, would suggest the necessity for a go-slow policy for satellite integration in the immediate future. The Soviet leaders were caught between their attempt to win popularity by dissociating themselves from Stalin's sins, and their determination, simultaneously, not to relinquish any of Stalin's ill-gotten gains. When the relaxation of Moscow's pressure contributed to the Poznan riots of June, 1956, the Kremlin tried to mark out its limits of toleration. Speaking in Warsaw on July 22, 1956, Bulganin declared frankly that the Soviet regime could not countenance "an attempt to weaken the international ties of the socialist camp under the pretext of respecting so-called 'national peculiarities,' or an attempt to undermine the authority of the people's democratic state under the pretext of some supposed 'extension of democracy.' "[49]

Similarly, the abandonment of Stalin's intransigence toward Tito and Khrushchev's endeavor to make a virtue out of necessity by recognizing that there are many roads to socialism, presented the new Soviet leadership with the dilemma of having to appear to de-Stalinize the satellites without installing new Titos. If the Soviet leaders could have confined the "many roads" doctrine to saying that it is, after all, the seizure and consolidation of power that counts and not the uniformity of method by which it was achieved, without, at the same time, materially weakening their control over their satellite puppets, then this policy might have permitted the non-Russian Communists to adjust more flexibly to local conditions, thereby strengthening the position of their satellite regimes. When extended to the Communist Parties outside the Soviet orbit, the "many roads" doctrine might have released hitherto suppressed independent sources of action and so served to revitalize and to intensify revolutionary movements. But again the Kremlin showed

[49] "Rech' tovarishcha N. A. Bulganina," *Pravda*, July 22, 1956, p. 3.

WAY STATIONS TO SOVIET WORLD STATE

that it was keenly aware of the dangers involved in giving greater play to these potentially centrifugal forces. In July, 1956, *Pravda* condemned those "politically immature people" who "rise to the bait of bombastic words about 'national communism.' "[50] "The diversity of the paths to socialism," *Pravda* insisted, "does not in the least mean that the great idea of proletarian internationalism has 'become obsolete,' as certain people try to suggest. . . . Different paths to socialism are by no means paths that diverge. On the contrary, all these paths lead to a single goal." The nations in the Soviet orbit were described as forming "a world socialist system . . . having a single, socialist pattern of state and social structure."[51]

By the fall of 1956 satellite de-Stalinization had acquired such popular momentum that it continued unabated in the face of these eminently clear warnings from Moscow. In late October and early November Soviet-satellite tensions erupted in the spectacular, open defiance of Moscow's will, first by the Poles and then by the Hungarians. In these crises the satellite armies proved their total unreliability as an instrument of Soviet power. Polish troops momentarily foiled Soviet troop movements in Poland, while Gomulka's "national communism" retained both enough popular support and enough communism to cause the Kremlin to retreat from a military showdown with a regime that might still be nudged back into the fold.

In Hungary the "national communism" of Imre Nagy was neither sufficiently popular nor sufficiently Communist to prevent the wholesale intervention of the Soviet Army. When Nagy announced the withdrawal of Hungary from the Warsaw Pact, in a desperate effort to save his tottering regime which was held up only by the bayonets of Russian soldiers, the Soviet arms were instantly turned on Nagy. Russian control of a de-Stalinized Hungary was restored with typical Stalinist brutality by means of a full-fledged civil war (if "civil" war can be extended to mean war between the Hungarian people and the Soviet Army of occupation seeking to reimpose a Hungarian puppet regime).

Even when apparently successful, as in Poland, national com-

[50] "Rastut i krepnut mezhdunarodnye sily mira, demokratii i sotsializma," *ibid.*, July 16, 1956, p. 2.
[51] "Nezyblemoe edinstvo stran sotsialisticheskoi sistemy," *ibid.*, July 24, 1956, p. 3.

munism remained a tense compromise that solved nothing. When a leader like Gomulka lessened his reliance upon Soviet support, he had to increase his reliance upon indigenous forces, and such new support was forthcoming only by offering significant concessions to his oppressed and disgruntled populace. But basic reforms of society have a corrosive effect upon the power monopoly of the ruling Communist apparatus. Thus, Tito, who was a more unchallenged master of his house than Gomulka, found it necessary to reward Djilas with three years in solitary confinement for suggesting that the ultimate destination of the Polish-Hungarian rebellions was the "withering away of contemporary communism." [52] During the first year after the "Polish October," Gomulka's conspicuous backing and filling between the "revisionists" and the "conservatives" demonstrated his dilemma of trying to satisfy popular demands for reform without sweeping away his own instruments of authority. Subsequently, under the combined pressure of the Polish "apparatchiki" and of Moscow, Gomulka was forced increasingly to come to terms with the "conservatives," who had rejected the reforms of the Polish rebellion.

The room for experimentation and maneuver in the external relations of Polish national communism, where Soviet power was more ominously apparent, was even more closely circumscribed. "We cannot always do what we like," Gomulka told a meeting of Poznan workers on the first anniversary of their memorable demonstration. "In the present political situation we are forced to abide by the Warsaw Pact." [53] Khrushchev was less delicate when, at a reception for Polish Premier Cyrankiewicz in April, 1957, he blurted out a warning ostensibly aimed at the West: "Don't trifle with us, don't test us with a provocateur's putsch, like the one organized in Hungary. . . . We are in a position to rap your knuckles." [54]

[52] Milovan Djilas, "The Storm in Eastern Europe," *New Leader*, Nov. 19, 1956, p. 6. This article was responsible for a three-year prison sentence, pronounced in December, 1956. The subsequent publication of his book, *The New Class*, resulted in another trial in October, 1957, and an additional seven-year term of imprisonment.

[53] Quoted in the Warsaw dispatch of Sydney Gruson, "Gomulka Terms Soviet Tie Vital," New York *Times*, June 6, 1957.

[54] "Rech' N. S. Khrushcheva na priëme v Posol'stve Pol'skoi Narodnoi Respubliki 19 aprelia 1957 goda," *Pravda*, April 21, 1957, p. 3.

WAY STATIONS TO SOVIET WORLD STATE 345

THE COSTS OF NATIONAL COMMUNISM

From Moscow's point of view almost every aspect of national communism has proven extremely distasteful. Just in terms of the tangible, material costs of economic disorganization in the Soviet orbit, the Soviet Union has sustained serious losses. The paralysis of the Hungarian economy resulting from the "civil war" and a prolonged general strike, the slackening in Polish production tempo because of relaxed political controls, Soviet emergency economic assistance, the reorientation of production goals to alleviate the economic plight of the satellite populations at the expense of production planned primarily for Moscow's benefit, Soviet cancellation of some sizable satellite debts, and the liberalization of terms of trade—all these form an impressive list of costly defeats and concessions which the Kremlin was compelled to tolerate.[55] The Soviet leaders have perhaps tried to recoup some of these losses by binding the economic resources of the subservient satellites even more closely to Moscow. This is evidenced by the Soviet-Czechoslovak economic agreement of January, 1957, and the Soviet-East German accord of July, 1958, which provided for the comprehensive integration of these two most highly industrialized satellites into the Soviet economy.[56] It is difficult to judge to what extent these arrangements have been offset by the multilateral trading system and payments union formed by the Council for Mutual Economic Aid in June, 1957, which seemingly pointed to an easing of the former direct economic dependence of the People's Democracies upon the Soviet Union.[57]

While some concessions may have been the price of pacification, is it conceivable that Moscow looks upon these arrangements as part of a permanent liberalization program, or as part of a transient period of adjustment before it is possible to move back toward "the good old days"? By the fall of 1957 it was revealed that the

[55] Harry Schwartz, "East Bloc Output in Industry Lags," New York *Times*, Dec. 2, 1957; Sydney Gruson, "Crises Disrupting East Bloc Trade," *ibid.*, Dec. 17, 1957; "October's Aftermath," *East Europe*, VI, No. 4 (April, 1957), 3-10.
[56] "Sovmestnaia Sovetsko–Chekhoslovatskaia Deklaratsiia," *Pravda*, Jan. 30, 1957, pp. 1-2; M. S. Handler, "Soviet Increases German Red Ties," New York *Times*, July 11, 1958.
[57] P. Nikitin, "Ekonomicheskoe sotrudnichestvo stran sotsialisticheskogo lageria," *Pravda*, July 14, 1957, pp. 4-5.

Council for Mutual Economic Aid was at work on a fifteen-year integrated economic plan for the Soviet Union and Eastern Europe, to run from 1961 through 1975.[58] A Soviet announcement of May, 1958, which spoke of the "drafting of long-range plans for the economic development of the socialist countries" aimed at "perfecting the forms of economic cooperation among them based on the more intensive specialization and coordination and production of the interrelated branches of the economies of the socialist camp countries," also noted that representatives from Communist China, North Vietnam, North Korea, and Outer Mongolia would increasingly participate in these joint economic arrangements.[59]

In the military field, experience with national communism has demonstrated that the sole guarantee of the Warsaw Pact is the Soviet Army. Consequently, agreements for the continued stationing of the Soviet Army in Rumania, Poland, East Germany, and Hungary were announced in the months following the 1956 rebellions.[60] While these agreements also introduced some concessions to placate the aroused national sensitivities of the peoples involved, it was obvious that Moscow would not countenance the evacuation of its troops from the satellites, as it was supposedly willing to contemplate, if one is to take seriously various frantic Soviet and Hungarian declarations issued in the course of trying to extinguish the fires of revolt. On May 24, 1958, Marshal Konev did announce the intention of the Soviet government to withdraw its troops from Rumania "in the near future," [61] but the qualified nature of this, or any other Soviet troop withdrawal, was made clear a few weeks prior when Khrushchev toured Hungary. Addressing himself to a misunderstanding that had apparently arisen

[58] Harry Schwartz, "East Bloc Binding Economies Anew," New York *Times*, Dec. 1, 1957; Stefan C. Stolte, "Soviet Economic Integration Plans for the Communist Bloc," *Bulletin of the Institute*, V, No. 9 (Sept., 1958), 31–38; Alfred Zauberman, "Economic Integration: Problems and Prospects," *Problems of Communism*, VIII, No. 4 (July–Aug., 1959), 23–29.
[59] "Kommiunike o Soveshchanii predstavitelei kommunisticheskikh i rabochikh partii stran—uchastnits Soveta Ekonomicheskoi Vzaimopomoshchi," *Pravda*, May 25, 1958, p. 1.
[60] Agreements sanctioning the continued "temporary" stationing of Soviet troops were announced on December 3, 1956, with Rumania; on December 17, 1956, with Poland; on March 12, 1957, with East Germany; and on May 27, 1957, with Hungary.
[61] "Kommiunike o Soveshchanii Politicheskogo Konsul'tativnogo Komiteta gosudarstv—uchastnikov Varshavskogo Dogovora o druzhbe, sotrudnichestve i vzaimnoi pomoshchi," *Pravda*, May 27, 1958, p. 1.

WAY STATIONS TO SOVIET WORLD STATE 347

concerning the use of Soviet troops to suppress any future revolts within any of the People's Democracies, Khrushchev warned:

We declare that if a new provocation is unleashed against any socialist country, the provocateurs will have to deal with all the countries of the socialist camp. The Soviet Union is always ready to come to the aid of its friends, to give the proper rebuff to the enemies of socialism when they try to violate the peaceful labor of the peoples of the socialist countries.[62]

Doubtless the most costly aspect of national communism for Moscow has been an intangible one. This has involved the shattering of Soviet prestige and political authority, in both the Soviet and the non-Soviet worlds, and at least a temporary displacement of Moscow's formerly unquestioned ideological supremacy in the People's Democracies. The long-range danger of ideological nonconformity, as Benjamin Schwartz has aptly emphasized, is that the toleration of ideological autonomy stimulates organizational independence.[63] This, in turn, could serve to disintegrate the whole totalitarian power complex of the Soviet orbit.

REAPPRAISAL BY MOSCOW OF THE "MANY ROADS" DOCTRINE

If, in his flamboyant and somewhat impetuous manner, Khrushchev seemed to embrace Tito too vigorously in their original accords of June, 1955, and June, 1956,[64] the Polish-Hungarian revolts made the Kremlin keenly aware of the connection between ideological autonomy and organizational independence and produced a series of explicit redefinitions of what the "many roads to socialism" doctrine was *not* intended to mean. To pursue one's own path to socialism, *Pravda* rebuked Yugoslavia's Kardelj in December, 1956, does not allow one to "adopt some sort of 'middle position' in the struggle that is now taking place." To give an independent evalua-

[62] "Rech' tovarishcha N. S. Khrushcheva na mitinge v gorode Tataban'e," *ibid.*, April 9, 1958, p. 2. The New York *Times* dispatch quoted Khrushchev as using more explicit language: "I say to you here that all the socialist countries and the armed forces of the Soviet Union are always prepared . . . to answer the provocation as it deserves to be answered." (Elie Abel, "Khrushchev Vows to Fight Revolts," New York *Times*, April 9, 1958.)

[63] Benjamin Schwartz, "Ideology and the Sino-Soviet Alliance," in *Moscow-Peking Axis*, pp. 117-20.

[64] "Declaration of the Governments of the FPRY and the USSR," June 2, 1955, *Review of International Affairs* (Belgrade), VI, No. 124 (June 1, 1955), 1-2; "Joint Yugoslav-Soviet Statement," June 20, 1956, *ibid.*, VI, No. 149 (June 15, 1956), 2-6.

tion of "the Hungarian events, to present some sort of a 'third line' . . . can actually only mean a concession in a greater or lesser degree to the ideology of reaction."[65] Even the Yugoslav formula, reiterated by the Poles, advocating "the peaceful coexistence of socialist countries" was bluntly rejected. Coexistence between the socialist and capitalist camps was a disagreeable fact that nonetheless demands recognition, but "how," *Izvestiia* scolded, "can we speak of mere 'coexistence' among countries of the socialist camp, when they are linked to each other above all by common goals and tasks and by fraternal friendship and cooperation! . . . To substitute the principle of coexistence for the principle of proletarian internationalism . . . leads directly into the morass of reactionary nationalist ideology."[66] "The propounders of 'national communism,' hiding behind demagogic phraseology," Moscow elaborated,

put all the emphasis not on the things that *unite* the socialist countries and the international worker's movement, but on the things that could divide them. They try to use the correct thesis about taking into account the individual and specific conditions of each country as an excuse for revising the basic principles of Marxism-Leninism, obligatory upon all countries taking the road to socialism.[67]

In prohibiting the revision of the basic principles of Marxism-Leninism, what, then, was the approved scope for taking account of the individual and specific conditions of each country on its road to socialism? On November 23, 1956, *Pravda* enumerated several mistakes of the Rakosi administration, which had not shown sufficient respect for national peculiarities and had thereby "injured the national self-respect of the Hungarian people." These included "the introduction of a military uniform resembling the uniform used in the Soviet Union." Also, "the same haircut in the army or the same system of grading in schools" is not required to prove the unity of the socialist countries. "It is impossible to cut everyone's hair in the same style," *Pravda* concluded.[68]

While generously allowing non-Russian nations to dress themselves and style their hair as they might wish, Soviet spokesmen

[65] Iu. Pavlov, "Komu eto vygodno?" *Pravda*, Dec. 18, 1956, p. 2.
[66] N. Vasil'ev, "Protiv izvrashcheniia printsipov proletarskogo internatsionalizma," *Izvestiia*, March 9, 1957, p. 3.
[67] T. Timofeev, "O fal'shivykh lozungakh 'natsional-kommunizma,'" *Sovetskaia Rossiia*, Feb. 3, 1957, p. 2.
[68] "Za dal'neishee splochenie sil sotsializma na osnove Marksistsko-Leninskikh printsip," *Pravda*, Nov. 23, 1956, p. 2.

simultaneously affirmed that the basic aspects of the Soviet Russian experience are mandatory for all socialist countries. Lenin's statement that "some of the basic features of our revolution have not only local, specifically national, or Russian significance, but an international significance," was conspicuously resurrected.[69] Similarly, Khrushchev told the Czechs on his visit to Prague in July, 1957, that the Soviet Russian brand of socialism was good not because it was Russian, but "because it is the only socialist system possible. . . . That brand is good for the Soviet people, the Czechs, the French and even the Americans." [70] The Soviet claim to ideological preeminence and the priority of Moscow's guiding role was thus repeatedly reaffirmed in the immediate aftermath of the national Communist rebellions. "The tremendous international significance of the experience of the Communist Party of the Soviet Union," *Pravda* pontificated, "consists in the fact that the experience of the Soviet Union, which was the first country to build a socialist society, helps the entire worker's movement to single out that which is essential, general, and basic in the building of socialism in each country." [71] The "many roads" doctrine was soon pared down to the proposition that each country shall adapt those "forms and methods" that prove most conducive to implementing the basic features of the Soviet system, with Moscow remaining the judge of what are the "essential, general, and basic" features that must be universally respected.

In August, 1957, Khrushchev again met Tito, this time in Bucharest. An uninformative official communiqué on this meeting [72] did not reveal Khrushchev's major aim, which, in retrospect, seems to have been to warn Tito that he must persist no longer in his disappointingly stubborn and independent behavior. "During the Bucharest meeting," Khrushchev later acknowledged, "we openly declared to the Yugoslav leaders that if they continued to indulge

[69] This is quoted, for example, in "39-ia godovshchina Velikoi Oktiabr'skoi sotsialisticheskoi revoliutsii, doklad tovarishcha M. A. Suslova na torzhestvennom zasedanii Moskovskogo Soveta 6 noiabria 1956 goda," *Pravda*, Nov. 7, 1956, p. 1; Timofeev, "O fal'shivykh," *Sovetskaia Rossiia*, Feb. 3, 1957, p. 3.
[70] Quoted in the Prague dispatch of Sydney Gruson, "Khrushchev Says Eisenhower Talks Bomb 'Stupidities,'" New York *Times*, July 12, 1957.
[71] "Edinstvo sotsialisticheskogo lageria—uslovie postroeniia sotsializma," *Pravda*, March 6, 1957, p. 5.
[72] "Soobshchenie o vstreche delegatsii TsK KPSS i Pravitel'stva Soiuza SSR i TsK SKIu i Pravitel'stva Federativnoi Narodnoi Respubliki Iugoslavii," *ibid.*, Aug. 4, 1957, p. 1.

in attacks against the countries of the socialist camp and the fraternal parties, not a single such statement would remain unanswered by us." [73]

A showdown came in Moscow, on the fortieth anniversary of the Bolshevik Revolution, in November, 1957, when representatives of the Communist-controlled world gathered to issue a joint Declaration. According to a Yugoslav source, Khrushchev announced that the time had come to choose between East and West. "How long can you go on sitting in two chairs?" he reportedly demanded of the Yugoslav delegates.[74] The price of sitting in the Soviet chair, the Yugoslavs judged, was exorbitant. The Declaration, which the Yugoslavs refused to sign, was aimed at contracting the non-Soviet roads to socialism, while it exalted the "basic laws applicable to all countries embarking upon the socialist path." The general laws of a socialist society, which were elaborated in some detail, admittedly required "a creative application," so as to take account of "the specific features of a given nation." But a regard for national peculiarities must not obscure the crucial issue. "At the present time, the main danger is revisionism," that is, a revision of those unchallengeable norms of Soviet society which all non-Russian socialists must emulate, and which serve as a constant reminder that Moscow is the leading center of the socialist camp. "The invincible camp of socialist states," the Declaration specified, is "headed by the Soviet Union." [75]

During the spring of 1958 the campaign against "revisionism" burst into full view. In April Moscow commenced by attacking the Yugoslav Party Program. The draft of the Yugoslav Program "defends 'national communism,' which, as is well known, emphasizes the national features in building socialism while it rejects the important and universally significant aspects" of a socialist society.[76] By the tenth anniversary of the original Soviet-Yugoslav break, Khrushchev was affirming that the 1948 Cominform Resolu-

[73] "Rech' tovarishcha N. S. Khrushcheva na VII s"ezde Bolgarskoi kommunisticheskoi partii 3 iiunia 1958 goda," *ibid.*, June 4, 1958, p. 2.
[74] Quoted in the Belgrade dispatch of Elie Abel, "Soviet Warning to Tito Revealed," New York *Times*, July 15, 1958.
[75] "Deklaratsiia Soveshchaniia predstavitelei kommunisticheskikh i rabochikh partii sotsialisticheskikh stran, sostoiavshegocia v Moskve 14–16 noiabria 1957 goda," *Pravda*, Nov. 22, 1957, p. 1.
[76] P. Fedoseev, I. Pomelov, and V. Cheprakov, "O proekte programme Soiuza kommunistov Iugoslavii," *Kommunist*, No. 6 (April, 1958), p. 34.

tion had been "basically correct." [77] This was followed by the execution of Imre Nagy—a dramatic object lesson on the fate of "revisionists" who would disrupt the unity of the "socialist commonwealth of nations."

THE COMMONWEALTH OF SOCIALIST STATES

The Moscow Declaration of November, 1957, referred to the Soviet orbit variously as "the socialist camp," "the world socialist system," and "the commonwealth of socialist states." Some observers have concluded that the commonwealth idea, connoting a loose grouping of sovereign, independent socialist states, effectively negates the goal of a single supranational Soviet world state. It would seem to be a gross misreading of the evidence, however, to identify the "commonwealth of socialist states" with the ideas clustered about "commonwealth" as it is used, for example, in the British Commonwealth of Nations. "The world camp of socialism," a Soviet spokesman has explained, "is a *monolithic* commonwealth of free and sovereign states with common interests and purposes, in which there is not and cannot be antagonism." [78]

The commonwealth idea, in Soviet usage, is of Stalinist origin. Far from negating the world state idea, the term "commonwealth" had been used to describe the future organization of mankind, which, in the same Stalinist tract, was alternately characterized as "a single World Socialist Republic." [79] Similarly, the present basically confederal pattern for East Central Europe goes back to Stalin's proposal of 1920, when it was clearly understood that this transitional form of interstate relations in no way contradicted the idea of a world state.[80]

In the post-Stalinist period the "commonwealth" term first came into prominence with the Soviet Declaration of October 30, 1956, issued at the height of the Hungarian revolt. As has already been noted, the Declaration, claiming that "the great commonwealth of socialist nations" was founded upon "the principles of complete equality, of respect for territorial integrity, state independence

[77] "Rech' tovarishcha N. S. Khrushcheva . . . 3 iiunia 1958 goda," *Pravda*, June 4, 1958, p. 2.
[78] S. Sanakoiev, "The Basis of the Relations Between the Socialist Countries," *International Affairs* (Moscow), No. 7 (July, 1958), p. 27 (italics added).
[79] See chapter 2, p. 47 above.   [80] See chapter 11, pp. 337-38 above.

and sovereignty, and of noninterference in one another's affairs," was followed almost immediately by the brutal and massive Soviet armed intervention in Hungary.[81] Soviet theorists then upheld these acts as examples of fraternal Soviet aid and respect for the national independence and sovereignty of Hungary. It must be recalled that national independence and national sovereignty, according to Soviet theory, are attained in their most perfect form when a nation finally achieves statehood as a Union Republic in an expanding USSR.[82]

"The participants in the great commonwealth of socialist nations," the Soviet ideologue Korovin asserted in 1958, see that "the consolidation and unity of the socialist countries is a sure guarantee of their national independence and sovereignty." This is manifested, for example, in "the selfless support and help typical of economic relations between the countries of the socialist commonwealth," based on the "socialist division of labor" and "the long-term joint coordination of plans for economic development."

All this is an illustration of the masterly prophecy made by Lenin when he spoke of a "tendency toward the creation of a single world economy, regulated" in accordance with a general plan "by the proletariat of all nations" and which "should certainly be further developed and fully consummated under socialism." [83]

The further development and full consummation of the existing socialist "commonwealth" is still explicitly found in Lenin's vision of 1920, as codified in the Theses of the Second Comintern Congress. The lives of all nations, Lenin had specified, would come to be regulated by a single common world economic plan operating within the framework of a Soviet world state.[84]

Another of Lenin's theoretical prescriptions of 1920 has obviously served to guide Khrushchev's seeming improvisations. Though Khrushchev has not succeeded in his gambit to win over Tito, it is enlightening to recall the initial Soviet explanation of its entente with Yugoslavia of June, 1955, as an indication of how Khrushchev hoped to deal with national differences within the various Com-

[81] See chapter 4, p. 121 above.   [82] See chapter 4, pp. 122-24 above.
[83] E. Korovin, "Proletarian Internationalism in World Relations," *International Affairs* (Moscow), No. 2 (Feb., 1958), pp. 26-28. The same prophecy is also quoted in Sanakoiev, "The Basis," *ibid.*, No. 7 (July, 1958), p. 29. This article further specifies that it was Lenin's ultimate aim to achieve a "union of nations" (*ibid.*, p. 32) as part of the fulfillment of his prophecy.
[84] See chapter 7, p. 233 above.

munist-controlled states. In an official clarification of its recently signed accord with Tito, Moscow granted that, "given unity in the most important and basic matter of guaranteeing the victory of socialism, different forms and methods for deciding the concrete problems of socialist construction can be applied in different countries, depending upon historic and national peculiarities." [85] Subsequently, it seems to have been impossible to achieve unity in those matters which Khrushchev deemed "important and basic," but this formula has supposedly found its application within the socialist "commonwealth," where, it is claimed, a basic unity of views exists.

Khrushchev's formula would appear to be little more than a paraphrase of Lenin's admonition of 1920 that "national and state differences exist among peoples and countries, and these differences will continue to exist for a very long time, even after the dictatorship of the proletariat has been established on a world scale." What was required of the working class movement in all countries, therefore, was "not the elimination of variety, not the abolition of national differences (that is a foolish dream at the present moment), but such an application of the *fundamental* principles of communism ... as will *correctly modify* these principles in *certain particulars*, correctly adapt and apply them to national and national-state differences." [86] Although the post-Stalinist Soviet leadership was forced to moderate Stalin's senseless demand for a rigid, mechanical imitation of the Soviet Russian pattern in its every aspect, Khrushchev could conveniently hark back to Lenin's pragmatic, flexible approach that would sanction the play of national variations within the general framework of the "valid" Russian pattern.

Khrushchev was also unquestionably aware of Lenin's fundamental purpose in taking account of national peculiarities. By so doing he hoped to neutralize and minimize national resentments and antagonisms so that, as Lenin added in the next breath, Moscow could "create a really *centralized*, leading center, capable of directing international tactics of the revolutionary proletariat in its struggle for a World Soviet Republic." [87] Lenin's ultimate image of a world society was totally centralist, and he wanted the tightest possible

---

[85] "Za razvitie druzhestvennykh otnoshenii mezhdu Sovetskim Soiuzom i Iugoslaviei," *Pravda*, July 16, 1955, p. 1.
[86] Lenin, "Detskaia bolezn' 'levizny' v kommunizme," April–May 1920, in *Sochineniia*, XXV, 227.
[87] *Ibid.*, XXV, 227 (italics added).

integration of all nations into a Soviet world state. While he condemned the imposition of a centrally devised plan upon all nations as "a foolish dream *at the present moment*," it was precisely this dream that lay at the end of his intended historical journey.

From Lenin's point of view, Stalin could not be censured for the *direction* in which he was moving by imposing an increasingly uniform pattern on all nations under his control, but only for the miscalculation of time required for such national refashionings to take hold. Within the Soviet Union it took several decades of terror, mass purges, deportations, and even repressions of open armed rebellion to install the Soviet system of controls in the rimlands surrounding Great Russia. The constant struggle against "nationalist deviations" in the Ukraine; prolonged guerrilla warfare with the Basmachi in Soviet Central Asia; armed uprisings in the Transcaucasus, such as the Azerbaijani riots of May, 1920, the Armenian rebellion of February, 1921, that drove the Soviet administration out of the capital of Erivan and the August, 1924, national uprising in Georgia that temporarily paralyzed Soviet rule, an uprising whose reverberations were apparently still being heard in the Tiflis riots of March, 1956; all these are but samplings of the encounters that Moscow had with non-Russian nations long before the Polish and Hungarian rebellions of 1956. Viewed in this perspective, the rebellion of the East European satellites is hardly novel. Stalin's innovation was his attempt to compress the process of assimilating the People's Democracies into the Soviet body politic in a briefer span than had been required for the non-Russian nations of the former Russian Empire, where the imprint of political independence was more remote and less well established than in the newly acquired East European satellites.

It is little wonder that the relaxation of Stalinist pressures following his death set loose rebellious elements that lay beneath the veneer of imposed conformity. Stalin's embarrassing failure to master the forces of Yugoslav communism, compounded by the Polish and Hungarian explosions, made the Kremlin painfully aware that it needed time to digest recalcitrant nations successfully. The "many roads" theory, it would seem, was devised as a calculated play for time, to entice, cajole, and finally to attempt to coerce deviants back onto the single, ever-narrowing path marked out by Moscow. Although Khrushchev has only met with partial success

WAY STATIONS TO SOVIET WORLD STATE 355

in this program, can it be doubted that his ultimate "solution," like Stalin's, is the total subservience of the peripheral nations to the Russian center? If there must be an uncomfortable, unavoidable, even prolonged interim before achieving this acceptable "solution," it must still be considered an interim.

One of the requirements for charting a steady course in the desired direction is the absence of serious dissension among the top policy makers in the Kremlin. When the power struggle among Stalin's heirs was aggravated by the vacillation and confusion of the de-Stalinization process, the satellite leaders were emboldened to weaken Moscow's channels of control. As might be expected, the resolution of factional differences in the Kremlin, such as resulted from the purges and demotions of Khrushchev's major rivals (Malenkov, Molotov, Kaganovich in June, 1957, Zhukov in October, 1957, and Bulganin beginning in March, 1958), have helped remove the restraints and indecision that had momentarily stayed the hand of the strong centralized authority over the outlying satrapies.

In the future, Khrushchev predicted in 1959, the importance attached to state borders in Ceneral and Eastern Europe will progressively diminish, after the pattern already in evidence among the Republics of the multinational USSR. He cited the controversies over the borders of a divided Germany and over the territorial lines between Poland and the Soviet Union, Yugoslavia and Hungary, Rumania and Hungary, and Rumania and the Soviet Union as examples of the legacy of capitalism which is doomed to extinction. Then going beyond the further integration of European states, he announced flatly: "With the victory of communism on a worldwide scale, borders among states will disappear." [88]

EXPANSION OF THE SOVIET FEDERATION IN ASIA

The expansion of the Soviet federation in Asia presents tantalizing problems, largely because of the prospective relationship between the Soviet Union and Communist China. Before the Communist conquest of the Chinese mainland in 1949, Moscow sought to detach borderland areas over which China had traditionally claimed authority with the object of making them wholly depend-

[88] "Rech' tovarishcha N. S. Khrushcheva na deviatoi obshchegermanskoi rabochei konferentsii v gorode Leiptsige 7 marta 1959 goda," *Pravda*, March 27, 1959, p. 2.

ent upon and finally attaching them to the Soviet Union. Diminutive Tannu Tuva, in which Soviet behavior was under least restraint, was the first region to complete the cycle from Chinese dependency to the "independence" of a "People's Republic" to outright annexation by the Soviet Union. On August 17, 1944, the "People's Republic" of Tannu Tuva petitioned Moscow for incorporation into the Soviet Union. The Presidium of the Supreme Soviet of the USSR quietly granted the request on October 11, 1944, and Tannu Tuva became the Tuvinian Autonomous Region of the RSFSR.[89] This first became known to the outside world when, a year later, the region was listed inconspicuously as an election district within the USSR.[90]

The "People's Republic" of Outer Mongolia meanwhile had been moving at a slower pace in the same direction. Ever since 1924 the Soviet Union had held to the ambiguous formula that Outer Mongolia was an "independent" country under Chinese "sovereignty." In reality, the Mongolian People's Republic was an early precursor in Asia of the Eastern European "People's Democracies." The purely nominal reference to Chinese "sovereignty" was retained out of consideration for Sino-Soviet relations. A plan for drawing Outer Mongolia closer to the Soviet Union was reportedly under consideration when the Second World War disrupted its implementation.[91] At Yalta Stalin secured agreement from the United States and Britain that Outer Mongolia would become independent of China in law as it was in fact. The Sino-Soviet Treaty of August 14, 1945, pledged China to "recognize the independence of Outer Mongolia in her existing boundaries," with a face-saving provision that this status be confirmed by plebiscite. On October 20, 1945, a Soviet-supervised plebiscite rendered 100 percent approval for the complete separation of Outer Mongolia from China. For all practical purposes Outer Mongolia might as well have been a Union Republic of the USSR. When the Soviet Union declared war on

[89] S. Toka, "Prazdnik tuvinskogo naroda," *Pravda*, Aug. 17, 1946, p. 2; Walter Kolarz, *The Peoples of the Soviet Far East* (New York, 1954), pp. 161–68.
[90] "Ukaz Prezidiuma Verkhovnogo Soveta SSSR ob izbiratel'nykh okrugakh po vyboram v Sovet Soiuza," *Pravda*, Oct. 17, 1945, p. 3.
[91] Nicholas Poppe, a leading Soviet expert on Mongolian affairs until his departure from the Soviet Union in 1943, testifies that "on the eve of World War II the Mongolian People's Republic was ripe for incorporation in the U.S.S.R., and a plan was under discussion to merge it with the Buriat-Mongolian Autonomous Soviet Socialist Republic." (Nicholas Poppe, "The Facts on Outer Mongolia," *New Leader*, Feb. 20, 1956, p. 14.)

Japan, the Soviet-equipped Mongolian army moved under Soviet command in perfect coordination with the Red Army of the Soviet Union.[92] Following the war, Soviet troops remained in Outer Mongolia under the February, 1946, Soviet-Mongol Treaty that provided for total cooperation in every important field of activity. In 1949 the Mongolian People's Republic redrafted its constitution along lines barely distinguishable from that of a Union Republic of the USSR.[93]

Soviet penetration into Sinkiang (Chinese Turkestan) dates from the early 1930s. By the middle of 1937 Soviet-sponsored troops, together with Red Army units in various disguises, had combined to bring all of Sinkiang under Soviet control, where it remained until the Nazi invasion of the Soviet Union in 1941. During the war Soviet influence waned, but by the end of 1944 a group of Soviet-backed Turkic tribesmen had proclaimed an "East Turkestan Republic" over Sinkiang's mineral-rich three northern provinces.

With the founding of the Chinese People's Republic in 1949 Moscow was faced with a dilemma: retain and extend Soviet control over the border areas at the risk of alienating Peking, or come to a working arrangement with China by subordinating the issue of Soviet influence in these areas to the larger and more vital needs of Sino-Soviet cooperation. In 1949, with the imminence of a Chinese Communist victory, the Turkic rebels in Sinkiang proclaimed the adherence of all Sinkiang to Communist China.

Former Soviet interests in Sinkiang were revived when Mao Tse-tung agreed to the operation of Soviet-controlled joint stock companies for the extraction of the oil and metal resources of Sinkiang. In October, 1954, Moscow recognized the increased stature of Communist China by abandoning the Soviet share in these enterprises, and by agreeing to help China build a railway linking Urumchi with central China.[94]

[92] Gerard M. Friters, *Outer Mongolia and Its International Position* (Baltimore, 1949), pp. 148-50, 284-87, 293-97; David J. Dallin, *Soviet Russia and the Far East* (New Haven, 1948), pp. 203, 353-58; Aitchen K. Wu, *China and the Soviet Union* (London, 1950), pp. 227-30; Herbert Feis, *The China Tangle* (Princeton, 1953), pp. 316-20.
[93] Kolarz, *Soviet Far East*, pp. 142-46.
[94] Dallin, *Far East*, pp. 361-68; Wu, *China*, pp. 231-33; Max Beloff, *Soviet Policy in the Far East, 1944-1951* (London, New York, Toronto, 1953), pp. 97-101; Li Chang, "Soviet Grip on Sinkiang," *Foreign Affairs*, XXXII, No. 3 (April, 1954), 491-503; Oleh S. Fedyshyn, "Soviet Retreat in Sinkiang?" *American Slavic*, XVI, No. 2 (April, 1957), 127-45; Howard L. Boorman, "The

Soviet retreat from exclusive control over Outer Mongolia proceeded more slowly, but Moscow recognized that maintaining its former position of dominance without regard for Chinese sensitivities would be foolhardy and provocative. In their desire to penetrate Outer Mongolia the Chinese Communist leaders had long shared with their non-Communist compatriots the traditional view that Outer Mongolia belongs to China. For example, in an interview of July 19, 1936, Mao Tse-tung stated that, "when the people's revolution has been victorious in China, the Outer Mongolian Republic will automatically become a part of the Chinese federation." [95]

In June, 1950, Communist China established an embassy in Ulan Bator, and during 1952 Mongolian delegations began visiting Peking where various economic and cultural agreements were signed. Then Moscow openly acknowledged China's interest in Outer Mongolia in the Sino-Soviet accords of October, 1954. By the beginning of 1956 a railway had been completed from Soviet territory to Ulan Bator and on through to Tsining in China proper, a line symbolizing the new position of Outer Mongolia as a link between the world's two great Communist powers. Peking has subsequently strengthened its hand at Ulan Bator by concluding agreements to send in 10,000 Chinese technicians and to construct a large number of industrial and cultural projects in Outer Mongolia.[96] The ultimate disposition of Outer Mongolian statehood is now obviously a matter to be settled jointly by Moscow and Peking.

The growth of the Soviet federation in Asia, then, revolves about the central question of the affiliation of Communist China. Of one

---

Borderlands and the Sino-Soviet Alliance," in *Moscow-Peking Axis*, pp. 173-89; Allen S. Whiting and General Sheng Shih-ts'ai, *Sinkiang: Pawn or Pivot?* (East Lansing, Mich., 1958).

[95] "Interviews with Mao Tse-tung, Communist Leader, by Edgar Snow," in *China, the March Towards Unity* (New York, 1937), p. 41. The exact date of this interview was supplied by Mr. Snow in a personal communication to the present writer. In the 1930s it was assumed that Communist China would be a federal state on the pattern of the USSR. Following the creation of the Chinese People's Republic in 1949, Communist China established areas of national autonomy for non-Chinese minorities, but it did not adopt a federal system.

[96] Kolarz, *Soviet Far East*, p. 156; Owen Lattimore, "Mongolia's Relations with Russia and China," *Manchester Guardian Weekly*, Dec. 4, 1952; Boorman, "The Borderlands," in *Moscow-Peking Axis*, pp. 166-73; the dispatches of Jack Raymond, based on his trip to Ulan Bator, New York *Times*, Aug. 28, 29, and Sept. 8, 1956.

thing we can be sure: the Chinese Communists have consistently viewed China as a future constituent member of a World Federation of Soviet Republics. When, in the early 1930s, the Chinese Communists were carving out a "Soviet Republic" on the territory of central and southern Kiangsi and western Fukien provinces, this tenuous state was glorified as the "second Soviet Republic, second in the world after the U.S.S.R.," and its destiny was linked to the ultimate goal of a Soviet world state. The Chinese delegates to a Comintern gathering in December, 1933, held that the Chinese Communist stronghold must be considered a shield protecting the Soviet Union against war in the Far East, as this would be a war "directed against the world proletarian revolution and the struggle for a World-wide Soviet Republic." [97]

At the time of the Communist victory on the Chinese mainland in 1949, Liu Shao-chi acted as the spokesman for China in reaffirming the orthodox Leninist view of the two-phased process of development that stretched out before the former dependent areas of the world: first their secession from the non-Soviet world and the attainment of national "independence," and then their integration into an ever-growing federation of Soviet Republics. On June 7, 1949, Liu wrote in *Pravda*:

The proletariat demands the full equality and free unification of all nations . . . on an international scale. The proletariat insists upon the idea of the gradual movement toward world unity through the different concrete paths of free secession (having as its aim to smash the yoke of imperialism and provide independence for the large majority of the nations of the world), and of free federation (the unification of different nationalities on an absolutely voluntary basis, after the yoke of imperialism has been destroyed).[98]

This was the same Liu Shao-chi who had announced to the Communist leaders of Asia and Australasia at their "trade union" conference in November, 1949, that "armed struggle is the main form of struggle in the national liberation movement in many colonies and semicolonies," and that it was therefore "necessary to create, wherever and whenever possible, strong people's armies of liberation." The two ideas were obviously connected: the secession of

[97] Wang Ming, "Revolution, War and Intervention in China and the Tasks of the Communist Party," Dec., 1933, in Wang Ming and Kang Sin, *Revolutionary China Today* (Moscow, 1934), p. 29.
[98] Liu Shao-chi, "Ob internatsionalizme i natsionalizme," *Pravda*, June 7, 1949, p. 3.

WAY STATIONS TO SOVIET WORLD STATE

nations from the non-Soviet world was to be accomplished in large measure by the use of armed force as the first step toward their "free federation" in a World Soviet Federation.

THE ASIAN CHALLENGE TO SOVIET RUSSIAN CENTRALISM

The accession of China and the rest of Communist Asia to the Soviet federation presents an intriguing prospect. In the period immediately following the Communist victory in China, the resources and the strategic aims of the Soviet Union and Communist China proved to be largely complementary.[99] China was compelled to lean heavily upon Soviet industrial development for the effective mobilization of the huge reserve of Chinese manpower. Soviet Russia found it profitable to provide China with a heavy industrial base that could sustain a modern military machine, as well as to arm directly the legions of Chinese soldiers with the latest military equipment. The military adventures in which Communist China has been involved, either directly or indirectly, have served the mutually compatible aims of undermining the power of Moscow's principal antagonists in the non-Soviet world and of aggrandizing Chinese power in Asia. Chinese armed assistance to the Vietminh in Indochina, for example, both helped to shake France to its very foundations, with all the ensuing recriminations and dissension among the NATO powers, and at the same time raised Chinese prestige to new heights in Asia. As the price for this immensely profitable collaboration Moscow could well afford to placate Chinese sensitivities over such traditional Sino-Russian bones of contention as Outer Mongolia, Sinkiang, and Manchuria.

Since a major weakening of one partner in the Sino-Soviet alliance would adversely affect the power position of the other, it would seem that the advantages that presently accrue to both from maintaining a close working arrangement far outweigh the disadvantages

[99] Eckstein demonstrates that the development of a high level of Sino-Soviet trade will be uneconomic, since the structure of their trading capacities is more competitive than complementary. In the short run, it is difficult to estimate whether these relations place a burden of any consequence upon the Soviet economy. But "even if its expanded trade with China should prove to be disadvantageous to the Soviet Union, Moscow may conclude that the political gains to be reaped outweigh the economic losses which must be absorbed in the process." (Alexander Eckstein, "Moscow-Peking Axis: The Economic Pattern," in *Moscow-Peking Axis*, pp. 75-88, 100.)

WAY STATIONS TO SOVIET WORLD STATE   361

of each partner's attempting to pursue its own narrowly defined objectives without regard for, or perhaps at the expense of, the interests of the other.

The cooperation and mutual accommodations required of the Moscow-Peking partnership transcend short-range material benefits, for the fundamental bond cannot adequately be explained in terms of the power position of each state. Both the Soviet and the Chinese leaders share a general Marxist-Leninist image of the future "liberation" of all mankind, and feel that their destinies are enmeshed in the universal refashioning of all nations into a socialist world state. A great deal would seem to depend upon what happens to this intangible, but supremely important, ideological factor. "If the ideological link has been a crucial one in Sino-Soviet relations," Benjamin Schwartz shrewdly conjectures, then "the constant wearing away of the core of shared ideological beliefs must inevitably weaken that core, and the alliance must come to rest more and more on the shifting sands of power interest." [100]

Mao Tse-tung has already contributed a number of ideological innovations, such as the theoretical justifications for seizing power in the name of a proletarian movement that was almost totally devoid of a proletariat, progressing toward "socialism" under the official auspices of a "bloc of four classes," constructing a singular, Chinese version of a "People's Democracy," using a peculiar combination of coercion and persuasion, such as the theory of "Let the hundred flowers bloom," and establishing a system of "people's communes." [101] All of these seemingly academic, opaque doctrinal refinements tend to accumulate a vast significance in a totalitarian system, because the ideological factor weighs heavily in a society that both pretends to explain and seeks to control every aspect of life.

[100] Schwartz, "Ideology," in *Moscow-Peking Axis*, p. 139.
[101] Schwartz develops Mao's ideological contributions in *ibid.*, pp. 123-41; *Chinese Communism and the Rise of Mao* (Cambridge, Mass., 1951); "China and the Soviet Theory of People's Democracy," *Problems of Communism*, III, No. 5 (Sept.-Oct., 1954), 8-15; "On the 'Originality' of Mao-Tse-tung," *Foreign Affairs*, XXXIV, No. 1 (Oct., 1955), 67-76; "New Trends in Maoism?" *Problems of Communism*, VI, No. 4 (July-Aug., 1957), 1-8. For some attempts to deny or to underestimate the innovations pointed up by Schwartz, see Peter S. H. Tang, "Stalin's Role in the Communist Victory in China," *American Slavic*, XIII, No. 3 (Oct., 1954), 375-88; Lucian W. Pye, *Guerrilla Warfare in Malaya* (Princeton, 1956), pp. 17-43; Harold R. Isaacs and David Nelson Rowe, "Mao's '100 Flowers,'" *New Leader*, Aug. 12, 1957, pp. 13-15; Karl A. Wittfogel, "Peking's 'Independence,'" *ibid.*, July 20-27, 1959, pp. 12-17.

To the end, Stalin stubbornly refused to credit Mao with any theoretical contributions. Following the creation of the Chinese People's Republic in 1949, Stalin treated Peking essentially as a junior partner, although he exercised more circumspection than in his relations with Eastern Europe, perhaps profiting from his encounter with Tito in 1948. The relations between Stalin and Mao must have generated considerable tension, although adequate documentation is not yet available. Soviet economic and political concessions to Peking following Stalin's death have relieved some of these grievances, while Khrushchev's de-Stalinization policy launched at the Twentieth Party Congress was accompanied by an explicit Soviet approval of the "Chinese road to socialism."

Chinese ideological innovations were finally recognized. In his speech in Peking to a Communist Party gathering in September, 1956, for example, Mikoyan praised unstintingly the Chinese Communists, and Mao in particular, because they

> have made a major contribution to Marxist-Leninist theory.... The Chinese Communist comrades, proceeding from the fundamental principles of Marxist-Leninist theory, applied them creatively to the concrete conditions of China and were able to find distinctive new forms and methods of building socialism very suitable to Chinese conditions, including forms and methods which although they have not been tried in other countries have yielded rich fruits on Chinese soil.[102]

Similarly, Khrushchev reiterated in November, 1956, that "I personally admire very much the wisdom of our Chinese comrades who are solving the question of the methods of building socialism and overcoming many difficulties in a creative and extremely original way by taking account of the specific conditions in their country." [103]

Superficially, it would seem that Khrushchev's generous attitude would reduce Sino-Soviet frictions. Perhaps he has only recognized that he was incapable of preventing Mao from taking the "Chinese road," and has therefore capitalized on his weakness by appearing to make a virtue out of events beyond his control. But might not the Soviet leaders still have to pay a dear price for this short-range harmony in the coin of long-range disintegrative pulls within the Soviet world? By raising Chinese prestige, and by sanctioning Peking as a new fountainhead of orthodoxy, especially as Marxism

[102] "Rech' tovarishcha A. I. Mikoyana na VIII Vsekitaiskom s"ezde Kommunisticheskoi partii Kitaia," *Pravda*, Sept. 18, 1956, p. 2.
[103] "Rech' tovarishcha N. S. Khrushcheva," *ibid.*, Nov. 19, 1956, p. 2.

can be applied in Asia, has not Moscow done irreparable damage to the single, universally valid core of doctrinal beliefs?

It was soon apparent that the impact of Peking's newly acclaimed doctrinal pronouncements could not be confined to Asia. The "revisionist" segment of the Polish Party in particular seized upon some of the "liberal" Chinese theoretical innovations in the hope of finding ideological justifications for asserting Polish political positions that diverged from those of Moscow. Mao's supposedly secret speech of February 27, 1957, advocating a controlled, "free" competition of "nonantagonistic contradictions" in a Communist state, was avidly discussed in the Polish press before an expurgated text was published in Peking and Moscow in June, 1957. Mao's theories that sanctioned freer discussion and encouraged persuasion in place of Stalinist-type coercion, a Warsaw journal declared in May, 1957, offered conclusions that are "important not only for China, but for all countries which are building socialism." [104] Moscow showed its anxiety over the extension of a disrupting Chinese influence into Eastern Europe, and replied through its pliant Czech and Hungarian puppets that Mao's doctrine was considered applicable only to the Afro-Asian countries.[105]

Chinese influence, however, was already conspicuously at work in Eastern Europe, having been called upon in the first instance by Moscow itself in an effort to bolster Soviet authority following the Polish and Hungarian revolts of 1956. Peking, whose position was also endangered by the threatened disintegration of the Communist camp, dutifully condemned Imre Nagy and Tito for their attempts to weaken the Warsaw Pact. Significantly, it was only *after* the sharp Chinese declaration of December 29, 1956, striking out at Tito and reaffirming "socialist unity," followed by Chou En-lai's reassuring visits to Moscow, Warsaw, and Budapest in January, 1957, that Soviet spokesmen began reverting to a tougher, more confident pose.

At the November, 1957, Moscow gathering of Communist Parties, the Soviet effort to fight "revisionism" and to tighten its controls over Eastern Europe was likewise strongly supported by Mao. For reasons of his own, Mao seemed to force Khrushchev's hand in the spring of 1958 when the Chinese press launched a campaign against

[104] *Sztandar Mlodych* (Warsaw), May 7, 1957; quoted in *East Europe*, VI, No. 7 (July, 1957), 49.
[105] Elie Abel, "Czech Reds Bar Mao's Doctrine," New York *Times*, June 25, 1957; Abel, "Hungary Rejects Mao, Tito Theses," *ibid.*, June 30, 1957.

Tito that was noticeably more vituperative than the previous Soviet attack.[106]

By relying upon the Chinese Communists to salvage and then help reassert Soviet authority in Eastern Europe, Moscow unavoidably has elevated Peking's status and bargaining power to that of a moderator, or perhaps even an arbiter, in the affairs of the entire Soviet world. Peking's increasingly independent political role has similarly reinforced and enhanced its position as a fountainhead of doctrinal orthodoxy for world communism. The initial key Chinese pronouncement of December, 1956, for example, simultaneously sat in judgment of Tito, condemned "counterrevolutionary" Hungarian nationalism, and pointedly lectured Moscow on the dangers of "great-power chauvinism." "Stalin had displayed a certain tendency toward great-power chauvinism," Peking recalled, "in the relations with fraternal parties and fraternal countries." Then addressing themselves to the present Soviet and satellite leaders in the paternalistic manner reminiscent of the warnings that Moscow had once issued to the Russian and non-Russian nations of the Soviet Union, the Chinese spokesmen continued: "Therefore, in the interests of strengthening international proletarian solidarity, there is not only the primary task of overcoming the tendency toward great-power chauvinism in the larger countries, but it is also necessary to overcome the tendency toward nationalism in the smaller countries." [107]

These warnings were accompanied by a growing tendency for Peking to voice its independent political judgment of Soviet be-

[106] Compare the opening Soviet critique of the Yugoslav Party Program in *Kommunist*, No. 6 (April, 1958), pp. 16–39, with the *Jen Min Jih Pao* editorial, May 5, 1958; reprinted as "Sovremennyi revizionizm dolzhen byt' osuzhden!" *Pravda*, May 6, 1958, p. 3. The Chinese, for example, were the first to justify the 1948 expulsion of Yugoslavia from the Cominform. Among the speculations on why the Chinese had assumed such a harsh position, Tito suggested, in a speech of June 15, 1958, that China sought to increase international tensions as a means of prying more economic and military aid from Moscow, which might be done, in part, at the expense of Yugoslavia. On May 28, 1958, the Soviet Union suspended credits worth $285,000,000 to Yugoslavia, which conceivably could be redirected to China. On May 27 an important, high-level Sino-Soviet military conference opened in Peking and remained in session until July 22. (A. M. Rosenthal, "Warsaw Reports Soviet-China Pact," New York *Times*, August 7, 1958.) In addition, Mao's stern position on "revisionism" coincided with his own domestic campaign of intense political repression, since his "Let the hundred flowers bloom" experiment had produced a generous crop of "weeds."

[107] *Jen Min Jih Pao* editorial, Dec. 29, 1956; reprinted as "Eshchë raz ob istoricheskom opyte diktatury proletariata," *Pravda*, Dec. 30, 1956, p. 4.

havior. Behind the public façade of Sino-Soviet unity on Soviet actions in Hungary, there were rumblings of recriminations. According to the version of Mao's speech of February 27, 1957, which was circulated in Warsaw, Mao identified the Soviet intervention in Hungary as a specific example of the general Chinese injunction against "the mistakes that spring from great-power feelings and chauvinism." Ultimately, there was no choice but to intervene, Mao conceded, since the Hungarian Communist Party "simply disappeared in a matter of a few days," and there was justifiable fear that the disintegration would extend "to the whole state." Nevertheless, it was a "tragedy" that Soviet policy had brought the situation to such a pass.[108] On the heels of this revelation General Lung Yun, Vice Chairman of Peking's National Defense Council, publicly demanded that Peking be reimbursed for the "huge quantities of industrial equipment" that the Soviet Union had removed from Manchuria at the end of the Second World War. Similarly, he held that it was "totally unfair" for Peking to bear the expenses of fighting the Korean War when it was "fighting for world socialism." [109] While it is true that General Lung was soon branded a "right deviationist," the fact that these criticisms were even allowed to appear in the official Chinese Communist press was itself significant.

Another striking display of independence and perhaps the boldest bid for ideological preeminence came in 1958 when Peking announced its campaign to organize the Chinese people into communes.[110] This gigantic program of social engineering, begun within a decade after the Communist conquest of the Chinese mainland, was represented as a primitive, egalitarian short cut to communism. The Soviet Union, meanwhile, admittedly still remained far distant from achieving the ultimate communal forms of life after more than forty years of experience with state power. "It is evident," the Central Committee of the Chinese Communist Party stated in

[108] Excerpts from Mao's speech quoted in the Warsaw dispatch of Sydney Gruson, "Mao Text Shows Reds 'Liquidated' 800,000 Since '49," New York Times, June 13, 1957.
[109] Official release of the New China News Agency quoted in the Hong Kong dispatch of Greg MacGregor, "Peiping General Criticizes Soviet on Seized Plants," ibid., June 24, 1957.
[110] On the origin and nature of the people's communes, see Stanley Rich, "The Communes—Mao's 'Big Family,'" Problems of Communism, VIII, No. 1 (Jan.-Feb., 1959), 1-5, and David Rousset, "The New Tyranny in the Countryside," ibid., pp. 5-13.

its resolution of August 29, 1958, "that the realization of communism in our country is already not something far off. We must actively use the form of the people's commune and through it find the concrete road for the transition to communism." [111] Moscow's distaste for this Chinese initiative was reflected in an almost total silence in the Soviet press on the sensational speed with which the Chinese peasantry was herded into communes during the fall of 1958. Far from greeting Peking's claim of spurting ahead toward the attainment of communism (ahead of the Soviet Union), an authoritative article in the October, 1958, issue of the Soviet philosophical journal held: "It must be assumed that the European socialist countries . . . will be the first to enter communism." The Asian countries were said to "constitute another regional zone," which, by implication, meant that they would enter the period of communism after the European nations.[112]

On December 1, 1958, Khrushchev was prodded for his views on the commune system during an interview with Senator Hubert H. Humphrey. Khrushchev is reported to have said: "They are old-fashioned, they are reactionary." Referring to the early Soviet experience of "war communism," when the egalitarian principle of distribution was introduced at a time of great scarcity, he continued: "We tried that right after the revolution. It just doesn't work. . . . You know, Senator, what those communes are based on? They are based on that principle 'from each according to his abilities, to each according to his needs.' You know that won't work. You can't get production without incentive." [113] In Soviet doctrine true communism must be based upon the prior attainment of an abundant society. This, in turn, Khrushchev held, could only be created by an enormous increase in production which must be stimulated by allocating material incentives according to one's ability to produce. Mikoyan repeated these ideas in some detail during the course of a public interview while on his trip through the United States in January, 1959.[114]

[111] The resolution was reprinted as "O sozdanii narodnykh kommun v derevniakh, Reshenie TsK Kompartii Kitaia," *Pravda*, Sept. 11, 1958, p. 3.
[112] Ts. A. Stepanian, "Oktiabr'skaia revoliutsiia i stanovlenie kommunisticheskoi formatsii," *Voprosy filosofii*, No. 10 (1958), p. 34.
[113] Senator Hubert H. Humphrey, "My Marathon Talk with Russia's Boss," *Life*, XLVI, No. 2 (Jan. 12, 1959), 86.
[114] Harrison E. Salisbury, "Mikoyan Declares Communes Failed in Soviet Practice," New York *Times*, Jan. 13, 1959. Similarly, the East German Am-

Peking soon retreated from its extremist claims. A new resolution of the Central Committee of the Chinese Communist Party, issued on December 10, 1958, warned "overeager" comrades that the ultimate goal of communism was not as near nor as easily attained as they seemed to think. On purely pragmatic grounds it was necessary to slow down and consolidate the rapid reorganization of the peasantry. Moreover, "we should not be in a hurry to set up people's communes on a large scale in the cities," although this goal was maintained from some future time. But there was also a withdrawal on the ideological front which seemed to bring the Chinese views into line with Khrushchev's. Peking scolded its zealots who "think that ownership in the rural people's communes is even now of the nature of ownership by the whole people, and that very soon or even now they can dispense with the socialist principle of 'to each according to his work' and adopt the Communist principle of 'to each according to his needs.'" No longer did Peking appear to ignore, if not reject, Soviet experience and ideological guidance on basic questions of socialist construction. Instead, the Chinese viewed as a "complex task" the creation of a highly productive socialist economy which "will take fifteen, twenty or more years to complete, counting from now." Then "the socialist system will have to continue for a very long time," while the achievement of communism was relegated to the still farther distant future.[115]

Khrushchev used the occasion of his address to the Twenty-first Party Congress in January, 1959, to stress his accord with Peking.

We are in full and complete agreement with the fraternal Communist Party of China, although in many respects its methods of building socialism do not resemble our own. We know that China has its specific features of historical development, size of population, level of production, and national culture. Therefore it would be a mistake to ignore these specific features and to copy what is good for one country but unsuitable for another.[116]

---

bassador in Peking derogated the communes by writing that they may be all right for China, but not for anywhere else. ("German Reds Limit Communes to China," *ibid.*, Jan. 14, 1959.)

[115] "Resolution on Some Questions Concerning the People's Communes," adopted by the CC of the CPC, Dec. 10, 1958, *World Marxist Review*, II, No. 3 (March, 1959), 73–75.

[116] "Doklad tovarishcha N. S. Khrushcheva," *Pravda*, Jan. 28, 1959, p. 9. Shortly thereafter Khrushchev felt compelled to denounce Humphrey as a

At the same time Khrushchev explicitly warned against a revival of the heresy of Chinese zealotry. Stung, no doubt, by Chinese audacity, he found it necessary to lecture at some length on the process of making the transition to communism. The ultimate goal of communism remains, "but society cannot leap from capitalism to communism," he protested, "skipping the socialist stage of development." Furthermore, "to pass prematurely to distribution according to needs when the economic conditions for this have not yet been created, when an abundance of material goods has not yet been achieved, when people have not been prepared to live and work in a Communist way would only harm the cause of building communism."

After Khrushchev made certain that Peking would not claim to have reached communism before Moscow, he offered to concede that neither would Asia enter communism after the Soviet Union and the countries of Eastern Europe, as some Soviet theorists had speculated.

How will the further development of the socialist countries proceed toward communism? Can one imagine one of the socialist countries attaining communism and introducing Communist principles of production and distribution, while other countries are left trailing somewhere behind in the early stages of building socialist society? This prospect is highly improbable. . . . Socialist countries will enter the higher phase of Communist society more or less simultaneously.[117]

Khrushchev had placed restraints upon the Chinese ambition to grasp the ideological leadership of the Communist world, but only at the cost of a certain embarrassment to Soviet pretentions. By granting that all socialist countries will enter the higher phase of Communist society more or less simultaneously he admitted that, however great the achievements of Soviet society, Moscow would have to wait until the poverty-stricken millions of China had created an abundant society before the Soviet Union could advance into the period of full communism. The uneasy nature of his ideological

"fabricator of fairy tales," although the ideas reported in the Humphrey interview had already been substantiated by the shift in the Chinese position as well as in Khrushchev's Party Congress speech. See "Khrushchev Makes Denial," New York *Times*, Feb. 6, 1959, and Russell Baker, "Humphrey Hints at Red Axis Rift," *ibid.*, Feb. 7, 1959. Then on his tour of Poland in July, 1959, Khrushchev publicly condemned the commune system in much the same terms as Humphrey had reported. ("Khrushchev Says Moscow Found Communes Futile," *ibid.*, July 22, 1959.)

[117] "Doklad tovarishcha N. S. Khrushcheva," *Pravda*, Jan. 28, 1959, pp. 8–9.

WAY STATIONS TO SOVIET WORLD STATE   369

accord with Peking also becomes evident if one realizes that at no time during these discussions did the Chinese discredit or abandon the ideal of the people's communes as the basic social and economic form of Chinese life. Peking only decreed a slower pace in their formation and acknowledged that it was a mistake to view them as the means for an immediate advance toward communism. Thus a superficial Sino-Soviet agreement has not reached the source of latent differences. It would therefore be rash to predict that Peking has made its last challenge to Soviet ideological and political supremacy.

What, then, of the long-range prospects, when Communist China has grown into a giant industrial power in its own right, pursuing the "Chinese road" to socialism and communism without the restraints that Moscow can presently impose? Should the day ever arrive when Peking has become militarily stronger than Moscow, to what extent will the Chinese be the willing handmaiden of Russian policy? Already the expansion of Chinese power has produced intoxicating visions, which may come to pass if China is endowed with the capabilities to implement them. C. L. Sulzberger, touring Southeast Asia in the spring of 1955, reported:

> Not long ago Indonesian security police confiscated a secret shipment of Communist textbooks. These featured maps of the "New China." Included in Chinese territory were the following: Burma, Thailand, Laos, Cambodia, Vietnam, Malaya, Singapore, Borneo (at present divided between Indonesia and Britain) and the Indonesian Islands of Sumatra and Celebes. Southeast Asia was not depicted as politically *Communist* but as geographically *Chinese*.[118]

Moreover, might not an overpopulated, land-hungry China someday gaze longingly at the vast expanses of Soviet Central Asia and

[118] C. L. Sulzberger, "Techniques of Expansion in Southeast Asia," New York *Times*, March 5, 1955. See also "Map of the People's Republic of China," *People's China* (Peking), II, No. 7 (Oct. 1, 1950), 16–17. This official 1950 map incorporates as Chinese territory northeastern Burma (the area Chinese troops invaded in force at the end of July, 1956), the eastern tip of Afghanistan, the watershed of the Indus River and parts of Kashmir, the northern strip of India's Assam province, the entire South China Sea including Taiwan and all the offshore islands and the Philippine territorial waters. All of Korea, then in the midst of war, was depicted as "the Korean Democratic People's Republic." The Chinese invasion of Indian border regions in the summer and fall of 1959 not only alarmed the Indians, but embarrassed and irritated Khrushchev, who was then in the midst of a renewed "peace offensive." For the Kremlin, this lack of coordination in Sino-Soviet policies must have appeared as another ominous symptom of Chinese independence.

Soviet Siberia as an outlet for its masses? By Russian standards these stretches may be considered difficult to colonize, but Chinese living standards have traditionally been so depressed that, to a Chinese, these areas may appear attractive. It is not beyond the realm of possibility that Communist Russia may yet have to defend itself against Communist China.

This is to suggest that Communist nations may be no more immune to the virus of nationalism than non-Communist nations. Prior to the victory of the Chinese Communists the differences in resolving these conflicts in the Soviet and non-Soviet worlds could be explained by the totalitarian nature of the Soviet regime, and by the imbalance of national populations in the Soviet orbit. The non-Soviet world is not molded into a single authoritarian pattern, nor is any single nation in vast numerical disproportion to all the others. There is, in short, neither the desire nor the ability to put the diverse nations of the non-Soviet world into a single national strait jacket. The Soviet world had "solved" its national problem by progressively Russifying all of the non-Russian nations. This was possible because of the coercive instruments of a Russian-centered totalitarian regime in which all non-Russian groups constituted national minorities vis-à-vis the Russians. As we have indicated in our discussion of Soviet Russian nationalism, this has resulted in the image of a Russified world state.

When it is asked how China, and all the multitudes of Asia, fit into this picture, it must be recognized that they do not. In terms of sheer numbers there are presently almost six times as many Chinese as Russians. Should a Communist victory sweep India and the rest of Asia, the Asians would reduce the Russians to a still less significant position. When these peoples join the Soviet state, would the Russians become a helpless minority, unable to maintain their goal of a Russified Soviet world state? Would the affiliation of a by-then industrialized, powerful China and of other Asian nations with an expanding Soviet Union cause the center of the state to shift to Asia? Or would several world centers arise? But the very core of the Soviet system is its centralism. There cannot for long be two or more equally powerful world centers in a Soviet world state without vitally altering the foundation stone of Leninist centralism.

For the present, Peking's public declarations continue to speak of the camp of "the world proletariat with the Soviet Union at its center."[119] But as it becomes increasingly possible to assert the specifically Chinese features of Chinese communism, may not the Chinese begin to revive the age-old claim that Peking is the center of the world? The Communist victory in China, reveling in the ejection of Western influence and Western values, has already produced a selective renaissance and reinforcement of customary Chinese values and ancient modes of expression.[120] Basic to these traditional Chinese values is an assumed uniform superiority of Chinese civilization and culture and, consequently, the right to consider China the political center of the world. "The Chinese long held it as an ideal," comments a distinguished Sinologue, "that there should be only one political administration for civilized mankind and regarded their own as that government."[121] Hence the most widely used designation for China, "Chung Kuo," means literally "The Middle Kingdom," or the kingdom at the center of the civilized world, which should naturally receive political tribute from the "barbarians" who surround it. During the Stalinist era, it is conceivable that the chafing position of a junior partner, in which the Chinese Communists lacked recognition for innovations that departed significantly from Stalin's repeatedly disastrous guidance, might have created a secret resentment, if not a feeling of contempt, on the part of the Chinese leaders toward their "barbarian" Russian protectors. Will the post-Stalinist recognition of the Maoist contributions dispel such contempt, or will it merely accentuate it, since Moscow has finally come to acknowledge the cleverness, if not

[119] *Jen Min Jih Pao* editorial, Dec. 29, 1956; reprinted as "Eshchë raz," *Pravda*, Dec. 30, 1956, p. 4. In a like manner, when Chou En-lai arrived in Moscow, he spoke of "the camp of socialism, headed by the great Soviet Union." ("Rech' tovarishcha Chzhoi En'-laia," *ibid.*, Jan. 18, 1957, p. 2.) The Chinese also approved of this formula in the Moscow Declaration of November, 1957. ("Deklaratsiia Soveshchaniia," *ibid.*, Nov. 22, 1957, p. 1.) Chou En-lai's speech to the Twenty-first Congress of the CPSU was again studded with the phrases: "the countries of the socialist camp, headed by the Soviet Union," and "the international Communist movement, of which the Communist Party of the Soviet Union is the center." ("Vystuplenie tovarishcha Chzhoi En'-laia," *ibid.*, Jan. 29, 1959, p. 4.)
[120] On the fusion and integration of Communist and traditionally nationalist elements in China, see David S. Nivison, *Communist Ethics and Chinese Tradition* (MIT Center for International Studies, Cambridge, Mass., 1954); Amaury de Riencourt, "Communism and the Traditional Culture of China," *Orbis*, I, No. 2 (Summer, 1957), 199–210.
[121] Kenneth Scott Latourette, *The Chinese, Their History and Culture* (New York, 1946), p. 3.

the superiority, of the Chinese over their erstwhile Russian teachers? As the Chinese feeling of self-confidence grows with the expanding role of Peking, how can the Chinese permanently humble themselves before their "barbarians"?

If, then, Moscow should be reduced to but one among several world centers would this not so distort, and possibly mellow, the present image of a Soviet world state that some entirely new configuration would emerge? Or, should a struggle develop between several of these world centers, is it not possible that this internecine battle might disintegrate the prospective Soviet world state from within? These are, of course, long-range problems not clearly discerned today; yet the existence of a Communist China and the possible extension of Communist power in Asia inevitably push these questions to the surface.

XII. Soviet Reactions to Supranational Plans from the Non-Soviet World

THE Soviet design for a world state is but one of many. The dream of all mankind united in a single world community antedates by far both the Communist movement and the Soviet regime. How have the Soviet leaders regarded plans other than their own for the transformation and integration of man's basic institutions into a higher unity? Is there any hint that such plans might be reconciled with the Soviet design for a world state? Or does the Soviet leadership rigidly reject compromise solutions and proclaim the inevitability of a death struggle between rival and mutually incompatible schemes? Forthright answers to these questions are needed for the benefit of those in the non-Soviet world who would wrestle with the critical problem of adapting an archaic nation-state system to the stresses of modern life.

EARLY DEBATES OVER A CAPITALIST UNITED STATES OF EUROPE

One of the earliest expressions on the subject of a capitalist United States of Europe came from Trotsky, who so often sounded the keynote for themes that were later developed by a chorus of Soviet theorists. The specter of a proletarian revolution, Trotsky recorded in 1906, was causing the capitalist states of Europe to seek ways of preventing their national rivalries from erupting into war.

A European war inevitably means a European revolution. . . . It is precisely this fear of the revolt of the proletariat that compels the bourgeois parties, even while voting monstrous sums for military expenditure, to make solemn declarations in favor of peace, to dream of International Arbitration Courts and even of the organization of a United States of Europe. These feeble declamations can, of course, neither abolish the antagonism of states nor armed conflicts.[1]

[1] Trotsky, "Europe and Revolution," 1906, in *A Review and Some Perspectives* (Moscow, 1921), pp. 79–80.

Trotsky's early rejection of a capitalist United States of Europe was matched by his enthusiasm for a proletarian United States of Europe as an essential first step toward a socialist United States of the World. The outbreak of the First World War caused Lenin to examine the idea of a capitalist United States of Europe. In September, 1914, he felt that this idea might be used to foster the overthrow of the monarchies of Europe as a preliminary link in a chain reaction that would end in a proletarian revolution. Lenin therefore advocated "as one of our most immediate slogans, propaganda in favor of republics in Germany, Poland, Russia, and other countries, and in favor of transforming all of the separate states of Europe into a Republican United States of Europe." [2] Again, in October, 1914, he advanced this slogan in the name of the Central Committee of his Party.[3] The Bolsheviks soon found themselves in strange company, for the Socialists of the Second International, whom Lenin roundly condemned as "social-chauvinists," likewise pressed for a United States of Europe, and even for a world federation. The London Conference of the Second International of February, 1915, resolved: "The victory of the Allied powers must be a victory of popular liberty, for unity, independence and autonomy of the nations in the peaceful federation of the United States of Europe and the world." [4] At the Bern Conference of the foreign sections of the Bolshevik Party, in March, 1915, where the question was again discussed, Lenin reported that "the discussion took a one-sided political turn, and it was decided to postpone the question pending an analysis of its *economic* side in the [Party] press." [5] By August, 1915, Lenin had concluded that while this idea was "entirely impregnable as a political slogan," from an economic point of view, "the United States of Europe under capitalism is either impossible or reactionary." [6]

[2] Lenin, "Zadachi revoliutsionnoi sotsial-demokratii v evropeiskoi voine," Sept., 1914, in *Sochineniia*, XVIII, 46.
[3] Lenin, "Voina i rossiiskaia sotsial-demokratiia," Oct., 1914, in *ibid.*, XVIII, 65.
[4] "Resolution Adopted at the London Conference, February 14, 1915"; quoted in Olga Gankin and H. H. Fisher, *The Bolsheviks and the World War* (Stanford, 1940), p. 279.
[5] Lenin, "Konferentsiia zagranichnykh sektsii RSDRP," March 29, 1915, in *Sochineniia*, XVIII, 124.
[6] Lenin, "O lozunge Soedinënnykh Shtatov Evropy," Aug. 23, 1915, in *ibid.*, XVIII, 230-31.

NON-SOVIET SUPRANATIONAL PLANS

This demand is either unrealizable under capitalism, with its assumption of the creation of a planned world economy under the conditions of the devision among separate states of the colonies, spheres of influence, etc., or this slogan is reactionary, signifying a temporary union of the great powers of Europe for the more successful oppression of the colonies and a joint plundering of the more rapidly developing states of Japan and America.[7]

This brought the Bolshevik view into line with Trotsky's original position, which he reaffirmed at the end of 1915: "A halfway complete economic union of Europe *coming from the top* by means of an agreement of the capitalist governments is sheer utopia." [8] The shift in Lenin's position, however, was more probably due to Bukharin's long pamphlet *Imperialism and World Economy*, written during 1915, which Lenin studied with care and to which Lenin himself contributed an introduction.

THE ATTACK ON ULTRA-IMPERIALISM

Bukharin argued that the struggle among national states for markets, raw materials, and spheres of capital investment represented an irreconcilable conflict between the growth of productive forces and the outmoded "national" limits in which production was organized. Under such conditions conflicts are inevitably "settled through extending the state frontiers in bloody struggles, a settlement which holds the prospects of new and more grandiose conflicts." [9] As the arena of this conflict is the world economy itself, "its economic and political limits are a world trust, a single world state obedient to the finance capital of the victors who assimilate all the rest." [10] During 1914 and 1915 Karl Kautsky cautiously advanced the proposition that the world might be moving into a period of "ultra-imperialism," marked by the disappearance of competition, in which the various national states might merge on a world scale without war. Bukharin denounced this as an "opportunist deviation," and found "no reason to expect, at least in the more or less near future, an agreement or a merging of the state capitalist trusts and their transformation into a single world trust." Bukharin did

[7] Lenin, "O lozunge Soedinënnykh Shtatov Evropy," Aug., 1915, in *ibid.*, XXX, 235.
[8] Trotsky, "Programma mira," 1915–1916, in *Sochineniia*, III, Part I, 85.
[9] Bukharin, *Imperialism*, 1915, p. 106.   [10] *Ibid.*, p. 120.

not deny that, "in the historic process which we are to witness in the near future, world capitalism will move in the direction of a universal state capitalist trust by absorbing the weaker formations." However, this will not bring peace, for "new problems will have to be 'solved' by the sword." [11] It is left to the proletariat alone to organize all nations into a peaceful world economy and a single world state.[12]

Lenin's introduction to this essay boldly affirmed Bukharin's conclusions. It is only by reasoning "in the abstract," only by entering the realm of dreams, he said, that one could grant the logic of Kautsky's suggestion. Lenin likewise conceded that "there is no doubt that the development is going *in the direction* of a single world trust that will swallow up all enterprises and all states without exception." But like Bukharin he insisted that

the development in this direction is proceeding under such stress, with such a tempo, with such contradictions, conflicts, and convulsions—not only economic, but also political, national, etc., etc.—that *before* a single world trust will be reached, before the respective national finance capitals will have formed a world union of "ultra-imperialism," imperialism will inevitably explode, capitalism will turn into its opposite.[13]

During 1916 Lenin stepped up his attack on the idea of a peaceful supranational union of capitalist states. His Theses of March, 1916, on the national question dismissed "the idea of a peaceful union of equal nations under imperialism" as a "philistine, opportunist utopia." [14] At the Kienthal Conference in April, 1916, he introduced a resolution denouncing as "a mirage" all proposals for "a United States of Europe, compulsory courts of arbitration, disarmament, democratized diplomacy, etc." [15] Then in his much-celebrated work, *Imperialism, the Highest Stage of Capitalism*, written during the first half of 1916, Lenin went to considerable lengths to "prove," with the aid of his usual invective, that Kautsky's "ultra-imperialism" was "ultra-nonsense." [16] Again at the beginning of 1917 he branded

[11] *Ibid.*, pp. 135-39.   [12] *Ibid.*, p. 167.
[13] *Ibid.*, p. 14; Lenin, "Predislovie k broshiure N. Bukharina 'Mirovoe khoziaistvo i imperializm,'" Dec., 1915, in *Sochineniia*, XVIII, 357.
[14] Lenin, "Sotsialisticheskaia revoliutsiia i pravo natsii na samoopredelenie," March, 1916, in *Sochineniia*, XIX, 40.
[15] Lenin, "Proekt rezoliutsii, vnesennyi tsimmerval'dskoi levoi po voprosu ob otnoshenii sotsial-demokratii k voprosu o mire," April, 1916, in *ibid.*, XIX, 436.
[16] Lenin, "Imperializm, kak vysshaia stadiia kapitalizma," Jan.-July, 1916, in *ibid.*, XIX, 141-70.

NON-SOVIET SUPRANATIONAL PLANS 377

the general phrases about "a federation of nations," "flaunted" by what he called "bourgeois nationalists," as "disgusting hypocrisy."[17] It was abundantly clear, even before the Bolsheviks had seized state power, that the Soviet theorists were convinced that only their kind of a world state was either desirable or possible. They consistently rejected any suggestions that this world state might be consummated in any other form or under any other aegis.

SOVIET REACTION TO THE LEAGUE OF NATIONS

Following the Bolshevik Revolution the Soviet leaders looked upon the newly formed League of Nations as a sinister, but stillborn attempt to create a capitalist world state. On October 24, 1918, Chicherin addressed a note to Woodrow Wilson in which he suggested how this organization might be "improved." "The League of Nations should not only liquidate the present war, but also make impossible any wars in the future.... We propose, therefore, Mr. President, that the League of Nations be based on the expropriation of the capitalists of all countries." This would have the happy effect of producing a condition of plenty for all nations so that "the League of Nations will be a League of mutual aid of the toiling masses."[18] Lenin countered the formation of the League of Nations with the founding of the Comintern, an organization committed to the fundamental aim of creating a Soviet world state. As the aims of these two world organizations were mutually exclusive, Lenin inserted in the conditions for affiliation to the Comintern the requirement that each affiliating party "must systematically explain to the workers that, without the revolutionary overthrow of capitalism, no international courts of arbitration, no talk about reducing arms, no 'democratic' reorganization of the League of Nations will save mankind from new imperialist wars."[19]

During 1919 Bukharin and Preobrazhenskii expounded the nature of the League of Nations in their *ABC of Communism*, which they

[17] Lenin, "Patsifizm burzhuaznyi i patsifizm sotsialisticheskii," Jan. 1, 1917, in *ibid.*, XIX, 374.
[18] "Note from Chicherin, People's Commissar for Foreign Affairs, to Woodrow Wilson, President of the United States of America, October 24th, 1918"; quoted in *The Soviet Union and Peace*, Intro. by Henri Barbusse (New York, 1929), pp. 53-54.
[19] Lenin, "Ob usloviiakh priëma v Kommunisticheskii Internatsional," July, 1920, in *Sochineniia*, XXV, 577.

described as "an elementary textbook of Communist knowledge." The League's principal advocate was President Wilson, "that clever and cunning knave," who in reality had set up a "League of Bandits" for the purpose of founding a world state capitalist trust.

The League of Nations is something in the nature of an attempt to create a monstrous world-wide trust, that would embrace our entire globe and exploit the whole world and which, on the other hand, would everywhere crush the working-class movement and its revolution with utmost ferocity. All talk to the effect that the League was established to insure peace is so much trash. . . . However the League of Nations will not be able to fulfill its two aims: the organization of the whole world economy into a single trust and the universal suppression of revolution. The great powers do not have sufficient unity to accomplish this.[20]

The Manifesto of the Second Comintern Congress of July, 1920, elaborated this theme:

Under the flag of the League of Nations, the United States made an attempt to extend its experience with a federal union of large, multinational masses to the other side of the ocean, to chain to its golden chariot the peoples of Europe and of other parts of the world, and to bring them under the rule of Washington.

That the United States was not only incapable of implementing this "plot," but even prevented from joining the League of Nations was explained by the contradictions among the "imperialist" powers. Wilson, "the American messiah," had found it necessary to renounce the League of Nations "which England had converted into one of her diplomatic chanceries."[21] More than that, the Versailles settlement, of which the League was an integral part, had not produced a further integration of capitalist states, but had brought about a disintegration of the existing state boundaries. As the Comintern Theses of July, 1921, noted, despite "the demands of the productive forces to eradicate the framework of national states and to convert Europe and the rest of the world into one economic territory, the result of the clash between the hostile imperialist powers was only to set up in Central and Eastern Europe a whole series of new boundaries, new customs barriers, and new armies." Instead of advancing toward a world union, capitalism had "thrown Europe back to the Middle Ages."[22]

[20] Bukharin and Preobrazhenskii, *Azbuka*, 1919, pp. 92–93.
[21] "Manifest II kongressa Kommunisticheskogo Internatsionala," July 19–Aug. 7, 1920, in *Kom. Int. v dok.*, pp. 140–41.
[22] "Mirovoe polozhenie i nashi zadachi: tezisy," June 22–July 12, 1921, in

At the Genoa Conference of European powers, held in April, 1922, the chief Soviet diplomat, Chicherin, continued his undiplomatic leg pulling about the League of Nations. He asserted that the Soviet government was willing "to review the Covenant of the League of Nations, in order to transform it into a real league of peoples, where there will not be domination of some nations by others, and where the existing division between victors and vanquished will be eliminated." [23] As no capitalist state showed any interest in exploring this offer, Chicherin did not pursue the idea further. What he apparently had in mind is elaborated by Alexander Barmine, who at the time served as a personal secretary in Chicherin's office. "He proposed to set up, under the protection of the Soviets, a League of Peoples, in which the wronged, the oppressed, the exploited, and members of ethnic minorities should be included on exactly the same footing as the dominant powers." [24] In short, he intended to turn the League of Nations into a gigantic Soviet propaganda platform to exploit to the fullest the strife and the conflicts in the non-Soviet world.

During the early 1920s the eminent Soviet legal authority, Pavel Stuchka, examined the probability of the League of Nations developing into a world state capable of enforcing the rule of world law. Plans for strengthening contemporary international law through "leagues of nations with special coercive authority" were "fantasies." While he acknowledged a certain basis for bourgeois authority organized on an international scale, this authority was "ephemeral and rapidly fades away." On the other hand, "such authority possesses complete reality for the proletariat where it becomes dominant. The Soviet form of state is *per se* an international unification of mankind (or of a portion of mankind)." This authority "upon an international scale is being generated in the Communist International." [25] "The League of Nations cannot be transformed into a superstate, or a federation of states, or even into a

---

ibid., pp. 173-74. See also D. Manuil'skii, "Report on the National and Colonial Question," June 30, 1924, in *Fifth Congress of the Communist International*, p. 185.
[23] Speech by Chicherin, April 10, 1922, in G. Bardi, ed., *Les Documents de la Conférence de Gênes* (Rome, 1922), p. 29. Chicherin spoke in French.
[24] Alexander Barmine, *One Who Survived* (New York, 1945), p. 117.
[25] P. I. Stuchka, "The Revolutionary Part Played by Law and the State—A General Doctrine of Law," 1921, in *Soviet Legal Philosophy*, Hugh W. Babb, trans., Intro. by John N. Hazard (Cambridge, Mass., 1951), p. 66.

confederation, because of the irreconcilable contradictions among the different capitalist states that constitute the League's membership."[26]

THE PAN-EUROPE SCHEME OF THE 1920S

Renewed interest in a non-Soviet United States of Europe resulted from Count Coudenhove-Kalergi's *Pan-Europe*, published in October, 1923. The idea in this work stimulated the formation of a Pan-Europe Movement, which held its first Congress in Vienna in October, 1926. Bukharin defined the Communist position on this movement in a speech to the Comintern Executive Committee in November, 1926. Even the most enthusiastic advocates of Pan-Europe, Bukharin noted, sought to exclude Great Britain and the Soviet Union. (It would be more accurate to say that the Soviet Union was not invited into this proposed union, while the British excluded themselves.) The true purpose of this union, Bukharin concluded, was to create a European military machine to challenge other world powers in the struggle for world hegemony. Even granting "the very improbable supposition that the unification of the whole of Western Europe, including Great Britain, had come about," the only result would be to intensify the conflict with America, Japan, and the Soviet Union. "It is not very difficult to realize that such a state of affairs would not mean cessation of the struggle and disappearance of the menace of war, but . . . the reproduction of the struggle at its highest stage, wars of a much more monstrous character and a colossal increase in their destructive power."[27] In response to such plans,

the Communist Parties should put forward, as against the slogan of the League of Nations, the slogan of a federation of Socialist Republics, against the slogan of Pan-Europe, the slogan of the United States of Socialist Europe, against the chatter about a new phase of capitalism without wars, the harsh truth about the monstrous wars which are being prepared by the bourgeoisie.[28]

[26] P. I. Stuchka, ed., *Entsiklopediia gosudarstva i prava* (Moscow, 1925–1926), II, 759.
[27] N. Bukharin, *Capitalist Stabilization and Proletarian Revolution: Report to the 7th Enlarged Plenum of the Executive Committee of the Comintern*, Nov. 22–Dec. 16, 1926 (Moscow, 1926), p. 60.
[28] *Ibid.*, p. 91. See also H. Gunter, "Glossary of the Pan-European Congress," *Communist International*, III, No. 3 (Nov. 15, 1926), 23.

The Sixth Comintern Congress of August, 1928, reaffirmed: "A United States of Europe or a United States of the World is a utopian dream under the capitalist system. . . . All tendencies operating in this direction (the Pan-Europe Movement, for example) are outright reactionary."[29]

The Pan-Europe Movement soon found an official sponsor in the person of the French Premier and Foreign Minister, Aristide Briand, who proposed the formation of a European Union in a speech of September 5, 1929, before the Assembly of the League of Nations.[30] This gesture was the high-water mark of the Pan-Europe Movement. In May, 1930, Briand revealed his concrete plan for European Union, but it amounted to little more than a proposal for a European league of sovereign nations operating within the League of Nations. The concessions he made were a response to the outcry of the French nationalists. Great Britain remained implacably opposed to any union on the European continent which would remove the British balance wheel from the European political mechanism. The precipitous rise of the Nazis and the tide of aggressive German nationalism, which itself was hostile to European federation, pushed France toward increased reliance upon British military and political support. The idea of European Union, for the time at least, was dead.

Despite the obviously unpromising prospect for a European Union, the idea continued to evoke sharp reactions from the Communists. The scheme for Pan-Europe, Stalin said in a speech of

[29] "Mery bor'by s opasnost'iu imperialistskikh voin: tezisy," July 17-Sept. 1, 1928, in *Kom. Int. v dok.*, p. 824. See also "Programma Kommunisticheskogo Internatsionala," Sept. 1, 1928, in *ibid.*, pp. 8, 37; N. Bukharin, "Speech in Reply to the Debate on the Program Question," *International Press Correspondence*, VIII, No. 59 (Sept. 4, 1928), 1036. Despite Bukharin's orthodox views on the impossibility of creating a capitalist world state, he was soon brought under attack for identifying himself with the theories of Kautsky and Hilferding on "ultra-imperialism." This was part of a general attack which Stalin launched to eliminate Bukharin as a rival for state power in the USSR. See "O t. Bukharine," July 3-19, 1929, in *Kom. Int. v dok.*, p. 912; Heinz Neumann, "Concerning a Revisionist Theory of Comrade Bukharin," *Communist International*, VI, No. 22 (1929), 848-57.

[30] On the relations between Briand and the Pan-Europe Movement, see Richard N. Coudenhove-Kalergi, *Crusade for Pan-Europe* (New York, 1943), pp. 114-38. Pan-Europe was not, of course, the only such plan advanced in the decade following the Bolshevik Revolution, though it was the most prominent. We shall confine our attention to those proposals that drew the most fire from Moscow. For a comprehensive survey of federalist plans, both regional and world-wide, see Edith Wynner and Georgia Lloyd, *Searchlight on Peace Plans* (New York, 1949).

June 27, 1930, was the latest expression of the desire to undertake a renewed capitalist intervention against the Soviet Union under the leadership of France.[31] Then Stalin sent Litvinov to Geneva in order further to disrupt and embarrass the League's consideration of the question of a European Union. The Soviet Union, Litvinov insisted, was also part of Europe. Even though the Soviet Union was not a member of the League of Nations, Moscow demanded full Soviet participation in the League's European Union Commission. Within the League, the German and Italian delegates pressed for the participation of the Soviet Union and Turkey to counterbalance what they suspected was a French attempt to dominate Europe. France was unable to prevent the dispatch of an invitation to Moscow, but, under a compromise formula, the role of the Soviet delegation was confined to deliberations on European economic problems. In meetings held from May, 1931, until October, 1932, Litvinov took advantage of this limited opportunity to oppose the formation of any European customs unions or tariff walls that would discriminate against the Soviet economy. The Soviet Union, then in the midst of a gigantic economic upheaval of rapid industrialization and collectivization of agriculture, was badly in need of access to foreign markets. Consequently, Litvinov proposed an economic nonaggression pact, which the conference debated but did not adopt. On the other hand, the League's deliberations made no progress toward the economic and political unification of Europe.[32]

THE SOVIET UNION'S ENTRANCE INTO THE LEAGUE OF NATIONS

The military threat posed by Hitler Germany caused Stalin to reconsider the use to which he might put the League of Nations. On December 25, 1933, he noted that the renunciation of League membership by Germany and Italy had made the League a logical focus of opposition to the expansionist designs of the Axis powers. Fearing that the Soviet Union would sooner or later become a victim of

[31] Stalin, "Politicheskii otchët Tsentral'nogo Komiteta XVI s"ezdu VKP(b)," June 27, 1930, in *Sochineniia*, XII, 255-56. See also articles by A. De Vries: "Pan-Europe," *Communist International*, VII, No. 7 (1930), 6-8; *ibid.*, VII, No. 10 (1930), 171-76.
[32] For Litvinov's major statements on European Union, see Degras, ed., *Soviet Documents*, II, 470-72, 492-94, 541-43. See also V. P. Potëmkin, ed., *Istoriia diplomatii* (Moscow, Leningrad, 1945), III, 413-16; Davis, *Soviets at Geneva*, pp. 223-43.

NON-SOVIET SUPRANATIONAL PLANS 383

Axis aggression, Stalin forecast that "it is not impossible that we should support the League of Nations, despite its colossal defects." [33] At the same time, he indicated a readiness to come to terms with Hitler, presumably in the hope of side-stepping the path of Axis assault. The offer of an olive branch was apparent in Stalin's public pronouncement of January 26, 1934. He objected to the view held by "certain German political leaders" that

> the USSR is now orienting itself toward France and Poland, that it has shifted from an opponent to a supporter of the Versailles Treaty, and that this change is to be explained by the establishment of a Fascist regime in Germany. This is not true. Of course, we are far from enthusiastic about the Fascist regime in Germany. But the question here is not one of fascism, because fascism, in Italy, for example, did not prevent the USSR from establishing the best relations with that country.[34]

Hitler's complete lack of interest in Stalin's plea for friendship settled the orientation of Soviet foreign policy.

In September, 1934, the Soviet Union joined the League of Nations and soon became the outstanding spokesman for making effective the existing Covenant provisions regarding collective security, by which the "satisfied" powers could defend the status quo.[35] In a sharp reversal of the traditional Soviet attitude, Litvinov even demanded that the League be endowed with additional authority. He proposed that it adopt a detailed definition of aggression, so that when aggression occurred no League member could be in doubt as to its obligation to jump to the defense of the victim. Litvinov concentrated his efforts on bolstering the effectiveness of Article 16 in the League's Covenant, under which military sanctions could be launched. In response to those who wished to confine or eliminate the use of Article 16, Litvinov insisted that, in the event of aggression, members must live up to the intent of the Covenant, and make its application automatic and obligatory for all League members. This view was not accepted by the so-called "Committee of Twenty-Eight," set up during 1936–1938 to study the various

---

[33] Stalin, "Beseda s korrespondentom gazety 'N'iu-Iork Taims' g. Diuranti," Dec. 25, 1933, in *Sochineniia*, XIII, 280. See also *Foreign Relations of the United States: The Soviet Union, 1933–1939* (Washington, 1952), pp. 53–54.
[34] Stalin, "Otchëtnyi doklad XVII s"ezdu partii o rabote TsK VKP(b)," Jan. 26, 1934, in *Sochineniia*, XIII, 302.
[35] On the other strain of Soviet policy allegedly running counter to Litvinov's role in the League of Nations, see chapter 4, footnote 3.

proposals advanced for the reform of the League of Nations.[36]

Litvinov found himself fighting a rear-guard action to prevent the adoption of a flood of amendments that would weaken the League's authority. On August 22, 1936, he proposed a comprehensive eleven-point program which would "contribute to the more precise and effective application of the principles of the Covenant in the sphere of collective security." The most radical of these proposals, which also failed of adoption, would have permitted the League Council to recommend military sanctions by a three-fourths majority instead of relying upon its usual principle of unanimity. In polling this vote both the attacking and the attacked states would be excluded, so that the aggressor state could not veto a majority recommendation.[37] Litvinov was perfectly aware that he was arguing for an infringement of the national sovereignty of the member states. "An end must be put to the situation wherein pleas of sovereignty and constitutional formalities are an obstacle to the performance of international obligations." [38] How radical this departure was from the previous Soviet position may be judged by citing Chicherin's objection, as stated in 1924, to the concept underlying Article 16: "The Soviet government rejects every plan for an international organization which anticipates eventual measures of constraint being applied by any international authority whatsoever against any particular state." [39] A similar contrast was evident in the Soviet attitude toward national sovereignty. Korovin's textbook on international law in 1924 held: "At a time when the general development of European international law moves in the direction of draining sovereignty of its content, in the name of contemporary interdependence of states . . . the Soviet government is recognized as the champion of the doctrine of 'classical' sovereignty." [40]

[36] "Final Report of the Committee of Twenty-Eight," Sept. 30, 1938, *League of Nations Official Journal, Special Supplement 183* (Geneva, 1938), p. 143.

[37] M. Litvinov, "Pis'mo general'nomu sekretariu Ligi Natsii ob uluchshenii printsipov pakta Ligi," Aug. 22, 1936, *Vneshniaia politika SSSR, rechi i zaiavleniia, 1927–1937* (Moscow, 1937), pp. 419–21.

[38] Litvinov, "Speech on the Indivisibility of Peace and the Strengthening of Collective Security Delivered at the XVI Plenum of the League of Nations," July 1, 1936, in *Against Aggression*, p. 43.

[39] "Nota Narodnogo Komissara po Inostrannym Delam Soiuza SSR Chicherina na imia general'nogo sekretaria Ligi Natsii Drummonda po povodu vyrabotannogo Ligoi proekta dogovora o vzaimnoi pomoshchi ot 12 marta 1024 g.," in Kliuchnikov and Sabanin, eds., *Mezhdunarodnaia politika*, III, Part I, 303.

[40] E. A. Korovin, *Mezhdunarodnoe pravo perekhodnogo vremeni* (Moscow, 1924), p. 43.

NON-SOVIET SUPRANATIONAL PLANS

Despite the apparent dissimilarity of these positions, the underlying Soviet motivation was very much the same. In 1924 Korovin emphasized the principle of unlimited national sovereignty as a means of discrediting any renewed attempt at capitalist intervention against the Soviet Union, in this instance by the victors of the First World War. A dozen years later Litvinov was calling for the sacrifice of national sovereignty to prevent another threatened capitalist assault on the Soviet Union, in this instance by the vanquished of the war. This manipulation of the doctrine of national sovereignty has already been noted in our discussion of Soviet Russian nationalism, where the main purpose was to demonstrate that there is no contradiction between Soviet solicitude for national sovereignty and the goal of a Soviet world state. The point to be emphasized at this juncture is the converse; namely, that Soviet acrobatics regarding the principle of national sovereignty have never reflected a belief that it was either desirable or possible for any international organization such as the League of Nations to grow into a world state. At the height of Litvinov's effort to strengthen the League, Andrew Rothstein, the Geneva correspondent for the Soviet news agency, Tass, sounded a warning to this effect in a speech of August, 1937, to the Geneva Institute of International Affairs:

> The Soviet Union did not enter the League of Nations because it thought that the League was some new panacea, some heaven-sent remedy for settling the affairs of this wicked world. . . . The Soviet conception of how the affairs of this world can be settled goes very far beyond such an instrument as the League of Nations. It does not believe, it has never believed, that the League of Nations can guarantee final peace. . . . There is no final guarantee against war until the causes for war have been eliminated—the struggle for markets, the exploitation of man by man. To that belief the Soviet Union holds as strongly as it did in 1917.[41]

The same theme was sounded by the Soviet theorist, Pavel Iudin, in September, 1937. Iudin took issue with the statement of Karl Kautsky that the League of Nations was needed "not only to avert the danger of war, but also to build the new society which must take the place of capitalist society." It was impossible, Iudin insisted, "to consider the League of Nations an international organization guar-

---

[41] Andrew Rothstein, "Soviet Policy and the Reconstruction of the League," Aug., 1937, in Geneva Institute of International Affairs, *Problems of Peace, Twelfth Series: Geneva and the Drift to War* (London, 1938), pp. 179, 188.

anteeing the transformation of capitalism to socialism."[42] This was merely a reformist, utopian illusion.

THE SOVIET ATTITUDE TOWARD THE FEDERATION OF THE WESTERN DEMOCRACIES

In addition to governmental schemes for avoiding war, there were many private proposals to limit or remove the rule of anarchy from the nation-state system. One of the most important proposals, resulting from a thorough disillusionment in the League of Nations, was Clarence Streit's *Union Now*, published in March, 1939. The democracies of the Western world were threatened by war, Streit argued, because of their weak and divided stand against the forces of aggression. Such weakness was inherent in any league system, where concerted action was dependent on the continual, unanimous agreement of every state asserting its sovereign rights as a member of an atomistic society. Only by forming a common government capable of taking positive, united action could Western democracy be adequately defended. In addition, a federation of the Western democracies around the core of the North Atlantic basin (the United States, members of the British Commonwealth, the democracies of continental Europe and Scandinavia) would enormously strengthen the democratic institutions within the Western world, unleash new productive forces in the enlarged framework of a giant common market, and provide a more adequate environment for the flourishing of individual freedom. This union of free peoples could serve as the nucleus for an eventual world union of democratic states.[43] With the signing of the Nazi-Soviet Pact and the outbreak of the Second World War, the British publicists Patrick Ransome and Sir Norman Angell proposed that a plan of this nature should be advanced as the basic war aim of the Western democracies.[44]

[42] P. Iudin, "Socialism and Law," Sept. 1, 1937, in *Soviet Legal Philosophy*, p. 283.
[43] Clarence K. Streit, *Union Now* (New York, 1939). This book was first distributed in a private edition of 300 copies in September, 1938, and following Hitler's conquest of continental Europe it was reissued in 1941 as *Union Now with Britain*. After American entry into the war and the brightening of the prospect for liberating continental Europe, subsequent editions, starting in 1943, reverted to the original proposals in *Union Now*.
[44] Patrick Ransome, "Plan for Permanent Peace," *Time and Tide*, XX, No. 34 (Aug. 26, 1939), 1144–45; Sir Norman Angell, "How Counter the Russian Move?" *ibid.*, XX, No. 38 (Sept. 23, 1939), 1249–50.

NON-SOVIET SUPRANATIONAL PLANS

By September, 1939, the Soviet Union was no longer interested in preventing a war against the Western democracies, and certainly had no sympathy with any plans that might serve to strengthen them, especially if such plans pretended to be the nucleus of a non-Soviet world state. The Soviet reaction was stated in familiar Leninist terminology:

> The "ideologists" of big capital now try to convince the peoples that the war must be waged in order to federate all the "democratic" states into a super-empire and thereby produce the basis for lasting peace. This idea put on the market as a brand new product, is in reality an old, unsaleable product of imperialism. . . . Any such super-empire would not be an insurance of peace, but right from the start machinery producing new wars.[45]

Less ambitious plans for the federation of Western Europe, built around a union of Britain and France, likewise came under attack. In February, 1940, the British Labor Party and the Socialist Party of France held a joint conference at which they proclaimed, as their common aim, the objective of a federated Europe. Then in June, 1940, Winston Churchill sent his dramatic offer of a Franco-British Union to French Premier Paul Reynaud. Had the French government accepted this offer, it would have laid the basis for overhauling the anachronistic political structure of the Western world. It is on this very point of British ties with the Continent that so many postwar attempts at European federation have foundered. Despite Reynaud's enthusiastic support, Churchill's project met with contempt on the part of the defeatist leaders Marshal Pétain and General Weygand, who carried the day in making peace with Hitler rather than fight on as a member of a newly born Franco-British Union.[46]

THE SOVIET VIEW OF FRIEND AND FOE AT THE TIME OF THE NAZI-SOVIET PACT

The Communist press uniformly inveighed against these approaches toward Western European unity. Especially noteworthy is a long article in the August, 1940, issue of *The Communist Inter-*

---

[45] "In Search of War Aims," *Communist International*, XVI, No. 11 (Nov. 1939), 1112.

[46] Winston S. Churchill, *Their Finest Hour* (Boston, 1949), pp. 205-15. The plan, originally conceived by the Frenchman, Jean Monnet, was presented to

national. As could be expected, the plans for a Franco-British Union were denounced as an attempt to create a European Empire for the conquest of the rest of Europe and for their joint exploitation of the colonial world. What is surprising is the following attack on Nazi Germany, with whom the Soviet Union was, at the time, an active partner: "The same idea of a 'New European Order' may be found in National Socialist newspapers. . . . In Germany, Schacht is working on a plan for a 'directed continental economy, an amalgamated European economy directed from one center, a planned economy for the whole of Europe.'" Both the Allied and Axis plans were dismissed as equally objectionable manifestations of "capitalist imperialism." In the eyes of the Allies, "England and France were to form the 'nucleus'; in Schacht's plan of Europe this was reserved to Germany and Italy." Even more astonishing is an attack on Japan with whom Soviet leaders were desperately trying to arrange a nonaggression pact (concluded only in April, 1941). In Asia, Japan's program for a "New Order" was but another symptom of the final stages of "aggressive capitalism." Nor did the United States escape criticism for its alleged imperialist designs, under the slogan of "Pan-America." Once each continent was organized by its respective master, then the struggle would be transferred to an intercontinental level, since "the European imperialists reject the idea of a 'Pan-America,' the American imperialists reject the idea of a 'Pan-Asia,' and the Asiatic imperialists likewise reject a 'Pan-America.'" "Indeed," the article concluded, "the system of small states is antiquated," but capitalism is incapable of forming stable supranational unions. "Only socialism can build a world of universal prosperity and peace based on the fraternal collaboration of peoples and nations." [47]

Soviet objections were not confined to schemes of vast proportions, aiming, supposedly, at the unification of entire continents and

---

Churchill by General de Gaulle. See Clarence Streit, "De Gaulle Urged Federal Union on Churchill in 1940," *Freedom & Union*, XIII, No. 7-8 (July-Aug., 1958), 14-16.

[47] J. Revai, "A 'Federated Europe,'" *Communist International*, XVII, No. 8 (Aug., 1940), 506-15. See also "May Day Manifesto of the Communist International," *ibid.*, XVII, No. 5 (May, 1940), 286; A. Meunier, "Who Betrayed the French People?" *ibid.*, XVII, No. 5 (May, 1940), 293-94; D. Manuil'skii, "Lenin vs. Social-Democratism," *ibid.*, XVII, No. 6 (June, 1940), 367. For a recent, comprehensive Soviet survey of supranational plans for Europe dating from the First World War to 1940, see V. B. Knaizhinskii, *Proval planov ob"edineniia "Evropy"* (Moscow, 1958).

NON-SOVIET SUPRANATIONAL PLANS 389

hemispheres. Equally bitter was the Soviet reaction toward attempts to create modest regional federations.

THE SOVIET VETO OF A FINNO-SWEDISH FEDERATION

Finland sought to protect itself against a renewed Soviet assault, following the Soviet-Finnish Peace of March, 1940, by inviting Sweden and Norway to form a joint defense pact. The Finns received a favorable response, but Moscow at once protested that such an alignment would be directed at the Soviet Union. The only sense in which a close military alliance of these three Scandinavian powers could "threaten" the Soviet Union lay in their increased strength to resist contemplated aggression by the Nazi-Soviet partnership. The proposed alliance was abandoned in the face of Soviet objections. On April 9, 1940, Germany invaded Norway. As only a small German force was involved, it is possible that the attack might not have been undertaken, had the Scandinavian military alliance been in force. In view of the renewed peril, Finland again turned to Sweden—this time with a proposal for political federation. By September, 1940, Finno-Swedish negotiations were under way to explore the problem of forming a federal government. Again Moscow protested against an alleged anti-Soviet "conspiracy," and Molotov threatened dire consequences if these designs were not abandoned. As a result, the plan was dropped, and Finland remained isolated until it was drawn into the Soviet-German war in June, 1941.[48] If Moscow had not interposed its objection, a Finno-Swedish federation would have benefited the USSR by keeping Finland neutral in the ensuing war.

SOVIET REACTION TO FEDERALIST PLANS IN EAST
CENTRAL EUROPE

During the Second World War the Soviet leadership also expressed strong opposition to forming regional groupings in East Central Europe. As early as November 11, 1940, the Polish and Czechoslovak governments in exile announced their intention of forming a confederation after the war, and a more concrete statement of this plan was signed in London on January 23, 1942. Just

[48] John H. Wuorinen, ed., *Finland and World War II, 1939–1944* (New York, 1948), pp. 88–91.

previously, the Greek and Yugoslav governments in exile had agreed, on January 15, 1942, to cooperate in forming a Balkan Union.[49]

Eduard Táborský, the political secretary to President Beneš of Czechoslovakia, recalls the aspirations embodied in these plans. The agreements were

intended to create the nuclei of two larger federations, one including also Austria and Hungary, the other one comprising also Bulgaria, Albania and possibly Turkey, while it was projected that Rumania would join either one of the two. Thus two regional federal blocs, one Central European and one Balkan, were to be created and to include all the countries of the broad belt between the Baltic and the Aegean, cooperating closely with one another, until they would be ready to merge into one big Eastern European Federal Union.[50]

Beyond that, Beneš himself asserted, "Our final aim must be the confederation of Europe as an element in some sort of world commonwealth." [51]

Moscow's hostility toward the Polish-Czechoslovak Confederation project of January 23, 1942, became evident within a week of its announcement, and on July 16, 1942, the Soviet envoy to the Allied governments in exile in London informed Czech Foreign Minister Masaryk that the Soviet Union would definitely veto any plan for a merger with Poland. Beneš then tried to obtain Soviet approval for the conclusion of a Polish-Czechoslovak mutual assistance pact, as a step in the same direction, but this too was firmly rejected in a Soviet message delivered on January 28, 1943.[52]

The Soviet press soon renewed its protests against all non-Soviet plans for the integration of European nations, "starting with the plan for the creation of a United States of Europe, Pan-Europe, and ending with the plan for the creation of a Europe divided into

[49] Documents reproduced in Feliks Gross, *Crossroads of Two Continents: A Democratic Federation of East-central Europe* (New York, 1945), pp. 102–7.
[50] Eduard Táborský, "A Polish-Czechoslovak Confederation: A Story of the First Soviet Veto," *Journal of Central European Affairs*, IX, No. 4 (Jan., 1950), 380.
[51] Eduard Beneš, "The Organization of Postwar Europe," *Foreign Affairs*, XX, No. 2 (Jan., 1942), 234.
[52] Táborský, "Polish-Czechoslovak," *Journal of Central European Affairs*, IX, No. 4 (Jan., 1950), 390–93; Jan Ciechanowski, *Defeat in Victory* (New York, 1947), pp. 93, 102–3; Piotr S. Wandycz, *Czechoslovak-Polish Confederation and the Great Powers, 1940–43* (Bloomington, Ind., 1956), pp. 71–99. The Wandycz study provides a comprehensive review of all the problems involved in the Polish-Czech project. See also Ladislav Feierabend, "Polish-Czechoslovak Negotiations in London During World War II," *Central European Federalist*, VI, No. 2 (Dec., 1958), 11–21.

NON-SOVIET SUPRANATIONAL PLANS 391

federations, confederations and regional blocs of states." In this regard the projected Polish-Czechoslovak Confederation came in for especial criticism.[53] Following the three-power Moscow Conference (United Kingdom, United States, and USSR) of October, 1943, *Izvestiia* took issue with the view being expressed in some Western circles "that the Declaration on Austria might be a forerunner to the formation of a Danubian Confederation." An *Izvestiia* editorial of November 18, 1943, wanted to know what phrases in the Declaration could possibly justify such an interpretation. For the small countries of Central Europe, "the restoration of their independence and sovereignty is one of the most important tasks of postwar reconstruction." The formation of any sort of supranational union, not under direct Soviet control, was automatically condemned as an anti-Soviet plot.

The Soviet point of view decisively rejects every sort of attempt to revive the policy of *cordon sanitaire* against the USSR, in whatever form it might be masked. It is only just to say that some of the projected federations recently coming from the West clearly emit the foul smell of this long bankrupt policy, hostile to the Soviet Union.

Here was the beginning of the theme, which was to reach a tremendous crescendo in postwar years, of protecting the sovereignty and independence of nations. Under the guise of defending itself from the supposed threat of a federation of non-Soviet nations, the Soviet Union sought to keep the nations of the non-Soviet world isolated from each other so as to render them more susceptible to Soviet domination. Wherever possible this Soviet control would be established through direct bilateral arrangements between Moscow and the country in question. It was evident that Moscow was operating simultaneously on two different levels. On the one hand, the *Izevestiia* editorial of November, 1943, protested that "it would be premature to consider, and thus artificially encourage, the creation of any sort of federation, or any sort of union of small states" because any agreement among the émigré governments in London could not be made "without the risk of violating the will of the people" who were living under German occupation.[54] On the other hand, Moscow had approached some of these same governments in

---

[53] "What is Behind the East European Federation Scheme?" *Information Bulletin, Embassy of the U.S.S.R.* (Washington, D.C.), No. 94 (Aug. 24, 1943), p. 6.
[54] "K voprosu o federatsiiakh 'malykh' gosudarstv v Evrope," *Izvestiia*, Nov. 18, 1943, p. 3. See also *The Memoirs of Cordell Hull* (New York, 1948), II, 1298–99.

exile as early as February, 1942, with an offer of a twenty-year treaty of alliance with the Soviet Union. Nothing came of the negotiations with Yugoslav and Polish émigrés, but a Soviet-Czechoslovak Treaty was actually signed in December, 1943, and it became the basis for the postwar Sovietization of Czechoslovakia.

SOVIET PARTICIPATION IN THE UNITED NATIONS

It was also during the war years that the Soviet Union agreed to become a charter member of the proposed United Nations organization, in keeping with its wartime collaboration with the Western Allies. But since the Soviet Union conceived of the UN as an exclusive, big-power club, in which the USSR would be one of the big powers, Moscow clearly anticipated that it could exercise its authority to prevent outside interference in Soviet affairs, while using the forums of the UN to extend Soviet influence into the non-Soviet world. The keystone of the UN, in Soviet eyes, is the unanimity principle of the great powers, which is embodied in the rules of the Security Council. The Soviet Union has therefore bitterly opposed all efforts of other states to get around the veto-locked Security Council as, for example, in the creation in 1947 of the so-called "Little Assembly," or in the adoption in 1950 of the "Uniting for Peace" resolution whereby the General Assembly declared itself competent to handle security questions originally thought to be the prerogative of the Security Council. Soviet opposition to endowing other UN organs with greater authority can be explained, in part, by the fact that in these other bodies the Soviet bloc, by itself, is relegated to a permanent numerical minority, whereas in the Security Council the Soviet Union can counter the moves of the majority with its own veto. But the basic Soviet objections to the UN go beyond this distaste for the mechanics of voting. The Soviet leaders did not conceive of the UN as a hopeful beginning of some future grand design, as an emergent world state capable of expressing a general consensus of the interests of the world community.

During Stalin's lifetime, Soviet participation was conspicuously absent from those community-building aspects of international life such as take place in the various UN specialized agencies and other international organizations. The Soviet Union belonged only to the most apolitical of these agencies: the Universal Postal Union, the International Telecommunication Union, and the World Meteorological Organization. The USSR was also an inactive member of the World Health Organization (WHO) until it withdrew early in 1949. Following Stalin's death a new flexibility in Soviet foreign policy was reflected in the Soviet decisions, in the spring of 1954, to accept membership in the International Labor Organization and the United Nations Educational, Scientific, and Cultural Organization. During 1955 the Soviet Union resumed its place in WHO and became a member of the International Bureau of Education and the Inter-Parliamentary Union. In April, 1957, the Kremlin deposited its ratification of the Statute of the International Atomic Energy Agency, which was established to develop the peaceful uses of atomic power. The post-Stalinist shift toward wider participation in such bodies has demonstrated a more imaginative approach toward the non-Soviet world. Instead of an implacable Stalinist hostility toward all countries not under Soviet control, with the consequent isolation of the Soviet bloc from most of the UN agencies, there has been a decided effort to champion the "neutralist" Afro-Asian cause against the NATO powers, as well as the perennial effort to separate the NATO powers from each other, so that the latter now find themselves under the shadow of a potential Soviet-Afro-Asian majority. By joining the ideological battle on new fields of international organization, Moscow has discovered additional weapons for achieving its old aim of driving wedges between non-Soviet member nations.

The only realm in which the Soviet UN delegates have consistently pressed for an extension of UN authority is within those agencies dealing with the administration of colonial and trusteeship areas. Again, the transparent motive in this instance was not to endow the UN with superstate powers, but to use the UN agencies to exploit the cry of the dependent nations for self-determination, assume the mantle of leadership of the anti-Western nationalist movements in Asia and Africa, and thus exacerbate strife and hasten disintegration within the non-Soviet world.[55] The objective of this

[55] Various aspects of Soviet policy toward the United Nations are treated by: John N. Hazard, "The Soviet Union and the United Nations," *Yale Law Journal*, LV, No. 5 (Aug., 1946), 1016–35; Philip E. Mosely, "Soviet Policy in the United Nations," *Proceedings of the Academy of Political Science*, XXII, No. 2 (Jan., 1947), 28–37; L. B. Schapiro, "Soviet Participation in International

disintegration is a future reintegration of the nations of the world, not in a predominantly non-Soviet league, such as the UN, but in a Soviet world state.

From the first days of the UN's existence the Soviet leaders have not concealed their hostility toward all proposals aiming to remodel the UN along supranational lines. "The United Nations Organization has not yet really begun to function," objected a Soviet publication in December, 1945, "but certain impatient politicians are already busying themselves with plans for its radical reconstruction." This protest was directed against those who held that the UN could effectively guarantee peace "only if it is converted into something in the nature of a 'world federation' in which the status of the present independent countries would be roughly equivalent to that of the individual states of the U.S.A." But these spokesmen in the non-Soviet world who called for "a 'world state' are least of all concerned to abolish the social and national oppression existing in the world today. The value of these widely boasted remedies is therefore nil." [56] Vyshinsky's repeated defense of the veto power

---

Institutions," in George W. Keeton and Georg Schwarzenberger, eds., *The Year Book of World Affairs, 1949* (London, 1949), pp. 205-40; C. Dale Fuller, "Soviet Policy in the United Nations," *The Annals,* CCLXIII (May, 1949), 141-51; P. D. Morozov, "Soviet Policy Towards Revision," *ibid.,* CCXCVI (Nov., 1954), 147-50; Philip Martin, "Soviet Russia and the ILO," *New Leader,* July 12, 1954, pp. 13-14; Philip Martin, "Who Will Win in the ILO?" *ibid.,* Jan. 24, 1955, pp. 22-23; Alvin Z. Rubinstein, "The U.S.S.R. and the I.L.O.," *Russian Review,* XIV, No. 1 (Jan., 1955), 11-18; Alexander W. Rudzinski, "The Influence of the United Nations on Soviet Policy," *International Organization,* V, No. 2 (May, 1951), 282-99; Rupert Emerson and Inis L. Claude, Jr., "The Soviet Union and the United Nations, an Essay in Interpretation," *ibid.,* VI, No. 1 (Feb., 1952), 1-26; John A. Armstrong, "The Soviet Attitude Toward Unesco," *ibid.,* VIII, No. 2 (May, 1954), 217-33; Alvin Z. Rubinstein, "Soviet Policy Toward Under-developed Areas in the Economic and Social Council," *ibid.,* IX, No. 2 (May, 1955), 232-43; "The Soviet United Nations Association," *International Affairs* (Moscow), No. 6 (June, 1956), pp. 157-60; Robert Loring Allen, "United Nations Technical Assistance: Soviet and East European Participation," *International Organization,* XI, No. 4 (Autumn, 1957), 615-34; V. Nesterov and B. Topornin, "Against Revision of the U.N. Charter," *International Affairs* (Moscow), No. 1 (Jan., 1958), pp. 114-15; Harold Karan Jacobson, "The Soviet Union, the UN and World Trade," *Western Political Quarterly,* XI, No. 3 (Sept., 1958), 673-88; Alvin Z. Rubinstein, "Soviet Policy in ECAFE: A Case Study of Soviet Behavior in International Economic Organization," *International Organization,* XII, No. 4 (Autumn, 1958), 459-72; Alexander Dallin, *The Soviet View of the United Nations* (MIT Center for International Studies, Cambridge, Mass., 1959); Elliot R. Goodman, "The Cry of National Liberation: Recent Soviet Attitudes Toward National Self-Determination," *International Organization,* XIV, No. 1 (Winter, 1960), 92-106.

[56] "A Cardinal Condition of Lasting Peace," *New Times,* No. 14 (Dec. 15, 1945), p. 1.

NON-SOVIET SUPRANATIONAL PLANS

was sometimes made in the name of protecting the UN from evolving toward a world state. For example, on November 21, 1947, he recalled a declaration by former Secretary of State Edward R. Stettinius that "the United Nations is neither a federal union nor a world state and that voting procedures among its sovereign member nations cannot necessarily be judged on the same basis as voting procedures in a state legislature or in the Congress." Efforts of the United States to restrict what it considered the abusive use of the veto caused Vyshinsky to charge that "this view is now being changed. The U.S. representatives are now actually doing all they can to repudiate the obligations assumed by the United States of America two or three years ago in the matter of the unanimity rule." [57]

THE ATOMIC BOMB, WESTERN FEDERALISM, AND SOVIET DERISION

Although no American spokesman in the UN has ever suggested the abolition of the veto or the transformation of the UN into a world state, such demands have been made with increasing frequency from men of high station in the non-Soviet world. The principal cause of these dramatic appeals, it would seem, came from the invention of the atomic bomb and the prospect of the total annihilation of mankind in a new atomic holocaust. In a debate in the House of Commons on November 22, 1945, Prime Minister Clement Attlee said that he conceived of the United Nations as "an instrument which, if all nations resolved to use it, can establish a rule of law and prevent war." Speaking for the opposition, Anthony Eden concurred. The discovery of atomic energy, he held, "has placed us several laps ahead of our international political development, and unless we can catch up politically to the point we have reached in science, and thus command the power which at present threatens

[57] *United Nations, Official Records of the Second Session of the General Assembly, Plenary Meetings*, Nov. 21, 1947, II, 1244–45. In a similar vein, Bulganin rejected President Eisenhower's proposal of January 12, 1958, which urged that some restrictions be imposed on the use of the veto in the UN Security Council: "The UN is not some kind of world government which could enact laws and adopt decisions that would be binding on all states. . . . Is it possible to forget that states which are members of the UN are sovereign and independent states and cannot permit themselves to be saddled with decisions which are incompatible with their sovereignty?" ("Premier Bulganin to the President," Feb. 1, 1958, *Department of State Bulletin*, XXXVIII, No. 976 [March 10, 1958], 378.)

us, we are all going to be blown to smithereens." The traditional concept of national sovereignty is now outmoded, yet national sentiment is as strong as ever. How, Eden asked, can this contradiction be resolved?

> I have thought much of this business of atomic energy . . . and for the life of me I have been unable to see—and I am still unable to see—any final solution that will make the world safe from atomic power other than that we all abate our present ideas of sovereignty. We have got somehow to take the sting out of nationalism.[58]

The following day Foreign Minister Ernest Bevin vowed: "I am willing to sit with anybody of any party of any nation to try to devise a franchise or a constitution for a world assembly of limited objective, the objective of peace." Such a world assembly would substitute for conventional international law a system of world law, enforced by a world police, and interpreted by a world judiciary.[59]

The Soviet reaction was, as usual, one of derision. E. A. Korovin commented, in an essay on international law:

> The dreams of Eden and Bevin are quite removed from reality; they bring to mind the talk at the end of the First World War about "superimperialism" and "superstate," about the gradual development of the League of Nations into a "world parliament" and so on—these were the arguments with which journalists and publicists, predominantly of the social reformist type, used to console both themselves and others. The chief fault of these theories lies in their authors' inability, either willingly or unwillingly, to understand the simple truth that the roots of aggressive nationalism which the "world parliament" would supposedly check, lie in the very nature of capitalist society.

These noble sentiments were, in reality, a cynical cover for a capitalist conspiracy. "It is scarcely possible that the contemporary gravediggers of sovereignty are so naive as to believe in earnest that peace and harmony on earth can be obtained by the creation of a world parliament." Is it not true, Korovin queried, that "at the bottom of these political fantasies lies an extremely shrewd calculation—in the realm of political arithmetic and voting games?" With the prevailing minority position of the Soviet bloc in the UN in mind, he concluded that "the eager troubadours of a world parliament are inspired by the thought of the voting majority in this new

---

[58] "Speech of Prime Minister Attlee in House of Commons"; "Speech of Anthony Eden," New York *Times*, Nov. 23, 1945.
[59] "Speech by Foreign Secretary Ernest Bevin," *ibid.*, Nov. 24, 1945.

NON-SOVIET SUPRANATIONAL PLANS

organ through which they can dictate their will to the rest of mankind." [60]

A large proportion of the scientists who developed the atomic bomb have looked upon their handiwork with a deeply troubled conscience. The only sure way of preventing its renewed use in wars between nation-states, they have reasoned, was to create a supranational body capable of preventing such wars. Among these scientists, the late Albert Einstein succeeded in developing a limited correspondence with some of his scientific counterparts in the Soviet Union, in an effort to clarify the nature of this demand. In an open letter of September 22, 1947, to the UN General Assembly, Einstein expressed his fears about the continuation of the armaments race, and held that "there is no compromise possible between preparation for war on the one hand, and preparation of a world society based on law and order on the other." The world must choose between the two. If every citizen could be made to realize that "the only guarantee for security and peace in this atomic age is the constant development of a supranational government, then he will do everything in his power to strengthen the United Nations." Einstein did not conceive of such a body as hostile to Soviet interests, and said hopefully: "It is by no means certain that the U.S.S.R.—which is often represented as the main antagonist to the idea of world government—would maintain its opposition if an equitable offer providing for real security were made." In the event that the Soviet Union could not be persuaded to join, the other nations would have to proceed on their own, but "only after all efforts have been made in utmost sincerity to obtain the cooperation of Russia and her allies." Even then, Einstein emphasized, "such a partial world government should make it clear from the beginning that its door remains wide open to any non-member, particularly Russia—for participation on the basis of complete equality." [61]

A response was soon forthcoming from four distinguished Soviet scientists; the late Sergei Vavilov, A. N. Frumkin, A. F. Joffe, and N. N. Semënov. "The advocates of a 'world government,'" they noted, "make wide use of the seemingly radical argument that in this atomic age state sovereignty is a relic of the past.... It would be hard to imagine an allegation that is farther from the truth." The

[60] E. A. Korovin, *Mezhdunarodnoe pravo na sovremennom etape* (Moscow, 1946), pp. 7–8.
[61] Albert Einstein, *Out of My Later Years* (New York, 1950), pp. 157-59.

idea of a "super-state" is not a product of the atomic age, but is a "reflection of the fact that the capitalist monopolies, which dominate the major industrial countries, find their own national boundaries too narrow." The demand for a world state is nothing but an expression of their search for world-wide markets, sources of raw materials and spheres of investment. The Soviet Union represents a radical break with the world capitalist system, "and now the proponents of a 'world super-state' are asking us voluntarily to surrender this independence for the sake of a 'world government' which is nothing but a flamboyant signboard for the world supremacy of capitalist monopoly. It is obviously preposterous to ask of us anything like that."

Einstein's solicitous attitude toward giving the Soviet Union every opportunity to join this world government was also firmly rebuffed. Essentially Einstein's proposal "differs very little from the suggestion of frank advocates of American imperialism, however remote Dr. Einstein may be from them in reality." All of these schemes were designed to wreck the UN and form a new organization directed against the Soviet Union. "We believe that Dr. Einstein has entered a false and dangerous path; he is choosing the mirage of a 'world state' in a world where different social, political and economic systems exist." [62]

In a letter of reply, Einstein pointed out what appeared to him as an inconsistency: "You are such passionate opponents of anarchy in the economic sphere, and yet equally passionate advocates of anarchy, e.g., unlimited sovereignty, in the sphere of international politics." He also expressed deep disappointment that the Soviet scientists had put so much emphasis upon economic questions, observing that "the controversies and differences of opinion which we have touched upon in our strange exchange of letters are insignificant pettiness compared to the danger in which we all find ourselves." He advocated world government solely because "there is no possible other way of eliminating the most terrible danger in which man has ever found himself. The objective of avoiding total destruction must have priority over any other objective." [63] This letter went unanswered, and here the correspondence ended.

The threat of atomic annihilation has not moved the Soviet leaders to visualize a compromise formula for a world state. There

[62] Quoted in *ibid.*, pp. 162–63, 166–67.   [63] *Ibid.*, pp. 171, 175.

NON-SOVIET SUPRANATIONAL PLANS

will either be a Soviet world state, or there will be no world state. To Bertrand Russell's cry, "We must create a world state or perish," *Pravda* replied: "Russell is shouting about the inevitable end of the world unless nations give up their national sovereignty and replace it by a world state headed by the U.S.A. and Britain." Similarly, *Pravda* distorted the views of Arnold Toynbee: "Scaring the weak-nerved with the horrors of atomic war and elaborating, for their benefit, the prospects of annihilation of the human race, Toynbee proposes that nations should voluntarily surrender to Anglo-American domination 'to avoid catastrophe.' " [64]

THE DEBATE OVER INTERNATIONAL CONTROL OF
ATOMIC ENERGY

The Soviet leaders were not impressed with the urgency of creating a supranational body, together with non-Soviet states, for the purpose of mastering the threat of atomic power. Consequently, Soviet spokesmen flailed and ridiculed the American proposal for the international control of atomic energy that had within it the seeds of a supranational organization.

The basic American position, set forth in the Acheson-Lilienthal Report of March, 1946, held that the only way to eliminate the dangerous uses of atomic energy among nations was to remove its development from national hands and place it under the auspices of an international body capable of controlling and supervising the exploitation of atomic energy within each nation. "National rivalries in the development of atomic energy readily convertible to destructive purposes are the heart of the difficulty." [65] It would be fatal to endow national governments with the primary responsibility for the development of atomic energy, supplemented only by an international system of inspection. The problems facing an international inspectorate would be insurmountable. The inspectors would be unable to confine their activity to a relatively few, clearly designated atomic enterprises, as would be the case if they were members of a single international authority that would know of every atomic installation because it controlled and authorized every

[64] P. Fedoseev, "Ideologii imperializma—vragi mira i progressa," *Pravda*, Sept. 19, 1950, p. 3.
[65] *A Report on the International Control of Atomic Energy*, Dept. of State Pub. 2498 (Washington, D.C., 1946), p. 5.

stage of atomic development throughout the world. In order to approximate such inspection, should the basic atomic energy processes be left to each nation, it would be necessary to recruit an impossibly large inspectorate of great scientific competence to play hide-and-seek with national governments for possible clandestine atomic operations. In addition, these inspectors would be unqualified to detect all of the processes related to atomic energy unless they were supplied with the latest technical information by their own international agency, which would be aware of all atomic developments throughout the world. The development of atomic energy must therefore be entrusted to a single world atomic authority that would control all aspects of atomic energy literally from the ground up.

These conclusions of the Acheson-Lilienthal Report were incorporated in the American plan for the international control of atomic energy, first presented to the UN by Bernard Baruch on June 14, 1946. Baruch, on his own initiative, added the condition that the operation of this international agency must not be subject to the veto power of any state, so that punishment for violation of its rules could not be avoided or obstructed. These proposals were substantially adopted as the majority plan of the UN Atomic Energy Commission, later approved by the UN General Assembly, with the Soviet minority dissenting.

Because of the prolonged, vitriolic attack which this plan drew from Soviet spokesmen, it is of interest to know the precise scope of activity proposed for the international Atomic Development Authority. The powers of the control agency were neatly summarized by Frederick Osborn, who succeeded Baruch as the chief American negotiator in matters of atomic energy:

These powers of control would include: (a) ownership by the agency of source material and all unclear fuel; (b) ownership, management, and operation by the agency of all dangerous facilities, that is, facilities which use or produce quantities of nuclear fuel sufficient for bombs; (c) licensing by the agency of all non-dangerous facilities which would be operated by nations; (d) inspection by the agency to prevent or detect clandestine activities. The agency's rights of inspection must be so broad as to give it access to any part of a nation's territory, subject, of course, to appropriate rights of appeal and the proper judicial procedures. (e) The agency would carry on, in its facilities and with its own personnel, research on all phases of atomic energy in order that it

NON-SOVIET SUPRANATIONAL PLANS

might keep abreast of new developments. Nations would be free to carry on research, provided, however, dangerous quantities of material were not required and subject always to appropriate supervision by the agency from which nations would get the small quantity of nuclear fuel required for their research activities.[66]

The American delegates never concealed the fact that this plan stood in contradiction to the traditional concept of national sovereignty. In the words of Ambassador Warren Austin, "no effective solution to this problem can be found without some delegation of sovereignty." The nations backing the majority proposal recognized that "the need for security against atomic warfare cannot be met without deputizing an international agency of control to make decisions in this matter. . . . If national sovereignty is put up as a barrier against international control it is a foregone conclusion that no effective control can be devised." [67]

Gromyko retorted for the Soviet Union that these proposals were "thoroughly vicious and unacceptable," posing an intolerable threat to the "internal affairs and internal life of states." [68] This plan, Vyshinsky explained, "speaks with great eloquence of the powerful appetites of the American monopolists striving, under cover of the United Nations and all kinds of 'international agencies,' for actual domination not only over all world supplies of atomic energy, but also over the economic development of every country." It is, therefore, "not a question of relinquishing a certain part of a nation's sovereignty . . . but of totally liquidating the state sovereignty, as such, of all other states." [69] Specifically, this was an atomic wedge to pry into the vital affairs of other countries, undermine their authority and lay the basis for an American-controlled world state. "The advocates of a 'world state' attempt with all their might to provide a 'theoretical' basis for the well-known Baruch Plan for the

---

[66] *International Control of Atomic Energy: Policy at the Crossroads*, Dept. of State Pub. 3161 (Washington, D.C., 1948), p. 146. For a summary of Osborn's experience with the Soviet delegates on the question of atomic energy, see Fredrick Osborn, "Negotiating on Atomic Energy, 1946-1947," in Raymond Dennett and Joseph E. Johnson, eds., *Negotiating with the Russians* (Boston, 1951), pp. 209-36.

[67] Warren Austin, Speech of Dec. 8, 1947; quoted in *Atomic Energy*, Dept. of State Pub. 3161, p. 133.

[68] Andrei Gromyko, Speech of March 5, 1947; quoted in *ibid.*, p. 132. See also *ibid.*, pp. 78-83.

[69] "O zapreshchenii atomnogo oruzhiia i o mezhdunarodnom kontrole; rech' A. Ia. Vyshinskogo v spetsial'nom politicheskom komitete, 10 noiabria 1949 goda," *Pravda*, Nov. 17, 1949, p. 4.

control of atomic energy," a Soviet pamphleteer asserted. This American proposal, advanced "as an 'international plan' defending the supposed 'universal interests of mankind' against the narrow interests of the separate states," is a means of hiding the "real aims of American world domination." The fact that there was "excessive praise of the Baruch Plan from the partisans of a 'world state'" showed conclusively that the plan was designed as an unlimited interventionist policy, "including subversive, diversionary, and spying activities practiced by the American imperialists and ther hirelings." [70]

What basis in fact is there for the Soviet assertion that the Baruch Plan would have totally undermined the sovereignty of the Soviet Union and have been but a short step to the creation of an American-dominated world state? Compared to the usual proposals made by national governments in the arena of international diplomacy, it must be conceded that the Baruch Plan frankly acknowledged the need for world order in the atomic age. It was an imaginative gesture in the direction of modifying the archaic structure of the international community, which fosters disorder by sanctioning the sovereign egotism of its members. It was a step toward world order, but it was a half-step that fell between two stools, for the Baruch Plan did not envisage the creation of a world state. On the one hand, Baruch recognized that "just outlawing the atomic bomb will not get us anywhere. . . . We must outlaw war itself." On the other hand, he believed "that this can be done by placing in the constitution of each country the pledge that it will not go to war. A system of inspection of the forces and arms allowed each country can be devised that will keep countries from going to war." [71]

National rivalries in the realm of atomic energy were to be eliminated by entrusting the development of atomic resources to a single world authority, while national rivalries in the other warmaking capacities of states were to be eliminated by relying upon the pledged word of each state to keep its arms at an agreed level and not to use them in war. This would put an intolerable strain on the good faith of each nation-state in a world community rife with distrust. Even within each nation-state, where the level of shared values is considerably higher, the pledged word of the individual

[70] Polents, "*Vsemirnoe gosudarstvo*," pp. 14–15.
[71] Letter from B. M. Baruch to Representative John M. Vorys, Aug. 2, 1946; quoted in *Common Cause*, III, No. 7 (Feb., 1950), 358.

NON-SOVIET SUPRANATIONAL PLANS

citizen is not relied upon to maintain an orderly way of life. Individual citizens or groups of citizens within each state are constrained from making war on each other by the various organs of state power, which have a monopoly on the weapons of mass coercion and provide machinery for the peaceful adjudication of disputes. The Baruch Plan excluded a comparable transfer of the weapons of coercion from nation-states to a world state endowed with the necessary mechanisms of government to attempt the peaceful settlement of disputes.

Baruch's hope of arriving at agreed levels for the comprehensive reduction of national armaments was equally illusory. This would mean that all states could agree upon fixing their ratio of military power in relation to all other states. This, in turn, presupposed agreement upon the reduction of each individual item in the national armory and the exact weight to be given to the innumerable and ever-changing elements that comprise the national military potential of each state. Past experience has shown that this is an impossible task: naval powers are prone to accept the reduction of land forces, land powers are willing to reduce the strength of naval forces, and all states evaluate differently the factors in their national economy which can be considered "war potential" according to the endowments of their natural resources and their degree of economic development. There is little likelihood that a comprehensive reduction of arms among sovereign nation-states can ever be achieved. The term "disarmament" is a misnomer if it refers to the problem of *reduction* of armaments among sovereign nations. If "disarmament" refers to the process of transferring the possession of arms from several state units to a newly created supranational state (leaving the constituent units with sufficient arms for internal policing, of course), then disarmament is a meaningful idea. The creation of larger political units with common armed forces has repeatedly occurred in many different ways, and it is entirely conceivable that it may occur in the future.

Because the "disarmament" of the Baruch Plan left the powers of the individual nation-states substantially intact, these separate states could still initiate wars with other weapons, seize the atomic installations of the international atomic authority located within their territories, and promptly begin the manufacture of atomic weapons for war. Chester Barnard, a member of the committee that wrote the original Acheson-Lilienthal Report, frankly acknowledged that the Baruch Plan was not designed to prevent war, but only to prevent the use of atomic weapons in the initial phase of a war. This plan "does not prohibit the use of atomic bombs once war breaks out." Barnard summarized the basic thinking behind the Baruch Plan in these unpretentious terms: "The difference between having no international agreement and having one, if you assume that the next war will involve the use of atomic bombs, is solely a difference in the speed with which we attempt to make ourselves less vulnerable." [72]

The hope that there would be a period of grace before atomic bombs began to fall was based on the assumption that the United States had a monopoly on the manufacture of atomic weapons. This would supposedly give the United States an opportunity to disperse the large concentrations of its population during the time that enemy states were learning how to make the atomic bomb. This modest benefit, as envisaged by the Baruch Plan, is now completely gone. With all major states possessing the knowledge of nuclear warfare, a "safe" nuclear stockpile seized from the international authority by any of these states could be converted into lethal weapons overnight. Moreover, the enormously increased destructive power of bigger and "better" nuclear weapons, and the as yet undetermined effects of radioactive fall-out from the explosion of a large number of nuclear bombs, raises the question of whether there will be any place to hide, even if population dispersals should be undertaken in peacetime. It would seem that any international plan for the control of nuclear energy that permitted the use of nuclear weapons at any stage of war is really no plan at all.

The Baruch proposal for the elimination of the veto in the punishment of states breaking the rules of the world atomic authority was equally faulty—again for the stubborn reason that the Baruch Plan did not seek to create a world state. Modification of the voting procedures in the world atomic authority could not alter the hidden veto of each sovereign state to take whatever action it wished in violation of the agreed rules of an atomic control treaty. If a certain state were found guilty of preparing for nuclear warfare, what body would punish it? Neither the world atomic authority nor the

[72] Chester I. Barnard, "Atomic Energy Control," *Dartmouth Alumni Magazine*, XL, No. 5 (Feb., 1948), 14.

NON-SOVIET SUPRANATIONAL PLANS   405

Security Council would have any means of its own to enforce punishment. A violation by any state could only be punished by the armed coercion of other states, namely by war. This type of enforcement action is radically different from the police action of a world state enforcing a rule of law upon individuals guilty of specific violations, as this would not involve the coercion of one segment of humanity, of guilty and innocent alike, by another collective body in the mass slaughter of war. Again Barnard frankly admitted that "the question of veto is irrelevant." When the veto question was first raised, "Mr. Lilienthal and I personally begged Mr. Baruch not to introduce the veto problem in connection with his presentation of the plan." Barnard told Baruch that "all you are doing is creating a blind-alley which will give the Russians their opportunity to dance up and down indefinitely." [73]

And dance the Russians have. Soviet spokesmen repeatedly played upon the veto provision of the Baruch Plan to discredit the whole scheme. "What are we doing here?" Vyshinsky demanded, in reply to the proposals for a veto-free international control organ, capable of taking punitive action. "Is this a world government? This is an assembly of sovereign states in which the will, interests, desires and views of each must be respected." [74] At the same time, Soviet terminology has sought to accommodate the clamor for a world atomic authority by conceding that a "strict international control is necessary" (the Soviet stock phrase first used by Stalin on October 23, 1946).[75] These protestations served to belittle the fact that the Soviet Union never at any time accepted the control provisions at the heart of the Baruch Plan which, at least, bordered upon the creation of a supranational institution: namely, the ownership and managerial control by the world atomic authority of nuclear facilities in all states. Soviet rejection of these provisions was so adamant and so persistent that a hopeless stalemate ensued. Finally in June, 1954, the United States consented to back a Franco-British compromise plan that omitted the international ownership and operational features. The Soviet Union, in turn, made a number of concessions on related issues, including the nature of the international inspec-

[73] *Ibid.*, pp. 35–36.
[74] *United Nations General Assembly, Ninth Session, Official Records, First Committee*, 692d Meeting, Oct. 18, 1954, p. 107. Vyshinsky again buttressed his position by quoting the Stettinius statement cited on p. 395 above.
[75] *Atomic Energy*, Dept. of State Pub. 3161, p. 79.

torate. But control plans confined to inspection lose sight of the unanimous conclusion of the original Acheson-Lilienthal Report "that international agreements to foreswear the military use of atomic weapons cannot be enforced solely by a system of inspection—that they cannot be enforced in a system which leaves the development of essentially dangerous activities in the field of atomic energy in national hands and subject to national rivalry." [76] This was written at a time when only the United States had a small atomic stockpile, which, it was assumed, would be turned over to the world atomic authority in good faith. In the intervening years enormous stockpiles of atomic material and finished nuclear weapons have been accumulating in a number of states, so that the only "foolproof" inspection system once possible is now impossible. A reliable inspection system might have been feasible if the inspectorate were part of a world atomic authority that knew of the precise location of every nuclear activity throughout the world because of its ownership and managerial functions. Today, even if such world atomic authority were set up, there would be no way of locating every last one of the nuclear weapons already manufactured, unless the inspectors were led to their hiding places by the authorities within each state. That all states would presently trust all other states to do this seems most unlikely. Moreover, for all its talk about broadening the powers of the inspectorate, would the Soviet Union grant these international agents unlimited access to its slave labor camps, which might serve as excellent storage depots for nuclear bombs? In the words of Eugene Rabinowitch, an editor of the *Bulletin of the Atomic Scientists*, these facts lead to "the sad recognition that effectively controlled atomic disarmament has ceased to be possible and that all attempts to find a compromise solution leading to such disarmament are therefore bound to remain futile." [77]

This gloomy conclusion about the attempted negotiation between the Soviet and non-Soviet worlds on the effective international control of atomic energy is but another case history documenting the schism in the world community. Here was a concrete effort to reach a compromise solution on a matter posing a mortal threat to all mankind. The Western proposals involved certain innovations of a mildly supranational character, but they did not com-

[76] *Atomic Energy*, Dept. of State Pub. 2498, p. 39.
[77] Eugene Rabinowitch, "The Danger of Nuclear Weapons," *New Leader*, Jan. 10, 1955, p. 6.

prise a demand for the creation of a world state. Had they received a sympathetic Soviet hearing, however, they might have served as a beginning for the future growth of a stable world order. Moscow is interested in a world order, that of a Soviet world state, but not in a compromise world order, regardless of its nature or of the quarter from which it is advanced.

THE SOVIET ANTICOSMOPOLITAN CAMPAIGN

The ideological setting for the categorical Soviet rejection of postwar proposals of a supranational character originating in the non-Soviet world is to be found in the heavy-handed campaign against "cosmopolitanism." *Pravda* explained to its readers that the word "cosmopolitan" comes from the Greek and means "citizen of the world." "Cosmopolitanism is the gospel of the so-called 'world citizenship,' the abandonment of allegiance to any nation whatsoever, the liquidation of the national traditions and the culture of nations under the screen of creating a 'world' culture." Its real purpose was to serve as "an ideological cover for the policy of the bourgeoisie aimed at the seizure of alien territories and new colonies and markets." The capitalists "recognize only the interest of their moneybags; for their sake they shamelessly sell out and betray national interests," disregard the patriotic feeling of the "popular masses," and trample on the independence of nations for the further exploitation of the toilers. This led to the conclusion that "cosmopolitanism is the reverse side of bourgeois nationalism." [78] The anticosmopolitan campaign, in effect, reduced the struggle between two concepts of a world society to the struggle between two types of nationalism. It cast all ideas and all phenomena in terms of national symbols. We have already noted, in our examination of Soviet Russian nationalism, how the fight against "cosmopolitanism" was associated with a strident, chauvinistic assertion of Russian nationalism and a clever manipulation of the concept of national sovereignty. But as we have also noted, Soviet Russian nationalism is a universal nationalism, a nationalism aiming to encompass the universe. This universal nationalism, which Moscow calls "proletarian internationalism," represents the Soviet concept of a world society.

[78] Iu. Pavlov, "Kosmopolitizm—ideologicheskoe oruzhie amerikanskoi reaktsii," *Pravda*, April 7, 1949, p. 2.

In contrast to this, every non-Soviet proposal for the abatement of nationalism and the creation of supranational institutions is dismissed by Soviet theorists as the artful disguise of "bourgeois nationalists" seeking to intensify national conflicts and national oppression. Here is another curious example of Soviet camouflage and projection. The universal aims of Soviet policy are largely camouflaged in national symbols, as in the glorification of the Russian nation and the "defense" of national sovereignty. On the other hand, Soviet-style motives of national aggrandizement are attributed to all non-Soviet schemes for the creation of a universal order.

CHARACTERIZATION OF AMERICAN-SPONSORED SUPRANATIONAL PROJECTS

Since the United States is the most powerful non-Soviet state, it has been singled out as the chief advocate of a "cosmopolitan" integration of the world. "The preaching of cosmopolitanism and the idea of establishing a 'world state,'" *Izvestiia* has declared, "only conceal brutal bourgeois nationalism and the predatory aims of American imperialism." [79] This theme was first prominently sounded at the founding Cominform Conference in September, 1947, by Andrei Zhdanov, who likewise sparked the anticosmopolitan campaign. "The idea of world government," he said, "has been taken up by bourgeois intellectual cranks and pacifists," and is being used to weaken the defenses of all nations "against the encroachments of American imperialism." World government was "a slogan especially directed against the Soviet Union." [80] In the Soviet view,

the American imperialists consider that a "world commonwealth of nations" might be achieved only under the supremacy of the U.S.A. Following the model of the Hitlerite racists, the American imperialists are exalting the Anglo-Saxons as a "superior race" and referring to other peoples contemptuously. They extol the so-called "American way of life," with its lynch-laws, Ku Klux Klan, and cruel terrorism against progressive leaders, as the supreme model of "democracy," in the endeavors to impose it on other countries.[81]

Moscow pointed to scattered statements on the desirability of a world federation by former President Truman as evidence of the

[79] E. Dunaeva, "Kosmopolitizm na sluzhbe imperialisticheskoi reaktsii," *Izvestiia*, April 18, 1950, p. 3.
[80] A. Zhdanov, "O mezhdunarodnom polozhenii," Sept., 1947, in *Informatsionnoe soveshchanie*, p. 34.
[81] Dunaeva, "Kosmopolitizm na sluzhbe," *Izvestiia*, April 18, 1950, p. 3.

desire to create an American dictatorship of the world. For example, in June, 1945, Truman told a Kansas City audience that some day "it will be just as easy for nations to get along in a republic of the world as it is for you to get along in the Republic of the United States." [82] The Soviet press pounced upon this as a piece of "cosmopolitan trickery and political falsification" hiding American intentions of world conquest.[83] Moscow held that Truman was by no means the first American President to harbor this design, which was always advanced in the name of world peace.

To the theories of a "world state," used as weapons by the American expansionists, there have always been joined false phrases of the bourgeoisie in favor of peace and cooperation among peoples. The combination of hypocritical "pacifist" phrases with cosmopolitan ideas was long ago practiced by the U.S. President Woodrow Wilson. An organization of U.S. cosmopolitans, formed during the First World War by such reactionary die-hards as another American, President Taft, even considered it essential to appropriate for itself the camouflage appellation of "The League to Enforce Peace." [84]

A number of prominent American officials, such as Supreme Court Justice William O. Douglas, Governor Harold Stassen, Senator Hubert H. Humphrey, and Ambassador Philip C. Jessup, have all come under attack for having, at one time or another, expressed a positive attitude toward the idea of world government. Despite the considerable differences in their views, they have all been indiscriminately lumped together as "homeless cosmopolitans."

Perhaps the most interesting polemic has been aimed at Jessup, who, in his capacity as a professor of international law, has suggested various approaches toward the strengthening of the international community and the development of enforceable world law. Jessup

---

[82] "The President's Speeches at Kansas City," *New York Herald Tribune*, June 29, 1945. In an interview Truman revealed that he had carried in his wallet for some fifty years Tennyson's verse about the "Parliament of Man, the Federation of the World," and added: "That's what I'm working for. I guess that's what I've been really working for ever since I first put that poetry in my pocket." (John Hersey, "Profiles: Mr. President," *The New Yorker*, XXVII, No. 8 [April 7, 1951], 49–50.) Truman affirmed this in a public address: "I am fully convinced that if we keep working at it the United Nations will become what it is intended to be—the parliament of man and the federation of the world. That's what we are looking forward to." ("Text of President's Address Presenting Stevenson to Convention," *New York Times*, July 26, 1952.)

[83] E. A. Korovin, "Za sovetskuiu patrioticheskuiu nauku prava," *Sovetskoe gosudarstvo i pravo*, No. 7 (July, 1949), p. 7.

[84] E. Cherniak, "Amerikanskie kosmopolity-podzhigateli voiny," *Novyi mir*, No. 10 (Oct., 1950), p. 268.

acknowledged that "sovereignty has been the chief obstacle in the way of the elimination of war. . . . It may be said that at this present stage the immediate dangers are so great that we must take the risk of too much rather than too little government on the international scale." [85] Nevertheless, he warned against the expectation of precipitous progress in this direction, and proposed that the present system of international law be revised gradually in two fundamental respects. First, "international law, like national law, must be directly applicable to the individual." Second, breaches of international law by any one state should become the concern of the whole international community, "in which the community as such brings its combined power to bear on the violator," thus pointing the way toward the "possibility of substituting some kind of joint sovereignty, the supremacy of the common will, for the old single-state sovereignty." [86]

The Soviet legal theoretician D. B. Levin stigmatized these proposals as "clearly absurd and spurious concepts." The suggestion that the individual should be recognized as a subject of international law was advanced "not to protect the rights and freedoms of individuals, but to overthrow national sovereignty, to legalize interference by American and other imperialists in the internal affairs of states . . . to destroy their national statehood." [87] States alone are the subjects of international law. Conveniently forgotten was the position previously taken by his colleague E. A. Korovin, who advocated that Communist-sponsored, nonstate bodies, such as the Comintern and the World Federation of Trade Unions, be accorded recognition as subjects of international law.[88] Apparently Soviet theorists are not opposed to developing international law if they believe it can further Soviet designs. As to the suggestion of developing collective responsibility for punishment of international crimes, Levin held that "Jessup has in mind the forcible suppression of all popular movements. This is to be the chief function of

[85] Philip C. Jessup, *The International Problem of Governing Mankind* (Claremont, Calif., 1947), p. 6.
[86] Philip C. Jessup, *A Modern Law of Nations* (New York, 1952), pp. 2, 13.
[87] D. B. Levin, "Falsifikatsiia poniatiia mezhdunarodnogo prava burzhuaznoi lzhenaukoi," *Sovetskoe gosudarstvo i pravo*, No. 4 (April, 1952), p. 58.
[88] E. A. Korovin, *Das Voelkerrecht in der Uebergangszeit*, 1924 (Berlin, 1929), and "The Second World War and International Law," *American Journal of International Law*, XL, No. 4 (Oct., 1946), 745; cited in Hans Kelsen, *The Communist Theory of Law* (New York, 1955), pp. 156, 164, 176.

NON-SOVIET SUPRANATIONAL PLANS

the American 'New Order,'" which would be "very much akin to Hitlerite plans for a 'New Order.'" The supremacy of the common will of the international community would amount to "decisions forced on the UN by American imperialists with the aid of the machine votes of the American satellites." [89]

The writings of Professor Frederick Schuman perhaps represent the ultimate in the attempt to reconcile the advocacy of world government with an "understanding" attitude toward the Soviet Union. But as the world government Schuman has in mind is a union of the presently existing Soviet and non-Soviet states, he has received small gratitude for his effort to reconcile the irreconcilable. For one who has often heard the charge of being an apologist for the Soviet Union, it must provide little comfort to be labeled by *Pravda* as an "apologist for imperialism," and to read the following gross misrepresentation of his book, *The Commonwealth of Man:* "The work urgently preaches the idea of setting up a 'world government' by means of conquest, of course, under U.S. leadership." [90]

The strange case of "world citizen" Garry Davis presented Moscow with a dilemma. Here was an American who dramatically renounced his American citizenship, and was therefore a potential source of anti-American propaganda. The tremendous popular sympathy that Davis aroused in Europe—a phenomenon that Americans totally failed to appreciate—also prevented the Communists from denouncing him without first attempting to use him for their own cause. But Davis insisted upon remaining apart from both the American and the Russian camps, and this aloofness finally brought Soviet wrath upon his head, as Moscow ultimately recognizes no middle way. More damaging, in Soviet eyes, was his determination to carry his plea for world government into the Soviet orbit. Davis deplored the defeatist attitude of anyone who "says that, if a real peace movement swept the world, world government might result, but that the Soviet fortress cannot be penetrated with such an

[89] D. B. Levin, " 'Mezhdunarodnoe pravo' amerikanskikh imperialisticheskikh razboinikov," *Sovetskoe gosudarstvo i pravo*, No. 3 (March, 1951), pp. 78, 80. For similar Soviet attacks on other American professors of international law, see W. W. Kulski, "Soviet Comments on International Law and International Relations," *American Journal of International Law*, XLVII, No. 1 (Jan., 1953), 128; *ibid.*, XLVIII, No. 2 (April, 1954), 311.
[90] E. Mamedov, "Otkroveniia apologeta 'politika sily' i voiny," *Pravda*, Oct. 30, 1953, p. 5.

idea."[91] Soon after his unauthorized balcony speech to the UN General Assembly and his subsequent interview with Assembly President Evatt in November, 1948, Davis indicated that he was receiving favorable mail from behind the Iron Curtain. On April 22, 1949, he attempted, without success, to read this simple message to a Communist-sponsored Partisans of Peace Congress in Paris: "In the West there are citizens of the world who are calling to all men beyond frontiers and barriers to construct a World Law."[92] The controversy aroused by this incident then forced *Pravda* to blast "that debauched American maniac, Garry Davis, styling himself a 'citizen of the world,' this preacher of the idea of 'world government,' a notion exported from the U.S. to Europe along with powdered eggs and gangster novels."[93]

The largest of the American federalist organizations, the United World Federalists, advocates the immediate transformation of the United Nations into a world federation with powers "limited but adequate" to maintain peace. These powers would presumably be minimal, such as control over armaments, leaving the internal order of each state otherwise untouched. The "limited but adequate" formula was controverted by the Committee to Frame a World Constitution, a group of scholars drawn largely from the University of Chicago. They believed that no limited world government could be adequate, as the price of peace was justice. This meant that the problem of world security could not be solved unless a world government also vigorously attacked the causes of social and economic unrest. These scholars looked forward to a world unified on the basis of democratic socialism as the eventual meeting ground of East and West.

Moscow was totally disinterested in these doctrinal squabbles and attacked both groups with equal venom. The United World Federalists were dismissed as "agents of Wall Street" because the late W. T. Holiday, President of Standard Oil of Ohio, once served as a UWF Vice President.[94] This member of the business community was actually the exception in UWF ranks. More representative was the young liberal, Cord Meyer, Jr., author of *Peace*

[91] "From Two Letters of Garry Davis," *Common Cause*, II, No. 8 (March, 1949), 284.
[92] "World Federalism vs. Communism," *ibid.*, II, No. 12 (July, 1949), 441.
[93] Iu. Zhukov, "Zhany ne pomniashchie rodstva," *Pravda*, May 4, 1949, p. 4.
[94] Polents, "*Vsemirnoe gosudarstvo*," p. 7.

NON-SOVIET SUPRANATIONAL PLANS 413

or Anarchy. He was called a "cosmopolitan gangster" for expounding the UWF position that a less-than-universal federation within the framework of the UN should be formed if a sincere effort to bring the Soviet Union into a world federation met with persistent failure. Moscow took this to mean that "the USSR must be forced to join a 'world government' under the threat of 'total destruction' of Soviet cities and industries." Similarly, Emery Reves, the author of the federalist best seller, *The Anatomy of Peace*, was labeled a "fascist degenerate," and Vernon Nash's *The World Must Be Governed* was referred to as "that vile little book" by a "cosmopolitan Judas."[95]

Of the group of Chicago scholars, Robert Hutchins, at the time Chancellor of the University of Chicago, was singled out as a "cosmopolitan ringleader," and accused of conducting a "malicious campaign" against peaceful coexistence for asserting that the competitive anarchy of sovereign states could not long remain peaceful.[96] The draft constitution of the Chicago group was condemned because "all power in this 'world government' would, in fact, devolve upon a president who would be a solitary and all-powerful dictator, elected in such a way that the countries of the Anglo-Saxon bloc will have a guarantee that the president's office will always be occupied by one of their stooges."[97] The plan, on the contrary, provided for a world government based on nine regional groupings, arranged in such a way that it would be very difficult for any one group to dominate the others.

Clarence Streit's proposal for a nuclear union of democratic states, rechristened the Atlantic Union Committee, also came in for renewed attack. First criticized by Moscow in 1939, when it was aimed at stopping Axis aggression, it was understandably treated with even less tenderness now that it was aimed at stopping Soviet aggression.[98]

The Soviet press has likewise not overlooked the Peoples' Convention Movement. This movement seeks to attain world government by appealing directly to the people of the world and by organizing elections for a Peoples' Convention authorized to write a world constitution, which would then be ratified by the existing national states. Because of the numerous difficulties involved in by-

---

[95] Cherniak, "Amerikanskie," *Novyi mir*, No. 10 (Oct., 1950), pp. 268–70.
[96] *Ibid.*, p. 269.   [97] Polents, "*Vsemirnoe gosudarstvo*," p. 9.
[98] Cherniak, "Amerikanskie," *Novyi mir*, No. 10 (Oct., 1950), p. 268.

passing existing institutions, not to mention the impossibility of holding free elections in large parts of the world, this approach, at best, represents an educational movement for the idea of world government. Nevertheless, Fyke Farmer, the leader of the Peoples' Convention Movement in the United States, succeeded in holding elections, officially sponsored by his native state of Tennessee, for delegates to a world constitutional convention. Il'ia Erenburg drew this picture of Farmer, whom he encountered on a trip to the United States:

I met Mr. Farmer in Tennessee. He was modest and embarrassed; he showed me the pitiful hovels in which the peasants live. Blushing with embarrassment, he told me that there is much savagery and darkness in Tennessee. . . . It might be supposed that the government of Tennessee, aware of its guilt before its fellow citizens and before the whole world, rather than teach the formation of a "world state," would set to work to bring the life of its state closer at least to the standards of the nineteenth century.[99]

European federalists are uniformly depicted as lackeys of American federalists and Wall Street, the latter two being one and the same in Moscow's eyes. A large portion of European support for supranational integration comes from the non-Communist left, whom the Communists designate "right socialists." These "traitors" to the cause of socialism are considered purveyors of the bourgeois ideology of an "imperialist" union of the world. In Britain, in addition to the previously noted attacks on Laborites Attlee and Bevin, Henry Usborne, a Labor M.P. active in the cause of world government, and Laborite theoreticians Kingsley Martin and the late Harold Laski have all been the recipients of choice Soviet epithets. No matter that the vision of a socialist world society painted by Martin and Laski played up, and perhaps magnified, the shortcomings of capitalism.[100]

Of the continental European Social Democrats, the Germans

[99] Il'ia Erenburg, "Sud'ba kultury," *Kultura i zhizn'*, Dec. 31, 1949, p. 3.
[100] P. N. Fedoseev, "*Manifest kommunisticheskoi partii*" *Marksa i Engelsa i materialisticheskoe ponimanie istorii* (Moscow, 1948), pp. 25-26. For the views criticized, see Harold J. Laski, "The Crisis in Our Civilization," *Foreign Affairs*, XXVI, No. 1 (Oct., 1947), 36-51; Kingsley Martin, "Marxism Reviewed," *The Political Quarterly*, XVIII, No. 3 (July-Sept., 1947), 240-49. The article of Martin, a "capitalist lackey," included the following: "I think the Communist is probably, but not certainly, right in believing that the inherent difficulties of capitalism will lead after many upheavals and great social misery to a socialist world state." (p. 247)

NON-SOVIET SUPRANATIONAL PLANS

have been least subject to criticism because of the patriotic pose they have assumed in opposition to Chancellor Konrad Adenauer's advocacy of supranationalism. Among those continental socialists selected for repeated attacks on the score of federalism have been Paul Henri Spaak of Belgium, Giuseppe Saragat of Italy, the late President of Austria, Karl Renner, and the late Léon Blum of France.

Blum, "that troubador of national treason," was, curiously enough, accused of forming a "touching alliance" with the Vatican. Together they fulfilled the "commands of the international imperialistic bourgeoisie behind the mask of pseudo-socialist and Christian phraseology." [101]

To call the Vatican a center of European socialism would be something more than an exaggeration. However, Pope Pius XII spoke approvingly of world federalism. On April 6, 1951, the Pope warmly endorsed this objective during a reception for a large delegation of world federalists.[102] The federalist ideal also apparently circulated freely in Church circles behind the Iron Curtain. The Soviet press specifically attacked the Catholic hierarchy of Poland for popularizing the "propaganda of Papal 'universalism,'" indicating that a Church magazine had published a "subversive" article entitled "The Anachronism of Sovereignty." [103]

WORLD FEDERALISTS CONFRONTED WITH THE ISSUE OF COMMUNISM

In August, 1947, the various national federalist groups formed a world-wide coordinating body known as the World Movement for World Federal Government. Moscow's awareness of the activities of the World Movement is fully reflected in a Soviet article on this subject, which accurately describes its founding and structure. But the groups in this movement,

> despite their effort to create the appearance of some sort of "international" movement for "world government," do not have any influence among the masses, but are only a mob of reactionaries of all tints and

---

[101] Polents, "*Vsemirnoe gosudarstvo*," pp. 7-8.
[102] "Pope's Message Gives Distinction to Fourth Congress of WMWFG," *World Government News*, IX, No. 98 (May, 1951), 3-4.
[103] I. Narskii and Iu. Geivish, "Bor'ba protiv burzhuaznoi ideologii v Pol'she," *Literaturnaia gazeta*, July 22, 1950, p. 3.

colors. Deprived of support of the broad popular masses, these groups exist and function chiefly on the dollars that Wall Street sends them.[104]

It is true that the World Movement was not too effective, partly because of a desperate lack of funds and, ironically, because the World Movement had a league structure. It has been justly criticized for not being able to create a powerful and coherent program, that is, to "federate the federalists," which is seemingly a prerequisite for those who hope to federate national governments.

Some of the federalist organizations in the World Movement have been especially intent on presenting their case to the Communists. One such group known simply as "The Federalists" has printed an accurate and precise exposition of the case for world federal government in a number of languages. The author of these pamphlets tells of his experience with them in Italy:

When the Communists see federation explained in their own language they feel at once it is what they want. But when they inquire of higher echelons in the Communist organization of what they ought to think about world federation . . . they are warned off and dare not go any further.[105]

These same pamphlets are printed in Russian, and as the occasion permits, they are put on board Russian ships in Western ports and have been distributed to Soviet occupation troops in such Western outposts as Berlin and Vienna. Not only the difficulty of crossing political barriers, but also inadequate finances have so far kept this operation on a very modest scale.

The issue of reaching the Communists came to a head at the Fourth World Congress of the World Movement for World Federal Government, held in Rome in April, 1951. This crisis was precipitated by a shift in the Communist Party line, as reflected in the tactics of the Communist-sponsored Partisans of Peace. In November, 1950, the Partisans of Peace held a Congress in Warsaw where a resolution was adopted advocating "cooperation" with world government groups. This decision was reaffirmed by a February, 1951, resolution of the World Peace Council (the executive body of the Partisans of Peace Congress). The resolution proposed "to continue discussions with the world government movement in different countries, to seek for points of agreement and joint

[104] Polents, "*Vsemirnoe gosudarstvo*," p. 7.
[105] Letter from Noel Rawnsley to this writer, June 14, 1950 (used with consent of author).

activity, and to encourage participation by both movements in their respective conferences and congresses." [106]

The reasoning behind this tack toward a "united front" with world federalists was not altogether clear. It may have been tied to the Communist "peace offensive," designed to slow down Western rearmament. Or the Communists may have felt that their other attempts to exploit the word "peace," such as the campaign for the Stockholm Peace Petition, had worn thin, while the world government movement still offered a fresh and attractive approach to the problem of peace. Consequently, the Communists may have reasoned, they should somehow infiltrate or compromise the world government movement. In any event, the magazine *Peace* for February, 1951, issued in ten languages by the Communist World Peace Council, published an astonishingly objective presentation of the case for world government, written by Jean Diedisheim, a member of the Executive Council of the World Movement for World Federal Government.[107]

Partly by way of reciprocation, the Executive Council of the World Movement invited the Partisans of Peace to send observers (with the right to speak but without voting privileges) to a so-called "Conference of Organization." This Conference, held in conjunction with the Fourth World Congress of the World Movement, was composed of organizations not members of the World Movement, but considered in some way sympathetic to it. It was felt that such a meeting could help spread an understanding of the world government idea.

The invitation to the Partisans of Peace threatened to wreck the World Movement and did in fact considerably upset the proceedings of the Rome Congress. The largest American world government organization, the United World Federalists, threatened to resign from the World Movement unless the invitation was immediately withdrawn and the Congress was held without the presence of any Communist group.

Following this mild flirtation with the world government move-

---

[106] "Speech by Pietro Nenni, November 17, 1950, at the Second World Peace Congress, Held in Warsaw," *Polish Facts and Figures* (Polish Embassy, London), No. 226 (Nov. 25, 1950), p. 5; "Communist 'Peace' Group Seeks New 'United Front,'" *World Government News*, IX, No. 98 (May, 1951), 8–9.

[107] Jean Diedisheim, "The Case for World Government," *Peace: A World Review* (Paris), II, No. 23 (Feb., 1951), 6–10.

ment, Moscow reverted to its generic hostility toward Western federalists.[108]

The incident of the Rome Congress crystallized the impasse that exists for the world federalist movement. Groups like the United World Federalists must face the fact that they are pursuing two incompatible goals. On the one hand, they claim to seek a *world* government, that is, a government that would include the Communists and necessarily accord them a conspicuous role. On the other hand, they dare not deal with Communists for fear of having a Red label pasted on them, a stigma that they know would promptly ruin the standing of their organization in the West. If it is held dangerous or impossible to deal with Communists, then it must be concluded that campaigning for a *world* government can no longer be a meaningful activity.

SOVIET HOSTILITY TO RECENT FEDERALIST DESIGNS WITHIN THE NON-SOVIET WORLD

By way of contrast, federalist activity within the non-Soviet world offers some possibility of tangible results. Because efforts to unify and strengthen the non-Soviet world are very much in the realm of practical politics, Moscow has desperately sought to disrupt every conceivable attempt at Western integration at every possible level.

A prodigious amount of Soviet energy has been directed toward perpetuating the disunity of Western Europe, which has been the most active postwar arena for the circulation of concrete supranational proposals. A variety of arguments has been advanced to discredit European union. Winston Churchill's advocacy of a United States of Europe simply reflected the desire of an "inveterate archzealot of imperialism" to bring Europe under British domination. His proposal of a Franco-British Union during the Second World War was cited as "evidence" of his attempt "to annex France to

---

[108] An exception to this occurred in the wake of the "Geneva spirit" created by the Big Four Summit Conference in July, 1955. Four prominent Soviet scientists attended a World Conference of Scientists in London, August 3–5, 1955, sponsored by the World Association of Parliamentarians for World Government. The Soviet delegates ignored the issue of world government and confined their participation to advocating the peaceful uses of nuclear energy, in conformity with the then-current Soviet "peace" campaign. For a full report of the Conference, see *World: for World Trade and World Law* (London), No. 1 (Winter, 1955–56), pp. 9–34.

NON-SOVIET SUPRANATIONAL PLANS 419

England."[109] A European federation, always designed to increase the exploitation of the toiling masses of Europe, became especially urgent after the Second World War, it was alleged, as a means of prolonging the exploitation of the colonial areas of the world, newly caught up in the movement for national liberation. The campaign for European unity represented "the yearning for a Holy Alliance of colonial slave holders which would guarantee them the possibility of exploiting the colonial peoples as of old."[110]

The most prevalent Soviet propaganda theme attributed the desire for European union, not to the European "imperialists," but to their more powerful counterparts in the United States. All the American efforts to resuscitate Western Europe and promote its political and economic integration were supposedly undertaken for the sole purpose of enriching the "monopolists of Wall Street," who transmit their orders through their "errand boys" in Washington. The Marshall Plan, the Organization for European Economic Cooperation, the European Payments Union, Benelux, the European Coal and Steel Community, the proposals for a European Defense Community and a European agricultural "Green Pool," the Council of Europe, and the proposed European Political Community were all "intended to curtail to the utmost the national sovereignty of the historically formed European states, to establish the domination of the ruling circles of the U.S. in all spheres of the economic, political and cultural life of the peoples of Western Europe, and to make it possible for their territories to be used as war bases and their youth as cannon fodder in the war that is being plotted against the Soviet Union and the People's Democracies."[111]

The idea that some of these attempts at integration originated in Europe for the purpose of benefiting Europeans has been rudely rejected. "The European Army scheme is sometimes referred to as the Pleven Plan, though it actually originated in Washington.

[109] "Protiv burzhuaznoi ideologii kozmopolotizma," *Voprosy filosofii*, No. 2 (1948), p. 15.
[110] A. Leontev, "Behind the Screen of 'European Unity,'" *New Times*, No. 12 (March 16, 1949), p. 6.
[111] A. Erusalimskii, " 'European Federation' of American Quislings," *ibid.*, No. 42 (Oct. 15, 1952), p. 15. The same arguments were repeated against the subsequent plans for a European Atomic Energy Community and a European Economic Community. See Iuri Rubinskii, "Euratom and Europe," *News*, No. 8 (April 16, 1956), pp. 18–19; Zigbert Kan, " 'Obshchii rynok' i Germaniia," *Pravda*, Aug. 5, 1957, p. 3; N. B. S. Scott, "The Soviet Approach to European Economic Integration," *Soviet Studies*, IX, No. 3 (Jan., 1958), 292–98.

So did the Schuman Plan."[112] In the case of the Coal and Steel Community, "Bidault and Schuman only translated into French what had been worked out and compiled across the ocean."[113] The West Germans have been depicted in these schemes as America's favorite "junior partner." It is still "the fondest dream of the German cosmopolitan to control Europe." As a step in this direction, "the German monopolists hope to play the role of manager for the American monopolies." It is conceded that this involves, "at least in the beginning, a subordinate status for the German capitalists, but they are quite amenable."[114] The fruit of this partnership would allegedly be the full-fledged revival of a Nazi-dominated Europe, under the general supervision of the American overlords. All of these various integrative arrangements are part of "a preparatory stage toward the formation of an American world empire in the form of an Atlantic Union."[115]

The most bitterly fought plan for Western integration was the proposed supranational European Defense Community (EDC), which would have permitted the controlled rearmament of Western Germany. As the moment for French ratification approached, Moscow advanced one ingenious counterproposal after another. On February 10, 1954, at the Big Four Conference in Berlin, Molotov presented a draft of an all-European collective security treaty, as a substitute for EDC, which was accused of splitting Europe into two opposing blocs. Molotov vehemently denied that the Soviet orbit already comprised a distinct military bloc. The security of Europe, Western Europe included, could only be assured by an all-inclusive treaty of sovereign European states, "without regard to their social systems."[116] On March 31 Moscow went one step further. The United States was invited to join in this general European treaty, and, in turn, the Soviet Union declared its readiness "to examine, in conjunction with the governments concerned, the question of the participation of the USSR in the North Atlantic

[112] I. Nezhdanov, "Behind the Scenes of the Schuman Plan," *News*, No. 19 (Oct., 1952), p. 13.
[113] M. Marinin, " 'Total'naia diplomatiia' v deistvii," *Pravda*, May 24, 1950, p. 4.
[114] L. F. Denisova, "Novaia lichina nemetskoi burzhuaznoi reaktsii," *Voprosy filosofii*, No. 3 (1948), p. 244.
[115] Marinin, " 'Total'naia diplomatiia,' " *Pravda*, May 24, 1950, p. 4.
[116] "Texts of Soviet Proposals on Europe and Remarks by Molotov and Dulles," New York *Times*, Feb. 11, 1954.

Treaty." [117] The advantage of this arrangement, it was stressed, lay not only in the destruction of an exclusive military bloc, but in the full protection of the sovereign rights of all states participating in the treaties. On April 26 Premier Malenkov denounced those who circulated

> the fashionable so-called theory, which is an enormous distortion of the truth, according to which the era of sovereign states is a thing of the past. No, the era of sovereign states is not past. It is in full bloom. . . . European security can become a reality only as a collective security of sovereign European states.[118]

When the French National Assembly rejected EDC on August 30, Moscow hailed the repudiation as "a deeply patriotic action" that permitted France to "maintain its national independence." [119] But Soviet jubilation was short-lived, for Western Germany was soon brought into NATO through an old-fashioned military treaty, misnamed a Western European Union. Although it could not prevent Western Germany from joining this alliance, Moscow did its share to forestall the creation of an effective supranational institution that could avoid the cumbersome procedures and the dangers of independent action endemic to treaty arrangements among sovereign states.

The same obstructionist Soviet tactics toward regional integration have been repeated in other areas of the non-Soviet world. In Scandinavia the Nordic Council was condemned because it was allegedly created as a means of bringing Sweden and Finland into NATO. When the Council considered proposals for Scandinavian union, common citizenship, a customs union, the joint working of ore deposits, and so forth, it was said to trample on the freedom of its various peoples. By way of contrast, "the true movement for Northern cooperation develops in the popular movement defending peace and the independent, sovereign existence of all the North European countries." [120] The formation of the Central African Fed-

---

[117] "Nota Sovetskogo Pravitel'stva Pravitel'stvam Frantsii, Velikobritanii, SShA," *Pravda*, April 1, 1954, p. 2.
[118] "Rech' Predsedatelia Soveta Ministrov SSSR, deputata G. M. Malenkova," *ibid.*, April 27, 1954, p. 6.
[119] "Text of Moscow Statement on European Security," New York *Times*, Sept. 10, 1954.
[120] P. Rysakov, "Dva vida 'severnogo sotrudnichestva,'" *Izvestiia*, April 10, 1953, p. 4. See also P. Rysakov, "Komu i zachem nuzhen Severnyi Sovet,"

eration was attributed to the desire of "British imperialism to consolidate its shaken position in Central Africa," as well as "to hold back the development of the national liberation movement and step up the exploitation and enslavement of the Africans." [121] The Federation, in addition, reflected growing contradictions in the capitalist camp, since it was designed to stop encroachments of "American monopolies, which have already won quite strong positions for themselves in Central Africa." [122] In the Middle East, a rumored proposal for a Turkish-Arab federation, attributed to Turkish Foreign Minister Köprülü, was castigated as an effort to lure the Arab League states into an Anglo-American Middle East Command and so destroy Arab sovereignty.[123]

The only exception to this otherwise monotonous record came with the Soviet support for the formation of the United Arab Republic in January, 1958. This new state, built around the merger of Egypt and Syria, but infused with Nasser's limitless Pan-Arabic if not Pan-Islamic ambitions, presented Khrushchev with a variant of an old problem. In the past Moscow had uniformly denounced Pan-Islamic movements, most of which were of Turkic origin, in large measure because it feared the creation of a competing center of loyalty for the Turkic peoples of the Soviet Union. Such movements were also censured on the grounds of diverting the Islamic peoples from a class struggle against their own reactionary religious leaders. The case of Nasser, Khrushchev judged, could be viewed somewhat differently. His movement was Pan-Arabic, not Pan-Turkic, and the Soviet Union contains no significant number of Arabs. As for Pan-Islamism, after forty years the Soviet regime need no longer fear the domestic strength of Islam as a religion.

---

ibid., Aug. 17, 1954, p. 3; Iakov Segal, "Nordic Council and National Interests," *News*, No. 3 (Feb., 1955), pp. 18–20. Following the Finno-Soviet negotiations in Moscow in September, 1955, the Finns apparently obtained Soviet consent to join the Nordic Council in the hopes that Finland would exert a strong neutralist influence in the Council, thereby weakening its ties with NATO. (Harry Schwartz, "Finns Due to Sit in Nordic Council," New York *Times*, Oct. 26, 1955; E. Ambartsumov, "Soviet-Finnish Relations," *International Affairs* [Moscow], No. 10 [Oct., 1955], p. 52; László Hámori, "The Soviets Woo Scandinavia," *New Leader*, Feb. 20, 1956, p. 9.)

[121] I. Potekhin, "Imperialisticheskie plany Anglii v tsentral'noi Afrike," *Izvestiia*, Jan. 15, 1953, p. 4.

[122] P. Niororo, "Narody tsentral'noi Afriki v bor'be za svoi prava," *Pravda*, April 4, 1953, p. 4. See also S. Datlin, "Central African Scheme," *News*, No. 10 (May 15, 1953), pp. 20–22.

[123] M. Mikhailov, "Obsnovannaia trevoga," *Izvestiia*, Feb. 28, 1953, p. 4.

Moreover, it was possible for Moscow to obscure the suppression of Islamic institutions at home, while penetrating the Islamic communities in the Arab world abroad through its skillfully directed foreign propaganda.

Nasser's position was perhaps thought to be somewhat analogous to that of Turkey's Kemal in the early 1920s (although Kemal did not indulge in Pan-Islamic dreams). Lenin had preferred to support Kemal as a native antifeudal, but more importantly, anti-Anglo-French leader, rather than work for an immediate Communist-led class struggle against the ascendant force of "bourgeois" nationalism. The Soviet ambition to use and then ultimately to subvert Kemal's regime backfired within a short time. The verdict is not yet in on Khrushchev's capacity to use and then destroy Nasser. In July, 1958, Khrushchev remarked candidly, "The Arabs are not Marxists. They fight under another flag—under the flag of nationalism. We hail them. National liberation is the first step." [124] The second step, not too widely advertised for the moment, would obviously consist of the next "higher" stage of "inevitable" historical development, requiring the installation of a system of Soviet controls and, ultimately, the integration of Nasser's Pan-Arabic union into an expanding Soviet federation.

From the beginning, an authoritative Soviet source revealed the conditional and expedient nature of Soviet support for Nasser's Pan-Arabism. "The Soviet Union welcomes the establishment of the United Arab Republic," and considers it "an historically important practical step towards Arab unity." However, "being Marxists, we are by no means inclined to make a fetish of Arab unity as such." Rather, Nasser's movement was deserving of Soviet assistance because it was a vehicle for displacing the influence of the NATO powers from the Arab world, or put in Soviet terminology, because it "has been seized by currents intimately connected with the anti-imperialist struggle." [125]

Nasser's uneasyness about the ambivalent attitude of his Soviet benefactors was first aired publicly toward the end of 1958, that

[124] Quoted in the Moscow dispatch of William J. Jorden, "Khrushchev Sees Need for Caution," New York *Times*, July 23, 1958.
[125] K. Ivanov, "A New Arab State," *International Affairs* (Moscow), No. 3 (March, 1958), p. 57. On an earlier Soviet flirtation with Pan-Arabism, see Walter Z. Laqueur, *The Soviet Union and the Middle East* (New York, 1959), pp. 94-96.

is, within a year of the formation of the United Arab Republic. His disillusionment with Moscow was undoubtedly accelerated by fear of the deep Communist inroads that were evident in the newly formed revolutionary government of Iraq. Nasser rightly regarded a Communist-controlled Iraq as a mortal challenge to his pretentions of leadership in the Arab world.

The ill-fated Iraqi-Jordanian federation of February, 1958, had found no favor with the Kremlin. Iraq, then tied to the NATO powers through the Baghdad Pact, could only play an "unprogressive" role by forming a union with another Arab state. The anti-Western Iraqi coup d'état of July, 1958, led by Abdul Karim Kassim, therefore received Moscow's enthusiastic support. Sobolëv, the chief Soviet spokesman in the United Nations, promptly and gleefully read into the record the declaration of the revolutionary junta dissolving the Iraqi-Jordanian Union: "The old regime was not a true federation with an aim of benefiting the people of the two countries, but had been proclaimed to strengthen a corrupt monarchy and to destroy the unity of the Arabs." [126]

Following the July revolution the Iraqi Communists emerged from their underground existence and promptly entrenched themselves in influential positions in the Kassim regime. They then apparently proceeded to encourage the Syrian Communists to pull away from Cairo. Nasser struck back sharply in his Port Said speech of December 23, 1958, in which he publicly accused the Syrian Communists of attempting to disrupt the United Arab Republic and the drive for Arab unity in general.[127] This was quickly followed by a widespread crackdown on Communist activities in the United Arab Republic, while Nasser sympathizers were increasingly harassed in Iraq. For several months an uneasy truce seemed to prevail, but in March, 1959, the conflict again burst into the open when Kassim suppressed a revolt staged at Mosul by pro-Nasser detachments of the Iraqi army.

After the failure of the Mosul revolt Nasser charged that the Communists in Iraq were not only trying to detach Syria from the United Arab Republic, but were also seeking to annex it to Iraq as the nucleus of a "Communist Fertile Crescent." [128] Khru-

[126] "Excerpts from the Statements in the U.N. Security Council on the Mideast Situation," New York *Times*, July 19, 1958.
[127] "Nasser Charges Syrian Reds Aim to Cut Cairo Ties," *ibid.*, Dec. 24, 1958.
[128] Richard P. Hunt, "Nasser Declares Enmity to Kassim," *ibid.*, March 14,

shchev then personally entered into the polemics. At a Moscow reception in honor of the government of Iraq on March 16, he praised Kassim because "we consider that in the Iraqi Republic progressive changes are under way and a more advanced system is being established than in the neighboring countries of the Arab East." Nasser's Pan-Arabic dreams were now labeled "delusions." Noting that "Nasser insists on annexing the Iraqi Republic to the United Arab Republic," Khrushchev warned that such a union would be "untimely" and threaten the rights and independence of the Iraqi people. While it was good that many Arab states had ejected their former Western rulers, "this does not mean that countries that have broken the fetters of colonialism must necessarily join some federation of states, be subject to one government or follow one leader, one head." [129] Not, that is, if that leader has become an obstacle to the realization of the Soviet grand design.

The evidence accumulated in this chapter should permit the formulation of several broad conclusions. No meaningful accord with the Soviet regime for the higher integration of nations is presently conceivable. This prospect can be altered only by an abandonment of the basic tenets of the Soviet regime, which rigidly maintains that nothing but a Soviet world state is either desirable or possible. The values upon which the Soviet and non-Soviet worlds rest are so incompatible that it is not possible to form even that minimal sense of community indispensable to the successful operation of any institution of world government. Consequently, all plans for a world state originating in the non-Soviet world, even the most moderate compromise proposals, are viewed by the Soviet leaders as a mortal threat to their own design for a world state. Furthermore, it is evident that the needed reorganization of the nation-state system in the non-Soviet world can only be undertaken without Soviet participation, and in the face of intense hostility from the Soviet leaders.

1959. Nasser soon renewed this charge. ("Nasser Accuses Arab Reds Again," *ibid.*, April 17, 1959.)

[129] "Rech' tovarishcha N. S. Khrushcheva," *Pravda*, March 17, 1959, pp 1-2. See also Obozrevatel', "Edinstvo arabskikh narodov v bor'be za nezavisimost'—zalog pobedy," *ibid.*, March 30, 1959, pp. 3-4.

XIII. The World State of No State

ANY analysis of the Soviet design for a world state would be incomplete without a brief account of that apocalyptic vision of the ultimate stage of world communism in which "world state" becomes "no state."

THE WITHERING OF THE SOVIET WORLD STATE AS THE
ULTIMATE GOAL OF WORLD COMMUNISM

The Marxist heritage of the Soviet leaders relegated all forms of the state to the category of a transient historical phenomenon. A Soviet world state could not therefore be considered an eternal institution. Since the state had supposedly arisen as an organ of oppression, following the division of society into antagonistic classes, it was destined to wither away, together with the disappearance of class exploitation, in the blissful era of a future classless society.

"The United States of the World," Lenin remarked in 1915, "is that state form for the unification and freedom of nations which we identify with socialism, while the full victory of communism will only make its appearance with the elimination of the state in its every aspect, its democratic form included." [1] (Lenin held that "democracy is also a state form which must disappear when the state disappears, but this will taken place only in the process of transition from completely victorious and consolidated socialism to complete communism.") [2]

Following the Bolshevik Revolution, the objective of transforming the Soviet world state into "no state" was again explicitly affirmed. The 1920 Comintern Statutes proclaimed that it was the aim of the Communist International "to create the International

[1] Lenin, "O lozunge Soedinënnykh Shtatov Evropy," Aug. 23, 1915, in *Sochineniia*, XVIII, 232.
[2] Lenin, "Sotsialisticheskaia revoliutsiia i pravo natsii na samoopredelenie," March, 1916, in *ibid.*, XIX, 37.

Soviet Republic as a transitional stage moving toward the complete abolition of the state."[3] A Communist handbook, written in 1923 under Bukharin's editorship, predicted that "Communist society will be organized on an international or world scale, uniting in itself all humanity, independent and without distinction of race or nationality. This society will have no internal state boundaries, nor will it as a whole constitute a state."[4] The 1928 Comintern Program stated: "The ultimate aim toward which the Communist International strives is to replace the world capitalist economy by a *world system of communism*. . . . State power, as the first among the organs of class domination, will vanish."[5] Similarly, in 1934 Bukharin projected this vision of a stateless world: "The dictatorship of the proletariat in its perspective is oriented towards a *world Communist community*—towards a huge organized economic whole, without exploitation and without classes—which would be the basis of the true brotherhood of all mankind."[6]

AN ALL-ENCOMPASSING PLAN FOR A CENTRALIZED,
STATELESS WORLD SOCIETY

Along what lines will this sublime brotherhood of man be organized, once the organs of a world state have withered away?

The shape of the ultimate world society as developed by Soviet theorists adheres closely to the position of Marx and Engels.[7] As Marx and Engels saw it, the elimination of anarchy in production, through the operation of a single, vast, centralized economic plan, would coincide with the elimination of state power. The resulting world society would be highly centralized but without any organs of political power; its basis would be centralization without compulsion.

Soviet theorists embraced fully the prospect of a centralized, stateless world society. Soviet centralism is presently overlaid by a thin veneer of federalism, and the World Federation of Soviet

[3] "Ustav Kommunisticheskogo Internatsionala," July 19–Aug. 7, 1920, in *Vtoroi kongress Kommunisticheskogo Internatsionala*, p. 535.
[4] Berdnikov and Svetlov, Bukharin, general ed., *Elements*, 1923, p. 236. See also *ibid.*, p. 282.
[5] "Programma Kommunisticheskogo Internatsionala," Sept. 1, 1928, in *Kom. Int. v dok.*, pp. 14–15.
[6] Bukharin, *Culture*, 1934, p. 15.   [7] See chapter 1 above.

Republics is expected to give way to a unitary, completely centralist Soviet world state. According to the Theses of the Second Comintern Congress, "Federation is the transitional form to the complete unity of the toilers of the different nations." A unitary world state would be consonant with the "creation of a single world economy regulated by the proletariat of all nations according to one common plan." [8] This unitary world state, in turn, was considered a transitional form to "no state," leaving behind a highly centralized Communist world society, which was to remain forever. Bukharin, whose writings are particularly fruitful regarding the ultimate stage of world communism, asserted flatly that "stateless centralization will be possible and historically inevitable, for the growth of productive forces leads to centralization." [9]

Conversely, stateless centralism would be necessary to sustain the maximal growth of the productive forces, upon which the Marxian nirvana of full communism was premised. Only an economy of perpetual, overwhelming abundance would allow man to be rewarded according to his needs, rather than according to his ability. Bukharin drew this picture of the condition of abundance required for communism: "All products under communism, created by the labor of all the workers, will come into the central distributing warehouses whence any member of society, without any money and without any exchange, may take quite freely, and in whatever quantity he wishes, everything that he requires for the complete satisfaction of his needs." [10] "When we are victorious on a world scale," Lenin said in reference to this society of abundance in which money will have lost all meaning, "I think we shall use gold for the purpose of building public toilets in the streets of some of the largest cities of the world." [11] The fact that it might not be possible to provide every individual with the complete satisfaction of all of his needs upon all occasions was dismissed as a bourgeois prej-

[8] "Natsional'nyi i kolonial'nyi voprosy," July 19–Aug. 7, 1920, in *Kom. Int. v dok.*, p. 127.
[9] N. Bukharin, "Marx's Teaching and Its Historical Importance," in *Marxism and Modern Thought* (New York, 1935), p. 78.
[10] Berdnikov and Svetlov, Bukharin, general ed., *Elements*, pp. 230–31. Elsewhere Bukharin suggests the use of consumer's communes for the distribution of this cornucopia (Bukharin, *Programma*, May 1918, pp. 50–51).
[11] Lenin, "O znachenii zolota teper' i posle polnoi pobedy sotsializma," Nov. 5, 1921, in *Sochineniia*, XXVII, 82. One wonders if Lenin had read Sir Thomas More's *Utopia*, in which life was also based on a community of goods and where (Bk. II, ch. 6) "of gold and silver they commonly make chamber pots and other vessels that serve for the most vile uses."

udice. It was assumed that capitalism was responsible for depressing production, and the mere fact of communal ownership would unleash hitherto unheard of productive impulses. As Stalin explained in an essay of 1906: "At present the development of productive forces is hindered by the existence of capitalist property, but if we keep in mind that capitalist property will not exist in the future society, it is self-evident that the productive forces will increase ten-fold." [12]

To sharpen the outlines of this immensely productive, centralist society Bukharin recalled Marx's attack on the anarchists. "The difference between the anarchist structure and that of the Communists is not that one has a state while the other does not; for neither has a state." Rather, the two images of a future society differed in that "the anarchist structure, instead of strengthening, centralizing, and disciplining production, will disperse it, thus *diminishing* man's domination of nature. There will be no common plan, no gigantic organization." World stateless communism would be organized in precisely the opposite manner:

There must be a single working *plan*. The more *comprehensive* the better. The whole world must finally become one great workshop, where all mankind works for itself according to a single, stringently executed plan, without employers and capitalists, but with the best machines and best factories. *To give production a push forward, it will be necessary not only to prevent the dispersal of gigantic production, which was inherited from capitalism.* On the contrary it will be necessary *to increase* it still more. . . . In other words, the more *centralization* the better.[13]

How will this massive centralized plan be operated in a world devoid of all organs of state power? In Stalin's 1906 essay it was suggested that "there will have to be a central statistical bureau, in addition to local bureaus, which will collect all sorts of information about the needs of the entire society, and then parcel out dif-

---

[12] Stalin, "Anarkhizm ili sotsializm?" 1906, in *Sochineniia*, I, 338.

[13] Bukharin, *Programma*, pp. 7–9. Stalin echoed that with the disappearance of the state the workers "will manage their economic affairs as a free association of toilers," and their economy "organized according to plan, will be based on the highest technique in both industry and agriculture." (Stalin, "Beseda s pervoi amerikanskoi rabochei delegatsiei," Sept. 9, 1927, in *Sochineniia*, X, 134.) Similarly the Comintern Program held that in "the world system of communism" there will be "planned utilization of all material resources and a painless economic development on the basis of an unrestricted, smooth, and rapid growth of the productive forces." ("Programma," in *Kom. Int. v dok.*, p. 15.)

ferent tasks among the toilers." These bureaus would apparently be responsive to some broadly based authority since "conferences and especially congresses will also be necessary, the decisions of which will be unconditionally obligatory upon those comrades remaining in the minority until the next congress." [14] The words "unconditionally obligatory" have a strange ring in a society without any organs of coercion. It would seem that the social consciousness of each worker would be expected to be so highly developed that he would voluntarily consider himself obliged to carry out the decisions of these congresses. Stalin evidently remained attached to elements of this scheme, since his last theoretical work, written in 1952, anticipated the advent of a Communist society of abundance in which

the distribution of labor among the branches of production will be regulated not by the law of value, which will have ceased to function by that time, but by the growth of society's demand for goods. This will be a society in which production will be regulated by the needs of society, and the calculation of society's needs will acquire preeminent significance for the planning bodies.[15]

The heir of public property then will not be the state, which will have withered away, but society itself in the shape of a central, directing organ.[16]

Bukharin agreed that the direction of this gigantic "workshop" would have to be entrusted to some central economic organ, since "the broader and more comprehensive the general plan, the more gigantic the dimensions of the organization of production, the more necessary it will be to get all data from a single center of accounting and control." [17] At the base of this economic pyramid Bukharin foresaw mass organizations somewhat like Stalin's suggested conferences and congresses: "The basis of the organization of future Communist society will be the unions and groups of workers in all forms . . . amalgamated on a world scale, with their congresses and other institutions." As in the case of Stalin's scheme,

---

[14] Stalin, "Anarkhizm," in *Sochineniia*, I, 336.
[15] Stalin, "Zamechaniia po ekonomicheskim voprosam, sviazannym s noiabr'skoi diskussiei 1951 goda," Feb. 1, 1952, in *Ekonomicheskie problemy*, p. 23.
[16] Stalin, "Otvet tovarishcham Saninoi A. V. i Venzheru V. G.," Sept. 28, 1952, in *ibid.*, p. 88.
[17] Bukharin, *Programma*, pp. 8–9. See also *ibid.*, pp. 28, 57–58; Bukharin and Preobrazhenskii, *Azbuka*, 1919, pp. 46, 48, 233; Berdnikov and Svetlov, Bukharin, general ed., *Elements*, p. 229.

the exact relationship between the single controlling summit and these undergirding mass congresses and "other institutions" is completely undefined. In an uncharacteristic fit of modesty Bukharin admitted that "it is possible that in a highly developed Communist society there will arise some other organizations and institutions, unlike any known to us until now, built upon completely different foundations." [18]

In May, 1918, Lenin hazarded the prediction that the future administrative institutions would be a direct extension of the newly created economic organs of the Soviet state. He anticipated an increasingly important "role for the Councils of the People's Economy which alone of all the state institutions are destined to occupy a permanent place." After the withering away of the old apparatus of state, the central directing and planning organ could be likened to "the apparatus of the type of the Supreme Council of the People's Economy, which is destined to grow, to develop and become strong, and to perform all the main activities of organized society." [19]

One assumption was stated without hesitation: namely, the more *comprehensive* the plan, the *easier* it would be to operate. Bigness was not considered an impediment to smooth administration. Once the contradictions and the anarchy of the capitalist system had been eliminated, gigantic economic operations would be an unmitigated blessing. (At least, this was the opinion offered before the Soviet leaders had had any experience in the administration of state power.) When questions were raised about the planning of production, the distribution of labor, and the keeping of accounts, Bukharin replied lightly: "It is not difficult to answer these questions." The people in the statistical bureaus would neatly resolve all these operations within the framework of a single plan, which would be simplicity itself. Everyone would become accustomed "from childhood onward" to live according to this plan, would understand that "life goes easier when everything is done according to a prearranged plan," so that the social order moved "like a well-oiled machine." Every worker would thoroughly understand the general plan, for in "the entire mechanism of social production there will no

---

[18] Berdnikov and Svetlov, Bukharin, general ed., *Elements*, pp. 236–37.
[19] Lenin, "Rech' na I s"ezde sovetov narodnogo khoziaistva," May 26, 1918, in *Sochineniia*, XXIII, 36.

longer be anything mysterious, incomprehensible, or unexpected." [20]

Thanks to the heritage of capitalist large-scale production, Lenin said prior to the Bolshevik Revolution, "the great majority of the functions of the old 'state power' have become so simplified and can be reduced to such simple operations of registration, filing, and checking that they will be quite within the reach of every literate person." [21] An argument could be made that Lenin was anticipating the wonders of the age of electronics, automation, and mechanical brains, in which fantastically complicated operations can be conducted with a minimal amount of human effort. This reasoning would be in line with the expectation that every aspect of Communist society would make use of the most advanced techniques available. But Lenin was apparently thinking in terms of the technology and administrative apparatus then at hand. For example, he thought that the big capitalist banks could be instantly transformed into an apparatus of "general state *accounting* of the production and distribution of goods, that is, so to speak, something in the nature of the *skeleton* of socialist society." All that need be done was to take over the bank mechanism *"ready-made* from capitalism" and then *"chop off* that which capitalistically disfigures this otherwise excellent apparatus and make it even *larger* . . . as huge as possible." From the first, these regulatory operations would be conducted by any ordinary literate person, "since the actual work of bookkeeping, control, registration, accounting, and summation is now carried out *by employees,* most of whom are proletarians or semi-proletarians." [22] The Program of the Russian Communist Party, adopted in March, 1919, anticipated that in the era of statelessness this huge socialist bank would "become the central bookkeeping establishment of Communist society." [23]

THE OMNICOMPETENT FUTURE MAN

The belief that simplicity was an inherent part of large-scale operations was but one of a cluster of illusions that came straight from Marx and Engels. An equally astonishing Marxist dictum held that this superbly mechanized world economy would destroy an

[20] Bukharin and Preobrazhenskii, *Azbuka,* pp. 48–49, 176.
[21] Lenin, "Gosudarstvo i revoliutsiia," Aug.–Sept., 1917, in *Sochineniia,* XXI, 399.
[22] Lenin, "Uderzhat li bol'sheviki gosudarstvennuiu vlast'?" Oct. 14, 1917, in *ibid.,* XXI, 260.
[23] "Vos'moi s"ezd RKP(b)," March 18–23, 1919, in *KPSS v rez.,* I, 427.

WORLD STATE OF NO STATE

institutionalized division of labor with its permanently specialized occupations, which are the basic ingredients of mass production and modern technology. As man was liberated from the slavery of a single repetitive function, the difference between mental and manual labor would vanish and he would become omnicompetent. This would permit a tightly integrated world society to be administered by an endless rotation of ordinary workers. Lenin was confident that the mass entry of workers into the administration of an economy "founded on large-scale production, of itself, leads to the gradual 'withering away' of all bureaucracy, to the gradual creation of a new order . . . in which the more and more simplified functions of control and accounting will be performed by each in turn, will then become a habit, and will finally die out as a special function of a *special* stratum of the population."[24] Lenin apparently thought that it would be easier to run a Communist world society than the Russian Communist Party, since the administration of a world society could be entrusted to any ordinary worker, while the Party apparatus was controlled by a tiny elite that placed no faith in the average man. In the future society Lenin predicted that "*all* will take a turn at managing, and will soon become accustomed to the idea of no managers at all."[25] That is, this global, centralized economic machine would be run by no one in particular and by everyone in general. Lenin explained that this would be quite possible because communism leads to "the abolition of the division of labor among people, to the education, schooling, and training of people with an *all-around* development," producing in short, "people *able to do everything*."[26]

Bukharin pictured the rotation of an omnicompetent worker:

Today a man may work in an administrative capacity, calculating how many felt boots or French rolls will be required during the coming month; tomorrow he will work in a soap factory, next week perhaps in a public laundry, and three days later in an electric power station.[27]

Stalin continued to uphold the idea of an omnicompetent man.[28] As late as 1952 he spoke of the need of introducing universal poly-

[24] Lenin, "Gosudarstvo i revoliutsiia," in *Sochineniia*, XXI, 403.
[25] *Ibid.*, XXI, 452.
[26] Lenin, "Detskaia bolezn' 'levizny' v kommunizme," April 27, 1920, in *Sochineniia*, XXV, 194.
[27] Bukharin and Preobrazhenskii, *Azbuka*, p. 47.
[28] Stalin, "Rech' na pervom vsesoiuznom soveshchanii stakhanovtsev," Nov. 17, 1935, in *Voprosy Leninizma* (11th ed., Moscow, 1945), p. 495.

technical education so that members of society might be "in a position freely to choose their occupations and not be tied all their lives, owing to the existing division of labor, to some one occupation." [29] Similarly, Khrushchev reaffirmed in 1958 that "in the course of building communism . . . man himself changes." He approvingly cited Lenin's image of the future, in which the abolition of the division of labor and the subsequent benefits of an all-round education and training would produce " 'people *able to do everything.* Communism is moving toward this, must move toward it and *will arrive* at it, though it will take many years.' " [30]

The future world society is supposed to be highly organized, centralized, planned, and yet the continual movement from place to place and job to job of the entire population of the world could just as easily be a description of anarchy. The more so since all organs of coercion will have withered away so that the observation of accepted norms and the performance of required duties would be left entirely to the conscience of each individual. Bukharin tried to reconcile the process of continual upheaval with the orderly administration of the world plan. The operation of "the bureaus, in which there will be one set of workers today, another tomorrow," would resemble the performance of an orchestra. "Just as in an orchestra all the performers take their cue from the conductor, so all members of society will read the instructions of the bureaus and direct their work accordingly." [31] The metaphor of an orchestra raises more problems than it solves. Presumably this orchestra would not play a single tune, since the future society is not to be static, but rather dynamic by constantly developing its productive forces. Will this orchestra's constantly changing personnel be able to master these constantly changing tunes without producing a good many

[29] Stalin, "Ob oshibkakh t. Iaroshenko L. D.," May 22, 1952, in *Ekonomicheskie problemy*, p. 69. *Izvestiia* added: "As Marx pointed out, the nature of large-scale industry requires movement of labor, changing of jobs, general mobility of workers. Under capitalism, however, the need for job change and for maximum adaptability of workers cannot be met, inasmuch as this runs contrary to the interests of the capitalists." (M. Skatkin, "O politekhnicheskom obuchenii v obshcheobrazovatel'noi shkole," *Izvestiia*, Nov. 21, 1952, p. 2.) If permanent division of labor is not inherent in large-scale industry, but only inherent in capitalism, then why has the worker in the Soviet Union been more strictly tied to his job than a worker in capitalist United States?
[30] "Kontrol'nye tsifry razvitiia narodnogo khoziaistva SSSR na 1959–1965 gody (Tezisy doklada tovarishcha N. S. Khrushcheva na XXI S"ezde KPSS)," *Pravda*, Nov. 14, 1958, p. 7.
[31] Bukharin and Preobrazhenskii, *Azbuka*, p. 49.

sour notes? Even granting that man will be transformed into superman so that he will be able to play every instrument interchangeably, will every individual be *such* a superman that he will also be capable of *conducting* this grandiose orchestra when it comes his turn?

Bukharin apparently had some second thoughts that caused him to introduce certain qualifications. "The totality of the most indispensable sciences is so vast," he admitted, "that no individual can grasp it in its entirety." He recognized that "in certain cases, where persons of unusual talent are concerned," it would be desirable to encourage the mastery of a specialized field of knowledge.[32] This would perhaps make allowance for an elite group even in the ultimate, fully automated society where machines run machines, since a separate corps of highly trained specialists would still be needed to invent, repair, and regulate these delicate and precise instruments.[33] To admit that certain people might have "unusual talent" also implied that certain individuals might be more suited than others to conduct the "orchestra" of a Communist world society. Bukharin even went so far as to suggest that the practice of "subordinating the minority to the majority will disappear . . . in developed Communist society, and that all questions and matters will be decided by science, on the basis of the *superior weight of the better-founded and more scientific opinions, even though in the minority*." This would be the type of relationship that exists "between a physician and a patient, or the leader of a study circle and the students," in which the multitude of ordinary layman voluntarily accepts the opinions of the few who possess superior knowledge and superior wisdom.[34] The prospect is thus raised of rule by a permanently entrenched minority, rather than by an endless rotation of ordinary workers. But Bukharin stubbornly refused to draw this logical conclusion. In another passage in which he mentioned "inequality in talent" as well as "in the social role," Bukharin maintained that "the withering away of the state involves also the elimination of all social and political hierarchies in general."[35] This ap-

[32] *Ibid.*, pp. 164-65.
[33] For an interesting speculation on the effects of introducing automation into the Soviet economy, see Geoffrey Ashe, "Industry," *New Leader*, Aug. 9, 1954, pp. 19-22.
[34] Berdnikov and Svetlov, Bukharin, general ed., *Elements*, p. 237 (italics added).
[35] Bukharin, *Culture*, p. 23.

parent contradiction was "solved" by reference to Marxist dogma which makes all social and political hierarchies dependent upon the existence of society rent by antagonistic classes. A permanent bureaucracy was solely an instrument of class exploitation, so that in a classless society, which by definition would have eliminated exploitation, a permanent bureaucracy could not exist. Since exploitation was explained by economics, it was impossible to visualize the exploitation of the masses by a permanently entrenched few who would administer this socially owned property. The fetish of economic determinism therefore prevented a frank examination of the possibility that power might forever devolve upon a tiny minority of mankind.

Stalin's final theoretical pronouncement in 1952 also contained some conspicuous backsliding on the prospect of the complete interchangeability of occupations. Stalin hedged on the question of obliterating the distinction between mental and manual labor: "The essential distinction between them, the difference in their cultural and technical levels, will certainly disappear. But some distinction, even if inessential, will remain, if only because the conditions of labor in the managerial staffs and those of the workers are not identical." [36] This view has been explicitly upheld in post-Stalinist ideological pronouncements.[37] The prospect of perpetuating the differences between the managers and the common workers certainly suggests that even in the ultimate stage of world communism there might be permanent "managerial staffs."

THE MERGING OF TOWN AND COUNTRY

A similar erasure of distinction was to occur between town and country. In 1926 Stalin described this future equalization as "a condition where workers and peasants will cease to exist as completely distinct economic groups. They will be transformed into toilers on the land and in the factories, i.e., it will be possible to equalize their economic position." [38] Bridging the gulf between town and country was to occur, in Bukharin's phrase, by "the development

[36] Stalin, "Zamechaniia," in *Ekonomicheskie problemy*, p. 29.
[37] K. Ostrovitianov, "Tovarnoe proizvodstvo i zakon stoimosti pri sotsializme," *Kommunist*, No. 13 (Sept., 1957), p. 89.
[38] Stalin, "O krest'ianstve, kak soiuznike rabochego klassa," Feb. 9, 1926, in *Sochineniia*, VIII, 92.

of an industrial regime in the rural economy."[39] In his 1952 essay, Stalin evinced great interest in the problem of how "to raise collective farm property to the level of public property," that is, how to reduce the collective farmer to the status of a factory worker.[40] The Soviet regime, he averred, had already laid the groundwork for eliminating "the antithesis between town and country, between industry and agriculture." But just as he had introduced reservations concerning the retention of certain "inessential" distinctions between mental and manual labor, so he now held that "the abolition of the essential distinction between industry and agriculture cannot lead to the abolition of all distinctions." He foresaw the persistence of "inessential" distinctions "due to the difference between the conditions of work in industry and in agriculture," again suggesting limitations on the interchangeability of occupations.[41] On this occasion he also openly controverted Engels's assertion that the leveling process between town and country would entail the destruction of the great urban centers. "Not only will the great towns not perish, but new great towns will appear as centers for the maximum development of culture, not only in the form of large industrial centers, but also as centers for the processing of agricultural produce and for the powerful development of all branches of the food industry."[42]

Post-Stalinist experimentations with the forms of Soviet agriculture have not altered the ultimate Stalinist objective of destroying the collective farm system and introducing an industrial regime in the countryside. The goal remains despite Khrushchev's apparent strengthening of the kolkhozes by such moves as the transfer of agricultural machinery to them from the machine tractor stations, a program which specifically runs counter to Stalin's proscription of 1952. However, the long-range significance of such innovations, *Kommunist* explained in April, 1958, must not be misunderstood. Under communism, both kolkhoz and state property will merge

[39] Bukharin, *Culture*, p. 15.
[40] Stalin, "Zamechaniia," in *Ekonomicheskie problemy*, pp. 16–17, 27–28; "Ob oshibkakh," in *ibid.*, pp. 66–67; "Otvet tovarishcham," in *ibid.*, pp. 93–94. See also Stalin, "Otchëtnyi doklad XVII s"ezdu partii o rabote TsK VKP(b)," Jan. 26, 1934, in *Sochineniia*, XIII, 351–53, on the transition from artel to commune.
[41] Stalin, "Zamechaniia," in *Ekonomicheskie problemy*, p. 29.
[42] *Ibid.*, p. 26.

into an "all-inclusive form of public, Communist property." Then, "together with the obliteration of differences between the two forms of property, the class boundaries will finally be eradicated between the working class and the kolkhoz peasant; workers and peasants will become the toilers of a unified Communist society." [43] Khrushchev specifically reaffirmed this prospect in his speech to the Twenty-first Party Congress in 1959: "In the future it is quite clear that the kolkhoz-cooperative and state forms of property will merge fully into a single Communist form of property. . . . Agricultural labor will gradually be transformed into a variety of industrial labor." [44]

THE STATUS OF WOMEN

Another phase of the original egalitarian vision was the promise to destroy "all traces of social inequality due to sex." [45] In keeping with the Marxian premise that the bourgeois family was designed to degrade women to the status of chattel, the future society would completely "liberate" women by breaking the shackles of that family structure. Women would be extricated from "domestic slavery" and drawn into socially productive labor through the creation of communal kitchens, laundries, nurseries, and so forth. The care and particularly the education of children would become the responsibility of the entire society.[46]

Subsequent developments witnessed a reversal of the early Soviet attitude of sneering at the sanctity of the bourgeois marital bond. But neither Stalin nor his successors abandoned their aim of transforming most of the other aspects of the bourgeois family pattern. In 1959 Khrushchev was continuing to call for the creation of conditions that will "enable all women to make greater use of their rights, their knowledge, and their talents in productive, socially useful activities." This will be facilitated "by enlarging the network of boarding schools, kindergartens, nurseries, public catering enterprises, and service establishments. . . . In the future," he predicted, "it is planned to provide the possibility of raising all children in

[43] I. Glotov, "Reorganizatsiia MTS i kolkhoznaia sobstvennost'," *Kommunist*, No. 5 (April, 1958), pp. 53-54.
[44] "Doklad tovarishcha N. S. Khrushcheva," *Pravda*, Jan. 28, 1959, p. 9.
[45] "Programma," in *Kom. Int. v dok.*, p. 15.
[46] Clara Zetkin, *Lenin on the Woman Question* (New York, 1934), pp. 10, 20, 28-30; Bukharin and Preobrazhenskii, *Azbuka*, pp. 161-63.

boarding schools. This will help solve the tasks of a Communist rearing for the growing generation and of drawing fresh millions of women into the ranks of active builders of a Communist society." [47]

THE FUSION OF NATIONS

The final annihilation of distinctions was to occur in the realm of nationality, with the fusion of nations and national cultures into a single, world-wide homogeneous entity. The steps envisioned for reaching this ultimate fusion and the possible shape of this entity have already been discussed at some length.[48]

THE TRANSFORMATION OF HUMAN NATURE

The sum total of all these transformations was supposed to produce a new man, requiring a *"mass change in human nature."* [49] This new man, living in a stateless world, would know how to do everything, be capable of perceiving that his every act was in perfect harmony with the requirements of the single world plan, and be the acme of moral rectitude, since his behavior would not be guided or constrained by any coercive authority. He would, in brief, be technically omnicompetent, socially omniscient, and morally unimpeachable.

The magnitude of the changes required in human nature as we know it can best be measured by contrasting the new Communist man with an individual who lives in a contemporary Western nation-state. The theory of the state with which we are familiar makes rather modest demands upon man's "human nature." It assumes that man is not perfect, and that he cannot be relied upon to govern himself without the aid of external restraint. Alexander Hamilton formulated the classic reply to the question: "Why has government been instituted at all? Because the passions of men will not conform to the dictates of reason and justice, without constraint." [50]

Recent Western psychological findings have confirmed Hamil-

[47] "Doklad tovarishcha N. S. Khrushcheva," *Pravda*, Jan. 28, 1959, p. 6.
[48] See especially chapter 7, pp. 209–11, 232, chapter 8, pp. 247–55, 262–63, and chapter 9 on world language.
[49] "Programma," in *Kom. Int. v dok.*, p. 28.
[50] Alexander Hamilton, "The Federalist, No. 15," 1787, in *The Federalist* (New York, Modern Library ed., 1937), p. 92.

ton's venerable judgment. Dr. Ranyard West, a British psychiatrist, has devoted particular attention to the relationship between man's basic make-up and his political order. He has concluded that

the field in which society can rely upon man's conscience to make him do the right thing is a very small one. The psychological mechanisms of fantasy-identification, selective remembering and projection (all of them devices for shelving responsibility for anti-social action) have left only a very limited sphere of *reliable* action under the sway of the moral law. . . . Men need law in their established societies, not so much because their consciences are weak as because their consciences serve prejudices that are strong.[51]

Human nature is such that, in all its most necessary social relationships, it is subject to the permanent threat of the self-assertive impulse, which misinterprets facts, mis-judges events, and then through consequent self-justificatory passion, breaks the social bond unless it be externally restrained.[52]

. . . .

Law becomes an *external support for man's social instinct against the anti-social activities of his self-assertive instinct.* In this function law and government may truly be regarded as an *extension of self-control.*[53]

Just as no individual can safely be relied upon to judge his own cause, so it is with nations living in a lawless world. The only successful way to control the passions of nations is by creating a world state and a common rule of enforceable law. "We cannot control the other party except by submitting to a like control ourselves." A world state would be compatible with man's basic nature since "human nature *is* naturally susceptible to external control, expects it, and can readily adjust itself to a change in the directing authority. Parents, school, national government, world government, lie psychologically along a straight-forward progression." [54] Nowhere does Dr. West suggest that human nature would permit this world state, once achieved, to wither away.

A. D. Lindsay supplies another valuable insight on the basic function of coercive law. "Force is needed to maintain common rules," he observes, "because there are rules which have little value unless everyone keeps them, and force is needed to fill the gap between

[51] Ranyard West, *Psychology and World Order* (New York, 1945), p. 39.
[52] Ranyard West, *Conscience and Society* (New York, 1945), p. 240.
[53] *Ibid.*, p. 168.
[54] Ranyard West, "A Plea for a Rational Approach to the Problem of War and Peace," *University of Chicago Law Review*, XVI, No. 3 (Spring, 1949), 394–95.

most people usually and all people always obeying." A special function of state power arises from "the necessity of assuring that some rules are universally and automatically obeyed, if they are going to be of any use at all." [55]

From the foregoing description of human nature as it now appears, the transformations required for man to live in a world stateless society are indeed formidable: he must be able to rely completely upon his own conscience, which would be undistorted by "fantasy-identification, selective remembering and projection"; he must be without prejudice, or without any antisocial "self-assertive impulses"; he must never misrepresent facts or misjudge events, especially must he be able to judge his own case without bias and without "self-justificatory passion"; and finally, he must always obey those rules of life that are without value unless obeyed universally and automatically. In the light of our present knowledge of man it would seem that no one could attain such perfection, let alone everyone. And the functioning of a world stateless society is premised upon the attainment of this condition of perfection by everyone.

The Soviet theorists have not provided the answers as to how changes of such magnitude in man's nature are to occur. More significantly, they have not even asked the questions that would indicate an awareness of the complexity of the human nature they intend to transform. They are able to assert with confidence that the needed changes will be possible, and what is more, that they will not be difficult, because they have avoided plumbing the murky depths of the human personality. The Soviet leaders have couched their prognosis in the simplified, optimistic frame of reference inherited from Marx and his nineteenth-century contemporaries. There were no heights that man could not scale, and progress toward these lofty peaks was inevitable. Te be detained by doubts that man might be incapable of living in this rarified atmosphere was to hold back the march of history and become a counterrevolutionary. For a revolutionary it was convenient to think that one could take man and do what one wanted with him.

In this context man appeared as a psychologically uncomplicated human being. Correct behavior would be simple to define and no

---

[55] A. D. Lindsay, *The Modern Democratic State* (New York, London, 1947), I, 205-7.

one would have any difficulty in living by these simple rules. "The new culture of humanity united for the first time without any sort of state boundaries," the Comintern Program declared, "will be based upon clear and transparent human relationships."[56] Bukharin felt sure that the basic rules of life would be observed unquestioningly, since "it will not occur to any healthy and normal person to oppose these rules." Should society occasionally turn up "unhealthy" individuals, they would be made to conform, not by the use of the police and jails, which would have disappeared, but by "hospitals and other educational institutions to which there might be sent any particularly incorrigible and abnormal persons."[57]

Like Pavlov's dogs, man could easily be trained to respond to certain approved patterns, which would become the habitual behavior of the new man. Lenin predicted that the *"necessity* of observing the uncomplicated, fundamental rules of human intercourse will become a *habit.*"[58]

People will gradually *become accustomed* to the observation of the elementary rules of social life that have been known for centuries and repeated for thousands of years in all school books; they will become accustomed to observing them without force, without compulsion, without subordination, without the *special apparatus* for compulsion which is called the state.[59]

ALL SOCIETY RUN BY A SINGLE "VALID" WILL

All life could be reduced to a few uncomplicated rules of behavior because Communist society would have eliminated all contradictory desires and selfish egotisms. In the terminology of the Jacobins, the will of each individual would be perfectly expressed in the single, general will of world society. Bukharin illustrated this fusion of wills by saying that if a group of people wished to sing a song or lift a heavy stone, they would enhance the possibility of fulfilling the will of each by acting in unison, that is, by fulfilling the will of the collective. "The case will be the same—but on a more magnificent scale, and in more intricate form—in Communist society. . . . In such a society, all the relations between men

[56] "Programma," in *Kom. Int. v dok.,* p. 16.
[57] Berdnikov and Svetlov, Bukharin, general ed., *Elements,* p. 241.
[58] Lenin, "Gosudarstvo i revoliutsiia," in *Sochineniia,* XXI, 441.
[59] *Ibid.,* XXI, 431.

will be obvious to each, and the social volition will be the *organization* of all their wills." [60]

Lenin added that "large-scale machine industry—which is precisely the material productive source and foundation of socialism—demands the absolute, strictest possible unity of will, to direct the joint labor of hundreds, thousands, and tens of thousands of people." This absolute unity of will would necessarily continue to exist in the era of full communism which would be founded upon the highest possible development of large-scale machine industry. "But how can strict unity of will be insured?" Lenin asked. "By thousands subordinating their will to the will of one." Here Lenin abandoned his customary phrases about the dictatorship of a class, or even the dictatorship of the Party acting in the name of a class, and spoke explicitly about the dictatorship of a single individual. He squarely faced the question: "Is the appointment of individual persons, dictators with unlimited powers, in general, compatible with the fundamental principles of Soviet power?" He answered this in the affirmative with equal forthrightness: "The irrefutable experience of history has shown that in the history of revolutionary movements the dictatorship of individual persons was very often the expression, the bearer, the vehicle of the dictatorship of the revolutionary classes." The will of the dictator expresses the will of the multitude; "hence there is absolutely no contradiction in principle between Soviet (i.e., socialist) democracy and the exercise of dictatorial powers by individual persons." [61]

[60] Bukharin, *Historical*, 1922, p. 41.
[61] Lenin, "Ocherednye zadachi sovetskoi vlasti," March–April, 1918, in *Sochineniia*, XXII, 461–62. Lenin reaffirmed the validity of this specific statement on several occasions. He recalled that "Soviet socialist democracy is in no way contradictory to one-man rule and dictatorship, that a dictator sometimes fulfills the will of a class." ("Rech' o khoziaistvennom stroitel'stve," March 31, 1920, in *ibid.*, XXV, 119.) Or again, Lenin noted that in 1918 "I had pointed out the need of one-man rule, the need of recognizing full dictatorial powers for a single person from the point of view of fulfilling the Soviet idea. All phrases about equal rights are nonsense." ("Rech' na III vserossiiskom s"ezde professional'nykh soiuzov," April 7, 1920, in *ibid.*, XXV, 144.) Lenin's demand for placing dictatorial powers in the hands of individual leaders was maintained even at the height of the attack on Stalin's "cult of the individual" in 1956: "The cult of the individual and the practice of leadership which developed under its influence in the last period of Stalin's life and activity produced great harm.... 'But this does not in the least mean that the process of collective labor can be left without definite leadership, without a precise definition of the responsibility of the leader, without the strictest order, created by the unity of will of the leader.' (Lenin,

Lenin was firmly in the Marxist tradition when he echoed Marx's belief that the successful operation of any joint labor process requires "one commanding will" like that found in the "director of an orchestra." [62] But the demand for a single commanding will was based upon more than a consideration of the economic necessities that Marx found inherent in any large-scale productive process. Lenin was also clearly invoking the shade of Robespierre, whose political ideas and methods of organizing society provided such striking precursors of Bolshevik concepts and techniques. The identity between Jacobinism and Leninism was astonishingly broad, running all the way from the assumption that an individual dictator might legitimately embody the will of all society to the ultimate vision, common both to Jacobin and to Marxist thought, of the withering away of coercive political authority. As Talmon reminds us: "It is vital for the understanding of Jacobinism to remember all the time that the Jacobins sincerely and deeply believed that their terrorist dictatorship, even when maintained for no compelling reason of defense, was nothing but a prelude to a harmonious state of society, in which coercion would become unnecessary." [63]

TODAY'S DICTATOR IS TOMORROW'S "CONDUCTOR"

What did Lenin think would become of the individual dictator in the future harmonious society, when all organs of coercion had withered away? Lenin made it clear that today's ugly reality and tomorrow's bliss would differ in the way the multitude subordinated themselves to the dictator, rather than in the abolition of the role of the dictator. Today the attainment of a unity of will "may assume the sharp forms of a dictatorship if ideal discipline and class consciousness are lacking." In the future society the masses would continue to subordinate themselves to a dictator, but, "given ideal

---

Sochineniia [4th ed.], XXVII, 186.) Combating the cult of the individual one must remember that Marxism-Leninism has nothing in common with petty-bourgeois anarchist views that deny the role of leaders and organizers of the masses." ("Pochemu kul't lichnosti chuzhd dukhu Marksizma-Leninizma?" *Pravda*, March 28, 1956, p. 3.) *Pravda* also quoted Lenin's words about the need to combine elements of tempestuous democracy "with *iron* discipline during work, with *unquestioning* obedience to the will of one person, of the Soviet leader." ("Kommunisticheskaia partiia—vdokhnovitel' i vozhd' sovetskogo naroda," *ibid.*, July 6, 1956, p. 3.)

[62] See chapter 1, p. 18 above.
[63] Talmon, *Totalitarian Democracy*, p. 132. See also *ibid.*, pp. 139–43, 195, 240.

class consciousness and discipline on the part of those participating in the common labor, this subordination would more than anything remind one of the mild leadership of the conductor of an orchestra." [64] Now Lenin filled out the meaning of the orchestra metaphor that we encountered first in Marx and then in Bukharin, who specifically employed it to describe the future administrative apparatus of a world stateless society. Lenin first used the orchestra metaphor in 1902, significantly enough, to idealize the functioning of a centralized, authoritarian Party apparatus.[65] It is clear that, when applied to the society of world communism, Lenin was also trying to depict a highly authoritarian system. (And in fact, an orchestra is highly authoritarian, for no one blows his horn or strings his bow until the split second that the conductor lowers his baton.) *The apocalyptic vision of the orchestra of world communism, then, amounts to a stateless totalitarian society, subject to the will of an individual dictator.* This somber picture is somewhat relieved by the promise that everyone will be eligible to fill the job of world dictator in the course of rotating from one occupation to another, but the reservations on this score introduced by the Soviet theorists themselves have gone a long way to cancel out this prospect.

THE MEANING OF FREEDOM

The Soviet theorists grace this condition of abject servitude with the label of freedom. To those who insist that freedom entails the opportunity to chose between alternate courses of action, and who deny that it is neither desirable nor possible to express the will of all men in the will of a single dictator, this condition denotes the perfect denial of freedom. But in Bolshevik eyes man finds "freedom" when he acts in the one "right" way, in accordance with the single will and single plan of society. There can be no conflict, Bukharin insisted, between individual freedom and the execution of a single all-encompassing plan. "The fulfillment of the plan is the personal, internal aim of these people; their *creative freedom can develop only on this basis.*" [66] When Engels predicted, Bukharin continued, that "humanity, in its transition to communism, makes a 'leap' from

[64] Lenin, "Ocherednye zadachi," in *Sochineniia*, XXII, 462.
[65] Lenin, "Pis'mo k tovarishchu o nashikh organizatsionnykh zadachakh," Sept., 1902, in *ibid.*, V, 190.
[66] Bukharin, *Culture*, p. 26.

the realm of necessity into the realm of freedom," he was describing a leap into a totally planned society of a "consciously organized character." He therefore recommended the definition of freedom that Engels had accepted from Hegel, namely that "freedom is the recognition of necessity." [67] Stalin specifically reiterated approval of this definition in his 1952 essay.[68]

If freedom is a recognition of necessity, what then distinguishes the era of necessity from the era of freedom? No difference can be found in terms of a strict and total subordination of the individual to a single central authority, since that is required in both eras. "Freedom" appears when the totalitarian behavior pattern occurs automatically, out of habit, out of the "free will" of the individual, without the aid of any coercive organs of state. That is, "freedom" consists of "freely" doing the necessary. But what kind of a man will this be? The Soviet theorists have dehydrated man of his human qualities, his very soul, and left the hulk of an automaton.

LENIN'S STRANGE PRESCRIPTION FOR TRAVELING THE PATH TO PARADISE

In order to reach this grotesque paradise Lenin prescribed a baffling formula. He demanded the creation of the strongest possible proletarian state that would turn into no state, *beginning immediately*. Writing on the eve of the Bolshevik Revolution, Lenin insisted that "the proletarian state will begin to wither away *immediately* after its victory, since a state is unnecessary and impossible in a society devoid of class antagonisms." [69] Or again, "the proletariat only needs a state in the process of withering away, i.e., so constituted that it will *begin to wither away at once*, and cannot help but wither away." [70] *At the same time*, in an article dated October 14, 1917, Lenin predicted that immediately after the revolution, "when the state has become proletarian, when it has become the coercive mechanism of the proletariat over the bourgeoisie, then we shall be fully and unreservedly for *a strong state* power and centralism." [71] It would be "extremely stupid and absurdly utopian,"

[67] Bukharin, *Historical*, p. 42.
[68] Stalin, "Zamechaniia," in *Ekonomicheskie problemy*, p. 6.
[69] Lenin, "Gosudarstvo i revoliutsiia," in *Sochineniia*, XXI, 388 (italics added).
[70] *Ibid.*, XXI, 385 (italics added).
[71] Lenin, "Uderzhat li bol'sheviki," in *Sochineniia*, XXI, 268 (italics added).

Lenin echoed in the spring of 1918, "to imagine that the transition from capitalism to socialism would be possible without coercion and dictatorship." And dictatorship means "iron rule, power that is revolutionary, bold, quick, and ruthless. . . . Our rule is too soft," Lenin complained; "very often it is more like jelly than iron." [72] This formula might be explicable to those initiated into the rites of dialectical materialism. To others, the demand for a state that should simultaneously maximize and minimize its powers would seem to be an expression of schizophrenia.

THE GEOGRAPHICAL EXTENT OF A WITHERING STATE

Neither were the Soviet theorists very clear about the geographical extent of state power that the proletariat would have to hold before this strange transformation could begin. Generally, Lenin seemed to expect that the process would commence at once in any isolated country in which the proletariat had staged a successful revolution. In July, 1919, however, he suggested that proletarian state power might not disappear until the proletariat had first established a world state. In the midst of a long, discursive passage he noted casually that "when there will no longer be the possibility of exploitation in the world . . . only then . . . will we hand over this [state] machine for destruction. Then there will be neither state nor exploitation." [73] In 1926 Stalin explicitly reverted to the view that the destruction of state power was dependent solely upon the elimination of class contradictions within each individual country: "The state is first of all the weapon of one class against other classes, and it is self-evident that as soon as classes disappear there can be no state." He acknowledged that this might lead to the withering away of the existing Soviet state *before* it had become a world state: "One must concede the possibility of a future classless society, having neither classes nor a state, which may nevertheless need a socialist militia to defend itself against foreign enemies." However, Stalin considered the continued isolation of the Soviet state an unrealistic contingency, since the Russian revolution "cannot fail to evoke revolutionary explosions in other countries." [74]

[72] Lenin, "Ocherednye zadachi," in *ibid.*, XXII, 458–59.
[73] Lenin, "O gosudarstve," July 11, 1919, in *ibid.*, XXIV, 377.
[74] Stalin, "Zakliuchitel'noe slovo," Dec. 13, 1926 in *Sochineniia*, IX, 129–30.

TIME ESTIMATES FOR THE WITHERING PROCESS

Precise estimates of the timing of the withering process have varied considerably. On the eve of the Bolshevik Revolution Lenin only ventured to assert that the process would begin from the moment the proletariat had seized power. As to when it would end, he cautioned: "We have the right to speak solely of the inevitable withering away of the state, emphasizing the protracted nature of this process . . . leaving completely open the question of time or the concrete forms of withering, since material for the solution of these questions is *not yet available*." [75] Flushed with victory, the Soviet leaders became bold and impatient. At the Seventh Party Congress in March, 1918, Bukharin complained that he could not yet see signs of the Soviet state withering away. Lenin, who was then immersed in the practical struggle of maximizing rather than minimizing state power, none the less agreed that the state was moving toward its own destruction. "The name of our Party indicates clearly enough that we are going toward full communism, that we stand for . . . a society without any sort of coercive control or force." Then facing up to Bukharin's question, "When will the state begin to wither away?" Lenin replied:

We still have time for at least two more Party Congresses before we can say: see how our state is withering away. Until that time, it is too early to speak of it. To proclaim the withering away of the state prematurely would destroy the historical perspective.[76]

As it was then customary to convene a Party Congress annually, Lenin apparently thought that the state might begin to wither away in 1920. In another statement of March, 1918, Lenin indicated that once the withering process was under way it might proceed very rapidly. The Soviet state, he observed, was engaged in leaping from the realm of necessity to the realm of freedom, and "leaps of this kind extend over periods of ten years or even more." [77] In 1919 Bukharin himself offered a more "conservative" estimate, predicting that "two or three generations will have to grow up under new conditions before the power of the working class state will be unnecessary. . . . Within a few decades there will be a new world

[75] Lenin, "Gosudarstvo i revoliutsiia," in *Sochineniia*, XXI, 436.
[76] Lenin, "Vystupleniia protiv popravki Bukharina k rezoliutsii o programme partii," March 8, 1918, in *ibid.*, XXII, 365.
[77] Lenin, "Ocherednye zadachi," in *ibid.*, XXII, 466.

WORLD STATE OF NO STATE

with other men and other manners." [78] Lenin also stretched out this prospect in a May Day speech of 1919: "A majority of those present who are under thirty or thirty-five years of age will see the flowering of communism, from which we are still far." [79] In 1924 Stalin likewise calculated that "the transition from capitalism to communism must not be regarded as a fleeting period of 'superrevolutionary' acts and decrees, but as an entire historical era." He cited with approval a statement of Marx that the workers "will have to go through fifteen, twenty, or fifty years" of wars and conflicts to reshape both external conditions and themselves.[80] After the mid-1920s the game of predicting the exact date for the arrival of stateless communism appears to have gone out of fashion.

THE STATE DISSOLVES IN THE HANDS OF THE PEOPLE

The sanguine expectations of the disappearance of the Soviet state were based on the assumption, frequently expressed by the Soviet leaders during their first years of power, that their state was *sui generis*, so constructed that it would unavoidably bring about its own early destruction. "Soviet power is a *new type of state*," Lenin declared in March, 1918, "in which there is no bureaucracy, no police, no standing army and in which bourgeois democracy is replaced by a new democracy that brings to the fore the vanguard of the toiling masses, turning them into legislators and executives and a military guard, and which creates an apparatus capable of reeducating the masses." [81] Actually this was not a description of the existing structure of Soviet power, but a picture of what the Soviet state was supposed to look like. The institution of the soviets was theoretically modeled on the Marxian image of the Paris Commune. This was a state form born as a "semistate" because it had destroyed three main props of bourgeois society: the bureaucracy, the police, and the standing army. In the new proletarian semistate these functions would be performed interchangeably by the entire populace, thus preventing the formation of a separate governing caste. So that

---

[78] Bukharin and Preobrazhenskii, *Azbuka*, p. 49.
[79] Lenin, "Tri rechi na krasnoi ploshchadi," May 1, 1919, in *Sochineniia*, XXIV, 270.
[80] Stalin, "Ob osnovakh Leninizma," April, 1924, in *O Lenine i Leninizme*, pp. 64–65.
[81] Lenin, "Doklad o peresmotre programy i nazvaniia partii," March 8, 1918, in *Sochineniia*, XXII, 353 (italics added).

no privileged groups might entrench themselves in the seats of power, Lenin recommended the "infallible expedients" of the Commune: "(1) not only election, but also recall at any time; (2) payment no higher than that of ordinary workers; (3) immediate introduction of control and supervision by *all*, so that *all* shall become 'bureaucrats' for a time and so that, therefore, *no one* can become a bureaucrat." [82] The soviets would immediately draw the ordinary worker into the processes of government, and, being both legislative and executive bodies, would provide him with the all-around political education required for the era of statelessness. Just prior to the seizure of power Lenin estimated that by means of the soviets "we can *bring into action immediately a state apparatus* of about ten, if not twenty millions," thereby shattering the "prejudice of bourgeois intellectuals that only special officials can carry on the administration of the state." "We are not utopians"—Lenin was always highly indignant at the charge that his plans were utopian. "We know that just any laborer or any cook would be incapable of taking over immediately the administration of the state." But he demanded that, "starting immediately," every laborer or cook should learn how to administer the affairs of state, so that the masses would soon be able to govern themselves without any special apparatus standing apart from, and above, the people.[83]

This great surge of mass initiative was to obliterate every vestige of an elite group, so that it would not only destroy the Soviet state, but also the Communist Party. In 1924 Stalin asserted: "the Party is an instrument of the proletariat. From this it follows that when classes disappear and the dictatorship of the proletariat withers away, the Party will also wither away." [84]

The prospect of all special governing apparatuses dissolving in the hand of the people raised some of the same sharp questions posed by the ultimate image of world communism. Were all the functions of state really so simple, as Lenin had supposed, that every common laborer could administer its vast affairs? And even if this were so, could the Party, which was based on rule from above by a tiny elite, tolerate its own destruction, by stimulating the rule of the masses from below? The first doubtful proposition, that every common

---

[82] Lenin, "Gosudarstvo i revoliutsiia," in *ibid.*, XXI, 446.
[83] Lenin, "Uderzhat li bol'sheviki," in *ibid.*, XXI, 266–67.
[84] Stalin, "Ob osnovakh Leninizma," in *O Lenine i Leninizme*, p. 138.

laborer would be fit to run the affairs of state, was prevented from ever being put to a test by the failure to implement the second proposition, that elite rule should be overturned by the rule of the masses.

Early in 1918 Rosa Luxemburg, a Marxist who was at the same time a severe critic of Lenin's Jacobin principles of Party organization, set down a clear-sighted prophecy on the outcome of the conflict between preparing the masses to rule themselves through the use of the soviets and the needs of an autocratic Party to stifle mass initiative.

Lenin and Trotsky have laid down the soviets as the only true representatives of the laboring masses. But with the repression of political life in the land as a whole, life in the soviets must also become more and more crippled. . . . Only bureaucracy remains as the active element. Public life gradually falls asleep, a few dozen Party leaders of inexhaustible energy and boundless experience direct and rule. Among them, in reality only a dozen outstanding heads do the leading and an elite of the working class is invited from time to time to meetings where they are to applaud the speeches of the leaders, and to approve proposed resolutions unanimously—at bottom, then, a clique affair—a dictatorship, to be sure, not a dictatorship of the proletariat, however, but only the dictatorship of a handful of politicians, that is a dictatorship in the bourgeois sense, in the sense of the rule of the Jacobins.[85]

In the same work in which Stalin envisioned the withering away of the Party as a result of stimulating the mass activity of the soviets, he affirmed that non-Party organizations, such as the soviets, were only of secondary importance. "The Party is . . . the only organization capable of centralizing the leadership of the struggle of the proletariat, thus transforming each and every non-Party organization of the working class into an auxiliary body and transmission belt linking the Party with the class." [86] Similarly, a Comintern resolution of 1920 found it necessary to warn that "the Communist Party must constantly and systematically direct the work of the soviets. . . . The idea that the Communist Party should *dissolve itself* in the soviets, that the soviets can *replace* the Communist Party is profoundly mistaken and reactionary." [87]

[85] Rosa Luxemburg, *The Russian Revolution*, early 1918, trans. and Intro. by Bertram D. Wolfe (New York, 1940), pp. 47-48.
[86] Stalin, "Ob osnovakh Leninizma," in *O Lenine i Leninizme*, p. 135.
[87] "Rol' kommunisticheskoi partii v proletarskoi revoliutsii," July 19-Aug. 7, 1920, in *Kom. Int. v dok.*, p. 108.

As the permanent organs of the proletarian state became increasingly entrenched, Lenin became obsessed with the idea of stimulating mass initiative. The creation of a permanent Red Army and a police force—including the dreaded secret police—was largely rationalized as temporary expedients needed to defend the Soviet workers from attack. But the re-creation of a permanent bureaucracy was more difficult to explain. "A putrid bureaucratic bog," Lenin complained in 1922, "is *sucking us* into the scribbling of documents, the talking about decrees, and the drafting of decrees, while vital work is being submerged in this morass of paper."[88] Soon after Lenin's death, in 1925, Stalin echoed that "it is necessary to overhaul the state apparatus in such a way that it will guarantee the transformation of society based on the dictatorship of the proletariat into a stateless society, a Communist society." In order to do this Stalin said that it was imperative to "put new life into the soviets."[89]

From the first days of the Soviet regime until the present, the Party leaders have repeatedly and unsuccessfully launched campaigns to fight bureaucracy and "put new life into the soviets."[90] Apart from the possibility that some sort of bureaucracy may be an inherent part of every society, Lenin himself once provided a clue as to why these campaigns would be doomed to failure by acknowledging a special connection between bureaucracy and the basic organizational principle of Bolshevism. "Bureaucracy *versus* democracy is precisely the same thing as centralism *versus* autonomy; it is the organizational principle of revolutionary Social Democracy as opposed to the organizational principle of opportunist Social Democracy."[91] These significant words were written in the heat of a Party debate in 1904 in the course of Lenin's defense of an elitist conception of the Party. Here Lenin stumbled upon the organic connection between centralism and bureaucracy as opposed to initiative from below, which he called democracy and autonomy. Though Lenin later sought to disavow bureaucracy and to advance his cause in the name of democracy, Soviet society remained firmly

[88] Lenin, "O novoi postanovke raboty SNK i STO," Jan. 24, 1922, in *Sochineniia*, XXVII, 159.
[89] Stalin, "Voprosy i otvety," June 9, 1925, in *Sochineniia*, VII, 159.
[90] On the failure of the soviets to stimulate mass initiative and destroy bureaucracy, see Barrington Moore, Jr., *Soviet Politics: The Dilemma of Power* (Cambridge, Mass., 1950), pp. 128–38, 170–76, 277–97.
[91] Lenin, "Shag vperëd, dva shaga nazad," Feb.–May, 1904, in *Sochineniia*, VI, 313.

attached to autocratic centralism, both in the Party (where it was disguised as "democratic centralism") and in the Soviet state (where it was disguised as "federalism").

Following the revolution Lenin cast the Siamese twins of bureaucracy and centralism in opposing roles. He protested that "we are being eaten up by bureaucracy." Yet he insisted that this situation "can only be repaired by centralization," since it was impermissible to "abandon centralism for the quagmire of localism." [92] But was it really possible to separate these twins and then use one to destroy the other? The futility of this approach was matched by the attempt to infuse new life into the Commissariat of Worker's and Peasant's Inspection, which was supposed to activate and verify the work of the soviets. In April, 1923, this Commissariat was interlocked with the Party Control Commission, with the result that the Party extended its control ever deeper into the soviets, thereby further reducing initiative from below.[93]

THE RETREAT TO REALITY WITH STALIN'S REPUDIATION OF LENIN

As it became clear that the masses were not being prepared to take over and then dissolve the organs of state, the Soviet leaders were forced to place ever greater reliance upon the existing state apparatus. The demand for a proletarian semistate became an increasing liability with the launching of the first Five-Year Plan in 1928 and the subsequent collectivization of agriculture. To carry out these programs Stalin found that he had to create an immense, stable bureaucracy and to enlarge significantly the power of the secret police and the other organs of state coercion.

Stalin, who claimed to be "the Lenin of today," had to attack a basic tenet of Leninism without appearing to attack Lenin. A convenient scapegoat was provided in the person of Bukharin, whom Stalin was then vigorously attempting to discredit, since Bukharin had written extensively on the coming era of statelessness. In April, 1929, Stalin began drumming up respect for a full-fledged proletarian state by pointing his finger at the supposedly heretical "opinion of Bukharin that the working class should be hostile *in principle*

[92] Lenin, "Rech' na zasedanii moskovskoi obshchegorodskoi konferentsii," Jan. 18, 1919, in *ibid.*, XXIII, 472.
[93] Carr, *Bolshevik Revolution*, I, 225-28.

454 WORLD STATE OF NO STATE

to *every sort* of state, including the working class state." [94] He based this accusation on a misunderstanding that had occurred between Lenin and Bukharin as a result of Bukharin's writings in 1916. From these articles Lenin had received the impression that Bukharin was advocating the destruction of all forms of the state. Actually Bukharin had carefully specified that "in the growing revolutionary struggle the proletariat destroys the state organization of the *bourgeoisie,* makes use of the remaining material framework, [and] creates its own temporary organization of state power." [95] Bukharin later emphasized that "I have not made the mistake attributed to me, for I clearly saw the need for the dictatorship of the proletariat," and related that Lenin had withdrawn his criticism and had insructed Krupskaia to convey his regrets to Bukharin. "When I arrived in Russia from America and saw Nadezhda Konstantinovna," Bukharin recalled, "her first words were 'V. I. asked me to tell you that he has no disagreements with you over the question of the state.' " [96]

In 1929 Stalin was intent upon driving a wedge between the views of Lenin and Bukharin and then overturning Lenin's ideas on the state, on the pretext that these views belonged solely to Bukharin. Consequently, Stalin resorted to the additional startagem of citing the appraisal of Bukharin that Lenin had recorded in his Testament (omitting, naturally, the scathing criticism reserved for Stalin):

Bukharin is not only the most valuable and biggest theoretician of the Party but he may also legitimately be considered the favorite of the whole Party; but *his theoretical views can only with the very greatest doubt be regarded as fully Marxist, for there is something scholastic in him (he has never learned, and I think never fully understood dialectics).*[97]

[94] Stalin, "O pravom uklone v VKP(b)," April, 1929, in *Sochineniia,* XII, 72.
[95] N. Bukharin, "K teorii imperialisticheskogo gosudarstva," summer, 1916, in *Revoliutsiia prava, sbornik* (Moscow, 1925), I, 31–32 (italics added).
[96] *Ibid.,* p. 5; a footnote Bukharin added at the time of publication in 1925. When attacking Bukharin in 1929, Stalin accepted the veracity of this statement: "Very likely Nadezhda Konstantinovna did tell Bukharin what he writes here." But from this Stalin drew the very different conclusion that "Lenin had certain reasons for believing that Bukharin had renounced or was ready to renounce his mistakes. That is all." (Stalin, "O pravom uklone," in *Sochineniia,* XII, 77–78.)
[97] Stalin, "O pravom uklone," in *Sochineniia,* XII, 69. For the full text and details on Lenin's Testament, see E. H. Carr, *The Interregnum, 1923–1924* (London, 1954), pp. 258–60, 263, 359–61. Following Khrushchev's attack on Stalin, these letters were finally published in the Soviet press: "Neopublikovannye dokumenty V. I. Lenina," *Kommunist,* No. 9 (June, 1956), pp. 17–18.

Stalin soon used Lenin's remark about dialectics as the springboard for an unabashed revision of the Leninist doctrine of the withering away of the state. In July, 1930, Stalin told the Sixteenth Party Congress:

We stand for the withering away of the state. At the same time we stand for the strengthening of the dictatorship of the proletariat, which represents the most powerful and mighty authority of all forms of the state which have existed up to the present day. The highest possible development of state power, with the object of preparing conditions for the withering away of the state; that is the Marxist formula. Is this "contradictory"? Yes, this is "contradictory." But this contradiction is a living thing and completely reflects Marxian dialectics. . . . Whoever has failed to understand this peculiarity and "contradictoriness" of our transitional times has not understood the dialectical character of the historical process and is lost to Marxism.[98]

Apparently Lenin was lost to Marxism since he had explicitly asserted that the mighty apparatus of the dictatorship of the proletariat must be "so constituted that it will *begin to wither away at once.*" The game of setting a timetable for withering, in which Stalin had likewise indulged in the early 1920s, clearly reflected the expectation that there were to be finite limits to the life of a proletarian semistate, and not that there would be an indefinite period of strengthening such a state's authority for the equivocal purpose of *"preparing the conditions* for the withering away of the state." And Bukharin, "the most valuable and biggest theoretician of the Party . . . never fully understood dialectics." Who then is to say what Marxian dialectics really means? As Lenin once remarked: "Many times, even in the history of Greek philosophy, dialectics have served as a bridge to sophistry." [99] Under the dictatorship of the proletariat dialectics, it would seem, means precisely what the dictator decides that it means.

Vyshinsky, the Stalinist hatchet man assigned to chop down the theorists of a withering state, also unearthed a supposed divergence between Lenin and Bukharin on the state. In 1920, Vyshinsky recalled, Lenin had criticized an article in which "Bukharin assumed (1) that the proletarian state withers away from the first moment of its emergence and (2) that this withering occurs in the following order: first the army and the fleet begin to wither away as the weap-

[98] Stalin, "Politicheskii otchët Tsentral'nogo Komiteta XVI s"ezdu VKP(b)," June 27, 1930, in *Sochineniia*, XII, 369–70.
[99] Lenin, "O broshiure Iuniusa," Aug., 1916, in *Sochineniia*, XIX, 181.

ons of the most severe external coercion; then the system of punitive and repressive organs; finally the coercive character of labor and so on." Lenin's critique, to which Vyshinsky attributed a "devastating sarcasm," posed the question: "Is it not the other way around: the first 'finally,' then 'then,' and the last 'first'?" [100]

The prospect of the army and fleet withering away first would have been somewhat less ridiculous if Vyshinsky had taken the trouble to quote the sentence that prefaced Bukharin's statement, namely: "As soon as the decisive world victory of the proletariat is apparent, the distorted growth of the proletarian state begins to decline abruptly." [101] With the world victory of the proletariat in the offing it is understandable that the need for organs of external coercion might quickly disappear. Moreover, the idea of a proletarian semistate defending itself against the outside world without a regular army, which Vyshinsky claimed to assail, was expounded by none other than Lenin. On the eve of the revolution, Lenin detailed a plan for replacing immediately a standing army by "a real *people's militia* . . . one that consists of the entire population *without exception*." [102] As late as 1926 Stalin maintained that "theoretically we may fully allow for a conception of society in which there are no classes, no state, but where there is an armed people defending its classless society against foreign enemies." [103]

If Lenin subsequently came to the conclusion that a regular army and fleet were necessary, and could only be dispensed with in the final stages of withering, how did this disprove Bukharin's belief that "the proletarian state withers away from the first moment of its emergence"? Lenin took issue with the *order* in which the various organs of state should wither away, but not with the *principle of their progressive disappearance*. According to Lenin's revised view, the coercive character of labor and the internal organs of punishment and repression should be the first to wither away. Yet Vyshinsky twisted Lenin's critique of Bukharin to mean that those who "preach the withering away of the organs of punishment and repression represented an attempt to deliver us with our hands tied—our

---

[100] A. Ia. Vyshinsky, *Osnovnye zadachi nauki sovetskogo sotsialisticheskogo prava* (Moscow, 1938), p. 14.
[101] V. I. Lenin, "Zamechaniia na knigu N. I. Bukharina: 'Ekonomika perekhodnogo perioda,' " May, 1920, in *Leninskii sbornik* (Moscow, 1924), XI, 400.
[102] Lenin, "Pis'ma iz daleka," March 24, 1917, in *Sochineniia*, XX, 37.
[103] Stalin, "Zakliuchitel'noe slovo," Dec. 13 1926, in *Sochineniia*, IX, 129.

WORLD STATE OF NO STATE 457

entire country—into the robber clutches of wreckers, terrorists, and diversionists," and ended with a hymn of praise to "our remarkable Stalinist intelligence service," the NKVD, and the Procurator's Office.[104]

STALIN'S ABANDONMENT OF EGALITARIAN PRETENSIONS

The newly proclaimed veneration for the organs of the proletarian state were accompanied by profound changes in the fabric of Soviet society which likewise repudiated the vision of a stateless, classless society. Lenin had held that a thoroughly egalitarian society was necessary to prevent the restoration of special privileges for a bureaucratic caste, with a vested interest in preserving and strengthening the state. Following the revolution the Soviet government was temporarily forced to pay high wages to bourgeois specialists, due to the lack of skilled proletarian technicians. This caused Lenin to protest: "Clearly such a measure is a compromise, a departure from the principle of the Paris Commune and of every proletarian state, which calls for the reduction of all salaries to the level of the wages of the average worker."[105] In 1931 Stalin stated unequivocally: "Egalitarianism has nothing in common with Marxian socialism."[106] Stalin attempted to justify the systematic introduction of inequality of reward, with its resulting hierarchical stratification of society, by claiming that Marx foresaw continued inequalities during the first phase of communism, when people would be rewarded in accordance with their work, and that such inequalities would only vanish in the era of full communism, when people would be rewarded in accordance with their needs, irrespective of the work performed.[107] To be sure, Lenin recognized that remnants of the bourgeois state would have to remain during the first period of communism to enforce the "bourgeois right" of unequal possession of articles of consumption, until a society of plenty could reward people according to their needs.[108] But he was simply anticipating the gradual elimination of old inequalities arising out of an economy of scarcity, and never

[104] Vyshinsky, *Osnovnye zadachi*, pp. 14–15.
[105] Lenin, "Ocherednye zadachi," in *Sochineniia*, XXII, 447.
[106] Stalin, "Beseda s nemetskim pisatelem Emilem Liudvigom," Dec. 13, 1931, in *Sochineniia*, XIII, 119.
[107] *Ibid.*, XIII, 118; Stalin, "Novaia obstanovka—novye zadachi khoziaistvennogo stroitel'stva," June 23, 1931, in *Sochineniia*, XIII, 55–60.
[108] Lenin, "Gosudarstvo i revoliutsiia,' in *Sochineniia*, XII, 435–38.

advocated the introduction and the glorification of drastic new inequalities.

Stalin's frank abandonment of social and economic equality coincided with the abandonment of equal status for the various nations of the Soviet Union and the growth of Great Russian chauvinism. This brought in its wake the restoration of the traditional bourgeois family and an official toleration and limited support of religion.[109] The introduction of all of these "reforms" comprised different aspects of the same phenomenon: the repudiation of the original international class ideology and the assertion of the values of nation above class. Henceforth the world-wide objectives of Soviet society would be realized through the infinite strengthening of a caste-ridden Soviet state, increasingly nurtured by the values of Russian nationalism, instead of by an egalitarian, international class doctrine, which if implemented, would destroy both Russian nationalism and the Soviet state.

SOCIALISM "ACHIEVED" WHILE THE STATE GROWS STRONGER

In 1936, mid-stream in these developments, some of which were not to mature for another decade, Stalin announced that the Soviet Union had achieved "the complete victory of socialism," as the first stage of communism. "All exploiting classes have now been eliminated," Stalin declared. The absence of antagonistic classes had rendered obsolete the terms "proletariat" and "dictatorship of the proletariat," since "the proletariat is a class exploited by the capitalists. But in our country, as you know, the capitalist class has already been eliminated." Soviet society, Stalin indicated, now consisted of two "friendly classes" of workers and peasants, plus a special "stratum" of the intelligentsia. Here "class" and "stratum" denoted occupational differences, not classes in the traditional Marxist sense of those involved in a class struggle.[110]

---

[109] For detailed accounts of the abandonment of the original class ideology in the numerous aspects of Soviet society, see Nicholas S. Timasheff, *The Great Retreat: The Growth and Decline of Communism in Russia* (New York, 1946); W. W. Kulski, *The Soviet Regime: Communism in Practice* (Syracuse, 1954).

[110] Stalin, "O proekte konstitutsii Soiuza SSR," Nov. 25, 1936, in *Doklad o proekte*, pp. 14-15, 23, 38-39. The attainment of "socialism," Stalin said, meant that "the exploitation of man by man has been abolished, eliminated." (*Ibid.*, p. 14.) This utopian condition had supposedly come about from the introduction of gross inequality of rewards, and the use of the most despised aspects

In the mid-1920s Stalin thought that the cessation of the class struggle would inevitably foredoom the state, since "the state is first of all the weapon of one class against the other classes, and it is self-evident that as soon as classes disappear there can be no state." [111] Moreover, as "the Party is an instrument of the dictatorship of the proletariat," it follows that when "the dictatorship of the proletariat withers away, the Party will also wither away." [112] The advent of "socialism" in 1936 did not produce these anticipated results. In his report on the 1936 Constitution, which legitimized the continued existence of the Soviet state, Stalin commented, "We need stability of laws now more than ever." [113] It is interesting that Stalin called the intelligentsia, which formed the permanent bureaucracy of the Soviet state, a special "stratum" of society. It will be recalled that Lenin had denounced the idea of entrusting the administration of the state to a special stratum of society as a prejudice of bourgeois intellectuals. Following the adoption of the 1936 Constitution, Stalin said: "Our new intelligentsia demands a new theory, teaching the need for a cordial attitude toward it, solicitude and respect for it." [114] Nor did Stalin abolish the ruling position of the Party. Although he had declared the dictatorship of the proletariat nonexistent, he immediately replaced it by the "dictatorship of the working class" which "preserves unchanged the present role of the Communist Party of the USSR." [115]

How did Stalin explain the obvious discrepancy between these

---

of capitalist production, such as the speed-up, piece work, stringent labor discipline, company unions, and quasi-dictatorial powers for plant managers—all in the appropriate Soviet disguises. Stalin's assertion could also be tested by the Marxist belief that socialism would abolish exploitation because a socialist economy would produce, not for profit, but for use. Production for use meant an abundance of consumer's goods for everyone. This assumed that socialism would result from the overturn of a capitalist economy in the highest stage of its development. The attempt to build socialism in a capitalistically primitive society resulted in the forced rate of building of capital goods and a conscious restriction of the production of use (or consumer's) goods. Thus the exploitation which Marx associated with the early stages of capitalism was intensified under Soviet "socialism." This exploitation is all the more cruel when advanced in the name of the voiceless workers, whose "interests" are represented through the fiction of a class will interpreted by the Party elite. All this refers to the "free" labor in the Soviet Union, and says nothing of the millions who worked in the Soviet slave labor camps.

[111] Stalin, "Zakliuchitel'noe slovo," in *Sochineniia*, IX, 129.
[112] Stalin, "Ob osnovakh Leninizma," in *O Lenine i Leninizme*, p. 138.
[113] Stalin, "O proekte," in *Doklad o proekte*, p. 45.
[114] Stalin, *Otchëtnyi doklad na XVIII s"ezde*, March 10, 1939, p. 156.
[115] Stalin, "O proekte," in *Doklad o proekte*, p. 34.

two views on the withering away of all governing formations in a socialist society? In 1930 he played verbal tricks with dialectics, but that hardly comprised a satisfactory explanation for this *volte-face*. In 1933 he presented a somewhat more palatable rationalization: "The state will not wither away as a result of the weakening of state power, but as a result of its strengthening to the utmost, which is necessary for the purpose of finally crushing the remnants of the dying classes and of organizing a defense against the capitalist encirclement." [116] After 1936, when the remnants of the dying classes had supposedly been wiped out, the only remaining justification for a strong state was the capitalist encirclement.

NEW JUSTIFICATIONS FOR LEVIATHAN

It was this argument that Stalin emphasized in 1939 in a renewed effort to explain the persistence of the Soviet state. So long as Soviet society has not been victorious on a world-wide scale, "it must have its own state strong enough to defend the conquests of socialism from foreign attack." [117] Capitalist encirclement likewise was advanced as the pretext for retaining "the punitive organs and the intelligence service, which are indispensable for the detection and punishment of spies, assassins, and wreckers sent into our country by foreign espionage services. As for our army, punitive organs, and intelligence service, their edge is no longer turned toward the inside of our country, but toward the outside, against external enemies." This was possible since within the country "exploitation has been abolished, there are no longer any exploiters left, and so there is no one to suppress." Since the existence of the Soviet state was made dependent upon the capitalist encirclement, Stalin indicated that the state would be preserved even in the era of full communism, should the capitalist encirclement remain. Conversely, the Soviet state "will not remain and will wither away if the capitalist encirclement is liquidated and a socialist encirclement takes its place." [118] According to this formula, the end of capitalist encirclement, which would provide the opportunity for the birth of the Soviet world state, would, at the same time, render the Soviet world state unnecessary and thereby prevent its appearance.

[116] Stalin, "Itogi pervoi piatiletki," Jan. 7, 1933, in *Sochineniia*, XIII, 211.
[117] Stalin, *Otchëtnyi doklad na XVIII s"ezde*, p. 140.
[118] *Ibid.*, pp. 148–50.

WORLD STATE OF NO STATE

Stalin then promptly upset this rather clear-cut line of reasoning by introducing several functions of the Soviet state which were in no apparent way dependent upon the existence, or the nonexistence, of the capitalist encirclement. Casually intermingled with the above explanation, Stalin declared: "In place of the function of suppression, the state has acquired the function of protecting socialist property from thieves and pilferers of the people's property." In addition, "the function of economic organization and cultural education by the state organs has also remained, and has received its full development. Now the main task of our state inside our country consists of peaceful economic organization and cultural education." [119] The persistence of the punitive functions of state required to protect socialist property could only be connected with capitalist encirclement on the far-fetched supposition that every pilferer was in the employ of a foreign power. And the retention of coercive organs of state directed against Soviet citizens for the purpose of economic organization and cultural education was even less plausibly related to capitalist encirclement.

In 1938, a year prior to this exposition by Stalin, Vyshinsky had already expounded the need to develop the positive, creative functions of a socialist state vis-à-vis its own people. "Soviet laws are directed at strengthening the socialist economy and Soviet discipline, as well as at educating its citizens in the spirit of communism. . . . In the hands of a socialist state, these laws are a mighty instrument for reorganizing society, for refashioning the human consciousness." [120] The unfolding of these new functions of law in a socialist society flatly contradicted the original Leninist expectation that only a few miserable remnants of the bourgeois state would persist in the era of socialism to protect private rights in consumption goods. Nothing could have been more absurd than for Lenin to have demanded that the coercive organs of state concerned with economic organization and cultural education be developed to the fullest at the very moment that all class antagonisms and all exploitation had ceased to exist. Nor did Vyshinsky indicate that these positive functions would vanish overnight. "The creation of new forms of social life, of new orders of community living," he concluded, "is an *extremely protracted process*." [121]

[119] *Ibid.*, pp. 148–49.
[120] Vyshinsky, *Sovetskoe gosudarstvennoe pravo*, p. 577.
[121] *Ibid.*, p. 579 (italics added).

WITHERING PLACED AT THE END OF INFINITY

How long is this "extremely protracted process"? Would these new functions of a socialist state automatically cease with the liquidation of the capitalist encirclement so as to preclude the formation of a Soviet world state? Since the development of these new functions is essentially unrelated to the capitalist encirclement, there is no reason to expect that the end of the capitalist encirclement will also bring an end to the Soviet state. The disappearance of the Soviet world state had, instead, become dependent upon perfecting its economic organization and completing the reeducation of humanity. But who is to say at what point society will be satisfactorily organized and the people sufficiently educated to live in a stateless world? These answers would obviously be provided by the elite ruling formations of the Soviet world state, and until they so determined, the coercive organs of the world state would continue to operate full blast. Under these conditions it is not only conceivable but likely that the withering away of the world state could be postponed forever.

By a sleight of hand Stalin had shifted the justification for the continued existence of the Soviet state from the objective factor of capitalist encirclement to the subjective factor of the arbitrary judgment and willful decision of the masters of the Soviet state. This shift also involved a "reinterpretation" of a basic "law" of Marxism, namely the dependence of the superstructure upon the base, thereby providing an additional rationalization for an indefinite delay in the withering process. Marx held that the material base, i.e., the economic forces and relations of production, determines the superstructure, i.e., the ideas and institutions of any given society.[122] Foremost among these institutions was the state. According to the original Marxist conception, the changes in the forces and relations of production required to create a socialist society would automatically and inevitably wither away that relic of the bourgeois superstructure known as the state. When Stalin proclaimed the exist-

[122] Engels later modified this oversimplified explanation, and in doing so destroyed a good deal of the logic of the Marxian writings based on what appeared to be a clear-cut assumption of economic determinism and the unquestioned primacy of the base over the superstructure. Engels finally acknowledged an interaction between the base and superstructure, while still holding that the economic factors are "finally decisive," and that "ultimately" the base determines the superstructure. See *Selected Correspondence*, pp. 475–77, 517–18.

ence of socialism and simultaneously demanded the fullest development of every aspect of state power he cut the superstructure adrift from its base, with the result that a total transformation in the material conditions of life need have no effect upon the continued existence of the state.

An admission that the base no longer determined the superstructure led to the dialectically opposite idea that the superstructure determined the base. This innovation, which Stalin appropriately called "a revolution from above," was, no doubt, another example of Stalin's unique insight into Marxian dialectics. The phrase "revolution from above" first appeared, significantly enough, in 1938, in the official *History of the All-Union Communist Party (Bolsheviks), Short Course*.[123] Stalin did not fully elaborate its meaning until he resumed his theorizing after the war, in the linguistics controversy of 1950. Attempting to endow his innovations with the appearance of orthodoxy, Stalin began by asserting that "the superstructure is the product of the base." He then substantially negated this statement with the explanation that

this does not mean that the superstructure merely reflects the base, that it is passive, neutral, indifferent to the fate of its base. . . . On the contrary, no sooner does it arise than it becomes *an exceedingly active force*, actively influencing the formation and the strengthening of its own base, employing all measures to help the new system finish off and liquidate the old base and the old classes.[124]

The collectivization of agriculture in the Soviet Union was an example of this process, because the old bourgeois agricultural base was liquidated through the power of the proletarian state: "It was a revolution from above, because the revolution was accomplished on the initiative of the existing power, with the support," as Stalin alleged, "of the broad mass of the peasantry." Stalin conveniently restricted the meaning of the word "revolution." Revolutions in a non-Soviet society must take the form of an "explosion," that is, "by means of the overthrow of the existing power and the creation of a new power." But a "revolution from above" in Soviet society

---

[123] *Istoriia vsesoiuznoi*, pp. 291-92. See also *ibid.*, p. 125: "*The tremendous role* of new social ideas, of new political institutions, of new political power, whose mission is to abolish forcibly the old relations of production, stands forth in bold relief."

[124] Stalin, "Otnositel'no Marksizma v iazykoznanii," June 20, 1950, in *Marksizm i voprosy*, pp. 4-5 (italics added).

proceeds without an "explosion," thus precluding the possibility of destroying the Soviet state.¹²⁵

Pravda promptly affirmed that the use of state power to perform a "revolution from above" was not confined to the past, to the liquidation of an old base and old classes. Stalin's pronouncements had sanctioned "the special, creative role of the new, socialist superstructure, and first of all, the role of the socialist state as the principal weapon in the creation of the economic base of socialism." Nor would the need for the Soviet state diminish in the future: "Now, in the period of the gradual transition from socialism to communism, the role of the Soviet state is revealed in all its power and strength as the principal weapon for constructing communism." ¹²⁶ Soviet theory had endowed that state with an endlessly creative role, regardless of its base.

POST-STALINIST DOCTRINE ON THE WITHERING PROCESS

The passing of Stalin did not upset this belief, for in March, 1953, immediately after Stalin's death, *Pravda* echoed: "The Soviet state is the principal instrument for the construction of a Communist society." ¹²⁷ Nor did the campaign against the Stalin cult, which was fully unveiled at the Twentieth Party Congress in February, 1956, involve a repudiation of Stalin's demand for an ever-stronger state. "The great tasks that face our country," Voroshilov told the Congress, "demand a further strengthening of the Soviet state and a fortifying of socialist law in the activity of every link of the state apparatus." ¹²⁸

In November, 1957, Khrushchev appeared to sound a fresh note when, in response to a question about the withering away of the state, he boasted: "This process is in fact already under way. As the

¹²⁵ *Ibid.*, p. 24.
¹²⁶ Konsul'tatsiia, "O bazise i nadstroike," *Pravda*, Oct. 5, 1950, p. 3.
¹²⁷ D. Chesnokov, "I. V. Stalin o sovetskom gosudarstve," *ibid.*, March 18, 1953, p. 2. Subsequently, *Kommunist* made an effort to reaffirm "the determining role of the base" and to criticize "the exaggerated role of the superstructure." However, this article also demanded—on the very same page—that one pay great attention to the question "of the sources of strength and might of the socialist state, which is the principal weapon for the construction of socialism and communism." (Unsigned editorial, "Nasushchnye voprosy filosofskii nauki," *Kommunist*, No. 5 [March, 1955], p. 15.) The problem of the relation between base and superstructure was discussed further in *Kommunist*, No. 10 (July, 1956), pp. 42–58, and No. 4 (March, 1957), pp. 46–58.
¹²⁸ "Rech' tovarishcha K. E. Voroshilova," *Pravda*, Feb. 21, 1956, p. 6.

Soviet state develops, the functions of state administration change and so do some organs of coercion." The duties of the courts and regular police have been appreciably lightened, since "the number of criminals in the USSR has decreased considerably." It was now mostly a matter of dealing with "petty crimes," because "political crimes have become rarities in our country." At the same time Khrushchev warned: "It would be the gravest mistake, a leftist deviation, if we were now to weaken our state organs of administration or to abolish the organs of coercion, which . . . now are principally the organs of defense against the machinations of external enemies." Justification for strong state power, however, also continued to rest upon the need to fulfill certain domestic tasks, which were unrelated to the defense apparatus. "Our Soviet state and its organs conduct great educational work among the Soviet citizens. . . . We are struggling against the survivals of capitalism in the people's consciousness." Like Stalin, Khrushchev could not foresee an early victory over these domestic antisocial forces. "These survivals in a certain part of the population," he complained, "will obviously remain for a prolonged time, because the process of overcoming them is assuredly lengthy and complicated." [129]

Even though the fulfillment of the withering process was still held to be a matter of the far distant future, to say that "this process is in fact already under way" reflected a decided change of tone. It would appear that this newly found optimism was connected with another event of November, 1957, namely the public showdown in Soviet-Yugoslav relations. The rift was visibly reopened when the Yugoslavs refused to sign the Moscow Declaration of Communist Parties, while Moscow launched an attack on "revisionist" doctrine in general and on Yugoslav "revisionism" in particular. One major source of ideological discord centered about the Yugoslav critique on the nature of the Soviet state.[130]

As this critique was formulated in the Program of the Yugoslav Communists, published in the spring of 1958, the Soviet state was accused of displaying "manifestations of bureaucratic-statist tendencies . . . errors and distortions in the development of the political system

---

[129] "Beseda N. S. Khrushcheva s korrespondentom amerikanskogo agentstva Iunaited Press Genri Shapiro," Nov. 14, 1957, *ibid.*, Nov. 19, 1957, p. 1.

[130] The coincidence between Khrushchev's statement on the withering of the Soviet state and the Moscow Declaration of Communist Parties is striking, since the Shapiro interview took place November 14, 1957, the same day as the opening of the Moscow Conference.

of the state," which had resulted from Stalin's "great concentration of power in the state machinery." The Yugoslavs then retorted to Moscow that they were not "revisionists"; rather it was in Moscow that "a pragmatic revision of some of the fundamental scientific postulates of Marxism and Leninism was carried out."

The Marxist-Leninist theory of the dictatorship of the proletariat as a political system of power in the state which is withering away, and as an instrument of working class struggle in the process of the abolition of the economic foundations of capitalism and the creation of political and material conditions for the free development of new socialist relations, was gradually replaced by Stalin's theory of the state which does not wither away and which must strengthen itself in all fields of social life, the state whose machinery is given too great a role in the construction of socialism, in the solving of internal contradictions of a transition period, a role which sooner or later must lead to the fettering of the development of social and economic factors.[131]

The Soviet leaders, forced to pose as the true defenders of Marxism, apparently decided to parry this attack by claiming, as Khrushchev had already indicated, that the Soviet state was then in the process of planning its own demise. A Party resolution of December, 1957, predicted that "Soviet trade unions will further increase their role in state, economic, and cultural work." [132] "There is no doubt," the prominent Soviet ideologue Mitin explained, "that the role of trade unions and other of our public organizations will continue to grow, their activities will intensify and will increasingly assume various state functions." But what was given with one hand was instantly taken away by the other. "The decisive condition for our further successes on the road to communism is the all-round strengthening of the socialist state, its forces and power." Falling back upon Stalin's "dialectical" formula of preparing for the withering away of the state by strengthening it to the utmost, Mitin concluded: "The dialectics of life consist of this; the movement toward communism assumes that alongside the retention and strengthening of our state organs there is a gradual transfer of activities into the hands of public organizations which in the future will assume many functions of state." [133]

---

[131] "The Programme of the League of Communists of Yugoslavia," *Review of International Affairs* (Belgrade), IX, No. 196 (June 1, 1958), 15.

[132] "O rabote professional'nykh soiuzov SSSR, Postanovlenie Plenuma TsK KPSS, priniatoe 17 dekabria 1957 goda," *Pravda*, Dec. 19, 1957, p. 2.

[133] M. Mitin, "Sotsializm i demokratiia," *ibid.*, Feb. 11, 1958, p. 3.

WORLD STATE OF NO STATE 467

The "dialectics of life" was promptly elaborated by other Soviet theorists. In the first issue of an international Communist journal published in fifteen languages, which was launched following the Moscow Conference of November, 1957, the Yugoslavs were castigated for

> having revised the Marxist-Leninist doctrine of the state. . . . Revisionists, as orthodox metaphysicians, cannot understand that efforts to strengthen the socialist state are not in insoluble contradiction with preparing the conditions for its withering away. . . . The socialist state draws the people into the work of governing. . . . And the more they are drawn in, the more the conditions are created for the withering away of the state. When all members of society learn to run social production and deal with public affairs then there will be no more need for a special apparatus of political power. Thus, the withering away of the state is prepared for by its consolidation. The revisionists break this dialectical connection between the strengthening of the socialist state and the creation of conditions for its withering away.[134]

It was also incorrect to "claim that the declining economic role of the state, the strong anarchosyndicalist tendencies which are evident in the economic practice of Yugoslavia, are symptoms of the 'withering away of the state.'" On the contrary, "state planning and regulation in socialist economy build up the mechanism for management of production which will continue to be necessary even under communism." It was recalled that Lenin's conception of the ultimate society was cast in the image of a centrally planned, tightly organized, highly disciplined mechanism. "Communist society does not mean the rule of anarchy, but presupposes the highest degree of consciousness and organization on the part of the working people." The Yugoslavs are deceiving themselves when they point to the decentralization of power among so-called "social self-government bodies" as a sign of the disappearance of the state, since they are actually speaking of bodies of state power, but only on a local level. Then referring to the Yugoslav experiments with increasing the activity of various nonstate public bodies, it was held that "even the transfer of some state functions to social organizations is not in itself identical with the withering away of the state, if the function of political power—specific to the state—does not come to an end." [135] This last remark, of course, should be equally applicable to

---

[134] G. Glezerman and B. Ukraintsev, "Socialism and the State," *World Marxist Review*, I, No. 1 (Sept., 1958), 26.
[135] *Ibid.*, pp. 24–27.

the Soviet Union, where a somewhat similar experiment in transferring functions to nonstate bodies was claimed as evidence that the withering process was already under way.

Some indication of when the state might be expected to wither away was revealed in another phase of these polemics. The Soviet theorists twitted the Yugoslavs for their insistent demand that state independence be strengthened, "while at the same time they proclaim that the withering away of the state is a practical task. To be consistent, they would have to pose the question of the withering away of state boundaries." Khrushchev has reaffirmed the Leninist axiom that boundaries among all states in the world will someday disappear, but this was tied to the drawing together and fusion of nations. The Soviet spokesmen then made the withering away of the state dependent upon the completion of this very long-range prospect. "Thus, from Lenin's point of view, the drawing together and fusion of nations do not *begin* but *end* with the withering away of the state." [136] If the withering of the state will appear on the agenda of history only after the complete fusion of the nations of the world, it is understandable why the Soviet theorists have rebuked the Yugoslavs for viewing the withering process as "a practical task."

Finally, in his report to the Twenty-first Party Congress in January, 1959, Khrushchev provided a comprehensive theoretical survey of the problems connected with the disappearance of the state. At first he repeated his dictum of 1957: "It is already clear that many functions performed by state organs must gradually be transferred to public organizations." The possibility of this happening had resulted, he boasted, from the supposedly radical decline in the need for domestic organs of a coercive political character. "There are now no cases in the Soviet Union," he asserted unequivocally, "of people being tried for political crimes. . . . This testifies to an unprecedented unity of political convictions of our entire people, to their solidarity with the Communist Party and the Soviet government." Close on the heels of this remark, and strangely at odds with it, was his attack on the "anti-Party group of Malenkov, Kaganovich, Molotov, Bulganin, and Shepilov," who had "stubbornly resisted" implementation of the Party line and had "used the lowest methods of factional, schismatic struggle" to sabotage the policies of the

[136] P. Fedoseev, I. Pomelov, and V. Cheprakov, "O proekte programmy Soiuza kommunistov Iugoslavii," *Kommunist*, No. 6 (April, 1958), pp. 28–29.

Soviet state for industry, agriculture, and foreign affairs.[137] Also difficult to explain was the new legal code adopted immediately before the opening of the Congress. If political crimes against the state were now a thing of the past, one is forced to wonder at the characterization of the new code by the chairman of the legislative drafting committee: "The draft principles provide, on the one hand, for a restriction and lightening of criminal responsibility for acts that do not represent a great danger to the state . . . while, on the other hand, they significantly increase the responsibility for the more serious crimes against the state." [138]

Nevertheless Khrushchev insisted that "matters are approaching a situation in which public organizations, alongside and parallel to such state organs as the militia [regular police] and the courts, will perform the functions of safeguarding public order and security. This process is now under way." Of course, he warned, such state agencies will continue to exercise "definite functions," and "the transfer of some functions from state organs to public organizations must be carried out without undue haste."

The more the masses are drawn into the processes of managing their own affairs the more they will be prepared to live in a stateless Communist society. Here again he had serious reservations concerning the capacity of "people to acquire the inner need to work in accordance with their abilities. So long as this is lacking, society cannot dispense with definite regulation of working time in order that every able-bodied person contribute a definite amount of labor to the production of the goods and services that the community needs." Bolstering his position with a quotation from Lenin, Khrushchev continued: " 'Until the higher phase of communism arrives, socialists demand the *most stringent* control by society and *by the state* over the amount of labor and the amount of consumption.' " Until society could rely upon the perfect self-discipline of each of its members and trust that everyone had developed the inner need to work for the good of the entire society, the state would apparently have to continue to exist and to exercise "the most stringent control."

Khrushchev's emphasis on discipline was fully in line with the Leninist tradition. The present principle of distribution according to

[137] "Doklad tovarishcha N. S. Khrushcheva," *Pravda*, Jan. 28, 1959, pp. 9–10.
[138] "Doklad predsedatelia Komissii zakonodatel'nykh predpolozhenii Soveta Soiuza deputata D. S. Polianskogo," *ibid.*, Dec. 26, 1958, p. 7.

work "performs an important educational function by accustoming people to socialist discipline and by making labor universal and obligatory. . . . Communist society, of course, will have a planned and organized allocation of labor." But, he objected, "some persons have a vulgarized conception of Communist society as a loose, unorganized, anarchic mass of people. No, it will be a highly organized and closely coordinated community of men of labor. Operation of machinery requires that each person perform his job and meet his social obligations at definite times and in definite ways." Khrushchev underscored the strictly regulated character of the future society by declaring indestructible the role of the Party, which is the fountainhead of discipline and the source of totalitarian controls. "In the process of building Communist society the role of the Party must grow, and not decline, as today's revisionists maintain." It is evident that Khrushchev's vision of the ultimate Communist society is, like Lenin's, that of stateless totalitarianism.

In one respect, Khrushchev's image of the future is even grimmer than Lenin's. At least Lenin held out the promise of a Communist society founded upon an overwhelming abundance of material goods, so that everyone could be effortlessly rewarded in accordance with his needs. Khrushchev, however, qualified the satisfaction of people's needs in the future "within necessary and reasonable limits. . . . Of course, when we speak of satisfying people's needs we have in mind not whims or claims to luxuries, but the wholesale consumption of a cultured person." That is, in the future abundant society there will be plenty for everyone—provided one does not want too much. And the Party will always be available to guide man in the choice of how much he wants.

Until the achievement of stateless totalitarianism, a mighty Soviet state apparatus is considered indispensable. Khrushchev also found justification for this view by reverting to Stalin's "dialectical" explanation, which was so fully elaborated in the Soviet pronouncements preceding the Twenty-first Party Congress. "The question of the withering away of the state, if one understands it dialectically," Khrushchev repeated to the Congress, "is a question of the development of the socialist state toward the objective of Communist public self-rule." Therefore the growing activity of nonstate groups, when considered "dialectically," could only strengthen the Soviet state. "Obviously, the transfer to public organizations of some functions now performed by state organs does not at all mean weakening the role of the socialist state in the building of communism. The fact that public organizations will perform a number of the present functions of the state will expand and strengthen the political base of socialist society." [139] The text of the economic plan adopted by the Congress likewise insisted that "the most important condition for the successful fulfillment of the Seven-Year Plan . . . is the further strengthening of our state and the intensification of its economic-organizational and cultural-educational activities." [140] The continual strengthening of the Soviet state in its every aspect, internal as well as external, remains the order of the day, despite recent ideological window dressing that might convey the opposite impression.

While Soviet theorists persistently render lip service to the mirage of a withering state, the rationale of this objective has been totally undermined. The state has become a wholly benign instrument of salvation instead of a wholly contemptuous symbol of repression. In 1917 Lenin categorically affirmed: "So long as there is a state there is no freedom. There will be freedom when there is no state." [141] Stalin and his successors have transformed the state into an affirmation of freedom and made it the indispensable vehicle for riding to utopia.

As happens in those political systems where the drive toward a beatific future is justified by the use of any means, however ruthless and coercive, the means inevitably tend to distort, corrupt, and finally to replace the end. The evidence accumulated from the operation of the Soviet regime conclusively affirms this truism. Soviet preoccupation with the construction and indefinite expansion of an all-powerful, all-embracing state authority, while originally justified as a necessary, transitory means, has instead become the indestructible, unwithering end of Soviet society. The idea of the withering away of the state has itself withered away. In its place there has remained the goal of the Soviet world state, the most extravagantly coercive, caste-ridden world state ever conceived in the minds of men.

[139] "Doklad tovarishcha N. S. Khrushcheva," *ibid.*, Jan. 28, 1959, pp. 8-10.
[140] "Kontrol'nye tsifry razvitiia narodnogo khoziaistva SSSR na 1959–1965 gody (Utverzhdeny edinoglasno XXI s"ezdom KPSS 5 fevralia 1959 goda)," *ibid.*, Feb. 8, 1959, p. 8.
[141] Lenin, "Gosudarstvo i revoliutsiia," in *Sochineniia*, XXI, 436.

XIV. The Response of the West

SOVIET totalitarianism recognizes no legitimate bounds to its power. Within the confines of the existing Soviet state the Kremlin claims the right to direct and control man totally, in his body, mind, and spirit. The ambition of the Soviet regime is also total for the world beyond its borders. The conscious and continuing outward thrust of Soviet power maintains as its objective the absorption of all nations of the world into the Soviet body politic and, ultimately, the reshaping of their patterns of life into the single, all-embracing mold of a Soviet world state.

The evidence gathered in this study may provide the basis for appraising the nature of their intended world state. Ideally, Soviet theorists repeatedly affirm, the power of decision making will be highly centralized, the entire world will function as one vast workshop according to the directives of a common plan elaborated and controlled from a single world center of political authority. Prior to the seizure of state power in Russia there was no consensus as to the location of the political center of gravity. Even after the revolution, figures like Trotsky continued to assign a traditional Marxian priority to the advanced industrial countries and so looked toward Western Europe as the likely center of the future world state. But power was seized in Russia by a predominantly Russian-based Bolshevik Party that was increasingly impelled to come to terms with the pressing tasks of preserving and expanding the power of the Soviet Russian state. The initial identification of progress toward a world state with the defense and aggrandizement of Russian state power was soon supported by a selective Soviet revival of the Russian cultural heritage, which produced as a goal the amalgam of a Russified Soviet world state. The ideal, classless culture of the future world society would therefore be dominated by a Russian nationalism become universal, while the single, universal language of the future would likewise be Russian.

All means, including resort to naked military force, have been explicitly condoned as valid instruments for the attainment of the "inevitable" and "voluntary" world union of nations. Following the destruction of the non-Soviet world and its replacement by a Soviet world state, it was originally assumed, the coercive mechanisms of world state power would be destined to wither away. In its place there was to appear the ultimate, eternal stage of civilization, in which a highly centralized, harmoniously functioning world society would be populated by omniscient, omnicompetent man, who would be able effortlessly to administer "things" on a universal scale. Both postrevolutionary Soviet practice and Soviet doctrinal innovations make it apparent that it is the withering idea that has withered away. There remains only the less beatific, if more brutally realistic, goal of an omnipotent totalitarian Soviet world state, which the Soviet leadership continues to pursue relentlessly, and often skillfully. This, in crude capsule form, would seem to be the shape of the Soviet design for a world state.

In the course of piecing together the Soviet grand design, the author was increasingly conscious of the need for the West to articulate a response that would be in keeping with the dimensions of the Soviet challenge. He therefore felt impelled to formulate, if only briefly, a tentative outline of the personal beliefs that grew out of this study. The reader, it is hoped, will not take offense at a foray into the realm of personal conviction, which is offered with the aim of stimulating a rethinking of some of the basic issues that the Soviet leadership has posed for the West.

Western responses to the Soviet challenge are marked by a variety of conflicting attitudes. The prevailing one, perhaps, is a type of political schizophrenia. Both the general public and those entrusted with governmental responsibility in the West are abundantly aware that "Moscow wants to dominate the world," and that in some vague way this involves a radical refashioning of the entire world. But the acceptance of such a cliché is frequently without conviction, since there is little willingness to face up to the specific implications the Soviet design holds for the future of the non-Soviet world and the Western nation-state system. Undoubtedly many people secretly tell themselves that the Soviet leaders really cannot mean what they say. Widespread wishful thinking nurtures the hope that the challenge cannot be of such enormity as to threaten to uproot one's comfortably settled beliefs and attachment to long-established institutions. This frame of mind is easily disposed to being swayed by every gently warming political breeze, to interpret every Soviet concession or minor easing of tension as evidence of a fundamental transformation in the Soviet system. The self-deception of constantly hoping for the best in the long run while drifting in the present renders one incapable of devising and implementing any positive, sustained program of action.

Even among those who genuinely acknowledge that "the Kremlin wants to control the world" there is a common assumption that it is too difficult, if not impossible, to determine the concrete nature of the Soviet grand design and its far-reaching implications for the non-Soviet world, and that it is therefore useless to attempt to probe too far beyond the present. "Be practical," meet each issue as it arises, "solve" one emergency after another by clever, on-the-scene improvisation, by rushing from spot to spot to douse the flames of an "emergency" which is not exceptional but rather is recurrent and permanent in nature. As a result, the West is constantly placed on the defensive, taken by surprise, forced to react to Soviet initiatives spasmodically, without coordination, and, too frequently, without success. This may be due in good measure to the inability, perhaps inherent in a free society, to understand the totalitarian world view of the Soviet mentality. In it, every act, every event is related to the totality; there is no separate, autonomous sphere of life unrelated to the world struggle, no surcease of struggle in times of peace, since peace is but a continuation of war by other "peaceful" means, no isolated parts or regions of the world which are unrelated to the whole "inevitable" pattern of the future. The West, that is to say, seems unable to understand the central fact that a Soviet grand design really exists and that its existence exerts an unabating and many-sided challenge which, by its nature, requires the formulation of a long-range, integrated grand response on the part of the West.

There are, of course, some in the West who have thought seriously about grand designs for the entire world. They argue plausibly that the anarchy reigning among states and the threat of world war demand the creation of a world state capable of maintaining a dependable, universal peace. But such people likewise undervalue or misunderstand the implications of the Soviet mentality and Soviet intentions. The Soviet leaders, for their part, have made it quite

RESPONSE OF THE WEST

explicit that they are unwilling to envisage any world order other than their own exclusive design for a world state. One is reluctantly forced to conclude that there is no present possibility of developing any all-inclusive world order, except on Soviet terms.

Occasionally some are heard to say that the need for world peace is so urgent and the implications of present-day war so horrible that peace alone is the issue. If man's desire for world peace is so overwhelming that he is willing to sacrifice all else to its attainment, then the Soviet grand design has the merit of proposing a concrete plan that would instantly impose a world order upon the unruly chaos of the nation-state system. But throughout history the issue has seldom been peace at any price. While today the scope of war's destructiveness is approaching the ultimate limit, death still remains an individual experience. Those who died in the past in defense of their beliefs found death just as final as it would prove to be for each of the world's inhabitants, should world civilization now perish. Today the price of world peace on Soviet terms is obviously the drowning of the treasured freedoms of the West in a sea of Soviet totalitarianism. The West, it is hoped, will refuse to pay this price.

We are apparently faced with the unhappy alternative of an indefinitely disordered universe in which there is little prospect of mending the world's ills by sending appeals directly to Moscow. But if this is so, should not the West devote its principal energies to hastening the disintegration of Soviet power by attempting to sharpen and exploit all the internal strains and tensions in the Soviet orbit? In the future, it would doubtless be well to have a series of carefully thought-through plans to take maximum advantage of explosions within the Soviet empire in the event that new "Hungarys" should occur. It must be emphasized, however, that the Hungarian and other such rebellions were almost exclusively internal in origin, resulting from a malfunctioning of the levers of power within the Soviet orbit. For the West to rely primarily upon externally contrived, adventuristic efforts to disrupt the Soviet system would be to pursue a program both of inordinate costs and of inordinate risks.

The major relevant scope of action for the West, it would seem, is the curing of its own potentially fatal disorders within the confines of its own common civilization. The presence of Soviet power in our midst, ever prodding one member of the Western community to work at cross-purposes with another, ever willing to capitalize on the paralysis and self-destructiveness arising from Western policy differences, makes it imperative to reform and refashion the inherently chaotic, but now no longer tolerable, structure of Western interstate relations. The radical reduction of these Western vulnerabilities is at least one problem which is not contingent upon agreement with Moscow. Negotiations can be conducted among democratic nations committed to a common heritage for the purpose of introducing a kind of order that would be compatible with the preservation of the freedom of their own societies.

The West is called upon to solve a presently urgent but age-old problem of constructing a political framework that will be adequate for the protection and flourishing of free institutions and an open society. All antiquity was faced with this problem and failed to come up with a satisfactory answer. The Greeks, by limiting themselves to direct democracy, necessarily confined the areas of their government to small dimensions. While this provided for freedom and the operation of democratic institutions within some of these boundaries, it resulted in an interstate lawlessness that eroded those very freedoms. The wars and imperialist depredations conducted by the Greek city-states against each other, as well as those undertaken by strong external powers against the divided Hellenic city-states, contributed significantly to the undermining of their democratic institutions and to the destruction of the freedoms that had been so precariously developed. The Roman imperium sinned on the other side of the ledger by providing a bond of law for an extended geographical area while failing to develop widespread institutions of democratic self-government. The survival of the free West today is imperiled by its inability to solve precisely this two-pronged task: to develop an effective institution of representative government over an area coextensive with its civilization, in which the advantages of interstate order would be combined with the freedoms of democratic self-government.

All the leading statesmen of the Atlantic Community declare from time to time that the Western world must not be permitted to fall apart, since Moscow stands ready to pick up the pieces. It has also been increasingly acknowledged that organizations such as **NATO**, if confined to the half-life of a military alliance, traditionally tend to lose their cohesive character. It was with this in mind that a special committee appointed to study "Non-Military Cooperation in NATO" recommended to the NATO Council of Ministers in December, 1956, that "it was wise and timely to bring about a closer association of kindred Atlantic and Western European nations for other than defense purposes alone; that a partial pooling of sovereignty for mutual protection should also promote progress and cooperation generally." All were agreed that "closer unity was both natural and desirable" toward the end of strengthening "common cultural traditions, free institutions and democratic concepts." This report, which was adopted unanimously by the NATO Ministers, concluded that "there was, in short, a sense of Atlantic Community, alongside the realization of an immediate common danger."[1]

The realization of these professions of allegiance to a precious common heritage has been frustrated repeatedly by numerous failures to achieve effective collaboration among the members of the Atlantic Community. This may best be illustrated, perhaps, by the Suez crisis that came to its explosive culmination in October, 1956, while this very NATO report was in the writing. The fiasco of Suez simultaneously helped propel Moscow into the Middle East as a major power, cast Franco-British policy as a dying gasp of imperialism, and temporarily shattered the alliance among NATO's strongest powers. It would therefore be well to revive the painful memory of the Suez experience if it can provide an insight into ways of narrowing the gap that separates profession from practice.

Suez, first and foremost, stands as a classic example of the hazards and limitations inherent in pursuing intimate cooperation among members of an Atlantic Community through the diplomatic method. For several years before the crisis broke each NATO Foreign Office formulated its own estimate on a variety of topics that bore directly upon the security of the Atlantic Community in the Middle East. What should be the role of the Baghdad Pact as an instrument to forestall Soviet aggression, and who should join it? What attitude must be assumed toward the Arab-Israeli tensions, which were highly vulnerable to Soviet manipulation? More specifically, how did one evaluate Nasser, and to what extent was his regime being subjected to Soviet influence or control? How should conflicting interests over the Suez Canal be resolved, and to what point, if any,

[1] "Text of the Report of the Committee of Three," Dec., 1956, *NATO Letter*, V, Special Supplement to No. 1 (Jan. 1, 1957), 3.

could one justify the threat and use of force to protect what was considered a vital interest? The spectacular Suez crisis in the fall of 1956 did not come as a bolt from the blue, but was the result of pressures that had built up over a period of years because of the failure of the NATO partners to reach agreed policy positions on issues of common concern.[2]

When the Suez issue was thrown open for debate in the United Nations General Assembly, American policy pursued a course that was openly at odds with its major NATO allies, while it was curiously in harmony with another long-standing American attitude toward the larger society of states represented by the United Nations. From the beginning, American thought has been marked by a persistent confusion as to the nature of NATO and the United Nations. When the Senate Foreign Relations Committee recommended approval of the NATO Treaty in June, 1949, its reasoning reflected a peculiar ambivalence. On the one hand, paraphrasing the Treaty preamble, it affirmed:

The peoples of the North Atlantic area are linked together not only by the interdependence of their security but by a common heritage and civilization and devotion to their free institutions, based upon the principles of democracy, individual liberty and the rule of law. It is this common heritage and civilization and these free institutions which the signatories are determined to defend.[3]

On the other hand, it seemed that this common civilization would best be defended by a minimal intimacy among the treaty signatories. While Article 2 spoke of "strengthening free institutions" and eliminating conflict in the international economic policies of the Treaty members, the Senators noted somewhat triumphantly that "no new machinery is envisaged for these purposes. . . . The Committee is completely satisfied that this article involves no obligation on us to take any legislative action whatsoever."[4] Article 4, which provided for joint consultation on issues threatening the

[2] By the time the military attack was launched, the Anglo-French sense of frustration and alienation from American policy was so severe that there was almost a total diplomatic blackout between Washington and its major allies. President Eisenhower complained: "The United States was not consulted in any way about any phase of these actions. Nor were we informed of them in advance." ("Text of Eisenhower Broadcast on Mideast Crisis," Oct. 31, 1956, New York *Times*, Nov. 1, 1956.)

[3] *North Atlantic Treaty*, Executive Report No. 8, Committee on Foreign Relations on Executive L, 81st Congress, 1st Session (Washington, 1949), p. 7.

[4] *Ibid.*, p. 10.

political and military security of any signatory, was treated even more gingerly. "The Committee underlines the fact that consultation could be requested only when the element of threat is present and expresses the opinion that this limitation should be strictly interpreted."[5] Continuous, close consultation among NATO partners leading to the formulation of a common NATO policy was considered a threat to the functioning of the United Nations. "Clearly such a danger would exist if consultations under the pact became so frequent they tended to replace United Nations machinery, or if such consultations resulted in a crystallization of views in advance of United Nations meetings and encouraged pact members to vote as a 'bloc.' "[6] The Suez crisis, it would seem, was a perfect fulfillment of the Senators' expectations on how NATO and the United Nations should function. One could hardly accuse the NATO powers of consultation that produced a common NATO policy prior to the Suez crisis, and the spectacle of the United States voting in the United Nations with the Soviet Union against Britain and France was surely an example of pact members not voting as a "bloc." But obviously the Senators could not have wished for the Suez drama that brought the Atlantic alliance to the verge of destruction. What, then, was out of joint?

At the very time that Lenin was attempting to impose a new Soviet world order on the old system of interstate relations, Woodrow Wilson was articulating his own quite different formula for transcending the traditional European diplomatic game of power politics among states. On the whole, Americans still tend to remain under the spell of Wilsonian illusions about the nature of an attainable world society. Wilson's image, molded by nineteenth-century liberalism, envisioned a world of nations in which each nation would combine its sovereign independent statehood with voluntary membership in a harmonious world community. This vision assumed the rapid and inevitable spread of democracy to all countries, which, moved by a consensus of rational democratic values, could promptly provide solutions for all conflicts by exposing them openly to the forum of world opinion. The right answer would at once be made self-evident in a debate before the public opinion of the world community, which was bound together by moral law and the search for justice. For states to combine in "blocs" was regarded as a wicked

[5] *Ibid.*, p. 11.   [6] *Ibid.*, p. 12.

manifestation of "power politics," which, if tolerated, would destroy the potential harmony among nations and pervert the standards of universal justice.

Even if Wilson's hope for the rapid spread of republican nation-states had been realized, it was still naive to expect an automatic harmonious functioning of the world community without modifying the independent sovereign status of each democratic nation-state. The agreed-upon harmony that prevails in any community can serve as a dependable basis of life only if it is reinforced by the institutions of state power, and yet this was to be a world community without a world state. Today the inadequacy of the nation-state as the highest repository of sovereignty is more evident than in Wilson's day, while the hope that the United Nations can provide a world forum for the emergence of a single, self-evident truth is even more remote in a world shattered by sharply conflicting, if not irreconcilable, political systems.

Yet it was precisely to a Wilsonian image of the world community that President Eisenhower turned in the Suez crisis. The Anglo-French leaders, operating in the deplorable absence of an agreed NATO policy that might have averted disaster, felt driven to equally deplorable acts of desperation in rebellion against a, to them, capricious or inadequate American diplomacy. The United States then held Britain and France answerable for their acts by placing them before the bar of a universal moral law which was supposedly expressed in the forum of world public opinion in the United Nations. "It is our hope and intent," Eisenhower told the world, "that this matter [Suez] will be brought before the United Nations General Assembly. There, with no veto operating, the opinion of the world can be brought to bear in our quest for a just end to this tormenting problem." Eisenhower spoke hopefully of the United Nations "increasing its ability to secure justice under international law." [7]

Whether or not one agreed with the specific acts of the British government, it is at least arguable that Eden's defense of his policy reflected a view of world society that was more in tune with reality than Eisenhower's. "Those who suggest that by the action we have taken in the Middle East we are striking at the roots of international law," Eden cautioned, "should reflect on the fact that law is

[7] "Text of Eisenhower Broadcast," New York *Times*, Nov. 1, 1956.

always associated with order." During the Second World War plans were hopefully laid for creating a genuine world order. "Had our plans succeeded, the United Nations would have become what it was intended to be, the beginning of a world government based on collective security. But since this conception failed, it is folly to behave as though it had succeeded, and to shut our eyes to the fact that the United Nations is not the true world order it was originally intended to be." Glancing at the Russians who were then drenching Budapest with the blood of Hungarian patriots in complete defiance of a ream of United Nations resolutions, Eden observed that if the use of force is permissible only for those who wish to destroy whatever world order has been attained, then "we are leaving the world open to the lawbreakers." "It is wrong, both morally and politically, to pretend to ourselves that genuine peace and international law prevail where they do not." [8]

The "universal moral law," to which the United States abdicated its policy in the case of Suez, was formulated with the active and gleeful participation of the Soviet delegates who uncritically championed the cause of the Afro-Asian bloc. Whether or not the position of the Afro-Asian bloc was an expression of impartial, universal justice may be discovered by comparing its zeal in castigating the Anglo-French use of force with its great reluctance to acknowledge the incomparably more brutal Russian use of force in Hungary. The double standard of judgment may be expressed vividly in another way by examining the position of India. The same Indian spokesmen who led the outcry against the use of force at Suez have endlessly protested against any United Nations supervised plebiscite in Kashmir, which India seized and continues to hold by force.

If there are serious grounds for doubting the existence of a Wilsonian world community which can serve as an embodiment of universal justice, what, then, is the significant community of political loyalty to which we can realistically adhere? NATO's self-scrutinizing report of December, 1956, reaffirmed that "the nation-state, by itself and relying exclusively on national policy and national power, is inadequate for progress or even for survival in the nuclear age." [9] The relevant community of political loyalty today is more

[8] "Excerpts from Eden's Speech in London," Nov. 17, 1956, *ibid.*, Nov. 18, 1956.
[9] "Text of the Report," *NATO Letter*, V, Special Supplement to No. 1 (Jan. 1, 1957), 5.

than the nation-state, but not yet a world state. Between these two extremes lies the problem of finding the area in which it will be possible to extend an interstate order that will be compatible with the functioning of free institutions.

Put another way, it is the task of combining Wilson's commendable quest for the greater democratic society with an ability to take account, as Wilsonian theory did not, of the power realities of the international community in which these democratic values are to take hold. To counter Lenin's messianic, totalitarian vision of a world order one must stand with Wilson in condemnation of a system of interstate relations that has no greater purpose than carrying on the traditional game of forming diplomatic and military alliances for the limited aim of perpetuating the independent existence of the various sovereign state units. Soviet plans and techniques for reconstructing world society present a threat that far exceeds the accustomed diplomatic and military dimensions of interstate relations, and must be met by the growth of another international community that is consciously grounded in the ethical and moral commitments of a democratic society. But the power realities of the contemporary international arena indicate that such a greater democratic society can at first take shape only, if at all, among the like-minded nations of the Atlantic Community. An effectively functioning Atlantic Community, dedicated to the preservation and extension of human freedom, could conceivably be an adequate response to the Soviet challenge to the nation-state system.

NATO would seem to provide the nucleus, however fuzzy at the edges it may presently appear, for constructing a viable political community of free nations. NATO's scope and structure need not be regarded as immutable; rather it can be viewed as the framework around which a body politic may grow which will be adequate to defend the common civilization of the Atlantic Community.

Here again we encounter a formidable obstacle in American thought. When American leaders speak approvingly of strengthening the Atlantic Community, their concrete recommendations almost invariably boil down to urging greater political and economic union for Western Europe. But Western Europe is not the sole repository of Western civilization, nor is it the significant area into which a dependable order must be introduced if that civilization is to be preserved. However desirable political union may be for resolving some of the conflicts of continental Western Europe, the British and the Scandinavians have been understandably reluctant to commit themselves to such a limited political association, while the exclusion of NATO's North American partners omits those power centers whose participation is essential if the West is to devise effective common policies. Conceivably, a Western European union could have a harmful and divisive effect upon the welfare of the Atlantic Community if its policies did not develop in accordance with the objectives of the larger community.

The preoccupation of Americans with supporting the integration of Western European institutions to the exclusion of a similar interest in the more inclusive Atlantic Community reflects the absence of a genuine sense of involvement in the larger community to which we pay lip service. American support of Western European union has, no doubt, been based to some extent upon a form of wishful thinking, upon the wistful neoisolationist hope that if only Europe could be helped through an interim emergency until it could be made politically sound, militarily strong, and economically healthy, then the United States could reduce its involvement in the essentially distasteful "foreign" affairs into which it has been thrust. The disparity between the American attitudes toward European and Atlantic unity arises from the fact that American leadership, and the American people as a whole, have still to achieve a fundamental rethinking of the conditions required for the survival of the West. Yet it may be taken as axiomatic that there can be no substantial advance toward blowing life into a genuine Atlantic Community without an energetic and steady American leadership.

Progress, to be sure, has been made. The December, 1956, NATO report enthusiastically embraced the idea of full and timely political consultation among NATO members on a wide range of issues arising both within and beyond the NATO Treaty area. The realization has finally come home that NATO might disintegrate even as a military organization unless it was revitalized as a political conception. The crucial question is: how far can the presently conceived notion of diplomatic consultation carry the NATO powers toward working out common policy positions? The NATO report that spoke so glowingly of the benefits of early and constant political consultation also admitted that no power was under an obligation to consult with its allies in any particular circumstance if "circumstances make such prior consultation obviously and demonstrably impossible." Each member state will apparently be its own judge as to when a matter may be excluded from joint deliberation. One of the limitations of consultation, the report acknowledged, "is the hard fact that ultimate responsibiilty for decision and action still rests on national governments." [10] This being so, even when joint consultation occurs, each government must first consult with its own parliament on most issues, with the result that national policy tends to become fixed in the process and NATO "consultation" tends to be reduced to an exchange of information on the various national policy positions. In some limited areas, such as negotiation concerning disarmament, it has proved possible to evolve joint policy positions through an intensification of diplomatic interchange within NATO's Permanent Council. But even here, NATO's Secretary General Spaak acknowledged in September, 1958, "the practice of consultation as we know it has revealed to us its limitations." The most important matters requiring urgent attention are still frequently acted upon unilaterally, with only a nod toward the pledge of joint consultation. NATO has perhaps approached a spasmodically coordinated, but not a consistently common, policy. As Spaak concluded, an international organization of this type cannot live up to its expectations until its "member countries, large and small, accept some measure of supranational control." [11] Indeed, is it reasonable to assume that the Atlantic Community can create a reliable, continually effective common policy without creating a common policymaking body that goes beyond the processes of diplomatic consultations?

It may be argued that the national policies of the NATO members are so irreconcilably divergent that no common institution could be established. This may be so, but if it is, this is most likely equivalent to saying that, so long as Soviet power and purposes remain intact, the West has doomed itself by its own divisions and that nothing much can be done to avoid disaster. Is it not necessary to ask to what extent national policies in the Atlantic Community diverge because of irreconcilable attitudes and values, and to what extent because these divergent policies are allowed to develop unchecked, without first having to filter them through the

[10] *Ibid.*, p. 7.
[11] Speech of M. Paul-Henri Spaak, Secretary General of NATO, Sept. 27, 1958, *ibid.*, VI, Nos. 9, 10 (Sept.–Oct., 1958), 23.

strainer of a common political institution before giving them effect? The very existence of a reliable instrumentality for hammering out a common policy might, in turn, reduce the proliferation of conflicting national policies, or at least place restraints on conflicting policies which might otherwise grow willy-nilly into extremist positions not readily subject to negotiation. To say that a common policymaking body cannot be created because there are not in existence common national policies is to beg the issue. If there were perfectly coordinated common policies there would be no need for such a common authority in the first instance. This institution is needed both because of the present lack of common policies and because its successful operation might help form common attitudes and expectations within the Atlantic Community that would influence the formulation of more compatible national policies in the future.

One of the principal benefits of an agreed Atlantic policy would lie in the formulation of a sense of common purpose toward the uncommitted nations. The separation of the non-Soviet East from the West can ultimately prove as disastrous to the West as the estrangement of members of the Western Community from each other. However, the existence of a broad area of agreement within the West is a prerequisite to its effective approach toward the fence-sitting "middle world." The old colonial system is crumbling and yet the West has not evolved a coherent policy to take its place. If its influence among the uncommitted nations, which has been ebbing away at an alarming pace, is to be restored, the West must assume a stance which coincides with the basic aspirations of these peoples. This involves, first of all, a recognition that colonialism is morally indefensible and politically suicidal. Beyond that, it requires an open acknowledgment that the expectation of a decent standard of life is now undeniably universal. The West must therefore do its best to satisfy the legitimate yearning for a status of dignity and human equality, founded upon its willingness to support a rapid and sustained economic growth of the impoverished areas of the world.

On the other hand, an extension of human welfare will not result from an uncritically anticolonial platform. Encouragement and appeasement of indigenous demagogues waving the banner of anti-colonialism in a frenzy of nationalistic zenophobia and aiming to embark on their own aggressive, imperialist adventures is hardly an improvement on the past. What is required is a general commitment to find a liberal and constructive solution to the heritage of the colonial problem. This would assume in an issue involving colonialism that neither side is automatically right, but that the existence of a consistent sense of purpose in the West, arrived at through a common policymaking organ, could guide decisions based on the merits of the individual cases. General agreement on this issue will undoubtedly be extremely hard to come by, yet the extremist groups that discredit the West can only be isolated and their influence markedly diminished if the Atlantic Community as a whole attempts to come to grips with this problem forthrightly. Some encouragement can perhaps be gleaned from the accord on Cyprus reached in 1959. When NATO finally involved itself in this bitter and seemingly insoluble dispute, after years of attempting to ignore it, it was found possible to reconcile the strategic and economic interests of a colonial power with the anticolonial aspirations of a people seeking national self-determination, even though this was complicated by the presence of another, minority nationality. Is it possible that other situations involving this type of conflict of interests could be resolved as NATO increasingly develops as a forum for dealing with emergent nationalism in the non-Soviet world?

The West, at the same time, should neglect no opportunity to point up the dangers that face the leaders of the rising Afro-Asian nationalist movements, should they become too reliant upon Soviet support. It may be difficult to dispel the illusion that the Kremlin has a genuine interest in a national liberation movement for its own sake, rather than understanding it is a tactical weapon to be exploited for the advancement of Soviet power. The dramatic failure of the post-Stalinist Soviet leadership to accommodate itself to Tito's independence has perhaps awakened some Afro-Asians to the realization that ultimately Moscow can tolerate no movement of national independence, even if such a nation be Communist.

A strong and unified West, capable of discouraging Communist aggression and dedicated to a positive approach toward the uncommitted world, is the best hope both for an enduring world peace and for building a future democratic community of mankind. The realization of this dream admittedly lies in the distant future. But the first steps in this direction may be taken now if the West learns how to organize sufficient strength behind its freedoms so that it will be capable of confounding Soviet expectations over the long haul.

It is often objected that institutionalizing the differences between East and West will exacerbate tension and increase the likelihood of war. The action of one side undoubtedly provokes reaction by the other, but this interplay is not obliged to end on the field of armed conflict. The Cominform, for example, was created on the heels of the Marshall Plan.[12] Does that mean, then, that the Marshall Plan should not have been implemented because it "hardened the lines" between the Soviet and non-Soviet worlds? The alternative was to avoid "provoking" Moscow by permitting it to swallow up Western Europe as it sank into economic and political chaos. Saving Western Europe through a vigorous cooperative effort, however, did not provoke war.

A survey of Soviet foreign policy suggests that the Kremlin has acted cautiously when confronted by strong external power and aggressively when it has been tempted by weakness. If one of the principal sources of weakness of the contemporary non-Soviet world is its disunity, then the surest way to precipitate war is to provide seemingly easy targets of Soviet conquest through dissension or neglect on the part of the non-Soviet world to formulate unmistakably affirmative policies. War came to Korea, for example, not because South Korea was strong, but because it was left under a cloud of ambiguity in an apparently exposed and defenseless position. And when the West finally joined forces to repulse Communist aggression in Korea, did this collective action destroy or preserve the United Nations, and the universal aspirations for peace and human welfare which are recorded in its Charter?

Building a supranational Atlantic Community that can outlast the threat of Soviet totalitarianism would be likely to advance the prospects for the further integration of a democratic world community. "From the viewpoint of democracy," a distinguished student of nationalism observes, "genuine freedom and development within a limited block of countries should be preferable to stagnation within a larger area.... The larger the area, however, in which *genuine* integration and development can be carried on

[12] The Marshall Plan, to be sure, was originally conceived as an open-ended offer, but it was later pursued in the face of fierce Soviet opposition.

successfully, the greater will become the probability that eventually the challenge of world order and world government will be mastered." [13]

At the present juncture of history the Soviet design for world order has several distinct advantages. Despite the existence of serious internal tensions, Soviet totalitarianism manages to function with a good measure of brutal efficiency. The disintegrative pulls of nationalism, so evident in the non-Soviet world, are also present within the Soviet orbit, but an armory of Communist police state weapons can keep these disruptive forces within bounds more easily than in the West. And should a nation, such as Hungary, clearly overstep the tolerable limits of independent action, then Moscow does not hesitate to restore the broken lines of control by all means, including massacre. The existence of a clear-cut totalitarian ideology also has the advantage of presenting the Soviet leaders with an all-embracing dynamic view of the world. Seemingly fragmentary and unrelated happenings in all parts of the world can be related meaningfully when they are fitted against a broadly conceived design for refashioning humanity into a Soviet world state. The boastful self-assurance of the Soviet leaders is not simply a pose, but reflects a conviction that it is possible to move history in a desired direction through intelligent planning, purposeful manipulation of events, and a constant alertness to exploit unforeseen windfalls.

The non-Soviet world is in need of a democratic order and a sense of direction, without which its freedoms will not be likely to endure. In the absence of a positive program for reshaping national destinies, all too often the rudderless West is buffeted about by the uncharted political gales, while Soviet power capitalizes on the default of Western policy to move steadily toward its preconceived objective. As a result, apathy, indifference, and a feeling of despair that we are viewing an unavoidable "decline of the West" are more widespread attitudes than one likes to acknowledge. This trend can only be reversed if the West becomes self-conscious about its condition of disorder and resolves to gain control over its destiny. Instead of seeking merely bare survival and the avoidance of Soviet conquest, it is past time for the West to rejuvenate its will to live, to be infused with a new strength and sense of purpose that will lead to a new flowering of freedom.

[13] Karl W. Deutsch, *Nationalism and Social Communication* (New York, 1953), p. 167.

Principal Sources

References to works not included in this list are given in full in the footnotes at their first appearance in each chapter.

BOOKS

Batsell, Walter. *Soviet Rule in Russia.* New York, 1929.
Berdnikov, A., and F. Svetlov, N. I. Bukharin (general ed.). *Elements of Political Education.* Chicago, 1926, translated from 1923 Russian edition.
Boorman, Howard L., et al. *Moscow-Peking Axis.* New York, 1957.
Borkenau, Franz. *The Communist International.* London, 1938.
Bukharin, Nikolai. *Culture in Two Worlds.* New York, 1934.
—— *Historical Materialism.* New York, 1925.
—— *Imperialism and World Economy.* New York, 1929.
—— *Programma kommunistov* (Program of the Communists). Moscow, 1921.
Bukharin, Nikolai, and E. Preobrazhenskii. *Azbuka kommunizma* (The ABC of Communism). Moscow, 1919.
Caroe, Olaf. *Soviet Empire: The Turks of Central Asia and Stalinism.* London, 1953.
Carr, E. H. *The Bolshevik Revolution, 1917–1923.* 3 vols. London, 1950–1953.
Comintern (Communist International). *Kommunisticheskii Internatsional v dokumentakh, 1919–1932* (The Communist International in Documents, 1919–1932). Bela Kun (ed.). Moscow, 1933. Referred to in footnotes as *Kom. Int. v. dok.*
—— First Congress. *La IIIe Internationale Communiste: Thèses adoptées par le Ier Congès—Documents Officiels pour l'année 1919–1920* (The Third Communist International: Theses Adopted by the First Congress—Official Documents for 1919–1920). Petrograd, 1920.
—— Second Congress. *Vtoroi kongress Kommunisticheskogo Internatsionala: protokoly* (The Second Congress of the Communist International: Protocols). Moscow, 1934.
—— Third Congress. *Third World Congress of the Communist International: Theses and Resolutions, June 22–July 12, 1921.* New York, 1921.
—— Fourth Congress. *Fourth Congress of the Communist International: Abridged Report of Meetings Held at Petrograd and Moscow, Nov. 7–Dec. 3, 1922.* London, n.d. [1923].

Comintern (Communist International) (*Continued*)
——— Fourth to Fifth Congress. *From the Fourth to the Fifth World Congress: Report of the Executive Committee of the Communist International.* London, 1924.
——— Fifth Congress. *V vsemirnyi kongress Kommunisticheskogo Internatsionala: Tezisy, rezoliutsii i postanovleniia* (The Fifth World Congress of the Communist International: Theses, Resolutions, and Decrees). Moscow, 1924.
——— *Fifth Congress of the Communist International: Abridged Report of Meetings Held at Moscow, June 17th to July 8th, 1924.* London, n.d.
——— Sixth Congress. *Sixth World Congress of the Communist International, July–August 1928,* Imprecorr, Vol. VIII, Nos. 39–92. Vienna, 1928.
——— Seventh Congress. *VII Congress of the Communist International: Abridged Stenographic Report of Proceedings.* Moscow, 1939.
Davis, Kathryn. *The Soviets at Geneva: The USSR and the League of Nations, 1919–1933.* Geneva, 1934.
Degras, Jane (ed.). *Soviet Documents on Foreign Policy.* 3 vols. London, New York, Toronto, 1951–1953.
Dennis, Alfred L. P. *The Foreign Policies of Soviet Russia.* New York, 1924.
Dimitrov, G. *Nastuplenie fashizma i zadachi Kommunisticheskogo Internatsionala v bor'be za edinstvo rabochego klassa protiv fashizma* (Fascist Aggression and the Tasks of the Communist International in the Struggle for Unity of the Working Class Against Fascism). Moscow, 1935.
Dunaeva, E. A. *The Collaboration of Nations in the USSR.* Moscow, 1951.
Engels, F. *Herr Eugen Dühring's Revolution in Science.* New York, 1939.
——— *The Origin of the Family, Private Property, and the State.* New York, 1942.
——— *Socialism, Utopian and Scientific.* New York, 1945.
Eudin, Xenia Joukoff, and Harold H. Fisher. *Soviet Russia and the West, 1920–1927: A Documentary Survey.* Stanford, 1957.
Eudin, Xenia Joukoff, and Robert C. North. *Soviet Russia and the East, 1920–1927: A Documentary Survey.* Stanford, 1957.
Fischer, Louis. *The Soviets in World Affairs, 1917–1929.* 2 vols. Princeton, N.J., 1951.
Fischer, Ruth. *Stalin and German Communism.* Cambridge, Mass., 1948.
Informatsionnoe soveshchanie predstavitelei nekotorikh Kompartii v Pol'she v kontse sentiabria 1947 goda (Informational Conference of Representatives of Various Communist Parties in Poland at the End of September, 1947). Moscow, 1948.
Istoriia vsesoiuznoi Kommunisticheskoi partii (bol'shevikov) kratkii kurs (History of the All-Union Communist Party [Bolsheviks] Short Course). Moscow, 1938 and Moscow, 1952.

PRINCIPAL SOURCES 491

Kammari, M. D. *The Development by J. V. Stalin of the Marxist-Leninist Theory of the National Question.* Moscow, 1951.
Kliuchnikov, Iu. V., and A. B. Sabanin (eds.). *Mezhdunarodnaia politika noveishego vremeni v dogovorakh, notakh i deklaratsiiakh* (International Politics of Recent Times in Treaties, Notes, and Declarations). 3 vols. Moscow, 1925–1928.
Kolarz, Walter. *Russia and Her Colonies.* New York, 1952.
Kom. Int. v dok., see Comintern (Communist International). *Kommunisticheskii Internatsional,* etc.
Kommunisticheskaia Partiia Sovetskogo Soiuza v rezoliutsiakh i resheniiakh s"ezdov, konferentsii i plenumov TsK, 1898–1953 (The Communist Party of the Soviet Union in Resolutions and Decisions of Congresses, Conferences, and Plenums of the Central Committee, 1898–1953). 11th ed., 2 vols. Moscow, 1953. Referred to in footnotes as *KPSS v rez.*
KPSS v rez., see *Kommunisticheskaia Partiia,* etc.
Lenin, V. I. *Sobranie sochinenii* (Collected Works). 1st ed., 19 vols. Moscow, 1924–25.
—— *Sochineniia* (Works). 2d ed., 31 vols. Moscow, 1930–1935.
—— *Sochineniia* (Works). 3d ed., 31 vols. Moscow, 1934–1935.
—— *Sochineniia* (Works). 4th ed., 35 vols. Moscow, 1941–1952.
Litvinov, Maxim. *Against Aggression.* New York, 1939.
Lorimer, Frank. *The Population of the Soviet Union: History and Prospects.* Geneva, 1946.
Malenkov, G. M. *Otchëtnyi doklad XIX s"ezdu partii o rabote Tsentral'nogo Komiteta VKP(b)* (Report to the Nineteenth Party Congress on the Work of the Central Committee of the All-Union Communist Party [Bolsheviks]). Moscow, 1952.
Marx, Karl. *Capital.* Kerr ed., 3 vols. Chicago, 1906–1909.
—— *Civil War in France.* Intro. by F. Engels. New York, 1940.
—— *Critique of the Gotha Program.* New York, 1933.
Marx, Karl, and F. Engels. *The Communist Manifesto.* New York, 1939.
—— *The German Ideology.* New York, 1947.
—— *The Russian Menace to Europe.* Paul W. Blackstock and Bert F. Hoselitz (eds.). Glencoe, Ill., 1952.
—— *The Selected Correspondence of Karl Marx and Frederick Engels.* New York, 1942.
Pipes, Richard. *The Formation of the Soviet Union.* Cambridge, Mass., 1954.
Polents, O. E. *"Vsemirnoe gosudarstvo"—oruzhie amerikansikikh imperialistov v bor'be za mirovoe gospodstvo* ("World Government"— Weapon of the American Imperialists in the Struggle for World Hegemony). Moscow, 1950.
Social Contract: Essays by Locke, Hume, and Rousseau. Intro. by Sir Ernest Barker. New York, London, 1948.
The Soviet-Yugoslav Dispute. London, 1948.
Stalin, J. V. *Doklad o proekte konstitutsii Soiuza SSR* (Report on the Draft Constitution of the USSR). Moscow, 1936.

Stalin, J. V. (*Continued*)
—— *Ekonomicheskie problemy sotsializma v SSSR* (Economic Problems of Socialism in the USSR). Moscow, 1952.
—— *Marksizm i voprosy iazykoznaniia* (Marxism and Questions of Linguistics). Moscow, 1950.
—— *O Lenine i Leninizme* (On Lenin and Leninism). Moscow, 1924.
—— *Otchëtnyi doklad na XVIII s"ezde partii o rabote TsK VKP(b)* (Report to the Eighteenth Party Congress on the Work of the Central Committee of the All-Union Communist Party [Bolsheviks]). Moscow, 1950.
—— *Sochineniia* (Works). 13 vols. Moscow, 1946–1951.
Talmon, J. L. *The Rise of Totalitarian Democracy.* Boston, 1952.
Trotsky, Leon. *Europe and America.* Colombo, 1951.
—— *My Life.* New York, 1931.
—— *Nashi politicheskie zadachi* (Our Political Tasks). Geneva, 1904.
—— *Permanent Revolution.* Calcutta, 1947.
—— *Piat' let Kominterna* (Five Years of the Comintern). Moscow, 1924.
—— *The Real Situation in Russia.* New York, 1928.
—— *The Revolution Betrayed.* New York, 1945.
—— *Sochineniia* (Works). Vol. III, Part I. Moscow, n.d. [1924].
—— *Stalin,* New York, 1941.
—— *The Third International After Lenin.* New York, 1936.
Velikovskii, M., and I. Levin (eds.). *Natsional'nyi vopros: Khrestomatiia* (The National Question: An Anthology). Vols. I and II, Part II. Moscow, 1931.
Vyshinsky, A. Ia. *Sovetskoe gosudarstvennoe pravo* (Soviet State Law). Moscow, 1938.
Wollenberg, Erich. *The Red Army.* London, 1938.
Zinner, Paul E. (ed.). *National Communism and Popular Revolt in Eastern Europe.* New York, 1956.

NEWSPAPERS AND PERIODICALS

The following publications have been consulted extensively.

The American Slavic and East European Review (New York).
The Annals of the American Academy of Political and Social Science (Philadelphia).
Bol'shevik (Bolshevik); after No. 19, October, 1952, *Kommunist* (Communist) (Moscow).
Bulletin of the Institute for the Study of the History and Culture of the USSR; after September, 1955, *Bulletin, Institute for the Study of the USSR* (Munich).
The Central Asian Review (London).
The Communist International (Petrograd, London, New York).
East Europe, see *News from Behind the Iron Curtain.*
For a Lasting Peace, For a People's Democracy! (Belgrade, Bucharest).

PRINCIPAL SOURCES

Foreign Affairs (New York).
International Affairs (London).
International Affairs (Moscow).
International Press Correspondence (Berlin, Basle, Vienna); after July 2, 1938, *World News and Views* (London).
Izvestiia (News) (Moscow).
Kommunist, see *Bol'shevik*.
Kultura i zhizn' (Culture and Life) (Moscow).
Literaturnaia gazeta (Literary Journal) (Moscow).
The New Leader (New York).
News (Moscow).
News from Behind the Iron Curtain; after November, 1956, *East Europe* (New York).
New Times (Moscow).
The New York Times.
Novyi mir (New World) (Moscow).
Pravda (Truth) (Moscow).
The Russian Review (Hanover, N.H.).
Sovetskoe gosudarstvo i pravo (Soviet State and Law) (Moscow).
Soviet Studies (Oxford).
Uchitel'skaia gazeta (Teacher's Gazette) (Moscow).
The Ukrainian Quarterly (New York).
Voprosy ekonomiki (Questions of Economics) (Moscow).
Voprosy filosofii (Questions of Philosophy) (Moscow).
Voprosy istorii (Questions of History) (Moscow).
World Government News (New York).
World Marxist Review (Toronto).
World News and Views, see *International Press Correspondence*.

Index

Abai Kunanbaev, 109
ABC of Communism (Bukharin and Preobrazhenskii), 290, 377
Acheson-Lilienthal Report of March, *1946,* 399-400, 404
Adamic, Louis, quoted, 331
Adenauer, Konrad, 415
Afghanistan, 242, 369n
Africa: concept of sovereignty in, 113-14, 116-17; federation plans in, 421-22
Afro-Asian bloc, 481
Afro-Asian nationalist movements, 486
Aggression, and national sovereignty, 118-19
Agriculture: collectivization of, 41, 98, 135, 437, 453, 463-64; need for Western techniques in, 103; industry and, 436-38
Albania: and Eastern European federation, 331, 334, 335; People's Soviets in, 339; as Yugoslav satellite, 341; plans for non-Soviet federation, 390
Albanians in Serbia, 327
Aleichem, Sholom, 274n
Alsace-Lorraine, Engels's attitude toward, 10
America, *see* United States
Anarchism: differences between socialism and, 16-17, 429; and stateless society, 18, 434, 467; attitude of Anarchists toward Russian nationalism, 84; on "skipping stages," 230n
Anatomy of Peace, The (Reves), 413
Angell, Sir Norman, 386
Anti-Semitism, Russian chauvinism and, 110-12
Arab-Israeli tensions, 477
Arab League, 422-25
Armaments, 397; in Baruch Plan, 402-3; *see also* Disarmament
Armenia: nationalism in, 35; Soviet-Turkish territorial ambitions in, 59n; federalism in, 199-200, 202, 206; in USSR, 240-41, 256; rebellion in, 354
Army, standing, abolition of, 13-14, 449-50; *see also* Red Army
Asia: concept of sovereignty in, 113-14, 116-17; Soviet use of armed force in, 313-17; confederal pattern for, 337-38; expansion of the Soviet federation in, 355-60; as challenge to Soviet Russian centralism, 360-71; *see also* Afro-Asian entries; *and specific countries,* e.g., China
Asia, Southeast, 369
Asia, Soviet Central: Great Russian influence in, 66; interviews of refugees from, 85n; backward peoples of, 107, 108-9; rebuff to federalism in, 242-43; guerrilla warfare with the Basmachi in, 354; and China, 369
Asian Communist Parties, 313-17
Assam, 369n
Atlantic Community, 476-88 *passim*
Atlantic Union Committee, 413
Atomic bomb, danger of, and need for world federation, 395-99
Atomic Development Authority, proposed, 400-7
Atomic energy, debate over international control of, 399-407
Atomic warfare, 185, 317-20, 324-25, 395-99
Attlee, Clement, cited, 395, 414
"August Bloc," 202-3
Austin, Warren, quoted, 401
Austria, 390, 415; *see also* Austro-Hungarian Empire
Austrian Social Democrats, 207, 216n
Austro-Hungarian Empire, multinational nature of, 10-11, 21-22, 26, 35, 207; *see also* Austria; Hungary
Austro-Prussian War of *1866,* 23
Autonomous Regions, 256
Autonomous Republics, number of, in USSR, 255-56
Axelrod, Paul, 195
Azerbaijan, 109, 240-41, 256, 354

INDEX 495

Babeuf, F. N., 197, 255
Baghdad Pact, 424, 477
Bakunin, Mikhail, 7, 16, 192*n*
Balkan Communist Federation, 327
Balkan states, *see specific states,* e.g., Bulgaria
Balkan Union, 390
Balkan Wars of *1912–1913,* 326
Balkar people: national autonomy destroyed, 95; restored, 96-97
Baltic states, Soviet Union and, 33, 44, 97, 119, 230; *see also specific states,* e.g., Estonia
Bandung Conference (1955), 316
Barmine, A., cited, 269, 378
Barnard, Chester, cited, 403-4, 405
Baruch Plan, 400-7
Bashkir ASSR, 272
Bashkirs, 98
Bavaria, Soviet Republic of, 32, 33, 295
Bednii, Dem'ian, letter from Stalin to, 74
Belgium, federalists in, 415
Belorussia, Communist Party of, 68
Belorussia, Western, 44, 90
Belorussian SSR, 235; question of membership in UN, 261, 338
Benelux, 419
Beneš, Eduard, 390
Beria, L. P., 102-3, 124
Berlin blockade, 182
Bessarabia, 44, 328
Bevin, Ernest, 396, 414
Bidault, Georges, 420
Bled Agreement (Aug. 1, 1947), 333
Bloom, Solomon F., 17*n*; quoted, 1, 20
Blum, Léon, 115, 415
Bokhara, 230
Bol'shevik, cited, 92; quoted, 145, 149-50, 301-2; *see also Kommunist*
Bolshevik Party, 5*n*, 25-49; Great Russian nationalism and structure of, 67-74; federalism versus centralism in, 195, 196, 213-15; rebirth of, 203; on right of self-determination, 212; on nationality problem, 247-51; on United States of Europe, 374; *see also* Communist Party of the Soviet Union
Bolshevik Revolution: vision of human redemption in, 29; and imminence of world state, 30-36; Russian nationalism and, 65; and fostering of national languages, 265-67
Borkenau, F., 78, 335

Borneo, 369
Bosnia-Herzegovina, 332
Bourgeois society, 2, 5-6, 7, 82; *see also* Capitalism
Briand, Aristide, 381
Bridges, Styles, quoted, 317*n*
Britain: concept of sovereignty, 113-14; and Eastern European federation, 332; federalists in, 414-15; and UN, 480; *see also* England
Brotherhood of man, Communist idea of, 427-32
Brusilov, A. A., 55
Bukharin, N. I.: on world state, 31; on nationalism, 51; attitude toward Treaty of Brest-Litovsk, 54; move from left to right wing of Party, 56; Stalin and, 77, 157, 453-55; sentenced to death, 88; attitude toward peaceful coexistence, 164; centralist opposition of, 215, 218-19; on right of self-determination, 228; on use of force, 290, 297; on ultra-imperialism, 375-76; on League of Nations, 377-78; on Pan-Europe movement, 380; Communist handbook by, 427; on stateless world society, 427, 428-31 *passim;* on omnicompetent worker, 433-36 *passim;* on orchestra metaphor, 434-35, 445; on merging of town and country, 436-38; on "valid" will, 442-43; on freedom, 444-45; on dictatorship, 445; on "withering away" of state, 448
Bukovina, northern, 44
Bulganin, N. A.: on atomic war, 320; on Poznan riots, 342; demotion of, 355; letter to Eisenhower, 395*n*; Khrushchev's attack on, 468-69
Bulgaria, 11; Soviet control in, 46, 332-36 *passim,* 339; plans for non-Soviet federation, 390
Bulgarian Communist Party, 327, 329, 331, 332, 336
Bund (General Jewish Worker's League of Lithuania, Poland, and Russia), 198, 199, 201, 207, 210
Bureaucracy: abolition of, 14, 449-50; re-creation of permanent, 452-53
Buriats, 249
Burma, 369
Burmeister, Alfred, 45*n*

Calcutta, Communist conclaves held in, 313
Cambodia, 369

Campbell, Thomas D., 143
Capital (Marx), quoted, 17-18
Capitalism: law of uneven development and, 4, 154-55; Marx and Engels on, 5, 7, 8-9, 18; Trotsky on, 25-29 *passim;* Stalin on, 35-36, 149-53, 429, 460-62; self-determination of nations and, 216; supranationalist plans of states under, 373-425; *see also* Imperialism
Capitalist encirclement, 149-53, 460-62
Carr, E. H., 62
Caucasus, 107-8, 227-28
Celebes, 369
Centralism: Marx and Engels's advocacy of, 8-12, 16, 23-24; Marxist internationalism and, 68-69; versus Federalism, 190-263; struggle for, in Party, 197-203; plans for, in organization of state power, 203-6; Lenin's struggle with doctrinaire group on, 215-21; voluntary, 221-22; Asian challenge to Soviet Russian, 360-72; in stateless world society, 427-32
Chashnikov, I., quoted, 312
Chatara, D., 241*n*
Chauvinism, *see* Russian nationalism
Chechen-Ingush peoples: national autonomy destroyed, 95-96; restored, 96-97
Cherniak, E., quoted, 409
Chervenkov, premier of Bulgaria, quoted, 283
Chiang Kai-shek, 75, 76, 78, 84
Chicherin, G. V.: as Soviet Commissar of Foreign Affairs, 59, 60-61, 62; on agreements with Germany, 165, 166; on peaceful coexistence, 169, 170; on disarmament, 299-300; on League of Nations, 377, 379, 384
Chikobava, A., 281
Children, care and education of, 20, 438
China: Soviet relations with, 60-61, 75-76, 84, 306 (*see also under* Chinese People's Republic); capitalism in, 230*n*
Chinese Communist Party, 75, 78, 84, 314
Chinese Eastern Railway, 60-61
Chinese language in Marr's theory, 281
Chinese People's Republic: Soviet relations with, 150, 313-17, 339, 346, 355-72; creation of, 314, 362
Chinese Trade Unions, 314

Chou En-lai, 363
Church, the: Soviet government and, 91; and federation, 415
Churchill, Winston, 387, 418
Cities, *see* Urban economy
Civil War in France, The (Marx), 9
Civil wars, 290, 291, 300, 321-22; in China, 313-15; Khrushchev on, 321
Class, 1, 2; effect on the state of differences in society, 13; consciousness, 197-99; dictatorship of, 443; abandonment of original ideology, 457-58; *see also* Class struggle
Classless society, future, 12-20, 426-71
Class struggle, 1-2, 12; nationalism and, 54-62 *passim,* 70; international, 76, 292
Clausewitz, Karl von, 287
Clissold, Stephen, quoted, 329*n*
Coexistence, *see* Peaceful coexistence
Collective farm system, 41, 98, 135, 437, 453, 463-64
Colonialism, 34, 113-14, 485-86
Cominform, *see* Communist Information Bureau
Comintern, *see* Communist International
Commissariat of Foreign Affairs, 64, 169, 260
Commissariat of Nationalities, 68-69
Commissariat of Worker's and Peasant's Inspection, 453
Commissariats, three types of, 246
Committee to Frame a World Constitution, 412
Commonwealth of Man (Schuman), 411
Commonwealth of Socialist States, 351-55
Communes: Paris, 8, 9, 13-15, 449-50; Proudhon's, 16; in China, 365-66, 369
Communism: national, 2, 342-47; Marx and Engels on full, 12-17; confronted with issue of world federalism, 415-18; world, in which "world state" becomes "no state," 426-71
Communist Information Bureau (Cominform): founding and dissolution of, 46-47; founding Conference (1947), 117-18, 313, 408; Marshall Plan as major reason for the creation of, 117; Tito and, 121; peaceful coexistence and, 178-80
Communist International (Comintern): founding of, 31, 32, 47, 377; aim of, 31, 426-27; dissolution of, 44-

INDEX

45; conditions for membership in, 62; Fifth Enlarged Plenum (1925), 75; acceptance of idea of United States of Europe, 158; task of, 161, 232; centralism in, 237-38; in Eastern Europe, 326-28; Executive Committee of, 328-29; suggestion that recognition as subject of international law be accorded, 410
—— Congresses: First (1919), 31-32; Second (1920), 33-35, 57, 61, 231, 237, 296, 337, 352, 378, 428; Fourth (1922), 36, 158, 297; Fifth (1924), 75, 328*n*; Sixth (1928), 39, 40, 77, 299, 381; Seventh (1935), 42, 82-83, 188
—— Manifesto (1920), 34-35
—— Program (1928), 39-40, 138-39, 158, 172, 427
—— Statutes (1920), 35, 62, 237, 296-97, 426; Statutes (1928), 40
—— Theses (1920), 233; Theses (1928), 299-301, 302
Communist International, The, cited, 43, 44, 89, 387-88
Communist Manifesto, The (Marx and Engels), cited, 2, 3, 5, 15, 22, 27
Communist Parties: treatment of defections in, 75; Moscow Declaration of, 105, 465-66; *see also under specific countries*, e.g., German Communist Party
Communist Parties of Europe, 83, 310-13
Communist Party of the Soviet Union (CPSU): Bolshevik Party, 25-49 (*see also* Bolshevik Party); Central Committee of, 45*n*; non-Russian element, 67-69; Russian Communist Party (Bolsheviks), 75 (*see also* Russian Communist Party); and centralist-federalist controversy, 190-203 *passim*, 234-35, 253-55; Russian Social Democratic Labor Party, 204 (*see also* Russian Social Democratic Labor Party); expulsion from, 235-36; as arbiter of minimal right of national expression, 253; effect of, on meaning of "national in form, socialist in content," 253-55; organization on military lines, 288; dictatorship of, 443; "withering away" of, 459; role of, in Communist society, 470
—— Conferences: October Conference (1913), 211; Thirteenth (1924), 236; Fourteenth (1925), 134, 142

—— Congresses: Second (1903), 198-99, 200, 204; Third (1905), 201; Fourth (or Unity) (1906), 201; Fifth (1907), 202; Seventh (1918), 448; Eighth (1919), 32, 227, 234; Tenth (1921), 35, 148, 235, 247; Twelfth (1923), 37-38, 66, 70, 248; Sixteenth (1930), 73, 149, 267; Seventeenth (1934), 304; Eighteenth (1939), 144, 307; Nineteenth (1952), 124, 184; Twentieth (1956), 96, 103, 150, 185, 320-21, 322-23, 340, 464; Twenty-first (1959), 103, 151, 367, 438, 468, 470
Confederal pattern for outlying satellites, 337-38
Congress of Cultural Leaders in Defense of Peace (1948), 181*n*
Constantinescu, M., quoted, 322
Consumption, control by society and by the state over amount of, 469-70
Cooperative movements, 132
Cosmopolitanism, defined, 407, 408
Coudenhove-Kalergi, Richard N., cited, 380
Council for Mutual Economic Aid, 339-40, 345-46
Council of Europe, 182, 419
Council of Nationalities, 256
Council of People's Commissars, 223, 224-27
Council of the Union, 256
Councils of the People's Economy, 431
Courland, 227-28
CPSU, *see* Communist Party of the Soviet Union
Crimean Region, 259
Crimean Tatars, 95, 96, 97
Crimes, political, 468-69; *see also* Purges
Critique of the Gotha Program (Marx), cited, 4-5
Croatia, 328, 332
Cucchi, Aldo, 312
Cultural and Scientific Conference for World Peace (1949), 181*n*
Culture: Marx and Engels on, 6; Trotsky on nationalism and, 29; world, 99*n*, 100-2, 209-11, 247-51; non-Russian, 112; national, 262-63, 266, 439 (*see also* Language); Lebed's "theory of the struggle of two cultures," 272; *see also* National cultural autonomy
Cuno government, 57
Cyprus, accord on, 486

497

Cyrankiewicz, Premier of Poland, 344
Czechoslovakia, 10; nationalism in, 35; Cominform in, 46; Mutual Assistance Pact signed by Soviet Union with, 83; press on Russian language, 282; Red Army in, 322; federation projects, 334, 389-92; National Committees in, 339; Sovietization of, 392

Dagestan, 108
Danubian countries, federation with Balkan states, 327-28
Davis, Garry, 411-12
Declaration of Rights of the Peoples of Russia (Nov. 15, 1917), 222
Declaration of the Founding Cominform Conference, 117-18
Declaration of the Rights of the Toiling and Exploited People, 225
Declaration of Union of USSR, 37
Declaration on the Formation of the USSR, 168
Delgado, Enrique Castro, 45*n*
Democracy: meaning of Soviet, 116; Lenin's attitude toward, 200-1, 426
Democratic Centralism, 236
Denationalization, 21
Denisov, A. I., quoted, 256; cited, 337
Dennis, Eugene, 111*n*
Deutsch, Karl W., quoted, 487-88
Dialectics, 455, 460, 463, 466-67
Diaz, José, 83
Dictatorship, 443-45
Dictatorship of the proletariat: Marx and Engels on, 8, 10, 12, 13, 16; Trotsky on, 29; Bukharin on, 31; Stalin on, 70; Lenin on, 232, 287; Khrushchev on, 320-21; Rosa Luxemburg on, 451; obsolescence of term, 458-60
Diedisheim, Jean, 417
Dimitrov, G., quoted, 33, 42-43, 45*n*, 82-83; and federalist projects, 333-35
Disarmament, 291, 299-301; in Baruch Plan, 403-4, 406
Djilas, M., 344
Dostoevsky, F. M., 126
Douglas, William O., 409
Dunaeva, E. A., quoted, 47-48, 90, 262, 408
Dzerzhinskii, F., 70

East, the: First Congress of the Peoples of the East, 58; nationalism and, 244-45; *see also* specific countries, e.g., China; *and* specific peoples, e.g., Moslem peoples

—— Far East, 57-58, 60-61, 84
—— Middle and Near East: proletarian internationalism and Russian nationalism and, 57-60; national sovereignty in, 118; Soviet Union in, 325; federation in, 422-25; Atlantic Community and, 477-81
Eastern Europe, *see* Europe, Eastern
Eastern European Federal Union, 389-90
Eckstein, Alexander, cited, 360*n*
Economic determinism, 1, 6-7, 13, 50, 217, 436, 462-63
Economic Problems of Socialism in the USSR, The (Stalin), 183
Economic systems, existence of two, 138-39, 140
Economy, Soviet: national groups and, 247-51; and attainment of socialism, 458-59
Economy, Soviet bloc: integration of Eastern European satellites with Soviet Union, 339-40; cost of national communism in terms of, 345-47; Sino-Soviet trade and, 360
Economy, world, 5, 29, 233-34, 352; in stateless world society, 17-20, 428, 429*n*, 431-36
Eden, Anthony, cited, 395-96; quoted, 480-81
Education: national groups and, 247-51; obligatory teaching of Russian in all non-Russian schools, 273-76
Egalitarianism, Stalin on, 457-58
Egypt, 422; *see also* Nasser
Einikeit (Yiddish newspaper), 110
Einstein, Albert, quoted, 397-98
Eisenhower, D. D., Bulganin's letter to, 320, 395*n*; quoted, 478*n*, 480
Elite group, 229, 450-51, 452, 462
Encirclement, capitalist and socialist, 149-53
Engels, Friedrich: on leveling process between town and country, 437; on freedom, 444-45; on economic determinism, 462*n*; *see also* Marx and Engels
England: Marx's attitude toward English-Irish relations, 11-12; proletariat in, 22; as prototype of capitalist nation-states, 26; *see also* Britain
English language, role of, in struggle for world supremacy between East and West, 271-73
Enver Pasha, 242
Erenburg, Il'ia, quoted, 414
Erusalimskii, A., quoted, 419

INDEX 499

Esperanto, 269
Estonia: incorporated into USSR, 90, 119; peace treaty with, 166, 167; Red Army in, 294, 298
Ethnic problem, 1, 9-10, 21-23, 26*n*, 49, 207; federalism as attempt to solve, 247-51
Euratom, 182, 340*n*
Europe: Russia as vanguard of revolution in, 3; national sovereignty and, 115-18; and Soviet trade policy, 181-82; non-communist plans for unification in the 1920s, 380-82; Soviet condemnation of federalists in, 414-15; *see also* Europe, Eastern; Europe, Western; United States of Europe
Europe, Eastern: Engels and Marx on ethnic rights of peoples in, 10-11; multinational nature of, 26, 35; attack on "nationalist" Communists of, 106; Red Army in, 311; postwar transformation of, 321-22; Communist plans for federation of, 326-38; Chinese influence in, 363-64; Soviet reaction to federalist plans in, 389-92
Europe, Western: as prototype of capitalist nation-states, 26; Marshall Plan and, 117-18, 178, 182, 419, 487; need of advanced countries of, in completing victory of socialism, 131-34, 146-49; Red Army and, 311-12; Soviet attitude toward federalist plans for, 418; as likely center of future world state, 472; NATO and, 476; political and economic union for, 482-83
European Army, 419
European Coal and Steel Community, 419
European Defense Community, 182, 419, 420-21
European Economic Community, 182
European Federative Republic, 7
European Foreign Ministers, Paris Conference of, 117
European Payments Union, 182, 419
European Political Community, 419
European Republic Federation, 153
European Socialists, 115
European Union, 380-82
Exploitation, economic and political, 6-7, 458-59*n*
Extermination, national, 21

Family, the, 19-20, 458
Far East, *see* East, the, Far East

Farmer, Fyke, 414
Fatherland, *see* Nationalism
Federalism: Marx and Engels on, 8-12, 23-24; advocacy by anarchists, 16; versus centralism, 190-263; Party, and "August Bloc," 202-3; Bolshevik conception of, 213-15; Soviet adoption of, 224-27; and world state, 233-38; in RSFSR, 239-40; in Transcaucasus, 240-41; rebuff of, in Soviet Central Asia, 242-43; in 1923 Constitution of USSR, 243; in 1936 Constitution of USSR, 255-62
Federalists, The, 416
Federation, non-Soviet world plans for, 373-425; Soviet reaction to, 387-425; Western proposals in view of danger of atomic war, 395-99
Federation of Eastern Europe: Communist plans for, 326-38; Tito, Dimitrov, and Stalin sparring over, 332-36; Stalin's alternative of confederal approach, 337-38
Federation of Western democracies, Soviet attitude toward, 386-87
Fedotov, George, quoted, 73*n*, 105
Fedoseev, P., quoted, 399
Feng, General, 75
Finland: nationalism in, 35; Soviet Union and, 43, 119, 167-68, 222-23, 308, 337; exercise of self-determination in, 227-28, 229-30; and federation, 233
Finnish Communists, 229
Finnish Social Democratic Party, 222
Finnish Socialist Worker's Republic, 229
Finno-Swedish federation, 389
First International, meeting of General Council of, 23
Fischer, Louis, quoted, 58
Fischer, Ruth, quoted, 75; cited, 335*n*
Five-Year Plans, 41, 339, 453
Folks-Shtimme (Warsaw Yiddish-language paper), 111*n*
Force, Soviet theory on use of, 285-325, 354
Foreign agents, Soviet, 128
Foreign Communist movements, 84
France, 21; proletariat in, 22; as prototype of capitalist nation-states, 26; Soviet expectations for, 46; Mutual Assistance Pact signed by Soviet Union with, 83; concept of sovereignty, 113-14; federalists in, 415; and UN, 480
Franco-British Union, 387, 388, 418

Franco regime in Spain, 113
Freedom, Soviet meaning of, 445-46
French Revolution, Lenin, and Jacobin tradition of, 8-9, 192-97, 229, 444
Frumkin, A. N., cited, 397-98
Frunze, M. V., 59

Geneva Conference (1955), 103, 318, 320
Geneva Institute of International Affairs, 385
Genoa Conference of European powers (1922), 379
Genocide, 22
Georgia: nationalism in, 35; Soviet-Turkish territorial ambitions in, 59n; USSR and, 68, 240-41, 256; national uprising in, 354
Georgian Social Democrats, 199-200, 206
German Communist Party, 56, 75, 78-79
German Democratic Republic, "full sovereignty" granted to, 341
Germans, Marx and Engels on, 21-22
Germany: proletariat in, 22; as prototype of capitalist nation-states, 26; effect of rise of Hitler on Russian nationalism, 41, 80; Soviet Russia and Weimar Republic of, 54-57; invasion of Soviet Union, 93-94; Soviet Russia and, 165-66; rising menace of, 175-76; Stalin's suggested confederation for a Soviet, 233, 337; Nazi plan of dividing world with USSR, 309-10; Red Army in war with, 310-13; Soviet Army in East, 341, 346; renunciation of League membership by, 382; Soviet propaganda attack on Nazi, 388; federalists in, 414-15; *see also* Hitler, Adolf; Nazi-Soviet Pact
Gheorghiu-Dej, 339
Ghilan, Soviet Republic of, 59
Girondins, 194
Goebbels, P. J., quoted, 94
Gomulka, Wladyslaw, 104, 111, 343, 344; quoted, 338
Gotha Program, 4, 5, 15n
Gouzenko, Igor, 45n
Great Britain, *see* Britain; England
Great Purges of *1936-1938*, 45n, 88, 254, 255, 257
Great Russia: Bolshevik Revolution and, 51-53, 54, 64-65, 126; chauvinism of, 85-88, 92, 254 (*see also* Russian nationalism); domination by, 248
Greece, 11; Turkey and, 58-59; and Eastern European federation, 332-36 *passim*; plans for Balkan Union, 390
Greek Communist Party, 327, 329, 336
"Green Pool," 419
Gromyko, A., 401
Gsovski, Vladimir, quoted, 20, 246-47
Guerrilla warfare, 313

Hamilton, Alexander, quoted, 439
Hegel, G. W. F., on freedom, 446
Helfferich, German ambassador, 165
Hilferding, R., 381n
Historiography, Soviet, 86-87, 106-10, 341
History of the All-Union Communist Party (Bolsheviks), Short Course, The, 45-46, 144, 463
Hitler, Adolf: attack on Soviet Union in *1941*, 44, 176; Communist reaction to, 79; Stalin and, 81, 90, 305, 330, 383; Molotov and, 309; on national self-determination, 328
Ho Chi Minh, 317
Holiday, W. T., 412
Howard, Roy, 175, 304
Hull, Cordell, quoted, 261
Human nature, transformation of, 439-42
Humphrey, Hubert H., 366, 367n, 409
Hungary: Soviet Republic of, 32, 33, 295; Cominform in, 46; Russian use of force in, 104-5, 322, 346, 351-52, 481; Communists' rewriting of history of, 106; national revolt in, 121-22, 343-44; and federation, 233; and Eastern European federation, 334-36 *passim*; Stalin's suggested confederation for, 337; People's Soviets in, 339; economic costs resulting from "civil war," 345; Mao on revolt in, 365; plans for non-Soviet federation, 390; *see also* Austro-Hungarian Empire
Hutchins, Robert, 413

Imperialism: Lenin on, 34; "two camps" theory and, 168-89; attack on ultra, 375-77; *see also* Capitalism
Imperialism and World Economy (Bukharin), 375
Imperialism, the Highest Stage of Capitalism (Lenin), 376
India, position of, 481

INDEX

Indian Communist Party, Congress of, 313
Indochina, 182, 316-17
Indonesia, 369
Industrialization of Soviet economy, 98, 135, 248
Industry: revolution and, 2-6; agriculture and, 19, 436-38; revolution based on large-scale, 67; need for Western technique in, 103
Ingush, see Chechen-Ingush
Institute No. 205, 45n
International Association of Democratic Lawyers, 181n
International Atomic Energy Agency, 393
International brotherhood of workers, 33
International Bureau of Education, 393
International control of atomic energy, discussed, 399-407
International courts of arbitration, 377
International Economic Conference (1922), 170
International Economic Conference (1927), 172
International Economic Conference (1952), 181
Internationalism, Soviet attitude toward, 51, 53-54, 55; see also Proletarian internationalism
International Labor Organization, 393
International law, 410; see also Korovin, E. A.
International Organization of Democratic Journalists, 181n
International politics, Soviet Russian nationalism and, 63
International Republic of Soviets, 31-33, 50, 63, 188, 327, 426-27
International Telecommunication Union, 393
International Union of Students, 181n
Inter-Parliamentary Union, 393
Iraq, 424-25
Iraqi-Jordanian federation, 424
Ireland, relations with England, 11-12
Islamic peoples, see Moslem peoples
Israel, 110, 477
Italian Communist Party, 312
Italy: as prototype of capitalist nation-states, 26; Soviet expectations for, 46; renunciation of League membership by, 382; federalists in, 415
Iudin, Pavel, quoted, 385-86
Izvestiia, cited, 82, 121, 338-39, 348, 391

Jacobinism, Leninism and, 192-97, 229, 444
Japan: effect of rise of militarist, on Russian nationalism, 41; nationalism in, 80; Soviet Union and, 84, 306-7, 388
Jen Min Jih Pao editorial, 364n
Jessup, Philip C., quoted, 409-10
Jewish Anti-Fascist Committee, 110
Jewish workers, 201
Jews, 110-12, 207; see also Anti-Semitism; Bund
Joffe, A. F., cited, 61, 397-98
Joint Nuclear Research Institute, 340
Jordan, 424
Joshi, P. C., 313
Jouhaux, Léon, 173

Kabardinian-Balkar ASSR, 95
Kaganovich, L. M.: quoted, 189, 319-20; demotion of, 355; Khrushchev's attack on, 468-69
Kalmyk people: national autonomy destroyed, 95-96; restored, 96-97
Kamenev, L., 133
Kammari, M. D., quoted, 47, 262, 271
Karachai people: national autonomy destroyed, 95; restored, 96-97
Karakhan, L., 61
Kardelj, Yugoslav Foreign Minister, 329-30
Karelo-Finnish Union Republic, 258
Kashmir, 369n
Kassim, Abdul Karim, 424-25
Kasymov, Kenesary, 109
Kautsky, Karl: Stalin's use of, 266, 267-68; on ultra-imperialism, 375, 376, 381n; on League of Nations, 385
Kazakh SSR, 244n, 259
Kazakhstan, 98, 109
Kellogg-Briand Pact, 301
Kemal Pasha, 58-59
Khorezm, 230
Khrushchev, N. S.: on world state, 48-49; on nationalism, 95n, 96, 103; anti-Jewish bias of, 112; Tito and, 121, 347, 349-51, 352-53; on capitalist encirclement, 150-51; on socialism in one country, 151-53; coexistence doctrine of, 185-87; on atomic war, 319, 320; "revisions" of Lenin on use of force, 320-24; on Council for Mutual Economic Aid, 339-40; attitude toward Poland, 344; on withdrawal of Soviet troops from satellite countries, 346-47; on na-

Khrushchev, N. S. (*Continued*)
tional communism, 349-51, 352-55 *passim;* on Chinese communism, 362, 368; Humphrey's interview with, 366, 367*n*; and United Arab Republic, 422-25; on omnicompetent man, 434; strengthening of kolkhozes by, 437-38; on status of women, 438-39; on "withering away" process, 464-65, 468-70
Khvilevoi (Khvylovy), M., quoted, 72-73; suicide of, 74
Kienthal Conference (April, 1916), 376
Kirghiz SSR, 244*n*
Knowland, William, quoted, 317*n*
Koenigsberg Area of East Prussia, 259
Kolarov, Vasil, 327
Kolarz, Walter, 88; quoted, 254
Kommunist: cited, 105, 437-38; quoted, 108, 321, 322; *see also Bol'shevik*
Konev, I. S., 341, 346
Konstantinovna, Nadezhda, 454
Köprülü, Turkish Foreign Minister, 422
Korea, 346, 369*n*, 487
Korean People's Republic, 150
Korean War, 118-19, 182, 316, 317, 365
Korovin, E. A.: on international law, 116, 396, 410; on peaceful coexistence, 179; on national sovereignty, 352, 384-85
Kozhevnikov, F. I., 308
Kozlov, G. V., 188-89
Krasnaia zvezda, quoted, 105
Krivitskii, W. G., 81*n*
Kronstadt rebellion (March, 1921), 235
Kunanbaev, Abai, 109
Kuusinen, O., 78; quoted, 115, 119

Labor: in stateless society, 17-20; abolition of the division of, 19, 433, 434*n*; control by society and by the state over amount of, 469-70
Labor movement, national and international, 4-5, 62
Language: national groups and, 29, 247-51, 262-63, 264; Russian as future world, 88, 276-78, 281-84, 472; right of population to receive education in its native, 203; world state and, 264-84; Russification of, in Soviet Union, 273-76; Marr's theory of, 276-81; *see also* Culture
Laos, 369

Laski, Harold, 414
Lassalle, Ferdinand, 4
Latvia, and USSR, 90, 119, 167-68, 235, 294, 298
Latvian Communist Party, 235
Latvian Social Democrats, 201
Laufenberg, German Communist, 55
Lausanne Conference (1922-23), 59
Law in Soviet ideology, 112-13, 410; *see also* Korovin, E. A.
League of Nations, 81-82, 113; Soviet entry into, 174, 382-86; Soviet disarmament proposals in, 300; Soviet reaction to, 377-80
Lenin, V. I.: Marx and, 15*n*; on nationality problem, 25-29 *passim;* Trotsky and, 25-26*n*, 70, 145-47; on world peace, 30; on world state, 30-35 *passim,* 48, 353-54; Draft Resolution on the National Question, 34; death of, 38; on nationalism, 51-53, 55-56, 70, 103; attitude toward Treaty of Brest-Litovsk, 54; disagreement with Roy, 58; internationalism and, 61-62; Great Russia and, 66; on centralism, 68, 190-238 *passim;* Stalin and, 69-70, 132-33, 134, 354, 453-57; on United States of the World, 129, 426; on world state and socialism in one country, 129-33; on "final" victory of socialism, 141, 142-43; on "permanent revolution," 145-48 *passim;* slogan of "the democratic dictatorship of the proletariat and the peasantry," 147; discovery of law of uneven development, 154; attitude toward peaceful coexistence, 164-70 *passim,* 188; theory of general will, 196-97; on national self-determination, 204-6, 211-13, 215-24, 228-30; on national culture, 209-11, 247-53 *passim;* on federalism, 213-15, 224-27; struggle with ritualistic centralists, 215-21; resolution against factions in Party, 236-37; on national languages, 265, 267; theory on use of force, 286-89; on Balkan federation, 326; on United States of Europe, 374-75, 376-77; and Bukharin, 375, 376, 454; on League of Nations, 377; on administrative institutions, 431; on human nature, 433, 442; on dictatorship, 443-45, 447; orchestra metaphor, 444-45; prescription for traveling path to paradise, 446-47; on timing of "withering process,"

INDEX

448-50; on bureaucracy, 452-53; on standing army, 456; on egalitarian society, 457
Leninism, 100, 144, 444
"Lesser-evil" theory, 107-8, 109n
Levin, I. D., quoted, 113, 119-20, 124, 410
Liberation, wars of, 291, 304-5, 310, 313-17
Lindsay, A. D., quoted, 440-41
Lithuania: and USSR, 90, 119, 167-68, 234-35, 294; federalist sentiment in, 198-99; exercise of self-determination in, 227-28
Lithuanian Communist Party, 235
Lithuanian Resistance Movement, 95
Lithuanian Social Democrats, 201
Lithuanian SSR, 259, 261
Litvinov, Maxim: at League of Nations, 113, 174-76, 303, 382, 383-84; on disarmament, 300; on European Union, 382
Liu Shao-chi, 314, 315; quoted, 359-61
Lorimer, Frank, cited, 99n
Ludwig, Emil, Stalin's conversation with, 41
Lung Yun, 365
Luxemburg, Rosa: cited, 51, 215, 218, 223-24; quoted, 451

MacArthur, Douglas, 317
Macedonia, 327, 329-33 *passim; see also* Pirin Macedonia
Madison, James, quoted, 236
Magnani, Valdo, 312
Magyars, 10, 21-22
Makharadze, F., 241
Malaya, 369
Malenkov, G. M.: on peaceful coexistence, 184, 185; on third world war, 318, 319, 323; deposed, 320, 355; opposition to EDC, 421; Khrushchev's attack on, 468-69
Man: omnicompetent, 17-20, 432-36, 473; Communist idea of brotherhood of, 427-32; transformation of nature of, 439-42
Manchuria, 360
Manifesto, see *Communist Manifesto*
Manuil'skii, Dimitri, 45n, 78
"Many roads" doctrine, reappraisal of, 347-57
Mao Tse-tung, 314, 357, 358, 361-66 *passim*
Markos Vafiades, 333-35
Marr, Nicolai Ia., 276-81

Marriage: Engels on, 19-20; Soviet attitude toward, 438
Marshall Plan, 117-18, 178, 182, 419, 487
Martin, Kingsley, 414
Martov, Julius, 227
Marx, Karl, orchestra metaphor, 18
Marx and Engels: on world state, 1-24; on nationalism, 1-2; on non-socialist nations, 3; Communists distinguished from other working-class parties, 5; on capitalism, 5, 7, 8-9, 18; on form of proletarian world state, 8-12; centralist philosophy of, 8-12, 16, 23-24, 192, 214; on transformation of world state into no state, 12-17, 427; on law of uneven development, 154-55; *see also* Engels, Friedrich
Marxist-Leninist theory: Soviet elaboration of, 24; use of force in, 286-99; China's contribution to, 361-62; dialectics, 455, 460, 463, 466-67; "reinterpretation" of basic "law" of, on relationship between the state and material forces of society, 462-64
Masaryk, Jan, 390
Mdivani, Georgian Communist, 241
Mekhlis, Lev, 307
Mensheviks, 68, 195
Meyer, Cord, Jr., 412-13
Middle East, see East, the, Middle and Near East
Mikoyan, A. I.: cited, 150, 366; quoted, 323, 362
Military blocs, 186
Mitin, M., quoted, 466
Molotov, V. M., 78, 87; on Marshall Plan, 117; on attack on Finland, 119; on two economic systems, 173; on peaceful coexistence, 176; on national development, 260; Hitler and, 309; on Red Army, 310-11; on atomic war, 319, 320; demotion of, 355; on Finno-Swedish federation, 389; draft of all-European collective security treaty, 420; Khrushchev's attack on, 468-69
Mongolia, Outer, 60, 346, 360
Mongolian People's Republic, 150, 356-57, 358
Monnet, Jean, 387n
Montenegro, 327, 329, 332
Mordinov, A. E., quoted, 278-79
Morgen Freiheit (New York Yiddish-language Communist paper), 112n

Moscow: as core of Great Russia, 67; as capital of future Soviet world state, 161
Moscow Declaration of Communist Parties, 105, 465-66
Mosely, P. E., 333
Moslem peoples, 71, 98, 242, 272, 422-25
Mutual Assistance pacts, 83
Myerson, Golda, 110

Nagy, Imre, 343, 351, 363
Narodniki, 230*n*
Nash, Vernon, 413
Nasser, Gamal Abdal, 422-24, 477
National anthem, 91
"National Bolshevism," 55, 56, 57
National communism, 2, 342-47
National cultural autonomy, theory of, 206-9, 211, 216*n*; see also Culture
Nationalism: Marx and Engels's evaluation of, 1-2, 6, 8; two Soviet attitudes toward, 50-53; internationalism and, 53-54; in Germany, 80, 81; in Japan, 80, 81; bourgeois, 101-2, 407, 408; Soviet manipulation of the terminology of, 123-26; underestimation of strength of, 220; national culture and, 262-63, 266, 439; national languages and, 264 (see also Language); in Communist nations, 369-70; and threat of atomic bomb, 395-99; struggle between two types of, 407; see also Russian nationalism
Nationality: place in world revolution, 10; Marx on unimportance of, 21-23; Lenin on, 25-29 *passim*, 66; Stalin on problem, 25-29 *passim;* "counter-revolutionary deviations" in the Soviet policy, 71; federalism as attempt to solve problem, 247-51; fusion of nations as final task of socialism, 251-53; annihilation of distinctions of, 439
National Question and Leninism, The (Stalin), 40
National self-determination, see Self-determination
National sovereignty: manipulation of, 112-26; ultimate stage in "protection" of, 122-26; doctrine of, 384-85; Soviet attitude toward, in UN, 395-99 *passim;* and control of atomic energy, 399-407; and proposed Atomic Development Authority, 401

National symbols, use of, 49, 50, 79, 81, 82, 91, 125-26, 254, 338, 408
Nation-states: Marx and Engels on, 1, 6, 9, 20-24; fusion of, 20-24, 209-11, 439, 468, 473; Bolshevik prerevolutionary view of, 25-29; internationalism and, 63; system, 386, 481-82
NATO, see North Atlantic Treaty Organization
Nazi-Soviet Pact (Aug., 1939), 43, 83, 90, 305, 307, 308, 387-89
Near East, see East, the, Middle and Near East
Nechkina, M., quoted, 107
Nehru, J., Bulganin's and Khrushchev's meeting with, 320
New York *Herald Tribune,* quoted, 44
NKVD, 457
Non-military cooperation in NATO, 476-86
Non-Russian peoples in Soviet bloc, 65-74 *passim;* and nationality problem, 71-72; within USSR, 85-128 *passim;* disaffection and punishment of, 93-99; remodeling of history and national consciousness of, 107; Russification of, 248, 272, 370
Non-Soviet world: peaceful coexistence with Soviets, 164-89; war-producing tensions within, 169; in event of nuclear war, 324-25; Soviet reactions to supranational plans from, 373, 425; Soviet hostility to recent federalist designs within, 418-25; Soviet grand design and implications for, 472-88; need of, 488; see also specific countries, e.g., United States
Nordic Council, 421
North Atlantic Treaty Organization (NATO): Soviet attitude toward, 182, 185, 325, 340-41, 393, 421, 423; dissension in, 360; non-military cooperation in, 476-86 *passim;* United Nations and, 478-79
Norway, 217, 389
Novoe vremiia (periodical), 82
Nuclear Research Institute, 340
Nuclear warfare, see Atomic warfare

On the Foundations of Leninism (Stalin), 38
On War (Clausewitz), 287

INDEX

505

Orchestra metaphor: Marx on, 18; Bukharin on, 434-35, 445; Lenin on, 444-45
Ordzhonikidze, S., 240
Organization for European Economic Cooperation, 182, 419
Orgburo of Russian Communist Party, 237
Orwell, George, quoted, 63, 106
Osborn, Frederick, quoted, 400-1
Outer Mongolia, 60, 346, 360

Padev, Michael, quoted, 106
Palestine, see Israel
Pan-Americanism, 388
Pan-Asia, 388
Pan-Europe (Coudenhove-Kalergi), 380
Pan-Europe scheme of the 1920s, 380-82
Pan-Slav Movement, 21-22, 126-27
Paris Commune, 8, 9, 13-15, 449-50
Parker, John J., quoted, 125
Parties, foreign, 62; see also Communist Parties, *and specific parties*, e.g., Chinese Communist Party
Partisans of Peace, 181, 302, 412, 416-17
Party, see Communist Party of the Soviet Union
Patriotism, Soviet, 85; see also Russian nationalism
Pavlov, Iu., quoted, 407
Peace, see World peace
Peace (1917), Decree on, 285, 289
"Peace bloc," Soviet-sponsored, 321
Peaceful coexistence, 49; meaning of, 164-89; origin of theory, 164-66; "theory of two camps," 166-68; "perfect" and imperfect, 168-69, 175; and trade, 170-74; and politics, 174-76; anticipated end of, 187-89; among countries of socialist camp, 348
"Peace" movement of Soviet Union, 180-89, 288-89, 301-8
"Peace offensive," Communist, 417
Peace or Anarchy (Meyer), 412-13
Peasantry: and proletariat, 147-49; in stateless society, 436-38; see also Agriculture
Peasants' Soviets, 39
"People," the, evolution in meaning of, 223
Peoples' Convention Movement, 413-14
People's Democracies, 120, 150; discrepancies between state structures of, and those of Union Republics in USSR, 338-39; Chinese version of, 361
People's militia, 13-14
People's Republic of China, proclamation of, 314-15; see also China
People's Revolutionary Government of Outer Mongolia, 60
Permanent revolution, 5, 145-49
Persia, Russian national interests and, 59-60
Pétain, H. P., 387
Philippines, 369n
Philosophical Dictionary, Short, 48
Piatakov, Georgii: on nationalism, 51; centralist position of, 215, 218-19; on right of national self-determination, 228; extremist views of, 233-34
Pieck, Wilhelm, quoted, 79, 188
Pipes, Richard, quoted, 85n; cited, 241n
Pirin Macedonia, 331, 332, 333
Pius XII, pope, 415
Plekhanov, G. V., 204
Pleven Plan, 419
Podvoiskii, N., quoted, 293
Pogodin, N. F., 127
Pokrovskii, M. N., 86-87, 107
Poland: Marx and Engels on, 10, 21-22, 56; nationalism in, 35; Soviet Union and, 46, 104, 167-68, 295-96, 322, 346; Communists' rewriting of history of, 106; anti-Semitism in, 111-12; national revolt in, 121-22, 343-44; federalist sentiment in, 198-99; exercise of national self-determination in, 227-28; and federation, 233, 334, 336, 389-92; Stalin's suggested confederation for, 337; slackening of production due to revolt, 345; effect of Chinese doctrinal pronouncements on, 363
Police, 14, 449-50; Soviet secret, 452, 453
Polish Social Democrats, 201, 202n, 206, 215-18
Politburo of Russian Communist Party, 237, 314
Political power, Marx and Engels on, 6, 13, 15
Poole, DeWitt C., quoted, 94
Popov, N., quoted, 66-67
Poppe, N., quoted, 356n
Po Prostu (Warsaw paper), cited, 111
POUM, 84
Poznan riots (June, 1956), 342, 344

Prague Conference, 202
Pravda: cited, 104, 335, 347, 348, 349, 407, 464; quoted, 48, 109, 110, 277, 302, 317, 334, 340, 343
Preobrazhenskii, E., 161-62, 228, 290, 377
Principles of Communism (Engels), 2
Procurator's Office, 457
Program of the Communists (Bukharin), 31
Proletarian internationalism: definition of, 61-63; Soviet world state and, 63-65; and Russian hegemony in USSR, 65-74; perversion of, in late 1920s and early 1930s, 74-79; Stalinist concept of, 76, 80, 102; and national symbols, 82-83; Russian nationalism and, 101; post-Stalinist, 102-6; as "universal" nationalism, 407
Proletariat: Marx and Engels on, 2-12 *passim;* in First World War, 27-29; Great Russian nationalism and "other," 53; use of term, 82; and peasantry, 147-49; and right of national self-determination, 215-21; obsolescence of term, 458-60; *see also* Dictatorship of the proletariat; Proletarian internationalism; Revolution
Proudhon, P. J., 9, 16
Purges, 75, 254; *see also* Great Purges of 1936–1938

Rabinowitch, Eugene, quoted, 406
Radek, Karl, 55, 56, 57, 215, 217
Raditsa, Bogdan, 329*n*
Rakosi, Matyas, 105, 348
Rakovskii, Khristian, 243-45, 260
Ransome, Patrick, 386
Rapallo, 56
Raun, Alo, quoted, 275
Răutu, L., quoted, 120
Ravines, Eudocio, 45*n*
Rawnsley, Noel, quoted, 416
"Reactionary" wars, 291
Red Army, 72; in Finland, 119; extensive program of organization of, 293-96; world-wide mission of, 298-99; in "wars of liberation," 305; use of, in Europe, 307-8, 310-13; in Eastern European countries, 322; and national communism, 346; creation of a permanent, 452
Renner, Karl, 115, 415
Reston, James, 180
Reves, Emery, 413

"Revisionism," 350-51; in Yugoslavia, 465, 466, 467; impact of Chinese doctrinal pronouncements on, 363
Revolution: Marx and Engels on, 1-24; world, 1-2, 146; industry and, 2-6; and skipping of stages, 4*n*, 230-32; results of, 18-19; attitude of Stalin toward, 76; weakest link theory and, 157-59; *see* Russian Revolution
Revolution, permanent, 5, 145-49
Revolutionary wars, 55-56, 289, 290, 291, 292, 301-8
"Revolution from above," 463-64
Revolution of *1848*, 7, 8
Reynaud, Paul, 387
Ribbentrop, J. von, 309
Robespierre, M. M. I., 193-94; *see also* Jacobins
Roosevelt, Elliott, 177
Rothstein, Andrew, quoted, 385
Rousseau, J. J., 192-97
Roy, M. N., 58, 298
RSFSR, *see* Russian Socialist Federal Soviet Republic
Rudzinski, A. W., cited, 338
Rumania, 11; Cominform in, 46; Eastern European federation and, 333-36; People's Soviets in, 339; Soviet Army in, 322, 346; plans for non-Soviet federation, 390
Rumanian Communist Party, 120, 322, 327, 333
Rural economy, 19, 436-38; *see also* Agriculture
Russell, Bertrand, quoted, 399
Russia: potential for revolution in, 3-4; Bolshevik coup d'état in, 30-36; Germany and, 54-57; national interests in early 1920s, 54-61; Far East and, 60-61; hegemony of, in USSR, 65-74 (*see also* Russian nationalism); civilization of, 88; patriotism in, 91; claims of priority in science and inventions, 99*n*, 100-2; Soviet experiences in, and concept of a Soviet world state, 190-91; federalist sentiment in, 198-99; *see also* Great Russia; Russian Socialist Federal Soviet Republic; Union of Soviet Socialist Republics
Russian Communist Party: factional struggle within, 75, 78-79; Program of, 227, 233-34, 432; centralism in, 234-38; Party Control Commission, 453; *see also* Communist Party of the Soviet Union

INDEX

Russian Empire, multinational nature of, 26, 35
Russian language: use of, in non-Russian regions, 265; role of, in struggle for world supremacy between East and West, 271-73; as possible future world language, 281-84
Russian nationalism: rebirth of, 41; influence of, to *1934*, 50-79; proletarian internationalism and, 62, 63-65, 72-74; and world proletariat, 74-79; since *1934*, 80-128; within the Soviet Union, 85-88; within and beyond the Soviet Union after Second World War, 99-102; history and, 106-10; manipulation of concept of national sovereignty in, 112-26; Tsarist and Soviet, compared, 126-28; "base" for world socialism and, 159-63; and Great Purges, 254; as universal nationalism, 472
Russian Orthodox Church, 91
Russian Revolution of *1905*, 145, 196-97
Russian Social Democratic Labor Party: nature of Bolshevik faction of, 67; split into Bolshevik and Menshevik factions, 195; Tammerfors Conference (1905), 201; Program, 203-6; founding Congress in *1898*, 204; federalist circles of, 207; *see also* Communist Party of the Soviet Union
Russian Socialist Federal Soviet Republic (RSFSR): Constitution of, 30-31, 53, 226, 240; Congresses of Soviets, 30, 225-26, 227; Stalin on, 36; "entry" of non-Russian countries into, 69-70; relations with other Soviet Republics, 232; federalism in, 239-40
Russo-Japanese War, 92
Russo-Polish War of *1920*, 55
Ruthenia, Subcarpathian, 261
Rykov, Aleksei, 88

Sadchikov, Soviet Ambassador to Yugoslavia, 329-30
Safarov, G., 98, 242
Saragat, Giuseppe, 115, 415
Satellites: preparation for promotion to Union Republics, 338-42; upset of timetable with revolts in, 342-44; de-Stalinization of, 342-44; *see also* National communism

Scandinavia, 421; *see also specific countries*, e.g., Norway
Schacht, H. H. G., 388
Schlageter movement, 57
Schuman, Frederick, 411
Schuman, Robert, 115
Schuman Plan, 182, 420
Schwartz, Benjamin, 347; quoted, 361
Science, claims of Russian contribution to world, 99n, 100-2
Scotland, 21
Secession, right of, 211-13, 220, 224-25, 228, 245-46, 256-58, 285
Second International, 27-28, 52, 204, 374
Secretariat of Russian Communist Party, 237
Self-determination: right of national, 204-6, 215-21; Lenin's definition of national, 211-13; reinterpretation of national, 221-24; national, in practice, 227-33; Soviet theory of national, 285; and right of Red Army to conquer foreign nations, 296; UN and question of national, 393-94; in Cyprus, 486
Semenov, N. N., cited, 397-98
Serbia, 327, 332
Serbs, 11n
Seven-Year Plan, 471
Shamil, 108
Shapiro, Henry, quoted, 465
Shepilov, D., Khrushchev's attack on, 468-69
Shestakov, A. V., 87
Sholom Aleichem, celebration of centennial of, 274n
Shumskii, O., 72, 73
Siberia, 370
Singapore, 369
Sinkiang (Chinese Turkestan), 357, 360
Sino-Soviet accords (Oct., 1954), 358, 369
Sino-Soviet Treaty (Aug. 14, 1945), 356
Skrypnyk, M.: and Ukrainian nationalism, 73, 74, 86, 260; on federalism, 243-45
Slansky, Rudolf, 110
Slavophil-Westernizer controversy, 161
Slavs, 21; *see also specific countries*, e.g., Croatia
Slovenia, 328, 332
Smodlaka, Josip, 331

Snow, Edgar, cited, 358n
Sobolëv, A., quoted, 321, 322, 424
Social Contract (Rousseau), 192-97
Socialism: Marx and Engels on international, 1-6; and world peace, 6-8; differences between anarchism and, 16-17; metamorphosis of man under, 17-20, 432-36, 473; nationalism and, 50-53; complete and final victory, 131-45, 151-53; world, Russian socialism and "base" for, 159-63; "two camps" theory and, 168-89; economics and, 217; fusion of nations still final task of, 251-53; war for, 290; "many roads" doctrine and, 347-51; and strengthening of state, 458-62
Socialism in one country: Stalin on, 41, 133-63 *passim;* Lenin on, 129-33; Trotsky on, 133-36, 138-39
Socialism in one sphere, 138-40
Socialism, Utopian and Scientific (Engels), 16
Socialist encirclement, 149-53, 460
Social Revolutionaries, 67, 206
Sololev, Leonid, quoted, 109
Sosiura, V., 101
Southeast Asia, 369
Southeast Asia Youth Conference, 313
Sovereignty, *see* National sovereignty
Soviet Central Asia, *see* Asia, Soviet Central
Soviet-Czechoslovak economic agreement (Jan., 1957), 345
Soviet-Czechoslovak Treaty (Dec., 1943), 392
Soviet-Czechoslovak Treaty (June, 1945), 261
Soviet–East German accord (July, 1958), 345
Soviet–East German Treaty, 341
Soviet Encyclopedia, Large (1938), 43
Soviet Encyclopedia, Large (1947), 123
Soviet Encyclopedia, Small, 40
Soviet-Finnish Peace of March, *1940,* 389
Soviet-Japanese Neutrality Pact, 307
Soviet-Mongol Treaty (Feb., 1946), 357
Soviet-Polish War of *1920,* 295
Soviet press, 91, 101-2, 120, 319; *see also specific periodicals,* e.g., *Pravda*
Soviets, the, 451-53
Soviet State Law (Denisov), 337

Soviet-Turkish Treaties of Friendship (1921), 59
Soviet world state: as explicit Soviet goal, 1-49 *passim;* Bolshevik Revolution and imminence of, 30-36; important role of colonial and semicolonial areas in formation of, 34; Soviet Union as prototype of, 36-41; "socialism in one country" and, 41-49, 129-63; problems of nationalism and, 53-54; two approaches to Soviet, 63-65; Stalin's goal of, 80; Great Russian chauvinism and, 100-2; as major ingredient of Soviet ideology, 127, 128; Russification of, 128 (*see also* Russian nationalism); long-range goal of centralist, 233-38; World Communist Party and, 237-38; world language and, 262-84; role of war in building, 285-325; way stations to, 326-72; and nationalism in Asia, 370; "withering away" as ultimate goal of world communism, 426-71; appraisal of nature of, 472-73; *see also* World state
Soviet-Yugoslav relations, 328-31, 465-66; *see also* Tito; Yugoslavia
Spaak, Paul Henri, 115, 415, 484
Spain, 21, 113
Spanish Civil War, Soviet policy toward, 83-84
Spanish Communist Party, 83-84
Stalin, J. V., 5n; on nationality problem, 25-29 *passim;* on nationalism, 35-36, 38; on Soviet Union as prototype of world state, 36-41; theory of "socialism in one country," 41-49, 64-65, 133-63 *passim,* 354; Tito and, 46 (*see also* Tito); as Commissar of Nationalities, 68-69; Lenin and, 69-70 (*see also* Lenin); on Great Russian nationalism, 69-74, 85-102 *passim;* Trotsky and, 75 (*see also* Trotsky); definition of proletarian internationalism, 76; "leftism" of, 77-78; Hitler and, 81 (*see also* Hitler); attitude toward League of Nations, 81-82; rewriting of Soviet interpretation of history, 86-87; on Russo-Japanese War, 92-93; shattering of cult of, 103, 111, 464; anti-Semitism of, 110-12; on national sovereignty, 114; on world state, 139-40; on role of peasantry, 147; on capitalist encirclement, 149-53, 460-62; on the United States of Europe, 153-56; on

INDEX

"weakest link" theory, 157-59; on "two camps theory," 166-88 *passim;* on peaceful coexistence, 168-74 *passim;* on power of Party and Soviet state, 191, 236*n*, 451; controversy between centralism and federalism, 199-200, 214, 239-63; on right of national self-determination, 205, 222-23, 285; on national culture, 207-8, 251-53; on national development, 249-51; on national languages, 264-84 *passim;* on use of force, 289-90, 297-98, 304, 305, 306; on atomic war, 318; and federalist projects, 332-36; Zhdanov and, 335; on alternative of confederal approach, 337-38; on commonwealth idea, 47, 351; Mao and, 362; on stateless society, 429-30, 459; on omnicompetent man, 433-36; on the merging of town and country, 436-38; on status of women, 438-39; on freedom, 446; on destruction of state power, 447; on "withering away" process of state, 449, 450, 462-64, 466; abandonment of egalitarian pretensions, 457-58
Stassen, Harold, 177-78, 409
State, *see* Nation-states; "Withering away" of the state; World state
State and Revolution (Lenin), 214
Stateless totalitarianism, 445, 470-71
State planning, 467
Statistical bureaus, 431
Steklov, Iurii, quoted, 30
Stettinius, Edward R., 260-61; quoted, 395
Stockholm Congress, 201, 202
Stockholm Peace Petition, 181, 182, 417
Stoica, Rumanian Premier, 336*n*
Streit, Clarence, 386, 413
Stresemann government, 57
Stuchka, P. I., 53, 379-80
Suez crisis, 477-81 *passim*
Sultan-Galiev, 71
Sulzberger, C. L., quoted, 369
Sumatra, 369
Sun Yat-sen, 230*n*
Supranational plans of non-Soviet countries, Soviet rejection of postwar proposals of, 407-8
Supreme Soviet (bicameral body), 256
Sweden, 217, 389
Symbols, *see* National symbols
Syndicalists, 84
Syria, 325, 422, 424

Táborský, Eduard, 390
Tadzhik SSR, 244*n*
Taft, William H., 409
Taiwan, 369*n*
Talmon, J. L., cited, 194, 197, 229*n*; quoted, 444
Tammerfors Conference (1905), 201
Tannu Tuva, 356
Tass, quoted, 385
Tatar ASSR, 272
Tempo (Svetozar Vukmanović), 331
Territorial autonomy, 206-9
Terror, use of, 286
Thailand, 369
Third International, *see* Communist International (Comintern)
Thorez, M., 312
Thrace, 333
Tiflis riots, 354
Timofeev, T., quoted, 348
Tito: Stalin and, 46, 104, 311-12, 331, 336, 342; reopening of schism between Kremlin and, 105; and Comintern, 328-29; and federalist projects, 332-36; and Markos, 333; Kremlin's rapprochement with, 336; treatment of Djilas, 344; Khrushchev and, 347, 349-51, 352-53; Chinese press attack on, 363-64
Togliatti, P., 312
Tolstoy, Alexei, quoted, 91
Totalitarian ideology, 470-73 *passim,* 488
Towster, Julian, cited, 259*n*, 261
Toynbee, Arnold, cited, 399
Trade: coexistence and, 170-74, 181-82; between USSR and China, 360
Trade union organizations as agents of Russification, 72; *see also* World Federation of Trade Unions
Transcaucasian Social Democrats, 202
Transcaucasus: Soviet-Turkish territorial ambitions in, 59*n*; and nationalism, 72-74; ethnic stocks in, 207, 244*n*; federalism in, 240-41; *see also specific countries of,* e.g., Georgia
Treaty of Brest-Litovsk, 54, 165, 289, 292
Treaty of Sèvres, 58
Trotsky, Leon: theory of "permanent revolution," 5*n*, 145-49; on goal of world state, 25-30 *passim,* 139-40; Lenin and, 25*n*-26*n*, 70, 145-47; on national interests of Russia, 64; Stalin and, 75, 77, 133, 135, 140, 145, 147-

Trotsky, Leon (*Continued*)
49, 153-59; on dictatorship of proletariat supported by peasantry, 147; slogan of "United States of Europe," 153-59, 373-75; on Jacobinism, 196; organization of "August Bloc" by, 202; on Red Army, 295; on Balkan federation, 326-27
Truman, H. S., 317, 318, 408-9
Tukhachevskii, M. N., quoted, 296
Turco-Tatar "Latinizers," 273
Turkestan, 71, 98, 242
Turkestan, Chinese, *see* Sinkiang
Turkey, 58-59; Enver Pasha's plan for Pan-Turkic federation, 242; and Syria, 325; British attitude toward Eastern European federation, 332; plans for non-Soviet federation, 390
Turkic peoples in RSFSR, 242
Turkish-Arab federation, 422
Turkish Communist Party, 59
Turkish Empire, 11
Turkmen Socialist Soviet Republic, 231, 244*n*
Tuvinian Autonomous Region of the RSFSR, 356
"Two camps" theory, 166-68

Ukraine: Lenin's appeal to, 33; Western, joins USSR, 44, 90 (*see also* Ukrainian Soviet Socialist Republic); Great Russian influence in, 66; Communist Party in, 68, 235; "nationalist deviations" in, 72-74, 86, 94-95, 98-99, 354; armed revolt against Moscow, 94-95; Soviet-sponsored deportations from, 97; linguistic Russification in, 102-3*n*, 272, 273*n*; exercise of national self-determination in, 227-28; as separate Soviet Republic, 234-35; Ukrainian federalist proposals for 1923 Constitution for USSR, 243
Ukrainian Insurgent Army, 95
Ukrainian People's Republic (1917), 225
Ukrainian Soviet Socialist Republic: Crimean Region added to, 259; no rights resulting from "great expansion of rights of," 261; question of membership in UN, 261, 338
Ulam, Adam, quoted, 330
Union Now (Streit), 386
Union of Soviet Socialist Republics (USSR): as nation-state, 26*n*-27*n*; formation of, 36-39, 168; as prototype of world state, 36-41, 65-74, 80; commemoration of tenth anniversary of revolution, 39; foreign policy of, 54-61, 64-65, 74-79, 81-84, 85 (*see also specific countries*, e.g., Germany); Russian hegemony in, 65-74, 85-88 (*see also* Russian nationalism); and world proletariat, 74-79; membership in, as ultimate stage of "protection" of national sovereignty, 122-26 (*see also* National sovereignty); as "perfect" type of coexistence, 175 (*see also* Peaceful coexistence); federalism in, 224-27 (*see also* Federalism); relationship between Party and states within, 234-37; bicameral system in, 243-45; three types of Commissariats in, 246; state budget of, 246; number of types of republics in, 255-56; addition of new Union Republics to, 258-62, 308, 328, 338-42; prospect of carving up world with Nazis, 309-10; attitude toward nuclear war, 324-25, 395-99; gradual amalgamation of East European states into, 337-38; formation of unified military command for satellite states, 340-41; expansion in Asia, 355-72 (*see also* China); as member of UN, 392-95; *see also specific subjects*, e.g., War; *and specific persons*, e.g., Stalin
—— Congress of Soviets: First (1922), 36-37, 168; Second (1924), 37; Sixth (1931), 173
—— Constitutions: of *1923*, 37, 122, 123, 168, 243-47; of *1936*, 43, 48, 88, 123-24, 255-62; amendment of *1944*, 259-61, 262
Union Republics, *see* Union of Soviet Socialist Republics
United Arab Republic, 422-25
United Nations: East European satellites' indictments of genocide before, 97; question of Franco regime in Spain before, 113; intervention in Korean War, 118-19; question of membership in, for every Union Republic in USSR, 260-61, 338; Soviet disarmament proposals in, 300; Soviet participation in, 392-95; Suez issue and, 478-81; NATO and, 478-81
United Nations Atomic Energy Commission, 400

INDEX

United Nations Educational, Scientific, and Cultural Organization, 393
United States of America: proletariat in, 22; as nation-state, 26n-27n; Soviet regime's effort to separate its allies from, 113, 115; at head of non-Soviet camp, 172; Stalin's interview with newspaper editors from, 180; and League of Nations, 378; Soviet propaganda attack on, 388; Soviet characterization of supranational projects of, 408-15; effort to assist Western Europe, 419; and Suez crisis, 477-81
United States of Europe: as step in Soviet goal of world state, 28-29, 39; controversy over Soviet, 153-59; early debates over a capitalist, 373-75, 381; Churchill's advocacy of, 418
United States of the World, 28-29, 129, 426
United World Federalists, 412-13, 417, 418
Universal Postal Union, 393
Urban economy, 19; merging of rural and, 436-38; see also Industry
Usborne, Henry, 414
USSR, see Union of Soviet Socialist Republics
Uzbek Socialist Soviet Republic, 231, 244n, 257

Vafiades, Markos, 333-35
Varga, Eugene, 56, 172n, 313
Vatican, the, 415
Vavilov, Sergei, cited, 397-98
Vietnam, 317, 346, 369
Violence, use of, 286, 320-21; see also War
Vlasov, General, 93
Volga Germans, 95, 96, 97
Volga-Urals region, 272
Vollmar, Georg, 4, 155
Voprosy ekonomiki, 188
Voprosy filosofi, 100, 101, 275
Voprosy istorii, 100
Voroshilov, K. E., cited, 464
Vyshinsky, A.: on Indonesia, 114; on national sovereignty, 118; on Rousseau's general will, 194n; on centralism in Party, 255, 257, 259; attitude toward Ukrainian SSR, 261; defense of the veto power in UN, 394-95; on atomic control, 401; on Baruch Plan, 405; on Lenin and Bukharin, 455-56; on socialist state, 461

Wallace, Henry A., 180, 182
War: role of, in building Soviet world state, 285-325; and politics, 287-88; three approved types of, 290; for socialism, 305; Soviet position on, 380, 385; outlawing of, 402; sovereignty and, 410; destructiveness of, 475; see also Atomic warfare; Civil wars; Liberation, wars of; Revolutionary wars
Warsaw Pact, 344, 346
"Weakest link" theory, 157-59
Werth, Alexander, 177
West, Ranyard, quoted, 440
West, the: importance of, in proletarian revolution, 3-4; as prototype of capitalist nation-states, 26; use of national sovereignty as shield against, 116-17; Soviet attitude toward federation of democracies of, 386-87; response of, 472-88
Western Europe, see Europe, Western
Western European Social Democrats, 62
Weygand, Maxim, 387
Wieden, P., quoted, 89
Wilson, Woodrow, 377, 378, 409, 479-82 *passim*
"Withering away" of the state: Marx and Engels on, 12-20; Soviet theorists on centralized world plan following the, 426-32; transformation of man and society with, 432-42; personal dictatorship and, 442-46; geographical extent of, 447; time estimates for, 448-49; dissolution of state organs in hands of people, 449-53; retreat from, with Stalin's repudiation of Lenin, 453-57; placed at end of infinity, 462-64; post-Stalinist doctrine on, 464-71, 473
Wolffheim, German Communist, 55
Wollenberg, Erich, quoted, 295
Women, status of, 438-39
Workers: type of, in stateless society, 432-38; see also Proletariat
Workers' and Peasants' Soviets, 39
Worker's Opposition, 236
World Communist Party, 40
World federalism, confronted with issue of communism, 415-18; see also Federation
World Federal Republic of Soviets, 32, 33

World Federation of Democratic Women, 181*n*
World Federation of Democratic Youth, 181*n*
World Federation of Scientific Workers, 181*n*
World Federation of Soviet Republics, 64, 136, 326, 427-28
World Federation of Trade Unions, 181*n*, 314, 410
World Health Organization (WHO), 393
World language, world state and, 262-84; see also Language
World Meteorological Organization, 393
World mission, Slavophile dreams of, 126-27
World Monetary and Economic Conference (1933), 174
World Movement for World Federal Government, 415-18
World Must Be Governed, The (Nash), 413
World peace: Marx and Engels on condition for, 6-8; Lenin on, 30; need for, 475
World Peace Council, 181, 319, 417
World politics, 80, 174-76
World Proletarian Army, 293
World Republic, 8
World Socialist Republic, 31, 351
World Socialist Soviet Republic, 168
World social systems, two, 151
World society, stateless: plan for, 427-32; general will of, 442-44
World Soviet Federation, 232, 233, 234, 285, 360
World Soviet Labor Republic, 38
World Soviet Republic, 232, 234
World Soviet Socialist Republic, 37

World state: plans for, other than Soviet, 373-425; UN and, 395; need for, 395-99, 475, 481-82; see also Soviet world state
World Union of Soviet Socialist Republics, 40, 139
World War, First, 27, 44
World War, Second: Russian nationalism during, 88-93; end of, 92; Red Army in, 298; revival of Soviet federalist plans for Eastern Europe after, 328-32
World war, third, 184
World-wide Union of Soviet Socialist Republics, 43

Yiddish, 274
Youth organizations, 313
Yugoslav Communist Party, 105, 327, 331, 350
Yugoslavia, 11; nationalism in, 35; Cominform in, 46, 121; and Eastern European federation, 332-36; plans for Balkan Union, 390; revisionism in, 465-68; see also Tito

Zetkin, Clara, cited, 56
Zhdanov, A.: murder of, 110-11; speech to Cominform Conference, 179; on use of armed force, 313; Stalin and, 335; anticosmopolitan campaign and, 408
Zhukov, E. M., 316, 355
Zimmerwald Conference (1915), 219
Zinoviev, G. E.: on world state, 33; on national patriotism, 55, 62; and Stalin, 77, 133; on federalism, 238; on use of force, 297; on Balkan federation, 327
Žujović, Sreten, 330